Towards a Semantic Web

CHANDOS
INTERNET SERIES

Chandos' new series of books are aimed at all those individuals interested in the internet. They have been specially commissioned to provide the reader with an authoritative view of current thinking. If you would like a full listing of current and forthcoming titles, please visit our website www.chandospublishing.com or e-mail info@chandospublishing.com or telephone number +44 (0) 1223 891358.

New authors: we are always pleased to receive ideas for new titles; if you would like to write a book for Chandos, please contact Dr Glyn Jones on e-mail gjones@chandospublishing.com or telephone number +44 (0) 1993 848726.

Bulk orders: some organisations buy a number of copies of our books. If you are interested in doing this, we would be pleased to discuss a discount. Please e-mail info@chandospublishing.com or telephone number +44 (0) 1223 891358.

Towards a Semantic Web

Connecting knowledge in academic research

BILL COPE
MARY KALANTZIS
LIAM MAGEE

CP

CHANDOS
PUBLISHING

Oxford Cambridge New Delhi

Chandos Publishing
TBAC Business Centre
Avenue 4
Station Lane
Witney
Oxford OX28 4BN
UK
Tel: +44 (0) 1993 848726
Email: info@chandospublishing.com
www.chandospublishing.com

Chandos Publishing is an imprint of Woodhead Publishing Limited

Woodhead Publishing Limited
80 High Street
Sawston, Cambridge CB22 3HJ
UK
Tel: +44 (0) 1223 499140
Fax: +44 (0) 1223 832819
www.woodheadpublishing.com

First published in 2011

ISBN:
978 1 84334 601 2

Contents

List of figures and tables   *xi*

Authors   *xv*

1   Changing knowledge systems in the era of the social web   **1**

Bill Cope and Mary Kalantzis

From print to digital text   1

Distributed knowledge systems: the changing role of the university   7

About this book   10

References   12

2   Frameworks for knowledge representation   **15**

Liam Magee

Putting things in order   16

Introducing the semantic web   22

Towards a framing of semantics   33

References   33

3   The meaning of meaning: alternative disciplinary perspectives   **35**

Liam Magee

Linguistic semantics   37

Cognitive semantics   46

Social semantics   52

Computational semantics   67

References   73

4   What does the digital do to knowledge making?   81

    Bill Cope and Mary Kalantzis

    The work of knowledge representation in the age of its
    digital reproducibility   82

    The old and the new in the representation of meaning
    in the era of its digital reproduction   84

    Conclusions   119

    References   120

5   Books and journal articles: the textual practices of academic
    knowledge   123

    Bill Cope and Mary Kalantzis

    The role of knowledge representation in knowledge design   123

    The scholarly monograph   126

    The academic journal   132

    Future knowledge systems   135

    Conclusions   141

    References   143

6   Textual representations and knowledge support-systems in
    research intensive networks   145

    Richard Vines, William P. Hall and Gavan McCarthy

    Introduction   146

    Towards an ontology of knowledge   151

    The theory of hierarchically complex systems   161

    Research knowledge and the dynamics of hierarchically
    complex systems   164

    Implications for managing research enterprises in a
    knowledge society   172

    Conclusions   182

    Acknowledgements   184

    Appendix: a preliminary ontology for research knowledge support   184

    References   189

7	An historical introduction to formal knowledge systems	197
	Liam Magee	
	Pre-modernity: logical lineages	200
	Early modernity: the mechanisation of thought	202
	Crises in modernity: the order of logic and the chaos of history	205
	References	212
8	Contemporary dilemmas: tables versus webs	215
	Liam Magee	
	Ordering the world by relations	215
	Early threads of the semantic web	218
	Shifting trends or status quo?	221
	Systems of knowledge: modern and postmodern	222
	Knowledge systems in social context	229
	References	232
9	Upper-level ontologies	235
	Liam Magee	
	A survey of upper-level ontologies	237
	A dialogical account of ontology engineering	257
	Conclusions: assessing commensurability	271
	Appendix: upper-level ontologies—supplementary data	278
	References	285
10	Describing knowledge domains: a case study of biological ontologies	289
	Liam Magee	
	Biological ontologies	290
	Biological cultures, ontological cultures	296
	Ontological objects	298
	Towards compromise: ontologies in practice	299
	References	300

11 On commensurability   **303**

Liam Magee

A world of 'material intangibles': social structures,
conceptual schemes and cultural perspectives   305

De-structuring critiques: struggling with systems,
structures and schemes   319

Interlude: constructions of science   324

Elastic structures: linking the linguistic, the cognitive and the social   330

Towards a framework...   340

References   341

12 A framework for commensurability   **343**

Liam Magee

What to measure—describing 'ontological cultures'   344

Presenting a framework for commensurability   349

Applying the framework   369

References   370

13 Creating an interlanguage of the social web   **371**

Bill Cope and Mary Kalantzis

The discursive practice of markup   371

Structural markup   374

Metamarkup: developing markup frameworks   378

Developing an interlanguage mechanism   384

Schema alignment for semantic publishing: the example of
Common Ground Markup Language   389

What tagging schemas do   397

Interlanguage   404

References   425

14 Interoperability and the exchange of humanly usable digital content   **429**

Richard Vines and Joseph Firestone

Introduction   429

The transformation of digital content   435

The XML-based interlanguage approach: two examples   444

The ontology-based interlanguage approach: OntoMerge   453

Evaluating approaches to interoperability   462

Addressing the translation problem: emergent possibilities   477

Conclusions   484

Acknowledgements   487

References   487

15 Framing a new agenda for semantic publishing   **491**

Bill Cope and Mary Kalantzis

The academic language game   492

Disciplinarity, or the reason why strategically unnatural
language is sometimes powerfully perceptive   496

Towards a new agenda for semantic publishing   502

References   506

Index   **509**

List of figures and tables

Figures

4.1	SGML markup for the definition of 'bungler' in the Oxford Dictionary	93
4.2	Changes in textwork since Gutenberg	97
4.3	Parallels between old and new media	104
6.1	Popper's 'general theory of evolution'	153
6.2	Knowledge in the three worlds ontology	155
6.3	The contextual nature of personal knowledge	157
6.4	John Boyd's OODA loop concept	160
6.5	The systems triad in hierarchy of complex dynamic systems	162
6.6	The hierarchical levels of knowledge cycling in a research enterprise	164
6.7	General process for turning personal into explicit knowledge	166
6.8	Social construction and formalisation of knowledge	169
6.9	Socio-technical aspects of harmonising standards across different research communities	181
9.1	A representation of the top-level classes in the BFO ontology	278
9.2	A representation of the top-level classes in the DOLCE ontology	278
9.3	A representation of the top-level classes in the GFO ontology	279

9.4 A representation of the top-level classes in the PROTON ontology 279

9.5 A representation of the top-level classes in the SUMO ontology 280

12.1 Commensurability model 353

13.1 The interlanguage mechanism 386

13.2 CGML as an interlanguage 406

13.3 Language pairs—full interoperability of 17 schemas requires 272 crosswalks 408

13.4 The interlanguage approach to CGML 409

13.5 Fragment of the CGML Dictionary of Authorship and Publishing specifying the concepts of <creation> and <creator> 413

13.6 Fragment of the CGML Dictionary specifying the concept of <editor> 415

13.7 First to fourth level concepts of the CGML Taxonomy of Authorship and Publishing 420

13.8 Fragment of the CGML Taxonomy of Authorship and Publishing specifying the concept of <party> from the fourth to sixth levels 422

13.9 Fragment of the Dublin Core to CGML Thesaurus 423

14.1 Translation/transformation architecture 437

14.2 Outline of the technical design choice between different transformation architectures 442

14.3 Comparison of the CGML and COAX systems 445

14.4 XML content translation using the CGML transformation system 448

14.5 XML content translation using the COAX transformation system 451

14.6 XML content translation using OntoMerge 460

15.1 A schema of knowledge processes 500

Tables

8.1	Comparison of knowledge systems	228
9.1	Swoogle results for five search terms, 2007 and 2009	238
9.2	Google Scholar results for five search terms, 2007 and 2009	239
9.3	Ontology methodologies	241
9.4	Foundational ontologies and their ontological choices as assessed by Oberle et al. (2007)	248
9.5	Comparison of the number of classes, properties, concepts and ratios within ontologies	249
9.6	Summary of ontology orientation	257
9.7	Messages received on the Semantic Web Interest Group and Ontolog Forum, 2000 to May 2009	259
9.8	Author and subject counts on the Semantic Web Interest Group and Ontolog Forum, 2000 to May 2009	260
9.9	Joint contributors to the ontologies surveyed, and the Semantic Web Interest Group and Ontolog Forum	260
9.10	Ontology count for the Semantic Web Interest Group and Ontolog Forum	262
9.11	Ontolog Forum dialogue map	264–7
9.12	Ontology commensurability matrix	273–4
9.13	Conceptual distinctions between the ontologies	280–2
9.14	Word frequency analysis of the Semantic Web Interest Group and Ontolog Forum	283–5
12.1	Intrinsic dimensions of a knowledge system	359–61
12.2	Extrinsic dimensions of a knowledge system	362–4

Authors

Bill Cope is a Research Professor in the Department of Educational Policy Studies at the University of Illinois, where has been a faculty member since 2006. He is also Director of Common Ground Publishing, a company that develops mixed medium print and internet publishing software located in the Research Park at the University of Illinois. He is a former First Assistant Secretary in the Department of the Prime Minister and Cabinet and Director of the Office of Multicultural Affairs in the Australian Federal Government. His most recent books are edited collections: *The Future of the Book in the Digital Age* (Oxford: Chandos, 2006) and *The Future of the Academic Journal* (Oxford: Chandos, 2009). *http://wwcope.com*

Mary Kalantzis has been Dean of the College of Education at the University of Illinois, Urbana-Champaign, since 2006. Before then she was Dean of the Faculty of Education, Language and Community Services at RMIT University in Melbourne, and President of the Australian Council of Deans of Education. With Bill Cope she is co-author or editor of: *The Powers of Literacy* (University of Pittsburg Press, 1993); *Multiliteracies: Literacy Learning and the Design of Social Futures* (Routledge, 2000); *New Learning: Elements of a Science of Education* (Cambridge University Press, 2008); and *Ubiquitous Learning* (University of Illinois Press, 2009). *http://marykalantzis.com*

Liam Magee is a Research Fellow at the Global Cities Research Institute, RMIT University, Melbourne. His research interests include the philosophy of technology, social research methods, and questions of knowledge representation and reasoning inherent in the semantic web. He is currently involved in a multi-disciplinary project exploring the application of semantic technologies to organisational reporting on sustainability.

Contributors

Joseph M. Firestone is Managing Director and CEO of the Knowledge Management Consortium International (KMCI), and Director and co-Instructor of KMCI's CKIM Certificate Program, as well as Director of KMCI's synchronous, real-time Distance Learning Program. He is also CKO of Executive Information Systems, Inc., a knowledge and information management consultancy.

Joe is author or co-author of more than 500 articles, blog posts, white papers and reports on knowledge management, policy analysis, political science, information technology (distributed knowledge management systems, enterprise knowledge portals, web, enterprise and KM 2.0), adaptive scorecards, risk intelligence, social science methodology and psychometrics. He has also written several books and papers: *Knowledge Management and Risk Management: A Business Fable* (Ark Group, 2008); *Risk Intelligence Metrics: An Adaptive Metrics Center Industry Report* (Wilmington, DE: KMCI Online Press, 2006); *Enterprise Information Portals and Knowledge Management* (Burlington, MA: KMCI Press/Butterworth-Heinemann, 2003); *Key Issues in the New Knowledge Management* (Burlington, MA: KMCI Press/Butterworth-Heinemann, 2003); and *Excerpt # 1 from The Open Enterprise* (Wilmington, DE: KMCI Online Press, 2003); and co-edited 'Has Knowledge Management Been Done', special issue of *The Learning Organization: An International Journal*, 12, no. 2, April, 2005. Joe developed the websites *http://www.dkms.com*, *http://www.kmci.org* and *http://www.adaptivemetricscenter.com*, and the blog 'All Life is Problem Solving' at *http://radio.weblogs.com/0135950* and *http://www.kmci.org/alllifeisproblemsolving*. He has taught political science at graduate and undergraduate levels; he has a BA from Cornell University in government, and MA and PhD degrees in comparative politics and international relations from Michigan State University.

William (Bill) Hall began university in 1957 with a major in physics and subsequently transitioned to biology through biophysics (neurophysiology). As a biologist, Bill's first interests were in ecosystems and the early evolution of life. His PhD in evolutionary biology (Harvard, 1973) focused on systematics and the evolution and roles of genetic systems in species formation. He also spent two postdoctoral years studying epistemology and scientific revolutions. His physics and biophysics background exposed him to early generation computers.

When he left academia in 1981, Bill purchased his first personal computer, and was fascinated from the outset by the rapid evolution of computers and how these new cognitive tools would change humanity. Between 1981 and 1989 Bill was employed in computer literacy, software and banking industries, and since 1990 until his retirement in 2007 he worked in the defence industry for a major engineering project management company in various documentation and knowledge management roles throughout the life-cycle of Australia's largest defence contract.

In 2001 Bill started writing a book on technological revolutions in the coevolution of human cognition and tools for extending cognition, but could not make sense of the impacts of cognitive technology (e.g. computing) on social and organisational aspects of cognition. He felt there was a need to rethink organisation theory and the theory of organisational knowledge. To research this problem, in 2002 he returned part time to an academic research environment with an honorary fellowship in Monash University's Knowledge Management Lab in the Faculty of Information Technology. In 2005 he moved to the University of Melbourne as (Hon.) National Fellow in the Australian Centre for Science, Innovation and Society, where he is also associated with the eScholarship Research Centre and the Engineering Learning Unit. In this last role Bill gives occasional guest lectures on engineering knowledge management.

Bill's formal publications range from cytogenetics and evolutionary biology (where Cytogenetic and Genome Research has just published Bill's 35-year retrospective review of around 100 papers by others following on from his PhD thesis) through practical knowledge management in the engineering environment and the theory of living systems, organisations and organisational knowledge management. Understanding and solving socio-technical problems and issues relating to the production and use of scientific and technical knowledge has remained a core thread of his long career within and outside the academic environment.

Gavan McCarthy is a Senior Research Fellow and Director of the eScholarship Research Centre at the University of Melbourne. The position of Director was created in 2007 and builds on McCarthy's previous academic work as part of the Department of History and Philosophy of Science, first with the Australian Science Archives Project (ASAP; 1985–1999), and then with the Australian Science and Technology. During this time he has been at the forefront of the development of national information services and infrastructure to support the history of Australian science, technology, medicine and engineering through the use of the emerging digital technologies.

McCarthy is noted in Australia and overseas for his innovative and research-driven approach to the challenges posed by digital technologies for the support of scholarship and sustainable knowledge. In 1995 his work was recognised internationally, and he has since established a number of enduring collaborative partnerships, the link with Imperial College London being foremost. From 2002 until 2007 he worked as a consultant for the International Atomic Energy Agency (IAEA), where he developed a new conceptual approach to the immensely problematic issue of the long-term management of information about radioactive waste. This same epistemic approach to sustainable information infrastructure has led to many successful ARC projects either as a technical partner or more recently as a chief investigator. McCarthy was among the first humanities scholars to receive ARC funding to support information infrastructure development (1992–1994), and has been consistently successful in the years since. The most publicly successful of these projects was the collaborative partnership with the Australian National University (2004–2006) to transform the *Australian Dictionary of Biography* into an online research resource of world stature.

Richard Vines is Honorary Research Fellow at the eScholarship Research Centre structurally located within the library at the University of Melbourne in Australia. He has worked across a wide range of industries encompassing research and development, community services, wood and forest products, agribusiness, and environmental and international briefing program management. From 2000 until 2004 he was Consultant/Client Services Manager to AusIndustry and the Australian Printing Industries Association within the Enhanced Printing Industries Competitiveness Scheme. For Vines, this experience prised open some deep philosophical and practical questions about print and electronic convergence, some of which are explored in this book.

Subsequent to this Vines consulted and published on aspects of digital media convergence for a number of different clients. In 2008 he helped establish a small advocacy group within the Victorian Council of Social Service in order to focus attention on the problems of media convergence in the Victorian community services sector. Flowing from this advocacy work, the Victorian Office for the Community Sector has commissioned a number of research projects which, in principle, have the potential to lay a foundation for state and national reforms associated with burden reduction, service enhancement and coordination, records, archival and knowledge management practices.

Changing knowledge systems in the era of the social web

Bill Cope and Mary Kalantzis

From print to digital text

To a greater extent than is often acknowledged, modern knowledge is a creature of the society of the printing press. Until the turn of the twenty-first century, print was the medium of scholarly communication. It was the source of book learning. Then, quite suddenly at the turn of the twenty-first century, digital text began to displace print as the primary means of access to the knowledge of academicians, and as the dominant medium for the delivery of instructional content. This book explores some of the consequences of this change. To what extent do digital technologies of representation and communication reproduce the knowledge systems of the half-millennium-long history of the modern university? Or do they disrupt and transform them?

To answer these questions, this book will explore key aspects of contemporary transformations, not just in the textual forms of digital representation, but also in the emerging social forms that digitisation reflects, affords and supports. This we call the 'social web', a term we use to describe the kinds of relationships to knowledge and culture that are emerging in the era of pervasively interconnected computing.

The first printed book, Gutenberg's 1452 Bible, had no title page, no contents page, no page numbering. Extant copies show the signs of ecclesiastical, manuscript culture—the beautifully illuminated marginalia which, until the era of print, gave the written word an aura of authority that raised it above the spoken word of everyday experience. It took another 50 years for the textual architecture of the printed word to take its modern form and, with it, new forms of textual authority.

By 1500, the end of the period of 'incunabula', eight million books had been printed. It was not until then that printed text came to be marked by the structures of graduated type and spatial page design, and the information hierarchies of chapter headings, section breaks and subheadings. Navigational devices were added in the form of tables of contents and running heads. Alphabetically ordered indexes were added. And the text was divided into uniform and easily discoverable units by means of the most under-rated and revolutionary of all modern information technologies—the page number (Eisenstein 1979; Febvre and Martin 1976).

These textual forms became the ground for representations of knowledge in its characteristically modern form. Petrus Ramus, a professor at the University of Paris in the mid sixteenth century, could be regarded as the inventor of the modern textbook, laboriously laying out in print the content of what students were to learn by way of a sectionalised knowledge taxonomy. There were 1,100 editions of Petrus Ramus's texts published between 1550 and 1650. Walter Ong credits Ramus with no intellectual originality in the content of the texts, but with an ingenious sense for the emerging epistemic order in which knowledge was analytically laid out and spatially ordered, replacing the authority and pedagogy of rhetoric and dialogue with the atomistically compartmentalised and formally schematised knowledge of modern academe (Ong 1958).

Also characteristic of the textual forms of the emerging print culture was the premium it placed on accuracy, from the standardisation of spelling in vernacular languages, to the processes of editing, proofing and correction. Even after printing, errata were used to correct the text, and text was further corrected from edition to edition—a logic intrinsic to the fastidiousness for detail and empirical verity which marked the emerging lifeworlds of the thinkers and teachers of the early modern academy.

Not merely textual, printed texts came to be located in an intertextual universe of cross-referencing. The announcement of author and title did not just mark the beginning of a work. It situated that work and its author in a universe of other texts and authors, and marked this with the emerging conventions of librarianship, citation and bibliography. Moving away from the rhetorical tradition, authors used footnotes and referencing not only as a sign of the erudition on which authoritative text was necessarily grounded, but also to distinguish the author's distinctive and ostensibly original voice from those of the textual authorities or research data on which they were relying (Grafton 1997).

No longer simply a matter of identification of authorial voice, the new social conventions of authorship became the boundary markers of private intellectual property, the copyright of authors as originators of ideas being embodied in specific forms of words. Knowledge as intellectual property expressed in written text, owned by the individual author and alienable as a commodity, was to be found in incipient forms as early as the fifteenth-century in Venice (Rose 1993).

This regime of textual knowledge became a key foundation of the modern university, in a clear break from its medieval monastic origins. It was both a symptom and an enabler in the development of characteristically modern ways of attributing human origins to ideas and of ascribing authority to these ideas.

What is new and not new about the emerging regime of digitised text? Widespread digitisation of parts of the text production process began in the 1970s with phototypesetters driven by rudimentary word-processing programs (Cope 2001). During the 1980s and 1990s, word processing and desktop publishing became near-universal tools of authorship. Academics who had previously handwritten their articles, books and teaching notes, passing them on to typists, started to spend a good part of their working days keyboarding digital text. The logic of their work, however, remained to a large degree within the Gutenberg orbit, marking up the information architectures of their text in the typographic mode, designed to be printed or pseudo-printed in the form of PDF (Portable Document Format) digital replicas of the printed page. Even at the end of the first decade of the twenty-first century, most academic publishing still had not yet escaped the typographic practices of the Gutenberg era, with its unlinear and at times frustratingly manual processes of writing in a word processor, transfer to a desktop publishing program then freezing the typeset text in a print-lookalike page.

Three decades into the digitisation process, we may well still be in an era of what Jean-Claude Guédon calls 'digital incunabula', in which the full potentialities of digital text have barely been explored, let alone exploited (Guédon 2001). Information is locked up in PDFs, which are designed for printing out rather than the functionalities of search, access and reproduction offered by more advanced digitisation technologies. Such texts-for-print are not marked up by structure and semantics, so even the best search mechanisms offer little more than what can be achieved through word collocation algorithms, far less adequate even in some crucial respects than the traditions of indexing and cataloguing from the era of print.

Moreover, some things which are purported to be new about digital text are not so new at all. For all its apparent novelty, 'hypertext' is nothing other than a version of the process of referencing to be found in the tradition of page numbering and catalogue listing established over the past five centuries. What is the link other than a way of making the same old distinction of individual authorship, delineating the boundaries between one piece of intellectual property and the next, and a sign of deference to the authorities on which a text is based?

As for the much-vaunted novelty of the 'virtual', what more is the digital than a reincarnation of the modes of representation of distant people, places and objects that made books so alluring from the moment they became cheaply and widely accessible? Also, books and their distribution systems, no less than today's networked communities, allowed the creation of dispersed communities of expertise, mediated by local interlocutors in the form of pedagogues who gave specialised classes (Cope and Kalantzis 2004).

Some things about the world of digital communications, however, may turn out to be very different from the world of printed text. Just how different remains to be seen, and the full impact on the social processes of knowledge making may take decades to become clear. Or it may happen sooner. We're thinking it might happen sooner.

Several features of the new communications environment stand out. One is a change to the economies of cultural and epistemic scale. While something like 1,000 copies need to be sold to make a print run viable, there is no difference in the cost of one person or 1,000 reading a web page, or the per-copy production cost of a print-on-demand book. The immediate consequence is that the amount of published and accessible content is rapidly growing and the average number of copies accessed of each academic work is declining (Waters 2004). These are ideal conditions for the development of ever more finely grained areas of knowledge, cultural perspectives and localised applications of knowledge. So significant is this change that knowledge itself may change. What is the enduring validity of universal and universalising perspectives? How do they accommodate the particular? How does the local connect with the global? Furthermore, with the development of Unicode and machine translation, scholarly communication beyond the local may not for much longer have to be expressed in the language of global English, and if it is, it is in the specialised discourses of academic technicality less dependent for their aura of reliability on the 'good style' of native English speakers.

Another key feature is the intrinsic multimodality of the new media. The elementary modular unit of text manufacture in the Gutenberg (and then ASCII) era was the character. Digital texts make written words and images of the same stuff, pixels, and sound of the same stuff as pixels—the zeros and ones of semiconductor circuitry. In everyday life, we have experienced this radical conflation of modes throughout the media, from illustrated books and journals (previously, lithographic processes as a simple matter of technical convenience meant that images were mostly placed on pages of their own), to video, to the internet. Academe, however, has stayed steadfastly wedded to text, with the increasing incursion of diagrams and images into the text (Kress 2003). Will the new media destablise the traditional textual forms of book, article, essay, paper and thesis? In what other ways might knowledge be represented today, and particularly in the areas of the sciences, the arts (Martin and Booth 2007) and design?

Also significant is what we call a shift in the balance of textual agency between the author and reader (Kalantzis 2006b; Kalantzis and Cope 2008). Here are some examples and symptoms of this change. Whereas print encyclopedias provided us with definitive knowledge constructed by experts, Wikipedia is constructed, reviewed and editable by readers and includes parallel argumentation by reader-editors about the 'objectivity' of each entry. Whereas a book was resistant to annotation (the size of the margins and a respect for its next reader), new reading devices and formats encourage annotation in which the reading text is also a (re)writing text. Whereas the diary was a space for time-sequenced private reflection, the blog is a place for personal voice, which invites public dialogue on personal feelings. Whereas a handwritten or typed page of text could only practically be the work of a single creator, 'changes tracking', version control and web document creation such as Google Docs make multi-author writing easy and collaborative authorship roles clear. Whereas novels and TV soaps had us engaging vicariously with characters in the narratives they presented to us, video games make us central characters in the story where we can influence its outcomes. Whereas broadcast TV had us all watching a handful of television channels, digital TV has us choosing one channel from among thousands, or interactive TV in which we select our own angles on a sports broadcast, or make our own video and post it to YouTube or the web. Whereas broadcast radio gave listeners a programmed playlist, every iPod user creates their own playlist (Kalantzis 2006a).

We call this rebalancing of agency, this blurring of the boundaries between authors (and their authority) and readers (and their reverence), 'the social web'. If print limited the scope for dialogue, the electronic communications web opens up new conversational possibilities.

Each of these new media is reminiscent of the old. In fact, we have eased ourselves into the digital world by using old media metaphors—creating documents or files and putting them away in folders on our desktops. We want to feel as though the new media are like the old. In some respects they are, but in other respects they are proving to be quite different.

Things have changed in an homologous fashion in the broader social relations of representation. Audiences have become users. Readers, listeners and viewers are invited to talk back to the extent that they have become media co-designers themselves. The division of labour between the authors of culture or creators of knowledge and their users has been blurred. The direction of knowledge flows is changing. In fact, the flows are now multifarious and in many directions. Users are also creators, and creators are users. Epistemic authority is more contingent, conditional and provisional—grounded in statements of 'may' rather than 'is'. They are more open to contestation and to critical reading on the basis of personal experience and voice. Knowledge and culture, as a consequence, become more fluid.

This is what we mean by a shift in the balance of agency, from a society of command and compliance to a society of reflexive co-construction. It might be that the workers are now creating bigger profits for the bosses, that neoliberalism 'naturally' exacerbates disparities in social power, and that proclamations of diversity do no more than put a positive gloss on inequality. The social outcomes, indeed, may at times be disappointingly unchanged or the relativities even deteriorating. What has changed is the way these outcomes are achieved. Control by people in positional or epistemic authority has become internalised self-control; compliance is self-imposed. New media are one part of this wider equation. The move may be primarily a social one, but the technology has provided new affordances. Social aspiration has helped us conceive uses for available technologies even beyond the imaginings of their inventors.

Where does this leave the traditional sources of epistemic authority and, in particular, academic research? What is the status of Wikipedia, written by tens of thousands of unnamed persons who may or may not have passed the credentialing hurdles of higher education, without the authority of individual expert voice or institutional credentials? What is the status of an academic's blog? How do we reference mini-lectures on YouTube, and measure the validity of one YouTube video against the next or a refereed article? How do we assess practice-based and multimodal theses, publications and exhibitions?

The means of production of meaning in the social web are also deceptively different from what has preceded. This is the primary focus of this book, along with a critical exploration of possible trends. Eschewing the Gutenberg lookalikes of word processing, desktop publishing and postscript files is a new tradition of semantic and structural markup (as opposed to visual markup, for one rendering). This tradition originated in the IBM labs of the 1960s as Standard Generalised Markup Language, but rose to widespread prominence with Berners-Lee's Hypertext Markup Language (HTML) in the early 1990s, and subsequent refinement as Extensible Markup Language (XML) and more recently the Resource Definition Framework (RDF) and Ontology Web Language (OWL), these being the key features in the technical agenda of the 'semantic web'. More broadly, however, these foundational technologies triggered a slow shift from typographic to semantic markup or a set of principles and practices that might be called 'semantic publishing'. The specifics of the semantic web and the generalities of 'semantic publishing' are the primary concerns of this book.

These developments sit within the context of second generation internet development, dubbed Web 2.0 in 2005 by technical publisher Tim O'Reilly, and is manifest in widespread application web-based social networking technologies including wikis, weblogs, podcasts and syndication feeds (O'Reilly 2005). In the words of the un-named author or authors of the Wikipedia Web 2.0 entry, it is also a 'social phenomenon embracing an approach to generating and distributing Web content itself, characterized by open communication, decentralization of authority, [and] freedom to share and re-use'.

This book will explore the relationships between the emerging world of semantic publishing, and its consequences for knowledge work in universities.

Distributed knowledge systems: the changing role of the university

Universities today face significant challenges to their historical role as producers of socially privileged knowledge. More knowledge is being produced by corporations than was the case in the past. More knowledge is being produced in the traditional broadcast media. More knowledge is being produced in the networked interstices of the social web, where knowing amateurs mix with academic professionals, in many places without distinction of rank. In these places, the logics and logistics of knowledge production are disruptive of the traditional values of the university—the for-profit, protected knowledge of the corporation; the multimodal knowledge of audiovisual media; and the 'wisdom of the crowd', which ranks knowledge and makes it discoverable through the internet according to its popularity.

The new, digital media raise fundamental questions for the university. How can it connect with the shifting sites and modes of knowledge production? How can it stay relevant? Are its traditional knowledge-making systems in need of renovation? What makes academic knowledge valid and reliable, and how can its epistemic virtues be strengthened to meet the challenges of our times? How can the university meet the challenges of the new media in order to renovate the disclosure and dissemination systems of scholarly publishing? How can the university connect with the emerging and dynamic sources of new knowledge formation outside its traditional boundaries?

To a greater extent than is frequently acknowledged, the rituals and forms of print publishing have been integral to the modern republic of humanistic and scientific knowledge. Publication is contingent on peer review, representing a point of disclosure in which other scientists can replicate findings or verify sources. Until publication, academic knowledge is without status, unassimilable into the body of knowledge that is the discipline and without teachable value. Publication is an integral part of the academic knowledge system (Cope and Phillips 2009).

Pre-publication, peer review as a method of scientific knowledge validation began to evolve from the seventeenth century, with Oldberg's editorship of the Philosophical Transactions of the Royal Society (Biagioli 2002; Guédon 2001; Peters 2007; Willinsky 2006). Post-publication, bibliometrics or citation analysis emerged as a measure of ranking the value of a published piece. The more people who cited an author and their text, the more influential that person and their work must have been on the discipline. This thinking was refined in the work of Eugene Garfield and his Institute for Scientific Information.

The system of academic publishing, however, had reached a now well-documented crisis point at the beginning of the twenty-first century (Cope and Kalantzis 2009b). The bulk of academic journal and book publishing was still dominated by commercial publishers producing to the economies and production logics of print—even their electronic versions were by and large in print-reproduction PDF form. The commercial publishers came under increasing fire for the slowness of their publication processes contrasted with the immediacy of the web, the relative closure of their networks of editorial control contrasted with the more democratic open-ness of the web, but most importantly for the rapidly increasing cost of journal subscriptions and books contrasted to the free content on the web (Bergman 2006; Peters 2007; Stanley 2007; Willinsky 2006). The background to this growing critique was one of the most remarkable phenomena of the evolving world of the internet—freely accessible intellectual property in the form of software code (Raymond 2001; Stallman 2002; Williams 2002), content tagged with Creative Commons licences (Benkler 2006; Lessig 1999, 2001, 2004) and, more specific to the case of academic knowledge, the rise of open access journals (Bergman 2006; Peters 2007; Willinsky 2006).

These developments in an economic domain that Benkler calls 'social production' are not, however, without their own difficulties. John Willinsky speaks lyrically of a return to the days when authors worked beside printers to produce their books (Willinsky 2006). However, academics do not have all the skills or resources of publishers. Nor is playing amateur publisher necessarily the best use of their time. The new economy of social production, moreover, is removing the economic basis for publishing as a form of employment and as a way of helping fund professional associations and research centres which have historically gained revenue from the sale of periodicals and books. Tens of thousands of people used to work for encyclopedia publishers, even if some of the jobs, such as that of the proverbial door-to-door salesperson, were less than ideal. Everybody who writes for Wikipedia has to have another source of income to sustain themselves. What would happen to the significantly sized global scholarly publishing industry if academics assumed collective and universal responsibility for self-publishing?

Open access, moreover, does not necessarily reduce the points of closure in academic publishing its English language and developed world bias; the self-replicating logic which gives visibility to established journals and the insider networks that support them; its bias to the natural sciences at the expense of the social sciences and humanities; its valuing of journal articles over books; the intrinsic lack of rigour of most refereeing, without reference to explicit criteria for valid knowledge; and its logic of ranking in which academic popularity ranks ahead of academic quality, and self- and negative citation carries the same weight as positive external citation (Cope and Kalantzis 2009b; Peters 2007).

The internet in its initial forms, in fact, perpetuates many of these deficiencies. Google is the brainchild of the son of a professor who translated Garfield's citation logic into the page rank algorithm which weights a page according to its 'backward links', or the people who have 'cited' that page by linking to it. When is such a process unhelpful populism, mob rule even, in the newly democratised republic of knowledge? And what do we make of a knowledge system in which even the wisdom of the crowd can be trumped by the wisdom of the sponsored link?

In 1965 J.C.R. Linklider wrote of the deficiencies of the book as a source of knowledge, and imagined a future of 'procognitive systems' in the year 2000 (Linklider 1965). He was anticipating a completely new knowledge system. That system is not with us yet. We are still in the era of digital incunabula.

In semantic publishing technologies, however, we see possibilities not yet realised, in which all the world's knowledge is marked up within developing disciplinary discourses and meaningfully accessible. In the social web we can gain an inkling of dialogical processes in which academics, professionals and amateurs may advance knowledge more rapidly, take greater intellectual risks, and develop more creatively divergent and globally distributed bodies of knowledge and theoretical paradigms than was possible in the slower and more centralised knowledge production systems of print publishing.

If it is the role of the university to produce deeper, broader and more reliable knowledge than is possible in everyday, casual experience, what do we need to do to extend this tradition rather than to surrender to populism? What needs to be done about the knowledge validation systems of peer review and the dissemination systems of academic publishing? These are fundamental questions at this transitionary moment. Their answers will not just involve new publishing processes. They will entail the creation of new systems of knowledge production, validation and distribution. These will be built on the semantic publishing infrastructures we explore in this book.

About this book

This book starts with an analysis of the semantic web as one vision for the future of textual work in the era of the internet. It explores the difficulties and limitations of this vision, then proposes a more modest agenda for what we define as 'semantic publishing'. The semantic publishing agenda has two major aspects. The first is a paradigmatic shift from typographic markup in which textual architectures are rendered visually, to functional markup in which the architectonics of text are explicitly marked in the text formation process. The second is a supplementary layer of semantic meaning added to the flow of text, in which formalised knowledge schemas apply semantic tags that supplement the text in order to support more reliable discovery, data mining, machine-assisted analysis and machine translation.

Part 1 introduces the semantic web, and situates this in the context of alternative disciplinary perspectives on the nature of meaning itself. Part 2 examines the ways in which the digitisation of text impacts on the representation of knowledge. Part 3 explores formal knowledge systems in general, and the processes by means of which semantic publishing ontologies represent knowledge. Part 4 analyses the ways in which this schematising work can be translated into knowledge and textual practices, and in particular addresses the question of how schemas referring to overlapping aspects of knowledge might be brought into productive inter-relation.

By way of brief background, this book has developed at the confluence of four research endeavours. The first has been research over a fifteen-year period into the changing communications environment, and the consequences of these changes for literacy pedagogy (Cope and Kalantzis 2000, 2009a; Kalantzis and Cope 2008). The second is a substantial body of research undertaken by Common Ground Publishing in association with RMIT University in Melbourne, Australia, for the Australian Department of Industry in 2000–2003, 'Creator to Consumer in a Digital Age: Book Production in Transition'. This research has culminated in the production of a series of ten research reports in book format examining changing technologies, markets and human skills in the publishing supply chain (C-2-C Project 2001–2003). This was followed by a research project funded by the Australian Research Council, RMIT University, and Fuji-Xerox on the nature of semantic publishing and the future of the semantic web.

The third research endeavour is the Common Ground Markup Language project commenced by Common Ground in 2000 with the support of an AusIndustry Research and Development grant. This has continued in the form of the CGMeaning semantic publishing schema-making and dictionary building space, created in the Common Ground engineering department, now located in the Research Park at the University of Illinois. Using its semantic publishing technologies, Common Ground now publishes several thousand peer-reviewed articles per year. Most recently, we have commenced a fourth stream of research, extending and applying these technologies for writing in educational contexts, supported by research and development projects funded by the US Department of Education.

If this book speaks strangely at times, it is because it speaks in several, at times incongruent, voices based on these varied sources of interest, concern and inspiration. And if its agenda seems peculiar, it is because it crosses backwards and forwards between philosophical-historical reflection and a call to techno-social action.

References

Benkler, Y. 2006. *The Wealth of Networks: How Social Production Transforms Markets and Freedom*. New Haven: Yale University Press.

Bergman, S.S. 2006. 'The Scholarly Communication Movement: Highlights and Recent Developments', *Collection Building* 25, pp. 108–28.

Biagioli, M. 2002. 'From Book Censorship to Academic Peer Review', *Emergences: Journal for the Study of Media & Composite Cultures* 12, pp. 11–45.

C-2-C Project. 2001–2003. 'Creator to Consumer in a Digital Age: Book Production in Transition: A Research Project Investigating Future Technologies, Future Markets and Future Skills in the Book Production and Publishing Supply Chain'. Melbourne: Common Ground.

Cope, B. 2001. 'New Ways with Words: Print and Etext Convergence'. In B. Cope and D. Kalantzis (eds), *Print and Electronic Text Convergence: Technology Drivers Across the Book Production Supply Chain, from Creator to Consumer*, C-2-C Project book 2.1. Melbourne: Common Ground, pp. 1–15.

Cope, B. and M. Kalantzis. 2000. *Multiliteracies: Literacy Learning and the Design of Social Futures*. London: Routledge.

—. 2004. 'Text-Made Text', *E-Learning* 1, pp. 198–282.

—. 2009a. '"Multiliteracies": New Literacies, New Learning', *Pedagogies: An International Journal* 4, pp. 164–95.

—. 2009b. 'Signs of Epistemic Disruption: Transformations in the Knowledge System of the Academic Journal', *First Monday* 14(4), 6 April.

Cope, B. and A. Phillips. 2009. *The Future of the Academic Journal*. Oxford: Chandos.

Eisenstein, E.L. 1979. *The Printing Press as an Agent of Change: Communications and Cultural Transformation in Early-Modern Europe*. Cambridge, UK: Cambridge University Press.

Febvre, L. and H.-J. Martin. 1976. *The Coming of the Book*. London: Verso.

Grafton, A. 1997. *The Footnote: A Curious History*. London: Faber and Faber.

Guédon, J.-C. 2001. *In Oldenburg's Long Shadow: Librarians, Research Scientists, Publishers, and the Control of Scientific Publishing*, conference proceedings. Washington, DC: Association of Research Libraries.

Kalantzis, M. 2006a. 'Changing Subjectivities, New Learning', *Pedagogies: An International Journal* 1, pp. 7–12.

—. 2006b. 'Elements of a Science of Education', *Australian Educational Researcher* 33, pp. 15–42.

Kalantzis, M. and B. Cope. 2008. *New Learning: Elements of a Science of Education*. Cambridge, UK: Cambridge University Press.

Kress, G. 2003. *Literacy in the New Media Age*. London: Routledge.

Lessig, L. 1999. *Code and Other Laws of Cyberspace*. New York: Basic Books.

—. 2001. *The Future of Ideas: The Fate of the Commons in a Connected World*. New York: Random House.

—. 2004. *Free Culture*. New York: Penguin Press.

Linklider, J.C.R. 1965. *Libraries of the Future*. Cambridge, MA: MIT Press.

Martin, E. and J. Booth. 2007. *Art-Based Research: A Proper Thesis?* Melbourne: Common Ground.

O'Reilly, T. 2005. 'What Is Web 2.0? Design Patterns and Business Models for the Next Generation of Software', *http://oreilly.com/web2/archive/what-is-web-20.html* (accessed 19 July 2010).

Ong, W.J. 1958. *Ramus, Method and the Decay of Dialogue*. Cambridge, MA: Harvard University Press.

Peters, M.A. 2007. *Knowledge Economy, Development and the Future of Higher Education*. Rotterdam: Sense Publishers.

Raymond, E. 2001. *The Cathedral and the Bazaar: Musings on Linux and Open Source by an Accidental Revolutionary*. Sebastapol, CA: O'Reilly.

Rose, M. 1993. *Authors and Owners: The Invention of Copyright*. Cambridge, MA: Harvard University Press.

Stallman, R. 2002. *Free Software, Free Society*. Boston, MA: GNU Press.

Stanley, C.A. 2007. 'When Counter Narratives Meet Master Narratives in the Journal Editorial-Review Process', *Educational Researcher* 36, pp. 14–24.

Waters, L. 2004. *Enemies of Promise: Publishing, Perishing and the Eclipse of Scholarship*. Chicago, IL: Prickly Paradigm Press.

Williams, S. 2002. *Free as in Freedom: Richard Stallman's Crusade for Free Software*. Sebastapol, CA: O'Reilly.

Willinsky, J. 2006. *The Access Principle: The Case for Open Research and Scholarship*. Cambridge, MA: MIT Press.

2

Frameworks for knowledge representation

Liam Magee

An ontology is an explicit specification of a conceptualization (Gruber 1993, p. 199).

Moreover, I have always disliked the word 'ontology' (Hacking 2002, p. 1).

This chapter, along with several of those that follow, is directed towards the problem of representation and translation across knowledge systems and frameworks, with a particular focus on those used in the emerging world of the semantic web. Knowledge systems are all too frequently characterised in essentialist terms—as though, as the etymology of 'data' would suggest, they are merely the housing of neutral empirical givens. In this book we maintain, on the contrary, that systems always carry with them the assumptions of cultures that design and use them—cultures that are, in the very broadest sense, responsible for them. This is the case for knowledge systems in general, as well as the specifics of what has come to be called the 'semantic web', and the ontologies, schemas, taxonomies and other representations of knowledge it supports. This chapter begins by setting the scene for modern approaches to knowledge representation, constructing a broad historical frame which both inspired and motived these approaches. It then introduces the semantic web, arguably the most significant of these approaches. It describes both the affordances and challenges of the semantic web, and outlines several key concepts, which will be mobilised in later chapters—*semantics*, *ontologies* and *commensurability*. This chapter also outlines some of the claims and interventions this book intends to make about both the semantic web specifically, and knowledge representation, management and use generally.

Before the semantic web is described more formally, it is useful to try to articulate what it is in broad brush strokes. At its most general, it is an encompassing vision which imagines a network of connected, federated and integrated databases (Berners-Lee, Hendler and Lassila 2001). It is motivated by the desire to simplify the integration of information from the myriad variety of existing data sources and formats on the web. In the language of the semantic web these structured data sets are termed *ontologies*, picking up on the analogy with philosophical ontology—how a region of the world is explicitly conceptualised in a series of codified commitments (Gruber 1993). Semantic web ontologies use formal languages—the Resource Definition Framework (RDF) and Ontology Web Language (OWL) to express these commitments (Berners-Lee, Hendler and Lassila 2001).

Ontologies are taken here to be only an exemplary species of the broader genus of knowledge systems—a genus which can be extended to include other types of database models, Extensible Markup Language (XML) schemas, expert systems and electronic classification systems generally. So while the focus is often directed towards semantic web ontologies, since they are not yet as commonly used in organisations as other types of systems, casting a broader net aims to extend the generality of the research findings without loss of semantic specificity. As the argument goes on to show, moreover, even the different formal properties of rival system types— semantic web ontologies compared with older database information models, for instance—can involve important assumptions of a philosophical ontological kind as well.

While shared and standardised ontologies may simplify the job of system integrators connecting data services, without explicit acknowledgement of their epistemological assumptions and conditions—how it is that systems claim to know what they know—there will remain significant impediments to the realisation of the semantic web. By adopting the standpoint that knowledge is a culturally constructed and negotiated process, this book aims to find some heuristic guidelines for finding points of similarity and difference in the systems which codify knowledge. But first, it is helpful to understand something of the background against which the desire to codify, organise and construct baroque informatic systems arose to begin with.

Putting things in order

In *The Order of Things*, Foucault (1970) writes of the 'great tables of the seventeenth and eighteenth centuries, when in the disciplines of biology, economics and philology the raw phenomena of experience was classified, categorised, organised and labeled'. At the start of the twenty-first century, when the classificatory technologies of the file system, spreadsheet, database and internet search engine have superseded those of the ruler and pencil, these descriptions of 'great tables' and their accompanying heroic taxonomic enterprises can seem quaint and anachronistic. The experience of lists, tables, hierarchical trees and networks and other informational structures as organisational aids is now unremarkable, quotidian, a tacit quality of a modern sensibility, reflected in the acquired facility to navigate everything from baroque scientific taxonomies and global standards to organisational directories and personalised databases. Consumers of electronic devices invest heavily in their repositories of music, books, photos and film, marking individual entries with qualifications of genre, commentary, ratings, biographical snippets and a host of other conceptual distinctions and demarcations. Business, governments and other organisations are necessarily technocratic taxonomists on a grand scale, investing in and managing large knowledge bases, processes and infrastructure. Such fervent activity has even inspired the emergence of a dedicated industry and academic discipline—that of knowledge management. Biology, one of the fields of scientific enterprise Foucault himself analyses, features ever-expanding databases of proteins, genomes, diseases and other biological entities, so vast in size that any single human attempt to review the data would fail by orders of magnitude (Arunguren 2005). It is hard therefore to share Foucault's wonder at the ambition and scope of classical scholarship, without making an equally wondrously empathic leap back into the past. A modern-day reaction might instead regard these old classificatory systems as historical curiosities; at most, as experimental preludes, for better or worse, to the immense contemporary and global industries which serve an insatiable demand for information.

Yet our current age is also heir to the efforts of those classical scholars. Since Leibniz, the development of symbolic systems to represent knowledge has been a recurring motif of philosophy and, later, of other more applied disciplinary studies. From his universal symbolism, to Kant's categories, to Frege's descriptions of a formal logic, to the development of logical positivism in the 1920s, to, finally, the recent developments of the relational database, artificial intelligence and the semantic web, it is possible to trace a distinct and particular epistemological tradition. That tradition has sought to develop increasingly refined formal languages to represent statements about the world unambiguously. Rigorous empiricism—recording only observable facts—would, when coupled with an automatic deductive procedure based on a logical formalism, simplify the production of all knowledge to a series of mechanical acts. In Leibniz's famous dictum, once this point had been reached even philosophers would be able to settle arguments by appealing to machination: 'Let us calculate!' (Lenzen 2004).

There have been at least two notable impediments to the realisation of this vision up until the end of the twentieth century. The first is the development of feasible logic systems and technical implementations systems for representing these concepts. This has been the subject of considerable research and application in artificial intelligence, knowledge representation and broader information technology over the last 50 years. Such research, and the practical consequences of it, have produced in turn a series of pivotal technologies for the emergence of what Castells (1996) terms the 'Network Society': the relational database—the current paradigmatic means for storing structured organisational information; the spreadsheet—a metaphor which pervades the construction of tabular data in the personal computing era; XML—a near-ubiquitous format for describing and transmitting data on the internet; and semantic web ontologies, the emerging standardised mechanism for representing knowledge on the internet.

The second impediment is development of consensual arrangements of concepts against which facts can be faithfully recorded. As the many successful cases of technical standards ratified by the ISO and other bodies show, there has been considerable success in efforts to develop standards. However, unlike the production of logical systems and implementations, consensus over such arrangements is frequently a brittle social dynamic, reliant on what (Davidson 2006) terms 'the principle of charity' adopted between heterogenous cultures and actors, as they seek to exchange meaning with each other.

The development of computational classification systems and standards has experienced at least partial success because they facilitate a distinctly modern taxonomic impulse—an apparently unceasing desire to order, organise, catalogue, coordinate and control. What makes this desire distinctively modern? In response it could be argued, in a deflationary fashion, that the urge to put things in order is inherent in human language—nouns, and names particularly, express implicit taxonomies. However, natural languages are taxed with many functions other than that of articulating some state of affairs in the world—they must also issue imperatives, pose interrogatives, invoke vocatives and generally perform a host of more esoteric speech acts; and even in the case of assertoric utterances, they must also permit statement modulation according to tense, mood, aspect and a range of sociolinguistic inflections. In contrast, artificial formal languages are deliberately designed with both a minimal syntax—how statements can be expressed—and rigorous semantics—how those statements must be interpreted—in order to make electronic taxonomies easily constructible and unambiguously interpretable. These features are not coincidentally related to the rising informational needs of modern institutions, departments, bureaucracies and organisations. Indeed the tendencies of late capitalism suggest a self-reinforcing chain of multiple factors which stimulate this impulse towards order and categorisation: the operational benefits of the 'network externalities' brought about by global communication networks; legal directives towards greater transparency and accountability; competitive pressures towards greater efficiencies; and improved control and regulation of people and objects, effected through ever more fine-grained classificatory structures. These factors both motivate and, in turn, are facilitated by the great affordances of information technology in the post-industrial era.

At the same time, the modernist conception of an organisation as a highly regulated machine-like entity has been challenged by new, postmodern metaphors, which imagine the organisation as open, interconnected, self-reflexive, fluid, relational and networked (Ashkenas et al. 1995; Castells 1996). The organisation is tasked with new, contemporary demands: to be visible, transparent, connected and accountable. It is to be audited regularly and stringently; it must be open to public inspection and accountable to numerous stakeholders—not only its direct constituents or shareholders, but a complex network of those with 'stakes' in organisational governance and performance. It must also deal more directly with its members, constituents, customers, partners, employees, suppliers, regulatory bodies and press organisations, via a host of increasingly immediate, ubiquitous, connected and 'on-demand' technologies. Information is the pivotal part of this equation, the connection between the modernist imperative to control, order and organise, and the postmodern desire to connect what is controlled, both within and between organisational boundaries. Accordingly, the desire to organise large amounts of information has led to interest, funding and prestige to be associated with information technologies, processes and management. These in turn have been seen as central to development of more successful organisations—organisations at any rate capable of greater performativity in a capitalistic environment. The twin development of the modern organisation and information technologies has been mutually reinforcing, to the extent that neither could any longer be imagined without the other. They are both features of a distinct phase of modernity.

Yet, just as these developments show a trend towards ever greater adoption of common, standardised and homogenised technical artefacts—informational and otherwise—they do not preclude an inverse tendency towards greater differentiation, in which various organisational cultures, brought into engagement within a globalised electronic landscape, both recognise and indeed actively produce perspectival differences towards the world they share. Like painters describing a landscape from different angles, these diverse orientations found both the conditions and limitations of the kinds of facts and observations which can be asserted about the world. Accumulating a base of information—a database—enables organisations to retrieve and analyse data rapidly; yet the price of this is a certain rigidity or reification at work in the deployment of concepts used to structure the database. The record of a person in a database, for instance, captures only some facets, properties, attributes and variables about the person—those typically deemed salient for the use of the system. Moreover these properties 'slice' the person in predefined ways, based on assumptions held by the culture responsible for the database. As the system is used over time, as more records are added, and other systems are adapted to fit the particular conceptualisation employed by the system, it becomes increasingly difficult to re-engineer or 'refactor' it. Consequently the conceptualisation becomes reified—appearing naturalised through the resilience to change of the system it is deployed in. Lost, or at least obscured, is the potential for other kinds of descriptions of entities to emerge. Nothing indicates, with the passing of time, that this is only one possible way among many others of 'carving nature at its joints'.

Viewed from the standpoints of either relativism or stark realism, this is either tautologically true or oxymoronically false—*true* if all expressions of facts are regarded as at best a partial and fragmentary glimpse of things as they are; *false* if some objective measure is accepted for why one concept is used instead of others. The objective here is to avoid any concomitant commitments along these metaphysical lines, but rather to recognise that in practice social convention determines a range of intermediate possibilities. To take one example, which is examined in further detail in one of the case studies: electronic documents are cultural objects, which are described in a variety of ways—as official records in records management systems; as collectible items in bibliographic databases; as consumable objects in distribution systems like Amazon; and as complex textual objects in word-processing applications. All of these systems can be said to adopt a different standpoint—a metaphorisation of a different set of concepts and conceptual relations—of documents. Yet, equally, none of these views captures the whole truth of a particular document for its author (the possible difficulties of writing it), or a reader (the interpretive reading of it), or indeed the various features of a document required for many other purposes. Rather they capture the particular 'facticities'—to employ a Foucauldian term—needed to exercise socially instrumented practical functions around documents: to retrieve them, catalogue them, edit them, print and bind them, distribute them, sell them, account for them, and so on. However, the conceptualisations engaged to describe documents for various functions are not at the same time discrete and self-contained bundles of properties or, in philosophical jargon, *qualia*, separate and unrelated to each other. To retain the geometric and spatial metaphor which is used throughout the study, conceptualisations frequently connect at orthogonal conceptual junctions and splices. They may share common concepts and properties—in the same example, books, authors and titles might be common terms across different system conceptualisations—and yet they may stand in different configurations and relations, which more or less line up depending on the context of their translation and use. How to assess this 'more-or-less-ness', the degree of commensurability, between the conceptual configurations operationalised by different systems is then a question that information system 'translators'—system analysts, engineers and programmers—increasingly face in a world where the prolixity of systems and the range of functions performed by them is ever-growing.

Between these opposing trends—towards standardisation, regulation, connectivity and unification on the one hand, and differentiation, customisation and individuation on the other—the promise of knowledge systems for these organisations has only been partially fulfilled. The digitisation of records management, the development of sophisticated data warehousing tools, the agreement on protocols for transmission of data across networks—among other things—has led to vast increases of scale in both the amount of data captured and the level of analysis which can be performed on this data. And yet here, too, in the age of the internet, the quantitative problems—cost and complexity—of communicating meaningful information across organisational boundaries have remained prohibitive, frustrating the aims of these very organisations. The semantic web is a technology platform explicitly designed to overcome the dilemmas of inter-system translation: a set of standards designed to allow translation and migration of data between systems and applications with the minimum of cognitive impedance or dissonance. Conceptual schemes are rendered as 'ontologies', collections of concepts, properties and individual data records, which can be developed using the existing technical infrastructure of the World Wide Web. Even here, however, interpretation, translation, coordination and negotiation of meaning cannot be relegated to the domain of purely technical and engineering considerations. While the systems themselves are technological artefacts, assessment of their commensurability leads from a concern over purely technical compatibility to broader questions of social meaning—what background cultural beliefs and practices motivate, justify and orient these systems? Along what dimensions can systems be said to be commensurable? What must be investigated, negotiated and made explicit in order for systems to be commensurable, translatable and interoperable? What elements of meaning might be sacrificed or abandoned in these negotiations? Together these questions compose a frame for exploring the central concern of this study—whether a holistic notion of commensurability, embracing both sociological and technological dimensions, can be usefully applied to the translation and coordination of organising schemes in the digital age.

Introducing the semantic web

A web of meaning

The semantic web 'provides a common framework that allows data to be shared and reused across application, enterprise, and community boundaries' (W3C 2009b). It is constructed on the existing scaffolding of the World Wide Web: it makes use of the whole infrastructure of Extensible Markup Language (XML), Uniform Resource Identifiers (URIs) and, to a degree, Hypertext Markup Language (HTML). Two key formal language specifications for making and connecting assertions about the world comprise the foundational building blocks of the semantic web: the Resource Definition Framework (RDF) and Ontology Web Language (OWL). Several derivative standards describe rules, trust and proof conditions for reasoning and sharing the resulting assertional networks. Any system that supports these standards should be able to write and save data, which can in turn be processed and reasoned over by other compliant systems—bringing about, in theory, a level of interoperability not possible previously. Both RDF and OWL have been developed to be compatible with XML, another standard and common language for the encoding of data and documents (W3C 2009a). One way of viewing the relationships between these standards is that XML supplies a standardised syntax, and RDF and OWL supply standardised semantics for data. Other syntaxes are also available for encoding RDF and OWL (Berners-Lee 2009). However, widely available support, in the form of software tools and libraries, make XML a convenient choice for many purposes.

RDF is designed for describing resources—documents, images, audio and video files, as well as real-world objects which 'can be *identified*'— on the web (Miller and Manola 2004). Descriptions take the conventional logical form of subject–predicate–object, where the subject and object are generally identified via a web address or, more formally, a uniform resource identifier. RDF does not supply an explicit vocabulary of terms such as 'author', 'publisher' or 'creation date'. Instead it operates at a higher level of abstraction, 'specif[ying] mechanisms that may be used to name and describe properties and the classes of resource they describe' (Guha and Brickley 2004). In other words, it provides well-defined abstract and formal structures—such as 'class', 'property', 'string', 'date' and 'collection'—for composing such terms (Powers 2003). OWL, in turn, extends RDF to handle descriptions of ontologies—a central concept for this study, which warrants a more extended introduction below. Together RDF and OWL form a basis for the standardisation of structured data on the web, in such a way that human and machine agents can share, query, navigate, manipulate and conduct inferences with it.

The semantic web is typically explained in terms of consumer convenience. In a now famous statement heralding the advent of the semantic web, Berners-Lee, Hendler and Lassila (2001) describe how it makes possible, for example, the aggregation of book catalogue records across multiple websites, or the merging of contact information from one application with calendaring data from another. The same article, written in the promissory and optimistic tones of technology evangelism, outlines how the semantic web will, more broadly, simplify the electronic life of a prototypical user:

> The semantic web will bring structure to the meaningful content of Web pages, creating an environment where software agents roaming from page to page can readily carry out sophisticated tasks for users. Such an agent coming to the clinic's Web page will know not just that the page has keywords such as 'treatment, medicine,

physical, therapy' (as might be encoded today) but also that Dr. Hartman works at this clinic on Mondays, Wednesdays and Fridays and that the script takes a date range in yyyy-mm-dd format and returns appointment times. And it will 'know' all this without needing artificial intelligence on the scale of 2001's Hal or Star Wars's C-3PO. Instead these semantics were encoded into the Web page when the clinic's office manager (who never took Comp Sci 101) massaged it into shape using off-the-shelf software for writing semantic web pages along with resources listed on the Physical Therapy Association's site (Berners-Lee, Hendler and Lassila 2001).

Arguably, though, the semantic web has greater application to the costly problems of system integration which preoccupy organisational IT departments or enterprises: for example, how to get the accounts system to 'talk to' the human resources system, how to integrate two customer databases after a company merger, or how to represent transaction details across different national taxation regimes. These translation scenarios are common areas of complexity and cost in system integration, and stand to benefit from the kinds of interoperability at least promised by the semantic web. A key example of this use has been the widespread adoption of the semantic web, and of ontologies in particular, among the bioinformatic research community. Chapter 10, 'Describing knowledge domains', explores this usage in further detail.

It is worth adding a cautionary note: in the decade since the early euphoric pronouncements of the semantic web, its adoption has been heavily fragmented. Research communities, such as those of the life sciences mentioned above, have been quick to embrace it. But the broader enterprise and consumer markets, targetted in the pitch cited above for instance, have stumbled over the apparent complexity and acronymic soup of its many recommendations and proposals. More specific causes have also been raised within the informal channels of the blogosphere (Shirky 2003), some of which are discussed in more detail in the comparison of knowledge systems in Chapter 7, 'An historical introduction to formal knowledge systems'. Suffice to say, the degree to which the semantic web remains a research project, limited to scientific and academic applications, remains a highly contested issue. The recent more catholic usage of 'ontology', evident in the studies presented here, is indicative of a more general desire to explore possibilities of many semantic webs, and many ontologies, inspired but not necessarily constrained to the specific proposals of the Semantic Web—in its proper noun form.

Ontology—computing 'what is'

Bearing in mind the preceding exhortation, before describing how ontologies are represented in OWL specifically, it is useful to describe the term 'ontology' in its more general computer science usage. The term has been appropriated from its philosophical roots to describe knowledge systems. Despite the shift in meaning from its traditional moorings—where it is far from being an unambiguous term—this appropriation is not without basis: an ontology, for knowledge representation, is a series of statements which purport to describe how the world is. The canonical definition for computer science usage of 'ontology' comes from Gruber (1993): 'an ontology is an explicit specification of a conceptualization'. Elsewhere he elaborates: 'Pragmatically, a common ontology defines the vocabulary with which queries and assertions are exchanged among agents. Ontological commitments are agreements to use the shared vocabulary in a coherent and consistent manner' (Gruber 1995, p. 909).

'Ontology' is therefore, even in its computer science usage, conceived in broad terms. In this study, it is generally treated as an umbrella term for a range of electronic classification systems: from those with minimal explicit semantics through to ontologies developed in OWL with a highly explicit semantics. It therefore includes taxonomies, controlled vocabularies, thesauri, classification systems, catalogues, XML specifications, software designs, database and knowledge-base schemas, logical deduction systems and, finally, knowledge representation formats such as OWL. Unlike programs, ontologies or knowledge bases do not generally contain procedures, though they may include rules which can be processed by programs.

In its computer science usage, then, an ontology is a representation of some knowledge about a domain or field, sometimes also referred to as a knowledge base or database, and encoded using some derivative of a first-order logical formalism. Further, an ontology is typically composed of a series of logical axioms—the basic building blocks of the knowledge base:

- *classes*—names designating sets of objects (for example, 'cell')

- *properties*—names an attribute of a class (for example, 'label'), or a relationship between two classes (for example, 'is_contained_by')

- *individuals*—names an individual object (for example, 'genid7566'—'An enzyme complex which in humans and yeast consists of at least five proteins').

Briefly, these axioms can be related in various ways. Classes can be defined through relations of subsumption (parent–child relations) to form a traditional taxonomic hierarchy; properties can be assigned to classes as part of their definition in terms of 'necessary and sufficient conditions'; and individuals can be stipulated in terms of their class association (what classes they are members of), and their attributes and relations with other objects.

Over the kinds of entrenched data systems commonly used—relational databases or spreadsheets, for example—ontologies offer several advantages:

- Formal mathematical models provide the foundational semantic anchorings of ontologies, which allow unambiguous and—under certain conditions—tractable interpretation of ontological axioms.

- Existing internet infrastructure provides some of the technical plumbing of ontologies—for example, object references or identifiers use web addresses (URIs), while the canonical syntactic format for ontologies is XML, a well-supported data markup language.

- The underlying formalisms of ontologies also have well-defined means for stating relationships between them. One ontology can 'import', and subsequently reuse, definitions and data from another. Logical relationships of subsumption, equivalence and disjointness can be declared between axioms of different ontologies, as much as within a single given ontology.

These features make possible very large-scale reasoning over heterogenous data sets, which can improve structured searches, interoperability between research results and the automatic discovery of new relationships. There are particular trade-offs however—the particular pros and cons of ontologies, databases and other forms of knowledge representation are discussed further in Chapter 7, 'An historical introduction to formal knowledge systems'.

Ontologies, at any rate, form a cornerstone of the promise of the semantic web—that in a global world of federated data sets, properly organised under shared ontologies and underlying conceptual schemes, users can publish and query information more quickly, more reliably and with the added benefit of computer-aided inferencing. In the many diverse fields of knowledge and informatics, with very large and ever-growing data sets, active and growing amendments to taxonomic structures, and a globally distributed network of researchers, this promise holds a special allure.

The Ontology Web Language—a language for the semantic web

The Ontology Web Language (OWL) was developed—or, more accurately, was derived from several earlier language initiatives—in order to provide a standardised way of representing ontologies on the semantic web. OWL itself comes in three language variants: OWL Lite, OWL DL (Description Logic) and OWL Full (W3C 2009b). These variants exhibit increasing degrees of computational complexity and expressivity. All variants originate in a long tradition of research into knowledge representation and machine learning, culminating in Description Logics in the 1980s and 1990s. RDF was developed for different, more pragmatic purposes of sharing data between systems, and early in the history of the semantic web efforts were made to harmonise RDF with OWL—since RDF permits a wide range of constructs, it is more expressive than OWL Full, but also computationally intractable. Both OWL and RDF can be rendered in a variety of syntaxes, such as XML, N-Triples and Notation3 (Berners-Lee 2009). While all of these syntaxes are humanly readable and writeable, in practice RDF and OWL files are typically generated by ontology editing tools such as Protégé (Gennari et al. 2003).

The purpose of the resulting OWL ontology is to provide a standards-based model of some set of facts about the world. Precisely because it is a standard, other systems can process an OWL ontology and make inferences about it; importantly, not only about a particular ontology itself, but also about how that ontology might connect with others. The semantic web envisages a network of ontologies which function like a large, distributed database. The current web of course might be said to supply this in a more amorphous form—but the whole point of the semantic web is precisely that any facts in an ontology have a certain amount of context made *explicit*. *Sally* is a *Person*; a *Person* is a sub-class of *Animal*; a *Person* may own a number of *Pets*; and so on. Each of these concepts, properties and individuals are defined in the ontology; therefore systems with no prior knowledge of *Sally*, *Persons* or *Animals* can nonetheless infer the relations between these things automatically.

Put another way: the semantics of data are encoded in ways that are specific or unique to the organisations, people or agents generating them. Ontologies attempt to solve this problem in a general way. They supply the mechanism by which agents can understand the semantics of any given domain—*without prior knowledge* of this domain. Consequently agents can consume arbitrary data, expressed in an ontology, and then *infer* various characteristics about the data. Such *inferences* include whether the data is in fact *valid* according to the ontology in which it is declared; how the data, as a series of *statements*, may relate to other statements (by denying, confirming, extending or refining those statements); and what sort of *relations* exist in the data itself (where such relations may include instantiation, generalisation, specialisation, composition and attribution).

As an example, a minimal ontology which conforms to the definition above could include the following set of concepts, properties and individuals:

Concepts

```
Person

Cat

Dog
```

Properties

```
instanceOf

ownsPet

hasFurColour
```

Individuals

```
Sally

Samba

Fido
```

The individuals can be assigned properties as follows:

```
Sally instanceOf Person.

Samba instanceOf Cat.

Fido instanceOf Dog.

Sally ownsPet Samba.

Sally ownsPet Fido.

Samba hasFurColour 'Grey'.

Fido hasFurColour 'Blonde'.
```

This ontology now expresses seven statements about the world in a semi-formal way—formal enough that an algorithm could be devised to process the statements in some way. Compare this with the range of natural language expressions which could express the same statements, both more succinctly and more verbosely: 'Sally owns two pets, a grey cat called Samba and a blonde dog called Fido'; 'There exists in the world a person called Sally'; 'There exists in the world a cat called Samba', and so on. As a minimal ontology, it also establishes the primordially ontological distinctions between *classes*, *properties* and *individuals*. In practice these distinctions, while on the one hand being crucial for the performance of current state-of-the-art knowledge representation systems, are on the other not always very clear-cut or easy to disambiguate.

These constructs are, then, sufficient to develop a broad definition of an ontology. It is possible to add further constructs, such as the ability to specify subsumption relations between concepts (e.g. 'Person', 'Cat' and 'Dog' are all sub-classes of the more general concept 'Animal'). The subsumption construct in particular is integral to providing reasoning services over an ontology, which enables inference about the relationship between two objects in the world (e.g. Sally, Fido and Samba are all instances of the concept 'Animal'). As one of the aims of OWL is to enable these kinds of inferences, it includes the subsumption construct. However under this broader definition of ontology, it is also to include two of the more common formal models for knowledge representation: the relational database and XML Schema. As one of the purposes of the semantic web, and OWL in particular, is to provide a general way to express any data, it is useful to have just such a broad working definition for the time being.

Networked ontologies—towards the web of meaning

A key goal of ontologies is that they are shared, reuseable repositories of data. In the short history of the semantic web a large number of ontologies have been developed for a range of fields and disciplines. Some of these ontologies define generic concepts, so-called 'upper-level' or foundational ontologies. These are designed to be applied across many or all domains, and might include concepts such as Process, Object, Time and Space. Others are quite specific to a given domain, such as the life sciences or linguistics. Upper-level ontologies can be incorporated or imported into more specific ontologies, which can be imported by other ontologies again—forming a lattice-like network of interconnected concepts. Ontologies that import other ontologies can also reuse their conceptual definitions, analogous to the world of object-oriented programming, where programming structures are reused in a similar fashion (Booch et al. 2007). This is one way in which concepts and data can be put towards purposes their original authors would not have envisioned. However, this relies on explicit directives from the authors of the importing ontology, who also take responsibility for the explicit conceptual relations and translations they establish between their own and the imported ontology.

In other contexts, two ontologies which have been independently authored often need to be integrated, translated, aligned or merged. Developing points of connection between two ontologies can be a time-consuming and error-prone task, particularly if the ontologies are large—containing many concepts, relations or individual data records. A specific sub-disciplinary area, *ontology matching*, has been established to find automatic means of associating concepts from multiple ontologies. In addition to the explicit authoring of connections between ontologies described above, ontology matching holds promise for the explicitation of otherwise implicit connections between ontologies. Together these two approaches make it possible to envisage a global knowledge base—one of the declared aims of the semantic web. Chapter 3, 'The meaning of meaning', distinguishes several specific ontology matching approaches; in spite of these distinctions, though, the common underlying feature of these algorithms is the production of a set of individual concept matches. This set, referred to as an overall 'alignment' of the ontologies (Shvaiko and Euzenat 2005), can in turn be used to generate a translation from concepts in one ontology to concepts in another. Ignored in this translation process is the general degree of fit between the ontologies—how their overall conceptualisations are *commensurable*.

The question of commensurability—weaving ontologies together

Commensurability as a concept originates in the field of geometry, meaning 'of common measure'. Wikipedia (2009), for example, defines this mathematical usage as follows: 'If two quantities can be measured in the same *units*, they are commensurable.' Kuhn introduces the term to talk about scientific paradigms:

> The hypotenuse of an isosceles right triangle is incommensurable with its side or the circumference of a circle with its radius in the sense that there is no unit of length contained without residue an integral number of times in each member of the pair.
>
> The incommensurability of these quantities does not mean one cannot be derived from the other however. In these two cases, hypotenuse = the root of 2 × side and circumference = 2 × PI × radius express the relations of these quantities. Since in both cases there is a residue, i.e. the equation does not result in an integer, the quantities are incommensurable (Kuhn 1970, p. 189).

Kuhn (1970) makes use of commensurability as a metaphor for how scientific theories, 'conceived of as sets of sentences, can be translated without residue or loss'. Following Kuhn, the term 'commensurability' is used—in place of synonyms like compatibility, congruence or consistency—to connote a deeper level of cultural perspectival alignment between knowledge systems, while allowing for surface-level differences, such as differences in nomenclature. When faced with two matching ontologies, for instance, commensurability suggests there exists some deep conceptual equivalence between them, even if there are no shared terms or concepts. By contrast, *in*commensurability suggests substantial differences between their underlying cultural conceptions—differences requiring greater effort to effect translation between them. This study presents a similar argument to that of Kuhn's *Structure of Scientific Revolutions*: that semantic web ontologies and other formal representations of knowledge are not always commensurable, and that some form of social negotiation is needed to effect translation when this is the case.

Like scientific paradigms, ontologies can be treated as holding a particular orientation towards the slice of the world they describe. Such an orientation bears any number of assumptions which are properly *ontological* in the philosophical sense—assumptions about how the world is, derived from the cultural backdrop in which the orientation is formulated. Together these assumptions form the epistemic conditions under which ontologies—of the semantic web kind—can be developed. To give a hypothetical example, which is explored further in the work as a case study, two separate ontologies could be developed to describe the world of documents. The first ontology uses the term Author, while the second ontology uses the alternative of Collaborator. Authors are people specifically engaged in the creation of the document—they write the text, capture and insert the images, structure the document and so on. Collaborators have a looser relationship—they may edit, publish, translate, typeset or perform any number of other activities in relation to the document. At this stage—without further knowledge or recourse to context—it is possible to interpret the difference in at least two ways. On the one hand, the difference could be viewed as contingent and accidental—a question of near-synonymic variants. In the second case, a more general term was chosen, which includes the specific term of the first—all `Authors` are also `Collaborators`. On the other hand, the difference could also mark a more fundamental ontological difference. Here, in the second ontology, there is no suitable translation for `Author`. Instead `Collaborators` simply collaborate to create a document—which could mean writing it, editing it, typesetting it, and so on. Indeed, possibly the concept of authorship is explicitly denied; there are no `Collaborators` bearing the special distinction of authorship. The first interpretation suggests there is in fact some underlying commensurability between these ontologies, in spite of the different terms chosen. They share the same view of the world, in which documents have both `Authors` and `Collaborators`, and `Authors` are particular kinds of `Collaborators`. The second interpretation instead suggests that at least in relation to these particular concepts of the two ontologies, the question of translatability is ambiguous. Consequently, commensurability is a less settled question, requiring at the very least further supplementary information.

According to the literal meaning, it could be argued that all knowledge systems, insofar as they employ different conceptual schemes, are trivially incommensurable. In the sense used here, however, commensurability is a question of degrees rather than kind—what matters is the extent of difference and, by extension, the cost, time and effort of translation between those systems. To assess this means going beyond the explicit representations of the systems themselves, inferring something about the implicit background network of assumptions which underpin them—variously termed their 'world views', 'conceptual schemes', 'paradigms', 'epistemes', 'gestalts' or 'frames of reference'. This study aims to demonstrate that using the metaphor of commensurability is a helpful way to conceive of both the explicit and tacit differences in the design of knowledge systems; helpful insofar as it provides practitioners with ways of identifying and bridging those differences—or, just as importantly, identifying when such differences are not practically translatable. Here, incommensurability does not imply a slippery slope into relativism or solipsism—a world in which knowledge systems, no less than the cultures that construct and use them, forever remain trapped in their particular hermetic conceptualisations. On the contrary, proper analysis of ontologies can lead to productive insights into the sorts of differences between them, and whether such differences can be readily reconciled in a given situational context.

The question of commensurability is directed towards the same sorts of problems identified by field of ontology matching. Ontology matching approaches seek to develop algorithms to match the terms of two or more ontologies, based on exploitation of terminological similarities. As discussed further in Chapter 3, 'The meaning of meaning', concept-by-concept matches generated by these approaches are a necessary but insufficient means of solving certain problems of 'semantic heterogeneity' (Shvaiko and Euzenat 2005). The ontology commensurability framework developed here is intended to augment these approaches by considering translation from a semantic holistic perspective—where not only individual conceptual matches but overall schematic commensurability can be assessed.

Towards a framing of semantics

The semantic web makes bold claims about solving problems of system interoperability—a 'silver bullet' solution, in effect, for an industry in which software incompatibilities, project failures, patchwork solutions and 'semantic heterogeneity' are sources of significant costs (Shvaiko and Euzenat 2008). Moreover it provides a means for weaving together the rich tapestry of existing data on the internet, by providing transparent means for making the structure of that data explicit. A subsidiary discipline has developed, *ontology matching*, which has sought various algorithmic solutions to the problem of integrating related ontologies. Here, we argue that translation in some contexts needs a holistic regard for the general cultural conceptualisations underpinning ontologies, which can usefully augment concept-by-concept matching algorithms. The Kuhnian term *commensurability* has been introduced in order to describe the overall degree of fit between two ontologies, assessed across a range of cognitive, social and technical dimensions. The next chapter explores some of these dimensions as they are understood with various academic discursive fields, and how they variously understand and articulate the meaning of meaning.

References

Arunguren, M.E. 2005. 'Ontology Design Patterns for the Formalisation of Biological Ontologies', technical report, University of Manchester.

Ashkenas, R., D. Ulrich, T. Jick and S. Kerr. 1995. *The Boundaryless Organization: Breaking the Chains of Organizational Structure*. San Francisco: Jossey-Bass.

Berners-Lee, T. 2009. 'Notation3 (N3): A Readable RDF Syntax', *http://www.w3.org/TeamSubmission/n3/* (accessed 29 October 2009).

Berners-Lee, T., J. Hendler and O. Lassila. 2001. 'The Semantic Web', *Scientific American* 284, pp. 34–43.

Booch, G., R. Maksimchuk, M. Engle, B. Young, J. Conallen and K. Houston. 2007. *Object-Oriented Analysis and Design with Applications*. Indianapolis, IN: Addison-Wesley Professional.

Castells, M. 1996. *The Rise of the Network Society*. Cambridge, MA: Blackwell.

Davidson, D. 2006. *The Essential Davidson*. Oxford: Oxford University Press.

Foucault, M. 1970. *The Order of Things: An Archaeology of the Human Sciences*. New York: Vintage Books.

Gennari, J.H., M.A. Musen, R.W. Fergerson, W.E. Grosso, M. Crubézy, H. Eriksson, N.F. Noy and S.W. Tu. 2003. 'The Evolution of Protégé: An Environment for Knowledge-Based Systems Development', *International Journal of Human-Computer Studies* 58, pp. 89–123.

Gruber, T.R. 1993. 'A Translation Approach to Portable Ontology Specifications', *Knowledge Acquisition* 5, pp. 199–220.

—. 1995. 'Toward Principles for the Design of Ontologies Used for Knowledge Sharing', *International Journal of Human Computer Studies* 43, pp. 907–28.

Guha, R.V. and D. Brickley. 2004. 'RDF Vocabulary Description Language 1.0: RDF Schema'. W3C recommendation, W3C, *http://www.w3.org/TR/rdf-schema/* (accessed 29 October 2009).

Hacking, I. 2002. *Historical Ontology*. Cambridge, MA: Harvard University Press.

Kuhn, T.S. 1970. *The Structure of Scientific Revolutions*. Chicago, IL: University of Chicago Press.

Lenzen, W. 2004. 'Leibniz's Logic'. In *Handbook of the History of Logic*, vol. 3, 'The Rise of Modern Logic from Leibniz to Frege'. Amsterdam: North-Holland Publishing Company.

Miller, E. and Manola, F. 2004. 'RDF Primer'. W3C recommendation, W3C, *http://www.w3.org/TR/rdf-primer/* (accessed 29 October 2009).

Powers, S. 2003. *Practical RDF*. Sebastopol: O'Reilly Media.

Shirky, C. 2003. 'The Semantic Web, Syllogism, and Worldview', *http://www.shirky.com/writings/semantic_syllogism.html* (accessed 25 November 2009).

Shvaiko, P. and J. Euzenat. 2005. 'A Survey of Schema-Based Matching Approaches', *Journal on Data Semantics* 4, pp. 146–71.

—. 2008. 'Ten Challenges for Ontology Matching'. In *OTM 2008: Proceedings of the 7th International Conference on Ontologies, Databases, and Applications of Semantics (ODBASE)*. Berlin and Heidelberg: Springer, pp. 1164–82.

W3C. 2009a. 'Extensible Markup Language (XML)', *http://www.w3.org/XML/* (accessed 29 October 2009).

—. 2009b. 'W3C Semantic Web Activity', *http://www.w3.org/2001/sw/* (accessed 29 October 2009).

Wikipedia. 2009. 'Commensurability', *http://en.wikipedia.org/wiki/Commensurability* (accessed 29 October 2009).

3

The meaning of meaning: alternative disciplinary perspectives

Liam Magee

> The sentence 'Snow is white' is true if, and only if, snow is white (Tarski 1957, p. 190).

A guiding thread through discussions of the semantic web is the very general notion of *meaning*—as something which can be variously reasoned over computationally, generated or processed cognitively, expressed linguistically and transmitted socially. In order to understand how this broad thematic can be conceived in relation to the specifically technological construct of the semantic web, here it is classified and discussed under the following 'semantic' rubrics or frames:

- linguistic semantics
- cognitive semantics
- social semantics
- computational semantics.

This chapter develops the introduction to the semantic web given in the previous chapter by reviewing these frames of how meaning is variously construed; it further serves as a preliminary schematisation of the kinds of variables used to organise, cluster and describe knowledge systems generally.

The first of the disciplinary frames surveyed below considers semantics as a subsidiary linguistics discipline—as the study of meaning as it is expressed in language. A general discussion outlines some of the major conceptual distinctions in this field. Given the reliance of knowledge systems on formal languages of different kinds, work in the area of formal semantics is discussed specifically. Other kinds of research have been directed towards the interpretation and use of ordinary everyday language; these theories in related fields of hermeneutics and pragmatics are also reviewed briefly.

Another, closely related, frame concerns recent work conducted in cognitive science and psychology on concept formation, categorisation and classification. Examining recent models of cognition can provide clues as to possible causes and locations of incommensurability between conceptualisations made explicit in ontologies. Several recent theories have developed explicitly spatial models of mind and cognition, which provide helpful metaphorical support, at least, for a discussion of commensurability. A review of recent research in these fields is developed in the section on cognitive semantics.

As well as being amenable to algorithmic analysis, representations of cognitive phenomena and linguistic artefacts, ontologies are also social products—they are things produced and consumed within a broader marketplace of communicative practices. It is then useful also to look at social theoretic models of communication generally, to see how these devolve onto the specific concerns of ontology commensurability. Chapter 11, 'On commensurability', examines several social theorists in more detail, but here it is useful to survey a range of theoretical and empirical research conducted under the broad umbrella of the social sciences. Specifically, research in key fields—sociology of knowledge, studies of technology and science, knowledge management, IT standardisation and cross-cultural anthropology—helps to introduce certain concepts which emerge again in the development of the commensurability framework in Chapter 12, 'A framework for commensurability'. A review of these fields is provided in the section on social semantics below.

Extensive research has been undertaken in the field of computer science, notably in the area of ontology matching, but also in related areas of ontology and database modelling and design. Much of this research focuses on developing improved algorithms for concept translation between ontologies; as noted in the introduction, there has been relatively little attention to using background knowledge as a heuristic tool for augmenting ontology translation efforts. The section on computational semantics, below, surveys work in ontology matching, and also discusses related studies looking at ontology metrics and collaboration.

Finally, considerable work in philosophy of mind and language has been oriented towards problems of conceptual schemes, translatability and interpretation. However, this field is much too broad to survey even schematically here; Chapter 11, 'On commensurability', provides a further review of this tradition, within the specific context of outlining a theoretical background for a framework of commensurability.

Linguistic semantics

Semantics in language

As a subsidiary domain of linguistics, semantics is, as a textbook puts it, 'the study of the systematic ways in which languages structure meaning' (Besnier et al. 1992). Early in the history of linguistics, Ferdinand de Saussure established several foundational semantic distinctions: between *signifier* (a spoken or written symbol) and *signified* (a mental concept); and between *sign* (the combination of signifier and signified) and *referent* (the thing referred to by the sign) (Saussure 1986). Bloomfieldian research in the 1930s and 1940s emphasised structural, comparative and descriptive rather than semantic features of language; ironically it was the advent of Chomskyian generative grammar in the 1950s which, in spite of emphasising syntax, again paved the way for a more explicit focus on semantics in the 1960s (Harris 1993). Since then, numerous kinds, branches and theories of semantics have emerged: generative semantics, formal semantics (applied to natural languages), lexical semantics, componential analysis, prototype and metaphor theories, 'universal' semantics, cognitive semantics, hermeneutics, pragmatics and various theories of translation—not to mention the general interest in semantic computer applications and platforms such as the semantic web.

Linguistic meaning can be studied through several different lexical units or levels: words, sentences, groups of sentences, discourse or text, and a corpus of texts (Besnier et al. 1992). At each level, different types of meaning can also be distinguished. In the classical essay 'On Sense and Reference', Frege ([1892] 1925) distinguishes what objects in the world words refer to—their extensional or denotative meaning—from how those words are defined by other words—their intensional or connotative meaning. More recent analyses of meaning build on this primary distinction; for example, Chierchia and McConnell-Ginet (2000) distinguish denotational (or referential) from psychologistic (or mentalistic) and social (or pragmatic) theories of meaning, while Leech (1981) proposes a total of seven types of meaning: conceptual meaning, connotative meaning, social meaning, affective meaning, reflected meaning, collocative meaning and thematic meaning. Denotational or conceptual meaning is regarded as primary in most mainstream semantic accounts; since this referring capacity of language is essential for other types of meaning to be possible, 'it can be shown to be integral to the essential functioning of language in a way that other types of meaning are not' (Leech 1981, p. 9).

Approaches to understanding natural language meaning even in a denotational sense vary considerably. Common approaches include componential analysis, where semantic units—typically, words—are given positive or negative markers against a set of 'components' or 'dimensions' of meaning (Burling 1964; Leech 1981), and lexical analysis, where relations of units to each other are defined according to a set of rules: synonymy/antonymy (units with the same/opposite meanings to other units); hypernymy/hyponymy (units which are superordinate/subordinate in meaning to other units); holonymy/meronymy (units which stand in relation of wholes/parts to other units); and homonymy/polysemy (units which have one/multiple definitions) (Besnier et al. 1992; Cann 1993).

As an early critic of componential analysis noted, underlying 'dimensions' of meaning are not immediately obvious—they need to be explicitly theorised (Burling 1964). One effort to develop a core set of shared concepts which underpin all languages is Goddard and Wierzbicka's 'natural semantic metalanguage' (NSM). The 'metalanguage' proposes a highly abstracted lexical inventory of 'semantic primes' from which all lexical units in any language can be derived (Goddard 2002)—an idea which is related to Rosch's 'basic' categories, discussed below. Generation of such primes requires a 'trial-and-error' approach of postulating prime candidates (Goddard 2002), and mapping their derivation from the metalanguage into various natural language forms (Goddard and Wierzbicka 2002). As the authors suggest, the process is time-consuming and highly speculative, yet brought to fruition would provide a powerful device for, among other things, providing unambiguous rules for the translation of concepts across natural languages (Wierzbicka 1980). As the case-study on upper-level ontologies shows, the effort to develop a metalanguage for natural languages has its direct analogue in equivalent efforts to develop a set of foundational or core concepts for formal knowledge representations—with much the same difficulties and trade-offs.

The remainder of the review of linguistic approach to meaning moves in three directions, which roughly mirror the division suggested by Chierchia and McConnell-Ginet (2000): towards formal semantics, which seeks to describe meaning within a logic-based framework; towards hermeneutics, which understands meaning in a holistic and subjectively inflected way;

and towards pragmatics, which understands meaning as a kind of social practice. Each of these approaches has important implications for a theory of commensurability developed here, and while apparently contradictory, the aim here is instead to demonstrate broad lines of complementarity. As Chierchia and McConnell-Ginet (2000, p. 54) emphasise, in a related context:

> We believe that these three perspectives are by no means incompatible. On the contrary, meaning has all three aspects (namely, the denotational, representational, and pragmatic aspects). Any theory that ignores any of them will deprive itself of a source of insight and is ultimately likely to prove unsatisfactory.

What is 'representational' here is also given more expansive treatment in the section 'Cognitive semantics', and what is termed 'pragmatic' is also discussed further in the section 'Social semantics'. However, the hermeneutic and pragmatic traditions covered here provide the means for extending out from language towards those cognitive and social domains, and consequently provide important building blocks in the development of the theory of commensurability.

Formal semantics

A significant strain of semantic research arose from work conducted in logic and foundational mathematics in the early twentieth century—a tradition touched on in more, albeit still schematic, detail in Chapter 7, 'An historical introduction to formal knowledge systems'. Within this tradition, 'semantics' is interpreted truth-functionally—a statement's meaning is just whether the proposition it expresses is true or false. Formal semantics arose generally through the interests of logical positivism, but specifically through an ingenious response to the logical paradoxes which had beset the preceding generation of logicians in the early twentieth century. Tarski's semantic conception of truth, first published in 1933, provided a 'formally correct and materially adequate' basis for describing the truth conditions of a proposition (Hodges 2008). One of Tarski's innovations was to impose a condition on a formal language, L, that it cannot construct a sentence based on an existing sentence and the predicate 'is true'—such a sentence could only be constructed in a *metalanguage*, M, which contains all of the sentences of L and the additional 'is true' predicate. Consequently, a paradoxical statement like 'this sentence is false' becomes nonsensical—to make sense, it is split into two sentences, the first of which contains the sentence under consideration in the object language *L*, and the second of which defines the truth value of the first in the metalanguage *M* (Cann 1993; Hodges 2008). For Tarski, at least, this conception could apply to the kinds of statements common to the sciences:

> At the present time the only languages with a specified structure are the formalized languages of various systems of deductive logic, possibly enriched by the introduction of certain non-logical terms. However, the field of application of these languages is rather comprehensive; we are able, theoretically, to develop in them various branches of science, for instance, mathematics and theoretical physics (Tarski 1957, p. 8).

The formal semantic conception of truth strongly influenced Quine, Davidson and Popper, among others. Although directed specifically towards formal languages, Tarski's *Convention T* was applied first to natural languages by Davidson (2006). More systematic accounts of natural language as a derivative of formal logic, where sentential parts sit as truth-bearing components within a sentential whole, were developed by Tarksi's student Montague (1974), followed by Dowty (1979), Partee (2004) and Kao (2004). The guiding insight of formal semantics was the 'principle of compositionality': 'The meaning of an expression is a monotonic function of the meaning of its parts and the way they are put together' (Cann 1993, p. 4).

While Chomsky's generative grammar demonstrated how sentences could be syntactically 'put together', by the end of the 1960s rival generative (Lakoff, McCawley, Postal and Katz) and interpretivist (Jackendoff and Chomsky) semantic movements had as yet yielded no prevailing paradigm for accounting for how the meaning of sentential parts—individual words, as well as noun and verb phrases, for example—could account for the meaning of the sentence as a whole (Harris 1993). Montague grammar sought to provide a unified theory for the syntax and semantics of both natural and artificial languages (Kao 2004). In 'The Proper Treatment of Quantification in Ordinary English' (1974), the seminal account of such a theory, Montague presents a syntax of a fragment of English, a form of 'tensed intensional logic' derived from Kripkean possible world semantics, and, finally, rules for translating a subset of English sentences into the intensional logic. The role of the intensional logic is to handle certain classes of 'complex intensional locutions' using 'intensional verbs'. For example, the truth value of a sentence containing the verb 'seeks' can vary depending on the verb complement—resolving the truth value means knowing the state of affairs which pertain within a possible world at a particular point in time (Forbes 2008). By demonstrating how it was possible to translate a large group of natural language sentences into disambiguated propositions, analysable into parts with truth conditions and able to stand as premises in logical inferences, Montague opened rich possibilities for further research in formal semantics (Kracht 2008; Partee 2004).

Formal semantics inspired by Tarski's model theory has also been used in the construction of syntactically well-formed and semantically interpretable artificial languages for knowledge representation, including the languages of the semantic web, Resource Definition Framework (RDF) and Ontology Web Language (OWL) (Hayes 2004; Hayes, Patel-Schneider and Horrocks 2004). The somewhat arcane origins of this 'semantic' epithet—by way of the abstractions of model theory and description logics—has led, perversely, to several varying interpretations of the semantic web itself: as a process of incremental technological adaptation, or as a wholesale revolution of how knowledge is produced, represented, disseminated and managed. Both the development and subsequent interpretations of the semantic web are described in more detail in Chapter 7, 'An historical introduction to formal knowledge systems'.

Hermeneutics and semantics

Hermeneutics predates the scientific study of semantics described above by some historical distance, originating in German Enlightenment philosophy in the eighteenth and early nineteenth centuries (Mueller-Vollmer 1988). Etymologically derived from the Greek for 'translate' or 'interpret', it is similarly concerned with meaning in a very general sense. In its earliest incarnations, the aims of hermeneutics were broadly sympathetic with later waves of the epistemologically ambitious programs of logical positivism and the semantic web:

> Finally, with the desire of Enlightenment philosophers to proceed everywhere from certain principles and to systematize all human knowledge, hermeneutics became a province of philosophy. Following the example of Aristotle... Enlightenment philosophers viewed hermeneutics and its problems as belonging to the domain of logic (Mueller-Vollmer 1988, p. 3).

In the nineteenth and twentieth centuries, under the various influences of Romanticism, secularism, materialism, vitalism and phenomenology, hermeneutic studies became oriented towards psychological, historical and subjective aspects of interpretation. Although treatment of hermeneutics differs from author to author, it can be distinguished from semantics in being:

- oriented more towards the holistic meaning of texts, rather than the individual meaning of smaller linguistic units such as sentences or words

- focused on historical and humanist explanations of interpretation rather than scientific and objective, truth-functional accounts

- more closely connected with traditional approaches to language— rhetoric, grammar, biblical exegesis and language genealogy—than semantics (Leech 1981; Mueller-Vollmer 1988)

- directed towards the internal rather than external 'side of our use of signs'—towards how signs are *understood*, rather than, conversely, how concepts can be *signified* (Gadamer 2004)

- interested in disruptive semantic features of meaning—ambiguity, paradox and contradiction are not features to be 'explained away', but rather are intrinsic characteristics of an account of meaning.

Twentieth-century philosophers working in the hermeneutic tradition have also pointed to a necessary structural relationship between holistic understanding and atomistic interpretation, depicted by the 'hermeneutic circle' (Gadamer 1975; Heidegger 1962). It describes a virtuous rather than vicious circular pattern of learning in relation to a text, discourse or tradition—as individual parts are interpreted, so the understanding of the whole becomes clearer; and as the text as a whole is better understood, so new parts are better able to be interpreted. This broad structure describes in the large the kind of complementarity discussed earlier between two approaches to aligning ontologies: ontology matching—translating atomic concepts found within them—and assessing commensurability—comparing holistically the conceptual schemes underlying them. Similarly, where atomic interpretation works from the explicit features of the ontologies themselves, developing a holistic understanding also engages the implicit assumptions and commitments held by those who design and use them.

Although typically directed towards historical, literary or philosophical texts, then, hermeneutics makes several distinctions and claims which can be no less applied to the interpretation of ontologies and other information systems—as texts of a different sort. Whereas ambiguity in poetical texts is often intentional, it is an unhelpful side-effect of tacit assumptions in the case of ontologies—and a 'broad-brush' hermeneutic orientation, which seeks to examine texts against the background of historical and contextual conditions, can be useful in making such assumptions explicit.

Pragmatic semantics

Linguistic pragmatics considers meaning a function of how words and phrases are used, famously coined in the Wittgensteinian expression 'the meaning of a word is its use in the language' (Wittgenstein 1967). According to this view, language, as well as being a repository of lexical items arranged according to various syntactic rules, primarily functions as a tool in the hands of linguistically capable agents. Utterances can be understood as acts, and are best analysed in terms of their effects. The meaning of words cannot be abstracted from their embeddedness in utterances, in the broader situational context in which those utterances are made, and in the practical effects they produce. Assertoric statements—of the kind analysed by formal semantics, whose semantic import could be judged by the truth value of their propositional contents—are an unremarkable region in the broader landscape of linguistic utterances, which can be analysable against several other functional vectors (Austin [1955] 1975). Unlike formal semantics, pragmatics focuses on a broader class of linguistic phenomena; unlike hermeneutics, this focus is less directed towards subjective interpretation, and more towards the social and intersubjective aspects of language use: speech acts, rules, functions, effects, games, commitments, and so on.

In the 1950s, Austin ([1955] 1975) Wittgenstein (1967), Quine ([1953] 1980) and Sellars ([1956] 1997) collectively mounted a series of what can best be described as pragmatically inflected critiques against the naïve empiricism embedded within a logical positivist view of meaning, a view which can still be traced in the formal semantics tradition. Through a subsequent generation of philosophers, linguists and cognitive scientists, these critiques presented a range of new perspectives for understanding how semantic concepts are organised and used within a broader landscape of social practice.

In his landmark text *How to do Things with Words*, Austin ([1955] 1975) discusses sentences whose functional role in discourse is distinct from that of assertional statements—that is, sentences which are not directly decomposable into propositional form. Austin directs attention particularly towards 'performatives'—utterances which *do* things. Unlike descriptive statements, which can be analysed in terms of truth content, such performative sentences have to be assessed against different criteria: whether they are successful in their execution, or in Austin's vocabulary, 'felicitous' Austin ([1955] 1975). He eventually introduces a trichotomous schema to characterise how a sentence functions:

- as a *locutionary* act—'uttering a certain sentence with a certain sense and reference'

- as a *illocutionary* act—'informing, ordering, undertaking, &c., i.e. utterances which have a certain (conventional) force'

- as a *perlocutionary* act—'what we bring about or achieve *by* saying something, such convincing, persuading, deterring...'.

Searle (1969) elaborates a further, extended and systematic account of various kinds of such speech acts, as well as various means for understanding their function and effects in discourse.

Wittgenstein's account represents, in turn, a yet more radical departure from a view which sees statement making as the canonical and primary function of language—a view which was moreover emphatically outlined in his own earlier work (Wittgenstein 1921). Understanding language meaning, again, means understanding how it is used in practice. Wittgenstein introduces the idea of language 'games', to direct attention to the role utterances play as pseudo-'moves'. Such games need not have winners, losers or even outcomes—what is distinctive about any linguistic situation is that it conforms to rules understood—at least partially—by its interlocutors. Despite its presentation in an elliptical and short text, Wittgenstein's later work has been immensely influential. As well as motivating Rosch's studies of prototypes and family resemblances (Lakoff 1987; Rosch 1975), his work has also been influential in a range of intersecting disciplines: Toulmin's analysis of rhetoric and argumentation; Geertz' phenomenological anthropology, with an attentiveness to 'thick' description and language games (Geertz 2005); and different strains of French philosophy and social theory, stretching across Bourdieu (1990), Lyotard (1984) and Latour (2004).

Sellars' critique of empiricism broadly echoes those of Austin, Wittgenstein and Quine, but contains a more explicit and direct critique of empiricism (Sellars [1956] 1997). The 'Myth of the Given', like the 'Two Dogmas of Empiricism', forms part of the backdrop to the more recent pragmatist philosophy of Rorty, McDowell and Brandom. Sentential or propositional meaning is not ignored in all of these accounts. In *Making It Explicit*, for example, Brandom develops a monumental theoretical apparatus which connects a fine-grained analysis of assertions—the ground left behind by previous pragmatist accounts—with the social game of, as he puts it, 'giving and asking for reasons' (Brandom 1994). His brand of 'analytic pragmatism' provides one of the foundations for the ontology commensurability framework presented further on, and is discussed in more detail in Chapter 11, 'On commensurability'.

Several implications can be drawn from a general pragmatist orientation towards language for the commensurability framework developed here. First, the main unit of pragmatic analysis is the sentential utterance rather than the word—focusing on the whole rather than the part. Second, a pragmatic treatment of meaning needs to be attentive towards not only the utterance itself, but also the situational context in which it is made—who is speaking, who is listening, what conventions are in operation, in what sequence utterances are made, what effects utterances produce, and so on. Third, definitional meanings can be understood not only as compositions of atomic parts—a series of denotations—but also only as codifications of convention—a bundle of connotations, associations and cultural practices. Fourth, an utterance can be understood simultaneously at variegated, multi-dimensional levels of abstraction—as a direct assertion, a move in a dialogical sequence, a tactical move in a language game, or an act which conforms to understood social norms and conventions.

At first glance, a pragmatist orientation might appear irrelevant for the interpretation of ontologies and other information schemes. After all, knowledge systems are developed in formal languages precisely to sidestep the kinds of ambiguities and 'infelicitations' which plague natural language. While systems are *prima facie* expressions of definitions and assertions, however, they also serve other discursive roles—to persuade, convince, insinuate and facilitate further negotiation. Moreover they are used in quite specific *social* language games—as 'tokens' in various kinds of political and economics games, for example. Interpreting knowledge systems pragmatically therefore means not only understanding their explicit commitments, but the roles they play in these extended language games. What are they developed and used for? What motivates their constructions—as very particular kinds of utterance? How are they positioned relative to other systems—what role do they play in the kinds of games played out between organisational, governmental, corporate and inter-departmental, for example? Pragmatism therefore provides a useful 'step up' from viewing ontologies as representations of conceptual schemes to viewing them as social products—'speech acts', 'utterances' and 'moves' in very broadly conceived language games. It also underlines the contextual relevance of commensurability assessments themselves—that interpretation and translation are also linguistic acts, performed for particular purposes and goals.

Cognitive semantics

Theories of categorisation

One way of considering knowledge systems is as formal mechanisms for classifying and categorising objects. Graphically, a typical ontology resembles a hierarchical taxonomy—though, technically, it is a directed acyclic graph, meaning that concepts can have more than a single 'parent' as well as multiple 'siblings' and 'children'. (Ontologies also can support other sorts of conceptual relations, but the relationship of subsumption is axiomatised into the semantics of the OWL directly, as are several other relations.) In such systems, concept application relies on objects meeting necessary and sufficient conditions for class membership. This general model accords well with the broad tradition of category application stretching back to Aristotle. However, ontologies are intended to be machine-oriented representations of conceptualisations, with only an analogical relation to mental cognitive models. What, then, can be gleaned from contemporary theories of categorisation?

Since the 1960s alternative models have been proposed for how mental concepts are organised and applied. Like ontologies, semantic networks, pioneered by Quillian (1967), model cognitive conceptual networks as directed graphs, with concepts connected by one-way associative links. Unlike ontologies these links do not imply any logical (or other) kind of relation between the concepts—only that a general association exists. Semantic networks were adapted for early knowledge representation systems, such as frame systems, which utilise the same graphic structure of conceptual nodes and links: 'We can think of a *frame* as a network of nodes and relations' (Minsky 1974). Minsky also explicitly notes the similarity between frame systems and Kuhnian paradigms—what results from the construction of a frame system as a viewpoint of a slice of the world. By extension, semantic networks can be viewed as proto-paradigms in the Kuhnian sense, though it is not clear what the limits between one network and another might be—this analogy should not, then, be over-strained.

A feature of semantic networks is the lack of underlying logical formalism. While Minskian frame systems and other analogues in the 1970s were 'updated' with formal semantic layers, notably through the development of description logics in the 1980s, according to Minsky the lack of formal apparatus is a 'feature' rather than a 'bug'—imposition of checks on consistency, for example, impose an unrealistic constraint on attempts to represent human kinds of knowledge, precisely because humans are rarely consistent in their use of concepts (Minsky 1974). At best they are required to be consistent across a localised portion of their cognitive semantic network, relevant to a given problem at hand, and the associated concepts and reasoning required to handle it. Similarly the authors of semantic network models note the difficulty in assuming neatly structured graphs model mental conceptual organisation: 'Dictionary definitions are not very orderly and we doubt that human memory, which is far richer, is even as orderly as a dictionary' (Collins and Quillian 1969). Semantic networks represent an early—and enduring—model of cognition, which continues to be influential in updated models such as neural networks and parallel distributed processing (Rogers and McClelland 2004). Such networks also exhibit two features of relevance to the theory adopted here: first, the emphasis on structural, *connectionist* models of cognition—that concepts are not merely accumulated quantitatively as entries in a cognitive dictionary, but are also inter-connected, so that the addition of new concepts makes a qualitative difference in how existing concepts are applied; and second, the implied *coherence* of networks, which suggests concepts are not merely arranged haphazardly but form coherent and explanatory schemes or structures.

In the mid-1970s prototype theory, another cognitive model, was proposed for describing concept use. Building on Wittgenstein's development of 'language games' (Wittgenstein 1967), Rosch (1975) demonstrated through a series of empirical experiments that the process of classifying objects under conceptual labels was generally not undertaken by looking for necessary and sufficient conditions for concept-hood. Rather, concepts are applied based on similarities between a perceived object and a conceptual 'prototype'—a typical or exemplary instance of a concept. Possession of necessary and sufficient attributes is a weaker indicator for object inclusion within a category than the proximity of the values of particularly salient attributes—markers of family resemblance—to those of the ideal category member. For example, a candidate dog might be classified so by virtue of the proximity of key perceptual attributes to those of an ideal 'dog' in the mind of the perceiver—fur, number of legs, size, shape of head, and so on. Applying categories on the basis of family resemblances rather than criterial attributes suggests that, at least in everyday circumstances, concept application is a vague and error-prone affair, guided by fuzzy heuristics rather than strict adherence to definitional conditions. Also, by implication, concept application is part of learning—repeated use of concepts results in prototypes which are more consistent with those used by other concept users. This would suggest a strong normative and consensual dimension to concept use. Finally, Rosch (1975) postulated that there exist 'basic level semantic categories', containing concepts most proximate to human experience and cognition. Superordinate categories have less contrastive features, while subordinate categories have less common features—hence basic categories tend to be those with more clearly identifiable prototypical instances, and so tend to be privileged in concept learning and use.

While semantic network and prototype models provide evocative descriptive theories that seem to capture more intuitive features of categorisation, they provide relatively little causal explanation of how particular clusters of concepts come to be organised cognitively. Several new theories were developed in the 1980s with a stronger explanatory emphasis (Komatsu 1992). Medin and Schaffer (1978), for example, propose an exemplar-based 'context' theory rival to prototype theory, which eschews the inherent naturalism of 'basic level' categorial identification for a more active role of cognition in devising 'strategies and hypotheses' when retrieving memorised category exemplar candidates. Concept use, then, involves agents not merely navigating a conceptual hierarchy or observing perceptual family resemblances when they apply concepts; they are also actively formulating theories derived from the present context, and drawing on associative connections between concept candidates and other associated concepts. In this model, concept use involves scientific theorising; in later variants, the model becomes 'theory theory' (Medin 1989). As one proponent puts it:

> In particular, children develop abstract, coherent systems of entities and rules, particularly causal entities and rules. That is, they develop theories. These theories enable children to make predictions about new evidence, to interpret evidence, and to explain evidence. Children actively experiment with and explore the world, testing the predictions of the theory and gathering relevant evidence. Some counter-evidence to the theory is simply reinterpreted in terms of the theory. Eventually, however, when many predictions of the theory are falsified, the child begins to seek alternative theories. If the alternative does a better job of predicting and explaining the evidence it replaces the existing theory (Gopnik 2003, p. 240).

Empirical research on cognitive development in children (Gopnik 2003) and cross-cultural comparisons of conceptual organisation and preference (Atran et al. 1999; Medin et al. 2006; Ross and Medin 2005) has shown strong support for 'theory theory' accounts. Quine's view of science as 'self-conscious common sense' provides a further form of philosophical endorsement to this view.

For the purposes of this study, a strength of the 'theory theory' account is its orientation towards conceptual holism and schematism—concepts do not merely relate to objects in the world, according to this view (although assuredly they do this too); they also stand within a dynamic, explanatory apparatus, with other concepts, relations and rules. Moreover theories are used by agents not to explain phenomena to themselves, but also to others; concept use has then a role both in one's own sense making of the world, and also in how one describes, explains, justifies and communicates with others. In short, concepts are understood as standing not only in relation to objects in the world, as a correspondence theory would have it; they stand in relation to one another, to form at least locally coherent mental explanations; and they also bind together participating users into communities and cultures. The account presented here similarly draws on supplemental *coherentist* and *consensual* notions of truth to explain commensurability.

Semantics and the embodied mind

Various other influential cognitive models have also been proposed. Drawing together several diverse theoretical strains—generative semantics, phenomenology and Rosch's earlier work—Lakoff and Johnson (1980) suggest that analogical and associative processes of metaphorisation are central to describing concept use and organisation. Eschewing logically derived models popular in the 1960s and 1970s, Johnson and Lakoff contend that conceptualisation is at least strongly influenced, if not causally determined, by the cognitive agent's physical and cultural orientation. Rational minds are therefore subject to a kind of phenomenological embeddedness within a physical and cultural world— even the most abstract conceptualisations can be shown to 'borrow', in the form of metaphorical structures, from the perceptual and intersubjective worlds we inhabit. To take one of the case study examples presented later, 'upper-level' or 'foundational' ontologies are so-called because 'upper' refers to the head, the sky or the heavens—the phenomenological locus of conceptual abstraction—while 'foundational', though physically inverted, refers to structural support, substance—again, the phenomenological and etymological locus of conceptual 'depth'. Johnson and Lakoff seek to explain not only individual concept use by this kind of metaphorical reduction, but also larger conceptual clusters, which when transposed from the immediate and physical to some more abstract field provide a means of understanding that field economically and coherently.

Lakoff and others develop tantalising glimpses of a metaphorical account of cognition, grounded in the 'embodied mind', in several subsequent works, notably Lakoff (1987), Dennett (1991) and Varela, Thompson and Rosch (1992). In part Lakoff's critique—as with Rosch—is directed towards a mechanistic or computational theory of mind, which views cognition as a series of abstract operations which could be conceivably replicated on any suitable hardware—biological or otherwise. Implied in this view is a form of Cartesian mind–body dualism, a false dualism according to Lakoff (1987) and Dennett (1991). What can be extracted from these kinds of critique is a cautionary and corrective view that sees cognition as irretrievably bound to a physically and socially embedded agent, intent on making sense of new experience by drawing on an existing reserve of culturally shared, coherent conceptual constructs. Above all, both conceptual and physical experiences here are firmly oriented within a series of 'cultural presuppositions', as Lakoff and Johnson suggest:

> In other words, what we call 'direct physical experience' is never merely a matter of having a body of a certain sort; rather, every experience takes place within a vast background of cultural presuppositions. It can be misleading, therefore, to speak of direct physical experience as though there were some core of immediate experience which we then 'interpret' in terms of our conceptual systems. Cultural assumptions, values, and attitudes are not a conceptual overlay which we may or may not place upon experience as we choose. It would be more correct to say that all experience is cultural through and through, that we experience our 'world' in such a way that our culture is already present in the very experience itself (Lakoff and Johnson 1980, p. 57).

Lakoff and Johnson's metaphorical model, while clearly capturing some part of the way concepts are transferred over domain boundaries, nonetheless suffers from a problem of theoretical indeterminacy—it fails to account for why some metaphors are used and not others. Moreover, it arguably does not give sufficient agency to concept users—under their theorisation of cognition, it is not clear how concept users are any more than passive adopters of a shared collective cultural heritage. The creative use of metaphor—much less the range of other, non-metaphorical linguistic actions, such as various forms of deductive, inductive or abductive reasoning—is not explicitly treated in their account.

Geometries of meaning—the re-emergence of conceptual structure

In part to gather up traditional and more progressive theories of categorisation, several more recent models have been proposed. These are at once highly systematic, and tolerant of the problems of vagueness and fuzziness which had plagued older logistic approaches. Gardenfors (2000), for instance, proposes a sophisticated geometric model of cognition, which blends together more conventional cognitive elements—concepts, properties, relations, reasoning—with some of the suggestive elements proposed by Lakoff and others. Rogers and McClelland (2004) put forward what they term a 'parallel distributed processing' account of semantic cognition, which builds on the descriptive and explanatory strengths of 'prototype' and 'theory' theories, while attempting to remedy their defects. Goldstone and Rogosky (2002) propose an algorithmic approach to translation across what they call a 'conceptual web', presupposing holistic conceptual schemes and a quantifiable notion of semantic distance separating concepts within and across schemes. Although these recent accounts are themselves quite different in approach and findings, they share a greater willingness to use computational and geometrically inspired models to explore feasible modes of cognitive activity.

These kinds of studies are evidence of a kind of resystematisation taking place in the cognitive sciences, as (qualified) structural models once more come to the fore. Unsurprisingly, such models are also well suited to describing representations of conceptual systems in ontologies and schemas. At the same time, the model presented by Gardenfors (2000) in particular can be reconciled with the kinds of experiential phenomenology and cultural embeddedness which feature in the work of Lakoff and Johnson (1980). Chapter 11, 'On commensurability', employs Gardenfors' model of cognition directly in relation to the question of commensurability, connecting it to the pragmatist-infused account of language offered by Brandom, and the more general social theory of Habermas, as the basis for generating comparative views of conceptual schemes ('conceptual spaces' in Garderfors' vocabulary) across different cognitive, linguistic and cultural tiers.

Social semantics

The following section aims to sample some of the prevailing paradigms of sociological theory and research in relation to semantics, and specifically in its intersection with technological kinds of meaning formation.

Sociology of knowledge

The semantic models put forward so far consider the creation and dissemination of meaning to be first and foremost a concern of individual rational agents, in which the influence of culture is a secondary and frequently distorting feature. The sociology of knowledge, following Marx and Nietzsche—both suspicious of knowledge's purported independence from its conditions of production—attempts to explain how different epistemic 'perspectives' emerge (Mannheim [1936] 1998). A more modern rendering describes sociology of knowledge as an inquiry into how knowledge is constituted or constructed within a social or cultural frame of reference (Hacking 1999). That is, knowledge is taken within such inquiry as not only trivially social—in the sense that it typically involves more than a single actor—but also, and fundamentally, as a product of social forces and relations. While epistemological inquiry has always sought to understand the role of external influences—usually negative ones—on the development of knowledge—even Socrates' attack on the sophists can be read in this vein—nevertheless there is a specific trajectory that can be traced across twentieth-century thought. This trajectory leads from Mannheim's *Ideology and Utopia* in the 1930s (Mannheim [1936] 1998), through to a revival in Kuhn, Foucault, Bloor and Latour in the 1970s (Bloor [1976] 1991; Foucault 1970; Kuhn 1970; Latour and Woolgar [1979] 1986), up to a flurry of present-day sociological interest in the natural and social sciences—most notably in the field of science and technology studies (Hacking 1999; Keller 2005).

Sociology of knowledge proponents are frequently accused of 'relativising' knowledge, making it little more than a circumstantial side-effect of social or cultural context (Davidson 2006; Pinker 1995). As several authors note (Bloor 1991; Hacking 1999, 2002), however, discussing social constructions of knowledge need not imply adoption of a relativising stance. Rather it can involve understanding why particular problems of knowledge—and solutions—might present themselves at various times. Moreover such an approach can be open to a two-way, dialectic relationship between knowledge and society—arguing that society (however broadly construed) is equally formed through the production of ideas, theories, facts and statements, as much as knowledge artefacts themselves are formed by societal influences. Treating knowledge as a social construct need not therefore be a one-way descent into epistemic relativism, in which all 'facts' can be merely be explained away as by-products of cultural forces, power relations or other social entities.

Applied to contemporary knowledge representation systems, as a general rubric, sociology of knowledge has much to recommend it. It opens a way to investigate not only *which* perspectives emerge in relation to some domain of knowledge, but also *how* those perspectives are coordinated with respect to each other—how, for instance, one perspective within a given domain can cause others to emerge as well, in opposition, or sometimes, perhaps, in an uneasy alliance. It also provides a convenient lexicon to move from technical discussions of ontologies—as knowledge artefacts—through to a general cultural field of perspectives, orientations, world views and standpoints. Moreover it suggests that it is possible, when looking at an object like a formal knowledge system through a sociological historical lens, to see it neither in strictly idealist terms (as intellectual history pure and simple, as the production of useful theorems and theses by enlightened minds), nor in strictly materialist terms (as the net effect of particular economic, political, governmental or military forces), but rather as something like the dialectical and probabilistic outgrowth of both idealistic and materialistic forces. As the case studies demonstrate, while ascribing direct causal influence on the production of knowledge systems is inveterately difficult, it is still possible to paint a plausible—and epistemologically defensible—portrait of the complex interplay of these forces.

Swidler and Arditi (1994) note that considerable attention has been devoted to a 'sociology of informal knowledge'. As the survey of science and technology studies below shows, there have been many studies of various kinds of 'formal knowledge' too. However, the term 'sociology of formal knowledge' is an apt epithet for the kind of approach adopted here—the study of the perspectival standpoints which underpin formal knowledge systems, where 'formal knowledge system' specifically means the encoding of some knowledge (a series of concepts, relations and individual objects) in a formal language. One of the claims of the study is that studying knowledge systems as social or cultural artefacts is not only a matter of interest to a sociologist of knowledge, but also provides practical guidance to a systems analyst faced with 'day-to-day' problems of conceptual translation across perspectival divides—indeed the claim suggests, perhaps, that these two disciplinary roles increasingly converge in 'networked societies' (Castells 1996) where the technological and the anthropological are inseparably intertwined.

A fitting example of one such 'intertwining' is the term 'ontology' itself. Although it is introduced in its computer science appropriation in Chapter 2, 'Frameworks for knowledge representation', in its modernised philosophical sense 'ontology' can be understood as the historical and cultural ground against which conceptualisations are developed. This view of ontology, freeing it from its metaphysical roots as the study of 'what is', is succinctly encapsulated by Hacking:

> Generally speaking, Foucault's archaeologies and genealogies were intended to be, among other things, histories of the present… At its boldest, historical ontology would show how to understand, act out, and resolve present problems, even when in so doing it generated new ones. At its more modest it is conceptual analysis, analyzing our concepts, but not in the timeless way for which I was educated as an undergraduate, in the finest tradition of philosophical analysis. That is because the concepts have their being in historical sites. The logical relations among them were formed in time, and they cannot be perceived correctly unless their temporal dimensions are kept in view (Hacking 2002, pp. 24–25).

In Chapter 11, 'On commensurability', some of the 'sociologists of knowledge' introduced here—in particular, Kuhn, Foucault and Hacking—are discussed in more detail. For now, this introduction is intended to demonstrate how the tradition of the sociology of knowledge strongly informs the approach adopted in this study. It also suggests that an analysis of commensurability aims, ideally, to shed light on the historical and cultural conditions—to the degree that these can be ascertained—of ontology construction and design. What at a first glance can pose itself as a largely technical exercise, of mapping, matching and aligning ontological concepts, can at its further degree present itself instead as a complex task of translation across cultural conceptual schemes or, in Hacking's phrase, 'historical ontologies'; the aim of the framework presented here is, in part, to help analyse concepts and their schemes against a broader historical and cultural backdrop. Knowledge systems, no less than any other cultural artefact, 'cannot be perceived correctly unless their temporal dimensions are kept in view' (Hacking 2002).

Critical theory as a sociology of knowledge

The historical dimension to ontological standpoints is analysed further by the critical theory tradition. Developed out of the work of Marx, Weber and Lucáks, critical theory dispenses with what it sees as idealistic aspects of sociology of knowledge—or rather, reorients these on the materialist conditions of knowledge production (Popper and Adorno 1976). Different perspectival orientations, in more extreme variants of this view, are the apparent epiphenomena which develop out of the structural character of the economy at given moments in history (Horkheimer and Adorno 2002). While differences of opinion might always be free to circulate in any society, fundamentally incommensurable world views, irreconcilable through rational discourse, are the product of the alienating forces of modern capitalism, which rigidifies human relations in terms of class structure.

Habermas sought to free analyses of knowledge and communication from the more deterministic aspects of critical theory, while retaining its materialist foundations. His theory of communicative action points to several complex overlapping dimensions in post-Enlightenment society. For Habermas, the fundamental rift between objective system and subjective lifeworld can be attenuated through the intersubjective sphere of communication and discourse (Habermas 1987). Within this orbit, different knowledge formations are free to circulate, with the potential to reconfigure structural inadequacies in the growing systematisation of individual lifeworlds enacted by capitalism.

Luhmann provides a related frame of reference via systems theory (Arnoldi 2001; Baecker 2001). Not at all assimilable to critical theory, Luhmannian systems nevertheless provide some elaboration on the objectivist, 'system' side of the critical theoretical coin. For Luhmann, systems are 'autopoetic'—they engender their own frames of meaning around a critical 'distinction'. For economic systems, for example, the motivating distinction is the presence or absence of money. The distinction then structures the cluster of concepts which inform how those in the system operate. Luhmann's views have some analogies with the model of culture put forward in Chapter 12, 'A framework for commensurability'; however, for reasons of parsimony, the theoretical cues from Habermas' admittedly less developed account of the complex overlays of systems in contemporary society, which provide a plausible generative and sufficiently abstract account of the divisions that fissure through contemporary knowledge systems, are instead adopted here. I return to Habermas in more detail in Chapter 11, 'On commensurability', where his theoretical apparatus is woven in among more fine-grained analyses of language and cognition.

Globalisation and technologies of knowledge

Related forms of social theory and research have investigated the rise of information technology and the correlative phenomenon of globalisation. Castells (1996), for instance, documents exhaustively the emergence of the 'network society', in which traditional forms of labour, organisation, urban planning, travel, markets, culture, communication and, finally, even human subjectivity are transformed by the 'network'— a metonymic substitute for various kinds of physical and information networks that parallel the growth of globalisation and late or 'hyper' capitalism at the turn of the millennium. According to Castells, the ontological 'horizon' of modern times is *qualitatively* different partly as a result of *quantitatively* expansive affordances offered by network effects or externalities. This results not in a simple homogenising of cultural differences; rather, echoing the Frankfurt School and Habermas, the 'global network of instrumental exchanges' 'follows a fundamental split between abstract, universal instrumentalism, and historically rooted, particularistic identities. Our societies are increasingly structured around a bipolar opposition between the Net and the Self' (Castells 1996, p. 3).

Just as, for Habermas, radical ontological incommensurability arises between the system and the lifeworld, so Castells sees a similar structural schism between 'the Net and the Self', and its various conceptual analogues—culture and nature, society and community, function and meaning. The rise of the network society therefore produces incommensurability as an 'unintended consequence' precisely because of its globalising, standardising and homogenising character; it creates localised resistances in the fissures or lacunae of its network. However, for Castells as for Habermas, these differences can always be negotiated by the proselytising force of communication itself, with ambiguous effects:

Because of the convergence of historical evolution and technological change we have entered a purely cultural pattern of social interaction and social organization. This is why information is the key ingredient of our social organization and why flows of messages and images between networks constitute the basic thread of our social structure (Castells 1996, p. 508).

Studies on technology and science

Many of the preoccupations of the 'sociology of knowledge' have been inherited by more recently emergent disciplines, such as science and technology studies. Largely inaugurated through Latour and Woolgar's seminal anthropological study of a scientific laboratory (Latour and Woolgar [1979] 1986)—though equally influenced by earlier 'structural' histories of science and technology—science and technology studies work for the most part by examining the sites and practices of science and technology. A common feature of science and technology studies research generally, and of research inspired by the closely aligned actor-network theory (ANT) in particular, is the desire to show how clear-cut conceptual boundaries—even those apparently fundamental, between subject and object, nature and culture, and active and passive agents—become blurred in scientific practice (Latour 1993; Law 1992, 2004). Not a 'theory' in the usual sense, owing more to Geertz's 'thick' methodological approach to ethnography than explanatory sociological models (Latour 2004), ANT has nonetheless provided a broad rubric and vocabulary for researchers attempting to analyse how different knowledge formations are constructed socially, or, as Law puts it, 'scientific knowledge is shaped by the social' (Law 2004). And as information technology has began to play an important role in many scientific disciplines, many science and technology studies have increasingly paid attention to the social construction of computational systems of classification.

Bowker and Star (1999), for instance, examine how active political and ethical choices become invisible once encoded within classificatory schemes in a variety of bureaucratic contexts: medical, health and governmental demography. Adopting the term 'information infrastructures' to describe how such schemes facilitate organisational practices just as physical infrastructure might do, their analysis develops its own set of distinguishing—and inter-related—typological features. Classification systems can be:

- *Formal/scientific* or *informal/folk*—Formal systems are used in 'information science, biology and statistics, among other places', while informal systems are 'folk, vernacular and 'ethno-classifications'.

- *Pragmatic* or *idealistic*—Pragmatic systems tend to be oriented towards a limited set of contemporary goals; idealistic systems are future-oriented, trying to anticipate future uses.

- *Backwards-compatible* or *future-oriented* (related to the previous distinction)—Backwards-compatible systems endeavour to harmonise categories with pre-existing schemes and data-sets; future-oriented systems are developed from relatively new principles or methods.

- *Practical* or *theoretical*—Practical systems tend to evolve to meet the needs of new users and applications, and may lose original motivating principles; theoretical systems tend to retain such principles as endemic to their operation.

- *Precise* or *prototypical*—Prototypical taxonomies provide 'good enough' descriptive labels, rather than rigorous necessary and sufficient conditions, recalling Rosch's distinction outlined above (Rosch 1975).

- *Parsimonious* or *comprehensive*—Parsimonious systems capture only a limited number of fields; comprehensive systems aim to gather as much information as possible.

- *Univocal* or *multivocal*—Univocal systems tend to reflect a singular, authoritative perspective; multi-vocal systems tend instead to reflect multiple interests.

- *Standardised* or *eccentric*—Standardised systems reflect a mainstream view of field or domain; eccentric systems adopt idiosyncratic, unique or otherwise alternative organisations of concepts.

- *Loosely* or *tightly* regulated—Loosely regulated classifications systems develop *ad hoc*—through trial and error, and incremental revision; tightly regulated systems tend to have formal review processes and versioning systems. (Adapted from Bowker and Star 1999.)

As the authors make clear, many of these distinctions are of degree rather than kind—systems may be more or less formal in the above sense, for example. These distinctions motivate several of the second-order dimensions introduced in Chapter 12, 'A framework for commensurability'; there they are applied as a means of classifying classification systems themselves.

In a series of further case studies, Bowker and Star (1999) also demonstrate the complexity of factors that motivate particular categorial distinctions behind classification systems. They highlight the inherent fuzziness and historical residues that accrue to systems over time, demonstrating how, for instance, political and ethical values become embedded long past their historical valency. Such critical impulses can also be found in a number of more recent studies—Smart et al. (2008), for instance, look at how racial and ethnic categories become homogenised within scientific classification systems. Other studies have also described the complications arising from overlapping or conflicting methodological approaches to classification. Sommerlund (2006) demonstrates how conflicting genotypical and phenotypical methodological approaches impact on research practices in molecular biology. In another study, Almklov (2008) has shown how formal classification systems are supplemented in practice by informal heuristics, as 'singular situations' need to be interpreted against potentially incommensurable 'standardised' conceptualisations and data sets. The negotiated process of meaning making involved in devising classification systems between diverse disciplinary experts has also recently received attention, for example, in a study by Hine (2006) of 'geneticists and computer engineers' devising a mouse DNA database.

The desire to renovate classification systems—either through development of new systems, or refinements to existing ones—can, then, be motivated by numerous extrinsic social factors. As these various studies demonstrate, *individual* classifications systems can be shown to exhibit conflicting tensions and practical trade-offs in their design, construction and application. Seeking to understand the commensurability of *multiple* systems amplifies the potential noise generated by these tensions; tracing them in turn relies on examining each system against a matrix of inter-related dimensions—including both the kinds of distinctions outlined above, and also a further series of contextually determined and more or less implied distinguishing elements: political and ethical beliefs, disciplinary methodologies, theoretical–practical overlays, and vocational orientations. The resulting profiles can in turn be used for comparing and contrasting the systems concerned—or, in the language adopted here, for assessing their commensurability.

IT standardisation

Central to the rise of globalisation has been the phenomenal growth of standardisation, a process of negotiated agreement across many social layers—from common legislative frameworks, economic agreements, political affiliations and linguistic consensus, through to a myriad of ratified protocols, specifications and standards for mechanical, electrical, engineering, communications and information technology instruments. Considerable research has been directed towards standardisation in the information technology sector specifically, much of it published through a journal dedicated to the field, the *Journal of IT Standards and Standardization Research*. Unlike the preceding science studies, which for the most part adopt an anthropological orientation towards the production of technical artefacts, this research views standardisation as a predominantly economic phenomenon—though with important political, legal and cultural bearings. Where an anthropological view is useful in bringing out the internal perspectival character of knowledge systems, describing how and why these systems became widely used and adopted often requires a broader scope—looking at the complex interplay between individual actors, corporations, governments and multinational consortia, well beyond the laboratory or workplace setting—and commensurately, employing different research methods, examining the motivations and processes of standardisation primarily through historical and documentary evidence, rather than first-hand observation. From the point of view of developing a set of descriptive criteria or dimensions for describing the cultures responsible for knowledge systems, studies of standardisation provide a valuable supplementary source.

Standards exists for a wide range of technical formats, protocols, processes and applications, and studies of IT standardisation have been accordingly eclectic—covering style languages (Germonprez, Avital and Srinivasan 2006), e-catalogue standards (Schmitz and Leukel 2005), e-commerce (Choi and Whinston 2000), mobile platforms (Tarnacha and Maitland 2008), operating systems (Hurd and Isaak 2005; Isaak 2006; Shen 2005), project management (Crawford and Pollack 2008) and software engineering processes (Fuller and Vertinsky 2006). The term 'standard' itself is notoriously difficult to define. Kurihara (2008) points to its French etymological origins as a military 'rallying point'; it has since been co-opted into economic parlance as being 'required for communication between the labeled product and its user in order to win the fullest confidence of the market' (Kurihara 2008). Blum (2005) suggests standards can be divided into 'public' and 'industrial' types; 'public standards' can be further distinguished between national and sector-specific, while 'industrial standards' can be either company or consortia-based. Blum also suggests further criteria for considering standardisation processes: the 'speed of the process'; 'outcomes', in terms of the competitive conditions of market; 'legal status'; and the 'nature of the economic goods created'—whether they be closed or open, public or private.

Several motivations have been identified for the development and use of standards. Most commonly, authors point to one or more economic rationales. For example, Krechmer (2006) identifies three economic beneficiaries of standardisation: governments and market regulators looking to promote competition; lowered production and distribution costs for standards implementers; and user or consumer benefits brought about by a standard's adoption. Hurd and Isaak (2005) add a fourth group: individuals, usually professionals, benefitting by certain kinds of standards certification and professionalisation. In addition, they note that standardisation benefits companies at all stages of a product's lifecycle: by accelerating the initial rate of technology adoption and product diffusion; by expanding the functionality of a product as it matures; and by extending the lifetime of a product as it becomes obsolete or redundant in the face of new, emergent products. The personal motivation which accrues to individuals through their involvement in standards development and certification processes is further noted by Isaak (2006) and Crawford and Pollack (2008). Similarly, standardised quality processes accompanied by internationally recognised certification can help differentiate a company in a crowded market-place—as Fuller and Vertinsky (2006) observe, certification can, in some cases, even be a good market indicator of 'improved future revenues'. Moreover numerous authors have emphasised the direct and indirect benefits of 'network externalities' which technology process, product and platform standardisation bring to users (Katz and Shapiro 1985; Park 2004; Parthasarathy and Srinivasan 2008; Tarnacha and Maitland 2008; Zhao 2004).

The by-products of standardisation are not, however, always beneficial. Van Wegberg (2004) discusses the trade-offs between 'speed and compatibility' in the development of standards, focusing particularly on the problematics of competing standardisation efforts instigated by rival industrial consortia. The fractious effects of multiple standards are further studied by Tarnacha and Maitland (2008) and Schmitz and Leukel (2005)—though authors are divided as to whether such problems arise from excessive competition, over-regulation, or are in fact intrinsic side-effects of market dynamics. The costs of standards compliance and certification processes can also produce negative unintended consequences, operating as market barriers to entry, and limiting rather than fostering market competition (Tarnacha and Maitland 2008). Furthermore, consequences can be culturally discriminatory: as one study has shown, on a national level standardisation can lead to adverse effects for 'indigenous technology developments' (Shen 2005), as the dispersion of proprietary, closed standards, in particular, can inhibit local training, innovation and industrial development. Analysis of the rivalry between Microsoft and Linux operating systems in China points to potential negative normative and even imperialist implications of purely market-driven standardisation, if unattended by adroit legal and political policy. Even relatively benign professional bodies, with no direct economic or political mandate, can, in developing standards, implicitly promote national or regional agendas into global ones—at the potential risk of marginalising those with less resources or authority (Crawford and Pollack 2008; Parthasarathy and Srinivasan 2008). Moreover, corporations have become experts at 'gaming' the standards process, both by overt political and economic influence, and by covert 'patent ambush', in which 'submarine' patents are submitted as part of otherwise 'open' or 'fair and reasonable' technological provisions to standards, only to resurface at the corporate donor's leisure—if new products or technologies inadvertently infringe on the patents (Hemphill 2005). Market dynamics also often foster so-called 'standards wars', in which companies form competing consortia promoting rival standards—a process which fragments the market and dilutes the network externalities of standards, at least until a dominant candidate emerges (Parthasarathy and Srinivasan 2008).

Consequently, while many studies note the generally beneficial nature of standardisation, such processes—and the technical artefacts they produce—can be seen as part of a social negotiation between different kinds of co-operative and competitive agents, engaged in a series of complex trade-offs. In the case of ontologies and schemas, standardisation is often their very *raison d'être*—broad diffusion and adoption being key elements of their promise to deliver interoperability. Understanding commensurability of ontologies, then, can often involve understanding the methods and means by which their authors endeavour to make them standards. Of the studies surveyed, only Schmitz and Leukel (2005) offer something of a typology of distinguishing features of standards; they propose the following for the purpose of choosing e-catalogue standards:

- General:
  - What is the market penetration of the standard—current and future?
  - What is the quality of the standard?
- Specific:
  - *Standard organisation*—How long will it remain effective? What level of power and international exposure does it have? What is the level of user involvement?
  - *Methodology*—Is the underlying language of the standard highly formalised? Machine-readable? Sufficiently expressive?
  - *Standard content*—Is the standard at the right level? What objects are categorised? Is the coverage right and satisfying?

Some of these specific features are picked up and reworked as descriptive dimensions later in the framework presented in Chapter 12, 'A framework for commensurability'. More generally, this review of standardisation studies has extracted a number of dimensions which can be applied to knowledge systems, particularly to the areas of process and motivation of system design. These dimensions include:

- open versus closed process
- levels of *de facto* and *de jure* standardisation
- size and levels of community activity around standards
- adoption rates, industry support, levels of satisfaction with standards
- differing motivations—economic, political, legal, social and technical.

Knowledge management

Knowledge systems can also be studied through yet another disciplinary lens, that of knowledge management. Knowledge management approaches tend to discuss ontologies less as kinds of classification systems or standards, and more as a kind of intangible organisational asset (Volkov and Garanina 2007). This perspectival shift brings about yet further distinctions which can be used to compare and contrast ontologies. Moreover, the literature review now moves closer to dealing with ontologies as a subject proper—increasingly knowledge management has co-opted ontologies as an exemplary kind of knowledge representation, with numerous studies explicitly proposing or examining frameworks, processes and systems for handling ontologies in knowledge management journals (Bosser 2005; Härtwig and Böhm 2006; Lanzenberger et al. 2008; Lausen et al. 2005; Macris, Papadimitriou and Vassilacopoulos 2008; Okafor and Osuagwu 2007).

Much attention in knowledge management studies is devoted to describing the relationship between tacit and explicit knowledge in an organisational context. Nonaka and Takeuchi (1995) put forward a widely adopted model for describing this relationship, which follows a four-step process of 'socialization' (tacit-to-tacit), 'externalization' (tacit-to-explicit), 'combination' (explicit-to-explicit) and 'internalization' (explicit-to-tacit). Hafeez and Alghatas (2007) study how this model can be applied to learning and knowledge management in a virtual community of practice devoted to systems dynamics. They also demonstrate how discourse analysis of online forums can be employed to demonstrate a process of knowledge transfer between participants—a method increasingly used to capture features of 'virtual' communities generally. These communities are an increasingly prevalent cultural setting for knowledge dissemination, as Restler and Woolis (2007) show; similarly, discourse analysis is used in several of the case studies in this work. Other studies extend similar knowledge diffusion models to the whole organisation life cycle (Mietlewski and Walkowiak 2007), or examine the application of such models as specific interventions into organisations, in the form of an action research program aimed at improving knowledge elicitation processes (Garcia-Perez and Mitra 2007). Al-Sayed and Ahmad show how expert knowledge exchange and transfer is facilitated within organisations by 'special languages'—limited and controlled vocabularies—which represent 'key concepts within a group of diverse interests'. As the authors point out, while use of such languages can serve to further the political aims of a specialised group within an organisation, the primary aim is one of parsimony 'for reducing ambiguity and increasing precision' within a professional context (Al-Sayed and Ahmad 2003). Such 'languages for special purposes' can serve to reify a given set of lexical items into discourse, giving rise to particular conceptualisations within a knowledgeable community of practice. In turn, these are frequently codified into knowledge systems; understanding the practical generative conditions of such languages is one way, then, towards understanding and describing the assumptions behind these systems.

Several authors (Detlor et al. 2006; Hughes and Jackson 2004; Loyola 2007; Soley and Pandya 2003) have sought to analyse the specific roles played by context and culture—two notoriously ill-defined concepts—in the formation, elicitation and management of knowledge. Acknowledging the resistance of the term 'culture' to easy definition, much less quantification, Soley and Pandya (2003) suggest a working definition: culture is a 'shared system of perceptions and values, or a group who share a certain system of perceptions and values', which would include 'sub-groups, shared beliefs and basic assumptions deriving from a group'. This working definition arguably ignores an important dimension of shared or collective practice which, following Bourdieu (1990), would seem constitutive of any culture. Nonetheless the authors point to important ways in which various cultural attributes—technical proficiency, economic wealth, as well as linguistic, educational and ethical characteristics—impact on knowledge sharing, and suggest, anticipating some of the same points made in this study, that a certain degree of sensitivity and comprehension of culture has material consequences—although, in their case, these consequences are subject to the overall 'game' of corporate competition.

Both Detlor et al. (2006) and Loyola (2007) seek to understand the role that a similarly vexed concept, context, plays in knowledge management. Detlor et al. (2006) provide a structural account of the relationship between a 'knowledge management environment' and organisational and personal information behavioural patterns, using a survey-driven approach to show that indeed a strong causal relationship exists. In their analysis, four survey items relating to 'environment' (used interchangeably here with 'context') reference terms like 'culture', 'organisation', 'work practices, lessons learned and knowledgeable persons' and 'information technology'—as well as 'knowledge' and 'information'—which suggests the notion of 'context' here is synonymous with the modern organisational bureaucracy. Loyola (2007), on the other hand, surveys approaches which seek to formalise context as a more abstract 'feature' of knowledge descriptions. Building on earlier work in this area (Akman and Surav 1996; Bouquet et al. 2003), Loyola (2007) argues these approaches strive to describe context either as part of a logical language, or as part of a data, programming or ontological model. Recognising that context is frequently tacit in knowledge representations—that it 'characterises common language, shared meanings and recognition of individual knowledge domains'—Loyola examines attempts to make it explicit as a kind of knowledge representation itself. After a comparative review, he concludes that an ontology developed by Strang, Linnhoff-Popien and Frank (2003) is best suited to describing context, and sees the explication of context as itself a vital part of facilitating interoperability between conceptual, informational and social divides.

While no studies address the specific question posed here about the commensurability of multiple ontologies, the relationships sketched in this literature between knowledge assets, on the one hand, and cultures, contexts and processes of knowledge management, on the other, constitute a useful conceptual rubric for the model of commensurability presented in Chapter 12, 'A framework for commensurability'. Moreover, these studies bring forward several further salient dimensions which can be applied to ontologies:

- whether the ontology represents a relatively small and insular, or large and variegated 'community of practice'
- whether the ontology uses 'expert' or 'lay' vocabulary
- what sorts of cultural beliefs, values, assumptions and practices impact on an ontology's design
- what sorts of contextual factors can impact on an ontology's design, and how those factors can be best rendered explicit.

As the literature review moves from an engagement with various forms of understanding social semantics towards examining computational approaches to representing and reasoning with meaning—in particular how to align different systems of meaning—the following complaint, ostensibly concerning the cognitive dissonance between ontology and broader knowledge management processes, provides a convenient segueway into the challenges at the intersection of these two fields:

> Currently, none of the ontology management tools support social agreement between stakeholders, or ontology engineers. They most often assume one single ontology engineer is undertaking the alignment, and no agreement is therefore necessary. However, the whole point in ontology alignment is that we bring together, or align, ontologies that may have been created by different user communities with quite different interpretations of the domain. Social quality describes the relationship among varying ontology interpretations of the social actors. Means to achieve social quality are presentations of the alignment results in such a way that the different alignment types are explicitly distinguished and the location of the alignments from... a detailed and global perspective are highlighted (Lanzenberger et al. 2008, p. 109).

Computational semantics

The question of meaning is foundational for semantic web and broader computational research; indeed, the problems of how to represent and reason with concepts have been central preoccupations since the earliest days of research in artificial intelligence (Norberg 1989). Considerable attention has been devoted to the formal, logical mechanisms for representing meaning generally and to the construction of ontologies for representing meaning in specific fields or domains. Chapter 7, 'An historical introduction to formal knowledge systems', which examines different knowledge representation mechanisms, surveys some of these discussions. In the decentralised world of the semantic web, with no governing authority dictating which ontologies are useful, a corollary challenge of inter-ontology translation has led to the development of specific algorithmic techniques for automating the production of conceptual matches between ontologies. This field of ontology matching is explored in brief detail below. Related work in ontology metrics and collaboration are also relevant to the general approach and framework proposed here, and some recent findings are presented as well.

Matching ontologies

Ontology matching aims to find relationships between ontologies via algorithmic means, where no (or few) explicit relationships exist between them; according to a recent survey of ontology matching approaches, it 'finds correspondences between semantically related entities of ontologies' and the fundamental problem faced by ontology matching is one of 'semantic heterogeneity' (Shvaiko and Euzenat 2008). As Halevy notes:

> When database schemas for the same domain are developed by independent parties, they will almost always be quite different from each other. These differences are referred to as semantic heterogeneity. Semantic heterogeneity also appears in the presence of multiple XML documents, web services and ontologies—or more broadly, whenever there is more than one way to structure a body of data (Halevy 2005, p. 50).

When dealing with one-to-one semantic mappings between databases within an organisation—a familiar system integration scenario—semantic heterogeneity is typically met with round-table discussions between experts and stakeholders, who endeavour to engineer appropriate conceptual translations between schemas. This takes time: 'In a typical data integration scenario, over half of the effort (and sometimes up to 80 per cent) is spent on creating the mappings, and the process is labor intensive and error prone' (Halevy 2005). These twin motives—time and quality—have spawned fervent searches for highly precise automatic approaches to mappings. Moreover, in the open world of the semantic web, where collaboration by ontology authors is often impossible, and at any rate where mappings need to be many-to-many, humanly engineered translations may be necessary, but invariably are insufficient (Gal and Shvaiko 2009).

Ontology matching algorithms typically take two ontologies (and possibly external data sources) as inputs, and generate a series of matches as output. A *match* consists of a tuple <*id,e,e',n,R*>, where *id* is the identifier of the match, *e* and *e'* are the two concepts from the two respective ontologies, *n* is the (optional) level of confidence in the match, and *R* is the relationship (one of conceptual equivalence, subsumption or disjointness) (Shvaiko and Euzenat 2005, 2008). The resulting match series is termed an *alignment*. Evaluation of algorithms, given the plethora of possible inputs and evaluative dimensions, is a notably difficult task (Do, Melnik and Rahm 2003). Since 2004, an annual competition has been held to rate algorithms' outputs against expert humanly engineered alignments across a range of fields (Shvaiko and Euzenat 2009). Some of these approaches have demonstrated impressive precision and recall results against humanly engineered mappings (Lauser et al. 2008; Marie and Gal 2008), although, as Shvaiko and Euzenat (2008) note, no stand-out candidate approach has yet emerged.

In order to generate alignments, various approaches exploit the different syntactic, structural and semantic properties of ontologies. Several surveys of ontology and schema matching approaches have been conducted (Choi, Song and Han 2006; Do, Melnik and Rahm 2003; Halevy 2005; Noy 2004; Rahm and Bernstein 2001; Shvaiko and Euzenat 2005). Shvaiko and Euzenat (2008) provide a useful set of distinctions for grouping different approaches and methods. As with the metrics below, some of these distinctions resurface in the presentations of dimensions in Chapter 12, 'A framework for commensurability'; hence it is useful to summarise these distinctions briefly here (redacted from Shvaiko and Euzenat 2008):

- *Element* versus *structure*—Element-based comparison is the comparison of individual concepts. An element-based comparison might be expected to find any of the following results: that 'tree' matches 'tree'; that 'tree' also matches the French equivalent of 'arbre'; that 'leaf' is a part of 'tree'; that 'tree' and 'animal' are disjoint, and so on. A structural comparison, on the other hand, might instead compare the overall ontology graphs, or sub-graphs. Instead of relying on individual element matches, element *relations* are also analysed. A 'tree -> leaf' relation might be found to be equivalent to an 'arbre -> feuille' relation, for example.

- *Syntactic* versus *external* versus *semantic*—Both syntactic and semantic techniques use only the information contained in the ontologies themselves; external techniques may refer to other sources for information, for instance, a repository of previous matches in the same domain, or a structured dictionary like WordNet. Semantic techniques are further differentiated through the analysis of semantic relations between elements. In these cases the elements of each ontology are first normalised into a set of comparable logical propositions. If any two logical propositions from each ontology are found to have some valid semantic relationship (where a relation may be equivalent, disjointness, generalisation or specialisation), then a match is found. For example, ontology *A* may have some proposition 'entity -> organic entity -> tree' [*A1*] and ontology *B* may have some proposition 'thing -> life-form -> vegetable -> tree' [*B1*]. By reference to some independent set of axioms, such as a dictionary (WordNet is a common choice), it can then be determined that 'entity' is roughly synonymous with 'thing'; 'organic entity' is synonymous with 'life-form'; and 'tree' is synonymous with 'tree'. Hence the relation of equivalence is deemed to hold between concepts *A1* and *B1*.

- *Schema* versus *instance*-based inferencing—The approaches described above refer only to the structure of the ontologies themselves, and therefore are defined as schema-based. Instance-based inferencing in contrast infers from the contents of the data the correct concepts belonging to that data. For example, some data containing a name with the word 'tree'—as in 'tree #35'—might be inferred as an instance of the tree class.

- *Single* versus *hybrid/composite* techniques—Hybrid and composite techniques use a combination of the above approaches. Frequently such approaches use various weighting schemes to preference one match over others.

Since the approach adopted in this study is contrasted with algorithmic ones generally—as heuristic and holistically oriented, rather than deterministic and atomistic—how do these distinctions differentiate algorithms particularly? Broadly it suggests that algorithms can themselves be plotted on a spectrum of 'atomism–holism', the more 'holistic' being those which are structural, utilise external sources, analyse semantic over syntactic relationships, and exploit a hybrid of alternative techniques (including both schema and instance-based ones). One algorithm which would rate highly against these holistic criteria is *S-Match* (Giunchiglia, Shvaiko and Yatskevich 2004). However, the modes of analysis and outputs remain very different from what is proposed here, which is oriented towards the general cultural assumptions and beliefs, and produces a general commensurability assessment rather than specific alignments. Without prior humanly engineered mappings to go by, the application of a culturally oriented holistic framework is a helpful process to cross-check the alignment results generated by algorithms.

All of the algorithmic approaches discussed in the surveys so far use what Noy (2004) terms 'heuristic and machine learning approaches'. The other avenue towards semantic integration is through explicit mappings, where two ontologies share some common third ontology, typically asserting some set of generic and reusable conceptual axioms. Such 'foundational' or 'upper-level' ontologies show promise for by-passing both the time commitments and error-proneness of humanly engineered mappings, and the vagaries of algorithmically generated alignments. However, as Chapter 9, 'Upper-level ontologies', demonstrates, the proliferation of upper-level ontologies can create new sources of semantic heterogeneity or, in the language adopted here, incommensurability.

Why, across a given domain, are different ontologies ever produced? Relatively little account is given to the *causes* of semantic heterogeneity. Halevy (2005) offers: 'Differing structures are a by-product of human nature—people think differently from one another even when faced with the same modeling goal.' The resort to a kind of naturalistic individualism here underestimates socially and culturally *structural* distinctions—of the sorts discussed in the literature above—which also generate difference in conceptualisations in less stochastic ways. In the framework and case studies that follow, no single causal theory is provided to account for these differences. Nonetheless, in specific cases it is possible to hypothesise socially structural causal factors—distinctions in economic and political subsystems, epistemological assumptions, methodological practices, and the processes and uses to which these systems are put—which orient the categorial configurations of different ontologies one way or another, without reverting to a psychologism which suggests individual agents simply and inherently 'think[ing] differently'. By making these factors explicit, it might be possible to plot lines of potential translation and integration—or, conversely, to recognise obstacles to translation irreducible to individual idiosyncrasies.

Ontology metrics

Several further studies have explored metrics for describing, comparing and evaluating ontologies. Use of these metrics is 'expected to give some insight for ontology developers to help them design ontologies, improve ontology quality, anticipate and reduce future maintenance requirements, as well as help ontology users to choose the ontologies that best meet their needs' (Yao, Orme and Etzkorn 2005). Some of these metrics are brought into the framework in order to characterise internal features of ontologies.

Tartir et al. (2005) propose a more extensive model for describing different features of ontologies, similar in principle to the framework presented here. They distinguish *schema* metrics, which describe only the arrangement of concepts in an ontology, from *instance* metrics, which describe individual objects. The authors propose the following schema metrics:

- *relationship richness*—'reflects the diversity of relations', by comparing the number of non-subsumption relations to the number of subsumption relations (which stipulate specifically that one class is a sub-class of another)
- *attribute richness*—shows the average number of attributes defined per-class within the ontology
- *inheritance richness*—'describes... the fan-out of parent classes', in other words, whether the ontology graph is broad or deep.

The instance metrics are more extensive, but generally are less relevant for the kind of ontology comparison anticipated here. One exception is 'average population', which describes the average number of instances or individual objects per class.

Yao, Orme and Etzkorn (2005) introduce three metrics specifically for describing the cohesion of ontologies, 'the degree to which the elements in a module belong together'. The metrics are: the number of root classes (NoR), the number of leaf classes (NoL) and the Average Depth of Inheritance Tree of Leaf Nodes (ADIT-LN). Together these metrics provide a picture of the structure of an ontology—low numbers of root and leaf classes, relative to the total number of classes, and conversely high numbers of inheritance trees suggest a high overall degree of coherence, a 'deep' rather than 'broad' lattice of concepts. These metrics, then, can be used to further refine the metric of 'inheritance richness' presented by Tartir et al. (2005).

Other research has focused on different aspects and uses for ontology metrics. Alani and Brewster (2006), for instance, discusses four distinct measures for ranking ontologies based on their relevance to search criteria, while Vrandečić and Sure (2007) discuss how to develop semantic rather than purely structural metrics, by first normalising the structure. However, the research by Tartir et al. (2005) and Yao, Orme and Etzkorn (2005) has proven to be of greatest relevance to developing generalised features which can be used to compare, as much as to evaluate, the intrinsic features of different ontologies. These metrics correspond to a number of the dimensions of the framework presented in Chapter 12, 'A framework for commensurability', and can be used to supply quantitative values as part of the application of that framework.

Collaborative ontologies

As a coda to this literature survey, a recent strand of research has focused on the idea of social, collaborative ontology development and matching—an area which intersects with many of the concerns of this book. Several studies have investigated approaches and software systems for collaborative ontology development (Bao and Honavar 2004; Hayes et al. 2005; Sure et al. 2002). In a sign that researchers are increasingly aware of social dimensions of ontology development and matching, two noted contributors to the field have advocated: 'a *public* approach, where any agent, namely Internet user (most importantly communities of users, opposed to individual users) or potentially programs, can match ontologies, save the alignments such that these are available to any other agents' reuse' (Zhdanova and Shvaiko 2006, p. 34).

As we explore further, it is vital to the future of the web as a social knowledge sharing platform that the very formal structures of knowledge are fully explicit: that representations and translations are shareable, reusable, contestable and malleable.

References

Akman, V. and M. Surav. 1996. 'Steps Toward Formalizing Context', *AI Magazine* 17, pp. 55–72.

Al-Sayed, R. and K. Ahmad. 2003. 'Special Languages and Shared Knowledge', *Electronic Journal of Knowledge Management* 1, pp. 1–16.

Alani, H. and C. Brewster. 2006. 'Metrics for Ranking Ontologies'. In *EON 2006: Proceedings of the 4th International Workshop on Evaluation of Ontologies for the Web, at the 15th International World Wide Web Conference (WWW06)*. Edinburgh: Association for Computing Machinery.

Almklov, P.G. 2008. 'Standardized Data and Singular Situations', *Social Studies of Science* 38, p. 873.

Arnoldi, J. 2001. 'Niklas Luhmann: An Introduction', *Theory, Culture & Society* 18, p. 1.

Atran, S., D. Medin, N. Ross, E. Lynch, J. Coley, E.U. Ek and V. Vapnarsky. 1999. 'Folkecology and Commons Management in the Maya Lowlands', *Proceedings of the National Academy of Sciences* 96, pp. 7598–603.

Austin, J.L. [1955] 1975. *How to Do Things With Words*. Oxford: Clarendon Press.

Baecker, D. 2001. 'Why Systems?' *Theory, Culture & Society* 18, pp. 59–74.

Bao, J. and V. Honavar. 2004. 'Collaborative Ontology Building with WikiOnt—a Multi-Agent Based Ontology Building Environment', technical report, International Semantic Web Conference (ISWC) Workshop on Evaluation of Ontology-based Tools (EON).

Besnier, N., D. Blair, P. Collins and E. Finegan. 1992. *Language: Its Structure and Use*. Sydney: Harcourt Brace Jovanovich.

Bloor, D. [1976] 1991. *Knowledge and Social Imagery*, 2nd edn. Chicago, IL: University of Chicago Press.

Blum, U. 2005. 'Lessons from the Past: Public Standardization in the Spotlight', *International Journal of IT Standards & Standardization Research* 3, pp. 1–20.

Bosser, T. 2005. 'Evaluating User Quality and Business Value of Applications Using Semantic Knowledge Technology', *Journal of Knowledge Management* 9, p. 50.

Bouquet, P., F. Giunchiglia, F. Van Harmelen, L. Serafini and H. Stuckenschmidt. 2003. 'C-OWL: Contextualizing Ontologies'. In *Proceedings of the International Semantic Web Conference 2003*.

Bourdieu, P. 1990. *The Logic of Practice*. Stanford: Stanford University Press.

Bowker, G.C. and S.L. Star. 1999. *Sorting Things Out: Classification and its Consequences*. Cambridge, MA: MIT Press.

Brandom, R. 1994. *Making It Explicit*. Cambridge, MA: Harvard University Press.

Burling, R. 1964. 'Cognition and Componential Analysis: God's Truth or Hocus Pocus?', *American Anthropologist* 66, pp. 20–28.

Cann, R. 1993. *Formal Semantics: An Introduction*. Cambridge, UK: Cambridge University Press.

Castells, M. 1996. *The Rise of the Network Society*. Cambridge, MA: Blackwell.

Chierchia, G. and S. McConnell-Ginet. 2000. *Meaning and Grammar: An Introduction to Semantics*. Cambridge, MA: MIT Press.

Choi, N., I.Y. Song and H. Han. 2006. 'A Survey on Ontology Mapping', *SIGMOD Record* 35, pp. 34–41.

Choi, S.Y. and A.B. Whinston. 2000. 'Benefits and Requirements for Interoperability in the Electronic Marketplace', *Technology in Society* 22, pp. 33–44.

Collins, A.M. and M.R. Quillian. 1969. 'Retrieval Time from Semantic Memory', *Journal of Verbal Learning and Verbal Behavior* 8, pp. 240–47.

Crawford, L. and J. Pollack. 2008. 'Developing a Basis for Global Reciprocity: Negotiating Between the Many Standards for Project Management', *International Journal of IT Standards & Standardization Research* 6, pp. 70–84.

Davidson, D. 2006. *The Essential Davidson*. Oxford: Oxford University Press.

Dennett, D.C. 1991. *Consciousness Explained*. New York: Little, Brown and Company.

Detlor, B., U. Ruhi, O. Turel, P. Bergeron, C.W. Choo, L. Heaton and S. Paquette. 2006. 'The Effect of Knowledge Management Context on Knowledge Management Practices: An Empirical Investigation', *Electronic Journal of Knowledge Management* 4, pp. 117–28.

Do, H.H., S. Melnik and E. Rahm. 2003. 'Comparison of Schema Matching Evaluations'. In *Revised Papers from the NODe 2002 Web and Database-Related Workshops on Web, Web-Services, and Database Systems*. London. Springer, pp. 221–37.

Dowty, D.R. 1979. *Word Meaning and Montague Grammar*. Dordrecht: Kluwer Academic Publishers.

Forbes, G. 2008. 'Intensional Transitive Verbs'. In E.N. Zalta (ed.), *The Stanford Encyclopedia of Philosophy*. Stanford, CA: Metaphysics Research Lab, Center for the Study of Language and Information, Stanford University.

Foucault, M. 1970. *The Order of Things: An Archaeology of the Human Sciences*. New York: Vintage Books.

Frege, G. [1892] 1925. 'On Sense and Reference'. Wikisource, The Free Library, *http://en.wikisource.org/w/index.php?title=On_Sense_and_Reference&oldid =1868023* (accessed 14 August 2010).

Fuller, G.K. and I. Vertinsky. 2006. 'Market Response to ISO 9000 Certification of Software Engineering Processes', *International Journal of IT Standards & Standardization Research* 4, pp. 43–54.

Gadamer, H.G. 1975. *Truth and Method*, J. Weinsheimer and D.G. Marshall (trs). London: Continuum.

—. 2004. *Philosophical Hermeneutics*, D.E. Linge (tr.). Berkeley: University of California Press.

Gal, A. and P. Shvaiko. 2009. 'Advances in Ontology Matching'. In T. Dillon, E. Chang, R. Meersman and K. Sycara (eds), *Advances in Web Semantics*, vol. 1. Berlin and Heidelberg: Springer, pp. 176–98.

Garcia-Perez, A. and A. Mitra. 2007. 'Tacit Knowledge Elicitation and Measurement in Research Organisations: A Methodological Approach', *Electronic Journal of Knowledge Management* 5, pp. 373–86.

Gardenfors, P. 2000. *Conceptual Spaces*. Cambridge, MA: MIT Press.

Geertz, C. 2005. 'Deep Play: Notes on the Balinese Cockfight', *Daedalus* 134, pp. 56–86.

Germonprez, M., M. Avital and N. Srinivasan. 2006. 'The Impacts of the Cascading Style Sheet Standard on Mobile Computing', *International Journal of IT Standards & Standardization Research* 4, pp. 55–69.

Giunchiglia, F., P. Shvaiko and M. Yatskevich. 2004. 'S-Match: An Algorithm and an Implementation of Semantic Matching'. In J. Davies, D. Fensel, C. Bussler and R. Studer (eds), *The Semantic Web: Research and Applications*. Berlin and Heidelberg: Springer, pp. 61–75.

Goddard, C. 2002. 'NSM Semantics in Brief', *http://www.une.edu.au/directory* (accessed 23 October 2009).

Goddard, C. and A. Wierzbicka. 2002. *Meaning and Universal Grammar: Theory and Empirical Findings*. Amsterdam: John Benjamins Publishing Company.

Goldstone, R.L. and B.J. Rogosky. 2002. 'Using Relations within Conceptual Systems to Translate Across Conceptual Systems', *Cognition* 84, pp. 295–320.

Gopnik, A. 2003. 'The Theory Theory as an Alternative to the Innateness Hypothesis'. In L. Antony and N. Hornstein (eds), *Chomsky and His Critics*. New York: Wiley-Blackwell, pp. 238–54.

Habermas, J. 1987. *The Theory of Communicative Action*, T. McCarthy (tr.). Boston: Beacon Press.

Hacking, I. 1999. *The Social Construction of What?* Cambridge, MA: Harvard University Press.

—. 2002. *Historical Ontology*. Cambridge, MA: Harvard University Press.

Hafeez, K. and F. Alghatas. 2007. 'Knowledge Management in a Virtual Community of Practice using Discourse Analysis', *Electronic Journal of Knowledge Management* 5, pp. 29–42.

Halevy, A. 2005. 'Why Your Data Won't Mix', *Queue* 3, pp. 50–58.

Harris, R.A. 1993. *The Linguistic Wars*. New York: Oxford University Press.

Härtwig, J. and K. Böhm. 2006. 'A Process Framework for an Interoperable Semantic Enterprise Environment', *Electronic Journal of Knowledge Management* 4, pp. 39–48.

Hayes, P. 2004. 'RDF Semantics'. W3C recommendation, W3C, *http://www.w3.org/TR/rdf-mt/* (accessed 20 January 2010).

Hayes, P., P.F. Patel-Schneider and I. Horrocks. 2004. 'OWL Web Ontology Language Semantics and Abstract Syntax'. W3C recommendation, W3C, *http://www.w3.org/TR/owl-semantics/* (accessed 20 January 2010).

Hayes, P., T.C. Eskridge, R. Saavedra, T. Reichherzer, M. Mehrotra and D. Bobrovnikoff. 2005. 'Collaborative Knowledge Capture in Ontologies'. In *Proceedings of the 3rd International Conference on Knowledge Capture*. New York: Association for Computing Machinery, pp. 99–106.

Heidegger, M. 1962. *Being and Time*, J. Macquarrie and E. Robinson (trs). Oxford: Blackwell Publishing.

Hemphill, T.A. 2005. 'Technology Standards Development, Patent Ambush, and US Antitrust Policy', *Technology in Society* 27, pp. 55–67.

Hine, C. 2006. 'Databases as Scientific Instruments and their Role in the Ordering of Scientific Work', *Social Studies of Science* 36, p. 269.

Hodges, W. 2008. 'Tarski's Truth Definitions'. In E.N. Zalta (ed.) *The Stanford Encyclopedia of Philosophy*. Stanford, CA: Metaphysics Research Lab, Center for the Study of Language and Information, Stanford University.

Horkheimer, M. and T.W. Adorno. 2002. *Dialectic of Enlightenment: Philosophical Fragments*, E. Jephcott (tr.). Stanford: Stanford University Press.

Hughes, V. and P. Jackson. 2004. 'The Influence of Technical, Social and Structural Factors on the Effective Use of Information in a Policing Environment', *Electronic Journal of Knowledge Management* 2, pp. 65–76.

Hurd, J. and J. Isaak. 2005. 'IT Standardization: The Billion Dollar Strategy', *International Journal of IT Standards & Standardization Research* 3, pp. 68–74.

Isaak, J. 2006. 'The Role of Individuals and Social Capital in POSIX Standardization', *International Journal of IT Standards & Standardization Research* 4, pp. 1–23.

Kao, A.H. 2004. 'Montague Grammar', *http://www-personal.umich.edu/~akao/ NLP_Paper.htm* (accessed 18 January 2010).

Katz, M.L. and C. Shapiro. 1985. 'Network Externalities, Competition, and Compatibility', *American Economic Review* 75, pp. 424–40.

Keller, R. 2005. 'Analysing Discourse. An Approach from the Sociology of Knowledge', *Forum: Qualitative Social Research* 6, p. 32.

Komatsu, L.K. 1992. 'Recent Views of Conceptual Structure', *Psychological Bulletin* 112, p. 500.

Kracht, M. 2008. 'Compositionality in Montague Grammar', *http://wwwhomes .uni-bielefeld.de/mkracht/html/montague.pdf* (accessed 26 July 2010).

Krechmer, K. 2006. 'Open Standards Requirements', *International Journal of IT Standards & Standardization Research* 4, pp. 43–61.

Kuhn, T.S. 1970. *The Structure of Scientific Revolutions*, 2nd edn. Chicago, IL: University of Chicago Press.

Kurihara, S. 2008. 'Foundations and Future Prospects of Standards Studies: Multidisciplinary Approach', *International Journal of IT Standards & Standardization Research* 6, pp. 1–20.

Lakoff, G. 1987. *Women, Fire and Dangerous Things*. Chicago, IL: University of Chicago Press.

Lakoff, G. and M. Johnson. 1980. *Metaphors We Live By*. Chicago, IL: University of Chicago Press.

Lanzenberger, M., J.J. Sampson, M. Rester, Y. Naudet and T. Latour. 2008. 'Visual Ontology Alignment for Knowledge Sharing and Reuse', *Journal of Knowledge Management* 12, pp. 102–20.

Latour, B. 1993. *We Have Never Been Modern*. Cambridge, MA: Harvard University Press.

—. 2004. 'On Using ANT for Studying Information Systems: A (Somewhat) Socratic Dialogue'. In C. Avgerou, C. Ciborra and F. Land (eds), *The Social Study of Information and Communication Technology: Innovation, Actors and Contexts*. Oxford: Oxford University Press, pp. 62–76.

Latour, B. and S. Woolgar. [1979] 1986. *Laboratory Life: The Construction of Scientific Facts*, 2nd edn. Princeton: Princeton University Press.

Lausen, H., Y. Ding, M. Stollberg, D. Fensel, R.L. Hernandez and S.K. Han. 2005. 'Semantic Web Portals: State-Of-The-Art Survey', *Journal of Knowledge Management* 9, p. 40.

Lauser, B., G. Johannsen, C. Caracciolo, J. Keizer, W.R. van Hage and P. Mayr. 2008. 'Comparing Human and Automatic Thesaurus Mapping Approaches in the Agricultural Domain'. In *DCMI 2008: Proceedings of the 8th International Conference on Dublin Core and Metadata Applications*. Göttingen: Universitätsverlag Göttingen.

Law, J. 1992. 'Notes on the Theory of the Actor-Network: Ordering, Strategy, and Heterogeneity', *Systemic Practice and Action Research* 5, pp. 379–93.

—. 2004. 'Enacting Naturecultures: A Note from STS'. Centre for Science Studies, Lancaster University, *http://www.lancs.ac.uk/fass/sociology/papers/law-enacting-naturecultures.pdf* (accessed 9 February 2010).

Leech, G.N. 1981. *Semantics*. Harmondsworth: Penguin.

Loyola, W. 2007. 'Comparison of Approaches toward Formalising Context: Implementation Characteristics and Capacities', *Electronic Journal of Knowledge Management* 5, pp. 203–15.

Lyotard, J.F. 1984. *The Postmodern Condition: A Report on Knowledge*, G. Bennington and B. Massumi (trs), F. Jameson (foreword). Minneapolis, MN: University of Minnesota Press.

Macris, A., E. Papadimitriou and G. Vassilacopoulos. 2008. 'An Ontology-Based Competency Model for Workflow Activity Assignment Policies', *Journal of Knowledge Management* 12, pp. 72–88.

Mannheim, K. [1936] 1998. *Ideology and Utopia*. Abingdon: Routledge.

Marie, A. and A. Gal. 2008. 'Boosting Schema Matchers'. In *OTM 2008: Proceedings of the OTM 2008 Confederated International Conferences*. Berlin and Heidelberg: Springer, pp. 283–300.

Medin, D.L. 1989. 'Concepts and Conceptual Structure', *American Psychologist* 44, pp. 1469–81.

Medin, D.L. and M.M. Schaffer. 1978. 'Context Theory of Classification Learning', *Psychological Review* 85, pp. 207–38.

Medin, D.L., N.O. Ross, S. Atran, D. Cox, J. Coley, J.B. Proffitt and S. Blok. 2006. 'Folkbiology of Freshwater Fish', *Cognition* 99, pp. 237–73.

Mietlewski, Z. and R. Walkowiak. 2007. 'Knowledge and Life Cycle of an Organization', *Electronic Journal of Knowledge Management* 5, pp. 449–52.

Minsky, M. 1974. 'A Framework for Representing Knowledge', *http://dspace.mit.edu/handle/1721.1/6089* (accessed 19 January 2010).

Montague, R. 1974. 'The Proper Treatment of Quantification in Ordinary English'. In P. Portner and B.H. Partee (eds), *Formal Semantics: The Essential Readings*. Oxford: Blackwell Publishing.

Mueller-Vollmer, K. 1988. *The Hermeneutics Reader: Texts of the German Tradition from the Enlightenment to the Present*. New York: Continuum International Publishing Group.

Nonaka, I.A. and H.A. Takeuchi. 1995. *The Knowledge-Creating Company: How Japanese Companies Create the Dynamics of Innovation*. Oxford: Oxford University Press.

Norberg, A.L. 1989. 'Oral History Interview with Marvin L. Minsky', *http://www.cbi.umn.edu/oh/display.phtml?id=107* (accessed 19 January 2010).

Noy, N.F. 2004. 'Semantic Integration: A Survey of Ontology-Based Approaches', *SIGMOD Record* 33, pp. 65–70.

Okafor, E.C. and C.C. Osuagwu. 2007. 'Issues in Structuring the Knowledge-base of Expert Systems', *Electronic Journal of Knowledge Management* 5, pp. 313–22.

Park, S. 2004. 'Some Retrospective Thoughts of an Economist on the 3rd IEEE Conference on Standardization and Innovation in Information Technology', *International Journal of IT Standards & Standardization Research* 2, pp. 76–79.

Partee, B.H. 2004. 'Reflections of a Formal Semanticist'. In *Compositionality in Formal Semantics: Selected Papers*. Malden, MA: Blackwell.

Parthasarathy, B. and J. Srinivasan. 2008. 'How the Development of ICTs Affects ICTs for Development: Social Contestation in the Shaping of Standards for the Information Age', *Science Technology & Society* 13, pp. 279–301.

Pinker, S. 1995. *The Language Instinct*. New York: HarperCollins.

Popper, K.R. and T.W. Adorno. 1976. *The Positivist Dispute in German Sociology*. London: Heinemann.

Quillian, M.R. 1967. 'Word Concepts: A Theory and Simulation of Some Basic Semantic Capabilities', *Behavioral Science* 12, pp. 410–30.

Quine, W.V.O. [1953] 1980. *From a Logical Point of View*, 2nd edn. Cambridge, MA: Harvard University Press.

Rahm, E. and P.A. Bernstein. 2001. 'A Survey of Approaches to Automatic Schema Matching', *VLDB Journal* 10, pp. 334–50.

Restler, S.G. and D. Woolis. 2007. 'Actors and Factors: Virtual Communities for Social Innovation', *Electronic Journal of Knowledge Management* 5, pp. 89–96.

Rogers, T.T. and J.L. McClelland. 2004. *Semantic Cognition: A Parallel Distributed Processing Approach*. Cambridge, MA: MIT Press.

Rosch, E. 1975. 'Cognitive Representations of Semantic Categories', *Journal of Experimental Psychology: General* 104, pp. 192–233.

Ross, N. and D.L. Medin. 2005. 'Ethnography and Experiments: Cultural Models and Expertise Effects Elicited with Experimental Research Techniques', *Field Methods* 17, p. 131.

Saussure, F. 1986. *Course in General Linguistics*, C. Bally, A. Sechehaye and A. Riedlinger (eds), R. Harris (tr.). Chicago, IL: Open Court Classics.

Schmitz, V. and J. Leukel. 2005. 'Findings and Recommendations from a Pan-European Research Project: Comparative Analysis of E-Catalog Standards', *International Journal of IT Standards & Standardization Research* 3, pp. 51–65.

Searle, J.R. 1969. *Speech Acts*. Cambridge, UK: Cambridge University Press.

Sellars, W. [1956] 1997. *Empiricism and the Philosophy of Mind*. Cambridge, MA: Harvard University Press.

Shen, X. 2005. 'Developing Country Perspectives on Software: Intellectual Property and Open Source', *International Journal of IT Standards & Standardization Research* 3, pp. 21–43.

Shvaiko, P. and J. Euzenat. 2005. 'A Survey of Schema-Based Matching Approaches', *Journal on Data Semantics* 4, pp. 146–71.

—. 2008. 'Ten Challenges for Ontology Matching'. In *OTM 2008: Proceedings of the 7th International Conference on Ontologies, Databases, and Applications of Semantics (ODBASE)*. Berlin and Heidelberg: Springer, pp. 1164–82.

—. 2009. 'Ontology Alignment Evaluation Initiative', *http://oaei.ontologymatching.org* (accessed 22 February 2010).

Smart, A., R. Tutton, P. Martin, G.T.H. Ellison and R. Ashcroft. 2008. 'The Standardization of Race and Ethnicity in Biomedical Science Editorials and UK Biobanks', *Social Studies of Science* 38, p. 407.

Soley, M. and K.V. Pandya. 2003. 'Culture as an Issue in Knowledge Sharing: A Means of Competitive Advantage', *Electronic Journal on Knowledge Management* 1, pp. 205–12.

Sommerlund, J. 2006. 'Classifying Microorganisms: The Multiplicity of Classifications and Research Practices in Molecular Microbial Ecology', *Social Studies of Science* 36, pp. 909–28.

Strang, T., C. Linnhoff-Popien and K. Frank. 2003. 'CoOL: A Context Ontology Language to Enable Contextual Interoperability'. In *Distributed Applications and Interoperable Systems*, vol. 2893. Berlin: Springer, pp. 236–47.

Sure, Y., M. Erdmann, J. Angele, S. Staab, R. Studer and D. Wenke. 2002. 'OntoEdit: Collaborative Ontology Development for the Semantic Web'. In *ISWC 2002: Proceedings of the First International Semantic Web Conference 2002*, vol. 2342. Berlin: Springer, pp. 221–35.

Swidler, A. and J. Arditi. 1994. 'The New Sociology of Knowledge', *Annual Review of Sociology* 20, pp. 305–29.

Tarnacha, A. and C. Maitland. 2008. 'Structural Effects of Platform Certification on a Complementary Product Market: The Case of Mobile Applications', *International Journal of IT Standards & Standardization Research* 6, pp. 48–65.

Tarski, A. 1957. *Logic, Semantics, Metamathematics*. Indianapolis, IN: Hackett Publishing Company.

Tartir, S., I.B. Arpinar, M. Moore, A.P. Sheth and B. Aleman-Meza. 2005. 'OntoQA: Metric-Based Ontology Quality Analysis'. In *Proceedings of IEEE Workshop on Knowledge Acquisition from Distributed, Autonomous, Semantically Heterogeneous Data and Knowledge Sources*. IEEE Computer Society, pp. 45–53.

Van Wegberg, M. 2004. 'Standardization and Competing Consortia: The Trade-Off between Speed and Compatibility'. *International Journal of IT Standards & Standardization Research* 2, pp. 18–33.

Varela, F.J., E. Thompson and E. Rosch. 1992. *The Embodied Mind: Cognitive Science and Human Experience*. Cambridge, MA: MIT Press.

Volkov, D. and T. Garanina. 2007. 'Intangible Assets: Importance in the Knowledge-Based Economy and the Role in Value Creation of a Company', *Electronic Journal of Knowledge Management* 5, pp. 539–50.

Vrandečić, D. and Y. Sure. 2007. 'How to Design Better Ontology Metrics'. In *ESWC 2007: Proceedings of the 4th European Conference on The Semantic Web*. Berlin and Heidelberg: Springer, pp. 311–25.

Wierzbicka, A. 1980. *Lingua Mentalis: The Semantics of Natural Language*. London: Academic Press.

Wittgenstein, L. 1921. *Tractatus Logico-Philosophicus*. Mineola, IA: Dover Publications.

—. 1967. *Philosophical Investigations*, 3rd edn (first published 1953). Oxford: Basil Blackwell.

Yao, H., A.M. Orme and L. Etzkorn. 2005. 'Cohesion Metrics for Ontology Design and Application', *Journal of Computer Science* 1, pp. 107–13.

Zhao, H. 2004. 'ICT Standardization: Key to Economic Growth?' *International Journal of IT Standards & Standardization Research* 2, pp. 46–48.

Zhdanova, A.V. and P. Shvaiko. 2006. 'Community-Driven Ontology Matching'. In *ESWC 2006: Proceedings of the Third European Semantic Web Conference 2006*, vol. 4011. Berlin and Heidelberg: Springer, pp. 34–49.

4

What does the digital do to knowledge making?

Bill Cope and Mary Kalantzis

Just as a child who has learned to grasp stretches out its hand for the moon as it would for a ball, so humanity, in all its efforts at innervation, sets its sights as much on currently utopian goals as on goals within reach. Because... technology aims at liberating human beings from drudgery, the individual suddenly sees his scope for play, his field of action, immeasurably expanded. He does not yet know his way around this space. But already he registers his demands on it (Benjamin [1936] 2008, p. 242).

Representation is integral to knowledge making. It is not enough to make knowledge, as the prognosticating Darwin did for many decades before the publication of *The Origin of Species*. For knowledge to become germane, to attain the status of knowledge proper, it needs to be represented to the world. It needs, in other words, to be put through the peculiarly social rituals of publishing.

This chapter argues that changes in the modes of representation of knowledge have the potential to change the social processes of knowledge making. To be specific, we want to argue that the transition from print to digital text has the potential in time to change profoundly the practices of knowledge making, and consequently knowledge itself.

But, you may respond, representation is a mere conduit for the expression of knowledge. Having to write *The Origin of Species* did not change what Darwin had discovered. The process of discovery and the process of representation are separated in time and space, the latter being impassively subordinate to the former. The publishing practices that turn knowledge into scholarly journals and monographs are mere means to epistemic ends.

We want to argue that the practices of representation are more pervasive, integral and influential in the knowledge-making process than that. For a start, before any discovery, we knowledge makers are immersed in a universe of textual meaning—bodies of prior evidence, conceptual schemas, alternative critical perspectives, documented disciplinary paradigms and already-formulated methodological prescriptions. The social knowledge with which we start any new knowledge endeavour is the body of already-represented knowledge. We are, in a sense, captive to its characteristic textualities. (In the following chapter, we call these 'available designs' of knowledge.) Next, discovery. This is not something that precedes in a simple sequence the textual processes publication. Discovery is itself a textual process—of recording, of ordering thoughts, of schematising, of representing knowledge textually to oneself as a preliminary to representing that knowledge to a wider knowledge community. There can be no facts or ideas without their representation, at least to oneself in the first instance. How often does the work of writing give clarity to one's thoughts? (In the next chapter, we call this 'designing knowledge'.) Then, knowledge is of little or no import if it is not taken through to a third representational step. In the world of scholarly knowledge this takes the form of rituals of validation (peer and publisher review) and then the business of public dissemination, traditionally in the forms of academic articles and monographs. (In the next chapter, we will call this 'the (re)designed', the representational traces left for the world of knowledge, becoming now 'available designs' for the social cycle of knowledge making to start again.)

How could changing the medium of knowledge representation have a transformative effect on these knowledge design processes? We want to argue that when we change the means of representation, it is bound to have significant effects, later if not sooner. In this chapter, we explore the already visible and potential further effects of the shift to the representation of knowledge through digital media.

The work of knowledge representation in the age of its digital reproducibility

A new translation of Walter Benjamin's essay, 'The Work of Art in the Age of Mechanical Reproduction' has changed the rather inert phrase 'mechanical reproduction' in earlier translations to 'technological reproducibility' (Benjamin [1936] 2008). This shift poignantly speaks to possibility rather than technological inevitability, and affordance, which creates a space for meaning making instead of deterministic consequences. In his essay Benjamin argues that something in art changes once it becomes reproducible. This is the case not only for the tangibly new manifestations of representation that emerge, such as photography and cinema, but in the nature of art itself, even the nature of seeing. Painting has an aura of instance-specific authenticity such that copies present as forgeries, whereas the photographic image is designed for its reproducibility. Photography opens new ways of seeing accessible only to the lens, things not visible to the naked eye which can be enlarged, or things not noticed by the photographer but noticed by the viewer. Cinema substitutes for the theatre audience a group of specialist viewers—the executive producer, director, cinematographer, sound recordist, and so on—who may on the basis of their expert viewing intervene in the actor's performance at any time. Photography is like painting, and cinema is like theatre, but both also represent profound changes in the social conditions of the production and reception of artistic meaning (Benjamin [1936] 2008).

So it is in the case of the textual representation of knowledge. Here, we're in the midst of a broader revolution in means of production of meaning, at the heart of which are digital technologies for the fabrication, recording and communication of meaning. What does this revolution mean? What are its affordances? This is not to ask what consequences follow from the emergence of this new mode of mechanical reproduction. Rather it is to ask what are its possibilities? What does it allow that we might mean or do with our meanings? What new possibilities for representation does it suggest? What are the consequences for knowledge making and knowledge representation?

In answering these questions, our counterpoint will be the world of print. How might the textual representation of knowledge change in the transition from the world of print to the world of digital text? We will examine six areas of current or imminent change. Each of these areas brings potentially enormous change to the processes of knowledge creation and representation:

- A significant change is emerging in *the mechanics of rendering*, or the task of making mechanically reproduced textual meaning. In the world of print, text was 'marked up' for a single rendering. In the emerging world of the digital, text is increasingly marked up for structure and semantics (its 'meaning functions'), and this allows for alternative renderings (various 'meaning forms', such as print, web page or audio) as well as more effective semantic search, data mining and machine translation.

- A new *navigational order* is constructed in which knowledge is accessed by moving between layers of relative concreteness or abstraction.

- This is intrinsically *a multimodal* environment, in which linguistic, visual and audio meanings are constructed of the same stuff by means of digital technologies.

- It is an environment of *ubiquitous recording*, allowing for unprecedented access to potentially reuseable data.

- This environment has the potential to change the *sources and directions of knowledge flows,* where the sources of expertise are much more widely distributed and the monopoly of the university or research institute as a privileged site of knowledge production is challenged by much more broadly distributed sites of knowledge production.

- Whereas English and other large European languages have historically dominated scientific and scholarly knowledge production, this is likely to be influenced by the inherently *polylingual* potentials of the new, digital media.

But before we examine these axes of change, two diversions.

The old and the new in the representation of meaning in the era of its digital reproduction

In this chapter we are concerned to address the question of the nature and significance of the changes to practices of representation and communication for knowledge production in the digital era. Some changes, however, may be less important than frequently assumed. The 'virtual' and hypertext, for instance, are founded on practices and phenomena entirely familiar to the half-millennium-long tradition of print. They seem new, but from the point of view of their epistemic import, they are not so new. They simply extend textual processes which support knowledge moves which are as old as modernity.

The hyperbole of the virtual

The new, digital media create a verisimilitude at times so striking that, for better or for worse, the elision of reality and its represented and communicated forms at times seem to warrant the descriptive label 'virtual reality'.

However, there is not much about the virtual in the digital communications era which print and the book did not create as a genuine innovation 500 years earlier. As a communication technology, print first brought modern people strangely close to distant and exotic places through the representation of those places in words and images on the printed page. So vivid at times was the representation that the early moderns could be excused for thinking they were virtually there. So too, in their time, the photograph, the telegraph, the newspaper, the telephone, the radio and the television were all credited for their remarkable verisimilitude—remarkable for the 'real' being so far away, yet also for being here and now—so easily, so quickly, and so seemingly close and true to life.

Each of these new virtual presences became a new kind of reality, a new 'telepresence' in our lives (Virilio 1997). We virtually lived through wars per medium of newspapers; and we virtually made ourself party to the lives of other people in other places and at other times through the medium of the novel or the travelogue. In the domain of formal knowledge representation, Darwin transported us to the world of the Galapagos Islands, astronomers into realms of space invisible to the naked eye, and social scientists into domains of social experience with which we may not have been immediately familiar.

In this respect, digitisation is just another small step in the long and slow journey into the cultural logic of modernity. We end up addressing the same tropes of proximity, empirical veracity and authenticity that have accompanied any practice of representation in the age of mechanical reproduction of meaning. The significance of the virtual in representation has been multiplied a thousand times since the beginning of modernity, with the rise of the printing press and later the telegraph, the telephone, sound recording, photography, cinema, radio and television. However, digitisation in and of itself adds nothing of qualitative significance to this dynamic. It just does more—maybe even a lot more—of the same.

The hype in hypertext

Hypertext represents a new, non-linear form of writing and reading, it is said, in which readers are engaged as never before as active creators of meaning (Chartier 2001).

However, even at first glance, hypermedia technologies are not so novel, tellingly using metaphorical devices drawn from the textual practices of the book such as 'browsing', 'bookmarking', 'pages' and 'index'. Moreover, when we examine the book as an information architecture, its characteristic devices are nothing if not hypertextual. Gutenberg's Bible had no title page, no contents page, no pagination, no index. In this sense, it was a truly linear text. However, within half a century of Gutenberg's invention, the modern information architecture of the book had been developed, including regularly numbered pages, punctuation marks, section breaks, running heads, indexes and cross-referencing. Among all these, pagination was perhaps the most crucial functional tool (Eisenstein 1979).

The idea that books are linear and digital text is multilateral is based on the assumption that readers of books necessarily read in a linear way. In fact, the devices of contents, indexing and referencing were designed precisely for alternative lateral readings, hypertextual readings, if you like. This is particularly the case for knowledge texts rather than novels, for instance. And the idea that the book or a journal article is a text with a neat beginning and a neat end—unlike the internet, which is an endless, seamless web of cross-linkages—is to judge the book by its covers or the journal article by its tangible beginning and end. However, a book or a journal article sits in a precise place in the world of other books, either literally when shelved in a library, and located in multiple ways by sophisticated subject cataloguing systems, or more profoundly in the form of the apparatuses of attribution (referencing) and subject definition (contents and indexes).

As for hypertext links that point beyond a particular text, all they do is what citation has always done. The footnote developed as a means of linking a text back to its precise sources, and directing a reader forward to a more detailed elaboration (Grafton 1997). The only difference between the footnote and hypertext is that in the past you had to go to the library to follow through on a reference. This relationship to other writing and other books comes to be regulated in the modern world of private property by the laws, conventions and ethics of copyright, plagiarism, quotation, citation, attribution and fair use (Cope 2001b).

Certainly, some things are different about the internet in this regard. Clicking a hypertext link is faster and easier than leafing through cross-referenced pages or dashing to the library to find a reference. But this difference is a matter of degree, not a qualitative difference. For all the hype in hypertext, it only does what printed books and journal articles have always done, which is to point to connections across and outside a particular text.

These are some of the deeply hypertextual processes by which a body of knowledge has historically been formed, none of which change with the addition of hypertext as a technology of interconnection. From an intertextual point of view, books and journal articles are interlinked through referencing conventions (such as citation), bibliographical practices (such as library cataloguing), and the inherent and often implicitly intertextual nature of all text (there is always some influence, conscious or unconscious, something that refracted from other works notwithstanding the authorial conceit of originality). From an extratextual point of view, books and journal articles always have semantic and social reference points. Semantically, they direct our attention to an external world. This external reference is the basis of validity and truth propositions, such as a pointer to an authentic historical source, or a scientifically established semantic reality located in a controlled vocabulary, such as C = carbon. The subject classification systems historically developed by librarians attempt to add structure and consistency to extratextual semantic reference. From an extratextual point of view, texts also have an acknowledged or unacknowledged ontogenesis—the world of supporters, informers, helpers, co-authors, editors and publishers that comprises the social-constructivist domain of authorship and publishing. Not to mention those at times capricious readers—texts enter this social world not as authorial edict, but open to alternative reading paths, in which communicative effects constructed as much by readerly as they are by authorial agendas.

To move on now to things that, in some important respects, are genuinely new to the emerging digital media.

The mechanics of rendering

Many say that the invention of the printing press was unequivocally the pre-eminent of modernity's world-defining events. Huge claims are made for the significance of print—as the basis of mass literacy and modern education, as the foundation of modern knowledge systems, and even for creating a modern consciousness aware of distant places and inner processes not visible to the naked eye of everyday experience (Febvre and Martin 1976).

Print created a new way of representing the world. Contents pages and indexes ordered textual and visual content analytically. A tradition of bibliography and citation arose in which a distinction was made between the author's voice and ideas and the voice and ideas of other authors. Copyright and intellectual property were invented. And the widely used modern written languages we know today rose to dominance and stabilised, along with their standardised spellings and alphabetically ordered dictionaries, displacing a myriad of small spoken languages and local dialects (Phillipson 1992).

The cultural impact of these developments was enormous: modern education and mass literacy; the rationalism of scientific knowledge; the idea that there could be factual knowledge of the social and historical world (Grafton 1997). These things are in part a consequence of the rise of print culture, and give modern consciousness much of its characteristic shape.

What was the defining moment? Was it Johannes Gutenberg's invention of moveable type in 1450 in Mainz, Germany? This is what the Eurocentric version of the story tells us. By another reckoning, the defining moment may have been the invention of clay moveable type in China by Li Sheng in about 1040CE, or of wooden moveable type by Wang Zhen in 1297, or of bronze moveable type by officials of the Song Dynasty in 1341 (Luo 1998). Or, if one goes back further, perhaps the decisive moments were the Chinese inventions of paper in 105CE, wood block printing in the late sixth century and book binding in about 1000CE. Whoever was first, it is hard to deny that the Gutenberg invention had a rapid, world-defining impact, while the Chinese invention of moveable type remained localised and even in China was little used. Within 50 years of the invention of the Gutenberg Press there were 1,500 print shops using the moveable type technology located in every sizeable town in Europe; and 23,000 titles had been produced totalling eight million volumes (Eisenstein 1979). The social, economic and cultural impact of such a transformation cannot be underestimated.

We will focus for a moment on one aspect of this transformation, the processes for the rendering of textually represented meanings. In this analysis our focus will be on the tools for representation, on the means of production of meaning. For the printing press marks the beginning of the age of mechanical reproduction of meaning. This is new to human history and, however subtly, it is a development that changes in some important respects the very process of representation.

Gutenberg had been a jeweller, and a key element of his invention was the application of his jeweller's skills to the development of cast alloy moveable type. Here is the essence of the invention: a single character is carved into the end of a punch; the punch is then hammered into a flat piece of softer metal, a matrix, leaving an impression of the letter; a handheld mould is then clamped over the matrix, and a molten alloy poured into it. The result is a tiny block of metal, a 'type', on the end of which is the shape of the character that had been carved into the punch. Experienced type founders could make several hundred types per hour. The type was then set into formes—blocks in which characters were lined up in rows, each block making up a page of text—assembled character by character, word by word, line by line. To this assembly Gutenberg applied the technology of the wine press to the process of printing; the inked forme was clamped against a sheet of paper, the pressure making an impression on the page. That impression was a page of manufactured writing (Man 2002).

The genius of the invention was that the type could be reused. After printing, the formes could be taken apart and the type used again. But the type was also ephemeral. When the relatively soft metal wore out, it could easily be melted down and new types moulded. One set of character punches was all that was needed to make hitherto unimaginable numbers of written words an infinite number of alternative textual combinations: the tiny number of punches producing as many matrices as were needed to mould a huge number of types in turn producing seemingly endless impressions on paper saying any manner of things that could be different from work to work. Indeed, Gutenberg invented in one stroke one of the fundamental principles of modern manufacturing: modularisation. He had found a simple solution to the conundrum of mass and complexity. Scribing a hand-written book, or making a hand-carved woodblock (which incidentally, remained the practice in China, well after Gutenberg and despite the earlier invention of moveable type by the Chinese), is an immensely complex, not to mention time-consuming, task. By reducing the key manufacturing process (making the types) to the modular unit of the character, Gutenberg introduced a process simplicity through which complex texts could easily and economically be manufactured.

Gutenberg, however, had also created a new means of production of meaning. Its significance can be evaluated on several measures: the technology of the sign, epistemology of the sign and social construction of the sign. The technology of the sign was centred around the new science and craft of 'typography'. The practices of typography came to rest on a language of textual design centred on the modular unit of the character, not only describing its size (in points), visual design (fonts) and expressive character (bold, italic, book). It also described in detail the spatial arrangements of characters and words and pages (leading, kerning, justification, blank space) and the visual information architecture of the text (chapter and paragraph breaks, orders of heading, running heads, footnotes). Typography established a sophisticated and increasingly complex and systematised science of punctuation—a series of visual markers of textual structure with no direct equivalent in speech. The discourse of typography described visual conventions for textual meaning in which meaning function was not only expressed through semantic and syntactic meaning forms but also through a new series of visual meaning forms designed to realise additional or complementary meaning functions.

The new regime of typography also added a layer of abstraction to the abstraction already inherent in language. Representation of the world with spoken words is more abstract than representation through images expressing resemblance, and this by virtue of the arbitrary conventions of language. Writing, in turn, is more abstract than oral language. Vygotsky says that writing is 'more abstract, more intellectualised, further removed from immediate needs' than oral language and requires a 'deliberate semantics', explicit about context and self-conscious of the conditions of its creation as meaning (Vygotsky 1962). With printing, further distance was added between expression and rendering, already separated by writing itself. The Gutenberg invention added to the inherent abstractness of writing. This took the form of a technical discourse of text creation which was, in a practical sense, so abstracted from everyday reality that it became the domain of specialist professionals: the words on the page, behind which is the impression of the forme on the paper, behind which is the profession of typography, behind which is the technology of type, a matrix and a punch. Only when one reaches the punch does one discover the atomic element on which the whole edifice is founded. The rest follows, based on the principles of modularisation and the manufacturing logic of recomposition and replication.

The social construction of the sign also occurs in new ways, and this is partly a consequence of these levels of scientific and manufacturing abstraction. With this comes the practical need to remove to the domain of specialists the processes, as well as the underlying understanding of the processes, for the manufacture of the sign. Speech and handwriting are, by comparison, relatively unmediated. To be well formed and to take on the aura of authoritativeness, printed text is constructed through a highly mediated chain of specialists, moving from author, to editor, to typesetter, to printer, and from there to bookstores, libraries and readers. Each mediation involves considerable backwards and forwards negotiation (such as drafting, refereeing, editing, proofing and markup) between author, editor, typesetter, printer, publisher, bookseller and library. The author only appears to be the font of meaning; in fact texts with the aura of authority are more socially constructed than the apparently less authored texts of speech and handwriting. What happens is more than just a process of increasing social construction based on negotiation between professionals. A shift also occurs in the locus of control of those meanings that are ascribed social significance and power. Those who communicate authoritatively are those who happen to be linked into the ownership and control of the means of production of meaning—those who control the plant that manufactures meaning and the social relations of production and distribution of meaning.

What are the consequences for knowledge making? The world of scholarly publishing is profoundly shaped by the modes of textuality established by print. Knowledge texts establish 'facts' and the validity of truth propositions by external reference: tables of data, footnotes and citations referring to sources, documentation of procedures of observation and the like. These texts place a premium on accuracy through processes of proofing, fact-checking, errata and revised editions. They construct hierarchical, taxonomical information architectures through chapter ordering, multilevel sectioning and highlighting of emphasis words. They include managed redundancy which makes this taxonomic logic explicit: tables of contents, introduction, chapter and other heading weights, summaries and conclusions. This creates a visual compartmentalisation and didactic sequencing of knowledge (Ong 1958). These texts distinguish authorial from other voices by insisting on the attribution of the provenance of others' ideas (citation) and the visual differentiation and sourcing of other's texts (quotation). To authorship, biographical authority is ascribed by institutional affiliation and publishing track record. All text also goes through a variety of social knowledge validation processes, involving publishers, peer reviewers and copy editors, and post-publication reviews and citation by other authors. Not that these are necessarily open or objective—indeed, this system reinforces the structural advantages of those at the centres of epistemic power in a hierarchical social/knowledge system, whose shape is as often determined by positional circumstance as intellectual 'excellence'. From this a body of knowledge is constructed, powerfully integrated by citation and bibliography. Knowledge, once disclosed by publication, is discoverable through tables of contents, indexes, pagination and bookstore or library shelving systems. Print reproduction allows the replication of this body of language by considerable duplication of key texts in multiple libraries and bookstores.

None of this changes, in the first instance, with the transition to digital text. Rather, we begin a slow transition, which in some respects may, as yet, have barely begun. The first 50 years of print from 1450 to 1500 is called the 'incunabula'—it was not until 1500 that the characteristic forms of modern print evolved. Jean-Claude Guédon says we are still in the era of a digital incunabula (Guédon 2001). Widespread digitisation of part of the text production process has been with us for many decades. The Linotron 1010 phototypesetter, a computer which projected character images onto bromide paper for subsequent lithographic printing, was first put into use at the US Government Printing Office in 1967. By 1980 most books were phototypeset.

After phototypesetting, domestic and broad commercial applications of digitisation of text were led by the introduction of word processing and desktop publishing systems. However, it was not until the late 1990s that we witnessed the beginnings of a significant shift in the mechanics of digital representation. Until then, text structure was defined by the self-same discourse of 'markup' that typesetters had used for 500 years. Historically, the role of the typesetter had been to devise appropriate visual renderings of meaning form on the basis of what they were able to impute from the meaning functions underlying the author's text. Markup was a system of manuscript annotation, or literally 'marking up' as a guide to the setting of the type into a visually identifiable textual architecture. This is where the highly specialised discourse of typography developed.

The only transition of note in the initial decades of digitisation was the spread of this discourse into the everyday, non-professional domains of writing (the word processor) and page layout (desktop publishing software). Never before had non-professionals needed to use terminology such as 'font', 'point size' or even 'leading'—the spaces between the lines which had formerly been blocked out with lead in the formes of letterpress printing. This terminology had been an exclusive part of the arcane, professional repertoire of typesetters. Now authors had to learn to be their own typesetters, and to do this they had to learn some of the language of typography. As significant as this shift was, the discourse of typography remained essentially unchanged, as well as the underlying relations of meaning function to meaning form.

The Gutenberg discourse of typography even survived the first iteration of Hypertext Markup Language (HTML), the engine of the World Wide Web (Berners-Lee 1990). This was a vastly cut-down version of Standardised General Markup Language (SGML), which had originated in the IBM laboratories in the early 1970s as a framework for the documentation of technical text, such as computer manuals (Goldfarb 1990). SGML represents a radical shift in markup practices, from typographic markup (visual markup by font variation and spatial layout) to the semantic and structural markup which is now integral to digital media spaces. Figure 4.1 shows a fragment of SGML markup, the definition of 'bungler' for the 1985 edition of the *Oxford Dictionary*.

Figure 4.1 SGML markup for the definition of 'bungler' in the Oxford Dictionary

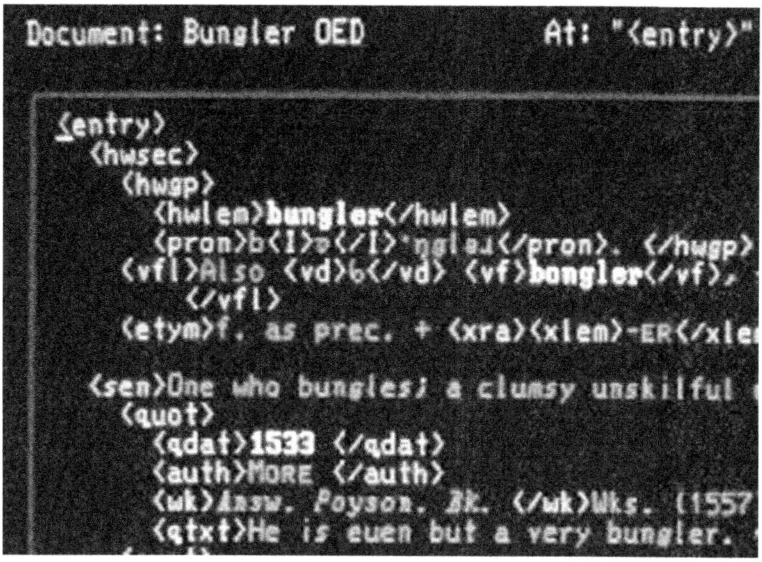

Particularly in its earliest versions in the first half of the 1990s, HTML was driven by a number of presentationally oriented 'tags', and in this regard was really not much more than a traditional typographic markup language, albeit one designed specifically for web browsers. Its genius was that it was based on just a few tags (about 100) drawn from SGML, and it was easy to use, accessible and free. Soon it was to become the universal language of the World Wide Web. However, Tim Berners-Lee bowdlerised SGML to create HTML, contrary to its principles mixing typographic with structural and semantic markup. The five versions of HTML since then have tried to get back closer to consistent principle. Tags mark up the text for its structural (e.g. <sen>) and semantic (e.g. <auth>) features, thus storing information in a way that allows for alternative renderings ('stylesheet transformations') and for more accurate search and discovery.

The next step in this (in retrospect) rather slow and haphazard process was the invention of Extensible Markup Language or XML in 1998. XML is a meta-space for creating structural and/or semantic markup languages. This is perhaps the most significant shift away from the world of Gutenberg in the history of the digitisation text. This, too, is a vastly simplified version of SGML, albeit a simplification more rigorously true to the original SGML insight into the benefits of separating information architecture from rendering. Within just a few years, XML became pervasive, if mostly invisible—not only in the production of text but also increasingly in electronic commerce, mobile phones and the internet. It may be decades before the depth of its impact is fully realised.

Unlike HTML, which is a markup language, XML is a framework for the construction of markup languages. It is a meta markup language. The common 'M' in the two acronyms is deceptive, because marking up markup is an activity of a very different order from marking up. XML is a simplified syntax for the construction of any markup language. In this sense XML is also a significant departure from SGML. Consequently, XML is a space where a plethora of markup languages is appearing, including markup languages that work for the activities of authorship and publishing, and a space for the realisation of ontologies of all kinds, including upper-level spaces for framing ontologies such as Resource Description Framework (RDF) and Ontology Web Language (OWL).

XML brackets the logistics of presentation away from the abstract descriptive language of structure and semantics. Take the heading of this section of this chapter, for instance. In traditional markup, we might use the typographer's analytical tool to mark this as a heading, and that (for instance) might be to apply the visual definition or command such as <14pointTimesBold>. We could enact this command by a variety of means, and one of these is the screen-based tool of word processing or desktop publishing. The command is invisible to the reader; but somebody (the author or the typesetter) had to translate the meaning function 'heading' into a visual meaning form which adequately represents that function to a community capable of reading that visual rendering for its conventionally evolved meaning. If we were to mark up by structure and semantics, however, we might use the concept <heading>. Then, when required, and in a rigorously separated transformational space, this tag is translated through a 'stylesheet' into its final rendered form—and this can vary according to the context in which this information is to be rendered: as HTML by means of a web browser, as conventional print (where it may happen to come out as 14 point Times Bold, but could equally come out as 16 point Garamond Italic, depending on the stylesheet), as a mobile phone or electronic reading device, as synthesised voice, or as text or audio in translation to another language.

The semantic part of XML is this: a tag defines the semantic content of what it marks up. For instance, 'cope' is an old English word for a priest's cloak; it is a state of mind; and it is the surname of one of the authors of this text. Semantic ambiguity is reduced by marking up 'Cope' as <surname>. Combined with a tag that identifies this surname as that of an <author> of this text, a particular rendering effect is created depending on the transformation effected by the stylesheet that has been applied. As a consequence, in the manufacturing process this author's surname is rendered in the place where you would expect it to appear and in a way you could expect it to look—as a byline to the title.

And the structural part of XML is this: a framework of tags provides an account of how a particular domain of meaning hangs together, in other words how its core conceptual elements, its tags, fit together as a relatively precise and interconnected set of structural relations. A domain of meaning consists of a system of inter-related concepts. For instance, <Person>'s name may consist of <GivenNames> and <Surname>. These three concepts define each other quite precisely. In fact, these relations can be represented taxonomically—<GivenNames> and <Surname> are 'children' of the 'parent' concept <Person>. Put simply, the effect of markup practices based in the first instance on semantics and structure rather than presentation is that meaning form is rigorously separated from meaning function. Digital technologies ('stylesheet transformations') automate the manufacture of form based on their peculiar framework for translating generalised function into the particularities of conventional understandings and readings of form. When 'Cope' is marked up as <surname> and this is also a component of <author> (the meaning function), then the stylesheet transformation will interpret this to mean that the word should be located in a particular point size at a particular place on the title page of a book (the meaning form). Meaning and information architecture are defined functionally. Then form follows function.

From this highly synoptic account of shifts in digital text creation and rendering technologies we would like to foreground one central idea, the emergence of a new kind of means of production of meaning: text-made text. Text-made text represents a new technique and new mechanics of the sign. Text is manufactured via an automated process in which text produces text. Text in the form of semantic and structural tags drives text rendering by means of stylesheet transformation. This is a technology for the automated manufacture of text from a self-reflective and abstracted running commentary on meaning function. It is a new mode of manufacture which, we contend, may well change the very dynamics of writing, and much more profoundly so than the accretion of typesetting language into everyday textual practices which accompanied the first phase of digitisation in the last quarter of the twentieth century.

Accompanying this new mechanics is a new epistemology of the sign. It is to be expected that the emergence of new representational means—new relations of meaning form to meaning function—will also entail new ways of understanding meaning and new ways of thinking. Writing acquires yet another layer of 'conscious semantics', to use the Vygotskian phrase, and one which Vygotsky could not possibly have imagined when he was working in the first half of the twentieth century. More than putting pen to paper, or fingers to keyboard, this new mechanics requires the self-conscious application of systematically articulated information architectures. In effect, these information architectures are functional grammars (referring to text structures) and ontologies (referring to the represented world).

However, even though we will soon be five decades into the development of digital text, digitisation still includes deeply embedded typographical practices—in word processing, desktop publishing, and the print-like Portable Document Format (PDF). These are old textual processes clothed in the garb of new technologies—and remain as barriers to many of the things that structural and semantic markup is designed to address: discoverability beyond character or word collocations, more accurate machine translation, flexible rendering in alternative formats and on alternative devices, non-linear workflow and collaborative authoring, to name a few of the serious deficiencies of typographic markup. Academic publishing, however, has yet barely moved outside the Gutenberg orbit.

Figure 4.2 shows the kinds of changes in textwork that are under way. The consequences for knowledge making of the shift to the third of these textual paradigms could be enormous, though barely realised yet.

Scholarly writers, more than any, would benefit from accurate semantic and structural markup of their texts, depending as they do for their knowledge work on finer and less ambiguous semantic distinctions than vernacular discourse. For instance, some domains are already well defined by XML schemas, such as Chemical Markup Language (ChemML). This is something they can most accurately do themselves, rather than publishers or automated indexing software. However their writing environments are still almost universally typographic. There is an urgent need for new text editing environments in whose operational paradigm might be called 'semantic web processing'. (Common Ground's CGAuthor environment is one such example.) When such a paradigm shift is made in the authoring processes of scholars, there will be a quantum leap in the accuracy and quality of search or discovery, data mining, rendering to alternative text and audio devices, accessibility to readers with disabilities, and machine translation.

| Figure 4.2 | Changes in textwork since Gutenberg |

Gutenberg's world	Moving the Gutenberg typographic paradigm onto the desktop	Text work using structural and semantic markup: semantic web processing
Penning the word	Keying the word: the word processor turns the author into an amateur typesetter	Building textual architectures [web pages, styled documents]
Typesetting	Desktop publishing and HTML [at first]; visual markup for a single rendering	Structural and semantic markup: separating text functions from text forms [stylesheets]
To print: letterpress and later lithographic	To print-like screens, and PDF as a postscript [printer] derivative	Multiple rendering paths: print, web, ubiquitous communications and reading devices, voice synthesis, translation engines
Respect the authority of text and its maker. Don't write on that book	Print facsimile pages over which it is hard for readers to write and interact with authors. Old relations of text production and use have barely changed. Mapping old textual practices into the digital media	Readers who write over texts: reviews, recommendations, wikis, annotations. They interact with authors. Exploring the social, dialogical affordances of digital media

A new navigational order

The digital media require users to get around their representational world in new ways. To be a new media user requires a new kind of thinking. In our textual journeys through these media we encounter multiple ersatz identifications in the form of icons, links, menus, file names and thumbnails. We work over the algorithmic manifestations of databases, mashups, structured text, tags, taxonomies and folksonomies in which no one ever sees the same data represented the same way. The person browsing the web or channel surfing or choosing camera angles on digital television is a fabricator and machine-assisted analyst of meanings. The new media, in other words, do just not present us with a pile of discoverable information. They require more work than that. Users can only navigate their way through the thickets of these media by understanding its architectural principles and by working across layers of meaning and levels of specificity or generality. The reader becomes a theoretician, a critical analyst, a cartographer of knowledge. And along the way, the reader can write as they read and talk back to authors, the dialogic effect of which is the formation of the reader who writes to read and the writer who reads to write. This is a new cognitive order, the textual rudiments of which arise in an earlier modernity, to be sure, as we argued earlier in the case of hypertext. However, what we have in the digital media is more than a more efficient system citation and cross reference—which is all that hypertext provides. More than this, we have processes of navigation and architectures of information design in the emerging digital regime that require a peculiarly abstracting sensibility. They also demand a new kind of critical literacy in which fact is moderated by reciprocal ecologies of knowledge validation and full of metadialogues around interest (the 'edit history' pages in wikis for instance). The resultant meanings and knowledge are more manifestly modal, contingent and conditional than ever before.

Let us contrast the knowledge processes of the traditional academic article or monograph with potential knowledge ecologies of the digital navigational order. With the increasing availability of articles in print facsimile PDF or other fixed digital delivery formats, nothing really changes other than a relatively trivial dimension of faster accessibility. Knowledge is still presented as linear, typographical text designed for conventional reading. We are presented with little or nothing more than the traditional typograhical or hypertextual navigation devices of abstracts, sectioning, citation and the like.

However, in the digital era it would be possible to present readers with a less textually mediated relation to knowledge. Data could be presented directly (quantitative, textual, visual) in addition to or even instead of the conventional exegesis of the scholarly article or monograph. Algorithmic 'mashup' layers could be added to this data. The assumption would be that readers of knowledge texts could construct for themselves more varied meanings than those issued by the author, based on their knowledge needs and interests. Also, the unidirectional knowledge flow transmitted from scholarly author to epistemically compliant reader could be transformed into a more dialogical relationship in which readers engage with authors, to the extent even of becoming the acknowledged co-constructors of knowledge.

Whereas print-facsimile publication has a one way irreversibility to it (barring errata or retractions in subsequent articles), scholarly authors would have the opportunity to revise and improve on already-published texts based on a more recursive knowledge dialogue. A scholarly rhetoric of empirical finality and theoretical definitiveness would be replaced by a more dynamic, rapidly evolving, responsive ecology of knowledge-as-dialogue. The mechanics of how this might be achieved are clearly manifest in today's wikis, blogs and social media. It remains for today's knowledge system designers to create such environments for scholarly publishing (Cope and Kalantzis 2009b; Whitworth and Friedman 2009a, 2009b).

Multimodality

The representational modality of written language rose to dominance in the era of print. However, a broad shift is now occurring away from linguistic and towards increasingly visual modes of meaning, reversing the language-centric tendencies of western meaning that emerged over the past half millennium (Kress 2001, 2009; Kress and van Leeuwen 1996). A key contributing factor to this development has been the potential opened by digital technologies. Of course, technology itself does not determine the change; it merely opens human possibilities. The more significant shift is in human semiotic practices.

Let us track back again to our counterpoint in the history of print, the moment of Gutenberg's press. In the Christian religion of medieval Europe, faith was acquired through the visual imagery of icons, the audio references of chant, the gestural presence of priests in sacred garb, and the spatial relationships of priest and supplicant within the architectonic frame of the church. The linguistic was backgrounded, an audio presence more than a linguistic one insofar as the language of liturgy was unintelligible to congregations (being in Latin rather than the vernacular). And the written forms of the sacred texts were inaccessible in any language to an illiterate population (Wacquet 2001). Gutenberg's first book was the Bible, and within a century the Reformation was in full swing. The Reformation sought to replace the Latin Bible with vernacular translations. These became an agent of, and a reason for, mass literacy. The effect of the printed Bible was to create congregations whose engagement with their faith was primarily written-linguistic—the sacred Word, for a people of the Book. The underlying assumptions about the nature of religious engagement were so radically transformed that Protestantism might as well have been a new religion.

So began a half-millennium-long (modern, Western) obsession with the power and authoritativeness of written language over other modes of represented meaning. One of the roots of this obsession was a practical consequence of the new means of production of meaning in which the elementary modular unit was the character. In a very pragmatic sense it was about as hard to make images as it had been to hand-make whole blocks before the invention of moveable type. Furthermore, with the rise of moveable type letterpress it was difficult, although not impossible, to put images on the same page as text—to set an image in the same forme as a block of text so that the impression of both text and image was as clear and even as it would have been had they been set into different formes. Until offset lithographic printing, if there were any 'plates' they were mostly printed in separate sections for the sake of convenience. If image was not removed entirely, text was separated from image (Cope 2001c).

So began a radical shift from image culture to the word culture of Western modernity (Kress 2000). This was taken so far as to entail eventually the violent destruction of images, the iconoclasm of Protestantism, which set out to remove the graven images of Catholicism in order to mark the transition to a religion based on personal encounter with the Word of God. This Word was now translated into vernacular languages, mass-produced as print and distributed to an increasingly literate populace. Gutenberg's modularisation of meaning to the written character was one of the things that made the Western world a word-driven place, or at the very least made our fetish for writing and word-centredness practicable.

By contrast with the Gutenberg technology, it is remarkably easy to put the images and words together when digitally constructing meaning, and this is in part because text and images are built on the same elementary modular unit. The elementary unit of computer-rendered text is an abstraction in computer code made up of perhaps eight (in the case of the Roman character set) or sixteen bits (in the case of larger character sets, such as those of some Asian languages). This is then rendered visually through the mechanised arrangement of dots, or pixels (picture elements), the number of pixels varying according to resolution—a smallish number of dots rendering the particular design of the letter 'A' in 12 point Helvetica to a screen, and many more dots when rendering the same letter to a printer. Images are rendered in precisely the same way, as a series of dots in a particular combination differentiated range of halftones and colours. Whether they are text or images, the raw materials of digital design and rendering are bits and pixels.

In fact, this drift began earlier in the twentieth century and before digitisation. Photoengraving and offset lithographic printing made it much easier to put images and text on the same plane. Print came to be produced through a series of photographically based darkroom and film composition practices which created a common platform for image and type. Evidence of this increasing co-location of text and image is to be found by comparing a newspaper or school textbook of the third quarter of the twentieth century with its equivalent 50 or 100 years ago (Kress 2009).

Digitisation merely opens the way for further developments in this long revolution, by making the process of assembling and rendering juxtaposed or overlaid text and images simpler, cheaper and more accessible to non-tradespeople. And so, we take a journey in which visual culture is revived, albeit in new forms, and written-textual culture itself is more closely integrated with visual culture. Digitisation accelerates this process.

One of the practical consequences of this development is that, among the text creation trades, typesetting is on the verge of disappearing. It has been replaced by desktop publishing in which textual and visual design occur on the same screen, for rendering on the same page. Even typing tools, such as Microsoft Word, have sophisticated methods for creating (drawing) images, and also importing images from other sources, such as scanned images or photographic images whose initial source is digital. Digital technologies make it easy to relate and integrate text and images on the same page. Complex information architectures and multimodal grammars emerge around practices of labelling, captioning and the superimposition of text and image.

In retrospect, it is ironic that in the first phase of digitisation, a simplified version of the discourse of typography is de-professionalised, and that this discourse was a quintessential part of the writing-centric semiotics of the Gutenberg era. Reading is actually a matter of seeing, and in this phase of digitisation the attention of the text creator is directed to the visual aspect of textual design.

Since the last decade of the twentieth century another layer has been added to this multimodal representational scene by the digital recording of sound. With this, music, speaking and video or cinema can all be made in the same space. The result is that we are today living in a world that is becoming less reliant on words, a world in which words rarely stand simply and starkly alone in the linguistic mode. Sometimes the communication has become purely visual—it is possible to navigate an airport by using the international pictographs. In fact, standardised icons are becoming so ubiquitous that they represent an at least partial shift from phonology to graphology—in this sense we're all becoming more Chinese.

There remains, however, a paradox, and that is the increasing use of written language tagging schemas for the identification, storage and rendering of digital media—visual and audio as well as textual. *Prima facie*, this seems to represent a setback in the long march of the visual. More profoundly, it may indicate the arrival of a truly integrated multimodality, with the deep inveiglement of the linguistic in other modes of meaning. Here, the linguistic is not just being itself, but also speaks of and for the visual.

The simple but hugely important fact is that, with digitisation, words, images and sound are, for the first time, made of the same stuff. As a consequence, more text finds its way into images with, for instance, the easy overlay of text and visuals, or the easy bringing together in video of image and gesture and sound and written-linguistic overlays. Television has much more writing 'over it' than was the case in the initial days of the medium—take the sports or business channels for instance.

Meanwhile, the world of academic knowledge remains anachronistically writing-centric (Jakubowicz 2009). It would add empirical and conceptual power, surely, to include animated diagrams, dynamically visualised datasets, and video and audio data or exegesis in published scholarly works. It would help peer reviewers see one layer beyond the author's textual gloss which, in the conventional academic text, removes the reviewer one further representational step from the knowledge the text purports to represent.

The ubiquity of recording and documentation

In the era of mass communications recording was expensive. It was also the preserve of specialised industry sectors peopled by tradespeople with arcane, insider technical knowledge—typesetters, printers, radio and television producers, cinematographers and the like. Cultural and knowledge production houses were owned by private entrepreneurs and sometimes the state. The social power of the captains of the media industry or the apparatchiks of state communications were at least in part derived from their ownership and control of the means of production of meaning—the proprietors of newspapers, publishing houses, radio stations, music studios, television channels and movie studios. Cultural recording and reproduction were expensive, specialised and centralised.

There were some significant spaces where modern people could and did incidentally record their represented meanings in the way pre-moderns did not—in letters, telegrams, photographs and tape recordings, for instance. However, these amateur spaces almost always produced single copies, inaccessible in the public domain. These were not spaces that had any of the peculiar powers of reproduction in the era of 'mass' society.

By contrast, the new, digital media spaces are not just sites of communication; they are places of ubiquitous recording. They are not just spaces of live communication; they are sites of asynchronous multimodal communication of recorded meanings or incidental recording of asynchronous communication—emails, text messages, voicemails, Facebook posts and Twitter tweets. The recording is so cheap as to be virtually free. And widespread public communication is as accessible and of the same technical quality for amateurs as it is for professionals.

Despite these momentous shifts in the lifeworld of private and public communications, most knowledge production practices remain ephemeral—conference presentations, lectures, conversations, data regarded as not immediately germane, interactions surrounding data and the like. Unrecorded, these disappear into the ether.

Now that so much can be so effortlessly recorded, how might we store these things for purposes ancillary to knowledge production? What status might we accord this stuff that is so integral to the knowledge process, but which previously remained unrecorded? How might we sift through the 'noise' to find what is significant? What might be released into the public domain? And what should be retained behind firewalls for times when knowledge requires validation before being made public? These are key questions which our scholarly publication system needs to address, but thus far has barely done so. They will surely need to be addressed soon, given the ubiquity of recording in the new, social media.

A shift in the balance of representational agency

Here are some of the differences between the old media and the new. Whereas broadcast TV had us all watching a handful television channels, digital TV has us choosing one channel from among thousands, or interactive TV has us selecting our own angles on a sports broadcast, or YouTube has us making our own videos and posting them to the web. Whereas novels and TV soaps had us engaging vicariously with characters in the narratives they presented to us, video games make us central characters in the story to the extent that we can even influence its outcomes. Whereas print encyclopedias provided us definitive knowledge constructed by experts, Wikipedia is constructed, reviewed and editable by readers and includes parallel argumentation by reader-editors about the 'objectivity' of each entry. Whereas broadcast radio gave listeners a programmed playlist, iPod users create their own playlists. Whereas a printed book was resistant to annotation (the limited size of its margins and the reader's respect for other readers), new reading devices and formats encourage annotation in which the reading text is also (re)writing the text. Whereas the diary was a space for time-sequenced private reflection, the blog is a place for personal voice which invites public dialogue on personal feelings. Whereas a handwritten or typed page of text could only practically be the work of a single creator, 'changes tracking', version control and web document creation spaces such as Google Docs or Etherpad make multi-author writing easy and collaborative authorship roles clear (Kalantzis 2006a).

Each of these new media is reminiscent of the old. In fact, we have eased ourselves into the digital world by using old media metaphors—creating documents or files and putting them away in folders on our desktops. We want to feel as though the new media are like the old. In some respects they are, but in some harder-to-see respects they are quite different. Figure 4.3 shows some apparent textual parallels.

The auras of familiarity are deceptive, however. If one thing is new about the digitised media, it is a shift in the balance of representational agency. People are meaning-makers as much as they are meaning-receptors. The sites of meaning production and meaning reception have been merged. They are writers in the same space that they are readers. Readers can talk back to authors and authors may or may not take heed in their writing. We are designers of our meaning-making environments as much as we are consumers—our iPod playlists, our collections of apps, our interface configurations. Blurring the old boundaries of writer–reader, artist–audience and producer–consumer, we are all 'users' now. And this, in the context of a series of epochal shifts which are much

Figure 4.3	Parallels between old and new media

Old media	New media
business card, resume	LinkedIn
broadcast TV	interactive TV, YouTube
manuscript	Google Docs
encyclopedia	Wikipedia
diary	blogs
scrapbook	Facebook, MySpace
novel, soap opera	video games
broadcast radio, playlists	podcast, iPod
photo album, picture book	Flickr
letter, memo	email
brochure	website
telegraph, telegram	Twitter

larger than digitisation: in post-Fordist workplaces where workers make team contributions and take responsibility measured in performance appraisals; in neo-liberal democracies where citizens are supposed to take increasingly self-regulatory control over their lives; and in the inner logic of the commodity in which 'prosumers' co-design specific use scenarios through alternative product applications and reconfigurable interfaces (Cope and Kalantzis 2009a; Kalantzis and Cope 2008).

This what we mean by the 'changing balance of agency' (Kalantzis 2006b; Kalantzis and Cope 2006). An earlier modern communications regime used metaphors of transmission—for television and radio, literally, but also in a figurative sense for scholarly knowledge, textbooks, curricula, public information, workplace memos and all manner of information and culture. This was an era when bosses bossed, political leaders heroically led (to the extent even of creating fascisms, communisms and welfare states for the ostensible good of the people), and personal and family life (and 'deviance') could be judged against the canons of normality. Now, self-responsibility is the order of the day. Diversity rules in everyday life, and with it the injunction to feel free to be true to your own identity.

Things have also changed in the social relations of meaning making. Audiences have become users. Readers, listeners and viewers are invited to talk back to the extent that they have become media co-designers themselves. The division of labour between culture and knowledge creators and consumers has been blurred. Consumers are also creators, and creators are consumers. Knowledge and authority are more contingent, provisional and conditional—based in relationships of 'could' rather than 'should'. This shift in the balance of agency represents a transition from a society of command and compliance to a society of reflexive co-construction. It might be that the workers create bigger profits for the bosses, that neoliberalism 'naturally' exacerbates disparities in social power, and that diversity is a way of putting a nice gloss on inequality. The social outcomes, indeed, may at times be disappointingly unchanged or the relativities even deteriorating. What has changed is the way these outcomes are achieved. Control by others has become self-control; compliance has become self-imposed. New media are one part of this broader equation. The move may be primarily a social one, but the technology has helped us head in this general direction.

What are the implications for our ecologies of knowledge production? Contrast traditional academic knowledge production with Wikipedia. Anyone can write a page or edit a page, without distinction of social position or rank. The arbiters of quality are readers and other writers, and all can engage in dialogue about the veracity or otherwise of the content in the edit and edit history areas, a public metacommentary on the page. The roles of writers and readers are blurred, and textual validation is an open, explicit, public and inclusive process. This represents a profound shift in the social relations of knowledge production.

This is a time when the sources and directions of knowledge flows are changing. The sites and modes of knowledge production are undergoing a process of transformation. The university has historically been a specialised and privileged place for knowledge production, an institutionally bounded space, the site of peculiarly 'disciplined' knowledge practices. Today, however, universities face significant challenges to their traditional position as knowledge makers and arbiters of veracity. In particular, contemporary knowledge systems are becoming more distributed. More knowledge is being produced by corporations than was the case in the past. More knowledge is being produced in the traditional broadcast media. More knowledge is being produced in the networked interstices of the social web. In these places, the logics and logistics of knowledge production are disruptive of the traditional values of the university—the for-profit, protected knowledge of the corporation; the multimodal knowledge of the broadcast media; and the 'wisdom of the crowd', which destabilises old regimes of epistemic privilege through the new, web-based media.

How can the university connect with the shifting sites and modes of knowledge production? How can it stay relevant? Are its traditional knowledge-making systems in need of renovation? What makes academic knowledge valid and reliable, and how can its epistemic virtues be strengthened to meet the challenges of our times? How can the university meet the challenges of the new media in order to renovate the disclosure and dissemination systems of scholarly publishing? How can the university connect with the emerging and dynamic sources of new knowledge formation outside its traditional boundaries?

The answers to these large questions are to be found in part in the development of new knowledge ecologies, which exploit the affordances of the new, digital media. This will involve collaborations which blur the traditional institutional boundaries of knowledge production, partnering with governments, enterprises and communities to co-construct distributed knowledge systems. Taking lessons from the emergence of social media, we need to address the slowness and in-network closures of our systems for the declaration of knowledge outcomes—peer review, and journal and book publication systems. In the era of the social web, we anachronistically retain knowledge systems based on the legacies of print. We must design knowledge systems which are speedier, more reflexive, more open and more systemically balanced than our current systems (Cope and Kalantzis 2009b).

A new dynamics of difference

A key aspect of Gutenberg's invention of letterpress printing was to create the manufacturing conditions for the mass reproduction of texts. This is another respect in which his invention anticipated, and even helped to usher in, one of the fundamentals of the modern world. Here, the idea of modularisation and the idea of mass production were integrally linked. The component parts of text were mass manufactured types assembled into formes. The atomic element of modularisation may have been reduced and rationalised; the process of assembly was nevertheless labour intensive. One printed book was far more expensive to produce than one scribed book. The economics of the printed book was a matter of scale, in which the high cost of set up is divided by the number of impressions. The longer the print run, the lower the per unit cost, the cheaper the final product and the better the margin that could be added to the sale price. Gutenberg printed only about 200 copies of his Bible, and for his trouble he went broke. He had worked out the technological fundamentals but not its commercial fundamentals. As it turned out, in the first centuries after the invention of the moveable type letterpress, books were printed in runs of about 1,000. We can assume that this was approximately the point where there was sufficient return on the cost of set up, despite their lower sale price than scribed books. Here begins a peculiarly modern manufacturing logic—the logic of increasing economies of scale or a logic which valorises mass.

Moreover, when culture and language are being manufactured, scale in discourse communities is crucial, or the assumption that there are enough people who can read and will purchase a particular text to justify its mass reproduction. At first, economies of scale were achieved in Europe by publishing in the *lingua franca* of the early modern cultural and religious intelligentsia, Latin. This meant that the market for a book was the whole of Europe, rather than the speakers of a local vernacular. By the seventeenth century, however, more and more material was being published in local vernaculars (Wacquet 2001). With the expansion of vernacular literacy, local markets grew to the point where they were viable. Given the multilingual realities of Europe, however, not all markets were of a sufficiently large scale. There were many small languages that could not support a print literature; there were also significant dialect differences within languages that the manufacturing logic of print ignored. Driven by economies of scale, the phenomenon that Anderson calls 'print capitalism' set about a process of linguistic and cultural standardisation of vernaculars, mostly based on the emerging metrics of the nation-state—marginalising small languages to the point where they became unviable in the modern world and standardising written national languages to official or high forms (Anderson 1983). This process of standardisation had to be rigorous and consistent, extending so far as the spelling of words—never such a large issue before—but essential in a world where text was shaped around non-linear reading apparatuses such as alphabetical indexing. With its inexorable trend to linguistic homogenisation and standardisation, print capitalism ushered in the modern nation state, premised as it was on cultural and linguistic commonality. And so 'correct' forms of national languages were taught in schools; newspapers and an emerging national literature spoke to a new civically defined public; government communications were produced in 'official' or 'standard' forms; and scholarly knowledge came to be published in official versions of national languages instead of Latin. As a consequence, a trend to mass culture accompanied the rise of mass manufacture of printed text, and pressure towards linguistic homogenisation became integral to the modernising logic of the nation-state.

However rational from an economic and political point of view—realising mass literacy, providing access to a wider domain of knowledge, creating a modern democracy whose inner workings were 'readable'—there have also been substantial losses as a consequence of these peculiarly modern processes. Phillipson documents the process of linguistic imperialism in which the teaching of literate forms of colonial and national languages does enormous damage to most of the ancestral and primarily oral languages of the world, as well as to their cultures (Phillipson 1992). Mühlhäusler traces the destruction of language ecologies—not just languages but the conditions that make these languages viable—by what he calls 'killer languages' (Mühlhäusler 1996).

And now, in the era of globalisation, it seems that English could have a similar effect on the whole globe to that which national languages had in their day on small languages and dialects within the territorial domains of nation-states. By virtue in part of its massive dominance of the world of writing and international communications, English is becoming a world language, a *lingua mundi*, as well as a common language, a *lingua franca*, of global communications and commerce. With this comes a corresponding decline in the world's language diversity. At the current rate, between 60 and 90 per cent of the world's 6,000 languages will disappear by the end of this century (Cope and Gollings 2001). To take one continent, of the estimated 250 languages existing in Australia in the late eighteenth century, two centuries later there are only 70 left possessing more than 50 speakers; perhaps only a dozen languages will survive another generation; and even those that survive will become more and more influenced by English and interconnected with Kriol (Cope 1998; Dixon 1980).

However, whereas the trend in the era of print was towards large, homogeneous speech communities and monolingual nationalism, the trend in the era of the digital may well be towards multilingualism and divergent speech communities which distinguish themselves by their peculiar manners of speech and writing—as defined, for instance, by technical domain, professional interest, cultural aspiration or subcultural fetish. None of these changes is technologically driven, or at least not simplistically so. It is not until 30 years into the history of the digitisation of text that clear signs of shape and possible consequences of these changes begin to emerge.

We will focus now on several aspects of these technological changes and changes in semiotic practice: new font rendering systems; an increasing reliance on the visual or the visually positioned textual; the emergence of social languages whose meaning functions have been signed at a level of abstraction above the meaning forms of natural language; machine translation assisted by semantic and structural markup; and a trend to customisable technologies which create the conditions for flat economies of scale, which in turn make small and divergent textual communities more viable. To denote the depth of this change, we have coined the word 'polylingual', foregrounding the polyvocal, polysemic potentials deeper than the simple language differences conventionally denoted by the word 'multilingual'.

The fundamental shift in the elementary modular unit of manufacture of textual meaning—from character-level to pixel level representation—means that platforms for text construction are no longer bound by the character set of a particular national language. Every character is just a picture, and the picture elements (pixels) can be combined and recombined to create an endless array of characters. This opportunity, however, was not initially realised. In fact, quite the reverse. The first phase in the use of computers as text-bearing machines placed the Roman character set at the centre of the new information and communication technologies. Above the 'bit' (an electric 'off' or 'on' representing a 0 or a 1), it was agreed that arbitrary combinations of 0s and 1s would represent particular characters, and these characters became the foundation of computer languages and coding practices, as well as digitised written-linguistic content. The elementary unit above the 'bit' is the 'byte', using eight bits to represent a character. An eight bit (one byte) encoding system, however, cannot represent more than a theoretical 256 characters, the maximum number of pattern variations when eight sets of 0s or 1s are combined (2^7, plus an eighth stop bit). The international convention for Roman script character encoding was to became the American Standard Code for Information Interchange (ASCII), as accepted by the American Standards Association in 1963. In its current form, ASCII consists of 94 characters in the upper and lower case and punctuation marks.

Although one byte character encoding works well enough for Roman and other alphabetic scripts it won't work for larger character sets such as the ideographic Asian languages. To represent languages with larger character sets, specialised two byte systems were created. However, these remained for all intents and purposes separate and designed for localised country and language use. Extensions to the ASCII one byte framework were also subsequently created to include characters and diacritica from languages other than English whose base character set was Roman. Non-Roman scripting systems remained in their own two-byte world. As the relationship between each character and the pattern of 0s and 1s is arbitrary, and as the various systems were not necessarily created to talk to each other, different computer systems were to a large degree incompatible with each other. However, to return to the fundamentals of digital text technology, pixels can just as easily be arranged in any font, from any language. Even in the case of ASCII, text fabrication seemed like just typing. Actually, it's drawing, or putting combinations of pixels together, and there's no reason why the pixels cannot be put together in any number of drawn combinations.

A new generation of digital technologies has been built on the Unicode universal character set (Unicode 2010). The project of Unicode is to encode every character and symbol in every human language in a consolidated two-byte system. The 94 ASCII Roman characters are now embedded in a new sixteen-bit character encoding. Here they pale into insignificance among the 107,156 characters of Unicode 5.2. These Unicode characters not only capture every character in every human language; they also capture archaic languages such as Linear B, the precursor to Ancient Greek found as inscriptions in Mycenaean ruins. Unicode captures a panoply of mathematical and scientific symbols. It captures geometric shapes frequently used in typesetting (squares, circles, dots and the like), and it captures pictographs, ranging from arrows, to international symbols such as the recycling symbol, to something so seemingly obscure as the set of fifteen Japanese dentistry symbols. The potential with Unicode is for every computing device in the world to render text in any and every language and symbol system, and perhaps most significantly for a multilingual world, to render different scripts and symbol systems on the same screen or the same page.

Unicode mixes ideographs and characters as though they were interchangeable. In fact, it blurs the boundaries between character, symbol and icon, and between writing and drawing. Ron Scollon speaks of an emerging 'visual holophrastic language'. He derives the term 'holophrastic' from research on young children's language in which an enormous load is put on a word such as 'some', which can only be interpreted by a caregiver in a context of visual, spatial and experiential association. In today's globalised world, brand logos and brand names (to what language does the word 'SONY' belong? he asks) form an internationalised visual language. A visual holophrastic sign brings with it a coterie of visual, spatial and experiential associations, and these are designed to cross the barriers of natural language (Scollon 1999).

These developments are but one aspect of the convergence of the visual-iconic and the linguistic-symbolic, discussed earlier in this chapter. And this, in turn, is one aspect of increasing polylingualism. The shift is in part a practical response to globalisation. Take the archetypical case of airport signage where it is simply impossible to operate in the language of every traveller. And take technical manuals—meaning is expressed primarily via image and diagrams; if in the design of the manual text is kept to a minimum, it is a relatively inexpensive task to translate labels and text and insert this into the digitised pages. Now that text and image are fabricated or rendered on the same plane, narrative text, captions and labels are easily translated and one language substituted for another in the source file. Communications, in other words, are increasingly built on visually structured templates, and the text is a secondary component.

Behind the multimodal semiotics of the visual, meaning functions are expressed via meaning forms in which natural language becomes genuinely arbitrary—or arbitrary in an additional sense to that originally proposed by founding linguist, Sassure, when he identified the arbitrary relation of the language signifier to its signified. Yet another layer of arbitrariness is added to the relation of forms of language to their meaning functions.

We will illustrate this additional layer of arbitrariness with a simplified example, e-commerce-enabled banking presenting itself to account holders in the machine interfaces of the automatic teller machine, internet banking or telephone banking. Banking involves what Scollon calls a 'chain of mediated action' (Scollon 2001). The bank is keeping my money, and in this context I approach it and I ask for some of it back. What follows is a formal interchange, and, if my request proves valid and is approved, the bank says so and gives me some of my money. My sequence of action and communication is motivated by a 'funnel of commitment', in which I attempt to realise my purpose, my meaning function. What follows from my commitment is a kind of narrative structure. In the traditional shopfront bank my purposes are served as I negotiate a complex array of printed forms that I need to fill out and sign, supported by oral conversations which frame the details of the transaction and give context to the written documentation. In the world of banking before electronic commerce, this was a heavily written and oral language-bound activity. You had to fill out a withdrawal slip that was almost invariably only available in the 'national' language of the bank and then speak to a teller in that language. Occasionally, in deference to multiculturalism and to break into niche markets, banks would make sure there were some multilingual withdrawal forms and bilingual tellers—that is if they wanted to conduct transactions with international tourists, or to serve immigrant languages heavily represented in a local neighbourhood, for instance. But there were practical limits to this, the principal of which was the limited number of languages that could realistically be serviced on one printed form or by the employees in a local branch.

E-commerce enabled banking—the ATM, online banking and automated phone banking—has the potential to change all of that. Various highly routine and predictable conversations, such as the 'I want some of my money' conversation, do not really (despite appearances) happen in English. They happen through a translation of the routine operation of withdrawing funds, or seeking an account balance, into a series of computer-generated prompts. The way these prompts are realised in a particular natural language is arbitrary. There is nothing peculiar or essential to the natural language of the banking conversation. Semantics and grammar, or meaning and information structure, are everything. The logic of the communicative exchange now operates below the level of natural language; it has been designed that way, and it works that way. Various 'banking conversations' are constructed as a universal, transnational, translinguistic code (actually, mediated computer code, because the customer is 'talking' to the bank's computer), in which the manifestation of that code in natural language is, in a communicative sense, arbitrary. You can choose any language you like at the beginning of the online banking session and the visible 'tags' describing the effect of pressing alternative buttons will be translated into your language of choice. There is nothing to stop this being in any script; or the screen swapping its directionality if you were to choose Arabic; or in non-visual interfaces, such as Braille; or interfaces translating text to audio. The ATM and voice-synthesised telephone banking do the same thing, working off the same e-commerce-abstracted text. The rendering of the meaning form can vary radically; but the meaning function remains constant. The business of making the banking service available in another language is as simple as translating the labels which represent the tagged information to the bank customer—a few hundred words at the most.

Once, the grammar of natural language was the entry point into the grammar of banking. Unless the customer and the bank were able to operate competently in the same conversational, written and thus cultural world, there could be no transaction. Banking was a language-delimited game, and the prescribed language or languages were a non-negotiable precondition for playing the banking game. However, in the world of e-commerce, the functional grammar of banking is created first, and this grammar can be realised in any natural language. This functional grammar does not only speak; it also invites a number of physical actions, such as pressing a particular button and taking the money.

Coming back to the questions of polylingualism, this example captures a quite contradictory tendency. On the one hand, billions of people have been drawn into the culture of ATMs since they were introduced in the last quarter of the twentieth century. To use a term defined and developed by linguist Jim Gee, they have become proficient speakers of a 'social language' (Gee 1996). In our example, we might want to call this social language 'global ATM' or 'electronic banking'. The particular natural language-form in which this social language is realised in the instance of a single transaction is measured in terms of human action and social meaning, an arbitrary and increasingly trivial accident of birth. Yes, the culture of electronic commerce and modern banking is taking over the world, spreading a certain kind of global sameness. Doing this sameness multilingually might be seen as a kind of ploy. But the facility also supports another kind of linguistic and cultural diversity, because it has reduced the need for speakers of smaller or locally marginal languages to move over into a dominant language, at least for the purposes of banking. Now you can play the global banking game, but you do not have to leave your culture and mother tongue behind to do it. You can be in a country where your language is not spoken in banks, and it does not matter because you can go to an ATM or ring telephone banking and deal with synthesised-audio, or if required be directed to a live operator in a call centre somewhere in the world who speaks your language. This is just one small and symptomatic example of the way in which new communications technologies may support language diversity, and make it less important in many settings to know a *lingua franca* such as English (Cope 2001a).

Behind this shift lie the ontology or schema-based 'tagging' technologies, tied together domain-specific ontologies. These tagging frameworks operate structurally and semantically. So, two of the tags behind our banking conversation may be: <customername>WilliamCope</customer name> and <withdrawalamount>50.00</withdrawalamount>. These tags sit within the domain of electronic banking. The data contained by tags can be any language or scripting system—and, for that matter, can be digitally recorded images or sound. However, a layer of arbitrariness is added to the tags themselves. The tags have a meaning function and, even in the computer code, they can be in any language and any script and still work as representation and communication within a particular social language. This is because meaning has been designed as a kind of functional map of that social language, the typical ways in which chains of mediated action play themselves out—the various conversational alternatives in the 'I want some of my money' dialogue, for instance.

The underlying design technique is based on the conceptualisation of meaning function. The practical solution is to stabilise each tag schema as a controlled vocabulary or ontology. This is supplemented by tag dictionaries that spell out in translation, across however many natural languages that may be required, the precise referents and the ontologically given structural and conceptual relations between the meaning functions to which the tags refer. Schemas are used to represent tags paradigmatically, typically presented in taxonomies. Tag relations can also be represented as narrative, as activity sequences of a syntagmatic variety, and these alternative conversational or narrative sequences may be represented in user stories and flow diagrams. These two devices represent meaning function at a level of abstraction beyond the level of natural language. They are tools for the construction of a relatively stable semantic ground below the level of natural language. Now, the primary basis for the design of meaning is not the instantiation of meaning in the meaning forms of language (although this is the equally important but now secondary concern of stylesheet transformations). The basis, rather, is the activity and conceptual structures of human intention and experience, or meaning functions.

Tag dictionaries representing ontologies and the linguistic elements of the façade of user interfaces for digital text may be created through human translation—a relatively easy and inexpensive process when the language elements of an interface, or printed text for that matter, have been designed to be substitutable. Marking up for meaning function, however, is an important basis for the increasingly sophisticated technologies of machine translation (Gerber 2001). It makes meaning functions less dependent on contextual markers and shared understandings between communicants. Mention of 'cope' would normally need to be contextualised in order to distinguish its particular meaning among its various meaning possibilities. But if we are working in a publishing schema in which the word is marked up semantically as <surname> and in a structural context where that surname refers to an <author> role, the markup will assist accurate translation.

One possibility created by these technologies is to reduce the relevance of language differences. It will be increasingly possible to participate in the all-encompassing world of global modernity without having to submit to one of its domineering language forms. We may all be able to speak with each other some day soon, and that capacity to communicate will be without prejudice to diversity.

There is still another profound way in which the post-Gutenberg technologies fundamentally shift the means of production of meaning and the ground of culture, and that is to reverse the logic of mass production and economies of scale. This is exemplified by the myriad websites (compare this to the number of 'publishers' in the world of print media), and the shift from the logic of broadcasting and mass media to the user-designed 'narrowcasting' or 'pointcasting' of syndication feeds.

Although it has none of the aura of newness of the digital electronic media, we will focus our attention for the moment on the less immediately obvious case of the printed book. In the Gutenberg era, letterpress, and later gravure and lithographic offset printing, involved the creation of plates, the cost of which have to be amortised over the length of a run (Dunn, Hester and Readman 2001). Typically, the set-up cost of creating a plate using traditional print technologies is between 200 and 1,000 times the cost of a single print in a viable print run. This means that the core commercial and cultural logic of traditional print manufacture centred around a process of reproduction. In its very nature it involves the replication of many copies of an identical original image. The effect is to favour markets and cultures of large scale. Jobs will only be printed if the run length can justify the cost per unit, and the longer the run, the lower the cost per unit. The bigger the culture, the more likely it is to get supported by traditional print. This fundamental commercial and cultural logic is at work in all technologies of reproduction. Although some aspects of the printing process have been digitised since the 1970s, it was not until the 1990s that digitisation was applied directly to the manufacturing process. This occurred through the application of laser technology to the older electro-magnetic technology of Xeroxography (Dunn, Hester and Readman 2001). This fully digital print constructs a final image directly on a substrate, or an impression medium, by arranging the elements of the image (pixels) dot by dot from computer code.

The most revolutionary feature of this technology is its variability. Rapidly printed consecutive pages can differ from each other with no fluctuation in speed and printing functionality. In other words, every new impression can be different from the previous impression as easily as it can be the same. A number of terms are frequently used to describe this technological shift including 'print on demand' and 'digital printing', but none of them capture the shift as appropriately as the notion of 'variable print'. In some respects, the term 'digital print' is a misnomer, for the reasons already discussed—almost all print was already digital in some respects. Only fully digitised print manufacture captures the dramatic potential of variability. Similarly, 'print on demand' is not strictly accurate or a particularly useful concept. Every commercial printer will tell you they print on demand in order to meet their customers' expectations as quickly and effectively as possible. And even fully digital presses need to go through a number of business systems and process steps (ordering, production, dispatch), which means that printing is never precisely on demand.

The commercial and cultural logic of fully digital or variable print begins with the fact that every print is an original. In the case of digitally rendered images, every one has been constructed, not from a reproduced original, but within a source file of ephemeral and unreadable computer code and the final print is the first and in this sense only rendering. There is no reason why it should be rendered in this particular form ever again, and if it is, technically speaking it is another original. This, in turn, engenders flat economies of scale. As every pixel is formed afresh in the rendering of each impression, there is no difference between the cost of rendering identical successive impressions and rendering different impressions. As there are no plates or set-up costs, one impression shares the same cost per unit as 1,000 impressions. As a consequence, there are no economies of manufacturing scale. Even in the case of print, then, this involves a paradigm shift beyond the system established by Gutenberg and dominant for half a millennium. The cultural as well as economic consequences are enormous. In the domain of manufacturing, long runs have no particular advantage over short runs; niche markets are no less viable than mass markets; small languages and cultures can be serviced as easily as large ones; and even the 'digital divide' can be bridged with a few computers combined with digital print.

This ensemble of changes opens the possibility (although by no means does it preordain the inevitability) of richer polylingualism. Returning to the spirit of our definition of this term, this applies not only to natural languages (conventional understandings of multilingualism), but also to the social languages of discourse communities, and these may be defined not only by knowledge community, but also by profession, ethnicity, subcultures, fashions, style, fad or fetish. The remarkable paradox of globalisation is that even when these social languages are expressed in the more and more extensive *lingua francas* of natural language (Chinese or English, for instance), social languages are diverging. They are, in fact becoming less mutually intelligible, and that reducing intelligibility is manifest in the likes of technicality and dialect (Cope and Kalantzis 2009a).

To these specific socio-technical developments we can now add a broader perspective by returning to the question of the shift in the balance of representational agency introduced earlier. We want to argue that the shift in the balance of representational agency opens the way for the development of a new dynamics of difference. The convenient aspirations to sameness and the pressures to acquiesce and conform in an earlier era, suddenly become anachronistic—mass consumer uniformity gives way to a myriad of niche markets; nationalistic (and at times racist) identities give way to a necessary global–local cosmopolitanism; mass broadcast media give way to constructing one's own, invariably peculiar take on the world across an uncountable number of new media spaces. Gone are the days when we had to become the same in order to participate as workers, citizens and community members. By opening new scope for agency in spaces that were previously structured as sites of compliance, opportunities emerge for the flourishing of differences. From each according to their identity and to each according to their proclivity.

The new media environment makes it possible for discourse communities to diverge, to find and develop voices that are truer to their evolving selves—identity-speak, profession-speak, peer-speak, diaspora-speak, fad-speak, affinity-speak. Knowledge and culture become more fluid, contestable and open. Discourses and the domains of culture and knowledge that they represent become less mutually intelligible, and we need to put more effort into cross-cultural dialogues in order to get things done (Cope and Kalantzis 2009a). In these ways, the rebalancing of agency in our epoch brings with it a shift away from a fundamental logic of uniformity in an earlier modernity, to a logic of difference.

In particular, the digital media provide channels for differences to represent themselves. After an era in which every pressure was to create homogeneity (the mass media with its one or two newspapers in every city, its half a dozen main television channels, its 'top 40' radio playlists), today's society and media provide spaces for divergence (the myriad of blogs and online newspaper offerings, the thousands of television channels and millions of YouTube offerings, and no two iPod playlists or iPhone app configurations are the same). Not only does difference come to light more vividly and poignantly given the easy useability and accessibility of the new media. Differences can auto recreate. Individuals and groups can become more different. The cost of entry for different ways of speaking, seeing, thinking and acting is lower. You don't need specialist trade skills or heavy duty infrastructure to be out there in your own voice—through the web, in video, or using digital print. The economies of scale of cultural production have been reversed. The logic of mass production (big production TV, long-print run books) is displaced at least in part by the logic of mass customisation (tens of thousands of widely divergent messages in YouTube, books where a print run of one costs the same per unit as a print run of ten or 10,000). So, too, this creates openings for new, highly specialised or hybrid interdisciplinary knowledge spaces, less viable in older publishing systems grounded in economies of scale or prohibitive charges for small scale.

What does this reading of the socio-technical conditions of text production and the cultural conditions of the digital world tell us about knowledge making? Formal academic knowledge making remains firmly and anachronistically located in the Gutenberg universe. The commercial logic of journals and monograph publishing still based on economies of large scale. 'Viable' translates into a subscriber base or book purchasing prospects of 1,000 or more. Our evaluation systems for 'impact' value popularity (in the form of the number of citations) over the quality of a piece of knowledge (Cope and Kalantzis 2009b). Specialist domains of knowledge and small cultures are devalued just because they will necessarily attract a low citation count, regardless of the quality of the knowledge itself. Meanwhile, imperial English dominates the scholarly publishing world in part because typographic markup does not support machine translation as well as it could. Content is neither written in readily translatable templates nor is it tagged in a way that supports the level of reliability required of machine translation in knowledge domains where precision and accuracy is a necessity.

This is all contrary to the emerging logics of the social media. Electronically delivered text and digital print allow for a viable production run in which one is as viable as many, assuming (as has always been the case) that the crucial publishing work is done in the honorary domain of peer review. One would think there to be a natural fit between the new socio-technical logic of digital text and an epistemic reality in which specialisation is one source of deep knowledge. You shouldn't have to write popularly and gain a wide readership to do powerful knowledge. We need to develop ways of measuring the value of knowledge in its own right, not by citation counts. The inexpensive reflexivity of the social media allows this. Only a few peers might read a piece of work, finding it powerful and influential in a specialist domain. It should be the credibility of their evaluations that measures the value of a work, not the breadth of its metaphorical sales (citations) in the marketplace of ideas. Unfortunately, however, even our bibliometrics is still caught in the Gutenberg logic of 'best sellers are better'. This may be a good thing for junk novels, but it is a particularly poor measure of knowledge. Finally, there need be no reason to write in English if semantic text editors are in place to support machine translation, and authors mark up their texts according to standardised translations of domain-specific tagging. For non-English speaking scholars, this would be better than writing in poor English, and at times having their work dismissed for the quality of its expression rather than the content of its ideas and findings.

Conclusions

In this chapter we have worked our way through a number of the enormous changes wrought by digitisation on the domains of culture and knowledge. We are today about half a century into the history of the digitisation of text. We have argued that only now are we on the cusp of a series of paradigm shifts in the processes of writing and, concomitantly, modes of cultural expression and social processes of knowing. We have described the transition under way in the fundamental mechanics of rendering, the new navigational order which is associated with this transition, the demise of isolated written text that accompanies the rise of multimodality, the ubiquity of recording and documentation, a shift in the balance of representation agency, and its correlate in the emergence of a new dynamics of difference.

The shape of these hugely significant changes is just beginning to become clear in the new, internet-mediated social media. The impacts of these changes on society, culture and economy are becoming more obvious. Their potential is to change our means of production of meaning, no less. This change is bound to change the ways we feel, act and think.

However, when we come to examine the domain of knowledge production, historically pivoting on the peer-reviewed journal and published monograph, there are as yet few signs of change. This chapter points in a tentative way to potentials for knowledge making which are as yet unrealised: semantic markup processes which will improve knowledge discovery, data mining and machine translation; a new navigational order in which knowledge is not simply presented in a linear textual exegesis; the multimodal representation of knowledge in which knowledge evaluators and validators gain a broader, deeper and less mediated view of the knowledge they are assessing; navigable databanks in which reviewers and readers alike can make what they will of data and interactions recorded incidental to knowledge making; co-construction of knowledge through recursive dialogue between knowledge creators and knowledge users, to the extent of eliding that distinction; and a polylingual, polysemic knowledge world in which source natural language is arbitrary and narrowly specialised discourses and bodies of knowledge can be valued by their intellectual quality instead of the quantitative mass of their readership and citation.

This suggests a large and ambitious agenda. However, it is one that is destined to effect the largest transformation in our social processes of knowledge making since Gutenberg's invention of the printing press.

References

Anderson, B. 1983. *Imagined Communities: Reflections on the Origin and Spread of Nationalism.* London: Verso.

Benjamin, W. [1936] 2008. 'The Work of Art in the Age of its Technological Reproducibility'. In M.W. Jennings, B. Doherty and T.Y. Levin (eds) *The Work of Art in the Age of its Technological Reproducibility and Other Writings on Media.* Cambridge, MA: Harvard University Press.

Berners-Lee, T. 1990. 'Information Management: A Proposal', *http://www.w3.org/History/1989/proposal.html* (accessed 26 July 2010).

Chartier, R. 2001. 'Readers and Readings in the Electronic Age', *http://www.text-e.org/.*

Cope, B. 1998. 'The Language of Forgetting: A Short History of the Word'. In M. Fraser (ed.), *Seams of Light: Best Antipodean Essays.* Sydney: Allen and Unwin, pp. 192–223.

—. 2001a. 'Globalisation, Multilingualism and the New Text Technologies'. In B. Cope and G. Gollings (eds), *Multilingual Book Production: Technology*

Drivers Across the Book Production Supply Chain, from Creator to Consumer, C-2-C Project book 2.2. Melbourne: Common Ground, pp. 1–15.

—. 2001b. 'Making and Moving Books in New Ways, From the Creator to the Consumer'. In B. Cope and D. Mason (eds), *Digital Book Production and Supply Chain Management: Technology Drivers Across the Book Production Supply Chain, from Creator to Consumer*, C-2-C Project book 2.3. Melbourne: Common Ground, pp. 1–20.

—. 2001c. 'New Ways with Words: Print and Etext Convergence'. In B. Cope and D. Kalantzis (eds), *Print and Electronic Text Convergence: Technology Drivers Across the Book Production Supply Chain, from Creator to Consumer*, C-2-C Project book 2.1. Melbourne: Common Ground, pp. 1–15.

Cope, B. and G. Gollings (eds). 2001. *Multilingual Book Production: Technology Drivers Across the Book Production Supply Chain, from Creator to Consumer*, C-2-C Project book 2.2. Melbourne: Common Ground.

Cope, B. and M. Kalantzis. 2009a. "Multiliteracies': New Literacies, New Learning', *Pedagogies: An International Journal* 4, pp. 164–95.

—. 2009b. 'Signs of Epistemic Disruption: Transformations in the Knowledge System of the Academic Journal', *First Monday* 14(4), 6 April.

Dixon, R.M.W. 1980. *The Languages of Australia*. Cambridge, UK: Cambridge University Press.

Dunn, R., R. Hester, and A. Readman. 2001. 'Printing Goes Digital'. In B. Cope and D. Kalantzis (eds), *Print and Electronic Text Convergence: Technology Drivers Across the Book Production Supply Chain, from Creator to Consumer*, C-2-C Project book 2.1. Melbourne: Common Ground, pp. 109–23.

Eisenstein, E.L. 1979. *The Printing Press as an Agent of Change: Communications and Cultural Transformation in Early-Modern Europe*. Cambridge, UK: Cambridge University Press.

Febvre, L. and H.-J. Martin. 1976. *The Coming of the Book*. London: Verso.

Gee, J.P. 1996. *Social Linguistics and Literacies: Ideology in Discourses*. London: Taylor and Francis.

Gerber, L. 2001. 'Translation in a Digital Environment'. In B. Cope and G. Gollings (eds), *Multilingual Book Production: Technology Drivers Across the Book Production Supply Chain, from Creator to Consumer*, C-2-C Project book 2.2. Melbourne: Common Ground, pp. 105–22.

Goldfarb, C. 1990. 'A Brief History of the Development of SGML', *http://www.sgmlsource.com/history/sgmlhist.htm* (accessed 26 July 2010).

Grafton, A. 1997. *The Footnote: A Curious History*. London: Faber and Faber.

Guédon, J.-C. 2001. *In Oldenburg's Long Shadow: Librarians, Research Scientists, Publishers, and the Control of Scientific Publishing*, conference proceedings. Washington, DC: Association of Research Libraries.

Jakubowicz, A. 2009. 'Beyond the Static Text: Multimedia Interactivity in Academic Publishing'. In B. Cope and A. Phillips (eds), *The Future of the Academic Journal*. Oxford: Chandos.

Kalantzis, M. 2006a. 'Changing Subjectivities, New Learning', *Pedagogies: An International Journal* 1, pp. 7–12.

—. 2006b. 'Elements of a Science of Education', *Australian Educational Researcher* 33, pp. 15–42.

Kalantzis, M. and B. Cope. 2006. *New Learning: Elements of a Science of Education*. Cambridge, UK: Cambridge University Press.

—. 2008. *New Learning: Elements of a Science of Education*. Cambridge, UK: Cambridge University Press.

Kress, G. 2000. 'Design and Transformation: New Theories of Meaning'. In B. Cope and M. Kalantzis, *Multiliteracies: Literacy Learning and the Design of Social Futures*. London: Routledge, pp. 153–61.

—. 2001. 'Issues for a Working Agenda in Literacy'. In M. Kalantzis and B. Cope (eds) *Transformations in Language and Learning: Perspectives on Multiliteracies*. Melbourne: Common Ground, pp. 33–52.

—. 2009. *Multimodality: A Social Semiotic Approach to Contemporary Communication*. London: Routledge.

Kress, G. and T. van Leeuwen. 1996. *Reading Images: The Grammar of Visual Design*. London: Routledge.

Luo, S. 1998. *An Illustrated History of Printing in Ancient China*. Hong Kong: City University of Hong Kong.

Man, J. 2002. *The Gutenberg Revolution*. London: Review.

Mühlhäusler, P. 1996. *Linguistic Ecology: Language Change and Linguistic Imperialism in the Pacific Region*. London: Routledge.

Ong, W.J. 1958. *Ramus, Method and the Decay of Dialogue*. Cambridge, MA: Harvard University Press.

Phillipson, R. 1992. *Linguistic Imperialism*. Oxford: Oxford University Press.

Scollon, R. 1999. 'Multilingualism and Intellectual Property: Visual Holophrastic Discourse and the Commodity/Sign', paper presented at Georgetown University Round Table 1999.

—. 2001. *Mediated Discourse: The Nexus of Practice*. London: Routledge.

Unicode. 2010. Unicode Consortium website, *http://unicode.org/* (accessed 26 July 2010).

Virilio, P. 1997. *Open Sky*. London: Verso.

Vygotsky, L. 1962. *Thought and Language*. Cambridge, MA: MIT Press.

Wacquet, F. 2001. *Latin, Or the Empire of the Sign*. London: Verso.

Whitworth, B. and R. Friedman. 2009a. 'Reinventing Academic Publishing Online. Part I: Rigor, Relevance and Practice', *First Monday* 14(8), 3 August.

—. 2009b. 'Reinventing Academic Publishing Online. Part II: A Socio-technical Vision', *First Monday* 14(9), 7 September.

5

Books and journal articles: the textual practices of academic knowledge

Bill Cope and Mary Kalantzis

The role of knowledge representation in knowledge design

The process of publication is an integral aspect of knowledge making. Far from being a neutral conduit for knowledge, the publication system defines the social processes through which knowledge is made, and gives tangible form to knowledge that would otherwise be relegated to the ephemeral. The message, of course, is by no means reducible to its medium. We take it for granted that there are knowledge referents external to knowledge representations, and that the representations are not ends in themselves. However, the representational media and the social norms of representation are as much the stuff of knowledge as the things those representations purport to represent (Cope and Kalantzis 2009).

But first, what is this thing 'knowledge'? What do we mean by specifically scientific, academic or scholarly knowledge? After all, people are 'knowing' in everyday life in a variety of ways. Academic or scholarly knowledge, by comparison, has some extraordinary features. It has an intensity of focus and a concentration of intellectual energies greater than that of ordinary, everyday, commonsense or lay knowing. It relies on the ritualistic rigour and accumulated wisdoms of disciplinary communities and their practices. It entails, in short, a kind of systematicity that does not exist in casual experience. Husserl draws the distinction between 'lifeworld' experience and what is 'transcendental' about 'science' (Cope and Kalantzis 2000a; Husserl [1954] 1970). The 'lifeworld' is everyday lived experience. The 'transcendental' of academic and scholarly knowledge stands in contra-distinction to the commonsense knowing of the lifeworld, which by comparison is relatively unconscious and unreflexive. Academic and scholarly knowledge sets out to comprehend and create meanings in the world, which extend more broadly and deeply than the everyday, amorphous pragmatics of the lifeworld. Such knowledge is systematic, premeditated, reflective, purposeful, disciplined and open to scrutiny by a community of experts. Science is more focused and harder work than the knowing that happens in and of the lifeworld (Kalantzis and Cope 2008).

Of course, scholarly knowledge making is by no means the only secular system of social meaning and knowing in modern societies. Media, literature and law all have their own representational protocols. However, we want to focus specifically on the knowledge systems of academe as found in the physical sciences, the applied sciences, the professions, the social sciences, the liberal arts and the humanities. We are interested in their means of production of knowledge, where the medium is not the whole message but where the textual and social processes of representation nevertheless give modern knowledge its peculiar shape and form.

Academic knowledge making is a kind of work, an act of epistemic design. 'Design' has a fortuitous double meaning. On the one hand, 'design' denotes something intrinsic to any found object—inherent patterns and structures irrespective of that object's natural or human provenance. Things have designs. Design is morphology. There is intrinsic design in the objects of knowledge, the stuff of the world on which scholars focus their attention. This is design, the noun.

On the other hand, design is an act of conception and an agenda for construction. This meaning takes the word back to its root in the Latin word *designare*, 'to mark out'. Design entails a certain kind of agency. In the case of scholarly knowledge work, researchers and thinkers make sense of the world using methods of observation and analysis, and applying and testing conceptual schemas. This is design, the verb. We can make this duality of meaning work for us to highlight two integral and complementary aspects of design.

The knowledge representation process is integral to the making of academic, scientific and scholarly knowledge. It is central to its business of epistemic design. This design process has three representational moments.

The first moment is what we would call 'available designs' (Cope and Kalantzis 2000b; Kress 2000). The body of scholarly literature—the five million or so scholarly articles published each year, the (probably) 100,000 books—is the tangible starting point of all knowledge work. These representational designs work at a number of levels, one of which is as textual practices of describing, reporting on observations, clarifying concepts and arguing to rhetorical effect (Bazerman 1988). They are also represented intertextually, at the level of bodies of knowledge, where no text sits alone but constantly draws on and references against other texts by way of conceptual distinction, or accretion of facts, or agreement on principle—among many of the possibilities that fuse a work into a body of knowledge. These representational designs are the fundamental ground of all academic and scholarly knowledge work. They give tangible form to fields of interest.

The second moment is the process of 'designing'. Available knowledge designs have a textual and intertextual morphology. These are the raw materials of already-represented knowledge or found knowledge objects. Designing is the stuff of agency, the things you do to know and the rhetorical representation of those things. It is also the stuff of communities of disciplinary practice. These practices involve certain kinds of knowledge representation—modes of argumentation, forms of reporting, descriptions of methods and data, ways of supplementing extant data, linking and distinguishing concepts, and critically reflecting on old and new ideas and facts. There is no knowledge making of scholarly relevance without the representation of that knowledge. And that representation happens in a community of practice: with collaborators who co-author or comment on drafts, with journal editors or book publishers who review manuscripts and send them out to referees, with referees who evaluate and comment, and then the intricacies of textual revision, checking, copy-editing and publication. Knowledge contents and the social processes of knowledge representation are inseparable.

And then there is a third moment of the process, 'the (re)designed', when a knowledge artefact joins the body of knowledge. Rights to ownership and attribution are established through publication. These do not inhere in the knowledge itself, but in the text which represents that knowledge (copyright) or through a mechanism that the representation describes (which may in the case of methods and apparatuses be captured in patents). Moral rights to attribution are established even when default private intellectual property rights are forgone by attaching a 'commons' licence. On the other hand, even the most rigorous of copyright licence allows quoting and paraphrasing in the public domain for the purposes of the discussion, review and verification. This guarantees that a privately owned text can be incorporated into a body of public knowledge and reported on again and credited via citation. This is the point at which the process of designing metamorphoses into the universal library of knowledge, the repository of publicly declared knowledge, deeply interlinked by the practices of citation (Quirós and

Martín 2009). At this point, the knowledge design becomes an 'available design', absorbed into the body of knowledge as raw materials for others in their designing processes.

The scholarly monograph

Along with the journal, the monograph or book is one of the two predominant media for the representation of academic knowledge.

So what is a book? Until recently, such a question would have seemed a good only for the kinds of epistemic games philosophers play. Unless this were a question intended to take us into some fraught metaphysical territory, the answer would have been a relatively simple and direct one— a volume of text, printed on 50 or more paper pages, bound between card covers, with certain generic features including a title page, contents, the sectioning of text around chapters, and the like. In this definition, the printed book is a tangible technological object, a means for rendering extended passages of text and images. It is the peculiar generic features of a book as an object that make it immediately distinguishable from other renderings of text or images, such as shopping lists or envelopes full of holiday snaps. And it is a technology that has proven especially helpful in the representation of academic knowledge, particularly in discipline areas which lend themselves to extended exegesis.

Technological developments since the beginning of the 1990s have thrown into considerable question traditional definitions of the book. Since then we have faced two powerful and seemingly contradictory lines of thought. Some commentators have predicted that the traditional form and function of books will be replaced by the internet and electronic reading devices. To some extent, current trends bear this out. Children writing school assignments used to have to borrow the relevant books from their school library. Now, they can get much of the information they need from the internet. More and more of the written material we need and want can be found on the internet. The direct competition between books and increasingly book-like internet-deliverable formats is manifest, notably the PDF. More recently, after a decade of promise, e-book readers seem to have taken off, notably Kindle, Nook and iPad. Some traditional forms of printed matter have been all but replaced by non-printed media. For instance, the encyclopedia and some technical manuals have virtually been replaced by electronic formats. As a technology, the internet has a number of distinct advantages over traditional books: all its available information is instantaneously available; it is more hugely expansive than any library or bookstore; it is readily searchable; it is mostly free or inexpensive; and it doesn't require as a precondition the environmentally deleterious practice of turning trees into pulp for paper. Surely, say the pundits who predict the end of the book, these new media provide superior technology for the transmission of text and images?

However, in an alternative view, the book is now everywhere. Despite predictions of the imminent demise of the book given the rise of the internet and electronic book reading devices, the book is now ubiquitous. The book is everywhere in another pervasive sense: its textual forms and communicative apparatuses are to be found throughout the new electronic formats. Computer renditions of text and images are looking more and more like books. Contrast, for instance, older word-processing systems with newer ones, and HTML files in the first generation of internet development with the proliferation of web-accessible PDF files. Much of the on-screen rendering of text and images is based on systems of representation derived from the book, including 'pages' of text, headings, systems for listing contents (buttons and navigation menus), referencing (links), cross-referencing (hypertext) and indexing (search). The rendering systems of Kindle, Nook and iPad all reproduce the logic of the book. The technology may differ, but these basic structures and functions are derived from the book, and were developed within the technology of the book over a 500-year period.

So, what is a book? Our old definition was focused on an object. Our new definition needs to focus on a function. A book is no longer a physical thing. A book is what a book does. And what does a book do? A book is a structured rendition of text and possibly also images, which displays certain generic features: it is an extended text (of, say, more than 20,000 words, and/or more than 50 or so pages of images), whose size means that for practical purposes the text needs to be formed around generic features, principally including cover, blurb, title, author, copyright statement, ISBN, table of contents, chapter headings, body text and images, and also, sometimes, a referencing apparatus, index, acknowledgements, foreword, author bio-note and introduction. Such a thing is recognisable in the world of text as a book, either by official allocation of an ISBN and registration as a book, or by cataloguing in the e-commerce universe of electronically downloadable books and online library catalogues.

Books are recognisable as such because they share a characteristic textual, and thus communicative, structure. They have book-like functions because they are defined, registered and recognised as books.

This means that when we need to 'do books', they can be found in bibliographical listings; they can be acquired through online or physical bookstores and libraries; and they can be referenced as books.

However, unlike the traditional definition, a book in this sense does not have to be printed. It can be rendered in many ways, including electronic-visual and audio (talking books). A book is not a thing. It is a textual form, a way of communicating. A book is not a product. It is an information architecture.

What then do the revolutionary transitions in the production and delivery of books that are currently under way mean for the scholarly book publishing business? We want to argue that enormous possibilities present themselves, but not without working our way through an at times traumatic transition in business models. The counterpoint for analysing this transition is the scholarly book-publishing processes of our recent past. Here we highlight the deficiencies of the print-publishing system.

Deficiencies of the print-publishing system

For scholarly authors

It seems to be becoming increasingly difficult to get academic work published in book format—whether because publishers are restricting their output to fewer, low risk, high margin, long-run items, or because there are more titles out there, and more authors are wanting to be published. Even university presses with a not-for-profit charter favour books that may also reach a trade publishing market, short introductions or textbooks over works judged purely on their scholarly significance. Then there is the issue of the kinds of royalties publishers pay—rarely above 10 per cent, and in some cases nothing or virtually nothing for books sold at sometimes exorbitant prices, which individuals cannot afford, whose marketing is targetted almost exclusively to institutional libraries.

For publishers

Margins seem to be dropping, particularly for small publishers and university presses. Yet the risks are as high as ever—large up-front investment in working capital, high distribution costs and retailing margins, as well as the unpredictable element of luck with any title.

For bookstores

Today's physical bookstores are the most capital intensive of all retail outlets, and this is particularly case for the spread of titles needed in a bookstore catering to an academic market. No other retail outlet would tolerate the amount of stock that is required, nor the average amount of time it sits on the shelf before it is sold. Even then, although the bookstore is a retail outlet, which works well for browsers, all but the very largest bookshops are notoriously frustrating places when you are looking for something specific. Even the largest bookstore can only stock a small fraction of books in print in a particular area of scholarly interest.

For readers

Academic books seem to be getting dearer all the time, and in a world which is fragmenting into ever more finely defined areas of knowledge focus the general academic bookstore is becoming less useful to its customers' interests and needs.

These dimensions of the scholarly book trade add up to bad business. This also means that this is a business ripe for change. One term that is regularly used to describe the direction of change in the supply chain is disintermediation: the collapse of one or more elements of the process into each other. Where have the typesetters, lithographers and platemakers gone in the digital printing process? The answer is just that they've gone, never to return except in the dioramas of industrial history museums. But it's not just a matter of collapsing some of the steps in the process; it's also a matter of creating new kinds of work, doing new things, things that were inconceivable in the old ecology of book production.

Promises of the new world of digitally mediated book production

Following are some of the promises of the new world of digitally mediated book production. We describe these processes not in some cases as they exist today, but as we imagine they may exist in the not too distant future, which we have been addressing in a practical way through the development of Common Ground's CGAuthor web environment.

For authors

Digital publishing ecologies are about content capture, in which the author does a greater proportion of the total work of the book production supply chain, yet does it with little additional effort. Authors do two main things—first, they typeset the text into fully designed book templates. This is not such a large request, as there is barely an author who does not work on a word processor these days. And second, through a series of online data capture mechanisms, they begin to build the metadata required for resource discovery on the internet and automatic insertion of the book into the world of digital books, so that once it is published it can be effortlessly ordered by any physical bookstore, and automatically put on sale in online bookstores.

Of course, publishers, reviewers and referees check and refine this metadata as well as the developing text, from proposal to final publication, but they do all of this online and while relating to a single, evolving source file stored on a webserver in a cloud computing environment. As the process is increasingly automated, productivity through the supply chain improves. The author becomes the primary risk taker (the largest investment in the whole process is the author's time), and so a substantial slice of the rewards of automation will go to them, be these the symbolic rewards of visibility within a knowledge ecology, or in the case of works that happen to be sold and sell well, a larger share of the sale price in the form of royalties.

This is the commercial outcome: workflow and production efficiencies that make scholarly writing a better business. But there's also a cultural outcome: that more people will be able to write—the Chinese poetry critic in Melbourne, Australia, writing in Chinese who knows there is a small market for her books not just in Melbourne but in Shanghai, Penang and San Diego; the academic educator writing about an obscure aspect of dyslexia, of enormous importance to the hundred or so academic experts in this field in the world; the Canadian indigenous elder who knows that the oral history of their community will become an important resource for the tourists of today and the scholars in the future. Call these niche markets if you like, but to get these works published will also be to create a more vibrant knowledge ecology, a healthy democracy and a place of more genuine cultural pluralism, and one that could never have been offered by the mass market.

For publishers

No prepayment for printing and no inventory—this is a publisher's dream. If a book sells in the online environment, either in an electronic format, or as a one-at-a-time print-on-demand product, all the better. If it doesn't, all that's lost from the publisher's point of view is the time they've spent reviewing, commenting and editing the author's successive drafts of their metadata and text. Or in the case of scholarly publishing this work may devolve largely to the unpaid reciprocal obligation of peers. Once the publisher has pressed the 'publish' button, the rest simply happens— physical books get printed and dispatched as they are ordered, and electronic books are downloaded by purchasers. What they get back is instant payment, and instant market information. They are relieved of the burden of discounting, remaindering and dealing with returns. And so publishers can stick at what they are good at, their core business, which is the location of valuable knowledge and cultural contents. They can focus their energies on finding, refining and placing content, instead of having to spend valuable time and resources managing the back end of an old fashioned mass manufacturing and warehousing business.

This is particularly good for small publishers who don't have the warehousing infrastructure and often pay 60 per cent or more of the book's sale price to outsource distribution. Many more small publishers may emerge in this environment, as smaller print runs become more economical and the entry point to the industry in terms of working capital is reduced. In Jason Epstein's words, book publishing 'is by nature a cottage industry, decentralised, improvisational, personal'. It is 'best performed by small groups of like-minded people, devoted to their craft, jealous of their autonomy' (Epstein 2001). This is the old ideal of publishing, which aligns perfectly with the knowledge ecologies of academe. The nice irony is that the new technologies and business processes will allow this old ideal to be realised, and far more effectively than was ever the case in the past.

For bookstores

Until it entered the electronic book market with Kindle, Amazon.com was but a thin veneer on an old economy—an economy of large inventories, of moving products from printer to distribution warehouse to bookstore dispatch. The printed book part of Amazon's business discounts to compete but has created few efficiencies in the supply chain. And even Kindle does not create efficiencies for the text-creation and knowledge ecologies, which still very inefficiently rely on a one-way file flow from word processor to desktop publisher, to print-alike PDF format, and then Amazon strips this back to its own, read-only proprietary format.

The fully digitised alternative is to build a back-end to Amazon, a book production process, which creates efficiencies, improves productivity, reduces costs and creates new products for new markets. So, where to, for that old and much loved institution, the physical bookstore? Are its days numbered? The answer is not necessarily. Bookstores of the future may provide consumers with a special experience, around a specialist area of knowledge, or the bookstore owner's eccentric sense of taste and style. You will visit the bookstore not because it can ever pretend to be comprehensive, but because you want to enter a space where the bookstore's selectivity has created a niche. Its range will be thorough for what it sets out to do, but with much less stock than the bookstores of the past. And its market will be the world, as the store's stock is reproduced in its online bookstore, its value being in its selectivity and the kinds of readers who write reviews in that space.

For readers

The world of scholarly reading is also certain to change, and for the better. Some forms of print will disappear, such as hugely expensive scholarly encyclopedias in which there is too much to read ever to want the whole volume, and where there is simply no need to purchase in print entries that you may never need to read. Chapter-by-chapter electronic access is much more resource efficient.

The academic journal

Just as academic book publishing is on the cusp of enormous change, so the academic journal system seems ripe for change, too.

Whereas in the scholarly book business, publishers employ commissioning editors who use reviewers to confirm their decisions regarding their lists, journal editing is devolved to academics, who in turn manage a peer-review process in order to vet article content. This process has come in for much criticism for its various flaws as a knowledge system.

To take the discursive features of the journal peer-review process, these track the linearity and post-publication fixity of text manufacturing processes in the era of print. Peer review is at the pre-publication phase of the social process of text production, drawing a clear distinction of pre- and post-publication at the moment of commitment to print. Pre-publication processes are hidden in confidential spaces, leading to publication of a text in which readers are unable to uncover the intertextuality, and thus dialogue, that went into this aspect of the process of knowledge design. The happenings in this space remain invisible to public scrutiny and thus unaccountable. This is in most part for practical reasons—it would be cumbersome and expensive to make these processes public. In the digital era, however, the incidental recording of communicative interchanges of all sorts is pervasive and cheap, suggesting in cases of public interest (of which knowledge making would surely be one) that these be made part of the public record or at least an independently auditable confidential record.

Then, in the post-publication phase, there is very little chance for dialogue that can have an impact on the statement of record, the printed article, beyond subsequent publication of errata. Reviews, citations and subsequent articles may reinforce, revise or repudiate the content of the publication of record, but these are all new publications equally the products of a linear textual workflow. Moving to PDF as a digital analogue of print does very little to change this mode of textual and knowledge production.

Key flaws in this knowledge system are the lack of transparency in pre-publication processes, lack of metamoderation or audit of referee reports or editor–referee deliberations, and the relative closure of a one step, one way publication process (Whitworth and Friedman 2009a, 2009b). If we posit that greater reflexivity and dialogue will make for more powerful, effective and responsive knowledge processes, then we have to say that we have yet barely exploited the affordances of digital media. Sosteric discusses Habermas' ideal speech situation in which both interlocutors have equal opportunity to initiate speech, there is mutual understanding, there is space for clarification, interlocutors can use any speech act and there is equal power over the exchange (Sosteric 1996). In each of these respects the journal peer-review process is less than ideal as a discursive framework. There are power asymmetries, identities are not revealed, dialogue between referee and author is prevented, the arbiter–editor is unaccountable, consensus is not necessarily reached, and none of these processes are open to scrutiny on the public record.

We can see some of what may be possible in the ways in which the new media integrally incorporate continuous review in their ranking and sorting mechanisms—from the simple ranking and viewing metrics of

YouTube to more sophisticated moderation and metamoderation methods at web publishing sites such as the web-based IT news publication Slashdot (*http://slashdot.org/moderation.shtml*). Social evaluations of text that were practically impossible for print are now easy to carry out in the digital media. Is it just habits of knowledge-making practice that prevent us moving in these directions? What about setting up a more dialogical relation between authors and referees? Let the author speak to referee and editor, with or without identities revealed: How useful did you find this review? If you did, perhaps you might acknowledge a specific debt? Or do you think the reviewer's judgement might have been clouded by ideological or paradigmatic antipathy?

Such dialogues are much of the time closed by the current peer-review system, and at best the author takes on board some of the reviewer's suggestions in the rewriting process, unacknowledged. Tentative experiments in open peer review, not too unlike post-publication review in a traditional publishing workflow, have been designed to grant greater recognition to the role of referees and create greater transparency, to discourage abusive reviews and to reduce the chances of ideas being stolen by anonymous reviewers before they can be published (Rowland 2002). Why should referees be less honest in their assessments when their identities are revealed? They may be just as honest. In fact, the cloak of anonymity has its own discursive dangers including non-disclosure of interests, unfairly motivated criticisms and theft of ideas.

In the new media, too, reviewers can be ranked by people whose work has been reviewed, and their reviews in turn ranked and weighted for their credibility in subsequent reviews. This is roughly how trusted super-author reviewers emerge in Wikipedia. There could also be multiple points of review, blurring the pre- and post-publication distinction. Initial texts can be published earlier, and re-versioning can occur indefinitely. In this way, published texts need not ossify, and the lines of their development could be traced because changes are disclosed in the public record of versions. These are some of the discursive possibilities that the digital allows, all of which may make for more open, dynamic and responsive knowledge dialogue, where the speed of the dialogue is not slowed down by the media through which it is carried.

Another major flaw in the traditional peer-review process, and a flaw that need not exist in the world of digital media, is in the textual form of the article itself. Here is a central contradiction in its mode of textuality: the canonical scholarly article speaks in a voice of empirical transparency, paradigmatic definitiveness and rhetorical neutrality—this last oxymoron capturing precisely a core contradiction, epistemic hypocrisy even. For the textual form of the article abstracts knowledge away from its reference points. The article does not contain the data; rather it refers to the data or suggests how the author's results could be replicated. The article is not the knowledge, or even the direct representation of knowledge—it is a rhetorical representation of knowledge.

This practically has to be the case for print and print look-alikes. But in the digital world there is no cost in presenting full datasets along with their interpretation, a complete record of the observations in point alongside replicable steps in observation, the archive itself alongside its exegesis. Referees, in other words, in the era of digital recording could not only review the knowledge representation, but come a good deal closer to the world to which those representations point in the form of immediate recordings of that world. This can occur multimodally through the amalgamation of datasets, still image, moving image and sound with text—along with captions, tags and exegeses.

Moreover, there are no page constraints (shape and textual form) or page limits (size and extent) in the digital record. This brings the reviewer into a different relation to the knowledge itself, more able to judge the relations between the purported knowledge and its textual forms, and for this reason also more able to make a contribution to its shaping as represented knowledge. This would also allow a greater deal of transparency in the dialectics of the empirical record and its interpretation. It may also lead to a more honest separation of represented data from the interpretative voice of the author, thus creating a more open and plausible environment for empirical work. In a provocative article, John Ioannidis argues that 'most published research findings are false' (Ioannidis 2005). Exposing data would invite critical reinterpretation of represented results and reduce the rates and margins of error in the published knowledge record.

Future knowledge systems

If today's knowledge systems are broken in places and on the verge of breaking in others, what, then, is to be done? Following is an agenda for the making of future knowledge systems that may optimise the affordances of the new, digital media.

Digital technologies and new media cultures suggest a number of possibilities for renovation of the knowledge system of the scholarly journal. Open peer review where authors and referees know each other's identities, or blind reviews that are made public, may well produce greater accountability on the part of editors and referees, and provide evidence of and credit the contribution a referee has made to the reconstruction of a text (Quirós and Martín 2009). Reviews could be dialogical, with or without the reviewer's identity declared, instead of the unidirectional finality of an accept, reject or rewrite judgement. The referee could be reviewed—by authors, moderators or other third party referees—and their reviews weighted for their accumulated, community-ascribed value as a referee. And whether review texts and decision dialogues are on the public record or not, they should be open to independent audit for abuses of positional power.

Then, instead of a lock-step march to a single point of publication, followed by an irrevocable fixity to the published record, a more incremental process of knowledge recording and refinement is straightforwardly possible. This could even end the distinction between pre-publication refereeing and post-publication review. Re-versioning would allow initial, pre-refereeing formulations to be made visible, as well as the dialogue that contributed to rewriting for publication. As further commentary and reviews come in, the author could correct and reformulate, thus opening the published text to continuous improvement.

One consequence of this shift will be that, rather than have the heroic author shepherding a text to a singular moment of publication, the 'social web' and interactive potentials intrinsic to the new media point to more broadly distributed, more collaborative knowledge futures. What has been called Web 2.0 (Hannay 2007), or the more interactive and extensively sociable application of the internet, points to wider networks of participation, greater responsiveness to commentary, more deeply integrated bodies of knowledge and more dynamic, responsive and faster moving knowledge cultures.

The effect of a more open system would be to allow entry points into the republic of scholarly knowledge for people currently outside the self-enclosing circles of prestigious research institutions and highly ranked journals. Make scholarly knowledge affordable to people without access through libraries to expensive institutional journal subscriptions, make the knowledge criteria explicit, add more accountability to the review process, allow all-comers to get started in the process of the incremental refinement of rigorously validated knowledge, and you'll find new knowledge—some adjudged to be manifestly sound and some not—emerging from industrial plants, schools, hospitals, government agencies, lawyer's offices, hobbyist organisations, business consultants and voluntary groups. Digital media infrastructures make this a viable possibility.

The possibility would also arise for more globally distributed sites of knowledge production, validation and dissemination. Approximately one-quarter of the world's universities are in the Anglophone world. However, the vast majority of the world's academic journal articles are from academics working in Anglophone countries. A more comprehensive and equitable global knowledge system would reduce this systemic bias. Openings in the new media include developments in machine translation and the role of knowledge schemas, semantic markup and tagging to assist discovery and access across different languages. They also speak to a greater tolerance for 'accented' writing in English as a non-native language.

In 1965 J.C.R. Linklider wrote of the deficiencies of the book as a source of knowledge, and imagined a future of 'procognitive systems' (Linklider 1965). He was, in fact, anticipating a completely new knowledge system. That system is not with us yet. In the words of Jean-Claude Guédon, we are still in the era of digital incunabula (Guédon 2001).

Escaping the confines of print look-alike formats, however, expansive possibilities present themselves. With semantic markup, large corpora of text might be opened up to data mining and cybermashups (Cope and Kalantzis 2004; Sompel and Lagoze 2007; Wilbanks 2007). Knowledge representations can present more of the world in less mediated form in datasets, images, videos and sound recordings (Fink and Bourne 2007; Lynch 2007). Whole disciplines traditionally represented only by textual exegesis, such as the arts, media and design, might be formally brought into academic knowledge systems in the actual modalities of their practice (Jakubowicz 2009). New units of knowledge may be created, at levels of granularity other than the singular article of today's journals system—fragments of evidence and ideas contributed by an author within an article (Campbell 2008), and curated collections and mashups above the level of an article, with sources duly credited by virtue of electronically tagged tracings of textual and data provenance.

Emerging knowledge ecologies: an agenda for transformation

What kinds of renewal do our academic knowledge systems require in order to improve their quality, effectiveness and value as an integral part of the research and knowledge building infrastructure of a peculiarly 'knowledge society'? The following ten points represent an agenda for further research. They are also a practical development agenda, suggesting that academic publishing, and the knowledge ecology which it supports, has a long way to go before it fully exploits the affordances of the internet. From the more specific to the more general, the key questions we propose towards the development of future knowledge systems are as follows.

Pre-publication knowledge validation

Whether it is commercial publishing or open access, the peer-review system is not working as well as it might. Peer review is not universal and it is not always clear which journals and book manuscripts are peer reviewed and which are not. In fact, the shift to digital repositories and rapid publication may be reducing the proportion of peer-reviewed academic articles and books. In open access and commercial models, however, commissioning editors in publishing houses and journal editors in universities have disproportionate influence, which may at times affect the quality of the knowledge systems they sustain: choosing reviewers who are likely to be sympathetic or unsympathetic to a particular work; general lack of a systematic, consistent and criterion-referenced review process; and an absence of reflexivity now characteristic of online 'social networking' environments—who reviews the reviewers (metamoderation) and how does the author enter dialogue with the reviewer? The key point here is that the current peer-review system has a tendency at times to conserve the boundaries of closed knowledge networks and to create an intellectual inertia which works against the publication of cross-disciplinary, substantially innovative or potentially paradigm-altering thinking. How, then, do we develop publication and knowledge systems which are more open and reflexive? What can be learnt from the logics of the 'social web'?

Post-publication knowledge validation

Today's systems of bibliometrics and impact assessment tend to favour traditional publishing models. Current validation processes (e.g. ISI or Web of Knowledge) are neither transparent nor reliable. They have notable and well-documented flaws (Lazaroiu 2009, pp. 62ff). The system neglects books and other media. Rejection rates are an arbitrary relation to the number of articles a journal publishes per year and the generality of its scope. Knowledge is measured by a form of 'popularity' rating, which works against small, specialised and emerging fields. Models of 'webometrics' are now appearing, but they are still crude. We need to investigate and develop more reliable ways of assessing the quality and impact of published knowledge. Furthermore, post publication, there is little opportunity for new and revised editions of articles to be published based on the ongoing dialogue of post-publication review. Post-publication knowledge validation needs to become more reflexive so that qualitative impact assessment feeds back into the knowledge system. (At the moment the main function it serves is as a career performance indicator.) Through an iterative process, readers could become more closely involved in the creation and refinement of knowledge.

Sustainability

Beyond the open access–commercial publishing dichotomy there is a question of resourcing models and sustainability. Academics' time is not best spent as amateur publishers. The main research question here is how does one build sustainable resourcing models which require neither cross-subsidy of academics' time, nor the unjustifiable and unsustainable costing and pricing structures of the big publishers? The key challenge is to develop new business models.

Intellectual property

How does one balance academics' and universities' interest in intellectual property with the public knowledge interest? At times, the 'gift economy' underwrites a 'theft economy' in which private companies profit from the supply content provided at no charge. Such companies copy content without permission or payment, and make money from advertising alongside this content. The key question here is how does one establish an intellectual property regime that sustains intellectual autonomy, rather than a 'give away' economy which may at times undervalue the work of the academy? When and to what extent are open access and 'commons' approaches to intellectual property appropriate and functional to creating socially productive knowledge systems? When are conventional licences appropriate?

Distributed knowledge

How do we open out academic knowledge systems so they can incorporate knowledge produced in other institutional sites—in hospitals, schools, industrial plants, government and the like? How can this knowledge be incorporated into meta-analyses by means of semantic publishing markup, tagging and data mining?

Disciplinarity and interdisciplinarity

How does publishing in different discipline areas reflect varied epistemological modes—from the social practices of citation and prepublication review to post-publication circulation? How is intellectual community created? We need to focus on lessons that may be learnt across disciplines for the creation of more resilient forms of knowledge, and to examine how new and cross-disciplinary knowledge systems emerge.

Modes of representation and signification

The digital media present new potentials for knowledge representation. Conventional scholarly publishing has not yet fully realised the multimodal affordances of the new media. What places do websites, video and datasets have in the new media? How might disciplinary practices traditionally represented only by second order exegesis, such as the arts, media, communications, design and architecture, be formally brought in less mediated ways into academic knowledge systems? How might they use forms of representation which are closer to their core professional and disciplinary practices?

Globalism

The key question here is how to achieve a more equitable global balance in scholarly publishing without prejudice to intellectual quality. There are also questions about how a more closely integrated global knowledge system would work. The answers lie in examination of the role of English as a *lingua franca* including articles written with a second language speaker's 'accent'; developments in machine translation; and the role of knowledge schemas, semantic markup and tagging to assist discovery and access across different languages.

Reconfiguring the role of the university

Underlying these research considerations is a larger question of the changing role of the university, from a place that supports a relatively closed knowledge system to one that serves more open knowledge architectures. How might a more participatory and inclusive knowledge culture be created, in which universities assume an integrating rather than exclusionary role?

Conditions of knowledge making for a 'knowledge economy'

Finally, there is an even larger question: how might renewed academic knowledge systems support a broader social agenda of intellectual risk taking, creativity and innovation? How is renovation of our academic knowledge systems a crucial aspect of meeting the heightened expectations of a 'knowledge society'? And what are the affordances of the digital media which may support reform?

Conclusions

Whatever the models of sustainability that emerge, knowledge systems of the near future could and should be very different from those of our recent past. The sites of formal knowledge validation and documentation will be more dispersed. They will be more global, in the *lingua franca* of English and also, as machine translation improves, not necessarily so. The knowledge processes they use will be more reflexive and so more thorough and reliable. Knowledge will be published more quickly. Through semantic publishing it will be more discoverable and open to aggregation and reinterpretation. There will be much more of it, but it will be much easier to navigate. The internet provides us these affordances. It is our task as knowledge workers to realise the promise of the internet and to create more responsive, equitable and powerful knowledge ecologies.

An information revolution has accompanied the digitisation of text, image and sound and the rapid emergence of the internet as a universal conduit for digital content. But the information revolution does not in itself bring about change of social or epistemic significance. Academic publishing is a case in point. The internet-accessible PDF file makes journal articles widely and cheaply available, but its form simply replicates the production processes and social relations of the print journal: a one-way production line which ends in the creation of a static, stable text restricted to text and still image. This change is not enough to warrant the descriptor 'disruptive'. The technological shift, large as it is, does not produce a change in the social processes and relations of knowledge production.

There is no deterministic relationship, in other words, between technology and social change. New technologies can be used to do old things. In fact, in their initial phases new technologies more often than not are simply put to work do old things—albeit, perhaps, more efficiently. At most, the technological opens out social affordances, frequently in ways not anticipated by the designers of those technologies. So what is the range of affordances in digital technologies that open new possibilities for knowledge making? We can see glimpses of possibility of new and more dynamic knowledge systems, but not yet captured in the mainstream academic journal or book publishing systems. For instance, in contrast to texts that replicate print and are structured around typographic markup, we can envisage more readily searchable and data mineable texts structured around semantic markup. In contrast to knowledge production processes, which force us to represent knowledge on the page, restricting us to text and still image, we can envision a broader, multimodal body of publishable knowledge which would represent objects of knowledge that could not have been so readily captured in print or its digital analogue: datasets, video, dynamic models and multimedia displays. The stuff that was formerly represented as the external stuff of knowledge can now be represented and incorporated within the knowledge. And in contrast to linear, lock-step modes of dissemination of knowledge, we can see signs of possibility for scholarly knowledge in the more collaborative, dialogical and recursive forms of knowledge making already to be found in less formal digital media spaces such as wikis, blogs and other readily accessible website content self-management systems. Even when it has moved to PDF or e-book reader formats, most book and journal content is still bound to the world of print-look-alike knowledge representation. However, a reading of technological affordances tells us that we don't have to be using digital technologies to replicate traditional processes of knowledge representation.

If trends can be read into the broader shifts in the new, digital media, they stand to transform the characteristic epistemic mode of authoritativeness of the heritage scholarly publishing. The historical dichotomy of author and reader, creator and consumer is everywhere being blurred. Authors blog, readers talk back, bloggers respond; wiki users read, and intervene to change the text if and when needs be; game players become participants in narratives; iPod users create their own playlists; digital TV viewers create their own viewing sequences. These are aspects of a general and symptomatic shift in the balance of agency, where a flat world of users replaces a hierarchical world of culture and knowledge in which a few producers create content to transmit to a mass of receivers (Cope and Kalantzis 2007).

What will academic publishing be like once it escapes its heritage constraints? There will be more knowledge collaborations between knowledge creators and knowledge users, in which user commentary perhaps can become part of the knowledge itself. Knowledge making will escape its linear, lock-step, beginning-to-end process. The end point will not be a singular version of record—it will be something that can be re-versioned as much as needed. Knowledge making will be more recursive, responsive, dynamic and, above all, more collaborative and social rather than it was in an earlier modernity, which paid greater obeisance to the voice of the heroically original author.

These, then, are some of the potentially profound shifts that may occur in the knowledge regime reflected in the representational processes of today's academic publishing. They could portend nothing less than a revolution in the shape and form of academic knowledge ecologies.

If it is the role of the scholarly knowledge system to produce deeper, broader and more reliable knowledge than is possible in everyday, casual experience, what do we need to do to deepen this tradition rather than allow it to break, falling victim to the disruptive forces of the new media? The answer will not just be to create new publishing processes. It will entail the building of new knowledge systems.

This inevitably leads us to an even larger question: how might renewed scholarly knowledge systems support a broader social agenda of intellectual risk taking, creativity and innovation? How is renovation of our academic knowledge systems a way to address the heightened expectations of a 'knowledge society'? And what are the affordances of the digital media which may support reform?

Whatever the models that emerge, the knowledge systems of the near future could and should be very different from those of our recent past. The sites of formal knowledge validation and documentation will be more dispersed across varied social sites. They will be more global. The knowledge processes they use will be more reflexive and so more thorough and reliable. Knowledge will be made available faster. Through semantic publishing, knowledge will be more discoverable and open to disaggregation, reaggregation and reinterpretation. There will be much more of it, but it will be much easier to navigate. The internet provides us these affordances. It will allow us to define and apply new epistemic virtues. It is our task as knowledge workers to realise the promise of our times and to create more responsive, equitable and powerful knowledge ecologies.

References

Bazerman, C. 1988. *Shaping Written Knowledge: The Genre and Activity of the Experimental Article in Science*. Madison, WI: University of Wisconsin Press.

Campbell, P. 2008. 'Escape from the Impact Factor', *Ethics in Science and Environmental Politics* 8, pp. 5–7.

Cope, B. and M. Kalantzis. 2000a. 'Designs for Social Futures'. In *Multiliteracies: Literacy Learning and the Design of Social Futures*, edited by B. Cope and M. Kalantzis. London: Routledge, pp. 203–34.

—. 2000b. *Multiliteracies: Literacy Learning and the Design of Social Futures.* London: Routledge, p. 350.

—. 2004. 'Text-Made Text', *E-Learning* 1, pp. 198–282.

—. 2007. 'New Media, New Learning', *International Journal of Learning* 14, pp. 75–79.

—. 2009. 'Signs of Epistemic Disruption: Transformations in the Knowledge System of the Academic Journal', *First Monday* 14(4), 6 April.

Epstein, J. 2001. *Book Business: Publishing Past Present and Future.* New York: Norton.

Fink, J.L. and P.E. Bourne. 2007. 'Reinventing Scholarly Communication for the Electronic Age', *CTWatch Quarterly* 3(3), pp. 26–31.

Guédon, J.-C. 2001. *In Oldenburg's Long Shadow: Librarians, Research Scientists, Publishers, and the Control of Scientific Publishing*, conference proceedings. Washington, DC: Association of Research Libraries.

Hannay, T. 2007. 'Web 2.0 in Science', *CTWatch Quarterly* 3(3), pp. 19–25.

Husserl, E. [1954] 1970. *The Crisis of European Sciences and Transcendental Phenomenology.* Evanston: Northwestern University Press.

Ioannidis, J.P.A. 2005. 'Why Most Published Research Findings Are False', *PLoS Med* 2, pp. 696–701.

Jakubowicz, A. 2009. 'Beyond the Static Text: Multimedia Interactivity in Academic Publishing'. In B. Cope and A. Phillips (eds), *The Future of the Academic Journal.* Oxford: Chandos.

Kalantzis, M. and B. Cope. 2008. *New Learning: Elements of a Science of Education.* Cambridge, UK: Cambridge University Press.

Kress, G. 2000. 'Design and Transformation: New Theories of Meaning'. In *Multiliteracies: Literacy Learning and the Design of Social Futures*, edited by B. Cope and M. Kalantzis. London: Routledge, pp. 153–61.

Lazaroiu, G. 2009. *Hyperreality, Cybernews, and the Power of Journalism.* New York: Addleton Academic Publishers.

Linklider, J.C.R. 1965. *Libraries of the Future.* Cambridge, MA: MIT Press.

Lynch, C. 2007. 'The Shape of the Scientific Article in the Developing Cyberinfrastructure', *CTWatch Quarterly* 3.

Quirós, J.L.G. and K.G. Martín. 2009. 'Arguments for an Open Model of e-Science'. In B. Cope and A. Phillips (eds), *The Future of the Academic Journal.* Oxford: Chandos.

Rowland, F. 2002. 'The Peer-Review Process', *Learned Publishing* 15, pp. 247–58.

Sompel, H. van de and C. Lagoze. 2007. 'Interoperability for the Discovery, Use, and Re-Use of Units of Scholarly Communication', *CTWatch Quarterly* 3.

Sosteric, M. 1996. 'Interactive Peer Review: A Research Note', *Electronic Journal of Sociology* 2(1), *http://socserv.socsci.mcmaster.ca/EJS/vol002.001/SostericNote.vol002.001.html* (accessed 25 July 2010).

Whitworth, B. and R. Friedman. 2009a. 'Reinventing Academic Publishing Online. Part I: Rigor, Relevance and Practice', *First Monday* 14(8), 3 August.

—. 2009b. 'Reinventing Academic Publishing Online. Part II: A Socio-technical Vision', *First Monday* 14(9), 7 September.

Wilbanks, J. 2007. 'Cyberinfrastructure for Knowledge Sharing', *CTWatch Quarterly* 3(3), August.

6

Textual representations and knowledge support-systems in research intensive networks

Richard Vines, William P. Hall and Gavan McCarthy

> The 'lifeworld' is everyday lived experience. The 'transcendental' of academic and scholarly knowledge stands in contradistinction to the commonsense knowing of the lifeworld, which by comparison is relatively unconscious and un-reflexive (Cope and Kalantzis, Chapter 5, 'Books and journal articles').

Serious consideration of this contradistinction between 'the lifeworld' and the more focused and harder work of science, as described in the previous chapter, poses some daunting intellectual and practical challenges. We aim to explore some of these challenges in this chapter. In so doing, we will cross over a multitude of perspectives and boundaries, many of which are discussed at length throughout this book. In doing this, we are interested in unpacking some of the theoretical inter-relationships between lifeworlds and science, and between constructivism and realism.

But first we ask—can these particular cross-paradigmatic perspectives be reasonably represented and reconciled in textual form? We think that attempts to do so are worthy of the greatest effort and that the reason for doing this is self-evident. Ideas are refined and improved through the process of writing. But beyond this, creation of textual representations of knowledge is of fundamental importance to the effective functioning of research intensive networks.

To support the increased efficacy and efficiency of research intensive networks and their impact in the world, we claim there is a need to expand the context of knowledge systems associated with research intensive networks. This idea for us involves the development of a public knowledge imperative. We suggest that textual representations expressed as knowledge claims can no longer be hidden away from the eyes of public scrutiny when there are important matters of public interest either implicitly or explicitly at stake. The recent catastrophe in the Gulf of Mexico provides an example of how particular types of knowledge, for example, procedures associated with offshore oil rigs, can rise up to become of the highest public priority almost overnight. To neglect the potency of such knowledge through a lack of public scrutiny can have devastating consequences, as the whole world has found out.

In this chapter we set out to provide a rationale as to why we think a public knowledge imperative is so important. To give expression to this imperative, we think there is a need for a new type of institutional and regulatory framework to protect and enhance the role of public knowledge. We call this framework a public knowledge space. It is public by virtue of the fact that it relies on semantic technologies and web-publishing principles. But more importantly, in order to understand the multiple functions of a public knowledge space, we suggest it is first necessary to develop a detailed ontology of knowledge itself. Our ontology outlined in this chapter is broadly based because we emphasise the value of experience and lifeworlds as much as we do the importance of rigorous critiquing and transparent review. By extension, our views are slightly orthogonal to prevailing perspectives of the semantic web.

In many ways, the underpinning of our notion of a public knowledge space is in alignment with the argument developed by Magee in chapters 11 and 12 of this book. Magee suggests it is possible to create a framework for commensurability which 'embraces correspondence, coherentist and consensual notions of truth'. Further, Magee's prominent referencing of the German sociologist and philosopher Jürgen Habermas and Habermas's interest in a 'public sphere' resonate strongly with what we develop in this chapter. It is interesting that we arrive at very similar conclusions but through quite a divergent intellectual pathway.

Introduction

Scholarly research is the primary driving force behind humanity's ever-increasing knowledge of the world. The utility of knowledge claims depends on how they are developed, refined and tested in the real world. The value of a claim is increased most through social processes of scholarly research involving cycles of knowledge sharing that includes individual creativity and inter-subjective criticism. We assert in this chapter that such scholarly research involves processes that occur within a hierarchically complex social system involving individual people, research teams, components at a research domain level, and the world in general, including consumers of research outputs. What makes these systems complex is that the patterns of behaviour across these varying levels of hierarchy are truly emergent in that they cannot be predicted. Thus, the impact of engaging in scholarly research work then is unpredictable.

Part of the reason for this lack of predictability we suggest is because all work is deeply grounded at the level of the lifeworld. All human beings bring their experience of the world to the context associated with their actions and to some extent we can never predict how people respond to any type of stimuli. This we suggest later in the chapter is fundamental to our understanding of knowledge itself. However, at a generalised level, we do suggest that scholarly work begins at the personal level with sense making, observation, creative thinking and self-criticism; and that this is entailed by commitments to the critiquing of preliminary ideas against existing knowledge, empirical data and more observations. This is followed by the individual's articulation and expression of knowledge claims. Such individual work is often conducted within a higher level social environment of collaboration with other people. Personal or small group expression of a knowledge claim is normally followed by inter-subjective activities within a research team, including further observation, data capture, analysis, group-orientated criticism and testing before a consensus about a collaboration is articulated and expressed. Through time, this creative work is then formalised at a discipline level through a publication process involving editorially managed peer reviews that may lead to reconsideration and revision by the authors prior to editorial acceptance and publication. Following publication of relevant research, interested communities in the broader world may further test, criticise, reshape and refine the knowledge claims through subsequent cycles of personal sense making, observation and publication.

From the establishment of scientific societies and the first journals in the Scientific Revolution in the 1660s until recently this process was relatively tangible, involving contacts and exchanges between participants that were either face-to-face or conducted via physical correspondence, leading up to the final printing and publication of the scholarly work (Fjallbrant 1997; Harkness 2007). The only technologies (other than observational instruments) involved in the process of building knowledge were those of writing (typing), duplication (printing) and the physical transport of paper manuscripts and documents between participants. Printing was a major revolution in its own right that made the Scientific Revolution possible (Eisenstein 1979, 1983; Fjallbrant 1997; Hall 2006b). For a time, printing made it possible for many peers to read and criticise the same version of a document. However, beyond this historical revolution, beginning with the exponential developments of computers in the 1950s and the internet in the 1970s, new technologies supporting scholarly research and communication are becoming more and more sophisticated and interconnected (ARL 2009; Lederberg 1991; Mackenzie Owen 2005; Maron and Kirby Smith 2008; Mukherjee 2009). These now are extending the capacity of human cognition for research in what Hall (2006b) claims is a revolution in our abilities to process codified knowledge (see also Carr and Harnad 2009; Dror and Harnad 2008).

In Chapter 4, 'What does the digital do to knowledge making?', Cope and Kalantzis describe six areas of current or imminent change that parallel Hall's views about a 'knowledge processing revolution'. These are discussed in detail under the descriptions of 'the mechanics of rendering'; the rise of a 'new navigation order'; the trend towards 'multimodal environments' and 'ubiquitous recording'; the 'change in sources and directions of knowledge flows'; and what Cope and Kalantzis describe as 'polylingual potentials' of the new digital media.

We think Cope and Kalantzis's descriptions offer a unique and significant insight into the nature of the changes emerging with the rise of digital media. However, we aim to reframe part of their and Magee's analyses by drawing on an extended theoretical filter. We do this by highlighting that research knowledge is developed, reviewed and disseminated in a hierarchy of subsystems comprising individual people, research teams and professional domains and the wider societal level. These subsystems involve the personal, social and intellectual interactions between people as well as the interactions mediated via technologies and the use of different types of *schemas* and standards.

We define a schema as the semantic and organisational structure of a cognitive process. Thus, schemas can be tacit, implicit and explicit. For example, we experience the tacit nature of schemas when working in cross-cultural contexts that are unfamiliar, where the ability to understand language and to accurately attribute meaning is far from certain. Tacit schemas are just that—they are deeply connected to the lifeworlds of actors. They cannot be made explicit and thus cannot be articulated within documents or database structures. By contrast, the semantics and structures diffusely embedded within documents, for example, can implicitly encode a schema that is representative of a person's personal knowledge of a particular domain. Such schemas are implicit to the extent that these schemas are not explicitly represented. However, given time, they can be made explicit and this is what distinguishes implicit schemas from tacit schemas.

There is a growing recognition that schemas associated with unstructured and semi-structured ways of thinking and expression need to be made explicit and published. This is because there is significant utility associated with the use of the internet and related technological systems to manage content exchanges.

For such benefits to be maximised, information systems need to be made interoperable by conforming to agreed standards. To reach negotiated agreements about such standards, reviews are undertaken by industry bodies which define, and then describe, the standard in question. These negotiated agreements are published as schemas. Such schemas 'express shared vocabularies and allow machines to carry out rules made by people' (Sperberg-McQueen and Thompson 2000–2007). The advantage of the process just described is that it allows an industry-standards body to agree on a schema which is sympathetic to the needs of that industry and declares it to be a standard for that industry.

The interactions that occur between the different subsystems involved in the creation of scientific and scholarly knowledge outlined above are reliant on the use of schemas ranging from tacit to explicit and formalised standards. Therefore, we think that these schemas and standards form part of what we call a 'knowledge support-system'. These support-systems are socio-technical in nature in that their functioning is reliant on networks of people, the mediation of person-to-person interactions through the use of technology, and individual people's interaction with computers and machines.

What makes these knowledge support-systems in the current era fundamentally different from the historical world of print is that the exchanges of bits and bytes of coded information can now occur more or less at light speed—and that these exchanges can be enacted simultaneously between the varying levels of hierarchy (for example, between individuals and research teams; individuals and teams and a research domain level; or between individuals, teams and research domain level and national or international standards body). Also, at least some components of the cognitive processing function are increasingly being assisted and automated or semi-automated by technology.

In our chapter we are interested in how people collectively harness and use these emerging knowledge support-systems to develop solutions to research problems. We consider these socio-technical activities as vital to the effective functioning of a 'research enterprise'. In using the term 'research enterprise', we are referring to both the internal and the extended networks that contribute to scholarly research globally. For example, it could refer to academic research institutions such as universities or other knowledge intensive organisations, or even commercial and semi-commercial research publishing enterprises where there is a high degree of reliance on research to support evidence-informed decision making.

The development and application of the knowledge support-systems described above is growing so rapidly that it is difficult for many to comprehend fully how these changes are affecting the socio-technical nature of the 'research enterprise' itself. For example, people in many different disciplines now routinely use knowledge support-systems to help them create and evaluate research knowledge. As part of these activities, these people are designing and implementing support-systems to process data and information in novel ways. In so doing, we claim a proliferation of subsystems is contributing to significant conceptual and terminological confusion when data is exchanged across system or discipline boundaries. When data crosses such boundaries, the differences in world views tacitly embedded within the social and professional languages used as part of the genre of these domains becomes evident. Therefore as the benefits of online data exchange grow, the need for conceptual and terminological clarity increases. Thus, in our chapter, we expose in some detail many of the challenges described by Cope and Kalantzis in Chapter 4, 'What does the digital do to knowledge making?', when they highlight the complexity of topics such as the emergence of a 'new navigation order' or the 'new dynamics of difference'.

A major barrier to the effective functioning of research enterprises is that of interoperability—a topic described in Chapter 14, 'Interoperability and the exchange of humanly usable digital content'. This problem emerges naturally because components of any system developed by stakeholders within a research enterprise may rely on different schemas and standards to support the exchange of data, information and knowledge. We think that consideration of the challenges associated with interoperability provides a concrete example of what Cope and Kalantzis calls the 'new dynamics of difference'.

Within this broad conception of the nature of the socio-technical research enterprise, we claim it will prove necessary to develop a deep epistemological and structural understanding of how research enterprises conceive, generate and use knowledge. We further claim that a semi-formal ontology is required to support enhanced communication across disciplinary boundaries. We aim to address some of the underlying epistemological and ontological confusion that we believe constrains the effective functioning of the modern day research enterprise.

Our central concern in writing this chapter is to show why we think the effective functioning of modern day research enterprises will increasingly rely on the emergence of an institutional framework we have previously referred to as a public knowledge space. We think these knowledge spaces are likely to emerge where multiple stakeholders, including government, are required to collaborate to solve problems. Central to addressing real-world problems is the willingness and ability of stakeholders to collaborate to create shared context. This ability can be facilitated by publishing and harmonising the different schemas and standards that are essential for online information sharing and monitoring.

We discuss how a public knowledge space can provide a range of services including providing pathways to access historical knowledge assets and related contexts. The need for this type of public infrastructure is likely to increase as the complexity of our knowledge-orientated society increases. A number of emergent projects are discussed.

Finally, the many challenges outlined are exacerbated by the fact that even professional knowledge managers—an emergent professional domain that could well do much to mediate paradigmatic differences—cannot agree on what it is they are supposed to be managing (Land 2009; Stenmark 2002; Wilson 2002).

To address this foundation problem, we begin our chapter by introducing a theory and ontology of knowledge derived from Karl Popper's evolutionary epistemology. We think this theory and ontology is necessary to explain the various forms of knowledge that emerge within a research enterprise. Popper's epistemology is combined with a theory of hierarchically complex systems to help understand the multiple layers of complexities within the research enterprise. We highlight that this application of a synthesis of theories has utility because it helps focus on interactions within and between the different levels of organisation—of individual researcher (and his or her lifeworld), research team, research community, research administration and worldwide.

Towards an ontology of knowledge

In this section we aim to outline an 'ontology of knowledge'. At base level here, we are interested in unpacking the theoretical questions and inter-relationships that arise when exploring the boundaries between lifeworlds and science; and between constructivism and realism. We do this first by discussing the notion that knowledge is an emergent property of evolutionary systems. We then describe the means by which different types of knowledge emerge through time within research enterprises. Finally, we refer to other types of cyclical models associated with the acquisition and growth of knowledge.

Knowledge as an emergent property of evolutionary systems

What do we mean by 'knowledge'? In knowledge management there are almost as many definitions of knowledge as there are practitioners, to say nothing of arguments about relationships between data, information and knowledge (e.g. Land 2009; Stenmark 2002). Here we adopt Karl R. Popper's (1972) concept that 'knowledge is solutions to problems'—or at least claims towards solutions. We choose to adopt this approach because it is grounded in an idea called an 'evolutionary epistemology' ('EE'). Donald T. Campbell (1974) first coined this term. However, Campbell credits Popper with its origination and with expressing its fundamental perspective in *Logik der Forschung* (1935). Both Campbell (1959, 1960, 1991) and Popper argued that knowledge emerges in living things as they adapt to the world. In his most complete explanation, Popper (1972, pp. 241–45) referred to this as his 'general theory of evolution'.

In this theory, outlined in Figure 6.1, P_n is a 'problem situation' the living entity faces and TS_m represents a range of 'tentative solutions', 'tentative hypotheses' or 'tentative theories' the living entity may propose or act on. *EE* ('error elimination') represents a process by which tentative solutions are tested or criticised to selectively remove solutions or claims that don't work in practice. Popper and Campbell are slightly different in their perspectives of EE in that Popper sees the selective forces of reality eliminating the failures, whereas Campbell sees selection leaving behind those tentative solutions that didn't fail. In either case, P_{n+1} represents the now changed problem situation remaining after a solution has been incorporated. As the entity iterates and reiterates the process (the arrow indicating iteration is added), it will construct increasingly accurate representations of and responses to external reality. These interconnected ideas formed the basis of Popper's (1972) 'general theory of evolution' and the 'growth of knowledge' that takes place in living entities. This idea of an evolutionary epistemology encompasses

Figure 6.1   Popper's 'general theory of evolution'

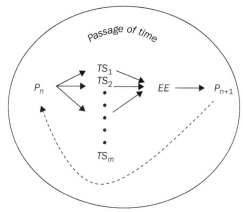

From Hall 2005, after Popper 1972, p. 243

what we mean when we say that *knowledge is an emergent property of an evolutionary system*. The arrows in Figure 6.1 indicate that these iterations through time are sequential processes and may involve self-observation. Some may suggest that such system attributes can result in a viciously circular and self-reenforced closed system (e.g., Luhmann 1995a, 1995b). But this is not the case, because the evolutionary system is open along the time axis (Hall and Nousala 2010). We suggest this latter point might be seen as slightly innocuous, but it could have significant ramifications for future research directions. For example, we think it opens up creative possibilities within the context of Cope and Kalantzis's juxtaposition of the realm of the lifeword against the harder work of science. It might also have the potential to create a pathway to be able to hold in balance constructivist, including radical constructivist, and realist perspectives. Thus we conclude the place of time within our ontology of knowledge is an exceptionally important one.

To fully comprehend what might be possible and what might become available through Popper's notion of an evolutionary epistemology it is necessary to consider additionally that Popper thought that knowledge grows through iterated interactions of three ontological domains or 'worlds' (Popper 1972). We contend this articulation of an ontology of knowledge is crucial in order to understand and explain the different types of knowledge that evolve through time.

Our ontology development therefore begins with defining these three distinct but interacting ontological domains or 'worlds' (Popper 1972, p. 107, etc., 1978, as extended by Hall 2005, 2006a). 'World 1' (W1) is 'the world of physical objects or of physical states', including the un-interpreted dynamics of everything physical. 'World 2' (W2) is the 'the world of states of consciousness, or of mental states, or perhaps of behavioural dispositions to act', which we extend to encompass the 'living' world of cybernetics, cognition and knowledge in the broad sense. Popper includes *'subjective' knowledge* (the subject's personal knowledge), which is an individual or subject's inherent propensity or disposition to 'behave or react' (1972, p. 108) in certain ways in particular circumstances in W2. This approximates Polanyi's (1958, 1966) personal and 'tacit' knowledge and we would suggest is inclusive of certain aspects of the lifeworld discussed in the previous chapter. 'World 3' (W3) includes all kinds of persistently encoded knowledge (e.g., the logical contents of written documents, electronically encoded information, sequences of nucleotides in a DNA molecule, etc.; Popper 1972, pp. 73–74). 'Knowledge in the objective sense is *knowledge without a knower*; it is *knowledge without a knowing subject*' (Popper 1972, p. 109). Codified knowledge is 'objective' because its logical content can exist in W3 logically encoded in the physical structure of a W1 container that can exist separately from the 'knowing subject', and can be decoded in W2 with similar subjective meanings by different subjects.

A fundamental question is: How does knowledge emerge when there are three ontological domains involved? Popper differed significantly from the logical positivists in that he argued no objective truth could be proved—only that certain claims could be shown to be in error through tests or criticisms of the claims as they impact reality (W1). He argued that knowledge claims may be aggregated and transformed, progressing from raw sense data registering impacts of the physical world on a living entity (for example, experience or observations of events), to well-tested and proven solutions for the major problems of life (Popper 1999). A theory referring to W1 can be constructed by people in W2 and (optionally) be expressed and shared in the form of W3 content. Through iterated cycles of hypothesising solutions, and testing and criticising them to eliminate errors, knowledge claims asserted in W2 or W3 can approach correspondence with W1's reality, as Popper (1972) explained in his 'general theory of evolution' (Figure 6.1).

Popper's ideas of the three worlds can be grossly misunderstood if one tries to interpret W3 from the viewpoint of Platonic idealism (Balaguer 2009), strict monism (Popper 1994; Schaffer 2009) or dualism (Robinson 2009). However, in Popper's interactionist concept (Popper 1994; see also Robb and Heil 2009 for interactionism), and as we use it here, the three worlds are constantly interacting, as shown in Figure 6.2. For example,

Figure 6.2 Knowledge in the three worlds ontology

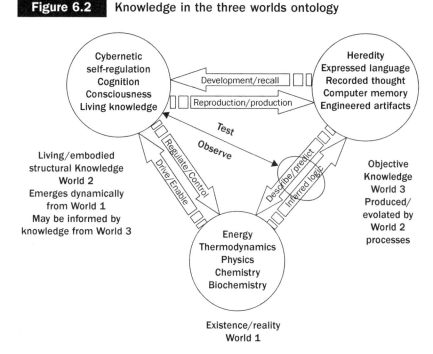

the dynamics of W1 drives life and its cyclical activities in W2, and these in turn contribute to the control of the physical dynamics of W1 through cybernetic regulatory processes. W2 processes in living entities can encode knowledge about W1 into objective knowledge that can persist in W3 over time and space. Or the inferred knowledge about W1 can be decoded from W3 and interpreted and acted on in W2, where it then serves to describe and predict dynamics in W1 (W1 and W2 do not interact directly, but only via cybernetic dynamics in W2).

Thus, we think that the interactions between these three worlds are as important as the epistemic distinctions between them. It is these interactions that differentiate Popper's approach from Plato's static approach or monistic or dualist approaches and that lies at the heart of our understanding of abstract objects that are textual representations of knowledge in W3.

The emergence of different types of knowledge through time

We have introduced the three-world ontology as above specifically because we claim it provides a foundation on which to understand the emergence of different types of knowledge through time. The reason we think the three world ontology is an important component of this theoretical framework is that it is the continuous interaction between the three ontological domains that give rise to the different types of knowledge we now describe. In the appendix to this chapter we provide a detailed summary of our ontology of knowledge as it relates to a research enterprise. We have documented this because it provides an understanding of our claim that different types of knowledge are continuously transformed into other types of knowledge. Later in our chapter we explain why we think this has important ramifications for knowledge support-systems within research enterprises and the functioning of a public knowledge space.

We start our description of knowledge by referencing Michael Polanyi (1958, 1966). Polanyi hypothesised that 'personal knowledge' encompasses several types of knowledge, and specifically includes what Popper (1972) described as 'dispositional' or 'subjective' knowledge. Dispositional knowledge is embodied in people's unconscious propensities to act in certain ways (as 'natural talent', habits and skills), while subjective knowledge lives in people's minds and together these contribute to personal knowledge in W2. The un-interpreted physical–chemical and dynamic structure of a person's brain exists in W1. However, the cybernetic control of that structure, whether it is physiological and reflexive or under the control of conscious decisions and the memory of history that together constitute the mind's knowledge, lives in W2 (Hall 2005, 2006a; Hall, Dalmaris and Nousala 2005; Popper 1978). Aspects of this personal knowledge can be encoded in W3 in inert and objectively persistent formats (as 'explicit' knowledge). Where the existence of this explicit knowledge is known only to the individual, we include this within 'personal knowledge'.

Personal knowledge emerges from cycles of natural selection and individual 'sense making'—encompassing activities in W2 that organise sensory impressions (data) of W1. Part of sense making may involve decoding W3 content and extracting and reformulating these materials to extend living knowledge—possibly to support immediate action and/or to create new content in W3 to support W2 memory or social processes of sense making and action.

In Figure 6.3 we adapt Nickols' (2000) terminology to highlight that personal knowledge is always contextualised. Knowledge initially emerges or is constructed as 'situational knowledge' in living entities—generally in response to situations and problems of existence. 'Tacit knowledge' (W2) is unconscious or inherent in a person and cannot be readily articulated. 'Implicit knowledge' also resides in W2, but is consciously available to the

Figure 6.3 The contextual nature of personal knowledge

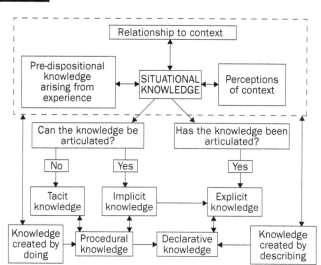

Adapted from Nickols 2000

person and can be articulated and may be codified for storage in W3. Tacit knowledge can become 'tacit procedural knowledge' if it becomes embodied in unconscious personal routines. Nelson and Winter (1982) argue that some competitive differences between (organisational) systems can be attributed to relatively stable capabilities expressed in the dynamic structures of these systems. These 'heritable' organisational capabilities include such things as undocumented 'routinization' of knowledge intensive processes at the organisational level, development of specific jargons, and the layout of plant and equipment. Nelson and Winter specifically called this 'tacit organisational knowledge' after Polanyi (1966). We think this contributes to cybernetic regulatory and control mechanisms (in W2) at the level of organisational knowledge systems and suggest this makes the knowledge of a research team, group, establishment or discipline something more than the sum of the personal knowledge of the networks' individual human members.

Personal knowledge may be shared with other people via conversation and articulation. Unless it has been shared and understood, tacit or implicit knowledge important to a research team or domain becomes 'lost knowledge' when links to it are broken (e.g., when people holding relevant personal knowledge leave that domain or network).

When knowledge is codified in an objectively persistent format (W3) it becomes 'explicit knowledge'. Explicit knowledge is 'objective' in

Popper's sense because it has been codified into or onto a persistent substrate, for example as sequences of letter marks on paper or polarisation domains on a magnetic surface. The logical and semantic content of the knowledge exists in W3. The atoms and molecules of the physically encoded form of that content exist in W1, but its meaning can only be made operational (Corning 2001) by a person's W2 processes to decode and act on the knowledge. Examples of explicit knowledge within a research enterprise include all documents, graphics, spreadsheet files, databases, emails, video clips, wikis and blogs, etc.

Even where important knowledge exists explicitly, access to that content may still rely on the personal knowledge of only one or two people (or no one). Thus, a research network may retain explicit knowledge generated by its members even after they leave, but in many cases the personal knowledge of other people, including tacit knowledge, is still required to access and apply it (Cowan, David and Foray 2000; Nousala et al. 2005; Tsoukas 2005). Where explicit knowledge is on paper, when personal knowledge about its existence and location is not available to a research network or is not available when and where it is needed, then such knowledge becomes 'orphaned explicit knowledge' and might as well not exist at all. Where explicit knowledge has been preserved in electronic formats, search capabilities in a technological support-system can minimise this kind of orphaning.

'Procedural knowledge' can often be both tacit and implicit and is created through learning by 'doing'. Procedural knowledge that is implicit in nature can be articulated to become 'declarative knowledge' and is created by describing things. 'Articulation' means putting ideas into words that may then be encoded into W3. We think there is some greyness and uncertainty about how to understand the ontological nature of articulated or declarative knowledge and when these types of knowledge are understood as explicit or objective. Some suggest that speech vanishes as it is articulated and leaves only subjective mental trace in the minds of those who hear it (Ong, 1982). But with the increasing ubiquity of mechanical recording devices this creates the potential to place recorded speech in W3. Thus, when recording of speech does occur, speech is fully explicit and objective.

'Common knowledge' is content that has been widely shared or is readily discoverable when needed using familiar retrieval methods. Personal tacit knowledge may be shared to become 'common tacit knowledge' (Nousala 2006; Nousala, Hall and John 2007). For example, apprenticeships, 'grapevines', 'rumour mills' and undocumented routines—'that's the way we do things here'—all provide examples of how 'personal knowledge' can be transferred and made 'common' without being made explicit. Similarly, explicit knowledge that becomes widely known or easily retrievable is termed 'common-explicit knowledge'. Consideration has been given to using the term 'shared' in these contexts instead of 'common', but sharing refers to a process and does not indicate how widespread the shared content might be. Only when the knowledge is widespread or easily discovered and accessed, and thus able to survive the absence of key individuals who know it, does the knowledge truly become available to members of a research network or enterprise rather than just a few individuals. Network protocols that limit access to particular files and documents or business practices that impede tacit sharing reduce the accessibility of knowledge, and hence the ability for it to become common rather than lost or orphaned.

'Formal knowledge' refers to 'authorised common knowledge'. Formal knowledge is that subset of common knowledge in W2 or W3 that has been socially critiqued and approved in an organisational context. Through the process of critiquing and reaching negotiated agreements, authorisation is given to use knowledge in appropriate contexts. Examples of formal knowledge include:

- negotiated schemas and industry based standards
- content of an industry training or university accredited training program
- knowledge transferred via apprenticeship programs
- instruction manuals, policies, procedures, engineering documentation, lessons-learned documents, research publications and so on, as formalised via release and publication workflows, acceptance by an organisational committee or a industry working party
- formally established business processes and workflows
- documented routines and processes, including plant and equipment layout, and so on, where people have authorised the implementation of chosen routines and processes.

Formal knowledge can be both tacit and explicit. For example, 'formal tacit knowledge' might refer to processes that are well-defined routines with these routines guiding how things are done in ways that are well known but not explicitly documented (after Nelson and Winter 1982). In contrast, 'formal explicit knowledge' refers to routines or policies that are developed as a result of research and are published in an objectively persistent format. Formal documents:

encompasses many categories of documents, including letters, notes, book reviews, conference papers, journal articles, responses and academic books. The common feature is that they have been subjected to formal review prior to publication, and hence carry some form of imprimatur recognized within the relevant scholarly community (Clarke and Kingsley 2008).

Other cyclical models associated with the acquisition and growth of knowledge

As represented at its most fundamental level by Popper's (1972) evolutionary epistemology (see Figure 6.1), the dynamics of knowledge acquisition and application is cyclical. Other cycles similar to Popper's have also been proposed, for example, SECI (Nonaka 1994; Nonaka and Takeuchi 1995), single and double loop learning (reviewed by Blackman, Connelly and Henderson 2004) or the knowledge life cycle (Firestone and McElroy 2003a). Because of its similarities to Popper's representation of the evolutionary theory of knowledge and the severe testing it has received in real-world conflicts (Mutch 2006), we find Boyd's (1976–1996) observe–orient–decide–act (OODA) cycle (Angerman 2004; Grant and Kooter 2004; Hall 2003, 2005, 2006a; Martin, Philp and Hall 2009; Philp and Martin 2009; Richards 2008) (see Figure 6.4) is suited to the discussion here.

Figure 6.4   John Boyd's OODA loop concept

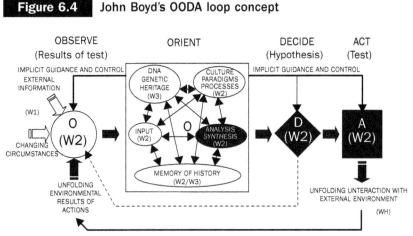

From Hall 2005 (after Boyd 1976–1996); Richards 2008

'Observe' and 'orient' involve the cybernetic processing of information in W2 (as shown in Figure 6.4) to collect and then contextualise observations of the world. In the generation of research knowledge, external information feeding into the cybernetic processing of observation and orientation includes knowledge extracted from the research literature. Then, in 'decide', decisions are made about what action to take—where 'decision' can involve anything from an instant gut response by an individual (W2) to deciding the results from the inter-subjective criticism of formal hypotheses (W3). Finally, the entity 'acts' to test its understanding and prior learning by observing results of action in the physical world. A new cycle begins with observing the results of prior action.

The theory of hierarchically complex systems

We have previously defined several knowledge related concepts and types of knowledge. We now add another dimension to this ontology by considering the functions of knowledge in the hierarchically complex systems of today's research enterprises.

It is easy for us to recognise and see complex system entities at our own human focal level or lower levels of organisation as through a magnifying glass or microscope (e.g., where most of us would know how to interpret what we see). On the other hand it is much more difficult for us to discriminate and 'see' complex entities at larger scales and higher levels of focus than our own, for example, entities such as the biological species we belong to (*Homo sapiens*), our solar system, or the Milky Way galaxy including our solar system (Chaisson 2001; Gould 2002; Hall 2005, 2006a; Salthe 1985, 2004). It takes the equivalent of looking through the 'wrong' end of a telescope and considerable mental effort and practice for us to recognise and focus on the boundaries of higher level systems that include us as components. However, many high-level systems including humans as components (e.g., knowledge-system networks) are bounded by the equivalent of a living cell's semi-permeable membrane that we can learn to recognise as 'permeable boundaries'. For example, members may be recruited on the basis of qualifications, there might be an allocation of passwords to allow authorised access to research data and research resources, and there might be some restrictions about communication of research findings etc). Following Simon (1962) such boundaries are normally reflected by a higher level of knowledge sharing interactions between people forming a system versus similar interactions with those outside the system. These considerations are clarified by hierarchy theory.

The theory of hierarchically complex dynamic systems derives from concepts of complexity (Simon 1962, 1973, 2002), control and causation (Corning 2001; Pattee 1973, 2000), and scalar levels of organisation and emergence (Hall 2006a; Salthe 1985, 1993, 2004). The dynamics of control and causation in a system are entropically driven by the dissipation of free energy in the transport of energy from a high potential source to a low potential sink (Prigogine 1955, 1981). 'Systems' are comprised of causally connected parts. In a 'complex system', where many parts interact non-linearly in ways such that even given the properties of the parts and the laws of their interactions, the properties of the whole are not easily predicted (Simon 1962). 'Hierarchically complex systems' are those where individual parts that interact to form a designated system at one 'level of focus' can be seen to be composed of several to many interacting components at a more detailed, 'lower', level of focus (Simon 1962, 1973); see Figure 6.5. Every entity that is a complex system can be seen to have a triadic existence (Koestler 1967, 1978; Salthe 1993): (1) as a component of and within a higher level system (e.g., a person working within a firm), (2) the existence of the

Figure 6.5 The systems triad in hierarchy of complex dynamic systems

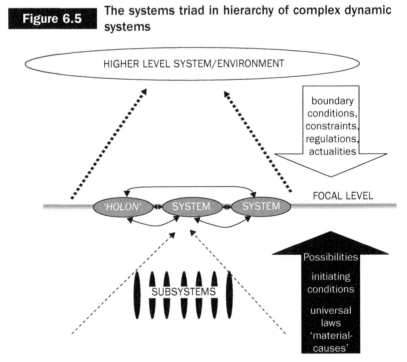

Hall, Dalmaris and Nousala 2005 (after Salthe 1985)

system itself (the person) at the focal level, called a 'holon', which in turn is comprised of (3), the collection of lower level systems serving as its components (the living cells comprising the person's body).

In general, by comparison to a specific holon or 'focal system' of interest that can be discerned at a given level of organisation, dynamic activities within the much smaller lower level components subsystems will be generally so much faster that they will appear to be in equilibrium—in effect defining the laws of interaction among the systems visible at the focal level and thus determining what it is possible for the holon to do. The dynamics of the much larger super-system, which includes the focal system as a subsystem, will be so much slower that they appear to provide a constant environment for the focal system—thus establishing constraints and boundary conditions on what the holon can do (Salthe 1985, 1993; Simon 1973, 2002). Constraints applying downward control may be negative (inhibitory) or positive (facilitative). The dynamic structure of a focal system (the specific states, interactions and trajectories of the components comprising the system) at a point in time establishes conditions that provide a downward control over the dynamic possibilities available to the subsystems comprising the focal system (Pattee 1973, 2000). The structures providing that control can be considered to embody 'control information' (Corning 2001; Pattee 2000).

Where the potential gradient in the energy flux between the source and sink across a given focal system is large enough (e.g., because the higher level super-system is 'inefficient') processes may emerge to form an additional dissipative system establishing an intermediate level of organisation in the complex systems hierarchy between the higher level system and the focal level (Salthe 2004).

These matters have relevance to the ontology of knowledge as this relates to research knowledge systems. For example, in large research enterprises, the formal processes surrounding applications for research funding are an example of one level of focus within the hierarchical complex system of academic research. At lower focal level individual researchers or research teams jostle to secure as much flexibility and adaptive capacity as possible, in order to respond to dynamics of these lower levels of hierarchy. The tension between these two levels of hierarchy, for example, has significant impact on the dynamics of the emergence and formalisation of knowledge. Downward causation, resulting in significant system constraints at lower levels of hierarchy, can prevent or facilitate the emergence of new knowledge claims. Going forward, one of the key skills will be to determine how and when system constraints should be applied (or relaxed) and on what basis.

Research knowledge and the dynamics of hierarchically complex systems

Modern-day research enterprises work to increase the formal knowledge available to a knowledge society (Lederberg 1991) and to solve pressing problems. We claim that the growth of knowledge in a knowledge society takes place in a hierarchically complex system comprised of at least four interacting levels of cyclical knowledge building. In what follows, we expand our ontology to discuss some of the processes through which research knowledge emerges and grows through time. We are particularly interested to highlight the dynamics through which research knowledge claims are constructed and evaluated and to show how the nature of knowledge that emerge from these varying levels of knowledge cycling. In outlining parts of our discussions we also refer to aspects of Popper's general theory of evolution (see Figure 6.1) and Boyd's OODA loop process (see Figure 6.4).

We will now proceed to examine the dynamics of the four levels of knowledge cycling in particular systems as shown in Figure 6.6 more closely.

Figure 6.6 The hierarchical levels of knowledge cycling in a research enterprise

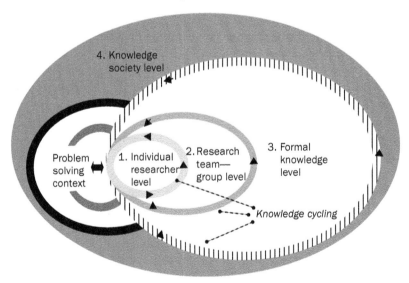

Individual researcher level (personal knowledge)

Scholarly research begins at the individual researcher level and involves sense making and associated cognitive activities of individual researchers. Individual researchers tend to follow a generic research cycle similar to the OODA cycle discussed above. They act by:

- observing (O) problems in the world (P_n), and the context within which the problem is manifest (problem solving context)

- orienting (O) to the observations through their awareness of prior explicit knowledge contained in the 'body of formal knowledge' (BoFK) as mediated by their innate cognitive capacities and constrained by cultural paradigms and processes (both corresponding to observation and orientation in the OODA cycle)

- formulating ideas and articulating claims or 'tentative theories' (*TT*—cf. decide in OODA cycle)

- eliminating errors (*EE*—cf. act in OODA) through criticising and testing them against the world

- observing the results (beginning the iteration of a new cognitive cycle at the researcher level).

While this process appears to be well structured and logical, significant amounts of tacit and implicit cognitive processing can be involved. That is, individuals may not be able to articulate what it is they do, why they make specific types of decisions or what types of schemas they apply in their work. We define a schema as the semantic and organisational structure of a cognitive process and thus at the individual researcher level schemas are mostly tacit and implicit in nature.

Figure 6.7 outlines the transformation of personal knowledge into explicit knowledge that occurs at the individual researcher level. Iterative interactions occur involving observing W1; mental processes, sense making, social languages and narrative exchanges in W2; and the coding and decoding of knowledge between W2 and W3. Part of the overall sense-making process may involve codifying empirical data and information into explicit knowledge objects (W3) as informed by cognitive processing in W2. An extension to existing research knowledge occurs when new knowledge claims are tested against W1 and the results are criticised in W2 against prior knowledge claims that exist in W3. It is the constant and cyclical interactions between these worlds that enable knowledge to be constructed tested, critiqued and refined. Through time, different versions of objective artefacts are produced.

Figure 6.7 General process for turning personal into explicit knowledge

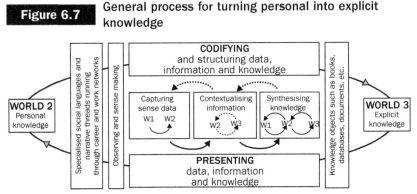

After Vines, Hall and Naismith 2007

Popper (1994, p. 13) makes an interesting statement:

> As for subjective knowledge [W2], much of it is simply taken over from objective knowledge [W3]. We learn a great deal from books, and in universities. But the opposite does not hold: although objective knowledge is man-made, it is rarely made by taking over subjective knowledge. It happens very rarely that a man first forms a conviction on the basis of personal experience, publishes it, and gets it objectively accepted as one of the things which we say 'it is known that…'.

What usually happens is that the knowledge claim is articulated and often written down in draft form for intersubjective criticism and testing long before it is accepted and approved for formal publication in a journal or book.

The exchange and sharing of personal knowledge often involves interactions that extend into team or group level interactions when a research claim or tentative theory is first being constructed. It is through these extended networks that personal knowledge begins to be articulated and tested in practice. One of the most important media through which such processes occurs is natural language conversation itself. There is, however, a risk that such personal knowledge sharing may have detrimental impacts because each person unavoidably constructs an understanding of the world within a personal frame of reference (Kuhn 1962, 1983). In effect, individual knowledge processing schemas as summarised in Figure 6.7 can be innate and tacit—corresponding to the culture, paradigms and processes of Boyd's OODA loop concept (Figure 6.4)—as well as implicit.

There are significant impediments to the transformation of personal knowledge into explicit knowledge. For example, solutions often emerge in a social environment, where personal knowledge can provide a tacit or implicit compass to guide action. Equally, attempting to use personal knowledge to create explicit knowledge so that such knowledge can be applied in other contexts by other people can also be problematic, because emergent knowledge might be highly context sensitive. Also, for various reasons, researchers may not want to explicitly advertise their expertise (Ardichvili 2008; Bock et al. 2005), because they may fear this might diminish their own particular position, they may not welcome critiquing of their professional expertise that could arise if they make their expertise explicit, or they simply may not wish to be bothered by people asking for help. On top of this, even where people are willing to share, there may still be limitations to sharing because of the principle of bounded rationality (Else 2004; Hall et al. 2007; Nousala 2006; Nousala et al. 2005, 2009; Simon 1979; Snowden 2002). That is, people cannot share all that they know, and sharing invariably results in some loss of knowledge. Workers also cannot write down everything they may be willing to share (Snowden 2002), although once codified, knowledge may be accessed and distributed more rapidly and widely than speech.

Research team or larger group level (common knowledge)

Today most research is done in a social environment of informal or formal collaboration. The second, higher level cycle shown in Figure 6.6 involves collaboration within a research team or larger group. This process may begin with:

- the sharing of articulated theories (Popper's *TT*) verbally or via draft papers, followed by
- collective orientation to the shared ideas and BoFK, followed by
- inter-subjective error elimination (*EE*), and concluding with
- collective criticism (c.f. 'act' in OODA) of the *TT*, leading to the authoring of an explicit knowledge claim or claims.

The development of higher levels of collaboration brings with it the challenge of enabling explicit knowledge artefacts to become more accessible, thereby gradually transforming explicit knowledge into common explicit knowledge. Online databases, enterprise web portals and document management systems with electronic workflows and search mechanisms (Hall et al. 2008) all help transform explicit knowledge into common knowledge. The challenge is to provide appropriate technologies, network architectures and process workflows to make this transformation easy and to limit the use of internal security controls that reduce the discoverability and accessibility of explicit knowledge as common knowledge.

Within a knowledge-system network, the shift from individual to collaborative decision making can never be assumed. There is a need to cultivate a level of shared context and language in order to support collaborative opportunities and directions. It is in understanding and managing the boundaries between personal knowledge and more communitarian understandings of knowledge where the complexities of the discipline of knowledge management arise. One of the purposes of the role of knowledge management and indeed of science education itself is to help individuals develop and expand their personal knowledge, and to facilitate rational knowledge sharing. We do not suggest this journey towards rational knowledge sharing is easy, because strong emotional responses can be unearthed in any journey that involves researching the unfamiliar.

Formal knowledge level

The third, higher level involves the development of formal knowledge. Within the research enterprise this can include formal publishing processes. In simplified form, at this level the knowledge cycle involves:

- submission of a paper by a researcher or group of collaborators to a publisher or authentication body
- initiation of a peer-review process by an editor working at the organisational level that involves observing and orienting to the paper and selecting appropriate reviewers for it
- individual peer reviewers at the researcher level each observing and orienting to the paper and in some cases testing the knowledge claims, criticising them and returning their explicit criticisms to the publisher or authentication organisation
- the editor at the organisational level either committing the paper to formal publication as an addition to the BoFK or returning it to the author(s) as a rejection or with a request for changes or improvement—which then initiates further cycles at the investigator and collaborator layers.

Within the research enterprise itself, the creation of formal knowledge can also involve various internal social processes of critiquing such as those that occur through supervision, community of practice reviews, committee structures and the like (Figure 6.8). We contend that this review of common knowledge is a knowledge quality-assurance process (Vines and Naismith 2002). Through such review processes, understandings and agreements are reached about the degree to which knowledge claims can be used to solve real-world problems (Firestone and McElroy 2003a, 2003b). Such agreements can be struck in a range of different contexts, including, for example, through staff supervision, formal research projects, formal committee structures or the journal publishing peer-review mechanism.

Part of any negotiation of 'agreements' involves dealing with the varying belief paradigms held by multiple stakeholders. What is needed is not a process of reaching 'shared or consensual truths' about a research domain's knowledge base, nor should decisions be made on the traditional hierarchical expression of power. Rather, the review process (and the role of the reviewer in the process) is to test knowledge claims against the real world (W1) and ensure that decisions reflect agreed views about what will

Figure 6.8   Social construction and formalisation of knowledge

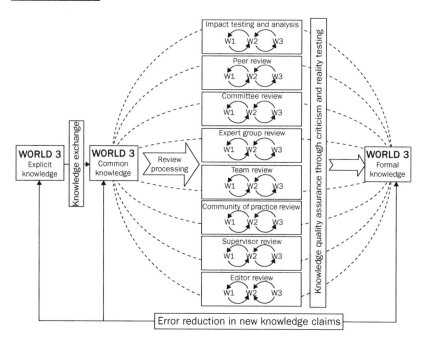

deal with real problems—until something else more pragmatically beneficial emerges (Firestone and McElroy 2003a). Ideally, reviewers, editors or those authorised to approve formal knowledge claims, such as technical committee chairpersons, should learn to make their observations taking into account multiple perspectives, to have their own underlying assumptions continuously tested (Firestone and McElroy 2003b), and to share this learning throughout any knowledge-system network.

Knowledge society level (acting on formal knowledge)

The highest layer of knowledge cycling occurs at the level of the knowledge society. The research enterprise incrementally contributes to better solutions to problems (P_n) by adding to a formalised BoFK. After formal publication of new or improved findings, these may well continue to be observed, oriented and criticised by an academy and may result in further cycles of research on new problems revealed by answers to the original problem (Popper's P_2). New research questions are posed, beginning again with individual investigators and research teams.

We claim later in this paper that new institutional mechanisms might well be required to support the acquisition and growth of knowledge at a knowledge society level. Preliminary ideas about such matters are introduced under the topic 'public knowledge space'.

The socio-technical aspects of schema interactions within research enterprises

As Cope and Kalantzis highlight, the knowledge practices embedded within the traditional paper journal and book publishing industries have emerged over the past five centuries. These knowledge processes involved simple exchange of text and recursive construction of textual knowledge. For example, tangible artefacts such as letters, draft manuscripts and publications were exchanged iteratively between authors, publishers and printers. The only technologies involved in the process of communicating knowledge were those of writing, typing and printing, and the ponderously slow physical transport of paper between participants.

However, with the advent of computers in the past several decades, digital technologies supporting scholarly work emerged and are becoming ever more sophisticated and interconnected, to the extent that these now form part of a research 'knowledge support-system'. These support-systems are being developed in such ways so as to enable larger and larger volumes of data and information to be exchanged and transformed virtually instantaneously via through online transactions. For example, up until the last decade or so, typesetting a paper from an author's manuscript required hours of work by people with specialised skills in a publishing house. Today, by clicking an Adobe PDF button in an Adobe Acrobat add-in to MS Word, an author can turn her MS Word manuscript into a typeset quality PDF e-print in seconds.

As the volume of data and information exchanges increase, a need emerges to structure data and information. This need arises from the benefits associate with the automated and semi-automated exchange of such data and information between different systems. When this need emerges, it is often only then that the extent of variation in the schemas held at different levels of focus (individual, team, organisational) comes into full view. At the individual level schemas are mostly often tacit and implicit in nature and form part of any individual's lifeworld. However, as the need for collaboration and coordination of research work increases, the need for what we call community-schemas emerges. These community-schemas emerge as explicit knowledge artefacts and as a form of common explicit knowledge. That is, they are usually published in formal ways, for example, through structured forms, data dictionaries or taxonomies. These explicit schemas are designed to facilitate a degree of mediation between the schemas tacitly and implicitly held by individuals and schemas relevant to the needs of a wider community of stakeholders within the research enterprise. In this way there is an ability to creatively harness the diversity and distributed nature of human cognition across the multiple levels of focus discussed in this section.

Where there is a need for the research enterprise to exchange data and information beyond its own boundaries to the wider world, a need for more formalised schemas declared as industry standards becomes more pressing. Such standards might be expressed as a formal specification in the form of an ontology, an industry or organisational specific XML standard, document type definitions (DTDs) or data dictionaries that the research enterprise needs to adopt or comply with. Such knowledge representations are emerging from a wide range of research domains including health and community services.

What makes these knowledge support-systems fundamentally different from the historical world of print is that the exchanges of bits and bytes of coded information can now occur more or less at light speed—and that these exchanges can be enacted simultaneously across varying levels of hierarchy (for example, those relevant to individuals, research teams, formal knowledge domains and a knowledge society). While this might be the case, we suggest that such support-systems are being developed and applied so rapidly that insufficient attention is being paid to the problems of conceptual and terminological confusion at different levels of organisation. There are two sources of such confusion. First, a wide range of personnel from different research domains are designing and enacting standards and schemas that reflect their own narrowly focused professional or social languages. Thus when exchanging information across professional boundaries the schemas used to support data and information exchange can often be incommensurable with other schemas. Second, and perhaps more importantly, insufficient attention is being paid to the challenges associated with harmonising variant schemas that emerge at different levels of hierarchy in the modern research enterprise (see Figure 6.6).

Implications for managing research enterprises in a knowledge society

The historical concern associated with 'open science'

In the final part of this chapter we want to draw out what we regard are the implications of our analysis thus far—particularly with respect to the future design of knowledge support-systems. Concerns are already being expressed as to whether the types of support-systems described in this paper are contributing to the continued strengthening of 'open science' for example:

> Provision of enhanced technical means of accessing distributed research resources is neither a necessary nor a sufficient condition for achieving open scientific collaboration... Collaboration technologies—both infrastructures and specific application tools and instruments—may be used to facilitate the work of distributed members of 'closed clubs,'... that work with proprietary data and materials, guarding their findings as trade secrets until they obtain the legal protections granted by intellectual property rights. Nor do researchers' tools as such define the organizational character of collaboration. This is evident from the fact that many academic

> researchers who fully and frequently disclose their findings, and collaborate freely with colleagues on an informal, non-contractual basis, nonetheless employ proprietary software and patented instruments, and publish in commercial scientific journals that charge high subscription fees (David, den Besten and Schroeder 2009, p. 2).

In the historical world of print-based journal publishing, many of the principles of open science emanated from tensions in the relationships between research and intellectual property. Boyle, for example, draws on significant historical analyses from Jefferson to the present day in order to tease out many of the complexities and intricacies of such matters: 'The general rule of law is that the noblest of human productions—knowledge, truths ascertained conceptions and ideas—become after voluntary communications to others, free as the air to common use' (2008, p. xv).

Within this broad context of common use, Merton ([1942] 1973) suggested a normative structure of science required commitments to ensure the advancement of reliable knowledge. He summarised these commitments using the acronym CUDOS. The production of reliable knowledge is reliant on the principle that research is a collective pursuit—thus the norm of (C)ommunalism. The norm of (U)niversalism entails that anyone can participate in the research process, thus the research field remains open to all competent persons. Commitments by (D)isinterested agents are required to ensure that findings are not skewed by the personal interests of researchers. The quality of knowledge is dependent on the (O)riginality of research contributions. A spirit of (S)cepticism and scrutiny is required to ensure claims are appropriately critiqued—thus safeguarding the quality of knowledge.

Merton was writing before the conception of the internet and semantic technologies. So, a relevant question is to ask whether a normative structure to science and the concern for the creation of 'reliable knowledge' still has currency in relation to the modern era, especially one where socio-technical systems are being deployed to support research activities. David, den Bestern and Schroeder think so, but that there might be a need to reconceptualise those norms to take into account the e of e-science:

> Questions concerning the actual extent of 'openness' of research processes identified with contemporary e-science, therefore ought to address at least two main sets of issues pertaining to the conduct of 'open science'. The first set concerns the terms on which individuals

> may enter and leave research projects. [...] The second set of questions concerns the norms and rules governing disclosure of data and information about research methods and results (2009, p. 7–8).

Part of the rationale underpinning this chapter is that we think the natural sciences and biology (B. McKelvey 1997, 2002a, 2002b; W. McKelvey 2003) offers a useful theoretical framework within which to consider contemporary e-research systems—and, specifically, socio-technical support-systems. The question of whether the widespread adoption of such systems is undermining the normative structure of research and commitments to open research as outlined by Merton ([1942] 1973) is a serious one. We contend that what is at stake is the 'reliability and diversity of research knowledge' itself. Thus, we claim, there is a public interest at stake.

Public knowledge space

If the reliability, diversity and integrity of research claims are to be safeguarded over time, ideally, we propose that such claims should be developed within the context of a new type of institutional space. The Director of the e-Scholarship Research Centre (eSRC) at the University of Melbourne in Australia, Gavan McCarthy, has called this space a 'public knowledge space'. We will elaborate on this topic briefly under three broad headings: examples of emergent public knowledge spaces; supporting the introduction of contextual information management practices; and harmonising variant schemas and standards.

Public knowledge and the notion of a public knowledge space

One of the central claims of our chapter is that socio-technical aspects of how knowledge emerges may well require commitments to public knowledge itself. The objective is to safeguard as much as possible the ongoing reliability of knowledge claim evaluations. To highlight this point, we now discuss three examples of initiatives that have the potential to evolve into what we are calling public knowledge spaces.

In 2002 the University of Melbourne's eSRC supported the establishment of the Agreements, Treaties and Negotiated Settlements (ATNS) with Indigenous Peoples in Settler States project. Early on the eSRC assisted this project to develop a public website that 'links together current information, historical detail and published material relating to agreements made between Indigenous people and others in Australia and overseas' (University of Melbourne 2007).

But the project was not just about making information resources public. The function of the site and the nature of the ATNS project have continued to evolve since its inception in 2002:

> The project's significance lies in its potential contribution to the social and economic fabric of remote and rural communities through enhanced planning and management of the implementation of agreements between Indigenous and local peoples and their government and Industry Partners in a range of jurisdictions. This new research proposal focuses existing expertise upon the investigation of four areas—legal, economic, governance and social/cultural sustainability—that we have identified as central research issues for examining agreement implementation and outcomes. More specifically, the project will investigate novel conceptual and practical issues related to agreements, including: Identification of Parties to an Agreement; Effective Legal Models for Implementation Economic Development; Governance; Communication Structures; Community Governance and Social Sustainability; and Biodiversity and Cultural Rights (University of Melbourne 2007).

We contend that the ATNS website represents an emergent public knowledge space, in that it services a wider function than just a website. The publishing of information that allows for the linking of current information with historical detail has helped catalyse and extend research and development activities. Indeed, the ATNS project has now drawn in ongoing commitments by various stakeholders, including the Australian Commonwealth government and corporates such as the Minerals Council of Australia and Rio Tinto Pty Ltd. A public knowledge space is being generated because a shared context is being generated to create effective links between research and policy formation and the ability to generate real-world impacts such as the reduction of poverty:

> In 2009/2010 a new ARC Linkage Project will commence entitled Poverty in the Midst of Plenty: Economic Empowerment, Wealth Creation and Institutional Reform for Sustainable Indigenous and Local Communities. The new research team comprises, Prof Marcia Langton, Assoc Prof Maureen Tehan, Prof Lee Godden,

Assoc Prof Miranda Stewart (all from the University of Melbourne), Prof Ciaran O'Faircheallaigh (Griffith University), Dr John Taylor (Australian National University) and Dr Lisa Strelein (AIATSIS). The industry partners for the new project are the Office of Indigenous Policy Coordination, Rio Tinto Ltd, Woodside Energy Ltd, Santos Ltd and Marnda Mia Central Negotiating Committee Pty Ltd. The new project aims to study the institutional, legal and policy reforms required to reduce indigenous people's poverty and to promote economic development for sustainable indigenous communities (University of Melbourne 2007).

In a different way, a second eSRC project has laid a foundation for the expression of a different type of public knowledge. In 2009 the eSRC commenced an Australian Research Council funded project in partnership with the University of Melbourne's Department of Social Work including a consortia consisting of the Australian Catholic University and several 'out of home care' providers in the state of Victoria. A critical component of the project was the creation of a public website within twelve months of the project commencing. This website provides a space where the history of the 'out of home care' sector in Victoria is made available to the general public. Pathways' *Historical Resources for People Who Have Experienced Out of Home 'Care' in Victoria* was launched publicly in December:

> Pathways is a resource for people who as children were in out-of-home 'care' in Victoria, including people known as 'care' leavers, Forgotten Australians, foster children, wards of the state, adopted children, Homies, child migrants, and members of the Stolen Generations. Some of these experiences overlap—for example, child migrants and the Stolen Generations usually grew up in Homes in Australia and many children were made wards of the state as well as being fostered or adopted. Only a small proportion of all these categories of children were legally orphans and for a time the term 'orphans of the living' was common—they had parents but were not able to be cared for by them for a variety of reasons.
>
> Pathways brings together historical resources relating to institutional 'care' in Victoria from its beginnings in the 1840s through to the present. You can use Pathways to find information, including documents and images, about institutions; organisations that managed children's institutions; policies; public figures, and legislation (Pathways 2009).

The Pathways project therefore is also creating a shared context for people who as children were in out-of-home care in Victoria. It is providing an opportunity for multiple stakeholders to create a public knowledge space to affect better linkages between research, policy and social work practice.

The potential utility of this embryonic idea of a 'public knowledge space' and its ability to facilitate effective linkages between research, policy and practice is significant. For example, in a recent report commissioned by the Victorian Government in Australia, it has been highlighted that the notion of a public knowledge space may well have a place in reducing the burden of uncoordinated regulatory interventions such as quality standards:

> What is now possible is the emergence of a new type of public knowledge space, similar to the Agreements, Treaties and Negotiated Settlements project referenced earlier in this document. A primary focus of this type of knowledge space is the continuous and relentless elimination of burden associated with collecting unnecessary data and information (Vines, McCarthy and Jones 2009).

Thus, we think there is potential to reduce the burden of government regulatory interventions if greater emphasis is placed on the idea that such interventions are expressions of 'public knowledge claims'. The notion of a public knowledge space, within this particular context, could do much to ensure that the reliability of such claims is continuously tested. For example, a public knowledge space might involve commitments to publish information that explicitly identifies relationship links with different instruments of regulation including:

- the acts of parliaments referenced within quality standards
- other types of published resources such as practice guidelines that form part of the basis of legislative intent or regulatory intervention such as the promulgation of quality standards
- detailed explanations of the role of corporate bodies involved in the conception, implementation and administration of quality standards and associated regulatory functions, including the changes to these over time
- the continued evolution through time of the evidence-base that forms the basis of any regulatory intervention such as the publishing of quality standard specifications
- publishing such information, to ensure there is public scrutiny of the effectiveness and reliability of the knowledge claims embedded across the different instruments of regulation just described.

In framing the notion of public knowledge in the way that we are doing here, we suggest this could do much to ensure that research challenges are continuously framed within the context of an emergent public interest. We emphasise that this notion of a public interest can be defined as widely or narrowly as the context might require. Therefore, these ideas have application where there is a public knowledge imperative within private sector, industry sector or scholarly community networks. A public knowledge agenda can do much to mediate cross-paradigmatic perspectives in order to solve pressing problems.

To support the advancement of these types of public knowledge commitments, we now extend our discussion by describing two overarching objectives that could do much to help secure the accessibility, diversity and reliability of public knowledge. These include 'enabling the introduction of contextual information management practices' and 'the role of knowledge brokering in harmonising variant schemas and standards'.

Public knowledge and contextual information management practices

When we suggest that a public knowledge space would provide a vehicle through which contextual information management practices could be supported, we are explicitly referring to three interacting challenges:

- the processes of documenting the context of research
- time persistence
- the exchange and interoperability of contextual information management.

We discuss these now in turn.

First, context. What does it actually mean to document context in a way that the records of a research enterprise can be situated in an information framework that will enable these records to be understood not just by the people intimately associated with their creation but by others who have an interest or need? For over a decade, this has been a fundamental challenge of the global archival community and has led to standards for archival description and management that include specific mention of context and its information components (ISAAR 2004). In Australia these standards have been used to map the socio-technical complexity of Australian science (McCarthy and Evans 2007).

By mapping the socio-technical complexity it is meant that there is a focus on mapping the relationship between information and archival resources created through time and the context within which such resources are created. The origins of this type of approach derive from the domain of archives management (Dryden 2007).

Documenting context is an evolving area of archival practice and this is a good time to start using a different term to cover this area. Context control seems to serve the purpose, and could tentatively be defined as:

> the process of establishing the preferred form of the name of a records creator, describing the records creator and the functions and activities that produced the records, and showing the relationships among records-creators, and between records-creators and records, for use in archival descriptions.

Second, time persistence. To be consistent with an evolutionary epistemology outlined in this chapter, we think a public knowledge space should include the publishing of research resources in a way that is consistent with the principles of contextual information management described above. The principle of persistence ensures evolutionary changes through time can be monitored and recorded systematically. Thus, part of the function of a public knowledge space should be concerned with how these spaces allow for—indeed captures—the evidence of evolution of these spaces through time. Such an approach is an essential characteristic of understanding the emergence of knowledge within an evolutionary framework.

Third, the exchange of contextual information. The People Australia project (2008) provides an example of the sorts of interoperability functionality a public knowledge space can facilitate. In late 2008 the National Library of Australia and the eSRC, using the data collected over an eight-year period in the Australian Women's register (Australian Women's Register 2009), exchanged rich and highly structured information using the Encoded Archival Context (EAC 2009) XML schema and the Open Archive Initiative—Protocol for Metadata Harvesting (OAIPMH undated). The boundary objects or points of interconnection were not publications or archival collections but context entities—information about historic people. Although still in testing and development, the success of the People Australia trials indicate it is possible to interconnect separate information systems in an open knowledge environment in a systematic and resilient manner. Thus the practice of contextual information management can be applied to support the interoperability of data and information exchange between different focal levels within a research enterprise. A vision of this type of approach is outlined in Vines, McCarthy and Jones (2009, pp. 25–33).

Interestingly these ideas and developments have parallels in the Netherlands. Wisse (2001) has outlined a foundation for a decade of conceptual thinking that has in effect tried to revolutionise how information systems are conceived and how they are constructed. He suggests that the systematic management and use of contextual information draws on relational theory, network theory as well as object and aspect orientated approaches. In Holland this conceptual work has led to the creation of 'Forum Standaardisatie' by the Dutch Minister of Economic Affairs in 2006 (Open Standaarden 2006). The intent of this initiative was to improve information interoperability not just between government agencies but also between government and citizens and companies. The Dutch experience highlights that if basic information registers do not sufficiently support semantic interoperability, the reuse of data (or knowledge) is compromised. Interoperability and reuse of data facilitate service improvement and reduce the administrative burden of government regulatory interventions.

Public knowledge and the role of knowledge brokering

We have previously highlighted that the widespread adoption of socio-technical support-systems is potentially having an unintended consequence of undermining the normative structure of research commitments as proposed by Merton ([1942] 1973). We think the notion of a public knowledge space could do much to address this problem. But, in thinking through the ways in which this can be done, we also claim it is necessary to take into account the synthesis of theoretical perspectives presented in this chapter including Popper's (1972) evolutionary epistemology and hierarchically complex systems (Corning 2001; Hall 2006a; Pattee 1973, 2000; Salthe 1985, 1993, 2004; Simon 1962, 1973, 2002).

The use of explicit schemas and standards that form part of a research enterprise's knowledge support-system is reflective of a normative approach to research: schemas and standards help establish practice norms. The problem with normative approaches to practice is that standards can easily become reified or excessively fixed. Thus, standards can provide a means of exerting centralised control over highly distributed activities.

In contrast, we claim it is necessary to support the continuous evolution of the variant schemas and standards that emerge at different levels of hierarchy. We have represented this challenge in diagrammatic form in Figure 6.9. In this diagram we represent the harmonisation of standards across two different research communities. To illustrate what this figure

Figure 6.9 Socio-technical aspects of harmonising standards across different research communities

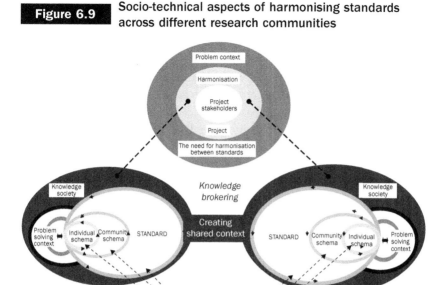

Knowledge cycling to support harmonisation of standards and schemas through time

means, we now refer to a particular example. One research community might be those with interests in understanding the outcomes for patients who are discharged from public hospitals. A second community might be those with interests in how best to reduce homelessness rates in the general population. A shared problem context might emerge in that research could identify potential benefits if hospital discharge units were able to refer at risk patients to those who provide homelessness services. The achievement of effective solutions would require the development of shared understandings between those involved in research, policy and practice. In order to achieve this, a type of knowledge brokering is required. This is likely to involve the integration of the case management schemas that pertain to hospital discharge units and those that provide homelessness services. Thus, in the process of facilitating more effective referral pathways, particularly e-referral pathways, between these different communities, there is a need to harmonise the variant schemas associated with each stakeholder group.

The topic of knowledge brokering is currently being given greater attention, particularly in its application to bridge the gaps between research, practice and policy (Bammer, Michaux and Sanson 2010). In contributing to this debate, we claim that the relationship between knowledge brokering and the idea of a public knowledge space has great utility. We suggest that the purpose of a public knowledge space is to create a shared context for problem definition and problem solving.

Our central claim is that in addressing the challenges of data and information sharing (interoperability), provision must be made to allow for significant amounts of tacit, implicit and explicit knowledge sharing and cycling. Knowledge brokering involves lifeworlds meeting science and the hard edge of evidence-based practice (realism) being continuously tested and modified as a result of feedback based on practitioners' personal knowledge and experience about what works in the world. We think that commitments to a public knowledge space could do much to mediate these often incommensurable positions.

Conclusions

The central concern in writing this chapter has been to show why we think the effective functioning of modern day research enterprises will become reliant on the emergence of a new type of institutional framework. We have called this framework a public knowledge space. In presenting this argument, we have attempted to highlight that the rationale for this public knowledge space may not be immediately apparent. This is because we suggest that there is widespread lack of agreement about the nature of public knowledge itself.

In unpacking this challenge, we first felt it necessary to address a foundation question about the very nature of knowledge itself. In doing this, we have been interested in unpacking some of the theoretical questions and inter-relationships that arise when exploring the boundaries between lifeworlds and science; and between constructivism and realism. We have done this by introducing a theory and ontology of knowledge derived from Karl Popper's evolutionary epistemology. We have combined Popper's epistemology with a theory of hierarchically complex systems to highlight that knowledge is an emergent property of complex systems and that it can emerge at any level of context—for example, at the individual level, the research team level, or at larger levels of complexity (termed the super-system level). We highlight that the dynamics of these super-systems which include the focal subsystems (such as a research team) are much slower. Thus they can exert significant constraints on any given subsystem. These constraints can be both negative (inhibitory) or positive (facilitative).

We claim that the synthesis of these different perspectives is required in order to understand the opportunities and constraints associated with the use of what we call 'knowledge support-systems'. Such support-systems are emerging within large complex research enterprises. They are socio-technical systems in nature in that they are reliant on networks of people, the mediation of person-to-person interactions through the use of technology and individual people's interaction with computers and machines. We claim that the design of any knowledge support-system must take into account the different types of schemas and standards that emerge at varying levels of hierarchy within any given research system. These schemas can be tacit, implicit or explicit. As we explain, there is increasing utility in being able to publish schemas in an explicit way, because of the benefits arising from being able to exchange content between multiple (electronic) information systems. But, in attending to these matters, we highlight that an increase in semantic technologies is giving rise to what Cope and Kalantzis have outlined in Chapter 4, 'What does the digital do to knowledge making?', as an emergence of a 'new navigation order' and 'new dynamics of difference'. Such dynamics include the means by which textual representations of knowledge in the form of schemas and standards are harmonised to help solve practical and real-world problems.

These are not small matters. They go to the heart of the future and effective functioning of a wide range of public–private service systems including, for example, the health and community service sectors. We have highlighted also in our introduction how the recent catastrophe in the Gulf of Mexico provides an example of the ways in which particular types of knowledge can rise up to become of the highest public priority almost overnight. To neglect the potency of such knowledge through a lack of public scrutiny can have devastating consequences as the whole world has found out.

Thus we conclude by outlining what we consider to be some of the key characteristics of a public knowledge space. We suggest that this notion can be defined as widely or narrowly as the context might require. Thus the principles have application within private sector organisations, industry representation bodies and within scholarly communities themselves. It is the potential function these institutional mechanisms offer that could prove to be decisively important. We claim such mechanisms will facilitate open access to important knowledge assets through time, thus allowing persistent access to such assets through time. We further suggest that they will include reference to the historical context of the emergence of these knowledge assets and their publication. If this is to be successfully achieved, we have shown why we think a public knowledge space would aim to facilitate the emergence of a 'shared context' among its various stakeholder groups in order to solve pressing problems in more efficient ways. Our ideas extend to the idea of harmonising variant schemas and standards as we have described in this chapter.

Many of these ideas are orthogonal to current and prevailing thinking about the future of the semantic web.

Acknowledgements

We acknowledge Dr Joe Firestone for his substantial and rigorous critiques of several versions of this paper. We also thank Luke Naismith from Dubai Futures for his contributions to earlier versions of this paper.

Hall wishes to acknowledge research facilities support from Dr Frada Burstein and an honorary fellowship from the School of Information Management and Systems from March 2002 through June 2005; the University of Melbourne's Australian Centre for Science, Innovation and Society for an honorary fellowship; and Prof. Liz Sonnenberg, Department of Information Systems, for research facilities support from December 2006.

Appendix: a preliminary ontology for research knowledge support

Worlds—ontologically separate domains relating to nature of knowledge and existence (Hall after Popper)	
	world 1 (W1)—W of physical and chemical dynamics, uninterpreted (mindless) existence of everything
	world 2 (W2)—W of cybernetic, cognitive and living phenomena; tacit, implicit and articulated knowledge
	world 3 (W3)—W of knowledge as physically codified into persistent objects and artefacts
Action relationships that facilitate interactions between worlds	
	encode or decode—(W2 to W3; W3 to W2) Knowledge is built into an inert and persistent object that living things can interact with at different times and places from the original encoding to decode the contained knowledge. Encoding moves knowledge from W2 to W3. Decoding moves knowledge from W3 to W2. Decoded knowledge is not necessarily immediately expressed in terms of development, behavior or action.

Appendix: a preliminary ontology for research knowledge support (*Cont'd*)

	embody—Knowledge is built into the dynamic structure of a W2 system. This corresponds more or less to Polanyi's tacit knowledge. The knowledge may not be expressed until required—we may not know what we know until we need to know it. (Note: there is a hint of W1 in this, as the embodiment of knowledge will affect the propensities of the physical structure to respond dynamically in certain ways.)	
	enact—'to act out'. The application of knowledge via actions on W1.	
Evolution—incremental accumulation of information in a system through time as a consequence of internal and external interactions (after Salthe 1993)		
Information—in (W2) a significant arrangement in the structure of a system that could have been different without any different expenditure of energy (after Salthe 1993) or a difference that makes a difference (Bateson 1972)		
Knowledge (broad sense)—in (W2) or (W3), information towards solving problems of life (after Popper)		
	degree of testing	
	idea—(W2) unexpressed thought that something might be so (or possible)	
	claim—(W2 or W3) articulated claim to know	
	tentative theory (Popper) or *hypothesis*—(W3) explicit expression of a claim open to testing	
	tested K—(W3) claim that has been criticised or tested against observation of predicted effects	
	reviewed K—(W3) claim or hypothesis that has been formally exposed to inter-subjective criticism	
	authorised or *published K*—(W3) claim that has been accepted and published via a formal editorial process	
	integrated or *working K*—(W2) knowledge that has become tacitly embodied in thinking or in working routines	
	sense of dispersion or spread of an idea, claim or knowledge as an object, etc. held by	
	individual, personal or *subjective* (Popper) *K*—(W2) knowledge of the world held by a single individual	
	common K—(W2 or W3) knowledge that is widely shared or easily discoverable by familiar retrieval methods	
	team, group or *community K*—knowledge that is common to members of a team, group or community	
	disciplinary K—knowledge that is common within a research discipline	
	world K—knowledge that is common across the global research enterprise	

Appendix: a preliminary ontology for research knowledge support (*Cont'd*)

	degree of expression	
		tacit—K held unconsciously by a living individual (W2)
		implicit—K that is consciously accessible to the individual but not articulated (W2)
		articulated—K that is expressed in words or speech (only) (W2) (Note: speech vanishes in the instant it is articulated. Its only record is in the W2 perceptions and memories of those who hear it.)
		explicit, *codified* or *objective* (Popper)—K expressed in an objectively persistent form that conveys the similar meanings when decoded at another time or by other individuals (W3)
		enacted, *integrated* or *embodied*—K internalised and embodied in the dynamic structure of a system (again tacit—W2)
		organic K—structurally determined propensities or dispositions to act in certain ways—knowledge that is tacit at a higher level of structure—see enacted, integrated or embodied (W2)
		procedural K—the organic K is explicitly defined and understood (W3 or W2)
	context	
		situational K—K formed by an entity in the context a particular situation
		procedural K (Nickols)—K created by doing
		declarative K (Nickols)—K created by describing (but see articulated, codified)
		lost or *orphaned K*—K that once existed but can now no longer be found, accessed or acted on because its links to situations and problems no longer exist
	types of knowledge by structural level of organisation	
		body of formal knowledge (BoFK)—the world repository of formalised knowledge available to the knowledge society (W3)
		cultural K—K embodied in the scientific and academic world in general (W2 and W3)
		organisational K—K controlling the functioning of higher level social, technical or socio-technical systems (e.g., university, scientific society, publisher) (W2 and W3)
		organismic or *tacit* (Polanyi) or *dispositional* (Popper) K—(W2) structural K controlling the functioning of individual organisms or people (e.g., as based on wiring of the nervous system—see tacit K)
		artifactual—explicit K expressed in technological artifacts, e.g., stored computer program (W3)

Appendix: a preliminary ontology for research knowledge support (*Cont'd*)

	cellular K—deeply organic forms of K passed on through cell lines controlling the development of cells and multicellular entities
	epigenetic K (heredity)—form of heredity based on the dynamic structure of cells (W2) and asexually reproducing multicellular organisms
	genetic K (heredity)—hereditary information encoded in DNA molecules (W3)
Hierarchy—a relationship in which each element is categorised into successive ranks or grades with each level contained within or governed by the one above	
	H theory—theory that identifies and maps the hierarchical structural organisation of the world
	natural or *scalar H*—representation of the world as composed of hierarchically organised levels of structure such that entities at a selected level of organisation can be seen as structural components contained within a higher level and that contains an assembly of several to many distinguishable entities at successively lower levels, down to the lowest level of organisation where entities can be distinguished
	specification H—a hierarchical classification, as in a taxonomic tree
	command or *governance H*—higher level entities control entities at lower levels in the hierarchy
Level of organisation—any particular level in a scalar hierarchy where an entity can be distinguished as a component of and within a higher level and can be seen to consist of components of a lower level of organisation	
	holon—a distinguishable entity at any level of organisation forming a component of an entity at the next higher level and containing within it several to many component entities at the next lower level
	focal level—a level of organisation designated for analysis
System—persistent assemblage of dynamically interacting components causally interacting with the world	
	S entity—set of components defined as belonging to a system or set of components more regularly interacting with one another than with elements in the rest of the world
	complex S—S comprising 'a large number of parts that interact in a nonsimple way' (Simon 1962)
	hierarchical S—S 'composed of interrelated subsystems, each of the latter being, in turn, hierarchic in structure until we reach some lowest level of elementary subsystem' (Simon 1962)
	social S—S comprising interacting living entities or people
	technological S—S comprising interacting logical or material artefacts

Appendix: a preliminary ontology for research knowledge support (*Cont'd*)

		socio-technical S—S comprising people and technology
		network—the graph of causal or information connections among components of a S
Research—consciously controlled or disciplined activities focused on extending knowledge of the world		
	research organisations at different levels of hierarchical organisation	
		knowledge society (Lederberg or Mukherjee) or *academia*—world interested in the results of disciplined R and formalised knowledge
		global R enterprise—the sum of all institutions directly concerned with carrying out R
		R domain—a broad area of common R interest
		R enterprise—a particular enterprise or large scale organisation devoted to R, specifically including people and their research knowledge support technologies
		R network—an extended group of investigators linked via direct person to person communications
		R group or *team*—individuals or co-investigators interacting around a particular research project
		R collaborators—individuals involved in authoring specific works
		individual researcher or *investigator*—a single individual involved in conducting R
	components of research enterprises	
		R knowledge support technologies—technological systems supporting the creation, management and communication of knowledge by humans (Note: concept specifically excludes data collection instruments (e.g., microscopes, telescopes, cyclotrons). E-science databases and data reduction systems (e.g., storage and pre-processing of terabytes of physical, astronomic and genomic data) represent a borderline.)
		Research establishment—system of people involved in R—investigators, technicians, administrators and other support personnel
		R paradigm—disciplinary matrix of shared vocabularies, exemplars and world views (Kuhn) that guides the enterprise's R activities and facilitates cognitive interactions among the enterprise's members
Schema—the semantic structure or dynamic organisation of cognitive processes, whether in the individual, mediated by technology or embodied at a higher level in the socio-technical research enterprise		
		incommensurable S—where there is a lack of direct equivalence between objects and functions between two different schemas (two paradigms may also be incommensurable)

References

Note: All URLs valid on 12 September 2010.

Angerman, W.S. 2004. 'Coming Full Circle With Boyd's OODA Loop Ideas: An Analysis of Innovation Diffusion and Evolution', MS thesis, Air Force Institute of Technology, Department of the Airforce, Air University, AFIT/GIR/ENV/04M-1, *http://tinyurl.com/ydgjuby*.

Ardichvili, A. 2008. 'Learning and Knowledge Sharing in Virtual Communities of Practice: Motivators, Barriers and Enablers', *Advances in Developing Human Resources* 10, 541–54.

ARL 2009. *The Research Library's Role in Digital Repository Services: Final Report of the ARL Digital Repository Issues Task Force*. Association of Research Libraries, Washington, DC, *http://tinyurl.com/cwyk5e*.

Australian Women's Register. 2009. National Foundation for Australian Women, and the University of Melbourne, *http://tinyurl.com/yec3u6p*.

Balaguer, M. 2009. 'Platonism in Metaphysics'. In E.N. Zalta (ed.), *The Stanford Encyclopedia of Philosophy*. Stanford, CA: Metaphysics Research Lab, Center for the Study of Language and Information, Stanford University, *http://tinyurl.com/y9hfexf*.

Bammer, G., A. Michaux and A. Sanson (eds). 2010. *Bridging the 'Know-Do' Gap: Knowledge Brokering to Improve Child Well-being*. Canberra: Australian National University E-Press.

Bateson, G. 1972. *Steps to an Ecology of Mind*. San Francisco: Chandler.

Blackman, D., J. Connelly and S. Henderson. 2004. 'Does Double Loop Learning Create Reliable Knowledge?', *The Learning Organization* 11(1), pp. 11–27.

Bock, G.-W., R.W. Zmud, Y.-G. Kim and J.-N. Lee. 2005. 'Behavioral Intention Formation in Knowledge Sharing: Examining the Roles of Extrinsic Motivators, Social-Psychological Forces, and Organizational Climate', *MIS Quarterly* 29(1), pp. 87–111.

Boyd, J.R. 1976–1996. Unpublished briefings under the name 'A Discourse on Winning and Losing': 'Introduction' (1996), 'Patterns of Conflict' (1986), 'Organic Design for Command and Control' (1987), 'Strategic Game of ? and ?' (1987), 'Destruction and Creation' (1976) and 'The Essence of Winning and Losing' (1996), *http://tinyurl.com/ykz3ayg*.

Boyle, J. 2008. *The Public Domain: Enclosing the Commons of the Mind*. New Haven and London: Yale University Press.

Campbell, D.T. 1959. 'Methodological Suggestions from a Comparative Psychology of Knowledge Processes', *Inquiry* 2(1), 152–82.

—. 1960. 'Blind Variation and Selective Retention in Creative Thought as in Other Knowledge Processes', *Psychological Review* 67, 380–400.

—. 1974. 'Evolutionary Epistemology'. In P.A. Schilpp (ed.), *The Philosophy of Karl R. Popper*. LaSalle, IL: Open Court, pp. 412–63.

—. 1991. 'Autopoietic Evolutionary Epistemology and Internal Selection', *Journal of Social and Biological Structures* 14(2), 166–73.

Carr, L. and S. Harnad. 2009. 'Offloading Cognition onto the Web', *IEEE Intelligent Systems* 24(6), *http://tinyurl.com/2dzhju*.

Chaisson, E. 2001. *Cosmic Evolution: The Rise of Complexity in Nature.* Cambridge, MA: Harvard University Press.

Clarke, R. and D. Kingsley. 2008. 'Epublishing's Impacts on Journals and Journal Articles', *Journal of Internet Commerce* 7(1), pp. 120–51.

Corning, P.A. 2001. '"Control Information": The Missing Element in Norbert Wiener's Cybernetic Paradigm?', *Kybernetes* 30, pp. 1272–88, *http://tinyurl.com/4vkk5k.*

Cowan, R., P.A. David and D. Foray. 2000. 'The Explicit Economics of Knowledge Codification and Tacitness', *Industrial and Corporate Change* 9(2), pp. 211–54, *http://tinyurl.com/27rabky.*

David, P.A., M. den Besten and R. Schroeder. 2009. 'Collaborative Research in E-science and Open Access to Information', Stanford Institute for Economic Policy Research Discussion Paper 08-21, *http://tinyurl.com/yc9jvr4.*

Dror, I.E and S. Harnad. 2008. 'Offloading Cognition Onto Cognitive Technology'. In I. Dror and S. Harnad (eds), *Cognition Distributed: How Cognitive Technology Extends Our Minds.* Amsterdam: John Benjamins, *http://tinyurl.com/2b85t27.*

Dryden, J. 2007. 'From Authority Control to Context Control'. In J. Dryden (ed.), *Respect for Authority: Authority Control, Context Control an Archival Description.* Binghamton, NY: Haworth Information Press.

EAC. 2009. 'Encoded Archival Context Corporate: Bodies, Persons, and Families (EAC-CPF)'. Society of American Archivists and Staatsbibliothek zu Berlin, *http://tinyurl.com/yjvsvkr.*

Eisenstein, E.L. 1979. *The Printing Press as an Agent of Change: Communications and Cultural Transformations in Early-Modern Europe.* Cambridge, UK: Cambridge University Press.

—. 1983. *The Printing Revolution in Early Modern Europe.* Cambridge, UK: Cambridge University Press.

Else, S.E. 2004. 'Organization Theory and the Transformation of Large, Complex Organizations: Donald H. Rumsfeld and the US Department of Defence, 2001–04'. PhD thesis, Faculty of the Graduate School of International Studies, University of Denver, *http://tinyurl.com/2e96xrk.*

Firestone, J. and M. McElroy. 2003a. *Key Issues in the New Knowledge Management.* Boston: Butterworth-Heinemann.

—. 2003b. 'Corporate Epistemology: Competing Philosophies of Truth in Business and How They Influence Knowledge Management'. Executive Information Systems, *http://tinyurl.com/3jmwrt.*

Fjällbrant, N. 1997. 'Scholarly Communication: Historical Development and New Possibilities'. In *Scholarly Communication in Focus: Proceedings of the 1997 International Association of Technology University Libraries (IATUL).* Trondheim: IATUL, *http://tinyurl.com/yk6hw4b.*

Gould, S.J. 2002. *The Structure of Evolutionary Theory.* Cambridge, MA: Harvard University Press.

Grant, T. and B. Kooter. 2004. 'Comparing OODA and Other Models as Operational View C2 Architecture'. In *10th International Command and Control Research and Technology Symposium: The Future of C2,* McLean Va., 13–16 June 2005, *http://tinyurl.com/6bb5ne.*

Hall, W.P. 2003. 'Organisational Autopoiesis and Knowledge Management'. Presented at ISD '03 Twelfth International Conference on Information Systems Development—Methods & Tools, Theory & Practice, Melbourne, Australia, 25–27 August 2003, *http://tinyurl.com/yehcqz*.

—. 2005. 'Biological Nature of Knowledge in the Learning Organization', *The Learning Organization* 12(2), pp. 169–88, *http://tinyurl.com/2lhs24*.

—. 2006a. 'Emergence and Growth of Knowledge and Diversity in Hierarchically Complex Living Systems' (working paper). Workshop 'Selection, Self-Organization and Diversity', CSIRO Centre for Complex Systems Science and ARC Complex Open Systems Network, Katoomba, NSW, Australia 17–18 May 2006, *http://tinyurl.com/2z4e9r*.

—. 2006b. 'Tools Extending Human and Organizational Cognition: Revolutionary Tools and Cognitive Revolutions', paper given at the Sixth International Conference on Knowledge, Culture and Change in Organisations, Prato, Italy, 11–14 July 2006, *International Journal of Knowledge, Culture and Change Management* 6, *http://tinyurl.com/qza7q*.

Hall, W.P. and S. Nousala. 2010. 'Autopoiesis and Knowledge in Self-sustaining Organizational Systems', paper given at the 4th International Multi-Conference on Society, Cybernetics and Informatics: IMSCI 2010, 29 June – 2 July 2010, Orlando, Florida, *http://tinyurl.com/yztsq4t*.

Hall, W.P., P. Dalmaris and S. Nousala. 2005. 'A Biological Theory of Knowledge and Applications to Real World Organizations'. Proceedings, KMAP05 Knowledge Management in Asia Pacific Wellington, N.Z., 28–29 November 2005, *http://tinyurl.com/qflam*.

Hall, W.P., P. Dalmaris, S. Else, C.P. Martin and W.R. Philp. 2007. 'Time Value of Knowledge: Time-Based Frameworks for Valuing Knowledge', paper given at the 10th Australian Conference for Knowledge Management and Intelligent Decision Support Melbourne, 10–11 December 2007, *http://tinyurl.com/25z68k*.

Hall, W.P., G. Richards, C. Sarelius and B. Kilpatrick. 2008. 'Organisational Management of Project and Technical Knowledge Over Fleet Lifecycles', *Australian Journal of Mechanical Engineering* 5(2), pp. 81–95, *http://tinyurl.com/5d2lz7*.

Harkness, D.E. 2007. *The Jewel House: Elizabethan London and the Scientific Revolution*. New Haven: Yale University Press.

ISAAR. 2004. *International Standard Archival Authority Record for Corporate Bodies, Perrsons, and Families*. 2nd ed. Paris: International Council of Archives, *http://tinyurl.com/yk6emcs*.

Koestler, A. 1967. *The Ghost in the Machine*. London: Arkana.

—. 1978. *Janus: A Summing Up*. New York: Random House.

Kuhn, T.S. 1962. *The Structure of Scientific Revolutions*. Chicago, IL: University of Chicago Press.

—. 1983. 'Commensurability, Comparability, Communicability'. In *PSA 1982: Proceedings of the 1982 Biennial Meeting of the Philosophy of Science Association*, vol. 2. Cited in Kuhn (2000). *The Road Since Structure*. Chicago, IL: University of Chicago Press.

Land, F. 2009. 'Knowledge Management or the Management of Knowledge?' In W.R. King (ed.), *Knowledge Management and Organizational Learning*. Boston, MA: Springer, pp. 15–25.

Lederberg, J. 1991. 'Communication as the Root of Scientific Progress', *http://tinyurl .com/yfx7flw*.

Luhmann, N. 1995a. 'Social Systems', J. Bednarz and D. Baecker (trs). In *Theories of Distinction: Redescribing the Descriptions of Modernity*. Stanford: Stanford University Press. (First published as *Soziale Systeme: Grundriss einer allgemeinen Theorie*, Frankfurt am Main: Suhrkamp, 1984.)

—. 1995b. 'The Paradox of Observing Systems'. In W. Rasch (ed.), *Theories of Distinction: Redescribing the Descriptions of Modernity*. Stanford: Stanford University Press, 2002, pp. 79–93. (Reprinted from *Cultural Critique* 31, pp. 37–53, 1995.)

Mackenzie Owen, J.S. 2005, 'The Scientific Article in the Age of Digitization'. PhD thesis, University of Amsterdam, *http://tinyurl.com/yhghgbd*.

Maron, N.L. and K. Kirby Smith. 2008. 'Current Models of Digital Scholarly Communication', results of an investigation conducted by Ithaka for the Association of Research Libraries. Washington, DC: ARL, *http://tinyurl.com/ 652euq*.

Martin, C.P., Philp, W. and Hall, W.P. 2009. 'Temporal Convergence for Knowledge Management', *Australasian Journal of Information Systems* 15(2), pp. 133–48, *http://tinyurl.com/yc7rba8*.

McCarthy, G. and J. Evans. 2007. 'Mapping the Socio-technical Complexity of Australian Science: From Archival Authorities to Networks of Contextual Information'. In J. Dryden (ed.), *Respect for Authority: Authority Control, Context Control an Archival Description*. Binghampton and New York: Hawarth Information Press.

McKelvey, B. 1997. 'Quasi-Natural Organization Science', *Organization Science* 8(4), pp. 352–80.

—. 2002a. 'Model-Centered Organization Science Epistemology'. In J.A.C. Baum (ed.), *Companion to Organizations*. Thousand Oaks, CA: Sage, pp. 752–80, *http://tinyurl.com/ygaqxql*.

—. 2002b. 'Postmodernism vs. Truth in Management Theory'. In E. Locke (ed.), *Postmodernism and Management: Pros, Cons, and Alternatives*. Amsterdam: Elsevier, pp. 113–68.

McKelvey, W. 2003. 'From Fields To Science: Can Organization Studies Make the Transition?'. In R. Westwood and S. Clegg (eds), *Debating Organization*. Oxford: Blackwell, pp. 47–73, *http://tinyurl.com/yg6uevp*.

Merton, R.K. [1942] 1973. 'The Normative Structure of Science'. In N.W. Storer (ed.), *The Sociology of Science: Theoretical and Empirical Investigations*. Chicago, IL: University of Chicago Press, pp. 267–78.

Mukherjee, B. 2009. 'Scholarly Communication: A Journey From Print To Web', *Library Philosophy and Practice*, *http://tinyurl.com/yatjwjd*.

Mutch, A. 2006. 'Organization Theory and Military Metaphor: Time for a Reappraisal?', *Organization* 13(6), 751–69.

Nelson, R.R. and S.G. Winter. 1982. *An Evolutionary Theory of Economic Change*. Cambridge, MA: Harvard University Press.

Nickols, F. 2000. 'The Knowledge in Knowledge Management (KM)'. In J.W. Cortada and J.A. Woods (eds), *The Knowledge Management Yearbook 2001-2002*. Boston: Butterworth-Heinemann, *http://tinyurl.com/34cafj*.

Nonaka, I. 1994. 'A Dynamic Theory of Organizational Knowledge Creation', *Organization Science* 5(1), 14–37.

Nonaka, I. and H. Takeuchi. 1995, *The Knowledge Creating Company: How Japanese Companies Create the Dynasties of Innovation.* Oxford: Oxford University Press.

Nousala, S. 2006. 'Tacit Knowledge Networks and Their Implementation in Complex Organizations'. PhD thesis, School of Aerospace, Mechanical and Manufacturing Engineering, RMIT University, *http://tinyurl.com/2feky6.*

Nousala, S. and W.P. Hall. 2008 'Emerging Autopoietic Communities— Scalability of Knowledge Transfer in Complex Systems'. Paper given at First IFIP International Workshop on Distributed Knowledge Management (DKM 2008), 18–19 October 2008, Shanghai, *http://tinyurl.com/25khr3o.*

Nousala, S., W.P. Hall and S. John. 2007. 'Transferring Tacit Knowledge in Extended Enterprises'. Proceedings, 2007 International Conference on Information and Knowledge Engineering, Las Vegas, Nevada, 25–28 June 2007, *http://tinyurl.com/5jb9jb.*

Nousala, S., A. Miles, B. Kilpatrick and W.P. Hall. 2005. 'Building Knowledge Sharing Communities Using Team Expertise Access Maps (TEAM)'. Proceedings, KMAP05 Knowledge Management in Asia Pacific Wellington, N.Z. 28–29 November 2005, *http://tinyurl.com/2ygh42.*

—. 2009. 'Building Knowledge Sharing Communities Using Team Expertise Access Maps (TEAM)', *International Journal of Business and Systems Research* 3(3), 279–96.

OAIPMH. Undated. 'Open Archive Initiative—Protocol for Metadata Harvesting'. Open Archives Initiative, USA, *http://tinyurl.com/29wud5j.*

Ong, W.J. 1982. *Orality and Literacy: The Technologizing of the Word.* London: Routledge.

Open Standaarden. 2006. Forum Standarrdisatie, *http://tinyurl.com/2da22kt.*

Pathways. 2009. 'Historical Resources for People Who Experience Out of Home "Care" in Victoria: The University of Melbourne and the "Who Am I?" Project', University of Melbourne.

Pattee, H.H. 1973. 'The Physical Basis and Origin of Hierarchical Control'. In H.H. Pattee (ed.), *Hierarchy Theory: The Challenge of Complex Systems.* New York: Braziller, pp. 71–108.

—. 2000. 'Causation, Control, and the Evolution of Complexity'. In P.B. Anderson, C. Emmeche, N.O. Finnemann and P.V. Christiansen (eds), *Downward Causation—Minds, Body and Matter.* Arhus: Arhus University Press, pp. 63–77, *http://tinyurl.com/42jksr.*

People Australia. 2008. National Library of Australia, Canberra, *http://tinyurl.com/yjusbx2.*

Philp, W.R. and Martin, C.P. 2009. 'A Philosophical Approach to Time in Military Knowledge Management', *Journal of Knowledge Management* 13(1), 171–83, *http://tinyurl.com/2bj7dxm.*

Polanyi, M. 1958. *Personal Knowledge: Towards a Post-Critical Philosophy*, [corrected ed., 1962]. Chicago, IL: University of Chicago Press.

—. 1966, *The Tacit Dimension.* London: Routledge & Kegan Paul.

Popper, K.R. 1935. *Logik der Forschung.* Vienna: Julius Springer. [1st English edition, *The Logic of Scientific Discovery*, published in 1959 by Hutchinson.]

—. 1972. *Objective Knowledge: An Evolutionary Approach*. London: Oxford University Press.

—. 1978. 'Three worlds'. Tanner lecture on human values: delivered at the University of Michigan, *http://tinyurl.com/57j86j*.

—. 1994. 'Knowledge and the Body-Mind Problem'. In M.A. Notturno (ed.), *Defence of Interaction*. London and New York: Routledge.

—. 1999. *All Life Is Problem Solving*. London and New York: Routledge, p. 192.

Prigogine, I. 1955. *Introduction to the Thermodynamics of Irreversible Processes*. Springfield, IL: C.C. Thomas.

—. I. 1981. *From Being to Becoming: Time and Complexity in the Physical Sciences*. New York: Freeman.

Richards, C. 2008. 'Crisis Management: Operating Inside Their OODA Loops. Defense and the National Interest', *http://tinyurl.com/yfkjdg7*.

Robb, D. and J. Heil. 2009. 'Mental Causation'. In E.N. Zalta (ed.), *The Stanford Encyclopedia of Philosophy*. Stanford, CA: Metaphysics Research Lab, Center for the Study of Language and Information, Stanford University, *http://tinyurl.com/ydkjm3p*.

Robinson, H. 2009. 'Dualism'. In E.N. Zalta (ed.), *The Stanford Encyclopedia of Philosophy*. Stanford, CA: Metaphysics Research Lab, Center for the Study of Language and Information, Stanford University, *http://tinyurl.com/yesrelu*.

Salthe, S. 1985. *Evolving Hierarchical Systems: Their Structure and Representation*. New York: Columbia University Press.

—. 1993. *Development and Evolution: Complexity and Change in Biology*. Cambridge, MA: MIT Press.

—. 2004. 'The Spontaneous Origin of New Levels in a Scalar Hierarchy', *Entropy* 6, 327–43, *http://tinyurl.com/3sb989*.

Schaffer, J. 2009. 'Monism'. In E.N. Zalta (ed.), *The Stanford Encyclopedia of Philosophy*. Stanford, CA: Metaphysics Research Lab, Center for the Study of Language and Information, Stanford University, *http://tinyurl.com/yan2bg8*.

Simon, H.A. 1962. 'The Architecture of Complexity', *Proceedings of the American Philosophical Society* 106(6), pp. 467–82.

—. 1973. 'The Organization of Complex Systems'. In H.H. Pattee (ed.), *Hierarchy Theory: The Challenge of Complex Systems*. New York: Braziller, pp. 1–27.

—. 1979. 'Rational Decision-Making in Business Organizations', *American Economic Review* 69(4), pp. 493–513, *http://tinyurl.com/27kkg85*.

—. 2002. 'Near Decomposability and the Speed of Evolution', *Industrial and Corporate Change* 11(3), pp. 587–99.

Snowden, D. 2002, 'Complex Acts of Knowing: Paradox and Descriptive Self-Awareness', *Journal of Knowledge Management* 6(2) 1–13.

Sperberg-McQueen, C.M. and H. Thompson. 2000–2007. 'XML Schema, World Wide Web Consortium (W3C)', *http://tinyurl.com/pkfh9* (ver 1.151, 12 January 2010).

Stenmark, D. 2002. 'Information vs. Knowledge: The Role of Intranets in Knowledge Management'. In *Proceedings of HICSS-35*, Hawaii, 7–10 January 2002, *http://tinyurl.com/5qwurc*.

Tsoukas, H. 2005. *Complex Knowledge: Studies in Organizational Epistemology*. Oxford: Oxford University Press.

University of Melbourne. 2007. 'The Agreements, Treaties and Negotiated Settlements Project', *http://tinyurl.com/26pynky.*

Vines, R. and L. Naismith. 2002. 'Exploring the Foundations of Knowledge Management Practice'. In B. Cope and R. Freeman *Developing Knowledge Workers in the Printing and Publishing Industries: Education, Training and Knowledge Management in the Publishing Supply Chain, from Creator to Consumer.* Melbourne: Common Ground, *http://tinyurl.com/5z2dgx.*

Vines, R., W.P. Hall and L. Naismith. 2007. 'Exploring the Foundations of Organisational Knowledge: An Emergent Synthesis Grounded in Thinking Related to Evolutionary Biology'. actKM Conference, Australian National University, Canberra, 23–24 October 2007, *http://tinyurl.com/3xpmbc.*

Vines, R., G. McCarthy and M. Jones. 2009. *Better Integrated Standards and Quality Assurance Programs. Reducing the Burden—Increasing the Impact: Enabling the Growth of Quality-Knowledge within the Victorian Community Sector.* Melbourne: University of Melbourne, *http://tinyurl.com/yjlu6bx.*

Wilson, T.D. 2002. The Nonsense of 'Knowledge Management'. *Information Research* 8(1), *http://tinyurl.com/2lupn.*

Wisse, P. 2001. *Metapattern: Context and Time in Information Models.* Boston, MA: Addison-Wesley.

An historical introduction to formal knowledge systems

Liam Magee

Kant moreover considers logic, that is, the aggregate of definitions and propositions which ordinarily passes for logic, to be fortunate in having attained so early to completion before the other sciences; since Aristotle, it has not lost any ground, but neither has it gained any, the latter because to all appearances it seems to be finished and complete. Now if logic has not undergone any change since Aristotle—and in fact, judging by modern compendiums of logic the changes frequently consist mainly in omissions—then surely the conclusion which should be drawn is that it is all the more in need of a total reconstruction; for spirit, after its labours over two thousand years, must have attained to a higher consciousness about its thinking and about its own pure, essential nature... Regarding this content, the reason why logic is so dull and spiritless has already been given above. Its determinations are accepted in their unmoved fixity and are brought only into external relation with each other. In judgements and syllogisms the operations are in the main reduced to and founded on the quantitative aspect of the determinations; consequently everything rests on an external difference, on mere comparison and becomes a completely analytical procedure and mechanical calculation. The deduction of the so-called rules and laws, chiefly of inference, is not much better than a manipulation of rods of unequal length in order to sort and group them according to size—than a childish game of fitting together the pieces of a coloured picture puzzle (Hegel 2004, p. 51).

Analysts discussing knowledge systems typically distinguish their *logical* (or procedural) and *ontological* (or data) components (Smith 1998; Sowa 2000). To employ another related distinction, the logical part can be termed the *formal* component of a system—what preserves truth in inferential reasoning—while the ontological part can be considered the *material* component—or what is reasoned about. Usually challenges of interoperability focus on the explicit ontological or material commitments of a system—what is conceptualised by that system. This is of course understandable; it is here where the authorial intent is to be divined, where the system design is manifest. However, as the history of knowledge systems demonstrates, the line between logical/ontological or formal/material is often blurred; as the mechanics of systems have evolved to provide different trade-offs between features and performance, so too have the kinds of implicit ontological assumptions embedded within the logical constructs of those systems. In less arcane terms, even the austere, content-less world of logic remains nonetheless a world—bare, but not quite empty. And since logics themselves are pluralised, it therefore makes sense that their worlds be plural too, with slight variations and gradations of difference between them. The next two chapters explore these differences, through the lens of the historical development of formal knowledge systems. This history stretches back beyond the information age to the earliest musings on the potential to arrive at conclusions through purely mechanical procedure; to deduce automatically and unambiguously.

This chapter, then, presents a general historical narrative, which plots the development of knowledge systems against three successive different waves of modernisation. This development is inherently tied to the rise of symbolic logic in the modern era, without which both computation generally, and knowledge systems specifically, would not be possible. A constant guiding goal, which can be termed, following Foucault, the pursuit of a '*mathesis universalis*' (Foucault 1970), motivates this development. At its most extreme, this goal represents a form of epistemological idealism; it imagines that all knowledge can be reduced to an appropriate vocabulary and limited rules of grammar and inference—in short, reduced to a *logical system*. The extent of this idealism is itself an important feature of the different formalisms surveyed.

To focus on this and other significant points of difference and similarity, the characterisation of the history of this development is intentionally schematic; it does not attempt a broad description of the history of logic, computers or information systems. It does, on the other hand, aim to illustrate the rough affinity between the specific history of knowledge systems and the much broader history of modern industrialisation and capitalism. This is in part to counter the tendency of histories of logic and computing to present them as purely intellectual traditions, with only coincidental application to problems of industry, bureaucracy and governance. Logical 'idealism' in fact arose specifically in those places and times which demonstrated a practical need for it—because, in a sense, both the quality and quantity demands of organisational knowledge management, traceable back to the rise of the bureaucracy in the nineteenth century, foreshadowed the emergence of information systems concurrently with the greater waves of modernity in the twentieth. The conclusion of the study, at the end of the next chapter, suggests that the nexus of tensions which arise in modernity play a structuring role in the production of incommensurability.

The structure employed here distinguishes between 'pre-modern', 'modern' and 'postmodern' development phases of knowledge systems. The 'pre-modern' and 'modern' periods cover, respectively, the scattered precursors and the more structured programs in logic and mathematics which pointed towards the development of knowledge systems. Early knowledge systems, such as the relational database, can be said to apply the results of 'modernist' logic in the form of highly controlled structures of knowledge. 'Postmodern' knowledge systems, on the other hand, arise out of the perceived difficulties of coercing all forms of knowledge into rigid structures. In particular, the era of the web has inspired the construction hybrid, semi-structured knowledge systems such as semantic web ontologies—combining some of the computational properties of relational databases with support for documents, multimedia, social networks and other less structured forms of data and information.

The next chapter shifts from an historical overview towards a more detailed examination of the question of commensurability of relational database and semantic web systems. In particular it looks at one stark area of potential incommensurability—that of so-called 'closed' versus 'open' world assumptions. While this area of incommensurability is well documented within the relevant literature (Reiter 1987; Sowa 2000), it resonates with several broader cultural distinctions between the two kinds of systems. These distinctions, along with several recent discussions of them, are then reviewed, followed by a suggestive assessment of commensurability between the two kinds of knowledge representation surveyed.

The conclusion of the two chapters recasts knowledge systems back into a broad historical frame, suggesting several causal factors behind the production of differences between them. These suggestive indications are further developed in later chapters in the book.

Pre-modernity: logical lineages

Retrospectively, it appears that modern knowledge systems are the culmination of a steady linear development in the field of logic. In the past century and a half, since Frege's efforts to systematise logic in symbolic form, progressive and continuous advancement is a plausible narrative line. Prior to Frege, however, logic appears at relatively brief intervals in the development of Western thought. A more fitting metaphor is perhaps that of an expanding series of fractal-like spirals—sporadic and incidental surges during the ancient, medieval and Enlightenment periods, before a sudden and sustained preoccupation from the nineteenth century onwards (Kneale 1984). Indeed, as the quote from Hegel suggests, at the start of the nineteenth century, logic was perceived to be a field for the most part exhausted by Aristotle's exposition of syllogisms. More recent histories have shown a somewhat more complex picture: important precedents to modern logic variants, such as predicate, modal and temporal logics, can be found in Aristotelian and later classical works on logic (Bochenski 1961), as well as in medieval scholasticism (Kneale 1984).

Notwithstanding these precursors, it is generally agreed that not until the seventeenth century was something like contemporary symbolic predicate logic, on which knowledge systems are based, conceived (Bochenski 1961; Kneale 1984). Largely the product of a solitary figure, Leibniz, this conception was of a universal symbolism—*universalis mathesis* (Foucault 1970)—which would provide both a standardised vocabulary and formal deductive system for resolving disputes with clinical and unambiguous clarity (Davis 2001). Leibniz dreamed of a process which could strip all argument from the vagaries and ambiguities of natural language, leaving only a pristine set of statements and rules of valid inference in its place:

> If this is done, whenever controversies arise, there will be no more need for arguing among two philosophers than among two mathematicians. For it will suffice to take pens into the hand and to sit down by the abacus, saying to each other (and if they wish also to a friend called for help): Let us calculate! (Lenzen 2004, p. 1).

Set in the context of Cartesian geometry, Newtonian physics, Copernican cosmology, the construction of the calculus, and a host of other mechanical formalisations of the seventeenth century, that mathematics should be seen to be the epistemological pinnacle towards which other kinds of thought might aspire—to reason 'clearly and distinctly', as another rationalist, Descartes, put it—is perhaps not surprising. At the time, consensual workings-out of 'controversies'—with or without the aid of a 'friend'—was an important intellectual concomitant to the preferences for personal introspection over traditional, largely clerical authority, for rationality over dogma, for individual decision making over ecclesiastical mandate, and for mechanical laws over divine decrees, all of which mark the emergence of the Enlightenment (Habermas 1989). The cry to resolve disputes by 'sitting down by the abacus'—or any of its contemporary analogues—was, however, to inspire a much longer and sustained wave of rationalist oneirism only by the middle of the nineteenth century. Arguably, Leibniz' fervour was not yet met by a sufficiently developed and broader need for rationalised and standardised communication in the social sphere at large. From the nineteenth century onwards, though, three further distinct points can be isolated within this historical trajectory: Frege's repudiation of German idealism and psychologism in the late nineteenth century, which paved the way for symbolic logic; logical positivism's rejection of metaphysics, and its search for a purified, foundational mathematics; and, most importantly, subsequent post-war exploration of computational methods to represent, refine and extend human knowledge, which gradually filtered down from 'pure' research to applied problem-solving in a myriad of practical contexts. What began as an individual exhortation, barely a rippling murmur in a sea of philosophical discourse, had, by the twentieth century, coalesced into a tradition of what Rorty (1992) termed 'Ideal Language Philosophy'—a putative, therapeutic program for extending the use of language, ultimately, from the selective company of human agents to that which would embrace a wider family of computational agents as well.

One of the foundational populist expressions of the ambitions of the semantic web, published in *Scientific American* in 2001, gives a modern rendering of this zeal for intellectual asceticism:

> The semantic web is not a separate Web but an extension of the current one, in which information is given well-defined meaning, better enabling computers and people to work in cooperation. The first steps in weaving the semantic web into the structure of the existing Web are already under way. In the near future, these developments will usher in significant new functionality as machines become much better able to process and 'understand' the data that they merely display at present... The semantic web, in

naming every concept simply by a URI [Uniform Resource Identifier], lets anyone express new concepts that they invent with minimal effort. Its unifying logical language will enable these concepts to be progressively linked into a universal Web. This structure will open up the knowledge and workings of humankind to meaningful analysis by software agents, providing a new class of tools by which we can live, work and learn together (Berners-Lee, Hendler and Lassila 2001).

As with the Enlightenment, these more recent moments have been accompanied by broader ideological trends. These are sketched out in more detail below—in part to emphasise the inter-dependent structural connections between the emergence of knowledge systems, on the one hand, and the rise of distinct styles of modern organisation and management—features of contemporary capitalism—on the other; and in part to help explain how variant knowledge formalisms—even at a level of abstraction from questions of conceptual content—still bear substantial epistemological assumptions. These assumptions, in turn, can have significant bearing on how systems based on these formalisms might be considered commensurable.

Early modernity: the mechanisation of thought

After Leibniz, the dream of a formal mechanism for 'calculating' the logical outcome from a set of premises was to remain dormant for a considerable period. Variants of Germanic idealism sought instead to emphasise the irreducibility of thought to pure procedure. Even the ostensibly logical works of Kant and Hegel differentiated the sphere of the rational from other modes of thought: practical/ethical and judgement/aesthetic categories were procedurally, not just substantively, differentiated. Foucault goes so far as to argue that the eighteenth and early nineteenth centuries, in the human sciences at least, are marked by a departure, at the level of method, from attempts at a common, universal and formal language:

In this sense, the appearance of man and the constitution of the human sciences... would be correlated to a sort of 'de-mathematicization'... for do not the first great advances of mathematical physics, the first massive utilizations of the calculation of probabilities, date from the time when the attempt at an immediate constitution of a general science of non-quantifiable orders was abandoned? (Foucault 1970, pp. 349–50).

It was not until the mid-nineteenth century, coincidentally when industrialisation, and the associated widespread mechanisation of industry, grew rapidly (Hobsbawm 1975), that logic began again to take on importance as an active field for new research in its own right. The incipient form of logic as a coherent and regulated, machine-like system began to take shape in four related British works around the middle of the nineteenth century: Richard Whately's *Elements of Logic* (1826), William Thomson's *Outlines of the Laws of Thought* (1842), John Stuart Mill's *A System of Logic* (1843) and, most significantly, George Boole's *An Investigation of the Laws of Thought* (1854). These developments, contemporaneous with the early computational designs of Babbage, mark a shift in the treatment of logic from a study of modes of argumentation (as a sibling discipline to rhetoric) to a study of a *system*, with strong affinities to mathematics—logic begins here to be considered as a kind of *calculus*, of the kind Leibniz envisioned, rather than a mere rhetorical aid (O'Regan 2008). This is especially evident in Boole's landmark text, which not only marks its discussion of logic with algebraic rather than verbal terms, but introduces for the first time a set of logical operations equivalent to those of arithmetic (logical product, sum and difference) (Bochenski 1961; Kneale 1984). Evidence of the radical nature of this effort is indicated by a prolonged defence in the introduction:

> Whence it is that the ultimate laws of Logic are mathematical in their form; why they are, except in a single point, identical with the general laws of Number; and why in that particular point they differ;—are questions upon which it might not be very remote from presumption to endeavour to pronounce a positive judgement. Probably they lie beyond the reach of our limited faculties. It may, perhaps, be permitted to the mind to attain a knowledge of the laws to which it is itself subject, without its being also given to it to understand their ground and origin, or even, except in a very limited degree, to comprehend their fitness for their end, as compared with other and conceivable systems of law. Such knowledge is, indeed, unnecessary for the ends of science, which properly concerns itself with what is, and seeks not for grounds of preference or reasons of appointment. These considerations furnish a sufficient answer to all

protests against the exhibition of Logic in the form of a Calculus. It is not because we choose to assign to it such a mode of manifestation, but because the ultimate laws of thought render that mode possible, and prescribe its character, and forbid, as it would seem, the perfect manifestation of the science in any other form, that such a mode demands adoption (Boole 2007, p. 11).

For Boole, rendering the laws of thought 'in the form of a Calculus' becomes 'perfect manifestation of the science', and a natural accompaniment to the greater scientific enterprise then burgeoning in mid-nineteenth century Britain. It is an undertaking which, moreover, fits comfortably with the broader economic and military aspiration of a global-looking empire (Hobsbawm 1975). Nevertheless, as the titles of these works indicate, logic remained a description of concomitant mentalistic 'laws of thought'—however much they may be 'mathematical in their form' (Boole 2007). That these laws themselves belonged to the domain of mathematics, or perhaps might found a new branch of 'metamathmatics', rather than psychology—and thus could be replicated by a machine—was an implication yet to be developed. For Frege, writing a little later in the nineteenth century, expressions such as 'laws of thought' were the last vestiges of a discipline about to be wrenched from its psychologistic origins (Kneale 1984). Subsequently, logic was to be reoriented onto new disciplinary foundations, not on the basis of a mere analogy or affinity with mathematics, but as no less than the very foundations of the mathematical enterprise.

The latter half of the nineteenth century witnessed the emergence of two new global powers which could compete with the military, economic and technological dominance of the British Empire—Germany and the United States (Hobsbawm 1987). Coincidentally these two countries also boast the two seminal logicians of this period, in Frege and Peirce. Quite independently and, in the case of Peirce, to relatively little initial acclaim, they worked to develop completely axiomatised logical systems, which in turn would form the basis for all modern-day formal knowledge systems (Davis 2001; Sowa 2000). Frege, in particular, developed three pivotal and influential innovations: the 'concept script' (*Begriffschrift*), a notational language of symbols with variables and constants with well-defined semantics; the vital conceptual distinction between connotational meaning (sense—*Sinn*) and denotational meaning (reference—*Bedeutung*); and, most notably, the formalisation of quantified predicate logic, which as one historian suggests 'was one of the greatest intellectual inventions of the nineteenth century' (Kneale 1984). While Frege's notation was never widely adopted, and presented considerable intellectual challenges to its early readers, the recognised flexibility of predicate logic allowed for an explosion of interest in 'metamathematical' problems—how to develop a foundational system from which all of mathematics could be derived (van Heijenoort 1967). Together with Cantor's set theory, at the turn of the twentieth century, it now appeared at least possible to unite mathematics under a single universal theory—indeed, the very desire to develop, for the first time, a unified coherent theory itself points to a uniquely modern epistemology of mathematics (Davis 2001). More ambitiously still, the challenge of erecting all knowledge on the rigorous epistemological foundations of logic and mathematics could now be conceived—a challenge which, around the turn of the century, was indeed posed by the mathematician Hilbert, and soon after was also accepted by Whitehead and Russell (van Heijenoort 1967).

Crises in modernity: the order of logic and the chaos of history

The fascination with propositional form, which characterises the enthusiasm for symbolic logic in the early twentieth century, has its suggestive cultural analogues in the geometric obsessions of cubism, the calculating devices of the new mass culture industries, modernist architecture, the ordered urban planning environments of Le Corbusier, and the shared desire and horror of order that is a continued motif of modernist art and literature (Adorno 2001; Hobsbawm 1994). It also parallels the development and interest in a host of more mundane technologies—double-entry book-keeping, time-and-motion studies, efficient transportation, assembly-line manufacturing, punch-card tabulation and the growth of explicit management techniques, to mention but a few (Hobsbawm 1994). The first half of the twentieth century was a highly productive period for the formalisation of logic, during which the foundations for contemporary research in artificial intelligence, cognitive science and a host of affiliated disciplines today were laid. It was during this period, too, that the latent potentials of logic began to coalesce with a fully fledged modernity to provide the kinds of technological instrumentation required to meet the demands of large-scale administrations and bureaucracies. Here the quantitative growth of organisational data collated would outstrip the capacities of pre-digital storage technologies—and companies quickly emerged to fill the breach: the late nineteenth century already witnessed the growth of one corporate entity willing to service government census needs with new tabulating machines, which by 1915 had, after a three-way merger, started to operate under the now familiar name of International Business Machines (IBM Corporation 2009). Yet formal logical systems were, by and large, still considered without direct regard for their applications. Prior to the elaboration of the first computers during and after the Second World War, the steady production of theorems in set theory, model theory, foundational arithmetic and mathematical logic formed the basis from which something like modern information and knowledge systems could emerge.

These innovations happen within an era of unprecedented political and economic crisis: two world wars, numerous political revolutions and the Great Depression (Hobsbawm 1994). The surrounding turmoil of Europe often appears eclipsed in the isolated intellectual histories of this period, which feature predominantly the relative sanctuaries of Cambridge, Oxford, Vienna, Warsaw universities, and eventually those of Berkeley, Harvard and Princeton too. Yet the application of logic in military, administrative and organisational context was to become an important factor in funding and direction of problem solving within these as yet relatively small academic circles (Ceruzzi 2003). Some of the key figures in the emergence of the information age—Turing and von Neumann—made vital contributions, respectively, in code breaking and the construction of the atomic bomb (O'Regan 2008). Notoriously, the Nazis used ever more efficient information systems for cataloguing concentration camp prisoners—recently, for instance, it has been claimed that this use of punch-card tabulators involved lucrative agreements and ongoing business with IBM subsidiaries (Black 2002). But on a more general level, systems for tabulating and calculating at high speeds for academic, governmental, commercial or military purposes meant that there was significant curiosity about the otherwise arcane results emerging from this form of theoretical enterprise, even if it did not hold the public attention in the way that, for example, theoretical physics did from the First World War onwards.

The following sections outline some of the salient developmental steps in the construction of both computers generally and knowledge systems in particular.

1910s—Mathematical principles

In *Principia Mathematica*, Whitehead and Russell (1910) endeavoured to refound the entirety of mathematics on the new 'meta-mathematics' of formal logic. This work developed on Frege's system, and was to prove instrumental in inspiring the development of the austere brand of philosophy by the Vienna circle in the 1920s, known as logical positivism (van Heijenoort 1967). *Principia Mathematica*, more than any other work, was responsible for directing Anglo-American philosophy away from metaphysics, idealism and the naïve empiricism of the nineteenth century, and towards an empiricism instead founded on the precise use of a language resolutely committed to describing facts—a language epitomised in the severe codes of symbolic logic. The impetus behind Russell and Whitehead's project remained that of Leibniz' dream, but phrased now in tones less of wishful thinking and more of matter-of-factual inevitability. The task of logical analysis, in Russell's telling introduction to Wittgenstein's work, is to show 'how traditional philosophy and traditional solutions arise out of ignorance of the principles of Symbolism and out of misuse of language' (Wittgenstein 1921). At the heart of this vision, in a reductionist form, is the idea that, once the appropriate logical vocabulary is supplied, and the concepts of a field made sufficiently clear, all knowledge can be reduced to empirical observation and data collection.

1920s—'Thereof one must be silent'

This vision, in the various imaginings of Frege, Russell and the logical positivists, receives its most incisive and forceful articulation in Wittgenstein's *Tractatus Logico-Philosophicus* (1921). Not a work on logic in the usual sense—it uses relatively little symbolism, almost no mathematics, and has none of the standard hallmarks of logical papers or textbooks—it nevertheless had great influence, and has continued to be read long after *Principia Mathematica* was relegated to relative obscurity of the history of logic. Indicative of what was deemed to be the new putative function of philosophy, the *Tractatus* took a long aim at the entire history of philosophy, portraying it as a discipline awash with metaphysical confusion. The following exemplifies this critique, but also suggests the putative manner in which philosophy ought to proceed—with surgical precision:

3.323 In the language of everyday life it very often happens that the same word signifies in two different ways—and therefore belongs to two different symbols—or that two words, which signify in different ways, are apparently applied in the same way in the proposition...

3.324 Thus there easily arise the most fundamental confusions (of which the whole of philosophy is full).

3.325 In order to avoid these errors, we must employ a symbolism which excludes them, by not applying the same sign in different symbols and by not applying signs in the same way which signify in different ways. A symbolism, that is to say, which obeys the rules of logical grammar—of logical syntax.

(The logical symbolism of Frege and Russell is such a language, which, however, does still not exclude all errors.) (Wittgenstein 1921, p. 41).

Wittgenstein's specific technical contribution to the discipline of logic in the *Tractatus* was limited to the construction of truth tables—a device for determining the truth function of a proposition given the truth values of its atomic parts. The broader influence of the *Tractatus* in philosophy, though, is inestimable—it completed the exercise instigated by Frege and Russell, of placing logic and linguistic analysis at the centre of contemporary philosophical discourse (Rorty 1992). Just as significantly, once sufficiently interpreted and translated by Carnap, Ayer, Popper and others, it emphasised just how the factual propositions constituting scientific knowledge, specifically, were to be articulated—as a system of concepts, relations and properties. This was to form the basis for how modern knowledge systems would develop. Of anything which could not be subsumed directly within this system, logical positivists, following Wittgenstein, might declare: 'thereof one must be silent' (Wittgenstein 1921).

1930s—Completeness, truth, decidability and computations

The 1930s witnessed a furious explosion of theoretical work in logic, and the first emergence of its practical application. In the early years, two of the most significant figures in the history of logic, Tarski and

Gödel, published vitally important results for the future evolution of knowledge systems. Neither's work is easily assimilable into a historical synopsis of this sort, so this section focuses only on two of their more significant results—published in Gödel's 'On Formally Undecidable Propositions of *Principia Mathematica* and Related Systems' ([1931] 1962) and Tarski's 'The Semantical Conception of Truth' (1944), respectively. These results were to have near-immediate impact on the development of computing—around the middle of the decade, Church and Turing delivered models of computation, and by the decade's end, quite independently, the first computer had been developed by Zuse in Germany (Lee 1995). Thereafter, the war was both to disrupt and furnish new opportunities for research in aid of the war effort, and, inadvertently, to establish a realignment of technological prowess with the diaspora of mathematical talent from the old to the new world.

In 1931 Gödel resolved the problem of providing a sufficient axiomatisation of the foundations of mathematics, albeit with a negative result. In his incompleteness theorem, he demonstrated that a logical system could not be both complete and consistent (Gödel [1931] 1962). A system could only describe a complete set of theorems, such as those of arithmetic, by also admitting contradictory theorems. This result was to have vital implications—in Turing's recasting of it several years later, the 'halting' problem indicated that in the context of a hypothetical Turing machine performing an algorithm, it was impossible to decide whether it would terminate or run forever. This insight, vital to the general notion of computability, would also eventually mature into different classes of logic-based knowledge systems, depending on the trade-off between expressivity—what kinds of facts such systems can represent and reason over—and tractability—what guarantees of performance and termination reasoning algorithms would have (Nagel and Newman 1959).

Tarski's work on formal languages has greater application still for the development of formal knowledge systems, and indeed has been highly influential in the philosophy of natural language. Although most of his work related to various fields in mathematics, several significant papers on logic published originally in Polish in the 1930s focus on the concept of truth in formal languages (Tarski 1957). These papers form the basis for the development of model theory, which aims to describe how linguistic models (expressed in either formal or natural languages) can be adequately interpreted in a truth-functional sense. Tarski's relevant work from this period is 'The Concept of Truth in Formalized Languages'. The aim of the paper is to 'construct—with reference to a given language—*a materially adequate and formally correct definition of the term "true sentence"* (Tarski 1957, p. 152, original emphasis). Tarski is careful not to offer a definition of truth itself—that task, he states, belongs to epistemology. Rather he is interested in answering the question: what is it for a sentence constructed in a given (formal) language to be true? An important step towards this result is the introduction of recursive languages, in which one language (a metalanguage) can be used to give the truth conditions of those in another (an object language). The metalanguage cannot however state the truth conditions of its own sentences—these conditions must be stated in yet another metalanguage. For Tarski, a sentence is true just in case there is a sentence in the metalanguage under consideration which is its translation. Tarski frames this result as a postulate known as *Convention T*. This semantic conception was eventually elaborated into model theory in the 1950s, and gave the precise semantic determination required for the construction of highly expressive formalisms, of which semantic web ontologies are a contemporary example.

Turing was another key figure who emerged in this period, building, as did Church, on Gödel's critical insights. Although Great Britain had a diminished role in the development of computing in the post-war period, Turing remained a significant and iconoclastic influence in this development until his death in 1954 (Hodges 2009). A member of the fervent Cambridge intellectual scene in the 1930s, Turing's work was to have greater practical consequence in the second half of the century than any of his contemporaries. The Turing machine, elaborated in an effort to solve the problem of mathematical decidability, was to form the basis of all of modern computers. Its key insight is that a machine can encode not only information, but also the very instructions for processing that information. This involved a virtualisation of the machine: from a predefined instruction set built into the machine itself, to one stored instead in 'software'—an erasable, manipulable tape or script which now programmed the machine. Critically, these instructions then could be modified, so that the underlying physical machine would effectively be reprogrammed using new algorithms to replicate any number of different 'logical' machines. In the same paper, Turing also applied Gödel's incompleteness theorem to demonstrate the undecidability of certain algorithmic classes. Just as the broad vista of the computer age was sketched out in intricate detail via a decidedly old-world metaphor of marked tape, ironically its theoretical horizon—the limits of computability—was also being discovered and announced.

1940s—Towards a computational world

The work of Whitehead, Russell, Wittgenstein, Gödel, Tarski, Church and Turing, among many others, were to have substantial implications for modern computing applications, but in the 1930s these remained confined to the small communities of mathematicians and logicians. The first computers were developed in the late 1930s and the early 1940s, in Germany and in Great Britain respectively (Metropolis, Howlett and Rota 1980), and hence theoretical work in this field was only tentatively being applied to practical applications. Although Great Britain and Germany continued to produce the predominant logicians of this period, the prominence of Tarski and others attested to the broader interest in logic across the European continent, and increasingly in the United States (Ceruzzi 2003; Davis 2001).

The advent of the Second World War had two significant effects on the further development of logic and its application. First, it brought greater attention and funding to a range of theoretical disciplines, which suddenly appeared to have tremendous military application. The most conspicuous example was the development of the atomic bomb, possible only because of the recently realised theoretical feasibility of splitting atoms. But there was also significant developing of computing applications, notably in Britain and the United States—Turing's enduring fame is partly as a result of his code-breaking work on the Enigma project (Metropolis, Howlett and Rota 1980). Germany could also have entered the computer age in this period; Zuse, an enterprising young engineer, built the first functioning computer in 1938, but ironically could not obtain funding from the Nazi party to further its development (Lee 1995; Metropolis, Howlett and Rota 1980). Second, with less immediate but equally great long term effect, the rise of Nazism and the war also stimulated the enormous migration of Jewish intellectuals to the United States in the 1930s and the early years of the war (Davis 2001). This included, along with many others, Gödel and Tarski, as well as von Neumann, a leading logician and economist, and also creator of the basic hardware architecture of the modern computer (Lee 1995). This influx of considerable talent provided an enormous stimulus to American universities, noticeably at Princeton, Berkeley and Harvard. The preponderance of these intellectuals led, in the post-war period, to a generation of students who had been trained and influenced within the relatively sedate academic climate of the wealthy American university system. In the context of the Cold War and burgeoning economic conditions of the 1950s, highly trained mathematicians and physicists were to be increasingly in demand for both industry and government. The United States, and to a much lesser extent Russia, were well placed, then, to capitalise on the influx of significant intellectuals like Gödel and Tarski—although their influence was equally likely to be felt indirectly, through the work of their students, and the subsequent dissemination of their results via translation.

Although they form only a small part of the broader work conducted in mathematical logic, or as it was then termed, 'metamathematics', the logicians introduced here still stand out as singularly responsible for the disciplinary orientations of philosophy and mathematics, and setting the foundations for the extraordinary rise of the computing industry in subsequent years. In the latter part of the twentieth century, this quantitative growth itself led to significant qualitative specialisation in computing science, to the extent that the number of conferences, papers and results has long since been impractical to survey single-handedly. Even this appreciable academic activity pales in comparison, however, to the extraordinary industrial investment in computing applications. The next section aims to chart the direction of this development in the latter part of the twentieth century, especially in the context of the rise of knowledge systems. Of these, the relational database has had the most spectacular rise, to the extent that it is now a pervasive part of any modern-day organisational infrastructure. The semantic web represents an effort to develop an alternative architecture for representing knowledge, featuring more expressive features than the set-theoretic models of relational databases. Collectively, however, they both represent species of a broader common genus, a family of formal knowledge systems which aimed to realise, with various inflections, the letter if not quite the spirit of Leibniz' much earlier utopic dreams.

References

Adorno, T.W. 2001. *The Culture Industry: Selected Essays on Mass Culture*. Abingdon: Routledge.

Berners-Lee, T., J. Hendler and O. Lassila. 2001. 'The Semantic Web', *Scientific American* 284, pp. 34–43.

Black, E. 2002. *IBM and the Holocaust: The Strategic Alliance between Nazi Germany and America's Most Powerful Corporation*. New York: Crown Publishing Group.

Bochenski, J.M. 1961. *A History of Formal Logic*, I. Thomas (tr.). Notre Dame: University of Notre Dame Press.

Boole, G. 2007. *An Investigation of the Laws of Thought*. New York: Cosimo Classics.

Ceruzzi, P.E. 2003. *A History of Modern Computing*. Cambridge, MA: MIT Press.

Davis, M. 2001. *Engines of Logic: Mathematicians and the Origin of the Computer*. New York: W.W. Norton & Company.

Foucault, M. 1970. *The Order of Things: An Archaeology of the Human Sciences*. New York: Vintage Books.

Gödel, K. [1931] 1962. *On Formally Undecidable Propositions of Principia Mathematica and Related Systems*. New York: Basic Books.

Habermas, J. 1989. *The Structural Transformation of the Public Sphere*, T. Burger (tr.). Cambridge, MA: MIT Press.

Hegel, G.W.F. 2004. *Science of Logic*, A.V. Miller (tr.). Abingdon: Routledge.

Hobsbawm, E.J. 1975. *The Age of Capital*. London: Weidenfeld & Nicolson.

—. 1987. The Age of Empire, 1875–1914. London: Weidenfeld & Nicolson.

—. 1994. *The Age of Extremes: The Short Twentieth Century, 1914–1991*. London: Michael Joseph and Pelham Books.

Hodges, A. 2009. 'Alan Turing'. In E.N. Zalta (ed.), *The Stanford Encyclopedia of Philosophy*. Stanford, CA: Metaphysics Research Lab, Center for the Study of Language and Information, Stanford University.

IBM Corporation. 2009. 'IBM Highlights, 1885–1969', *http://www-03.ibm.com/ibm/history/documents/pdf/1885–1969.pdf* (accessed 19 January 2010).

Kneale, M. 1984. *The Development of Logic*. Oxford: Oxford University Press.

Lee, J.A.N. 1995. *Computer Pioneers*. Los Alamitos: IEEE Computer Society Press.

Lenzen, W. 2004. 'Leibniz's Logic'. In *Handbook of the History of Logic*, vol. 3, 'The Rise of Modern Logic from Leibniz to Frege'. Amsterdam: North-Holland Publishing Company.

Metropolis, N.C., J. Howlett and G.C. Rota. 1980. *A History of Computing in the Twentieth Century*. Orlando: Harcourt Brace Jovanovich.

Nagel, E. and J.R. Newman. 1959. *Godel's Proof*. London: Routledge & Kegan Paul.

O'Regan, G. 2008. *A Brief History of Computing*. London: Springer.

Reiter, R. 1987. 'On Closed World Data Bases'. In M.L. Ginsberg (ed.), *Readings in Nonmonotonic Reasoning*. San Francisco: Morgan Kaufmann Publishers.

Rorty, R. 1992. *The Linguistic Turn: Essays in Philosophical Method*. Chicago, IL: University of Chicago Press.

Smith, B. 1998. 'Basic Concepts of Formal Ontology'. In *FOIS 1998: Proceedings of Formal Ontology in Information Systems*. IOS Press, pp. 19–28.

Sowa, J.F. 2000. *Knowledge Representation: Logical, Philosophical, and Computational Foundations*. Cambridge, MA: MIT Press.

Tarski, A. 1944. 'The Semantic Conception of Truth and the Foundations of Semantics'. *Philosophy and Phenomenological Research* 4.

—. 1957. 'The Concept of Truth in Formalized Languages'. In *Logic, Semantics, Metamathematics*. Indianapolis, IN: Hackett Publishing Company.

van Heijenoort, J. 1967. *From Frege to Gödel: A Source Book in Mathematical Logic, 1879–1931*. Cambridge, MA: Harvard University Press.

Whitehead, A.N. and B. Russell. 1910. *Principia Mathematica*. Cambridge, UK: Cambridge University Press.

Wittgenstein, L. 1921. *Tractatus Logico-Philosophicus*. Mineola, IA: Dover Publications.

8

Contemporary dilemmas:
tables versus webs

Liam Magee

This chapter picks up the narrative thread of the preceding one—telling the story of the rise of modern knowledge systems. It considers specifically two of the more perspicuous forms of these systems: the relational database and the semantic web. Even if at a technical level these kinds of systems appear congruous, without doubt they have followed different historical trajectories, leading to different cultures of designers and adopters. Latter parts of this chapter attempt to articulate some of these differences via a set of analytic categories, and, to test those categories, undertake a brief foray into the online world of technological commentary—to get a taste for how different kinds of systems are perceived in practice. It concludes by fanning back out to the broad historical context the previous chapter began with, to look at the suggestive correlations between these forms of structured knowledge representations, and the vast social webs which underpin particular knowledge practices, the complex strands of political and economic relations inherent in the late capitalist era.

Ordering the world by relations

After the Second World War, and partially in response to the emergence of a new kind of conflict in which information was to become a central rather than peripheral military asset, the United States embarked on a continuous and unabated course of research into a wide range of computing applications. At one end of the research spectrum was feverish, speculative and sometimes disappointing research into artificial intelligence, conducted by technology-oriented institutes like MIT. At the other end, companies and organisations like IBM, Xcrox, Digital Equipment Corporation (DEC) and the RAND Corporation developed their own more commercially oriented but still highly experimental research incubators, which frequently coordinated with their academic counterparts, often hiring bright PhD candidates with a firm eye on commercial applications. Government departments, particularly those associated with the military, often engaged researchers on various diverse computing projects, including cryptography, cybernetics, game theory and large-scale networking (Ceruzzi 2003). It was the work of the Defense Advanced Research Projects Agency (DARPA) in the 1960s which gave rise to the first widespread computing networks, forerunners of the modern internet. Frequently more prosaic areas of research, like networking, user interface development, typography and operating systems, yielded long-term and substantial gains. Attempts to emulate concepts as nebulous and little understood as human intelligence repeatedly hit low-lying hurdles—in the same period Chomsky was demonstrating just how complex one area of cognition, language acquisition and use could be (Chomsky 1965).

The rise of large commercial organisations operating over international territories increased the imperative to develop technologies for managing the expansive quantitative growth of information (Lyotard 1984). In the 1960s, as computers grew in processing power and storage capacity, different methods were developed for managing volumes of structured information. Principal users of these technologies were the banking and insurance industries, for whom the need to provide reliable and systematic information on customers and transactions was paramount. Data storage at this time used a network or hierarchical model, where data records were linked in a parent–child relationship. Navigating from parent records (for example, from a customer) to children (to the customer's transactions) was relatively simple programmatically. However, the *ad hoc* aggregation of records based on relations which had not been previously defined in this manner—for instance, a request for all successful transactions within a given period—was time-consuming and computationally expensive. An industry group, the Database Task Group, comprising a number of leading technology companies, but notably excluding the market leader, IBM, proposed a so-called 'network' model in the late 1960s. Both this approach and IBM's subsequent alternative hierarchical model nonetheless continued to suffer the same limitations of performance and feasibility (National Research Council 1999).

In 1969, in response to these limitations, an IBM employee, Edgar Codd, developed a rich algebra and calculus for representing data using what he termed a 'relational model' (Codd 1970). The model comprises several key concepts: *relations*, *attributes* and *tuples*—concepts which became known to designers and users of databases and spreadsheets under more familiar monikers of *tables*, *columns* and *rows*. Although this paper essentially proposes the application of set theoretical constructs to data models, it has a practical purpose—it explicitly aims to provide a better model for 'non-inferential systems', unlike the early progenitors of research into artificial intelligence. The principal benefits of this model were to provide a sufficiently abstract series of informational constructs which, once standardised, could allow for true data independence, and a rigorous axiomatic system which could ensure data consistency (although as subsequent database administrators would discover, many other factors intrude on the problem of maintaining a consistent data set). IBM itself was slow to follow up on the promise of its own innovation, and other elaborations of it which followed from its laboratories in the early 1970s. The company did develop a prototype system based on the relational model, called System R, but this failed to be adopted by IBM commercially (National Research Council 1999). It did however publish its research on the relational model; and in 1977, after reading some of this research, three entrepreneurs founded what was soon to become the largest database company in the world, and one of the largest in the information technology sector (Oracle 2007). Like Microsoft, Oracle's growth through the 1980s and 1990s was staggering—ironically, both companies profited from costly miscalculations at IBM. Though IBM was soon to catch up somewhat with its own commercial relational database system, Oracle's success was largely driven by, and indeed cleverly anticipated, the unrelenting drive of large organisations to manage enormous data sets. This was complemented by the increasing affordances of ever cheaper and more powerful hardware.

One of the principal advantages of the relational model is the provision of a standard and well-defined query language, Structured Query Language (SQL). In spite of fierce competition among database vendors, and a corresponding emphasis on product differentiation, SQL quickly became—and remained—an essential part of all modern database systems (Date 2007). SQL was ratified as a US ANSI standard in 1986, and an international ISO standard in 1987, ensuring a minimal base compliance for manipulating and querying data across rival systems (Wikipedia 2009). Unhappily for users of these systems, vendors like Oracle, IBM and Microsoft continued to extend the subsequent sequence of standards with various 'proprietary' extensions. The preponderance of industry support for SQL demonstrates that even in the heavily competitive and nascent database software industry, vendors were prepared to trade off short-term competitive advantage against the longer term positive network externalities of a larger marketplace built around selective feature standardisation and differentiation (Katz and Shapiro 1985). As SQL became an integral component of modern computing degrees and certification processes, it demonstrated that English-like formal languages could achieve widespread adoption, with the significant incentive of a burgeoning job market in the 1990s and early part of the twenty-first century. Moreover it was no longer just the domain of large organisations—small- to medium-sized businesses and even keen individuals increasingly adopted relational databases as the basis for data management, usually with convenient user interfaces overlaid. The permeation of the relational data model into all aspects of computing culture represents the overwhelming and ongoing success of this paradigm for managing structured data (National Research Council 1999). Indeed, in a very direct sense, the relational model represents the culmination and fruition of the modernist dream to order and organise knowledge systematically.

Early threads of the semantic web

The evolution of the semantic web, and its methods for representing knowledge, follow a decidedly different route. Since its earliest developments, when machines first replaced human 'computers' (Davis 2001), theorists and philosophers had been pondering the question of whether—and how—artificial intelligence was possible. The Turing Test, developed as early as 1950, suggested a range of criteria for determining how machine intelligence could be tested (Turing 1950). Research in artificial intelligence was to proceed down numerous different lines over the remainder of the century, in pursuit of the often elusive goal of emulating human behaviour and cognition. Frequently denigrated for not realising its lofty ambitions, many artificial intelligence innovations nevertheless filtered down from these comparatively abstract areas of research into everyday practical technologies. One area that received particular attention was the problem of modelling or representing knowledge—an essential step towards building computational equivalents of memory and reasoning processes.

In the 1960s Quillian (1967) pioneered the idea of 'semantic networks'—graphs of nodal concepts connected by associations, a precursor to neural networks. These were followed by more detailed models, such as semantic frames (Minsky 1974). Semantic frames added the notion of 'slots' to concepts, where their attributes could be stored. Abstractly, both attributes and relations could be considered as properties of a concept, distinguished only on the basis of whether a property could take a data value (attribute) or object value (relation). Semantic network and frame approaches were the basis of a number of early expert systems, with Minsky's proposals in particular galvanising interest in artificial intelligence circles about the possibility of engineering computational approximations to human cognitive processes (Sowa 2000). From another angle, there were various endeavours to instrumentalise theorem proving through use of declarative or logic programming languages (Colmerauer and Roussel 1996). For whatever reason—perhaps because it was easier to separate knowledge bases from the procedures which reasoned over them—logic programming approaches were to remain a niche market. On the other hand, it soon became apparent that the sorts of things which constitute an 'association' or 'relationship' between concepts need greater semantic specificity than existing semantic network or frame approaches allowed. In 1979 a new system, KL-ONE, emerged with more expressive semantics, where the kinds of relationships between conceptual nodes is explicitly stipulated (Brachman and Schmolze 1985). This was a step closer towards greater levels of interoperability between multiple knowledge systems; however, it was still possible to interpret constructs differently across different systems.

Over the course of the 1980s and 1990s, researchers began developing restricted forms of logic for representing knowledge (Sowa 2000). 'Terminological' or 'description logics', as they became known, were fragments of first order logic with specific constructs for representing *concepts*, *properties* and *individuals* (Brachman et al. 1991). Significantly, description logics were directly derived from Tarksi's work on model theory, discussed earlier, providing unambiguous interpretation of the effect of logical operations within conforming systems (Nardi and Brachman 2003). For example, if a concept is stipulated as being subsumed by two other concepts, its *extension*—the objects denoted by the concept—must be interpreted as the union of the objects denoted by the parent concepts. For systems implementing these semantics, and for users of these systems, this feature ensured consistency in the handling of queries, and remedied many of the derivative problems which emerged in the implementations of earlier models (Nardi and Brachman 2003).

Still, at this stage knowledge systems were invariably small scale— much too small to capture the many background facts assumed to sit behind the kind of commonsense reasoning humans typically undertake.

In 1984 Doug Lenat began a project called Cyc, which was intended to contain all of the facts which constitute an ordinary human's understanding of the world. Development of the Cyc knowledge base is still ongoing, part of the commercial intellectual property of its owner, Cycorp, and represents a substantial undertaking to codify knowledge under the auspice of a single overriding conceptualisation (Lenat 2001).

Proposals for the semantic web built on the work of description logics even more explicitly. Unlike Cyc, the vision of the semantic web involves *many* authors and conceptualisations, linked together by a common model-theoretic foundation in RDF and OWL, explicit references and shared pointers to web resources. The explicit design goals of the semantic web were to provide a very general mechanism by which knowledge could be represented, shared and reasoned over computationally. The first published version of OWL came with different description logic variants, with different levels of expressivity and tractability—as the logic becomes more expressive, there are fewer guarantees that in the worst case reasoning problems are tractable, or can be resolved in finite time (Levesque and Brachman 1987). Though its precursors Ontology Inference Language (OIL) and DARPA Agent Markup Language (DAML) were first motivated by a combination of academic and military research, OWL itself quickly became sold to the broader web community as a facilitator for a new range of 'intelligent' services—process automation, e-commerce, system integration and enhanced consumer applications (Berners-Lee, Hendler and Lassila 2001; Fensel et al. 2001). RDF had similar, if more pragmatic, origins as a language for data markup, with less emphasis on automated reasoning. It was, however, also motivated by the need to model information more flexibly than the highly structured models of preceding generations of data technology—notably the relational model—would allow. The document-centric nature of the World Wide Web suggested that significant amounts of information could not conform to the strictures of a relational view of the world. While being compatible with existing structured information sources was one constraint on the design of RDF, so too was the need to permit modelling of flexible, semi-structured, document-like and inter-connected data. The involvement of the World Wide Web Consortium (W3C) ensured that the semantic web architecture technically and philosophically built on the foundations of the already—by the late 1990s, when the first formal semantic web technical recommendations were drafted—hugely successful precursor of the World Wide Web.

Shifting trends or status quo?

Broadly, then, the semantic web can be seen as the consequence of three dominant broad trends in information technology and management over the later decades of the twentieth century. First, organisations had grown in size and, commensurately, the burgeoning fields of business, management and information studies had encouraged the use of disciplined techniques for obtaining greater predictability over key variables in organisational operations. From the 1970s onwards the explosive quantitative growth of data, the availability of and demand for computing resources for storing and processing it, and the increasing awareness of the opportunistic value of analysing it led in turn to enormous investments in scientific research and development, as well as considerable financial speculation in the data management industry. This was primarily oriented around the relational data model—although other data storage models continued to be prevalent in specific fields, the general applicability of the relational model led to its near ubiquity as a mechanism for storing structured information.

Meanwhile, a second, less perspicuous trend took place in the ongoing research in artificial intelligence and knowledge representation, which in turn made feasible a well-defined and consistent notation for describing facts and permitting sophisticated inferencing operations. In fields with large numbers of concepts and very large amounts of data, such as medical, financial and military applications, the need for expert systems had long been evident.

Finally, the rise of the World Wide Web—the third, and arguably most disruptive of these trends—also brought new applications and therefore greater commercial relevance for deductive reasoning systems. Where the relational model had typically been used in intra-organisational (or even intra-departmental) settings, the advent of a global network, and the academic, economic and political advantages to be gained through its exploitation, made more evident than ever the need to supply unambiguous definitions of data through a highly expressive formal notation. The application of deductive reasoning to information from a myriad of sources gave rise to new problems of trust, proof and authentication, but also provided the tantalising prospect of unprecedented data being accessible to reasoning algorithms. The development of RDF and OWL was driven by the competing demands of providing notations simple enough, on the one hand, to be used and developed by software engineers and web developers untrained in knowledge representation, and expressive enough, on the other, to permit the kind of deductive power envisaged by the pioneers of artificial intelligence, and indeed by their precursors, the foundational logicians.

In spite of these evolutions, it would be premature to conclude that the semantic web is in the process of replacing the relational database. In fact the relational model has proved remarkably resilient in an industry recognised for inevitable if not always planned technological obsolescence. The massive commercial database industries still dwarf the largely academic and entrepreneurial world of the semantic web, and considerable work has been devoted to building bridging technologies between the respective formalisms—to promote, in fact, further use of the semantic web through connections to existing relational repositories of data (Malhotra 2008). Meanwhile, many in the broader web community are also now examining alternatives to the semantic web itself, suggesting a more complex picture marked by overlapping, shifting trends rather than any clear pattern of technology phase-out (Khare and Çelik 2006). At this stage it is more likely that both relational databases and semantic web ontologies will continue to be developed—making the question of their commensurability, discussed in the section below, highly pertinent.

Systems of knowledge: modern and postmodern

These two models—the first, representing the fulfilment of modernist logicism, the second, a postmodern response and would-be successor—have special interest within a broader historical trajectory of formal systems. Relational systems hold, as mentioned above, a dominant position in the market of information systems. By one indicator—worldwide 'total software revenue' (incorporating licences, subscriptions, support and maintenance)—the relational database market grossed an estimated US$15.3 billion in revenue in 2006, US$16.8 billion in 2007 and US$18.8 billion in 2008, continuing to show strong growth rates in spite of a global economic downturn (Gartner 2007, 2009). While this figure includes immediately subsidiary revenues accompanying software, it does not include the many development and maintenance tools, services, related or derivative systems which depend on relational database systems—a value likely to be much higher. Moreover, even an eventual meteoric rise of the semantic web does not imply the eclipse of the database industry, since, as suggested above, logical semantic web data structures like ontologies can be physically stored in a relational database; however, as the analysis above shows, ontologies do present a rival conception of knowledge representation at a logical level, and a separate tradition in a historical sense. Although they represent different logical formalisms, with few ontological commitments, nevertheless they can be distinguished on the basis of certain minimal and abstract assumptions. Perhaps the most contentious of these concerns the use of so-called 'closed' versus 'open' world assumptions, a distinction which has received substantial attention in the literature on logic, databases and knowledge representation (Reiter 1987; Sowa 2000). The following review examines this distinction in greater detail.

Closed versus open world assumptions

Reiter (1987) introduced 'closed world' assumptions to describe the interpretation of an empty or failed query result on a database as equivalent to a negation of the facts asserted in the query: 'In a closed world, negation as failure is equivalent to ordinary negation' (Sowa 2000). In other words, the set of facts contained in a database are assumed to be complete descriptions of a given domain of discourse—any proposition not either directly stated or indirectly inferrable is interpreted to be false. In contrast, an assumption of an 'open world' interprets the absence of a proposition as indicating its truth value is unknown (Date 2007). One way of characterising this difference, then, is to say that a 'closed world assumption' interprets failure semantically—directly, as a false proposition—where an 'open world assumption' interprets failure epistemologically—indirectly, as a failure of knowledge about the semantic state of the proposition. An important consequence follows, related to the properties of the logics which underpin these interpretive systems. Under open world assumptions, reasoning is monotonic—no new information added to a database can invalidate existing information, and the deductive conclusions which can be drawn from it (Sowa 2000). Reasoning is essentially additive—new facts added to the database always increase the number of conclusions which can be drawn. In the extreme case, if a new proposition contradicts something already stated, every proposition is rendered provable. Conversely, nonmonotonic reasoning is revisionary—new facts can revise existing conclusions. Depending on the scope of new facts, the sum of conclusions derivable from a database can accordingly increase or decrease. In logical terms, if a conclusion

C is derivable from a premiss A, but not from the conjunction of A and a further proposition B, then the mode of reasoning must be nonmonotonic (Hayes 2004).

Matters are further complicated with the introduction of context:

> The relationship between monotonic and nonmonotonic inferences is often subtle. For example, if a closed-world assumption is made explicit, e.g. by asserting explicitly that the corpus is complete and providing explicit provenance information in the conclusion, then closed-world reasoning is monotonic; it is the implicitness that makes the reasoning nonmonotonic. Nonmonotonic conclusions can be said to be valid only in some kind of 'context', and are liable to be incorrect or misleading when used outside that context. Making the context explicit in the reasoning and visible in the conclusion is a way to map them into a monotonic framework (Hayes 2004).

Consequently it is possible to augment a set of propositions, interpreted under local closed-world conditions, with explicit contextual information—temporal, spatial, providential, jurisdictional, functional—to move towards an open-world interpretation essential to the unconstrained environment of the semantic web. Since specifying context is itself an open-ended affair, this suggests interpretation moves across a scale of 'closed-open worldliness'—a point also suggested by Sowa (2000): 'Reiter's two categories of databases can be extended with a third category, called semi-open, in which some subdomains are closed by definition, but other subdomains contain observed or measured information that is typically incomplete.' Conversely, Date (2007) disputes that anything approximating to open world reasoning ever takes place, even on the semantic web—this would entail an unacceptable ternary logic, as though the epistemic predicate 'unknown' could sit alongside the semantic predicates of 'true' and 'false'. It is worth noting that there is incommensurability here even at the level of definition—by, as it happens, noted authorities on the semantic web (Hayes) and the relational model (Date) respectively. Interpreting commensurability of systems distinguished by this assumption depends, then, on how the assumption itself is viewed: as an epistemological question over the nature of non-existent information; as a scale against which the state of information of a database can be measured; or as a nonsensical category.

Modern grids, postmodern webs

These properties of logical interpretation are not unconnected from the cultural environs in which database systems are used. Indeed, it is precisely because of the unusual usage conditions of the semantic web that 'open world assumptions' and non-monotonic reasoning are considered significant in this context. As Date (2007) notes, the 'closed' metaphor has unfortunately pejorative connotations—but ironically parallels the closedness of the cultural contexts in which systems with closed world assumptions are likely to be used. As the tracing of their respective evolutionary paths above suggests, the semantic web is largely derived from academic research; conversely, relational databases originate in commercial and organisational environments. The connotations of these institutional settings impacts on the contemporary reception of the formalisms themselves. The following section examines remarks made by online commentators in response to these cultural allusions.

Numerous media articles and bloggers have commented on the apparent threat and 'disruptive innovation' of the semantic web to the prevailing relational database paradigm. Familiar tropes heralding the 'shock of the new' are common in the more hyperbolic of media reports. Several blogs presage the 'death' of the relation database model (Lunn 2008; Williams 2008; Zaino 2008), while one blogger eulogises the rise of RDF and OWL, delivering an acute characterisation of the perceived distinction between old and new models:

> The single failure of data integration since the inception of information technologies—for more than 30 years, now—has been schema rigidity or schema fragility. That is, once data relationships are set, they remain so and can not easily be changed in conventional data management systems nor in the applications that use them.
>
> Relational database management (RDBM) systems have not helped this challenge, at all. While tremendously useful for transactions and enabling the addition of more data records (instances, or rows in a relational table schema), they are not adaptive nor flexible.
>
> Why is this so?
>
> In part, it has to do with the structural view of the world. If everything is represented as a flat table of rows and columns, with keys to other flat structures, as soon as that representation changes, the tentacled connections can break. Such has been the fragility of the RDBMS model, and the hard-earned resistance of RDBMS administrators to schema growth or change (Bergman 2009).

Other commentators portray the shift towards the semantic web in similarly revolutionary terms: 'To me, the Semantic Web is a fundamental shift in software architecture' (Kolb 2008) and 'The relational database is becoming increasingly less useful in a web 2.0 world' (Williams 2008).

On the other side of the coin, many voices have decried the complexity, redundancy and eccentric design of the semantic web, which intentionally introduces an 'impedance mismatch' with mainstream information technological infrastructure, notably the world of relational databases and associated tools and expertise. An early and infamous critique ironically postulated that the semantic web was a purist academic exercise designed to homogenise the world's information under an unduly complex architecture, requiring both a deductive logic and a single global ontology, and with little practical likelihood of adoption and uptake: 'This is the promise of the semantic web—it will improve all the areas of your life where you currently use syllogisms. Which is to say, almost nowhere' (Shirky 2003).

The rhetoric of these positions tend to congeal around several common metaphorical tropes. The semantic web is open, free, 'bottom-up', democratic. The relational database is closed, secure, solid, robust, 'top-down', controlled. The semantic web conveys a chaotic sprawling information network or graph, without apparent origin, centre or terminus. The relational database is housed within the 'back office' of the modern-day enterprise, whose grid-locked modernist architecture mirror structured data sets, with rectilinear tables, columns, rows and cells. The semantic web is broad, visionary, idealistic, experimental, revolutionary, part of Web 2.0, 3.0 or even some futuristic variant; the relational database is mature, well understood, pragmatic, workable, third or fourth generational technology, protected by corporate support. Where the semantic web famously envisions a world in which 'information wants to be free'—a phrase originating in an earlier period of computing infused with libertarian ethos (Clarke 2001), but often applied to the semantic web movement equally—relational databases are often portrayed as siloed repositories of hermetically sealed, 'closed' organisational data, carefully managed by government and corporate enterprises and departments; the catch-cry of this world might be instead 'no one ever got fired for choosing IBM'. The world of the database is a dehumanised, administered, bureaucratic, orderly, modernist *Gesellschaft*; the semantic web instead an interconnected, uncontrolled, chaotic and postmodern *Gemeinschaft*.

These metaphorical caricatures ignore numerous confounding elements: for example, semantic web data (RDF and OWL ontologies) are capable of being stored in relational databases, and relational databases have for some time supported a range of technical connectivity options. It might well be argued that benevolent synergies between styles of systems makes for less interesting debate, and less opportunity to differentiate products and services that depend on perceived friction and dissonance. More august commentary is provided by Tim Berners-Lee, suggesting, very early in the development of the semantic web, that the major differences are superficially syntactic, rather than semantic, ontological or epistemological: 'The semantic web data model is very directly connected with the model of relational databases... The mapping is very direct' (Berners-Lee 1998).

Considerable commercial and academic research has also been directed towards hybrid and bridging technologies between relational databases and the semantic web, as the report by Malhotra (2008) suggests. Some of these involve simply publishing relational data as RDF; others use relational models to capture RDF and OWL ontological axioms directly; still others provide mappings between proprietary XML and other formats and standard RDF. Current trends tend towards conciliation—perhaps as both positive and negative hysteria around the semantic web changes into a more mature recognition of its role, as something neither entirely central nor tangential in modern system engineering.

Assessing commensurability

Some points of historical, technical and sociological contrast have been elaborated in the discussion of knowledge systems above. What does this analysis imply for an assessment of the commensurability of the systems? Table 8.1 picks up several of the generic dimensions presented in Chapter 12, 'A framework for commensurability', to characterise at least what are perceived differences in the systems. These have been selected largely because they have emerged as distinctive in the analysis above. Several addition dimensions have also been added—'Open world assumptions', 'Interconnected with other systems', 'Trusting of other systems' and 'Multi-modal' (meaning multiple generic 'modes' of information are supported—qualitative or quantitative; structured or amorphous; textual or multimedia)—which are particularly relevant to this comparison. Each of the dimensions is rated only in approximated quantitative terms; since the assessment here is designed to exercise and explore the framework, and has no obvious practical assessment, there are no clear grounds to be derived from a situation context for weighting and valuing the dimensions more precisely. Nevertheless it is possible to see a general outline emerge in the evaluations shown in Table 8.1.

In terms of public perception and adoption, in particular, the analysis suggests the two systems are broadly incommensurable. One key dimension, 'Open world assumptions', suggests a potentially insurmountable difference in orientation between the two formalisms. As the analysis above suggests, evaluating the effect of this distinction in particular depends critically on how radically it is interpreted. Several interpretations were suggested. Date (2007), for example, views the distinction itself as the product of a confusion of semantic and epistemological boundaries; for Hayes (2004), the distinction can be

Table 8.1   Comparison of knowledge systems

Dimension	Relational model	Semantic web
Orientation		
Open world assumptions	Low	High
Interconnected with other systems	Low	High
Trusting of other systems	Low	High
Multi-modal	Low	High
Idealistic (vs pragmatic)	Low	High
Applied (vs academic)	High	Low
Grounded (vs speculative)	High	Low
Purpose		
Financially motivated	High	Low
Politically motivated	Low	Moderate
Process		
Distributed (vs central) design	Moderate	High
Tran	Moderate	High
Reception		
Adoption rate	High	Moderate
Technological maturity	High	Low
Backwards compatibility	High	Moderate
De facto standard	High	Low
De jure standard	High	High
Industry support	High	Moderate

erased through the explication of context; for Sowa (2000), the distinction is a gradual one, as system 'subdomains' can be either closed or open; for other commentators (Bergman 2009; Kolb 2008; Williams 2008), the division is instead indicative of more fundamental incommensurability. Assessing the very possibility of translation between systems falling on either side of this assumption depends, then, on which of these interpretations are adopted.

In relation to the broader social dimensions, the interest in the semantic web has paralleled the phenomenal growth of 'libertarian' technologies: commoditised computing hardware and connectivity, open source software, standards and protocols, and the World Wide Web itself. Sympathies with these ideals might emphasise stronger incommensurability with older, industrial and bureaucratic technological models like the relational database. However, the relation between the knowledge system and its field of application is far from a direct one—relational databases also benefit from open standards, and a number of database products have been released as open source. Equally, the semantic web has suffered from the perception that it is overly complex and immature relative to its older representational sibling. How much of this critique will endure in the face of further research and emerging industry supports remains to be seen.

As suggested much earlier in the historical account, lurking within the deep divisions of epistemological assumptions between these two formalisms is an even deeper epistemological affinity—a putative view that knowledge can be heavily structured, organised, cleaned and disambiguated from its natural language expression. Insofar as formalisms can be contrasted, the salient contrastive features necessarily suggest difference over similarity. It is only when positioned against broader epistemological frames—which might dispute the very project of rendering knowledge faithfully in denuded formalistic terms—that this deeper affinity is exhibited. In moving towards other, more fine-grained domains of comparison and commensurability, this irreducibly contextual aspect of assessment needs to remain prominent.

Knowledge systems in social context

To round out the discussion of knowledge systems, the following summary also teases out what was an underlying thread in the account above—the relationship between technological innovation and broader social shifts. These shifts exhibit a complex network of causal relationships to the general processes of technological design, development and innovation, and hence to the question of commensurability between rival systems that emerge from these processes. These relationships, tenuously charted in this study, are more explicit in the studies that follow.

In the last quarter of the twentieth century the development of formal knowledge systems has been precipitous. The preceding discussion showed how this ascent was premised on the foundational work in mathematical logic in the late nineteenth and early twentieth centuries. Leibniz's dream—of a single symbolic language in which thoughts and argument could be conducted without ambiguity—was a constant motif throughout the evolution of this tradition. Symbolic logic, then, represents a pristine formal component of a long-ranging historical epistemological ideal, while an endless accumulation of 'sense-experience' supplies the matter. The semantic web represents a modern-day recasting of this ideal, in which precise agreement about meaning forms the underlying substrate for sharing information and deducing inferences. It receives its most emphatic expression from Ayer, who envisioned philosophy and science of ardent empiricism: 'The view of philosophy which we have adopted may, I think, fairly be described as a form of empiricism. For it is characteristic of an empiricist to eschew metaphysics, on the ground that every factual proposition must refer to sense-experience' (Ayer 1952, p. 71).

The unfolding of this tradition in the account above describes three key phases—classicism, modernism and postmodernism. These phases show an increasing impulse towards the development of 'taxinomia'—indexable, searchable and interoperable knowledge systems which span from the globally networked enterprise down to the fragmentary databases of commercial and social interactions managed by individual consumers. By tracing this tradition through a purely intellectual history, it is possible to suggest several causal factors internal to the tradition itself: the production of particular fortuitous mathematical results, or a sense of exhaustion with the preceding metaphysical speculations of Kant and Hegel, for example. It is equally possible, though, to plot lines of concordance between this intellectual history and broader transitions in economic and political history. Is it purely fortuitous that the search for logic formalisms coincided with a reciprocal drive towards standardisation, in a host of technological, communicative and legal fields, that is related to modern capitalism—specifically, of its relentless need and demand for predictability and efficiency? For Foucault, the modern taxonomic impulse originates alongside the great social and political shifts of the Enlightenment:

What makes the totality of the Classical episteme possible is primarily the relation to a knowledge of order. When dealing with the ordering of simple natures, one has recourse to a mathesis, of which the universal method is algebra. When dealing with the ordering of complex natures (representations in general, as they are given in experience), one has to constitute a taxinomia, and to do that one has to establish a system of systems (Foucault 2002, pp. 79–80).

By the time of the emergence of formal logic in something like its rigorous modern form in the nineteenth century, the world was also undergoing a period of rapid economic expansion, industrialisation, scientific endeavour and technological innovation (Hobsbawm 1975). Already the opportunities of standardisation were being considered in a host of practical contexts—rail gauge standardisation, currency exchange, scientific notation, legal charters and academic disciplinary vocabularies. The counterweight to international and inter-corporate competition was the beneficial network externalities—greater efficiency, information transparency and intelligibility—these standards would bring. Since these first standards emerged, their growth has been rapid— the ISO website alone currently advertises 17,500 separately catalogued standards (ISO 2009).

While standardisation might rightly seem, then, to be an inextricable feature of modernity, coupled with economic globalisation and cultural homogenisation, it can equally be argued that capitalism also harbours countervailing trends towards systemic differentiation. Most notably in the case of the quintessential capitalist organisation, the company, product or service differentiation forms the foundation for market share, profit, and thus for increasing shareholder value. To take one metric of the extent of differentiation, at the level of invention and innovation: the US Patent Office has filed over seven million utility patents alone since 1836 (US Patent and Trademark Office 2009), with an average rate of increase in the number of patent applications between 1836 and 2008 of 23.5 per cent. There were 436 patent applications filed in 1838, and 158,699 applications filed in 2008, an overall increase of 36,399 per cent over 170 years (the raw data has been taken from the US Patent and Trademark Office (2009), while the percentile calculations are my own). Whatever explanation of drift towards standardisation can be drawn from modern capitalism, there is an equivalent burden for explaining a similar level of hyper-activity towards proprietary protection of intellectual capital and assets.

Equivalent, if more tenuous motives for differentiation can be found in other organisational types—political affiliations, methodological distinctions and sublimated competitive instincts exist in government, scientific and academic institutions as much as in corporate ones. The development and coordination of knowledge systems—formalised representations of meaning—has its origins, in one side of modern capitalism, in the impulse to order, organise and predict. The proliferation of multiple systems represents, then, another facet of capitalism—the need for differentiation and competition. Schumpeterian 'creative destruction', describing the process by which capitalism continually cannibalises its own monuments with successive waves of technological and procedural innovation, captures something of these apparently contradictory impulses towards both standardisation and differentiation at the level of systems of meaning. However, as this and the following studies show, other, less tangible vectors can also be seen influencing the mutations of these systems.

At this stage, though, it is perhaps sufficient to draw out the coincidental tendencies between the specific phenomenon of the emergence of knowledge systems and the much broader chameleonic shifts of capitalism, without pursuing too strong an attribution to determining causes. The following studies bring out other complicating and more fine-grained features of the contexts in which these systems emerge, and of the factors which influence their respective differentiation.

References

Ayer, A.J. 1952. *Language, Truth and Logic*. Mineola, IA: Dover Publications.

Bergman, M. 2009. 'Advantages and Myths of RDF', *http://www.mkbergman.com/483/advantages-and-myths-of-rdf/* (accessed 25 November 2009).

Berners-Lee, T. 1998. 'Relational Databases on the Semantic Web', *http://www.w3.org/DesignIssues/RDB-RDF.html* (accessed 25 November 2009).

Berners-Lee, T., J. Hendler and O. Lassila. 2001. 'The Semantic Web', *Scientific American* 284, pp. 34–43.

Brachman, R.J. and J.G. Schmolze. 1985. 'An Overview of the KL-ONE Knowledge Representation System', *Cognitive Science* 9, pp. 171–216.

Brachman, R.J., D.L. McGuinness, P.F. Patel-Schneider, L.A. Resnick and A. Borgida. 1991. 'Living with CLASSIC: When and How to Use a KL-ONE-like Language'. In *Principles of Semantic Networks: Explorations in the Representation of Knowledge*. San Mateo: Morgan Kaufmann Publishers, pp. 401–56.

Ceruzzi, P.E. 2003. *A History of Modern Computing*. Cambridge, MA: MIT Press.

Chomsky, N. 1965. *Aspects of the Theory of Syntax*. Cambridge, MA: MIT Press.

Clarke, R. 2001. 'Information Wants to be Free...', *http://www.rogerclarke.com/II/IWtbF.html* (accessed 25 November 2009).

Codd, E.F. 1970. 'A Relational Model of Data for Large Shared Data Banks', *Communications of the ACM* 13, pp. 377–87.

Colmerauer, A. and P. Roussel. 1996. 'The Birth of Prolog', In *History of Programming Languages—II*, pp. 331–67.

Date, C.J. 2007. *Logic and Databases: The Roots of Relational Theory*. Victoria, BC: Trafford Publishing.

Davis, M. 2001. *Engines of Logic: Mathematicians and the Origin of the Computer*. New York: W.W. Norton & Company.

Fensel, D., I. Horrocks, F. Van Harmelen, D. McGuinness and P.F. Patel-Schneider. 2001. 'OIL: Ontology Infrastructure to Enable the Semantic Web', *IEEE Intelligent Systems* 16, pp. 38–45.

Foucault, M. 2002. *Archaeology of Knowledge*. Abingdon: Routledge.

Gartner. 2007. 'Gartner Says Worldwide Relational Database Market Increased 14 Percent in 2006', *http://www.gartner.com/it/page.jsp?id=507466* (accessed 19 January 2010).

—. 2009. 'Market Share: Relational Database Management System Software by Operating System, Worldwide, 2008', *http://www.gartner.com/DisplayDocument?id=1018712* (accessed 19 January 2010).

Hayes, P. 2004. 'RDF Semantics'. W3C Recommendation, W3C, *http://www.w3.org/TR/rdf-mt/* (accessed 20 January 2010).

Hobsbawm, E.J. 1975. *The Age of Capital*. London: Weidenfeld & Nicolson.

IBM Corporation. 2009. 'IBM Highlights, 1885–1969', *http://www-03.ibm.com/ibm/history/documents/pdf/1885-1969.pdf* (accessed 19 January 2010).

ISO. 2009. 'ISO Store', International Organization for Standardization, *http://www.iso.org/iso/store.htm* (accessed 3 December 2009).

Katz, M.L. and C. Shapiro. 1985. 'Network Externalities, Competition, and Compatibility', *American Economic Review* 75, pp. 424–40.

Khare, R. and T. Çelik. 2006. 'Microformats: A Pragmatic Path to the Semantic Web'. In WWW 2006: Proceedings of the 15th International Conference on World Wide Web. New York: ACM, pp. 865–66.

Kolb, J. 2008. 'What Can the Semantic Web Do For Me?', *http://jasonkolb.com/weblog/2008/06/what-can-the-se.html* (accessed 25 November 2009).

Lenat, D.B. 2001. 'From 2001 to 2001: Common Sense and the Mind of HAL'. In *HAL's Legacy*. Cambridge, MA: Massachusetts Institute of Technology, pp. 193–209.

Levesque, H.J. and R.J. Brachman. 1987. 'Expressiveness and Tractability in Knowledge Representation and Reasoning', *Computational Intelligence* 3, pp. 78–93.

Lunn, B. 2008. '11 Things To Know About Semantic Web', *http://www.readwriteweb.com/archives/semantic_web_11_things_to_know.php* (accessed 25 November 2009).

Lyotard, J.F. 1984. *The Postmodern Condition: A Report on Knowledge*, G. Bennington and B. Massumi (trs), F. Jameson (foreword). Minneapolis, MN: University of Minnesota Press.

Malhotra, A. 2008. 'Progress Report from the RDB2RDF XG'. In *Proceedings of the International Semantic Web Conference 2008*.

Minsky, M. 1974. 'A Framework for Representing Knowledge', *http://dspace.mit.edu/handle/1721.1/6089* (accessed 19 January 2010).

Nardi, D. and R.J. Brachman. 2003. 'An Introduction to Description Logics'. In F. Baader et al. (eds), *The Description Logic Handbook: Theory, Implementation, and Applications*. New York: Cambridge University Press.

National Research Council. 1999. 'Funding a Revolution: Government Support for Computing Research', *http://www.nap.edu/catalog/6323.html* (accessed 19 January 2010).

Oracle. 2007. 'Oracle's 30th Anniversary', *http://www.oracle.com/oramag/profit/07-may/p27anniv.html* (accessed 18 January 2010).

Quillian, M.R. 1967. 'Word Concepts: A Theory and Simulation of Some Basic Semantic Capabilities', *Behavioral Science* 12, pp. 410–30.

Reiter, R. 1987. 'On Closed World Data Bases'. In M.L. Ginsberg (ed.), *Readings in Nonmonotonic Reasoning*. San Francisco: Morgan Kaufmann Publishers.

Shirky, C. 2003. 'The Semantic Web, Syllogism, and Worldview', *http://www.shirky.com/writings/semantic_syllogism.html* (accessed 25 November 2009).

Smith, B. 1998. 'Basic Concepts of Formal Ontology'. In *FOIS 1998: Proceedings of Formal Ontology in Information Systems*. Amsterdam: IOS Press, pp. 19–28.

Sowa, J.F. 2000. *Knowledge Representation: Logical, Philosophical, and Computational Foundations*. Cambridge, MA: MIT Press.

Turing, A.M. 1950. 'Computing Machinery and Intelligence', *Mind* 59, pp. 433–60.

US Patent and Trademark Office. 2009. 'Issue Years and Patent Numbers', *http://www.uspto.gov/web/offices/ac/ido/oeip/taf/data/issuyear.htm* (accessed 3 December 2009).

Wikipedia. 2009. 'SQL', *http://en.wikipedia.org/wiki/SQL* (accessed 13 November 2009).

Williams, H. 2008. 'The Death of the Relational Database', *http://whydoeseverythingsuck.com/2008/02/death-of-relational-database.html* (accessed 25 November 2009).

Zaino, J. 2008. 'Death of the Relational Database?', *http://www.semanticweb.com/main/death_of_the_relational_database_138938.asp* (accessed 25 November 2009).

9

Upper-level ontologies

Liam Magee

Expressions which are in no way composite signify substance, quantity, quality, relation, place, time, position, state, action, or affection. To sketch my meaning roughly, examples of substance are 'man' or 'the horse', of quantity, such terms as 'two cubits long' or 'three cubits long', of quality, such attributes as 'white', 'grammatical'. 'Double', 'half', 'greater', fall under the category of relation; 'in the market place', 'in the Lyceum', under that of place; 'yesterday', 'last year', under that of time. 'Lying', 'sitting', are terms indicating position, 'shod', 'armed', state; 'to lance', 'to cauterize', action; 'to be lanced', 'to be cauterized', affection (Aristotle 1994, p. 4).

This chapter provides a concrete case study of several overlapping ontologies with a particular field, that of 'upper-level', or foundational, ontologies. These ontologies aim to provide reliable and reusable definitions of abstract concepts and their relations: what, for instance, concepts like *space*, *time*, *particular* and *quality* mean, and how they relate. In the past ten years a number of upper-level ontologies have been developed to establish a set of concepts and definitions which could be shared by lower-level, domain ontologies. By establishing a core set of abstract concepts, use of an upper-level ontology by lower-level, domain-level ontologies is at least some guarantee of a shared metaphysical orientation. For example, several upper-level ontologies surveyed below make a fundamental distinction between 'endurants' and 'perdurants', or, in another vocabulary, 'occurrents' and 'continuants'. Roughly, this conceptual pair distinguishes things which take place *in* time—such as events—from those which exist *through* time—such as material objects. Domain-level ontologies which import an upper-level ontology making this conceptual distinction can be said to inherit the distinction too. So two such ontologies can at least be said to be commensurable insofar as their subordinate conceptual classes are distinguishable as either event-like endurants or object-like perdurants. Use of the OWL syntactic imports construct to import an ontology does not guarantee that all—or even any—of its semantic commitments are inherited in this way, but does provide a starting point for domain-level ontologies to establish points of connectivity and interoperability.

Inevitably there has been competition in the development of upper-level ontologies. Rather than answer questions of compatibility and commensurability among domain-level ontologies, then, this has served to redirect these question towards the upper-level ontologies themselves. In a scenario where two domain-level ontologies import and use different upper-level ontologies, a matching task may need to establish concordance between the concepts specified in both the domain-level and upper-level ontologies. Moreover, precisely because of the abstraction of conceptualisations specified in the upper-level ontologies, these matches become considerably more difficult to establish, especially by purely algorithmic means.

The first part of the study below surveys five ontologies developed in OWL over the past decade, to examine what sorts of evaluation of commensurability can be made about them. As well as using the framework established in Chapter 12, 'A framework for commensurability', this study also makes use of some earlier comparative work by Oberle et al. (2007). All of the ontologies were developed by academic groups, with some level of industry and government input. One side-effect of this method of development, and of the relative obscurity of upper-level ontologies, is that while there are more or less corresponding academic publications for each of the ontologies, it is comparatively difficult to understand many of the motivations, reasons and processes by which the ontologies are developed. To date, the ontologies are not widely used either, making it difficult to understand how they are used in derivative domain-level ontologies. To combat this, the second part of the study also examines two public mailing lists (the Semantic Web and Ontolog Forumlists), where many of the issues relating to upper-level ontologies are debated, and several of the ontology authors themselves also appear. A series of quantitative and qualitative techniques are used to elicit clarification of several of the distinctions developed in the review of ontologies. The study then concludes with a general assessment of the commensurability of the ontologies, and some notes on potential implications for the overall model of commensurability developed thus far.

A survey of upper-level ontologies

The following survey describes the ontologies in terms of five specific features:

- background *contextual information*
- stated or implied *methodologies*
- explicitly stated *assumptions*
- *structural* features
- key *concepts* and *categories*.

The survey covers five published upper-level ontologies which have been expressed in the Ontology Web Language (OWL), version 1.0 (Hayes, Patel-Schneider and Horrocks 2004). These ontologies are: Basic Formal Ontology (BFO) (Grenon 2003a), PROTo ONtology (PROTON) (Terziev, Kiryakov and Manov 2004), General Formal Ontology (GFO) (Herre 2009), Descriptive Ontology for Linguistic and Cognitive Engineering (DOLCE) (Masolo et al. 2002) and Standard Upper Merged Ontology (SUMO) (Niles and Pease 2001).

Background

The upper-level ontologies surveyed are developed within academic or joint academic–government initiatives, sometimes as part of larger projects. For example, the BFO ontology has been developed within the Institute for Formal Ontology and Medical Information Science (IFOMIS), utilising a grant to 'develop a formal ontology that will be applied and tested in the domain of medical and biomedical information science' (IFOMIS 2007). Similarly the DOLCE ontology has been developed as part of 'EU IST integrated project Semantic Knowledge Technologies (SEKT)', a project funded by the 'EU 6 Framework programme' (Semantic Knowledge Technologies 2007). Two of the ontologies—BFO and GFO—have been developed with specific focus on medical classification applications. The institutional nature of ontology engineering is common to domain-specific ontologies also, although several popular ontologies have been developed in the public domain, without any notable institutional involvement—the Friend of a Friend (FOAF) ontology is one such example (FOAF 2007).

All of the ontologies have been developed in Europe, with the exception of SUMO, developed in the United States. Each of the ontologies have been presented at semantic web-related conferences—suggesting that, at the time of publication, upper-level ontologies generally have been of greater interest to academic communities than to either commercial or software engineering communities. In addition, there are numerous academic publications which cite these ontologies or the papers describing them, either in the context of ontology engineering specifically, or in relation to broader ontological questions.

Many of the authors of findings actively contribute to public domain mailing lists where ontology engineering issues are discussed. For example, Barry Smith and John Sowa have been actively involved in the construction of two of the featured ontologies (BFO and SUMO respectively), and also have contributed extensively to mailing lists analysed further on in this analysis. In spite of the lack of mailing lists or other discursive sources dedicated to the surveyed ontologies themselves, there is active online debate about the sorts of concepts and distinctions that feature in upper-level ontologies generally. An analysis of these mailing lists is presented in detail below.

At the time of writing it is difficult to measure the relative impact of the ontologies quantitatively. For the purpose of the survey, two sources have been used to indicate the impact:

- results from Swoogle, a semantic web search engine (Ding et al. 2004)
- citation counts from Google Scholar in relation to the titles of key papers presenting the ontologies.

Results have been collated from Swoogle and Google Scholar searches conducted in October 2007 and October 2009. They are presented in tables 9.1 and 9.2.

Table 9.1   Swoogle results for five search terms, 2007 and 2009

Ontology	Search term*	2007	2009
BFO	'BFO'	10	135
PROTON	'Proto ontology'	5	10
GFO	'GFO'	10	38
DOLCE	'DOLCE'	108	157
SUMO	'SUMO'	92	121

* The 'search term' is the actual text searched for, in order to disambiguate ontology names or acronyms from other names. In the case of 'Proton', for example, the ontology title is also the name of a physical object (positively sub-atomic particle).

| Table 9.2 | Google Scholar results for five search terms, 2007 and 2009 |

Ontology	Search term**	2007	2009
BFO	'Spatio-temporality in Basic Formal Ontology'	11	13
PROTON	'Base upper-level ontology (BULO) Guidance'	9	19
GFO	'General Formal Ontology (GFO)'	2	12
DOLCE	'The WonderWeb Library of Foundational Ontologies'	71	168
SUMO	'Toward a standard upper ontology'	356	773

** In this case the 'search term' is the name of the main paper in which the ontology is presented. The same paper can be listed several times in results (for example, as both conference proceedings and technical reports); the citation counts have been totalled where this has occurred, and also where the citation count is greater than 1.

The comparison of the searches between Swoogle and Google Scholar show a positive correlation of 0.67 for the results in 2007, and a weaker correlation of 0.37 for those in 2009. With the exception of the large number of ontology references for BFO, DOLCE and SUMO have more ontology references and citations. This does not take into account private usage of these ontologies, but provides a useful heuristic of present adoption rates. It indicates also the increased use of upper-level ontologies over time, according to both of the metrics used, with numbers roughly doubling on average over the two-year period for all ontologies surveyed. As mentioned, the BFO ontology experienced a large surge in the number of ontology references—this abnormal jump appears to be the result of widespread references from newly developed biological ontologies housed by the OBO Foundry, which the BFO was designed to support (Grenon 2003a).

It is also worth noting that there have several prominent efforts at upper-level ontologies that predate the emergence of OWL as a standard for modelling ontologies:

- Cyc
- WordNet
- Standard Upper Ontology (SUO).

These are expressed in different formalisms, and so are not amenable to algorithmic comparison with those expressed in OWL. The SUMO ontology is explicitly indebted to the SUO ontology (Niles and Pease 2001), and most of the ontologies described have some level of mapping to WordNet, a publicly available online dictionary, which links words based on semantic relations (Miller 1995). Cyc is an older and well-established representation of upper-level and domain-level knowledge (Lenat 1995), developed privately by Cycorp. It is frequently cited in the literature on upper-level ontologies (and knowledge representation), but because of its proprietary nature and different formal structure it is not available for direct comparison.

Finally, as discussed at further length in the section 'Assumptions', below, several of the upper-level ontologies have been developed with awareness of competing ontologies, and so reference distinctions between them explicitly. For instance, the GFO ontology is compared with SUMO and DOLCE by its authors (Herre 2009); the BFO ontology is compared with DOLCE (Grenon 2003a); the PROTON ontology references WordNet and Cyc (Terziev, Kiryakov and Manov 2004); and the SUMO ontology, as mentioned, is itself compiled from SUO and a range of other sources:

> The SUMO was created by merging publicly available ontological content into a single, comprehensive, and cohesive structure. This content included the ontologies available on the Ontolingua server, John Sowa's upper level ontology, the ontologies developed by ITBM-CNR, and various mereotopological theories, among other sources (Niles and Pease 2001).

There has also been a certain amount of *post facto* literature comparing DOLCE and SUMO in particular, the innovatively entitled 'DOLCE ergo SUMO' (Oberle et al. 2007) and 'OntoMap' (Kiryakov, Simov and Dimitrov 2001) being two such examples. This activity suggests that ontology engineering is a highly dynamic social process, and at the present time, still far from finding agreement for the abstract concepts upper-level ontologies describe. The engagement with the mailing lists— the informal 'chatter' that sits behind the formal austerity of ontologies—explores this dynamic and dialogical process further.

Methodologies

The methodologies outlined in the literature surrounding upper-level ontologies vary from highly explicit (SUMO) to implicit (PROTON). Table 9.3 provides an overview of the methodological approach

Table 9.3	Ontology methodologies	
Ontology	Methodology	Degree of formality
BFO	Draws on an explicit account of philosophical ontology (BFO 2007; Smith 2004)	Moderate
DOLCE	Unknown (seems to rely on prior research)	Moderate
GFO	Draws on abstract conceptualisations presented in philosophical literature (Brentano, Husserl, Hartmann, Ingarden, Johansson, Searle)	Moderate
PROTON	Designed as a 'light-weight' ontology, modeled on 'common sense' (Terziev, Kiryakov and Manov 2004)	Low
SUMO	Identifies a range of prior ontologies, including SUO; ensures each identified ontology is syntactically compatible; performs a manual semantic merging of the ontologies	High

adopted—as best as can be inferred if not otherwise stated—and the degree of formality of process of ontology construction.

The variance in methodology (in terms of the adopted approach itself, and the degree of explicitness *about* the approach) is one indicator about the degree of commensurability between upper-level ontologies. How concepts are selected and arranged can divulge further assumptions not explicit in the conceptualisation. However, even in the case of the SUMO ontology, little is stated about how one concept was chosen over another, what leads to a particular arrangement of concepts, beyond an acknowledgement of certain existential assumptions, and what degree of detail is suitable. Arguably the criterion of methodology is harder to apply to upper-level ontologies especially, given the abstractions of the concepts concerned. Subsequent discussion returns to this variance, since it has a bearing on what can be said about the commensurability of these ontologies.

Assumptions

None of the upper-level ontologies surveyed lay great pretensions towards definitiveness; the authors of DOLCE for instance state: 'we do *not* intend DOLCE as a candidate for a "universal" standard ontology' (Masolo et al. 2002). In the literature showcasing the ontologies, their designers are overtly aware of the assumptions which characterise their construction (Masolo et al. 2002). Nevertheless there are clear differences in these assumptions, in kind and degree. The following section examines what assumptions are employed, and how they compare.

Basic Formal Ontology (BFO)

The Basic Formal Ontology (BFO) is by far the most explicit about the assumptions the authors employ in its design. The three papers outlining the BFO are presented alongside six other papers authored or co-authored by Smith, heavily directed towards justification of a philosophical orientation of 'realist perspectivalism' (BFO 2007; Smith 2004). This is characterised by 'the view that any given domain of reality can be viewed from a number of different ontological perspectives, all of which can have equal claim to veridicality' (Smith and Grenon 2004). Realist perspectivalism avoids two key fallacies of ontology engineering, in Smith's views: on the one hand, those inherited from 'idealist, skeptical, or constructionist philosophy', which 'appear commonly in the wider world under the guise of postmodernism or cultural relativism' (Smith 2004); and on the other, those incurred through too enthusiastic an adherence to predicate logic and the stark ontology of its formalism—a brand of philosophy described by Smith as 'fantology' (Smith 2005). This latter kind of fallacy has, for Smith, been perpetuated by logicians since Frege:

> But [Frege's] signal achievement was for a long time marred by its association with an overestimation of the power of a relatively simplistic type of logico-linguistic analysis to resolve ontological problems. Exposing some of the effects of this overestimation should allow us to understand the development of analytical philosophy in a new way, and to bring to light aspects of this development which are normally hidden (Smith 2005).

Smith's alternative, which forms the guiding principle of the BFO's construction, is admit perspectivalism only in *veridical form*, that is, only insofar as any given perspective is corroborated by natural science:

> But perspectivalism is constrained by realism: thus it does not amount to the thesis that just any view of reality is legitimate. To establish which views are legitimate we must weigh them against

their ability to survive critical tests when confronted with reality, for example via scientific experiments (Smith and Grenon 2004).

In this paper, the realist perspectivalist account is augmented with *fallibilist* and *adequetist* qualifiers. Smith names philosophical precursors to this account are Aristotle and Husserl—though, with similarities to the GFO assumptions discussed later, Husserl is mediated by Ingarden's *realist* phenomenology.

A pivotal difference between the approach promulgated by Smith and Grenon in their introductory paper to the BFO, and the unified reductivist ontology they critique, concerns the treatment of *time*, or in the more particular words of the authors, different 'Temporal Modes of Being' (Smith and Grenon 2004). Smith and Grenon devote considerable attention to the distinction between 3D and 4D perspectives (which they translate into the more convenient monikers 'SNAP' and 'SPAN'. According to the perspectivalist account, a generalised account must be capable of reflecting *both* perspectives (otherwise it falls on the side of a reductivist account, privileging a single perspective). The 3D/SNAP perspective treats entities in the world as *continuant* or *endurant* (entities which exist *wholly* at some point in time). The 4D/SPAN perspective treats entities as *occurrent* or *perdurant* (entities which exist only *in part* at any point in time). Each perspective is assumed to be valid and veridical, that is, verifiable via empirical evidence. Nevertheless 'they are incompatible' (Smith and Grenon 2004)—or in the terms familiar to this study, incommensurable. The authors deal with this troubling incompatibility by developing *two* ontologies, side by side, within the same overriding ontological scaffolding. The following quote highlights the role of this key assumption:

> In order to do justice to the entities of each type, we need to have two distinct ontologies. The ontology adequate for 3-D entities is analogous to a snapshot of the world, it accounts for the entities as they are now. That adequate for 4-D entities is more analogous to a videoscopic view taken upon reality. Basic Formal Ontology (BFO) is the complete and adequate ontology of reality which is divided into the two aforementioned ontologies. More precisely, there is, on the one hand, a succession of ontologies for substances and like 3-D objects, namely, a series of snapshot ontologies of the world at any given instant of time (Smith and Grenon 2004).

This distinction is found in several of the other ontologies, and is further pursued in the analysis below.

Descriptive Ontology for Linguistic and Cognitive Engineering (DOLCE)

The Descriptive Ontology for Linguistic and Cognitive Engineering (DOLCE) ontology devotes several of its 38 pages of its accompanying introductory paper to discussing assumptions. Like the PROTON ontology, it takes what might be termed a 'constructivist' stance, in which categories are chosen for their proximation to 'cognitive artifacts ultimately depending on human perception, cultural imprints and social conventions (a sort of "cognitive" metaphysics)' (Masolo et al. 2002). Moreover the authors of DOLCE confess their ontology is not intended 'as a candidate for a "universal" standard ontology', but rather 'has a clear *cognitive bias*, in the sense that it aims at capturing the ontological categories underlying natural language and human commonsense [sic]' (Masolo et al. 2002). The philosophical antecedents of their approach are motivated in part by the work of Searle, and his notion of 'deep background' (Searle 1983).

The authors also make use of the distinction between *endurant* (or *continuant*) and *perdurant* (or *occurrent*), as well as several other 'classical' concepts, which have been part of philosophical ontology since Aristotle's *Categories* (Aristotle 1994). Hence, categories like 'universal', 'particular', 'physical', 'abstract', 'qualities', 'time' and 'space' can be located within the upper taxonomic echelons in the ontology (Masolo et al. 2002).

General Formal Ontology (GFO)

The General Formal Ontology (GFO) is perhaps the easiest of the ontologies to examine in terms of assumptions, and they are discussed in section 2.1 of the GFO presentation. The authors initially take a 'realist position in philosophy', aware that 'there is the need to clarify more precisely the term "realism"' (Herre 2009). However, the actual *categories* employed, presented in the following section (2.1.1), 'are conceived in such a way that we are not forced to commit ourselves to realism, conceptualism, or nominalism' (Herre 2009). This is yet further complicated by the brief discussion in section 2.1.2, entitled 'Existence and Modes of Being'. It is worth quoting this section in full:

> In [32] a classification of modes of existence is discussed that is useful for a deeper understanding of entities of several kinds. According to [32] there are—roughly—the following modes of being: absolute, ideal, real, and intentional entities. This classification can be to some extent related to Gracia's approach and to the levels of reality in the

spirit of Nicolai Hartmann [29]. But, the theory of Roman Ingarden is not sufficiently elaborated compared with Hartmann's large ontological system. For Ingarden there is the (open) problem, whether material things are real spatio-temporal entities or intentional entities in the sense of the later Husserl. We hold that there is no real opposition between the realistic attitude of Ingarden and the position of the later Husserl, who considers the material things as intentional entities being constructed by a transcendental self. Both views provide valuable insights in the modes of being that can be useful for conceptual modelling purposes (Herre 2009; reference [32] in the text refers to Roman Ingarden. *Der Streit um die Existenz der Welt I (Existentialontologie)*. Tübingen: Max Niemeyer, 1964; reference [29] refers to Nicolai Hartmann. *Der Aufbau der realen Welt*. Walter de Gruyter and Co, 1964).

In contrast with other forms of realism related below, and with the exception of the BFO, this is a realism unusually highly inflected by the phenomenological tradition, established by Husserl, Ingarden, Hartmann and others.

PROTON (PROTo ONtology)

Opposed to the BFO and GFO, the PROTON (formerly 'BULO') ontology authors employ what may best be described as relativist, constructivist and pragmatist assumptions about the world they set out to model. They happily confess, 'Its common-sense basis is, of course, quite an arbitrary claim to deal with' (Terziev, Kiryakov and Manov 2004). Moreover 'the diversity of world knowledge... actually blur[s] the horizon of hope from a purely philosophical point of view if one wants an ontology that is... "compliant" with the common-sense of "everybody"' (Terziev, Kiryakov and Manov 2004). The authors are somewhat vague on the two pages on which they discuss the philosophical considerations of what constitutes the 'common-sense basis' of the ontology. The discussion presented concerns less the question of assumptions in the sense invoked here (what motivates the categories and distinctions of the ontology) than what might be termed a quasi-philosophical discourse on 'logicalized' ontology, existence, essence, meaning and cognition. For example, the authors claim 'the end users of PROTON are also humans and therefore it is all about everyone's personal cognition and perception of reality' (Terziev, Kiryakov and Manov 2004). In fact, as discussed below, the formalisation of the ontology presented in the subsequent 50 or so pages is anything but 'arbitrary'. The authors' conclusion suggests the aim is indeed to describe the 'very basic spatial, temporal, material ("physical"), and abstract concepts of world knowledge, which for the most part are independent of a particular problem or domain' (Terziev, Kiryakov and Manov 2004). There is little else in the text that suggests what sorts of principles or assumptions might guide the selection of such 'concepts'.

Suggested Upper Merged Ontology (SUMO)

The SUMO ontology is one of the two more widely used upper-level ontologies, and yet it is presented with minimal discussion of its assumptions. This is perhaps largely because of the syncretic nature of the ontologies; as the authors characterise its development, 'This content included the ontologies available on the Ontolingua server, John Sowa's upper level ontology, the ontologies developed by ITBM-CNR, and various mereotopological theories, among other sources' (Niles and Pease 2001). The hybridisation of other ontologies suggests that SUMO must in some sense inherit the assumptions of its sources. This becomes a question of methodology, which the authors discuss at some length: 'we were faced with the much more difficult task of the "semantic merge"—combining all of the various ontologies into a single, consistent, and comprehensive framework' (Niles and Pease 2001). The difficulties of reconciling different assumptions are clear from a later section of the paper—again worth citing at length, since it highlights a key distinction, which is discussed further below:

> Under the concept of 'Physical', we have the disjoint concepts of 'Object' and 'Process'. The existence and nature of the distinction between these two notions was the subject of much heated debate on the SUO mailing list. According to those who adopt a 3D orientation (or 'endurantists', as they are sometimes called), there is a basic, categorial distinction between objects and processes. According to those who adopt a 4D orientation (the 'perdurantists'), on the other hand, there is no such distinction. The 3D orientation posits that objects, unlike processes, are completely present at any moment of their existence, while a 4D orientation regards everything as a space-time worm (or a slice of such a worm). On the latter view, paradigmatic processes and objects are merely opposite ends of a continuum of spatio-temporal phenomena. The current version of the SUMO embodies a 3D orientation by making 'Object' and 'Process' disjoint siblings of the parent node 'Physical' (Niles and Pease 2001).

This passage echoes in almost identical terms Kuhn's concept of 'paradigms', describing the difficulties of assimilating two fundamentally distinct and incompatible 'orientations' towards the world. Unlike the BFO, SUMO's authors assume paradigmatic incommensurability presents even co-location of 3D and 4D perspectives.

Smart Web Integrated Ontology (SWIntO)— taxonomising ontological assumptions

One effort to make sense of the medley of assumptions made by upper-level or foundational ontologies is represented by the work of Oberle et al. As part of a broader effort to develop a 'demonstrator system which combines intelligent multimodal and mobile user interface technology with question-answering functionalities over both the open internet and specific thematic domains at the same time' (Oberle et al. 2007), the authors discuss their efforts to construct a hybrid foundational ontology as the basis for subsequent domain-level ontologies. As part of this work, they consider 'ontological choices' or 'meta-criteria', against which they rate many of the ontologies canvassed here. The 'choices' consist of the following distinctions:

- *Descriptive vs. revisionary*—Descriptive aims to capture intuitionist, 'common-sense' categories; revisionary aims to describe the 'intrinsic nature of the world' (Oberle et al. 2007).

- *Multiplicative vs. reductionist*—Multiplicative allows for the possibility of multiple, potentially competing ontological points of view; reductionist aims to reduce such perspectives to a unifying, single point of view.

- *Possibilism vs. actualism*—Possibilism allows for possible as well as actual entities (and typically requires some form of modal logical distinction between necessity and possibility); actualism admits only actual entities.

- *Endurantism vs. perdurantism*—As previously discussed, endurantism considers entities as wholly 'in time'; perdurantism considers entities as potentially containing temporal parts (and are therefore not 'in time', but persist 'through time').

Table 9.4 presents the assessment of Oberle et al. (2007) on foundational ontologies and their ontological choices. It is redacted here to eliminate other candidate ontologies not surveyed here, OpenCyc and OCHRE, neither of which is represented in OWL.

Table 9.4	Foundational ontologies and their ontological choices as assessed by Oberle et al. (2007)*

Requirement or alternative	BFO	DOLCE	SUMO
Descriptive	No	Yes	Yes
Multiplicative	No**	Yes	Yes
Actualism	Yes	No	Unclear
4D	Yes	Yes	Yes

* All figures have been derived by using the OWLAPI library (Horridge, Bechhofer and Noppens 2007) and some custom scripts. These ontologies are split across a series of physical files, and figures have been collated from all of the files.
** Given the discussion above, it might be argued that the BFO is similarly multiplicative, although it does indeed aim to be 'revisionary' in the sense used here.

The authors proceed to develop a hybridised upper-level ontology based on DOLCE and SUMO, SmartSUMO (Oberle et al. 2007), using a similar grafting method to that described by the authors of SUMO itself. I return briefly to this development in the final section below.

Extending the taxonomy

Based on the brief review above, several further salient dimensions can be added to the model for comparison:

- *Derived vs. original composition*—SUMO is explicitly derived from several existing ontological sources; the other ontologies appear to be constructed originally, with reference to other systems.

- *Realist vs. constructivist attitude*—SUMO and DOLCE have some constructs for representing a subjective point of view within the ontology itself, suggesting they support a 'constructivist' or nominalist standpoint. BFO, by comparison, is stridently realist (though with complications). The GFO leans strongly towards realism also, while the PROTON ontology, as best can be divined, also adopts a more constructivist attitude.

- *'Home-grown' vs. imported philosophy*—DOLCE explicitly acknowledges the work of John Searle and others as guiding the development of the ontology, and in a general sense can be said to use an 'imported' philosophy. The authors of the BFO, at the other extreme, spend considerable time in various publications justifying a 'home-grown' take on various philosophical issues. The other ontologies sit somewhere in between these two extremes.

Structural features

The most evident structural difference between the ontologies is in size. Table 9.5 compares the number of classes, properties and individuals contained in each of the ontologies.

As indicated, the PROTON and DOLCE ontologies have been constructed as a series of smaller ontologies, which are linked together via the `imports` construct. In contrast, the other ontologies are contained within single files.

The PROTON ontology has been separated into three separate ontologies: system, top and upper. The upper imports the top ontology, which in turn imports the system ontology. The DOLCE ontology contains eight separate subsidiary and interconnected ontologies, yielding a more complex structure:

- `SpatialRelations`

- `TemporalRelations`

- `ExtendedDnS`

- `ModalDescriptions`

- `FunctionalParticipation`

- `InformationObjects`

- `SocialUnits`

- `Plans`

To use the SocialUnits ontology, for example, means to import the classes and properties from `InformationObjects`, `ExtendedDnS`, `TemporalRelations`, `SpatialRelations` and `DOLCE-Lite` ontologies.

Table 9.5 Comparison of the number of classes, properties, concepts and ratios within ontologies

Ontology	Classes	Properties	Concepts	Ratio
BFO	36	0	36	36.00
DOLCE	159	280	439	0.57
GFO	78	69	147	1.11
PROTON	266	113	379	2.33
SUMO	630	236	866	2.66

It is also noticeable that the ontologies differ in the degree that they use classes over properties, expressed in the ratio figures above. In the case of DOLCE in particular, this suggests what might be termed a 'functional' or 'attributive' approach to the organisation of entities, since the majority of its conceptual constructs are properties rather than classes. This point is elaborated further in the discussion of categories below.

Categories

The preceding sections suggest the five upper-level ontologies employ somewhat different methods, assumptions and design strategies. How, then, do they compare in actual categorial or conceptual content? The following sub-section aims to compare only the most abstract, top-level concepts described in the ontologies. Diagrams of the top three or four graph layers (depending on visual clarity) of the five ontologies were generated using Protégé (Gennari et al. 2003) and the OWLViz plug-in (Horridge 2005)—these are shown in the appendix to this chapter. A subset of these graphs is presented for each of the ontologies below, showing the salient classes used in the following discussion.

BFO

```
Entity
  - Continuant
  - IndependentContinuant
  - DependentContinuant
  - SpatialRegion
  - Occurrent
  - ProcessualEntity
  - SpatiotemporalEntity
  - TemporalRegion
```

DOLCE

```
particular
  - spatio-temporal-particular
  - endurant
```

- quality

- physical-realisation

- perdurant

- abstract

- region

- proposition

- set

GFO

Entity

- Item

- Individual

—— Independent

—— Dependent

—— Abstract

—— Concrete

—— Discrete

—— Continuous

- Category

- Set

PROTON

Entity

- Object

- Statement

- Location

- Service

- Agent

- Product

- Abstract

- Language

- Topic

- Number

- GeneralTerm

- ContactInformation

- Happening

- TimeInterval

- Event

- Situation

SUMO

Entity

- Physical

- Process

- Object

- Abstract

- SetOrClass

- Quantity

- Attribute

- Relation

- Proposition

Even this schematic outline shows some initial points of similarity and difference between the five ontologies. Each starts with a common root concept, Entity, or its near-cognate: the DOLCE ontology has a root concept of particular, which it defines as 'entities which have no instances' (Masolo et al. 2002), distinguished from universals, which do not adhere to this constraint. The following conceptual distinctions, or near synonyms of them, are also common to at least three of the ontologies:

- *Spatial–Temporal*
- *Abstract–Concrete*
- *Collective–Individual*
- *Continuant–Occurrent* (or, alternatively, *Endurant–Perdurant*)
- *Independent–Dependent*
- *Conceptual–Physical.*

These distinctions can be mapped to specific concepts in each of the five ontologies; these are depicted in screen shots in the appendix to this chapter.

This comparison demonstrates that there is a high degree of overlap in the use of concepts across the ontology set and, equally, that these concepts are differently configured, so that establishing direct concordances between apparently synonymous concepts is risky. The interpretation of the above distinctions, when applied to particular ontologies, carry considerable ambiguity. For example, the *Conceptual–Physical* distinction aligns Concept (GFO), [GeneralTerm–Topic] (PROTON) and Proposition (SUMO, DOLCE) as all conceptual entities—clearly, however, they are not all synonymous terms. More tenuously, the meaning of *Dependent* might appear to be preserved by the [Relation–Attribute–Quantity] (SUMO) and quality (DOLCE) classes, since these have equivalently named terms in other ontologies which are sub-classes of kinds of *Dependent* entities: the DependentContinuant and Dependent classes of BFO and GFO ontologies respectively. The *Continuant–Occurrent* distinction is also difficult to interpret consistently across the ontologies. Broadly, continuant entities are those which 'are wholly present (all their parts are present) at any time at which they exist' while occurrent entities are those 'that extend in time and are only partially present for any time at which they exist because some of their temporal parts may be not present' (Bazzanella, Stoermer and Bouquet 2008). The GFO ontology synonym for this distinction, the *Continuous–Discrete* pair, nevertheless contains a mixture of both object-like and process-like classes within each of the Continuous and Discrete super classes—and the ontology also contains a sibling Presential class, which appears a more natural synonym for *Continuant*. The BFO ontology subsumes TemporalRegion under Occurrent and SpatialRegion under Continuant classes, but also adds SpatiotemporalRegion as a subclass of Occurrent, with the following extended note:

An instance of the spatiotemporal region [span:SpatiotemporalRegion] is a part of spacetime. All parts of spacetime are spatiotemporal region [span:SpatiotemporalRegion] entities and only spatiotemporal region [span:SpatiotemporalRegion] entities are parts of spacetime. In particular, neither spatial region [snap:SpatialRegion] entities nor temporal region [span:TemporalRegion] entities are in BFO parts of spacetime. Spacetime is the entire extent of the spatiotemporal universe, a designated individual, which is thus itself a spatiotemporal region [span:SpatiotemporalRegion]. Spacetime is among occurrents the analogous of space among continuant [snap:Continuant] entities (Grenon 2003a).

This confirms the point made earlier: two ontological perspectives are supported by the BFO—one sharply distinguishing spatial and temporal, continuant and occurrent entities, the other collapsing within a general occurrent, spatio-temporal conceptual apparatus. Habituation of two fundamental perspectives within the one ontological housing creates a point of dissonance with other ontologies which maintain a single viewpoint, preserving 'continuant' and 'occurrent' entities as primordially distinct and mutually disjoint. The SUMO and DOLCE ontologies are largely consistent in maintaining this distinction, while the PROTON ontology seems idiosyncratically to treat JobPosition—arguably a continuous entity—as a kind of Happening, while Service (in the sense of a service rendered) is a kind of Object.

The difficulty of drawing synonymous relations across ontologies is more notable still in a comparison of the summative effect of multiple conceptual distinctions. For example, while each of the ontologies has classes to represent the *Spatial–Temporal* and *Continuant–Occurrent* conceptual pairs, *how* these distinctions are organised differs markedly. The BFO ontology makes a *primary* distinction between Continuant and Occurrent classes. The distinction between spatial and temporal entities is then a subordinate one—more formally, the pair [SpatialRegion/TemporalRegion] is subordinate to the pair [Continuant/Occurrent]. The GFO ontology treats these distinctions as *equivalent*—both [Discrete/Continuous] and [Space_time/Space and Space_time/Time] class pairs are subsumed by the Entity/Item/Individual class. The PROTON ontology follows the BFO organisation: the pair [Object/Location and Happening/TimeInterval] is subordinate to the [Object/Happening] pair. Meanwhile, the SUMO ontology has an orthogonal relation between the equivalent pairs: while Object/Region is clearly subordinate to `Object`, the nearest temporal synonym, `TimeMeasure`, is treated as a kind of `Quantity`, not a subordinate of `Process`—the nearest SUMO synonym to the `Occurrent` concept used by the BFO. The DOLCE ontology pairs both sets of conceptual classes: the *Continuant–Occurrent* distinction is matched by the near-synonymous pair [`endurant/perdurant`], while the *Spatial–Temporal* distinction is matched by the [`space-region/temporal-region`] pair of classes. However, the latter pair is subordinate to a higher level class, `abstract`, which is distinguished from the *spatio-temporal-particular* class. Instances of the `spatio-temporal-particular` class (whether members of an `endurant`, `perdurant`, or of another class) are bound to space or time regions via properties, rather than through direct class subsumption relations. This suggests conversion between DOLCE and other ontologies would need to interpret and transform other kinds of relations into class subsumption ones.

Similar complexities can be found in other conceptual overlays. The BFO ontology has no class pair corresponding to the *Abstract–Concrete* distinction, yet synonymous class pairs are primary distinctions for the PROTON, SUMO and DOLCE ontologies (and a more subordinate distinction for the GFO ontology). Only one of the ontologies, DOLCE, reinforces this conception distinction with a logical constraint: the `abstract` class is declared logically disjoint from `endurant`, `perdurant` and `quality` subclasses of the `spatio-temporal-particular` class, and further annotates the `abstract` class: 'The main characteristic of abstract entities is that they do not have spatial nor temporal qualities, and they are not qualities themselves' (Gangemi 2006).

The five ontologies also have clear conceptual areas of what might be termed 'perspectival specialisation'—areas in which they move beyond upper-level abstractions towards domain-level specificity. The BFO ontology, with 36 classes and no properties, contains only abstract physical classes, roughly representative of the distinctions introduced above (*Continuant–Occurrent*, *Dependent–Independent*, *Collective–Individual*). The emphasis on supporting the mutually exclusive three- and four-dimensional perspectives is the main unusual feature of its categorial structure—although this feature is also supported by DOLCE and SUMO ontologies within a single perspectival view. The GFO ontology uses a number of specialised terms further down the class hierarchy which indicate a scientific or technical orientation: `Chronoid` ('Every chronoid has exactly two extremal and infinitely many inner time boundaries which are equivalently called time-points'), `Topoid` ('connected compacted regions of space'), Configuroid ('integrated wholes made up of material structure processes and property processes') and Situoid ('processes whose boundaries are situations and which satisfy certain principles of coherence, comprehensibility, and continuity') are examples (Herre 2009). The PROTON ontology contains Product, Service, Document, JobPosition and ContactInformation, which relate more specifically to organisational or commercial fields (Terziev, Kiryakov and Manov 2004). Moreover PROTON makes a first-order distinction between Entity, LexicalResource and EntitySource, suggesting a primary demarcation between entities in the world, and their discursive description and provenance.

The SUMO ontology explicitly incorporates the intentional or constitutive standpoint of an agent—a large number of agent actions, including *Guiding*, *Classifying*, *Listening*, *Looking* and *Meeting*, are subsumed within an *IntentionalProcess* class. These total 114 classes, or 20 per cent of the number of classes in the ontology as a whole, which is suggestive of an internalist or subjectively-oriented perspective towards ontological entities. Finally, the DOLCE ontology largely mirrors the kinds of distinctions maintained by SUMO, but models these as object properties between classes, rather than as class inheritance. Thus it sees entities as bound by mereological and functional, rather than by subsumption relations. This formalist perspective is mirrored by object property names such as parameterises, postconditions, preconditions, deputes and interprets. The SUMO ontology has a similarly large number of object properties, but uses more colloquial and lay terms such as causes, employs, larger and uses.

Table 9.6 summarises these underlying differences in orientation. These qualitative distinctions could be used to further form the basis of a set of quantitative valuations against the dimensions introduced in the commensurability framework chapter, as well as refinement of what those dimensions, in the case of the five upper-level ontologies, should be; at this stage, it is enough to demonstrate the utility of the kind of interpretative analysis employed here for teasing out what some of the salient distinctions between the ontologies are. The next section examines the sociological context in which these distinctions are voiced and debated, through an online content analysis of two mailing lists. This analysis also brings forward further suggestive extrinsic or social distinctions which mark these ontologies.

| Table 9.6 | Summary of ontology orientation |

Ontology	Orientation
BFO	Minimalist; supports mutually exclusive 3D/4D physical perspectives; continuant/occurrent distinction fundamental; scientific naturalist epistemology
DOLCE	Constructivist; scientific; theoretical; functional/attributive
GFO	Naturalist epistemology; uses scientific over 'folk' terms
PROTON	Focus on commercial/industrial terms; pragmatic
SUMO	Intentional; constructivist epistemology; pragmatic

A dialogical account of ontology engineering

> I think we're arguing about the definitions of our terms, here. My use of the term 'Truth' causes cognitive dissonance for you.

> Well, you haven't actually defined it: but I think I get your drift. It doesn't cause me cognitive dissonance (if it did, I might be more inclined to agree with it): I just think its mistaken (Ontolog Forum 2010, message 188).

The analysis of the five ontologies suggests that to some degree ontology development takes place in isolated engineering teams, drawing on disparate sources of inspiration, with different goals and perhaps some level of collegial overlap. In practice, this picture is distorted by the presence of public social media through which researchers openly debate many aspects of ontology design. These represent a fascinating insight of how debate and dialogue around ontologies take place.

The following sections present a brief analysis of some of the discussion on these lists in relation to upper-level ontologies. The Semantic Web Interest Group and Ontolog Forum mailing lists (hereafter referred to as Semantic Web Interest Group and Ontolog Forum) are reviewed in detail, since these include messages from a number of researchers who have worked on the ontologies listed above, or who contribute to the broader academic discussion around formal ontologies. Both lists are publicly available, and anyone can request subscription. In the case of the Semantic Web Interest Group, subscription is automatic (via *http://www.w3.org/Mail/Request*); Ontolog Forum requires an email request be sent to the forum convenor (via *http://ontolog.cim3.net/cgi-bin/wiki.pl?WikiHomePage\#nid1J*). The two lists have different objectives, and consequently different kinds of communities. The Semantic Web Interest Group covers all topics related to the semantic web, usually with a technological rather than philosophical focus. Subjects include discussion of semantic web architecture, terminology, application and specific ontologies, as well as frequent conference announcements and job advertisements. Ontolog Forum, by comparison, is concentrated on the construction of upper-level ontologies, with considerable reference to technological and philosophical aspects of this task. Both lists are attended by prominent contributors to academic and practical ontology engineering, and comprise what might be termed 'expert communities of practice' in these fields.

Analysis of mailing lists

To analyse the lists, a small software script was developed to harvest the contents of emails from their publicly available archives (Ontolog Forum 2010; W3C 2010). The script retrieved posts since their inception (March 2000 for the Semantic Web Interest Group and May 2002 for Ontolog Forum) until 18 May 2009. Mailing list archives typically employ the following structure:

- main index page, containing the months the list has been running, with links to posts listed by dates or by thread (subject)
- date pages, containing a list of posts for the month, organised by day
- thread pages, containing a list of posts for the month, organised by thread (subject)
- individual posts, containing the contents of a single message, including subject, date, author and message contents.

The script exploits this common structure (at least for the two archives in question) and, starting with the index page, follows links to the date and message pages automatically. On each of these pages it parses the contents for common elements, such as the date, author, subject and contents of the message. Importantly, message 'threads' retain the same subject heading for the most part, permitting analysis of common topics and keywords. The script then captures unique authors, subjects, messages and individual words in a database system. Care has been taken to ensure accuracy in the results; however, for various reasons, it is difficult to gain precision with subject, author and word counts—continuous subjects can be arbitrarily varied by authors or their mail clients; authors can post from different mail accounts, with different names or variants; word morphographic variants, aside from plurals, can be difficult to correlate automatically; email thread subject headings can be renamed by correspondents, to follow new 'threads' of conversation; and mailing lists can allow for the possibility of 'spoofing', faking email contents, due to lack of rigorous authentication methods. The last concern, given the specialised nature of these lists, is a relatively low risk in these particular cases.

Quantitative analysis

Table 9.7 summarises the number of messages received on the Semantic Web Interest Group and Ontolog Forum between 2000 and 2009. These figures show that there has been a rising interest in the forums in recent years—the Semantic Web list grew rapidly in 2005, the Ontolog Forum grew in 2007. The total number of messages is comparable, with indications in 2009 that Ontolog Forum experienced roughly twice the amount of activity.

A count of authors and subjects suggests that Ontolog Forum has a smaller and more focused community than the Semantic Web Interest Group (Table 9.8). These numbers indicate that each author contributes on average approximately 23 messages across the entire period surveyed (2000 through to May 2009), and each subject receives four messages on

Table 9.7 Messages received on the Semantic Web Interest Group and Ontolog Forum, 2000 to May 2009 (survey conducted on 19 May 2009)

Year	Semantic Web	Ontolog Forum
2000	26	N/A
2001	14	N/A
2002	11	220
2003	29	589
2004	52	577
2005	1,705	517
2006	2,072	619
2007	2,743	3,708
2008	2,962	2,548
2009 (to 18 May)	965	1,891
Total	10,579	10,669

Table 9.8	Author and subject counts on the Semantic Web Interest Group and Ontolog Forum, 2000 to May 2009

	Semantic Web	Ontolog Forum
Total messages	10,579	10,699
Total authors	1,361	461
Total subjects	4,487	2,649
Messages per author	7.77	23.12
Messages per subject	2.36	4.04

Ontolog Forum, compared with approximately eight and two messages respectively received on the Semantic Web list. This is confirmed by an analysis of the top 20 authors and subjects, which show higher message-to-author and message-to-subject ratios for Ontolog Forum.

Although the five ontologies and two comparative studies (OntoMap and SWIntO) analysed above are products of private development, and consequently do not have mailing lists or other public fora, several of the contributing authors featured in the lists surveyed. Table 9.9 shows each of the contributors featuring in the lists, along with the number of messages posted.

Table 9.9	Joint contributors to the ontologies surveyed, and the Semantic Web Interest Group and Ontolog Forum

Author	Ontology	Semantic Web	Ontolog Forum
Pierre Grenon	BFO	4	0
Barry Smith	BFO	2	68
Adam Pease	SUMO	0	172
Stefano Borgo	DOLCE	0	3
Aldo Gangemi	DOLCE	13	1
Nicola Guarino	DOLCE	0	1
Alessandro Oltramari	DOLCE	78	0
Marin Dimitrov	OntoMap	1	0
Philipp Cimiano	SWIntO	3	0
Pascal Hitzler	SWIntO	32	0
Daniel Oberle	SWIntO	1	0
Michael Sintek	SWIntO	2	0

These figures can be used as basic heuristics for some of the dimensions introduced for classifying the ontologies above. While over-extrapolation from these figures can be misleading—for instance, other relevant mailing lists are not included here, and there is no means of reviewing offline discussions—based on the characterisation of the lists themselves, it is possible to make several inferences:

- A contributor to each of the BFO and SUMO ontologies is also actively involved in Ontolog Forum, suggesting that these ontologies have a stronger philosophical orientation.

- DOLCE contributors were involved in both lists, although only to a minimal degree on Ontolog Forum, suggesting that DOLCE has a stronger technical orientation.

- No contributor to the GFO or PROTON ontologies participated in either of the lists, suggesting that authors of these ontologies are less active in the broader ontology community, and possibly that the ontologies themselves experience lower rates of adoption.

- Contributors to OntoMap and SWIntO comparisons had some involvement in the Semantic Web Interest Group rather than Ontolog Forum, suggesting that ontological comparison, even of upper-level ontologies, is regarded as more of a technical than abstract philosophical task.

These tentative observations are corroborated by a word frequency analysis of the ontology terms themselves. Fortuitously, each of the ontologies has an acronym that is unusual enough to make collision with quotidian usage quite unlikely. Table 9.10 shows the number of times each ontology is mentioned on the Semantic Web Interest Group and Ontolog Forum, along with their frequency relative to the most commonly cited ontology. Discussion on Ontolog Forum is predictably far more prolific, as it is dedicated to the establishment of foundational or upper-level ontologies. All of the ontologies are mentioned more often in absolute terms on Ontolog Forum, with SUMO, DOLCE and BFO cited more often by a factor of ten or more. Notwithstanding this absolute difference, in relative terms DOLCE is mentioned twice as often on the Semantic Web Interest Group list as SUMO, while SUMO is mentioned nearly three times more often on Ontolog Forum. Both GFO and PROTON are mentioned relatively infrequently, reinforcing earlier suggestions that these ontologies have low levels of interest and community engagement.

| Table 9.10 | | Ontology count for the Semantic Web Interest Group and Ontolog Forum (survey conducted on 19 May, 2009) | | | | |

Semantic Web	Frequency	Relative frequency	Ontolog Forum	Frequency	Relative frequency	Ratio
dolce	49	100.0%	sumo	1,730	100.0%	35.31
sumo	24	49.0%	dolce	592	34.2%	24.67
bfo	19	38.8%	bfo	176	10.2%	9.26
gfo	13	26.5%	proton	55	3.2%	4.23
proton	6	12.2%	gfo	8	0.5%	1.33

Word frequency analysis

A more general word frequency analysis table is shown in the appendix to this chapter. It displays the top 100 words for the Semantic Web Interest Group and Ontolog Forum. The frequencies were compiled by counting discrete words in every message across the corpus of each list, and eliminating prepositions, pronouns, common verbs and adjectives, HTML elements and entities (such as <span> and <font> tags), and certain template words which appeared in every message (such as 'unsubscribe'). The entire corpus was converted to lower case during extraction of these statistics. Morphological variants, such as plurals, have not been controlled for.

Both lists exhibit a large number of common words: 51 out of a possible 100. Terms like 'ontology', 'semantic', 'web', 'language', 'knowledge' and 'information' are clearly of central interest to both communities. However, there are pertinent differences, both in which terms are not common, and in how common terms are ranked. As expected, the Semantic Web Interest Group has a large number of technical terms, with 'rdf', 'owl', 'uri' and 'xml' all featuring in the top 20 results. None of these are in the top 20 results for Ontolog Forum, with only 'rdf' and 'owl' appearing in the top 100 results (each is mentioned approximately 10 per cent and 25 per cent as often, respectively). The Semantic Web list also contains a number of terms that relate to possible contexts for discussion and application of the technologies discussed: terms like 'workshop', 'conference', 'systems', 'applications', 'services', 'management', 'business' and 'social' are either ranked lower or do not appear at all in Ontolog Forum.

Conversely, Ontolog Forum contains many philosophical and mathematical terms which rank highly: 'ontology', 'time', 'language', 'logic', 'set', 'point', 'model', 'theory' and 'world' all appear in the first

30 most frequently used words. Despite the fact that real-world application of ontologies is a frequent topic of debate, these terms indicate a heavy orientation towards abstract and formal discussion. Less perspicuously, three proper names appear in the first 40 words—more often than words like 'meaning', 'list' and 'thing', for example—indicating that dialogue takes place among a more concentrated group of members. Still less conclusively, many terms refer to the epistemic conditions of the discussion itself—verbs like 'leave', 'say', 'know', 'agree', 'mean' and 'take'; adjectives like 'shared', 'real', 'true' and 'common'; and nouns like 'context', 'discussion', 'question' and 'view' all suggest a strong tendency towards self-referential discussion *about* the process of discussion on the list. This tendency, however tenuous, does correlate loosely to the larger average number of posts per subject (Ontolog Forum 4.03; Semantic Web Interest Group 2.36), and the substantially larger average number of posts per author featured on Ontolog Forum (Ontolog Forum 23.14; Semantic Web Interest Group 7.77).

The word frequency analysis shows some significant difference in the nature of the two list communities. But what can be inferred from this to the question of commensurability of the ontologies themselves? At most the results are suggestive: they show that the SUMO and BFO ontologies have contributors who are active on Ontolog Forum, which might suggest they are more oriented towards philosophical rather than technical issues of ontology composition, and more inclined to engage in active debate over these issues with a broader community over time. Potentially these two ontologies themselves are more commensurable also, or at least the differences between them more likely to have been made explicit in the course of discussion on the list. Similarly the kinds of concepts treated in upper-level ontologies—'time', 'set', 'process', 'context', 'thing' and so on—receive frequent attention on Ontolog Forum. Interestingly, many of the pertinent concepts and distinctions used in the five ontologies—such as 'entity', 'object', 'item', 'discrete', 'abstract' and 'individual'—do not appear in the top 100 words of either lists. This suggests that neither list is predominantly engaged in trying to determine, for instance, whether the *endurant/perdurant* distinction is foundational or not. Across both lists, considerably greater discussion centres rather around the formal aspects of knowledge representation. In the case of the Semantic Web Interest Group, these aspects are discussed in preponderantly technical terms: for example, how to construct and connect ontologies using constructs from OWL and RDF language specifications. On Ontolog Forum, this sort of discussion tends to be considerably more abstract, and is focused more on general issues of logical syntax and semantics.

Qualitative analysis

One conversational thread from Ontolog Forum has been selected for more detailed qualitative analysis. Entitled 'Two ontologies that are inconsistent but both needed', the conversation involves one of the authors of the BFO ontology (Barry Smith), and other influential participants—the author of the RDF specification, Pat Hayes; a frequently cited author on ontologies, John Sowa; and a number of contributors to various standards initiatives. Usefully, the subject matter covers both the general problem of commensurability between ontologies, as well as the specific question of interoperability between upper-level ontologies. The conversation takes place in June 2007, some time after the ontologies covered here were developed, so it does not directly relate to the background of their development. Nevertheless it elucidates many of the foundational issues involved in upper-level ontology engineering, which remain active subjects for debate, and brings into view a range of perspectives on the challenges of interoperability between multiple ontologies.

Ontological dialogue

The discussion in this thread principally involves the problem of reconciling two ontologies with potentially different presuppositions. As common with such discussions, it winds over a range of different subjects, however, and engages different disputants along the way. Table 9.11 summarises the major movements in the dialogue on Ontolog Forum. The message responsible for the change of topic (within the same subject heading) is indicated, along with a summary of the topic.

Table 9.11 Ontolog Forum dialogue map

Message ID	Date	Author	Summary
Preliminaries			
	27 April 2007	Di Maio	Announces invitation for participation in disaster management ontology.
54	7 June 2007	Barker	Problem of multiple ontological 'perspectives' raised.
59	7 June 2007	Andersen	'Perspectivalism' queried; two options proposed: either ontologies are 'incommensurable' or they are not (and 'perspectivalism' disappears).

Table 9.11   Ontolog Forum dialogue map (*Cont'd*)

Message ID	Date	Author	Summary
71	8 June 2007	Sowa	Preceding dichotomy queried, perspectivalism reintroduced; granular inconsistencies can dissolve under different perspectival orientations. Issue raised of work involved.
80	8 June 2007	Kusnierczyk	Expresses sympathy with message 59—either ontologies are consistent, or they are not.
81 (?)	8 June 2007	Smith	Offers evidence of logically consistent but philosophically incommensurable ontology (own work).
Perspectives on the continuant/occurrent distinction			
91	8 June 2007	Hayes	Argues for reconciliation of perspectives expressed in Smith's work. Multiple 'perspectives' can be reduced, simplified—issue one of terminological rather than ontological difference.
98	8 June 2007	Smith	Pragmatic rebuttal; BFO is successful in practice.
108	8 June 2007	Sowa	Claims informal, lay distinctions are susceptible to critique even when dressed in formal ontological axioms.
169	11 June 2007	Smith	Further pragmatic justifications—successful *use* justifies an ontology's design rationale.
?	12 June 2007	Hayes	Reiterates mutual translatability between continuant and occurrent 'perspectives'.
180	12 June 2007	Smith	Seeming agreement with Hayes' position.
181	12 June 2007	Conklin	Frustration at tenuous discussion, given its initial practical aims—to provide some consensus on whether multiple ontologies can be consistent, yet reflect different perspectives.

Table 9.11 Ontolog Forum dialogue map (*Cont'd*)

Message ID	Date	Author	Summary
Diversions			
182	12 June 2007	Laskey	Begins discussion on 'probabilistic' ontologies, where concept agreement is expressed as 'degrees of certitude'.
361	18 June 2007	Barkmeyer	Discusses distinctions between ontologies and data models.
Metaphysical dilemmas			
308	16 June 2007	Partridge	Reopens debate about continuants and occurrents—suggests distinction depends on metaphysical perspective rather than empirical evidence.
358	18 June 2007	Hayes	Disputes metaphysical bias; suggests that even upper-level ontologies can be constructed solely out of abstraction from empirical (scientific) observation.
378	19 June 2007	Laskey	Emphasises role of pre-existing cultural bias.
381	19 June 2007	Hayes	Reaffirms value of intuition and observation, rather than metaphysical speculation, as basis for ontology development.
383	19 June 2007	Laskey	Agrees on the value of observational starting points, on pragmatic grounds.
409	20 June 2007	Partridge	Parodies Hayes' comments re: metaphysics, by directing criticism instead towards unreflective logicism and empiricism.
411	20 June 2007	Sowa	Points towards continuous 'forgetting' of previous development in artificial intelligence and logic.
417	20 June 2007	Hayes	Emphasises that logic and science, unlike metaphysics, can be measured by demonstrable progress.

| Table 9.11 | Ontolog Forum dialogue map (*Cont'd*) |

Message ID	Date	Author	Summary
432	21 June 2007	Partridge	Critiques this view as being naïvely 'positivist', ignoring essentially Kuhnian 'paradigmatic'—and irrational—nature of scientific development.
433	21 June 2007	Hayes	Underscores distinction between progressive science and philosophy mired in 'opinion'.
Concluding remarks			
435	21 June 2007	Brown	Questions (similar to message 181) value of the preceding discussion.
448	22 June 2007	Partridge	Affirms need for metaphysical understanding when devising upper-level ontologies for use in large-scale, complex systems.
449	22 June 2007	Hayes	Affirms need to begin with user needs and observation to more abstract concepts ('bottom-up') rather than working down from metaphysical systems ('top-down').
454	23 June 2007	Sowa	Suggests 'middle-road'; metaphysical systems can be useful, but only when road-tested against 'observation and experiment'.

Positions and distinctions

This thread demonstrates the shifting sands that underpin the building of foundational, upper-level ontologies. The evident tensions between metaphysical speculation, of the kind which has always beset abstract philosophical ontological formulations, and pragmatic engineering concerns—how to construct workable ontologies of the technical kind which facilitate system and data-level interoperability—are drawn out but far from reconciled here. Readings of earlier and later threads, in this forum and others like it, show that similar tensions continually emerge. One of the unintended consequences, ironically, of attempting to focus on purely engineering concerns is the inevitable lapse—not always unwelcome, as this thread shows, but invariably protracted and inconclusive—into various forms of metaphysical speculation.

Equally evident are the various postures and positions adopted by those involved in the dialogue. The ontologies surveyed above have the appearance of being effected as a result of some purist intellectual effort, with only a handful of attendant publications describing the process. This debate makes evident, on the other hand, the communicative marketplace under which even the most abstract conceptualisations are formulated through the retail practice of what Brandom (1994) terms the practice of 'giving and asking for reasons'. In particular, several crucial distinctions in orientation towards the construction of upper-level ontologies can be drawn. These, in turn, can be applied as dimensions to the assessment of the commensurability of the ontologies themselves.

The first distinction, exhibited throughout the thread, concerns that between pragmatic, empirical, 'bottom-up' and metaphysical, speculative, 'top-down' approaches to upper-level ontological construction. While the majority of the voices on the list, particularly Hayes and Smith, have a noted aversion to 'philosophising' over categories, a minority point to the merit of engaging philosophy as means of avoiding errors in categorial construction. Even Hayes, at one stage, points to the need for some philosophical background: 'Just be aware of a few common mental traps, such as not making the use/mention confusion, and you should do OK' (Ontolog Forum 2010, message 358).

If a consensus emerges at all here, it is that some level of 'metaphysics is unavoidable'—the dispute is the degree to which abstract theorising of the philosophical kind is embraced or, alternatively, brought in as a last resort. The distinction hinges on the extent to which upper-level ontology construction is viewed as a purely engineering activity, or whether it is a continuation of a much longer philosophical activity—one in which Aristotle's categories are as relevant as contemporary technical artefacts. Partridge and Sowa, in particular, appear to hold some sympathy with the latter view.

The next distinction is between so-called '3D' and '4D' world views, and whether these are merely verbal transpositions of the same underlying 'view'. The dispute between Smith and Hayes essentially involves this question (Ontolog Forum 2010, messages 98, 108, 169, 358). For Hayes, 'continuants' are sometimes fortuitous, but always unnecessary ways of speaking about existential phenomena (Ontolog Forum 2010, message 91). Smith regards the relationship between 'continuants' and 'occurrents' as ontologically primary—a view that informs the BFO and DOLCE ontologies (Ontolog Forum 2010, message 98).

A further distinction is introduced by the 'Probabilistic Ontologies' sub-thread. Here the question is whether existing logical formalisms are sufficient to express degrees of certitude over the claims made in an ontology. Laskey suggests they are necessary refinement to connect machine reasoning, of the 'either/or' binary variety, with the kinds of everyday ambiguous reasoning human agents engage in (Ontolog Forum 2010, message 182). Sowa cautions that tradition logical expressions can be trivially extended to add modal and veridical meta-claims to ontological axioms (Ontolog Forum 2010, message 313). This conversation concerns whether modalities such as necessity and possibility ought to be first-order constructs of the logical formalism in which ontologies are expressed, or rather treated as axioms of the ontologies themselves. All of the ontologies surveyed above use canonical forms of OWL, and therefore represent necessary and possible modalities as postulated axioms, if at all.

Yet another distinction involves another sub-thread, 'Ontology-building vs. data modelling', where conventional data modelling is distinguished from ontology engineering (Ontolog Forum 2010, messages 339, 346, 361, 362, 394, 414, 420, 423, 424 and 425). The debate here centres on whether the distinction is one of kind (ontologies being of a different, conceptual order to their physical representation as data models) or of degree (ontologies are simply more refined sub-sets of a general vague category called 'data models').

It is worth noting the thread as a whole arose out of an introduction to participate in the development of a disaster management ontology. At least several participants express some frustration that the meandering threads never tie back to the originating subject, and note the difficulty of ever arriving at consensus over deep philosophical issues, while practical issues of (lower-level) ontology engineering remain. A further distinction can be introduced to capture these positions—about whether there is a need for upper-level ontologies at all.

Several distinct positions can be identified when considering the question of how to reconcile two potentially inconsistent ontologies, which can be transposed into the terms of this study as the question of commensurability. Hayes argues, at least for the 'potentially inconsistent' examples given, that this is a purely terminological issue, one in which one set of axioms can be rewritten into another trivially—at the cost of some effort, but without sacrificing integrity or consistency (Ontolog Forum 2010, message 91). Smith, at least in relation to the '3D/4D', argues for an essentially 'incommensurable' thesis—two inconsistent viewpoints can, however, be housed within the one ontological scaffold (Ontolog Forum 2010, message 98). Laskey and Sowa argue that commensurability is a question of degree rather than kind, with Laskey further insisting that probabilistic ontologies can best represent such degrees (Ontolog Forum 2010, messages 71 and 182). Partridge suggests that a common metaphysical foundation is essential—otherwise there is no means for establishing commensurability at the level of domain ontologies (Ontolog Forum 2010, message 448). The value of an upper-level ontology is therefore not its purely veridical status, but its usefulness as a means for making explicit what underlying assumptions those domain ontologies make. Hayes' response echoes obliquely the findings of the survey above—that the push for resolution at an 'upper-level' makes for further questions and yet further speculative 'levels' (Ontolog Forum 2010, message 449).

In addition to explicit positions adopted, there are implicit differences in how members of the list engage. While it is an 'expert' community, some members are more conciliatory to opposing positions than others. Where Hayes, Partridge and Smith—along with many others who post less verbosely and frequently—often happily engage in point-scoring, Sowa, in particular, generally adopts a strategy of qualified agreement, where the qualification attempts to extend a line of thought or embrace other contrary positions. For example, out of nearly 1,000 messages posted to the forum over the period surveyed by Sowa (nearly 10 per cent of the total number of messages posted), 264, or more than a quarter, include the exact construction 'I agree'. Elsewhere, authors use familiar tropes of informal online communication: irony, parody, questions (rhetorical and intentional), long interleaving responses and brief, dismissive rebuttals, exasperated summaries and erstwhile explanation. The performative flavour of individual contributions, and of the community as a whole, can be used to characterise particular ontological efforts, however tangentially—they are suggestive, at least, of the motivations, orientations and intentions under which such technological artefacts are produced. Directly, in this instance, Barry Smith's tone conveys a sense of hard ontological commitment to the categories posited in BFO; indirectly, the forum provides a sense of the 'behind-the-scenes' gerrymandering required to build consensus around ontologies, particularly those which are not subject to established disciplinary or community practices.

These distinctions can be summarised in the following set of dimensions of specific relevance to the ontologies in this study:

- role of metaphysics in ontology engineering: essential or accidental?
- '3D/4D' distinction: ontological or terminological?
- possible and necessary modalities: require first-order support in the formalism?

- ontologies and data models: different in degree or in kind?
- upper-level ontologies necessary?
- commensurability: multiple, potentially inconsistent viewpoints supported?
- viewpoint: negotiable or resolute?

With some modest adaptations, these in turn can be applied as interpretive dimensions to the surveyed ontologies as part of a general evaluation of their commensurability. The evaluation of the ontologies against these dimensions is presented in the concluding section below.

Conclusions: assessing commensurability

This analysis concludes with two sets of findings: one outlining what can be said about the commensurability of upper-level ontologies on the basis of the analysis above, the other reflecting on what the analysis might mean for a general theory of commensurability, based on the framework which has been applied.

Commensurability of upper-level ontologies

The exploration of the five 'upper-level' ontologies has suggested considerable areas of both similarity and difference. Structurally, the PROTON and DOLCE ontologies show greater modularisation, while PROTON, DOLCE and SUMO are considerable larger and semantically denser than GFO and BFO. The DOLCE ontology also favours use of object properties to relate entities functionally, rather than via class subsumption relations. This is carried over in the more scientific and theoretical orientation of DOLCE, evidenced by use of specialised terminology, a feature it shares with GFO, and to some extent with BFO. Comparatively, the PROTON and SUMO ontologies share a more pragmatic and vernacular orientation. The BFO, SUMO and DOLCE also permit multiple perspectives on physical entities. They can be described using spacetime coordinates (4D), or with clearly demarcated spatial and temporal characteristics (3D), along a more abstract distinction between 'Continuant' and 'Occurrent' categories. This is evident in the BFO ontology directly, but requires some reference to the surrounding literature for SUMO and DOLCE. It is unclear how the GFO and PROTON ontologies are positioned around this distinction, but since both support some variant of the *Continuant–Occurrent* distinction, it can be assumed they operate within a three-dimensional paradigm. The SUMO ontology, and to a much lesser degree the PROTON and DOLCE ontologies, also explicitly model an agent's intentional relation to entities in the world, permitting—though not necessarily insisting on—a constructivist rather than naturalist outlook. Despite considerable overlap, conceptual *equivalence*, or synonymy, is frequently hard to establish, because of the differing levels of terminological intersection, use of functional roles over class subsumption (in the case of DOLCE), greater conceptual density with the larger ontologies (in the cases of PROTON, SUMO and DOLCE) and a general lack of transparent isomorphisms between the conceptual graphs of the ontologies.

Table 9.12 summarises some of the findings of the exploration of the five 'upper-level' ontologies, using a combination of the dimensions introduced in the general model in Chapter 12, 'A framework for commensurability', and those which have presented themselves in the course of the analysis of upper-level ontologies particularly. In addition, I have added the SWIntO variables (Oberle et al. 2007) as supplementary dimensions, since these are largely specific to the upper-level ontologies described, and are not included in my general taxonomy. Valuations for each of the ontologies are relative—a low valuation on the 'small vs. large' dimension, for example, indicates a small number of logical axioms relative to the other ontologies considered. 'Low' and 'high' values reflect evaluations against the second term of each conceptual opposition expressed by a dimension.

From this matrix several patterns emerge. SUMO and DOLCE ontologies match up on a number of dimensions, and do not differ greatly on any. That they are broadly commensurable is further borne out in efforts to develop translations between them (Oberle et al. 2007). However, their relative size and complexity would suggest a large number of 'local' commensurability issues, at particular branches of their respective taxonomic structures. BFO seems to differ markedly from both of these, and indeed from the aims of PROTON as well. Since it is similarly designed for use in scientific and biological systems, it is perhaps unsurprising that the GFO ontology is closest, at least for dimensions where values can be meaningfully derived. Otherwise, the GFO and PROTON ontologies stand out as relatively idiosyncratic in terms of usage and available documentation—relatively little more can be inferred from the sources available. A large number of 'Unknowns' for these ontologies might imply either better commensurability—or,

Table 9.12   Ontology commensurability matrix

Dimension	BFO	DOLCE	GFO	PROTON	SUMO
Structure—How are the ontologies structured?					
Small vs. large	Low	High	Low	Low	High
Light vs. dense	Low	Moderate	Low	Moderate	High
Classificatory vs. attributive	Low	High	Moderate	Moderate	Moderate
Low vs. high modularisation	Low	High	Low	Moderate	Moderate
Semantics—How do the ontologies relate to 'real-world' objects?					
Possibilism vs. actualism	High	Low	Unknown	Unknown	Unknown
Simple—complex	Low	High	Moderate	Low	High
Subject—What sorts of objects do the ontologies describe?					
Concrete vs. abstract objects	High	High	Moderate	Low	Moderate
Natural vs. social objects	Low	Low	Low	High	Moderate
Style—How are the ontologies authored?					
Normative vs. descriptive	Low	Moderate	Moderate	Moderate	High
Tentative vs. committed	High	High	Moderate	Low	Moderate
Process—How are the ontologies developed?					
Derived vs. original composition	High	Low	Moderate	Moderate	Moderate
'Home-grown' vs. imported philosophy	High	Low	Moderate	Moderate	Moderate
Implicit vs. explicit assumptions	High	Moderate	Low	Low	High
Ad hoc vs. rigorous design methods	Moderate	Moderate	Moderate	Low	High
Practice—How are the ontologies are used?					
Low vs. high recognition	Low	High	Low	Low	High
Low vs. high usage	Moderate	High	Low	Low	High

Table 9.12 Ontology commensurability matrix (*Cont'd*)

Dimension	BFO	DOLCE	GFO	PROTON	SUMO
Purpose—What motivates the development of the ontologies?					
Low vs. high economic motivation	Moderate	Low	Low	High	Low
Low vs. high scientific motivation	High	High	High	Low	Moderate
Perspective—What perspective 'informs' the ontology?					
Realist vs. constructivist attitude	Low	High	Low	Moderate	High
Descriptive vs. revisionary	High	Low	Unknown	Unknown	Low
Multiplicative vs. reductionist	Moderate	Low	Unknown	Unknown	Low
Endurantism vs. perdurantism	High	High	Low	Low	High
Essential role of metaphysics	Moderate	Moderate	Unknown	Low	High
Importance of '3D/4D' distinction	High	Moderate	Unknown	Unknown	Low
Modalities supported	Moderate	High	Low	Low	High
Ontologies vs. data models	High	Moderate	Moderate	Low	Moderate
Necessity of upper-level agreement	High	High	High	High	High
Multiple viewpoints	High	Moderate	Low	Low	High
Negotiable viewpoint	Low	Moderate	Moderate	Moderate	Moderate

more likely, since they leave open large degrees of interpretative scope for different domain ontologies importing them, might imply 'hidden' pockets of potential incommensurability which might emerge only on further analysis. By contrast, the explicitness attached to BFO, SUMO and DOLCE ontologies suggests that areas of incommensurability are easier to locate up front.

While the mailing list analysis can be used to generate a series of evaluations of the ontologies themselves, this kind of exercise is perhaps more helpful for considering the question of commensurability of upper-level ontologies generally. In particular, the distinctions raised at the end of the analysis are perhaps questions more to be asked of the situational context in which upper-level ontologies are being considered. In some situations it might be useful to ask whether there are metaphysical issues important for the users, systems and requirements at hand; whether different systems must agree on their definition of abstract concepts; whether multiple viewpoints can be accommodated; and whether differences in viewpoints can be negotiated and, if so, how? In other situations, where an analyst needs to evaluate upper-level ontologies, the dimensions and distinctions outlined above could become a series of evaluative criteria. Here it might be useful to ask what it would mean to view the world as ontologically divided into objects and processes, or, on the other hand, to see all things as possessing 'object-like' and 'process-like' features in different measures—or, *pace* Smith, to ask whether both viewpoints can be housed in a single, logically consistent but philosophically incommensurable system. A further question might ask whether, from a procedural point of view, these kinds of distinctions ought to arise organically, through piece-meal observation and analysis, or alternatively ought to be imposed as a set of guiding metaphysical assumptions from above. And, finally, it might be asked what kinds of downstream commensurability issues arise by the assumptions made by upper-level ontologies, and the lower-level domain ontologies they are designed to support.

In short, these questions could be more useful as broader interpretive 'framings' for consideration of other, more fine-grained commensurability dimensions, such as whether the ontologies employ similar design methods. Consequently, while these dimensions are included under the 'Perspective' group in Table 9.12, they better reflect general aspects of the situation in which the ontologies are considered, rather than the ontologies themselves. This point is revisited briefly in the next section.

Implications for a general theory of commensurability

What do these findings suggest for a theory of commensurability? As indicated in Chapter 12, 'A framework for commensurability', commensurability is assessed against a contextual backdrop of a given scenario—typically, a project with requirements, aims and purposes. Since the development of upper-level ontologies is what might be described as a niche market, it is hard to characterise the sociological environment in which these ontologies are developed and used. However, the quantitative and qualitative analysis of two mailing lists—featuring some of the ontology contributors themselves, and many other developers and users of ontologies—are revealing. On the one hand, comparatively little discussion takes place over the actual categories of upper-level ontologies, in spite of the avowed purpose of the lists. On the other, the lists do discuss questions of mechanics—how to develop and deploy ontologies—and those of logical entailment within and between ontologies. The Semantic Web Interest Group list is on the whole dedicated to the technological and operational side of ontologies—announcements about conferences, workshops, specification releases, and so on—while Ontolog Forum focuses more on issues of ontology content, but nonetheless features many discussions around broadly logical and methodological issues, rather than those of substantive ontological content. As the thread described above shows, this coverage includes the very problem of ontology commensurability itself.

The lists proved useful as heuristic aids for understanding the general backdrop against which the surveyed ontologies can be understood. One immediate result is that what appear to be posited categories within those ontologies are still very much the subject of considerable contention. Further, what appear to be circumstantial deviations between ontologies—fortuitous reliance on one distinction over another—can be shown to be rooted in fundamental philosophical positions, which are not clearly evident in either the ontologies themselves, or their supporting literature. How vital differences in these positions are again is a matter for context—but clearly, in the case of BFO ontology, one of the key authors holds a resolute view as to the primacy of the top-level categories posited. Drafting connections from BFO to other ontologies based on purely lexical considerations is likely to obscure at least the authorial intent if not the actual extension of these categories to other domain-level ontologies in practice. How much adoption of an upper-level ontology implies a wholesale commitment to its claims is yet a further question, bearing here on the commensurability relation between importing domain-level and imported upper-level ontology. Concern over this question has, in turn, led some members of these lists to advocate either forms of ontological pluralism—in which multiple, incompatible conceptual schemes are happily co-opted—or abnegation—where talk of 'upper levels' is ignored altogether. Each of these options implies some weaker form of interoperability, where total agreement is passed over in favour of partial and local—but perhaps workable—agreements.

Practically, the absence of direct background material about the ontologies themselves led me to examine two mailing lists where the peculiar fusion of speculative philosophical and detailed technical subjects are discussed. This suggests that a range of approaches and data sources need to be considered when looking for commensurability 'clues'. Another consequence of this analysis was the addition of several further distinguishing dimensions to the commensurability evaluation model. However, these dimensions could relate better to the situational context in which commensurability is evaluated, rather than to the ontologies themselves—and suggests that, in terms of the commensurability model outlined in Chapter 12, 'A framework for commensurability', it may be important to model the context more stringently. In practice, the vagueness and open-endedness of 'context' make such a formal treatment a difficult prospect—despite some existing efforts to do this. I return to this subject in the conclusion to the study, as a candidate area for further refinements and research of the model.

Although the upper-level ontologies surveyed demonstrate impressive theoretical coherence, engaging with the public fora in which they are produced shows that for many questions of fundamental ontological importance—in philosophical and engineering senses—no kind of Platonic-level resolution is in sight. Rather the mailing lists evoke an atmosphere of endless dialogue, intractable positions and an endless recasting of distinctions. Nevertheless, engagement with these social networks provides a necessary warning against any superficial reconciliation between concepts which a purely technical review of ontologies might suggest. It indicates that the very question of commensurability itself is enmeshed within the broader, messy, retail world of discursive practices. By engaging with these practices, it is possible to succumb to a potentially interminable dialogue, far removed from the pristine conceptualisations of ontologies themselves, in which semantic equivalences and distinctions are endlessly debated. Conversely, that engagement reveals the contrived and fictional concordance, the illusory character of the harmonious, but purely formal translation of concepts. It serves as a reminder that knowledge systems are merely the latest emergent suburban region within the much broader metropolis of epistemic discourse.

Appendix: upper-level ontologies—supplementary data

Upper-level ontologies in Protégé

Figure 9.1 A representation of the top-level classes in the BFO ontology

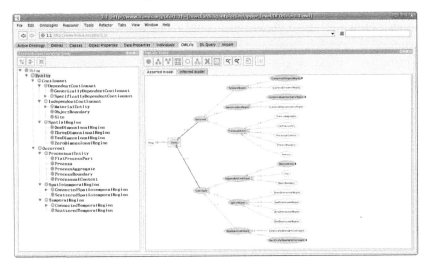

Figure 9.2 A representation of the top-level classes in the DOLCE ontology

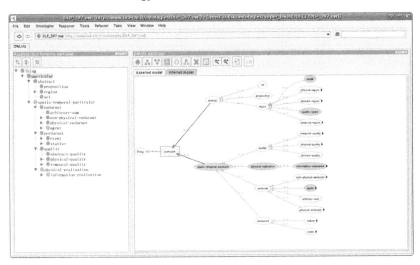

Figure 9.3   A representation of the top-level classes in the GFO ontology

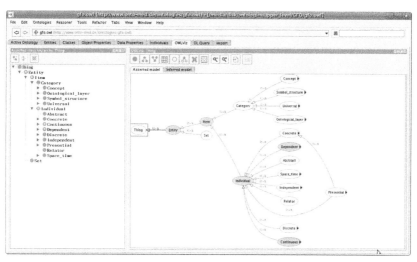

Figure 9.4   A representation of the top-level classes in the PROTON ontology

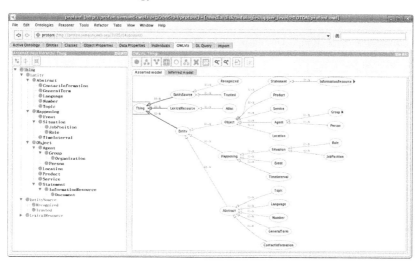

Figure 9.5 A representation of the top-level classes in the SUMO ontology

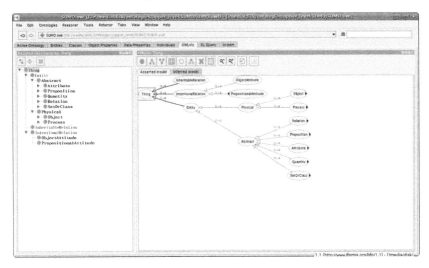

Conceptual distinctions between the ontologies

Table 9.13 Conceptual distinctions between the ontologies

Conceptual distinction*	Ontology	Concept
Spatial or temporal		
	BFO	/Entity/Continuent/SpatialRegion /Entity/Occurrent/TemporalRegion
	DOLCE	/particular/abstract/region/ physical—region/space—region /particular/abstract/region/ temporal—region
	GFO	/Entity/Item/Individual/ Spacetime/Space /Entity/Item/Individual/ Spacetime/Time
	PROTON	/Entity/Object/Location /Entity/Happening/TimeInterval
	SUMO	/Entity/Physical/Object/Region /Entity/Abstract/Quantity/Phys icalQuantity/ConstantQuantity/ TimeMeasure

Table 9.13 Conceptual distinctions between the ontologies (*Cont'd*)

Conceptual distinction*	Ontology	Concept
Collective or individual		
	BFO	`/Entity/Continuant/Independent Continuant/MaterialEntity/Object Aggregate` `/Entity/Continuant/IndependentCo ntinuant/MaterialEntity/ [Object—FiatObject Aggregate]`
	DOLCE	`/particular/abstract/set` `/particular/spatio-temporal- particular`
	GFO	`/Entity/Set` `/Entity/Item`
	PROTON	UNKNOWN
	SUMO	`/Entity/Abstract/SetOrClass` `/Entity/Physical`
Abstract or concrete		
	BFO	*UNKNOWN*
	DOLCE	`/particular/abstract` `/particular/spatio-temporal- particular`
	GFO	`/Entity/Item/Individual/Abstract` `/Entity/Item/Individual/Concrete`
	PROTON	`/Entity/Abstract` `/Entity/[Object|Happening]`
	SUMO	`/Entity/Abstract` `/Entity/Physical`
Continuant or occurrent		
	BFO	`/Entity/Continuant` `/Entity/Occurrent`
	DOLCE	`/particular/spatio-temporal- particular/endurant` `/particular/spatio-temporal- particular/perdurant`
	GFO	`/Entity/Item/Individual/ Continuous` `/Entity/Item/Individual/Discrete`
	PROTON	`/Entity/Object` `/Entity/Happening/Event`
	SUMO	`/Entity/Physical/Object` `/Entity/Physical/Process`

Table 9.13 Conceptual distinctions between the ontologies (*Cont'd*)

Conceptual distinction*	Ontology	Concept
Independent or dependent		
	BFO	`/Entity/Continuant/Independent Continuant` `/Entity/Continuant/Dependent Continuant`
	DOLCE	`/particular/spatio-temporal-particular/[physical-realization—endurant—perdurant]` `/particular/spatio-temporal-particular /quality`
	GFO	`/Entity/Item/Individual/ Independent` `/Entity/Item/Individual/ Dependent`
	PROTON	*UNKNOWN*
	SUMO	`/Entity/Physical` `/Entity/Abstract/[Relation| Attribute|Quantity]`
Conceptual or physical		
	BFO	*UNKNOWN*
	DOLCE	`/particular/abstract/proposition` `/particular/spatio-temporal-particular`
	GFO	`/Entity/Item/Category/Concept` `/Entity/Item/Individual`
	PROTON	`/Entity/Abstact/[GeneralTerm| Topic]` `/Entity/[Happening—Object]`
	SUMO	`/Entity/Abstract/Proposition` `/Entity/Abstract/Physical`

Note: Forward slash characters (/) are used to indicate subsumption conceptual relations; square brackets ([]) indicate sibling classes; pipe characters (|) indicate a sequence of two or more classes; and [A|B] means that A and B share the same parent class, and that collectively these both are suitable candidates for one side of the distinction in question.

Word frequency analysis details

| Table 9.14 | Word frequency analysis of the Semantic Web Interest Group and Ontolog Forum |

Rank	Semantic Web Interest Group		Ontolog Forum	
	Word	Frequency	Word	Frequency
1	rdf	35,104	ontology	28,507
2	web	35,042	community	22,013
3	semantic	25,767	shared	17,448
4	university	18,017	leave	14,464
5	data	15,991	time	11,591
6	owl	15,902	ontologies	10,759
7	information	13,291	different	9,311
8	ontology	11,245	language	8,907
9	papers	8,798	web	8,857
10	resource	8,769	logic	8,614
11	workshop	8,692	knowledge	8,448
12	uri	8,571	semantic	8,328
13	knowledge	7,667	people	8,054
14	research	7,587	work	8,008
15	systems	7,230	information	8,000
16	example	7,120	way	7,903
17	conference	7,011	set	7,894
18	people	6,426	pat	7,831
19	ontologies	6,147	john	7,705
20	xml	6,138	point	7,249
21	applications	6,138	model	7,235
22	usa	6,095	subject	6,972
23	class	5,816	things	6,898
24	new	5,600	theory	6,882
25	work	5,593	family	6,751
26	different	5,548	world	6,718
27	html	5,545	say	6,655
28	semantics	5,093	make	6,562
29	way	5,058	example	6,535
30	services	4,782	need	6,502
31	foaf	4,765	data	6,490
32	technology	4,751	systems	6,402
33	submission	4,680	two	6,309
34	uk	4,625	context	5,886
35	type	4,588	semantics	5,784

Table 9.14	Word frequency analysis of the Semantic Web Interest Group and Ontolog Forum (*Cont'd*)			
Rank	Semantic Web Interest Group		Ontolog Forum	
	Word	Frequency	Word	Frequency
36	list	4,572	system	5,711
37	rdfs	4,545	being	5,634
38	name	4,500	first	5,547
39	make	4,493	know	5,545
40	subject	4,448	peter	5,543
41	need	4,401	color	5,452
42	language	4,394	terms	5,439
43	paper	4,361	new	5,293
44	know	4,341	formal	5,242
45	technologies	4,341	open	5,222
46	want	4,293	part	5,115
47	time	4,292	something	5,073
48	international	4,252	meaning	5,053
49	uris	4,244	common	5,021
50	things	4,224	owl	4,863
51	two	4,209	discussion	4,646
52	first	4,174	original	4,639
53	content	4,123	list	4,637
54	thing	4,080	concepts	4,572
55	something	4,035	problem	4,506
56	application	4,010	thing	4,505
57	description	3,980	agree	4,497
58	open	3,957	join	4,474
59	world	3,911	possible	4,468
60	management	3,875	class	4,456
61	property	3,873	call	4,444
62	say	3,841	bounces	4,421
63	business	3,830	sense	4,371
64	model	3,700	sent	4,365
65	software	3,686	real	4345
66	sparql	3,605	each	4,344
67	service	3,596	session	4,336
68	germany	3,555	another	4,334
69	case	3,464	true	4,278
70	document	3,454	business	4,191
71	being	3,446	standards	4,175
72	system	3,434	process	4,147

Table 9.14 Word frequency analysis of the Semantic Web Interest Group and Ontolog Forum (*Cont'd*)

Rank	Semantic Web Interest Group		Ontolog Forum	
	Word	Frequency	Word	Frequency
73	problem	3,417	useful	4,124
74	point	3,407	project	4,117
75	tools	3,406	number	4,075
76	computer	3,353	mean	4,004
77	science	3,285	want	3,976
78	user	3,217	level	3,944
79	page	3,213	fact	3,904
80	set	3,199	rdf	3,871
81	context	3,186	why	3,818
82	submissions	3,178	question	3,793
83	query	3,153	find	3,778
84	original	3,100	word	3,634
85	following	3,082	case	3,633
86	reasoning	3,080	since	3,592
87	available	3,071	human	3,584
88	important	3,050	person	3,565
89	th	2,960	type	3,562
90	group	2,954	without	3,558
91	project	2,953	regards	3,529
92	person	2,930	concept	3,519
93	part	2,918	rather	3,517
94	really	2,917	view	3,504
95	question	2,902	order	3,501
96	each	2,899	take	3,499
97	languages	2,897	still	3,487
98	domain	2,882	axioms	3,479
99	find	2,881	logical	3,436
100	social	2,820	standard	3,425

References

Aristotle. 1994. *Categories*, E.M. Edghill (tr.), The Internet Classics Archives, *http://classics.mit.edu/Aristotle/categories.html* (accessed 20 March 2010).

Bazzanella, B., H. Stoermer and P. Bouquet. 2008. 'Top Level Categories and Attributes for Entity Representation'. Technical Report 1, University of Trento, Scienze della Cognizione e della Formazione.

BFO. 2007. Basic Formal Ontology (BFO) website, *http://www.ifomis.org/bfo* (accessed 22 July 2007).

Brandom, R. 1994. *Making It Explicit*. Cambridge, MA: Harvard University Press.

Ding, L., T. Finin, A. Joshi, R. Pan, R.S. Cost, Y. Peng, P. Reddivari, V. Doshi and J. Sachs. 2004. 'Swoogle: A Search and Metadata Engine for the Semantic Web'. In *CIKM 2004: Proceedings of the Thirteenth ACM International Conference on Information and Knowledge Management*. New York: Association for Computing Machinery, pp. 652–59.

FOAF. 2007. The Friend of a Friend (FOAF) Project website, *http://www.foaf-project.org* (accessed 22 July 2007).

Gangemi, A. 2006. 'The DOLCE and DnS ontologies', *http://www.loa-cnr.it/DOLCE.html* (accessed 22 February 2010).

Gennari, J.H., M.A. Musen, R.W. Fergerson, W.E. Grosso, M. Crubézy, H. Eriksson, N.F. Noy and S.W. Tu. 2003. 'The Evolution of Protégé: An Environment for Knowledge-Based Systems Development', *International Journal of Human-Computer Studies* 58, pp. 89–123.

Grenon, P. 2003a. 'BFO in a Nutshell: A Bi-Categorial Axiomatization of BFO and Comparison with DOLCE', technical report. Leipzig: Institute for Formal Ontology and Medical Information Science, University of Leipzig.

—. 2003b. 'Spatio-Temporality in Basic Formal Ontology (BFO)', technical report. Leipzig: Institute for Formal Ontology and Medical Information Science, University of Leipzig.

Grenon, P. and B. Smith. 2004. 'SNAP and SPAN: Towards Dynamic Spatial Ontology', *Event-Oriented Approaches in Geographic Information Science* 69, pp. 137–71.

Hayes, P. 2004. 'RDF Semantics'. W3C recommendation, World Wide Web Consortium, *http://www.w3.org/TR/rdf-mt/* (accessed 20 January 2010).

Hayes, P., P.F. Patel-Schneider and I. Horrocks. 2004. 'OWL Web Ontology Language Semantics and Abstract Syntax'. W3C recommendation, W3C, *http://www.w3.org/TR/owl-semantics/* (accessed 20 January 2010).

Herre, H. 2009. 'General Formal Ontology (GFO): A Foundational Ontology for Conceptual Modelling'. In R. Poli and L. Obrst (eds), *Theory and Applications of Ontology*, vol. 2. Berlin and Heidelberg: Springer.

Horridge, M. 2005. 'Protégé OWLViz', *http://protegewiki.stanford.edu/wiki/OWLViz* (accessed 10 February 2010).

Horridge, M., S. Bechhofer and O. Noppens. 2007. 'Igniting the OWL 1.1 Touch Paper: The OWL API'. In *3rd OWL Experiences and Directions Workshop (OWLED 2007)*. [Berlin]: Springer.

IFOMIS. 2007. IFOMIS website, *http://www.ifomis.org* (accessed 22 July 2007).

Kiryakov, A., K.I. Simov and M. Dimitrov. 2001. 'OntoMap: Portal for Upper-Level Ontologies'. In *FOIS 2001: Proceedings of the International Conference on Formal Ontology in Information Systems*. New York: Association for Computing Machinery, pp. 47–58.

Lenat, D.B. 1995. 'Cyc: A Large-Scale Investment in Knowledge Infrastructure', *Communications of the ACM* 38, pp. 33–38.

—. 2001. 'From 2001 to 2001: Common Sense and the Mind of HAL'. In *HAL's Legacy*. Cambridge, MA: MIT Press, pp. 193–209.

Masolo, C., S. Borgo, A. Gangemi, N. Guarino, A. Oltramari and L. Schneider. 2002. 'The WonderWeb Library of Foundational Ontologies', technical report,

LADSEB-Cnr. Padua: National Research Council, Institute of Cognitive Sciences and Technology.

Miller, G.A. 1995. 'WordNet: A Lexical Database for English', *Communications of the ACM* 38, pp. 39–41.

Niles, I. and A. Pease. 2001. 'Towards a Standard Upper Ontology'. In *FOIS 2001: Proceedings of the International Conference on Formal Ontology in Information Systems*. New York: Association for Computing Machinery, pp. 2–9.

Oberle, D., A. Ankolekar, P. Hitzler, P. Cimiano, M. Sintek, M. Kiesel, B. Mougouie, S.Vembu, S. Baumann and M. Romanelli. 2007. 'DOLCE ergo SUMO: On Foundational and Domain Models in SWIntO (Smartweb Integrated Ontology)', *Journal of Web Semantics: Science, Services and Agents on the World Wide Web* 5, pp. 156–74.

Ontolog Forum. 2010. Ontolog Forum Mail Archives, *http://ontolog.cim3.net/forum/* (accessed 18 January 2010).

Searle, J.R. 1983. *Intentionality: An Essay in the Philosophy of Mind*. Cambridge, UK: Cambridge University Press.

Semantic Knowledge Technologies. 2007. 'Welcome to SEKT—SEKT Portal', *http://www.sekt-project.com* (accessed 22 February 2010).

Smith, B. 2004. 'Beyond Concepts: Ontology as Reality Representation'. In A. Varzi and L. Vieu (eds), *FOIS 2004: Proceedings of the Third Conference on Formal Ontology in Information Systems*. Amsterdam: IOS Press, pp. 73–84.

—. 2005. 'Against Fantology'. In M.E. Reicher and J.C. Marek (eds), *Experience and Analysis*. Vienna: HPT & ÖBV, pp. 153–70.

Smith, B. and P. Grenon. 2004. 'The Cornucopia of Formal-Ontological Relations', *Dialectica* 58, pp. 279–96.

Terziev, I., A. Kiryakov and D. Manov. 2004. 'Base Upper-Level Ontology (BULO) Guidance', technical report, Semantic Knowledge Technologies (SEKT).

W3C. 2010. Semantic Web Interest Group Mail Archives, World Wide Web Consortium, *http://lists.w3.org/Archives/Public/semantic-web/* (accessed 19 February 2010).

10

Describing knowledge domains: a case study of biological ontologies

Liam Magee

In the past decade, the development of standardised and machine-processable controlled vocabularies has been a fertile field of research in the life sciences. Understandably, development of the semantic web has attracted significant attention from parts of the medical and life science community. A nexus of government, academic and corporate sources has funded the construction of semantic web ontologies for a range of biomedical and biological vocabularies, including: clinical terms (SNOMED), genetic sequencing (Gene Ontology), proteins (PRotein Ontology) and general ontology repositories (Open Biological and Biomedical Ontologies). Even several of the upper-level ontologies surveyed in the preceding chapter were the beneficiaries of bioinformatics funding. The nature and scale of the classificatory structures of life sciences makes the semantic web, and ontologies in particular, seem especially well suited.

A problem arises for the operationalisation of ontologies, however, due to the tendency for classificatory practices to engage multiple systems or conceptual schemes. As an example, sociologists have explored how microbial objects are frequently analysed through competing frames of physiological and genetic characteristics in laboratories (Sommerlund 2006). While the homogenisation of vocabularies holds promise for system-level interoperability across medical and life science industries, it risks the occlusion of practiced differentiation, in which biological objects are allowed to 'speak' through alternate and potentially inconsistent frames (Bowker and Starr 1999). Moreover the promulgation of institutionally invested ontologies has broader societal implications—as Smart et al. (2008) have shown, social categories of race and ethnicity are increasingly filtered through genetic codes, suggesting that biomedical categories are far from being innocent epistemological constructs.

This study seek to explore some of the trade-offs of taxonomic standardisation through a content analysis of ontologies and surrounding debates in the life science and bioinformatics communities. It begins by briefly examining some of the more successful ontologies used in biological research, including two of the most widely cited and noted: an umbrella biomedical ontology collaborative effort known as the 'OBO Foundry', and a particularly successful biological ontology, the Gene Ontology. These examples highlight 'state of the art', large-scale, interoperable biological classification systems, while also demonstrating some of the latent tensions in the move towards standardised representations of biological objects. This examination holds a secondary purpose—to consider also how new computational representations of biological objects themselves can be understood as 'second-order', discursive objects, reflecting the epistemological theories and methodological practices—the perspectival orbits—of their authors. This has bearing on the more general question of commensurability, posed in earlier chapters. Rather than attempt an explicit analysis of the commensurability of multiple ontologies here, however, the study discusses how some of the perspectival character of bioinformatic systems might be made more perspicuous in the process of ontology design and dissemination. This in turn can be viewed as a series of tentative suggestions for how it might be possible to reach at least partial commensurability and interoperability between ontologies and their underlying conceptualisations.

Biological ontologies

Developing formal ontologies which can be used and reused across biological research teams is a formidable undertaking, both technically and culturally. In many cases the advent of new standardised mechanisms like semantic web ontologies incur the familiar penalty of trading cost—of migrating existing information systems to yet another format—against technological obsolescence. Moreover ontologies are technically challenging to construct, presuming not only knowledge of the biomedical field, but also a new set of technical procedures and vocabulary.

In the biological field these challenges are partially mitigated by the kinds of advantages mentioned above—reusability, portability and interoperability of data, and the possibility of automatic inferencing across large conceptual taxonomies. Indeed, interest in ontologies has led to bioinformatic research groups funding much of the core semantic web research itself.

In the past decade there have been numerous efforts to construct ontologies and other highly structured bioinformatic taxonomies:

- The National Cancer Institute (part of the US National Institutes of Health) has developed a thesaurus and meta-thesaurus, covering a wide range of clinical, research and health administration terms.

- Systematized Nomenclature of Medicine-Clinical Terms (SNOMED-CT), funded by the US Federal Government, is a healthcare terminology covering over one million clinical terms; it is now moving towards management by an international standards development organisation.

- Unified Medical Language System (UMLS) was developed by the National Library of Medicine in the United States; it is another general purpose vocabulary for biomedical, healthcare and informatics terms.

- MedicalWordNet was an experimental extension of the Princeton WordNet thesaurus to the medical domain, distinguishing medical facts (determined by experts) from beliefs (held by lay users).

- BioCyc (Cycorp) is part of a large research knowledge base operated by Cycorp Inc., a private US company; it contains databases of 'pathways and genomes of different organisms'.

- Dumontier ontologies were developed by Michel Dumontier at Carleton University, Canada, to describe 'biological and scientific concepts and relations'.

- The Open Biological and Biomedical Ontologies (OBO) Foundry was hosted at Berkeley; it is an umbrella hosting environment and framework for independent ontology development and collaboration.

- There have been several smaller sub-disiplinary research taxonomies and ontologies, such as OpenGalen, BioPAX and Ecocyc (Aranguren 2005).

These initiatives, with varying degrees of cost and complexity, all aim to deliver standardised vocabularies of biomedical and biological entities to researchers and practitioners. The following sections review two of these in further detail.

OBO Foundry

The largest organisation of ontologies is housed by the Open Biological and Biomedical Ontologies (OBO) Foundry, hosted by Berkeley but with participants and funding from around the United States and Europe (OBO Foundry 2010). Several quotes from the OBO Foundry website highlight its aims and methods for designing and maintaining ontologies:

> The OBO Foundry is a collaborative experiment involving developers of science-based ontologies who are establishing a set of principles for ontology development with the goal of creating a suite of orthogonal interoperable reference ontologies in the biomedical domain (OBO Foundry 2010).
>
> It is our vision that a core of these ontologies will be fully interoperable, by virtue of a common design philosophy and implementation, thereby enabling scientists and their instruments to communicate with minimum ambiguity. In this way the data generated in the course of biomedical research will form a single, consistent, cumulatively expanding, and algorithmically tractable whole.
>
> The OBO Foundry is open, inclusive and collaborative. The contributors are those biological researchers and ontology developers who have agreed to work together on an evolving set of design principles that can foster interoperability of ontologies, and ensure a gradual improvement of quality and formal rigor in ontologies, in ways designed to meet the increasing needs of data and information integration in the biomedical domain (OBO Foundry 2010).
>
> Experience thus far confirms that adherence to OBO principles is largely self-policing because of the positive benefits that accrue to individual members. The task of the OBO coordinators is to help to build this community (OBO Foundry 2010).

As these quotes suggest, the OBO Foundry is structured very much like an open access academic journal, open to general contributions, with a group of editors responsible for outlining and enforcing 'a common design philosophy and implementation' (OBO Foundry 2010).

Presently the OBO Foundry lists around 60 discrete ontologies, which relate to a wide range of biomedical fields. Some of the ontologies are anatomical, describing parts of particular organisms such as spiders, mice and fungi; others are taxonomic, covering various species of, for instance, amphibians, flies and disease; others again are methodological, describing units of measure and biological instruments; and a final set of ontologies can be described as 'foundational', covering general spatial and temporal concepts, as well as biological processes, functions and components. According to its website, and several publications by its editors, the ontologies gathered in the OBO Foundry are intended to interoperate 'orthogonally'—meaning they need not fit together as an entirely consistent and comprehensive whole, but they ought not to contradict another ontology's definitional terms and, where possible, ought also to reuse more basic conceptual axioms declared in other ontologies.

Foundational principles

In a positioning paper published in 2007, members of the OBO Consortium claim:

> Our long-term goal is that the data generated through biomedical research should form a single, consistent, cumulatively expanding and algorithmically tractable whole. Our efforts to realize this goal, which are still very much in the proving stage, reflect an attempt to walk the line between the flexibility that is indispensable to scientific advance and the institution of principles that is indispensable to successful co-ordination (Smith et al. 2007).

In a set of associated publications, several of the editors have attempted to elucidate what these 'principles' might be. Aside from questions of naming conventions and design patterns applied to the ontologies, there are a number of what might be termed 'epistemological' recommendations—which pertain to just how biological objects are to be represented, understood and reasoned over within a conformant ontological representation.

The first suggestion relates to the compositing of class relationships. The key recommendation here is that ontologies ought to utilise 'two backbone hierarchies of "is_a" and "part_of" relations' (Smith et al. 2007). Class composition, the foundational activity of ontology modelling, should then be driven by finding relationships of specialisation–generalisation—where members of one class can be said to be members of another—and of part–whole—where members of one class can be said to parts of members of another.

In a series of further publications, Barry Smith—one of the foundry editors—and others have also attempted to define a so-called 'Basic

Formal Ontology' (BFO), which describes a metaphysical theory of reality in a formal ontology. The purpose of such an ontology would be that, if successfully adopted, domain-level ontologies such as biomedical ones would have commensurate views over foundational notions such as time and space, universals and particulars, substances and qualities, and so on. In the authors' terms, the underlying theory is one of 'naive realism', which eschews various conceptualised contaminants in favour of a kind of commonsense empiricism, founded on observational data furnished by the natural sciences. Perhaps its most controversial claim is a top-level distinction between 'occurents' (events or processing taking place 'in time') and 'continuants' (objects which endure 'through time'). Espousing what they call 'ontological pluralism', in a paper titled 'The Cornucopia of Formal-Ontological Relations', Smith and Grenon (2004) argue for a dualistic—and mutually incommensurable—view of objects. On the one hand, a three-dimensionalist view sees objects as occupying spatial locality within a series of temporal points; on the other, a four-dimensionalist view sees objects as mere apparitions of underlying processes which take place within a spatio-temporal continuum. Smith and Grenon (2004) further argue that neither view is independently sufficient to account for the kinds of descriptions and representations ontology modellers and designers need in practice. By co-ordinating incompatible perspectives within the same foundational ontology, multiple, equally viable, scientific descriptions can be housed in derivative ontologies, constrained only by veridicality. Moreover such descriptions have the advantage of making explicit their perspectival orientation towards the objects described.

The BFO has been explicitly referenced by around 10 per cent of the OBO ontologies (OBO Foundry 2010), suggesting its foundation definitions have been of some practical use in biomedical ontology design. How much this reflects commitments to its underlying theory of ontological pluralism is difficult to gauge.

The Gene Ontology

Of the 60 or so ontologies housed by the OBO Foundry, the Gene Ontology is its flagship one in size and usage. It has been under active and ongoing development since 2000, having originated as an effort to unite three existing genomic databases:

- the FlyBase project (cataloguing a particular species of fruitfly, *Drosophila melanogaster*)

- the Mouse Genome Informatics project (cataloguing the 'laboratory mouse')

- the Saccharomyces Genome Database project (cataloguing the budding yeast *Saccharomyces cerevisiae*) (Ashburner et al. 2000).

The US National Institute of Health provided the initial grant to consolidate these databases, which were then organised into the nascent Gene Ontology, with the much grander ambition of cataloguing general biological functions systematically. Currently the Gene Ontology is managed by the Gene Ontology Consortium, a loose group of US and Europe-based institutes, funded by a range of grants. The Gene Ontology website acknowledges several benefactors: 'Direct support for the Gene Ontology Consortium is provided by an R01 grant from the National Human Genome Research Institute (NHGRI) [grant HG02273]; AstraZeneca; Incyte Genomics; the European Union and the UK Medical Research Council' (The GO Consortium 2010).

The current Gene Ontology comprises approximately 22,000 concepts. These are organised into three separate—though related—sub-ontologies:

- the Biological Process—the 'biological objective to which the gene or gene product contributes'

- the Molecular Function—the 'biochemical activity... of a gene product'

- the Cellular Component—the 'place in a cell where a gene product is active'.

Genes, gene products and gene product groups can each be described by one or more attributes from each of these categories. The authors of Gene Ontology note:

> The relationships between a gene product (or gene-product group) to biological process, molecular function and cellular component are one-to-many, reflecting the biological reality that a particular protein may function in several processes, contain domains that carry out diverse molecular functions, and participate in multiple alternative interactions with other proteins, organelles or locations in the cell (Ashburner et al. 2000).

While these sub-ontologies are clearly related, the designers are restrained from defining any such relationships explicitly—this would complicate the overall ontological structure, lead to possible errors and hinder adoption among the bioinformatic community.

Factors in the success of gene ontology

In the comparatively obscure world of biological ontologies, the Gene Ontology has been incredibly successful. Its website lists 2,829 articles that cite or make use of the ontology, while Google Scholar suggests the positioning paper introducing the ontology has been cited 4,773 times since its publication in 2000 (The GO Consortium 2010).

A study by Michael Bada et al. titled 'A Short Study on the Success of the Gene Ontology'—some of the authors of which also collaborated on the Gene Ontology itself—concluded that seven factors contributed to its successful emergence as the *de facto* taxonomy for genetic coding:

1. community involvement
2. clear goals
3. limited scope
4. simple, intuitive structure
5. continuous evolution
6. active curation
7. early use (Bada et al. 2004).

Of these factors, 1, 5, 6 and 7 relate to extrinsic—or sociological—features, which help explain its adoption. Specifically, involving the bioinformatic community, whose members would ultimately use the ontology early in its development, and continuously improving and actively maintaining the ontology, has played a significant role in its success.

Another, underrated element is that the overarching policing of the ontology has balanced classificatory quality with community input. Other ontologies—and also thesauri, taxonomies and controlled vocabularies—have suffered either by being closed to diverse community input, or by being too open to community input, with quality being corroded as a result. Related to this, the very publication of the Gene Ontology itself, alongside supporting academic materials, encourages would-be users to browse, use and potentially extend the ontology, fostering further collaboration and adoption.

Biological cultures, ontological cultures

Ontologies, in spite of their formal rigour, remain intransigently cultural artefacts, and therefore reflect the cultural biases and assumptions of their authors. Unsurprisingly, given the complexity and field of these kinds of artefacts, they tend to be funded by a combination of well-heeled Western university, government and corporate sponsors. In their purely technical form, even accompanied by academic publications, relatively little can be gleaned about the perspectival assumptions that underwrite their construction. As ontologies like the Gene Ontology emerge as *de facto* standards, adopted by increasing numbers of bioinformatics researchers and, further downstream, medical practitioners, it becomes increasingly vital—and yet exceedingly difficult—to understand the motivating choices behind one particular method of 'carving nature at its joints'. As Bowker and Starr (1999) illustrate in their discussion of conceptual schemes in medical contexts, the process of standardisation inevitably tends towards ossification—where objects are demarcated within increasingly uncontested categorial boundaries.

The Gene Ontology exemplifies this positing of predefined categorial assertions. While the authors have published papers that discuss and justify distinctions, these too have the appearance of organic origin, as though this and no other conceptual scheme could meet a set of idealised scientific desiderata. The context of the production and dissimination of the ontology remains obscured in these discussions—indeed such considerations would appear out of place, unnatural, within the discursive constraints of biological scientific publications.

This contrasts with kind of picture Julie Sommerlund (2006), for instance, describes in relation to practicing scientists working with multiple microbial classification systems. She writes:

> When I first visited the Molecular Microbial Ecology Group, it struck me that everybody told me stories of conflict when they introduced me to their work. They told stories of historical conflicts (about earlier forms of science that had been difficult to get past) and stories of concurrent conflicts between traditions or paradigms that were still influential. These kinds of conflicts seemed very important to the researchers, presumably because their field is interdisciplinary, combining as it does molecular microbiology with microbial ecology (Sommerlund 2006).

By contrast, presented in their idealised formal state, ontologies and even associated published collateral demonstrate no such conflict. Indeed the 'resistible rise' and permeation of the Gene Ontology through bioinformatic discourse seems to take place without forcable opposition, though of course this opposition may well exist, both at a paradigmatic level—in the fundamental theoretical assumptions on which the design of the ontology rests—and the piece-meal level—in the individual concepts admitted to the ontology in the course of its various iterations. But the absence of visible contestation serves only to obscure just what perspectival characteristics the informational system has inherited from its authorial sources and context.

Ontological objects

In *The Order of Things*, Foucault writes of the 'great tables of the seventeenth and eighteenth centuries, when in the disciplines of biology, economics and philology the raw phenomena of experience was classified, categorised, organised and labelled' (Foucault 1970). In the twenty-first century, bioinformatics is reorienting the description of biological objects away from tabular and hierarchical structures, towards directed acyclic informational graphs of incomparably greater scale and sophistication, operated by multidisplinary and globally distributed teams of human and—increasingly—computational agents. The costs, expertise and resources for developing and maintaining these structures invariably constrains the number of rival ontologies, resulting in a kind of gradual 'merger and acquisition' activity as localised databases are rolled into umbrella frameworks like the OBO Foundry.

In this context, bioinformational objects tend to inherit some of the very characteristics of the biological objects they represent. Like genes, they codify complex sets of instructions; like viruses, they can proliferate across the unfettered 'body' of the internet; like cells, they can exist in complex interwoven structures and linkages with other objects; and like all organic materials they leave traces on the—in their case, purely digital—environment. And while in a mundane sense they are products of specifically research cultures, in another sense they operate increasingly like biological cultures—transmitting, consuming, adapting and evolving as if independent of the human agents responsible for them. In this sense they are active rather than passive; coupled with reasoning algorithms, they are able to grow and produce 'new information' or 'new knowledge' via deductive inferencing procedures. They are then to some extent self-explicating and self-analysing discursive artefacts, quasi-objects in the Latourian sense, cultural entitites, but also possessing a pecular nature of their own. However, the preceding analysis shows there is a risk of information objects becoming 'naturalised' in a different way, as the 'cultured' part of their nature—the particular material conditions, epistemological theories and methodological practices of the context in which they emerge—is occluded.

Towards compromise: ontologies in practice

As Bowker and Star (1999) suggest, information systems have the propensity to reify and rigidify disciplinary categories. In the case of biological ontologies, the formal rigour of these artefacts affords research groups powerful means for analysing and sharing scientific results. This comes at the cost, I would argue, of increasing difficulty of negotiating the conceptual boundaries under which biological objects are located. Moreover the pristine mathematical formalism in which these systems are described serves to obscure the messy contested practices of scientific discovery and definition, in favour of a definitive conceptualisation.

The examples of the OBO Foundry and Gene Ontology suggest some of these concerns can be mitigated by a number of policing determinations before and during the development of biological ontologies. Retaining a relatively open policy towards the ongoing development permits scientific innovations—both paradigmatic and piece-meal—to revise ontological structures, while preserving the kinds of quality characteristics that make the ontologies serviceable to a scientific community at all. Open access and publication of the ontologies encourages ongoing use and critical peer review. However, as standardised bioinformatic ontological structures become increasingly central to the practice of research, it becomes important to develop ways of describing the theoretical scaffolds that underpin these structures. This poses difficulties for the authors of ontologies themselves, and for sociological researchers who engage with ontologies from outside their disciplinary terrain, as cultured rather naturalised objects.

Part of the difficulty arises via a second-order, meta problem of commensurability, which can be posed as follows. While the ontology commensurability framework presented in earlier chapters provides a mechanism for comparing ontologies, what emerges from the case of the Gene Ontology in particular, in the conflicting accounts and styles of the authors of biological ontologies, on the one hand, and those of sociologists of biology—such as Sommerlund, and Bowker and Star—on the other, is the potential need to navigate between the respective advocatory and critical views of standardised knowledge systems. Here the question is less, then, one of commensurability between systems themselves than between the disciplines which propagate and dissect them. This requires a respect for the efforts of ontology developers, without losing sight of potential power effects within the epistemic frames they operate within—the propensity, for instance, for standardised vocabularies to eclipse rival theories, terms and conceptualisations. Equally, it requires avoiding lapsing into naïve forms of reconciliatory relativism and perspectivalism, in which all vantage points are accommodated, but in a manner that deflates them of critical resonance and impact.

A starting point towards this goal would follow the model already laid out in the commensurability framework—it involves identifying a set of salient distinctions in the respective viewpoints. These distinctions in turn can be evaluated for those viewpoints, quantified, weighted and subjected to further algorithmic treatment if necessary. This treatment fundamentally, though, would seek to develop an analysis of how ontologies are designed and used, both on their own terms—using the methodological and theoretical principles laid out by the authors themselves, where available—and within the broader epistemic fields in which they operate, using the critical evaluative apparatuses and conceptual distinctions operationalised by sociologists of science. From the point of view of users and adopters, this analysis provides a mechanism for what would at least be a preliminary evaluation of the trade-offs, assumptions and commitments entailed by usage of an ontology. This, in turn, makes for a critical rather than purely dogmatic or passive engagement to a particular set of ontological concepts, terms and corresponding practices.

References

Aranguren, M.E. 2005. 'Ontology Design Patterns for the Formalisation of Biological Ontologies', technical report, University of Manchester.

Ashburner, M., C.A. Ball, J.A. Blake, D. Botstein, H. Butler, J.M. Cherry, A.P. Davis, K. Dolinski, S.S. Dwight, J.T. Eppig, M.A. Harris, D.P. Hill, L. Issel-Tarver, A. Kasarskis, S. Lewis, J.C. Matese, J.E. Richardson, M. Ringwald, G.M. Rubin and G. Sherlock. 2000. 'Gene Ontology: Tool for the Unification of Biology: The Gene Ontology Consortium', *Nature Genetics* 25(1), pp. 25–29.

Bada, M., R. Stevens, C. Goble, Y. Gil, M. Ashburner, J.A. Blake, J.M. Cherry, M. Harris and S. Lewis. 2004. 'A Short Study on the Success of the Gene Ontology', *Web Semantics: Science, Services and Agents on the World Wide Web* 1(2), pp. 235–40.

Bowker, G.C. and S.L. Star. 1999. *Sorting Things Out: Classification and its Consequences*. Cambridge, MA: MIT Press.

Foucault, M. 1970. *The Order of Things: An Archaeology of the Human Sciences*. New York: Vintage Books.

The GO Consortium. 2010. The GO Consortium website, *http://www.geneontology.org* (accessed 16 June 2010).

OBO Foundry. 2010. 'The Open Biological and Biomedical Ontologies', *http://www.obofoundry.org* (accessed 16 June 2010).

Smart, A., R. Tutton, P. Martin, G.T.H. Ellison and R. Ashcroft. 2008. 'The Standardization of Race and Ethnicity in Biomedical Science Editorials and UK Biobanks', *Social Studies of Science* 38, p. 407.

Smith, B. and P. Grenon. 2004. 'The Cornucopia of Formal-Ontological Relations', *Dialectica* 58, pp. 279–96.

Smith, B., M. Ashburner, C. Rosse, J. Bard, W. Bug, W. Ceusters, L.J. Goldberg, K. Eilbeck, A. Ireland, C.J. Mungall, The OBI Consortium, N. Leontis, P. Rocca-Serra, A. Ruttenberg, S-A. Sansone, R.H. Scheuermann, N. Shah, P.L. Whetzel and S. Lewis. 2007. 'The OBO Foundry: Coordinated Evolution of Ontologies to Support Biomedical Data Integration', *Nature Biotechnology* 25, pp. 1251–55.

Sommerlund, J. 2006. 'Classifying Microorganisms: The Multiplicity of Classifications and Research Practices in Molecular Microbial Ecology', *Social Studies of Science* 36, pp. 909–28.

11

On commensurability

Liam Magee

The freedom with the constraints of ritual logic that comes from perfect mastery of that logic is what makes it possible for the same symbol to refer back to realities that are opposed in terms of the axiomatics of the system itself. Consequently, although it is not inconceivable that a rigorous algebra of practical logics might one day be written, it will never be done unless it is understood that logical logic, which only speaks of them negatively, if at all, in the very operations through which it constitutes itself by denying them, is not equipped to describe them without destroying them. It is a question of reconstituting the 'fuzzy', flexible, partial logic of this partially integrated system of generative schemes which, being partially mobilized in relation to each particular situation, produces, in each case, below the level of the discourse and the logical control that it makes possible, a 'practical' definition of the situation and the functions of the action (which are almost always multiple and interlocking), and which, with the aid of a simple yet inexhaustible combinatory, generates the actions best suited to fulfil these functions with the limits of the available means (Bourdieu 1990).

Several of the preceding chapters compared approaches to describing or representing knowledge within particular fields. One way of characterising these studies is that they are seeking to understand what might be termed, following Kuhn (1970), the commensurability of ontologies and their associated formalisms and frameworks. The present chapter discusses the question of commensurability in more theoretical terms, stepping through several philosophical positions to arrive at the basis for the framework presented in the next chapter. So far, commensurability has been about both the explicit conceptual commitments of knowledge systems, and an implicit 'something' which sits behind them. But what sorts of 'somethings' are these; what is it that can be said to be commensurable or otherwise? Not just the systems themselves, otherwise ontology matching techniques would presumably be sufficient—there would be no need to step outside the system to glean further information. Rather, it is the constellation of beliefs, assumptions, commitments, intentions, structures and practices held by the people responsible for those systems, who design and use them. Since people also engage in a range of other social constellations and configurations, it would be accurate to speak of the dedicated cultures—organisational, communal, national or global—responsible for knowledge systems. This amorphous kind of entity will be given greater specificity in Chapter 12, 'A framework for commensurability'; however, its description will invariably be indebted to, and share, many of the features exhibited by canonical 'structural' accounts of socialised knowledge: Kuhnian paradigms, Foucauldian *epistemes* and Quinean conceptual schemes.

The discussion of the present chapter begins, then, with a survey of these significant developments. It follows with an examination of several notable critiques of these different brands of conceptual relativism, made by Davidson and Derrida. These debates remain of central concern to contemporary theories of knowledge. Nonetheless they belong to a preceding generation of scholars; to counter with a more recent debate, the discussion embarks on an interlude examining the 'science wars' of the 1990s, via the series of critical analyses developed by Hacking. Returning to the formative problems of describing shared conceptual schemes, the discussion then presents recent theorisations by Habermas, Brandom and Gardenfors, in more detail than was afforded in the literature review. Together the positions outlined by these authors constitute an overarching theoretical scaffolding on which a framework can be erected, rehabilitated from the relativist critiques which beset their precursors. The resulting view of conceptual cultures, interconnected through predominantly communicative practices, is not so much 'poststructural'—through that epithet is employed below—as a more elastic and granular form of 'structuralism'. The critical resulting move is one from 'conceptual relativism'—the charge laid, variously, at Kuhn, Quine and Foucault—to a form of 'conceptual perspectivism', where concepts oriented within a culture do frame the view out onto the objects they observe, but critically permit a revisionary 'kick-back', both from the objects themselves, and from the intersubjective communicative sphere of other cultures and agents who also observe and engage them.

A full critical exposition of any of these authors might constitute a substantial study in itself. The apology for the abbreviated treatment offered here is only that these positions provide useful stepping stones towards the articulation of a theoretical position, which in turn provides greater specificity and robustness for the specific methods and dimensions offered in the framework description. The alternative—to do away with the theoretical artifice altogether—would set the framework adrift, as just another concocted instrument among others. It is intended that the discussion here offers the epistemological foundations, then, that orient the subsequent technical and empirical overlay that the framework and its application in the case studies provide.

A world of 'material intangibles': social structures, conceptual schemes and cultural perspectives

In Chapter 7, 'An historical introduction to formal knowledge systems', the historical survey of knowledge systems described the movement known as *logical positivism*, an intellectual tradition which emphasised rigorous logical analysis and an unwavering commitment to empirical observation. This line of thought, influential in the early half of the twentieth century, came under increasing critique in the post-war period. The later Wittgenstein relinquished his early normative analysis (Wittgenstein 1921) for a descriptive exploration of language games (Wittgenstein 1967); Austin suggested new lines of inquiry for analysing utterances beyond their purely truth-functional semantic content (Austin 1975), instigating new dimensions for gauging their practical effect; and Sellars demonstrated the implied metaphysics which dwelt within the purportedly pure observational propositions of empiricism (Sellars 1997). From other angles, Marxian, Saussurean and Freudian-fuelled critiques sought to expose the deep structures that lay beneath the apparent epiphenomena of social, linguistic and psychological life.

Kuhn, Foucault and Quine represent further, mature 'refractions' of the harsh critical light shone on the presuppositions of the positivists. Kuhn argued that science moved not due to the irrepressible spontaneity of genius, nor the industriousness of well-managed institutions, nor, even, the inherent corrective process of Popperian falsifications endemic to scientific practice. Instead, science is a puzzle-solving exercise conducted, under normal conditions, under a 'paradigm'—a set of core theoretical tenets which laid out the problems normal scientific practice could pursue (Kuhn 1970). Foucault in turn suggested that the human sciences operated under similar epistemic structures—'*epistemes*'—which gave rise to a set of broadly contiguous discursive practices (Foucault 1970). These discursive practices participate within, and help actively constitute, political structures and techniques. In short, knowledge is power in a literal sense—it is invariably imbricated in the 'political'. Quine, finally, put forward a variant of the 'theoretical underdetermination' thesis—that for any given set of observational data, more than one theory could be compatible with it, and therefore a theory would always remain critically underdetermined by its evidence. Prevailing theories instead do so because of the ease of their accommodation within an encompassing conceptual scheme. Each of these points to a *structural* feature in the production of knowledge: paradigms change when puzzles can no longer be solved; epistemic discursive practices operate within a mutually reinforcing synergistic dynamic with power structures; rival scientific theories win out because of their fortuitous affiliation with peripheral sets of beliefs. Narratives of either the heroic individual genius—the Darwin or Einstein of their field—or of the efficient managerial enterprise—of which IBM was an early progenitor—engaging in unencumbered hypothesis testing are exposed as mythological fictions, or, at best, as radically insufficient conditions for the production of knowledge.

These kinds of structural accounts of knowledge hold considerable appeal—they permit analysis to extend beyond the surface presentation of the practices, discourses and statements that constitute the tangible aspects of knowledge. At the same time, they are materialist rather than metaphysical, showing how epistemic conceptualisations are manifest through these very tangible elements. A paradigm is just the collection of shared theories, hypotheses, puzzles, problems, experiments and data that constitute 'normal science' at a point in time. An *episteme* is similarly only exhibited through the discursive practices which constitute it. A conceptual scheme is the shared beliefs held by a scientific or knowledge culture, manifest in both its utterances and practices. Yet these concepts are not mere relinquishable or interchangeable metaphors. They reference an importantly emergent property of knowledge, in which the whole is more than the sum of parts. Just as a portrait is more than the quantities and intensities of colour which compose it, these structures organise and formalise concepts, relations and properties into crystalline frames through which objects can be known. They constitute something like the perspective or world view through which objects can be observed, inspected, analysed, described and, ultimately, acted on. It is this material quality—that these structures allow their participating agents to reach out, through conceptual frames, to the world—that differentiates the epistemological bent of scientific and knowledgeable enterprises from other, purely metaphysical kinds of conjecture.

The next two chapters, then, introduce a vocabulary to capture the characteristics of this 'material intangible' thing which is both part of and more than the knowledge systems it sits behind. These first structural descriptions, invariably directed towards sweeping periods of history rather than the micro-cultures which produce particular knowledge systems, nevertheless pave the way towards the articulation of a framework for describing this elusive entity.

Kuhnian paradigms

Thomas Kuhn's *The Structure of Scientific Revolutions* systematised a thesis which had previously been only put forward informally in the earlier theories of authors such as Koyre, Polanyi and Feyerband. The proposition that science proceeds not as an accumulation of facts which serve to inductively corroborate some theory, the classical notion of science, but as a series of paradigms which instead determine what sorts of facts may be produced, was succinctly and compellingly elaborated here. Since its publication, it has tremendous influence in the history of science and, arguably, even greater appeal through the 'trickle-down' dissemination of key terms into the broader cultural lexicon. In the practice of historical and social studies of science, rival models such as Actor-Network Theory now hold sway. Nevertheless Kuhn's thesis is a pivotal moment in the widespread recognition that the movement of science is marked not only by quantitative epistemic growth but also, and more foundationally, through qualitative epistemic shifts. These qualitative shifts are described by two key concepts, which warrant further exploration: paradigms and incommensurability.

Paradigms are, for Kuhn, the epistemological conditions under which the normal enterprise of science operates. They are the 'ways of knowing' which make possible the posing and solving of puzzles: 'The existence of this strong network of commitments—conceptual, theoretical, instrumental and methodological—is a principle source of the metaphor that relates normal science to puzzle-solving' (Kuhn 1970, p. 42). While practitioners of science exhibit a kind of 'know-how' imparted by a paradigm, this does not necessarily constitute 'knowing-that' the paradigm exists; paradigms need not be, and only infrequently are, explicit: 'Scientists work from models acquired through education and through subsequent exposure to the literature often without quite knowing or needing to know what characteristics have given these models the status of community paradigms' (Kuhn 1970, p. 46). Paradigms are also the grounding conditions of the scientific practices they make possible, and cannot be made explicit as form of rules, statements or axioms: 'Paradigms may be prior to, more binding, and more complete than any set of rules for research that could be unequivocally abstracted from them' (Kuhn 1970, p. 46). As Kuhn notes elsewhere, paradigms have a very broad extensional definition—seeming to mean a set of both implied and explicit epistemic commitments; a meta-theoretical ground on which more granular theories and experimental practice can be constructed; a process of socialisation—what scientists do to become scientists; and an historically, spatially or epistemically bounded field, separated from others before, after or around it. In fact each of these definitional facets permit further generous extensions in the application of 'paradigm' (or its eventual cognate partner employed here) (Kuhn 2002).

On the one hand, following its popular usage there seems little reason to limit the use of paradigm to scientific forms of knowledge only. Other disciplinary fields—academic and industrial—seem to meet some if not all of the qualifying features of paradigms. Management practices, for instance, operate within broad cultural conceptual models, which seem to undergo more or less radical transitions when they lose their efficacy for problem solving. Moreover, often the distinction between a paradigm of rigorous science and, perhaps, a broader paradigm of the science and its applications are difficult to distinguish, particularly as science itself frequently bifurcates into sub-disciplinary and inter-disciplinary fields— ontology matching, introduced in earlier chapters, is a good example of a self-contained field that borrows approaches from beyond its computational science borders. Paradigms applied to clear historical revolutions—the Copernican turn in cosmology, Newton's laws of physics, Maxwell's thermodynamic equations, Darwin's theory of evolution, to take some of Kuhn's examples—show comparatively harsh lines of theoretical demarcation, and make a compelling narrative of different ways of seeing and knowing experienced through various paradigmatic lens. In the twilight world of less spectacular transitions— but no less revolutionary, for those who go through them—such lines are more blurry. Knowledge systems constitute ideal candidate expressions of more fine-grained paradigms, and these paradigms need considerably more elastic definition.

Similarly, for Kuhn—as for Foucault, further below—paradigms are invariably expressed in historical terms; paradigms succeed each other. Yet at a more granular level, different spheres of knowledge frequently coincide, compete, intersect and merge. Kuhn allows, for example, for a physicist and a chemist to provide different definitions of a molecule, based on the different paradigms they operate under (Kuhn 1970). However, even this example assumes too rigid a distinction around an agent's paradigmatic engagement—as though one can be either a physicist or a chemist, but not both. Paradigms operating at a useful enough level of granularity to be applied to knowledge systems need to be the sorts of structures which agents can belong to severally, and for limited durations—enough to allow self-conscious and self-reflexive examination of the key commitments belonging to one or another co-existing paradigm. This is not an arbitrary mandate imposed here, but rather a feature of the kinds of analysis which take place in the translation of knowledge systems. System analysts, at least on an implicit, phenomenological level, frequently operate within a cognitive geometry of rotating paradigms—figuring out how to describe a concept first one way, then another; how to classify an object one way, and then another; and so on. Kuhn's paradigms all but cover these scenarios, but need to be extended down towards the 'micro-paradigmatic' level to be useful here. I therefore look to carry across the insights of Kuhn's definition of 'paradigm', as a general set of epistemological commitments and practices, into the theoretical dimensions of the framework, while looking to refine it into a concept more applicable to more fine-grained knowledge structures.

Kuhn also introduces the even more critical term—in the context of the present study—of 'incommensurability'. This is used in the *The Structure of Scientific Revolutions* to describe how rival paradigms hold 'incommensurable ways of seeing the world and of practicing science in it' (Kuhn 1970, p. 4). As discussed below, incommensurability is a controversial term. Incommensurable paradigms suggest, literally, that propositions belonging to one are untranslatable into those of the other. By extension, these propositions are true or false only within the frame of reference of the current paradigm. Kuhn first depicts incommensurability in optical rather than linguistic metaphors. In a key chapter titled 'Revolutions as changes of world view', he works carefully to avoid the most obvious accusations of relativism:

> Do we, however, really need to describe what separates Galileo from Aristotle, or Lavoisier from Priestley, as a transformation of vision? Did these really see different things when looking at the same sorts of objects?' (Kuhn 1970, p. 120).

> I am... acutely aware of the difficulties created by saying that when Aristotle and Galileo looked at swinging stones, the first saw constrained fall, the second a pendulum. The same difficulties are presented in an even more fundamental form by the opening sentences of this section: though the world does not change with a change of paradigm, the scientist afterward works in a different world (Kuhn 1970, p. 121).

> Rather than being an interpreter, the scientist who embraces a new paradigm is like the man wearing inverting lenses (Kuhn 1970, p. 122).

Kuhn emphasises, over and over, how different paradigms cause scientists literally to see objects differently. The constellation of concepts which compose a given paradigm structure the observational work of science. Echoing Sellars' critique of empiricism in particular, Kuhn writes: 'The operations and measurements that a scientist undertakes in the laboratory are not "the given" of experience but rather "the collected with difficulty"' (Kuhn 1970, p. 126).

Moreover empirical data is experienced against a paradigmatic backdrop which provides a pre-existing construct for how the data can be organised and interpreted:

> All of this may seem more reasonable if we again remember that neither scientists nor laymen learn to see the world piecemeal or item by item. Except when all the conceptual and manipulative categories are prepared in advance... both scientists and laymen sort out whole areas together from the flux of experience (Kuhn 1970, p. 128).

As these visual cues suggest, Kuhn wants perspectives to be incommensurable to the extent that perceived objects are organised in different conceptual configurations and constellations. In a later postscript (written after, and in response to, Davidson's critique discussed below), Kuhn asserts this incommensurability is not merely terminological, and 'they cannot be resolved simply by stipulating the definitions of troublesome terms' (Kuhn 1970). There is, on the one hand, no immediate language capable of neutralising these conceptual and perspectival differences: 'The claim that two theories are incommensurable is then the claim that there is no language, neutral or otherwise, into which both theories, conceived as sets of sentences, can be translated without residue or loss' (Kuhn 2002, p. 36).

Yet, on the other, there must be a way out of the solipsistic world of a paradigm. There is both the direct 'stimuli' of experience, and a broader communal culture that agents under incommensurable paradigms share. This makes possible, not a neutral language, but translation between two paradigmatically committed languages: 'Briefly put, what the participants in a communication breakdown can do is recognize each other as members of different language communities and then become translators' (Kuhn 1970, p. 202).

Translation is then the vehicle which begins the process of persuasion and conversion to move from one paradigm to another. However, it is frequently insufficient: 'To translate a theory or world view into one's own language is not to make it one's own. For that one must go native, discover that one is *thinking and working in*, not simply translating out of, a language that was previously foreign' (Kuhn 1970, p. 204, my emphasis).

Paradigms are more, then, than use of a language—they are ways of knowing, 'thinking and working'. Until scientists are thinking and acting as though the world operates under Einstein's theory of relativity, they are not operating within the paradigm of relativity.

It is not clear, however, that these clarifications are adequate. In spite of Kuhn's caveats, the edges or boundaries of paradigms seem immutably hard, and nothing explains quite how, except by a process of gradual elision, an individual agent's views shift to the point of belonging to another paradigm. Yet this introduces the pain of regress to an infinity of intermediate paradigms along the way, unacceptably diluting the concept altogether. One of the steps through this difficulty is to suggest that paradigm are structures of considerably greater elasticity than Kuhn wants to allow—that 'scientific revolutions' represent simply quantitatively greater shifts than other, more fine-grained changes in perspectival position. Paradigmatic incommensurability then becomes a question of degree rather than kind—a measure of 'semantic heterogeneity' rather than a quality of conceptual structures.

Foucauldian epistemes

Foucault's notion of *episteme* is more difficult to trace and delineate than Kuhnian paradigms. As Hacking (2002) notes, Foucault rarely lays out explicit definitions of concepts, nor holds on to them for long. In one of his more programmatic declarations, *The Order of Things* introduces *epistemes* indirectly as a means for describing epistemological affinities between different strands of intellectual production. To characterise the sense of the modern *episteme*, Foucault describes the rise of the classificatory disciplines—biology, economics and grammar—in the late eighteenth century:

> We have now advanced a long way beyond the historical event we were concerned with situating—a long way beyond the chronological edges of the rift that divides in depth the episteme of the Western world, and isolates for us the beginning of a certain modern manner of knowing empiricities. This is because the thought that is contemporaneous with us, and with which, willy-nilly, we think, is still largely dominated by the impossibility, brought to light towards the end of the eighteenth century, of basing syntheses in the space of representation, and by the correlative obligations— simultaneous but immediately divided against itself—to open up the transcendental field of subjectivity, and to constitute inversely, beyond the object, what are for us the 'quasi-transcendentals' of Life, Labour and Language (Foucault 1970, p. 272).

In this and other descriptions, several qualities of the *episteme* emerge: it is historical and, unlike a paradigm, situated across rather than within particular knowledge fields. Here, an *episteme* appears resolutely structural—a broad, temporal swathe of beliefs and practices which constitute both our subjectivity and our concepts. For Foucault, as for Kuhn, these structures affect both ways of seeing and speaking: 'What came surreptitiously into being between the age of the theatre and that of the catalogue was not the desire for knowledge, but a new way of connecting things both to the eye and to discourse. A new way of making history' (Foucault 1970, p. 143).

Later, in the more programmatic text of *The Archaeology of Knowledge*, Foucault explicitly defines an *episteme*:

> The analysis of discursive formations, of positivities, and knowledge in their relations with epistemological figures and with the sciences is what has been called, to distinguish it from other possible forms of the history of the sciences, the analysis of the episteme... By episteme, we mean, in fact, the total set of relations that unite, at a given period, the discursive practices that give rise to epistemological figures, sciences, and possibly formalised systems (Foucault 2002, p. 211).

Further on, he elaborates:

> The episteme is not a form of knowledge or type of rationality which, crossing the boundaries of the most varied sciences, manifests the sovereign unity of a subject, a spirit, or a period; it is the totality of relations that can be discovered, for a given period, between the sciences when one analyses them at the level of discursive regularities.
>
> The description of the episteme presents several essential characteristics therefore: it opens up an inexhaustible field and can never be closed; its aim is not to reconstitute the system of postulates that governs all the branches of knowledge (connaissance) of a given period, but to cover an indefinite field of relations. Moreover, the episteme is not a motionless figure that appeared one day with the mission of effacing all that preceded it: it is a constantly moving set of articulations, shifts, and coincidences that are established, only to give rise to others. As a set of relations between sciences, epistemological figures, positivities, and discursive practices, the episteme makes it possible to grasp the set of constraints and limitations which, at a given moment, are imposed on discourse (Foucault 2002, p. 211).

In this later explication, the structural features of an *episteme* appear looser, more elastic. Moreover, an *episteme* is directed less towards the conceptual, and more towards the discursive properties of knowledge formation. An *episteme* here seems disembodied of the 'us' which figured heavily in the description above. Rather it operates as a sort of content-less grid, a network of rules which permits certain kinds of discourse to emerge and be treated as 'science' or 'knowledge'. Naturally there remain human agents in the background, enacting discursive practices, reading, writing and interpreting. However, these are extraneous to the construction of an *episteme*—what matters are the discursive 'relations', 'rules' and 'regularities'. These in turn stand in various relationships to other kinds of non-discursive practices, particularly those employed in the administration of power. For Foucault, clinics, asylums and prisons are the sites *par excellence*, where power-driven practices, discursive and otherwise, intersect—and where an analysis of these practices might lead to their revision or erosion. Since 'science', as a privileged form of epistemic practice, invests particular statements with a peculiar vindicating force for the exercise of power, making explicit the conditions that particularise and legitimate them also exposes them to critique: 'In the enigma of scientific discourse, what the analysis of the episteme questions is not its right to be a science, but the fact that it exists' (Foucault 2002, p. 212).

Elsewhere in interviews Foucault has also emphasised the constraining character of an *episteme*:

> If you like, I would define the episteme retrospectively as the strategic apparatus which permits of separating out from among all the statements which are possible those that will be acceptable within, I won't say a scientific theory, but a field of scientificity, and which it is possible to say are true or false. The episteme is the 'apparatus' which makes possible the separation, not of the true from the false, but of what may from what may not be characterised as scientific (Foucault 1980, p. 197).

In relation to Kuhnian paradigms, then, *epistemes* clearly have points of affinity and divergence. Among the more notable distinctions:

- *Epistemes* relate discursive practices of a science to other practices—both other discursive practices of other forms of knowledge, and other, non-discursive social practices; paradigms remain hermetically sealed structures of a singular science.

- *Epistemes*—at least in the more explicit articulation Foucault provides in later writings—are loose, permeable structures of discursive relations, not the shared perspectives or world views which constitute paradigms.

- *Epistemes* are framed as 'rules' and 'regularities' discerned by an *observer*—the 'archaeologist' of knowledge; paradigms are, while still unconscious to the practitioners of science, much closer to the surface, and at least partially describable by those practitioners.

- *Epistemes* function to make possible and legitimate certain kinds of *statements* within a broader nexus of power; paradigms function specifically for 'normal science' to solve puzzles—only indirectly, and coincidentally, do they engage with discourse.

There are, however, features common to paradigms and *epistemes*: they are largely unconscious for those who engage them, and require particular interpretive tools or methods to discover them; they are not purely conceptual constructs, but also are exhibited within social practices (discursive and otherwise); both reflect social features of a culture or community, rather than an individualistic psychological state of mind; and both involve some form of 'orientation' towards the objects under description—through orientation must be understood in an active sense, as actively constituting rather than merely passively observing those objects. These features carry over to the description of a more fine-grained construct in the framework ahead. Both also offer the problem of how statements can be translated across epistemic or paradigmatic boundaries—a theme returned to below.

Quinean conceptual schemes

Quine's notion of conceptual schemes fits within the generously extended family, which also includes Kuhnian paradigms and Foucauldian *epistemes*. As with *epistemes*, it is difficult to get a definitive view as to what a conceptual scheme is. In a late interview Quine admits: 'The only meaning I attached to it is a vague one. Namely, the conceptual scheme would be the more abstract general structure of one's overall theory' (Quine 1992).

Echoing a famous Quinean sentiment, that science is 'self-conscious common sense', conceptual schemes embrace theories of both scientific and everyday varieties (Quine 1964). While conceptual schemes might connote a sort of cognitive structure, for Quine, they are equally 'cultural posits'. As theories, ultimately they have an explanatory function:

> As an empiricist I continue to think of the conceptual scheme of science as a tool, ultimately, for predicting future experience in the light of past experience... For my part I do, qua lay physicist, believe in physical objects and not Homer's gods; and I consider it a scientific error to believe otherwise. But in point of epistemological footing the physical objects and the gods differ only in degree and not in kind. Both sorts of entities enter our conception only as cultural posits (Quine 1980, p. 44).

Conceptual schemes of all sorts are irretrievably bound to a language, for Quine: 'Conceptualization on any considerable scale is inseparable from language' (Quine 1964, p. 3). He is keen to show that linguistic translation generally, and the special kind of conceptual scheme inherent in scientific theory specifically, suffer the same fate of indeterminacy. For any set of sensory stimuli, there are many more or less meritorious theories to account for them; analogously, for any source language, there are many more or less adequate translations into a target language. For

Quine, the idea of a direct 'sense-datum language' capable of reporting just the facts is one of the two infamous 'dogmas of empiricism', which he attributes to the more naïve leanings of positivism (the other dogma is that there can be a strict separation between analytic and synthetic statements) (Quine 1980). Empiricism instead must be rehabituated to the *a priori* conceptual structures capable of organising perceptions, or else suffer a form of circularity: 'small wonder that the quest for sense data should be guided by the same sort of knowledge that prompts it' (Quine 1964, p. 2).

Unlike the rigid characterisation of paradigms, conceptual schemes admit of ongoing partial and 'self-conscious' revision. Scientific discovery differs in degree rather than kind from other kinds of belief, precisely because it accepts revisionary evidence. Rather than the relativism of pluralised conceptual schemes, though, Quine thinks it is possible to be epistemically committed to a set of beliefs when none better present themselves:

> Have we now so far lowered our sights as to settle for a relativistic doctrine of truth...? Not so. The saving consideration is that we continue to take seriously our own particular aggregate science, our own particular world-theory or loose total fabric of quasi-theories, whatever it may be. Unlike Descartes, we own and use our beliefs of the moment, even in the midst of philosophizing, until what is vaguely called scientific method we change them here and there for the better. Within our own total evolving doctrine, we can judge truth as earnestly and absolutely as can be; subject to correction, but that goes without saying (Quine 1964, pp. 24–25).

The problem of under-determination does not just relate to the relationship of data to theory—it equally applies to translation of one theory to another. Multiple viable translations are always possible: 'manuals for translating one language into another can be set up in divergent ways, all compatible with the totality of speech dispositions, yet incompatible with one another' (Quine 1980, p. 27). Here it is not that the languages or theories are untranslatable; rather, they are translatable in many different ways. And it is the translations themselves which are incommensurable—'incompatible', in Quine's words—with each other. He emphasises this point with a lengthy thought experiment—what happens when a linguist is faced with some unknown language presented by an informant? The preconditions of the experiment are that there is no interpreter, and the language is not a 'kindred' one for the linguist (bears no common cognates or derivations). The linguist is presented with a word, 'gavagai', in the presence of a rabbit. The linguist then employs a steady process of elimination, with the aim of deriving the translation 'gavagai = rabbit'. One of the eventually excluded possibilities is that of equivalence based on *stimulus meaning*, the sense derived from pure experience of the rabbit-phenomenon: perhaps the word 'gavagai' relates to this perception and not the actual animal? (Quine 1964, pp. 31–35). Another is that of occasion sentences, which refer to a particular circumstance of perceiving the rabbit—is the perceiver in a state of 'gavagai', then, on remarking of the rabbit? Or is the rabbit instead in a particular state indicated by 'gavagai', for example, that of being in position to be shot? (Quine 1964, pp. 35–41). Yet another possibility is that of observational sentences: does 'gavagai' relate instead to the phenomenological happening of an observation of a rabbit? (Quine 1964, pp. 41–46). Even after these possibilities are systematically eliminated under controlled circumstances, there is no guarantee of synonymity: 'Who knows but what the objects to which this term applies are not rabbits after all, but mere stages, or brief temporal segments, of rabbits?' (Quine 1964, p. 51). Even if the stimulus meaning—the responses of the informant hearing 'gavagai' on sight of the rabbit—is consistent with the linguist's interpretation of the word 'rabbit', Quine argues that the extra-stimuli requirements for understanding the use of a term differ radically: 'the whole apparatus [for using a term] are interdependent, and the very notion of term is as provincial to our culture as are those associated devices... Occasion sentences and stimulus meaning are general coin; terms and reference are local to our conceptual scheme' (Quine 1964, p. 53). There is ultimately no recourse to sense data or an ideal language for devising a singular mapping between sentences or theory-fragments:

> Sentences translatable outright, translatable by independent evidence of stimulatory occasions, are sparse and must woefully under-determine the analytical hypotheses on which the translation of all further sentences depends... There can be no doubt that rival systems of analytical hypotheses can fit the totality of speech behaviour to perfection, and can fit the totality of dispositions to speech behaviour as well, and still specify mutually incompatible translations of countless sentences insusceptible of independent control (Quine 1980, p. 72).

As noted earlier, conceptual schemes seem broadly contiguous with other structural notions of paradigms and *epistemes*. Quine's critique of positivism is derived from a logical rather than historical analysis, and consequently specific kinds of historical and cultural 'posits' are argued for analytically rather than demonstrated through cases. Consequently their definition is considerably abstract; nevertheless some concrete characteristics can be identified:

- Conceptual schemes are in the first instance *cultural* rather than cognitive entities.
- Conceptual schemes are *elastic*, and capable of endless revision.
- *More than one* conceptual scheme can arise to account for the phenomena being described.
- There can also be more than one *translation* between two conceptual schemes.

There are several implications of Quine's analysis for the treatment of knowledge systems: first, it admits the possibility both of multiple, equally valid knowledge systems in a given domain, and also, of multiple ways of aligning or matching these systems. Second, such systems do not describe the 'sense data', or objects belonging to a domain, neutrally, but bring to bear the background cultural 'posits' inherited by their authors. Third, these 'posits' invariably undergo revision—hence schemes should not be seen in rigid terms like the systems themselves, but as flexible networks which 'cohere' into reified form in systems. Hence uncovering background concepts is necessarily a more heuristic and interpretive exercise.

These three accounts—Kuhnian paradigms, Foucauldian *epistemes* and Quinean conceptual schemes—are now 'classic' structural treatments of knowledge systems in the broad sense, and deserve detailed coverage. The theoretical underpinnings of the ontology commensurability framework build on these treatments, but rely on more recent work of Habermas, Brandom and Gardenfors, which adds both greater descriptive precision about what schemes are, and causal suggestiveness for how it is that multiple schemes arise. In the meantime, the specifically structural character of conceptual schemes and its analogues was to receive significant critical attention in the 1970s; two of these critical lines are reviewed in the next section.

De-structuring critiques: struggling with systems, structures and schemes

What has been described as the 'structural' tendencies in Kuhn, Foucault and Quine is more by way of general shared analogical traits than any strong identifying ideological tenets. Only Foucault could be tentatively affiliated with the intellectual movement known as 'structuralism'—and was, in any case, progressively characterised as a post-structuralist in his later work. Nevertheless, as the discussion above shows, there are common threads between these authors, and indeed others of the same period. These in turn were to come under critical fire from various directions. The critiques by Davidson and Derrida are notable both from the prominence of their respective authors, and for the 'anti-schematic' and 'post-structural' movements to which they gave rise in various strains of linguistics, cultural studies and philosophy of language. The general outline of these critiques is traced in the next two sections.

'On the very idea'...

Davidson explicitly responds to the positions espoused by Kuhn and Quine, suggesting they represent various forms of *conceptual relativism*. Bracketing Whorfian languages and Kuhnian paradigms under the general heading of Quinean 'conceptual schemes', Davidson offers a basic outline of the conceptual relativist's position:

> Conceptual schemes, we are told, are ways of organizing experience; they are systems of categories that give form to the data of sensation; they are points of view from which individuals, cultures, or periods survey the passing scene. There may be no translating from one scheme to another, in which case the beliefs, desires, hopes, and bits of knowledge that characterize one person have no true counterparts for the subscriber to another scheme. Reality itself is relative to a scheme: what counts as real in one system may not in another (Davidson 2006, p. 186).

The inherent paradox involved in such as position is that explaining how conceptual schemes *differ* presupposes an underlying *common* language—and corresponding conceptual scheme. The act of description shows how the terms of both schemes can be mapped onto a higher level set of terms, the language of the description itself: 'Different points of view make sense, but only if there is a common co-ordinate system on which to plot them; yet the existence of a common system belies the claim of dramatic incomparability' (Davidson 2006, p. 197).

Davidson distinguishes between two 'failures of translatability'—complete and partial (Davidson 2006, p. 198). Complete untranslatability means no substantial translation between two languages; partial means some sentences can be translated, some cannot. In going after complete untranslatability, Davidson further distinguishes between the following two scenarios: the first, where speakers talk about *different* worlds using the *same* language; the second, where speakers talk about the *same* world using *different* languages. The first case makes the mistake of exercising one of Quine's dogmas of empiricism, relying on the distinction between analytic and synthetic truths. The second case, Davidson argues, commits an analogous though different sin of relying on a distinction between 'scheme' and 'content'. This so-called 'third dogma'—extending the two Quinean dogmas discussed above—is one which Quine himself is guilty of, as are Kuhn and other purveyors of conceptual relativism.

Davidson proceeds to argue that this dogma assumes conceptual schemes are seen as either 'organising' or 'fitting in' with some 'content'—in turn, such content is either 'reality' or 'experience'. Taken actively, schemes must organise pluralities of worldly or experiential content. But such pluralities must, for Davidson, consist of observable 'individualities', which in the final resort can be shown and demonstrated to other linguistic speakers, even when languages differ. In such cases, 'a language that organizes *such* entities must be a language very like our own' (Davidson 2006, p. 203). Taken passively, schemes must generate true statements of the content they purport to represent: 'the point is that for a theory to fit or face up to the totality of possible sensory evidence is for that theory to be true' (Davidson 2006, p. 204). For the thesis of complete untranslatability, it must be possible for two schemes both to be 'largely true but untranslatable' (Davidson 2006, p. 205). Davidson then invokes Tarski's *Convention T* to demonstrate that on 'our best intuition as to how the concept of truth is used', translation is in fact an 'essential notion':

> according to Tarski's Convention T, a satisfactory theory of truth
> for a language L must entail, for every sentence s of L, a theorem of
> the form 's is true if and only if p' where 's' is replaced by a
> description of s and 'p' by s itself if L is English, and by a translation
> of s into English if L is not English (Davidson 2006, p. 205).

Understanding that a sentence is true in another language involves being able to translate that sentence, or a description of it, into a native language. Consequently, a theory of schemes which are mutually and completely untranslatable (or incommensurable), yet which together contain large sets of true sentences, must lapse into incoherence.

The case for partial untranslatability (or incommensurability) rests on this first result. Davidson invokes what he terms a 'principle of charity'—we understand speakers of other languages (and scientific theories or conceptual schemes) by 'knowing or assuming a great deal about the speaker's beliefs' (Davidson 2006, p. 207). Accordingly, 'we make maximum sense of the words and thoughts of others when we interpret in a way which optimizes agreement (this includes room, as we said, for explicable error, i.e. differences of opinion)' (Davidson 2006, p. 207). On this view, substantial agreement needs to precede even the possibility of disagreement; rival conceptual schemes are deflated for local 'differences of opinion'. Less otiose, for Davidson partial untranslatability is nonetheless equally incoherent, and as a final consequence, the third dogma of empiricism—that of scheme and reality—can at this point be happily dispensed with: 'In giving up the dualism of scheme and world, we do not give up the world, but re-establish unmediated touch with the familiar objects whose antics make our sentences and opinions true or false' (Davidson 2006, p. 208).

The incommensurability of madness

Derrida's early critique of Foucault, written in 1963, is lengthy and complex, pivoting in part on a close reading and interpretation of Descartes, and of Foucault's reading of Descartes (Derrida 2001). In broad terms it mirrors the broad structure of the critique Davidson levies at Kuhn and Quine; it is also worth noting that this critique is directed towards an early variant of Foucault's 'structuralist' thought, which is revised heavily by the time of the works cited above. Rather than follow the argument in depth, I extract some salient lines of critique to demonstrate the analogy with Davidson; points which also go to the heart of the structuralist program.

In *Madness and Civilization*, Foucault attempted to mark an epistemic break in the eighteenth century in the dialogue between Reason and Madness (Foucault 1965). During the Middle Ages and the Renaissance, Foucault argues, Madness could be publicly paraded—literally and discursively—as evidenced in the texts of Rabelais, Shakespeare and

Cervantes. The Enlightenment marks the breakdown of this dialogue into two separate monologues; or rather, as madness became increasingly silenced through the general institutionalisation of rationality and the specific institutions of psychiatry, into the monologue of Reason and the silence of Madness. Foucault's project is to provide a history of that silence, to be the voice through which, retrospectively and belatedly, Madness can once again speak. Transposed to more convenient vocabulary, Reason and Madness are historically incommensurable, riven apart by the rationalist *episteme* since the Enlightenment.

Derrida's overt object of criticism is whether this project is possible and coherent—or whether, rather, in attempting to liberate Madness from its Enlightenment constraints, Foucault merely repeats the constraining gestures of Reason: 'Would not the archaeology of silence by the most efficacious and subtle restoration, the *repetition*, in the most irreducibly ambiguous meaning of the word, of the act perpetrated against madness—and be so at the very moment when this act is denounced?' (Derrida 2001, p. 41).

And later: 'Thus, not an expediency, but a different and more ambitious design, one that should lead to a praise of reason... but this time of a reason more profound than that which opposes and determines itself in a historically determined conflict [with madness]' (Derrida 2001, p. 51).

More obliquely, Derrida also critiques the historical structures Foucault erects to describe the broad epistemic transitions from a dialogical—if strained—relationship between Reason and Madness towards an exclusionary one marked by the advent of the Enlightenment. At one point Derrida directs attention to the apparent arbitrariness with which Foucault cites Descartes as an exemplar of a new, emerging and ominously silencing attitude towards Madness, precisely as Reason is receiving its definitive articulation: 'It is an example as sample, and not as model' (Derrida 2001, p. 51). What epistemic status, then, does this 'sample' have in a history of madness? Its representativeness of Enlightenment constructions of madness, at least, is for Derrida highly questionable.

Later, describing Foucault's project, Derrida writes: 'But I wonder whether, when one is concerned with history (and Foucault wants to write a history), a strict structuralism is possible, and, especially, whether, if only for the sake of order and within the order of its own descriptions, such a study can avoid all etiological questions' (Derrida 2001, p. 52).

Derrida wants to ask what relationship a singular passage from Descartes—later to be analysed in considerable depth—has to the broad historical structure Foucault seeks to account for: 'Is this "act of force" described in the dimension of theoretical knowledge and metaphysics [that of Descartes' *Meditations*], a symptom, a cause, a language?' (Derrida 2001, p. 53). If an example does not function as either cause or effect, but simply counts as a kind of suggestive evidence of the existence of a structure, what motivates its selection—and not others, in particular potential counter-examples? Although at some remove from Davidson's line of argument, there is a common concern with the relationship of the 'totality' of the structure to its parts—'individualities' for Davidson, the unspecified 'exemplarity' of Descartes for Derrida. A lack of methodological specificity regarding the role of exemplary parts is met by an equivalent concern voiced earlier: that different historical periods have complex, shifting and overlapping trajectories regarding the conceptual delineations they make. Consequently it is difficult to voice the history of a notion—'Madness'—which itself has undergone considerable transformation over time: 'Foucault, in rejecting the psychiatric or philosophical material that has always emprisoned the mad, winds up employing—inevitably—a popular and equivocal notion of madness, taken from an unverifiable source' (Derrida 2001, p. 49).

Just as, for Davidson, the attempt to separate content and scheme collapses—and along with it, the problem of schematic incommensurability—so, for Derrida, the various cases of conceptual and historical structures—between, respectively, the concepts of Madness and History, and medieval and classical periods of treatment of madness—are compromised. On the one hand the conceptual, structural opposition between Reason and Madness is shown to be more complicated—that trying to speak the history of a singularised entity called 'Madness' risks objectifying it as an object of an historicising and alienating Reason all over again. On the other hand, the historical 'structures' in which these concepts figure are shown to be less stable, and less demonstrable by way of exemplary cases, than Foucault's clear delineations might suggest.

Resurrecting structures

Davidson and Derrida's critiques are of the more strenuous variety directed towards the implied relativist tendencies in any talk of conceptual structure, in either abstract or concrete historical terms. It seems anachronistic, then, to commit to untranslatable 'ontological' entities such as paradigms, *epistemes* and schemes. Yet, as discussed below, geometric metaphorisations of cultural and cognitive structure continue to emerge in more recent theories. One way of avoiding the types of traps Davidson and Derrida might lay out for prospective structuralist tendencies of this sort would be to suggest such theories adopt the kinds of tempering characteristics at least implied in Foucault and Quine—to suggest that conceptual schemes are elastic, supple sorts of historical and cultural objects, without clear and rigid boundaries or demarcations. As if to help avoid this impasse, at one stage Davidson makes a crucial elision—caricaturing the relativist's position, he notes: 'the test of [schematic] difference remains failure *or difficulty* of translation' (Davidson 2006, p. 202, my emphasis). While Kuhn stresses complete untranslatability, Quine in particular wants to acknowledge that translation is a rough-and-ready, more or less inexact and partial process, where 'difficulty' need not necessarily elide into 'failure'. This arguably accords well with everyday intuitions about translation, even between the 'micro-languages' of various organisational and cultural settings, as well as, more concretely, between the various orientations adopted within knowledge systems. And it ought to be possible to continue to think 'schematically'—that is, retaining the language of conceptual schemes and structures—just so long as those schemes are treated in a suitable elastic sense. The question of commensurability can then be posed in many-valued *degrees* rather than two-valued *kind*—as a question of 'how' rather than 'whether' two schemes are commensurable. Moreover, schemes can be happily readopted having been denuded of any palpable and reified ontological form—and instead be treated as convenient bundles of particular concepts, beliefs, statements and practices of some more or less aligned group of actors. Schemes and structures, in a rehabilitated and analytical rather than ontological form, can serve a practical purpose in describing both the tacit and explicit statements of systems, and the notion of commensurability can further serve a derivatively useful function as a measure of the 'difficulty' translating one set of schematic commitments into another.

Interlude: constructions of science

In *The Social Construction of What?* Hacking provides a contemporary review on the kinds of positions reflected in the discussions above (Hacking 1999). He reviews not only the by now 'classic' articulations of what has become known as 'social constructionism'—through the work of Kuhn, Foucault and others—but also a series of more recent exchanges which took place over the course of the 1990s, in the course of the so-called 'Science Wars'. The Sokal hoax, in which a fictitious article, hyperbolically overblown with postmodern cliches, was published in a literary theory journal, supplied the catalytic impetus for the debate which followed. Hacking, in his account, is less interested in accounting for the specifics of the exchange than in endeavouring to reconfigure the crudely bifurcated divide of 'realist' and 'constructionist' camps into a more finely discriminated constellation of positions.

The purpose of covering Hacking's analysis here is to demonstrate the ongoing resonance of the theoretical issues canvassed so far, and to suggest some ways that the proposed framework can sidestep at least the more naïve excesses of relativism, if not several other related species of nominalism and constructivism. One of the risks of applying the sorts of terms adopted in this study is that it itself can be relativised to a particular cultural conceptual scheme—one which effectively mitigates its putative claims towards truth or, less ambitiously, towards usefulness. By sifting through the distinctions Hacking raises, the argument can escape with a lesser charge of 'conceptual perspectivism', a viewpoint which holds that correspondence theories of truth are usefully augmented, rather than replaced by, coherentist and consensual notions. As a consequence the theoretical underpinnings of the study would then be exonerated of the more exacting crimes of relativism and incoherence to which Davidson and others have charged some of the foundational structuralist claims laid out above.

Hacking begins by connecting the brand of conceptual relativism and social constructionism held by Kuhn, Foucault and others to an older philosophical position of nominalism:

> Constructionists tend to maintain that classifications are not determined by how the world is, but are convenient ways in which to represent it. They maintain that the world does not come quietly wrapped up in facts. Facts are the consequences of ways in which we represent the world. The constructionist vision here is splendidly old-fashioned. It is a species of nominalism. It is countered by a strong sense that the world has an inherent structure that we discover (Hacking 1999, p. 33).

Hacking wants to show that exploded out of epithetic form, 'realist' and 'constructivist' positions need not entail mutually exclusive propositions. He argues that while the natural sciences can be considered as describing reality compellingly, in ways which mesh with our practical efforts to orient ourselves to the world, a degree of social construction is frequently entailed as well. Aspects of the opposition degenerate into a 'two sides of the same coin' type of argument: for Hacking, rather, a scientific theory can be both the best account of naturalistic phenomena we have—it can even be 'real', 'as real as anything we know' (Hacking 1999)—and yet equally belong to a given historical *episteme* or paradigm, exist in a given conceptual scheme, and be socially constructed as much as any cultural or social—that is, as any identifiably unnatural—thing might be. This account explicates what is implicit in the theoretical overlays of Kuhn and Foucault in particular, and suggests they hold a more complicated relationship between 'scheme' and 'reality' than the charge of naïve, full-blown relativism often laid against them would indicate.

Elsewhere Rorty characterises this sentiment in perspicuous fashion:

> 'Relativism' is the view that every belief on a certain topic, or perhaps about any topic, is as good as every other. No-one holds this view. Except for the occasional cooperative freshman, one cannot find anybody who says that two incompatible opinions on an important topic are equally good. The philosophers who get called 'relativists' are those who say that the grounds for choosing between such opinions are less algorithmic than had been thought' (Rorty 1982, p. 166).

Rorty is here keen to separate pragmatism from the stigmatism of relativism and irrationalism. Hacking is broadly sympathetic with the kind of pragmatism Rorty advances; however he wants also to pursue a demarcation of these positions in more fine-grained terms. In circumscribing the field of positions identifiably constructionist, Hacking sets up a simple analytic schema of three independent variables: a theory is constructionist if it rates highly on scales of contingency, nominalism and external explanations of stability. For the adamant constructionist, scientific 'truths' are quintessentially contingent ones:

> The constructionist maintains a contingency thesis. In the case of physics, (a) physics (theoretical, experimental, material) could have developed in, for example, a nonquarky way, and, by the detailed standards that would have evolved with this alternative physics, could have been as successful as recent physics has been by its detailed standards (Hacking 1999, pp. 78–79).

The opposite side of this coin is inevitability—the idea of regardless who invented, discovered, studied or funded what, '*if* successful physics took place, *then* it would inevitably have happened in something like our way' (Hacking 1999, p. 79). The inevitabilist position would claim that even some alien species, following a separate historical, linguistic and cultural path, and having embarked on a project to discover physical laws, must necessarily have derived something like our physics; if this is the case, no amount of cultural deviation and contingency as to the superficiality of discovery change the substantive content of the discovery. Hacking cites 'Maxwell's Equations, the Second Law of Thermodynamics, the velocity of light' (Hacking 1999, p. 79) as particularly unshakeable discoveries. He then suggests that the position of the inevitabilists, unlike those of the discoveries themselves, is 'not derived by inference from experience' but rather is prompted by 'a sensibility that arises in a great many people in Western civilization who are attracted to scientific styles of reasoning' (Hacking 1999, p. 79). As this quote suggests, Hacking's analysis contains a sense that at heart both contingency and inevitability theses arise from a culturally instilled aesthetic sensibility, rather than from rational calculation. On the inevitabilist side, incompatible views are always trivially so—capable of reconciliation once the superficial contingencies of disparate lexical and observational items have been worked through by holders of those views. A believer in epistemic contingency permits of radically different conceptual organisations, though how this might be so would be difficult to determine in advance: 'Moreover—and this is something badly in need of clarification—the "different" physics would not have been equivalent to present physics. Not logically incompatible with, just different' (Hacking 1999, p. 72).

Nominalism, the second variable Hacking introduces, is also is best understood against its more familiar opposite, which supposes that reality has an *inherent* structure waiting to be discovered:

> Even if we have not got things right, it is at least possible that the world is so structured. The whole point of inquiry is to find out about the world. The facts are there, arranged as they are, no matter how we describe them. To think otherwise is not to respect the universe but to suffer from hubris... (Hacking 1999, p. 83).

Nominalism makes the opposite claim: 'the world is so autonomous, so much to itself, that it does not even have what we call structure in itself' (Hacking 1999, p. 72). Hacking argues that nominalists share Kant's distinction between phenomena and noumena—the world *in itself* is unknowable: 'We make our puny representations of this world, but all the structure of which we can conceive lies within our representations'

(Hacking 1999, p. 72). Words pick out groups of objects based on what appear to be their common properties. Science, as Quine would put it, 'is self-conscious common sense' (Quine 1980, p. 3)—in light of an ever-growing body of empirical evidence, new words are coined both to identify and differentiate that evidence. Concepts thus coined are related into structures which appear to lay bare the hidden organisations of things—but for a nominalist, these structures are not lasting reflections of the nature they mirror, they are pragmatic tools to convey a particular understanding, to achieve a given outcome. The indeterminacy of those structures—that they could be otherwise—does not necessitate perpetual and crippling doubt on behalf of the nominalist, however, unlike the caricature which would claim 'no one is a social constructionist at 30,000 feet' (Hacking 1999, p. 67); both Hacking and Pinker (Pinker 1995) quote Richard Dawkins as the original source of this anti-relativist quote. There is no inconsistency in holding that a given arrangement of concepts allows for considerable practical feats of engineering, for example, while questioning whether that arrangement is the only one given to adequate concordance with nature.

The final variable Hacking introduces concerns explanations of scientific stability. The constructionist position here is that science is alternatively *stable* or *volatile* at times depending at least in part on the social context in which they operate. For Hacking, the highly fluctuating states of the natural sciences in the early and middle parts of the twentieth century account for a view of science as volatile and erratic—Kuhn, Feyerabend, Popper and others were responding to unusual periods of scientific and political activity and turmoil, and consequently found discontinuities, anarchism and dialectic everywhere in what had previously been presupposed as a stable and cumulative exercise. The challenge now for sociologists and historians of science, states Hacking, is 'to understand stability' (Hacking 1999, p. 85), given recent decades have tended to reaffirm the glacial rather the volcanic terrain of scientific knowledge. This stability also plays into the hands of those who would like to affirm the 'objective nature of scientific knowledge [which] has been denied by Ross... Latour... Rorty and... Kuhn, but is taken for granted by most natural scientists' (Hacking 1999, p. 88, quoting Stephen Weinberg). Here 'stabilists' tend to corroborate a traditional view of science as progressionist, accumulative and rational; 'revolutionaries' of science affirm its epistemic and paradigmatic disruptions, generated not by internal discovery but by irrational external factors. Hacking connects these two trends with another classical distinction between rationalism and empiricism: 'Leibniz thinks that the reasons underlying truths are internal to those truths, while Locke holds that (our confidence in) truths about the world is always external, never grounded in more than our experience' (Hacking 1999, p. 91).

Hacking conveys a sense that, as with the previous 'variables', the choice here is one of temperament: 'rationalists, at least retrospectively, can always adduce reasons that satisfy *them*. Constructivists, with equal ingenuity, can always find to their own satisfaction an openness where the upshot of research is settled by something other than reason' (Hacking 1999, pp. 91–92). However, there is more at stake than a simple acknowledgement of the significance of aesthetics in determining positions on the variable scales Hacking identifies. The provocations of constructivism have an important deflationary role in the institutionalising and authoritarian tendencies of modern science. In other words, Hacking recognises the structural side-effects of Kuhn and Feyerabend's critiques (Hacking 1999)—and elsewhere, those of Foucault also (Hacking 2002)—which cause science to rethink its ontological foundations and perhaps accept, in Hacking's terms, a 'kind of objectivity... that strives for a multitude of standpoints' (Hacking 1999, p. 96).

What can be taken from this analysis for considering the commensurability of knowledge systems? It has already been emphasised that a simple binary opposition of commensurable–incommensurable is inadequate, and this assessment need to be treated more as scaled, multi-dimensional constructs. Hacking's three variables for describing a more general orientation towards science—contingency, nominalism and stability—also suggest a similarly scalar rather than binary application. Moreover, the variables themselves are useful in rating the standpoints of more fine-grained entities like knowledge systems; accordingly they will be carried over, in less abstract form, to the presentation of system dimensions in the next chapter. More generally, Hacking's analysis goes after what he terms elsewhere 'historical ontologies' (Hacking 2002)—positions which, though framed in contemporary dialogue, in fact exhibit historical resonances with earlier articulations, similarly locked into intractable dialogical structures with their contraries. Tracing such 'irresoluble differences', all the better to 'emphasize philosophical barriers, real issues on which clear and honorable thinkers may eternally disagree' (Hacking 1999, p. 68), is not, for Hacking, an exercise in intellectual vanity, but serves to exorcise both the implacable grand-standing and 'false positive' of facile reconciliations of various standpoints. There is an intrinsic sympathy, then, between his analysis here and the downstream exercise of assessing inter-system commensurability, by allowing differences to be exhumed in their various cultural refractions, and not to be merely reconciled algorithmically. The correcting factor in the case of system translation is that such differences are not presumed to be 'irresoluble' in anything like an ontological sense—this judgement, too, is one contingent on the conditions of particular situational contexts in which translation takes place.

Finally, Hacking has suggested some ways out of the impasse brought about by Davidson and Derrida, by replacing conceptual 'relativism' with a weaker variant of 'perspectivism'—an acknowledgement that potentially irreconcilable views are organised within a historical structure of interdependent standpoints, which can in turn be analysed and made explicit against adroitly selected dimensional criteria. This insight can be applied no less to fine-grained 'systems of knowledge', in the specific technical sense referred to here, as to scientific theories and indeed the whole of science itself. The next section develops this guiding insight through the theories of Habermas, Brandom and Gardenfors, who collectively provide a rehabilitated, elasticised structural account— covering social, linguistic and cognitive aspects—of conceptual schemes, which in turn paves the way for the elaboration of the framework in the next chapter.

Elastic structures: linking the linguistic, the cognitive and the social

Habermas outlines a complex diagnostic theory of modern society which locates social pathologies in the rise of instrumental reason since the Enlightenment, and its subsequent domination over ethical and aesthetic value spheres (Habermas 1987). Within the historical emergence of secularism and capitalism, this has led to the proliferation of social systems with competing ends. In the context of my argument, this proliferation spreads down to the conceptual schemes embedded within the information systems which aid in the procedural means needed to meet such ends, and is thus a major causative factor for creating conditions of incommensurability. Brandom offers an exacting analysis of language, which builds on the insights of analytic and pragmatist twentieth-century philosophy. He outlines a fine-grained theory of meaning which emphasises the normative, pragmatist, inferentialist and holist character of language (Brandom 1994). For Brandom, this account runs against the general grain of twentieth-century semantics, which he instead suggests offers a psychological, idealist, representational and atomistic theory of meaning. Gardenfors' work on conceptual spaces, which uses geometric metaphors to describe cognitive structures, at first glance seems incongruous against Brandom's predominantly socialised account of meaning (Gardenfors 2000). Gardenfors, however, carefully reconciles concept use in individuals with a pragmatist standpoint which leads back out to the social.

These accounts are correctively adjusted to the kinds of critiques laid at the 'classical' structures described above. Gardenfors' cognitive spaces are pliable and adaptable organisations of concepts, not, in this respect at least, dissimilar from Quine's conceptual schemes; Brandom's assertional structures are not the unmediated neutral language of description favoured by positivism, but sorts of trading tokens in a social 'game of asking for and giving reasons'. Habermas' social structures are unfortunate side-effects of an overly systematised modernity, but equally capable of interrogation and revision. These traits were certainly observable in generous readings of Kuhn, Foucault and Quine—though, as Davidson and Derrida's readings demonstrate, it is also possible to view paradigms, *epistemes* and schemes as overly reified, dogmatised and fossilised structures, which suffer incoherence under scrutiny. The second 'triumvirate' of theoretical positions, moreover, provides a suitable overlay of cognitive, linguistic and social structures through which conceptualisations can be viewed and described. For the purpose of establishing a theoretical basis for the framework which follows, then, Gardenfors provides a thorough-going and empirical theory of conceptual schemes which serves to ground the analysis presented here; Brandom develops the broad over-arching justification for connecting such schemes to the social context in which they emerge; while Habermas offers a partially causal explanation for the structural forms of these contexts, giving at least a generalised set of reasons for why rival, incommensurable conceptual schemes should arise at all in the modern era.

Spatialising concepts

In *Conceptual Spaces*, Gardenfors (2000) develops a theory of conceptual representation in the cognitive science tradition developed by Rosch, Lakoff and others (Lakoff and Johnson 1980; Medin 1989; Rosch 1975), surveyed earlier in Chapter 3, 'The meaning of meaning'. Gardenfors develops a 'conceptual framework', a constellation of concepts in which 'concept' itself figures prominently. In the first part of the book, Gardenfors presents a framework comprising:

- *Conceptual spaces*—A high level collection of concepts and relations, used for organising and comparing sensory, memory or imaginative experiences.

- *Domains*—A clustering of related concepts. Gardenfors (2000) suggests 'spatial', 'colors', 'kinship' and 'sounds' are possible concept domains.

- *Quality dimensions*—Generalised distinctions which determine the kinds of domains concepts belong to, such as 'temperature', 'weight', 'height', 'width' and 'depth'. Gardenfors states: 'The primary function of the quality dimensions is to represent various "qualities" of objects', and, more specifically, that they can be 'used to assign *properties* to objects and to specify *relations* among them' (Gardenfors 2000, p. 6). Dimensions can be either phenomenal (relating to direct experience) or scientific (relating to theorisations of experience); innate or culturally acquired; sensory or abstract.

- *Representations*—Gardenfors discriminates between three layers of representation: the symbolic (or linguistic), the sub-conceptual (or connectionist) and the conceptual, which Gardenfors claims mediates between the other two layers. Each layer—from sub-conceptual through to symbolic—exhibits increasing degrees of granularity and abstraction of representation. Gardenfors also notes that the conceptual mediates between the parallel processing of sub-conceptual neural networks and serial processing involved in the production and interpretation of symbolic language.

- *Properties*—'These are means 'for "reifying" the invariances in our perceptions that correspond to assigning properties to the perceived objects' (Gardenfors 2000, p. 59). They are specialised kinds of concepts which occupy a 'region' within a single domain, delineated within the broader conceptual space by quality dimensions. A feature of properties defined in this way is that they accord both with strict and vague or fuzzy borders between properties—objects can be permitted 'degree[s] of membership', depending on their proximity to the centre of the property region. Both classical and prototypical theories of classification can be accommodated.

- *Concepts*—General (non-propertied) concepts differ from properties in that they can belong to multiple domains, and different conceptual features can gain greater salience in different contexts. Concepts are in a constant process of being added, edited and deleted within new domain arrangements; consequently, concept meaning is transient. Conceptual similarity comes on the basis of shared or overlapping domains.

The resulting framework is pragmatic and 'instrumentalist'; the 'ontological status' of conceptual spaces is less relevant than that 'we can *do* things with them' (Gardenfors 2000, p. 31). Specifically, the framework ought to have 'testable empirical consequences' and, further, to provide a useful knowledge representation model for 'constructing artificial systems' (Gardenfors 2000, p. 31). One advantage of the use of geometric metaphors to describe conceptual arrangements is that it is possible to calculate approximate quantifications of semantic distance between individual concepts and concept clusters. However, the mathematisation of conceptual structures is to be taken as a heuristic rather than deterministic model—for Gardenfors, 'we constantly learn new concepts and adjust old ones in the light of new experiences' (Gardenfors 2000, p. 102). In light of this ever-changing configuration of concepts, any calculation of semantic proximity or distance is likely to be at best accurate at a point in time, although statistically—across time and users of conceptual clusters and relations—there may well be computable aggregate tendencies.

The arrangement of concepts and properties within conceptual spaces and domains depends on a coordinating principle of similarity:

> First, a property is something that objects can have in common. If two objects both have a particular property, they are similar in some respect... Second, for many properties, there are empirical tests to decide whether it is present in an object or not. In particular, we can often perceive that an object has a specific property or not (Gardenfors 2000, pp. 60–61).

Dimensions form the basis against which similarity is assessed—a single dimension for properties, multiple dimensions for concepts. Conceptual similarity for Gardenfors is intrinsically a cognitive and theoretical notion, however, which can consequently be varied as different dimensional properties are found to be more or less salient:

> For example, folk botany may classify plants according to the color or shape of the flowers and leaves, but after Linnaeus the number of pistils and stamens became the most important dimensions for botanical categorizations. And these dimensions are perceptually much less salient than the color or shape domains. Shifts of attention to other domains thus also involve a shift in overall similarity judgments (Gardenfors 2000, p. 108).

In the latter part of the book, Gardenfors then shows how his framework can be applied to traditional problems of semantics, induction and computational knowledge representation and reasoning (Gardenfors 2000). In particular he emphasises the relationship of conceptual structures to broader spheres of human action and practice. In what is an avowedly 'pragmatist account', meaning is put to the service of *use* within these spheres—though it is not equivalent to it. Unlike conventional semantics, the kind of 'conceptual semantics' Gardenfors espouses works down from social practice to fine-grained linguistics utterances: 'actions are seen as the most basic entities; pragmatics consists of the rules for linguistic actions; semantics is conventionalized pragmatics... and finally syntax adds markers to help disambiguate when the context does not suffice' (Gardenfors 2000, p. 185).

The pragmatist elements of this account fits well with the analysis of language Brandom undertakes, while the social orientation begins to bring concepts out of mind and language and into the intersubjective domain theorised by Habermas—points of accord succinctly encapsulated in the following quote: 'In brief, I claim that there is no linguistic meaning that cannot be described by cognitive structures together with sociolinguistic power structures' (Gardenfors 2000, p. 201). Applied to knowledge systems, Gardenfors supplies a convenient 'first tier' description of the kind of entity which includes the explicit conceptualisation of the system itself, and the tacit commitments which stand behind it. 'Conceptual spaces', standing here for Quine's 'conceptual schemes', are mentalist metaphors for describing at least part of what it is that a knowledge system represents. The remaining sections add further descriptive tiers on which the framework of the study can be mounted.

Practicing with concepts

Brandom develops a contemporary account of linguistic practices grounded in the pragmatist tradition of Sellars and Rorty. Unlike Rorty, for whom all kinds of linguistic utterance were of equivalent functional significance, Brandom privileges propositional *assertions* as 'fundamental speech acts', without which other speech acts—commands, interrogatives, exclamations—would not be thinkable (Brandom 2000a). Assertions are, for Brandom, tokens in a 'game of giving and asking for reasons', nodal components in a vast articulated web of *inferences* which constitute discursive practice. The primary role of assertions is not, as a correspondence theory of truth would have it, to represent an actual state of affairs, but rather to express, or, in Brandom's more canonical expression, to make '*explicit* what is *implicit*'. In a pivotal passage, he continues: 'This can be understood in a pragmatist sense of turning something we can initially only *do* into something we can *say*: codifying some sort of knowing *how* in the form of a knowing *that*' (Brandom 2000a, p. 8).

Where Gardenfors' primary linguistic unit of analysis is the word, for Brandom it is the sentential structure that provides the key to 'knowing *that*', to assertion making. An atomistic orientation towards concept-use might make it appear that concepts are accumulated, one after another. For Brandom, *contra* Davidson, the *scheme* necessarily precedes the individuated concept:

> One immediate consequence of such an inferential demarcation of the conceptual is that one must have many concepts in order to have any. For grasping a concept involves mastering the proprieties of inferential moves that connect it to many other concepts... One cannot have just one concept. This holism about concepts contrasts with the atomism that would result if one identified concepts with differential responsive dispositions (Brandom 1994, p. 89).

Brandom's implied broad swipe here is directed towards a whole semantically formalist tradition whose origin he locates in the work of the later Frege (his reading of early Frege is considerably more commensurate with the inferentialist, expressivist and pragmatist line Brandom himself adopts). Demonstrating how sentences, and sub-sentential devices such as anaphora, primarily function to relate concepts within an inferentialist network of reasons takes Brandom much of the 741 pages of his landmark *Making It Explicit* (Brandom 1994). At the heart of Brandom's enterprise is an attempt to reconcile the rigour associated with this formalist tradition with a more appropriate philosophically holistic orientation, which sees assertional speech acts within a broad tapestry of human action and 'social practice' generally. This has clear resonance with this particular project; although Brandom addresses neither the question of translation nor the question of knowledge systems specifically, several inferences can be drawn from his analysis:

- Knowledge systems utilise formal languages, which for Brandom differ by degree rather than kind from natural languages. A fundamental feature of a knowledge system remains that of making assertions and 'giving reasons'. The very purpose of employing such systems, with an underlying logical apparatus, is precisely that of deriving conclusions from a set of axioms using an explicit chain of reasoning.

- More generally, the systems themselves stand as discursive practices with a general game between, typically, more course-grained sociological entities than individual actors—organisations, departments and other cultural groups.

- The semantically holistic and expressive orientation towards knowledge systems can direct attention not only towards the existing 'knowing-thats' asserted by the systems themselves, but also towards the background 'knowing-hows' and 'knowing-thats'—the practices and as yet unexplicated conceptual commitments—of the cultures responsible for them.

- Finally, translation itself consists of a series of assertions, that concept A is synonymous with concept B, for example. The act of translation therefore entails its own 'circumstances and consequences of application' (to invoke another Brandom idiom). Recognition of the situational context of the translation directs attention towards just what circumstantial and consequential conditions impinge on those assertions.

A further note relates to the specific treatment of structure in Brandom's work. The entire practice of making, interpreting and reasoning with assertions stands within what he terms an 'I-thou deontic score-keeping' relation. This, for Brandom, is 'the fundamental social structure' (Brandom 1994). This base structure operates like a simplified, idealised model, in which two interlocutors are locked into a game, metaphorically tabulating each others' reasons offered for actions, practices, commitments, beliefs and attitudes. This theoretically endless activity does not yet offer an account for how some series of disagreements might grow into schemes which are incommensurable. To explain this—without falling prey again to Davidsonian lines of critique—requires a shift in registers, from what appears fundamentally a psychological intersubjective scenario—between two well-intentioned agents—to a sociological one—between two cultures, whose intentions are never quite irreducible to those of the agents who represent them. To make this shift the next section draws on an essential Habermasian distinction, between lifeworld and system, which offers explanation for how more fundamental rifts in the social tapestry might occur.

Socialising concepts

Where Gardenfors and Brandom acknowledge the role played by the social sphere in structuring conceptual arrangements, neither provide an account of what sorts of structure are germane to this sphere itself, nor what might cause rival conceptualisations to emerge. Kuhn and Foucault had developed explanatory theories of sorts but, at least in the case of Kuhn, these theories were limited to a particular domain of the social—the scientific domain. While no encompassing causal theory might adequately account for all variations in cultural conceptualisations—or, less abstractly, differences in how cultures see the world—a theory which at least makes perspicuous some common lines of demarcation would be helpful. Foucault's later analysis of 'micro-power' goes some way in this direction, yet he consciously abjures any abstract generalisable theorisation (Foucault 1980). Bourdieu's elaboration of 'habitus' is similarly useful at an intra-cultural level (Bourdieu 1990), but is not directed oriented towards an explanation of the sorts of inter-cultural differences which might arise, particularly within the 'networked societies' engaged in information system development and use (Castells 1996).

Habermas is sometimes taken as being either a theorist of 'incommensurability' (Latour 1993) or, at others, its exact opposite: a naïve advocate for an idealised 'communicative rationality' directed towards utopian understanding (Flyvbjerg 1998). The interpretation offered here suggests that he represents neither of these extremes, but rather a Kantian rationalism despondent—on the one hand—at the over-systematisation and objectification of modernity, yet conciliatory—on the other—towards the potentials of dialogue and communication for redressing this trend. As with the other theorists encountered here, there is insufficient scope for any kind of thorough treatment of Habermas' full theoretical apparatus. Instead I focus attention on a pivotal conceptual opposition between system and lifeworld, outlined in *The Theory of Communicative Action* (Habermas 1987).

For Habermas, the Kantian trichotomy of instrumental, ethical and aesthetic rationality is ontologically primary categories of modernity. These broadly correspond to objective, inter-subjective and subjective spheres of individual experience. Habermas inherits the critical lines of Weber, Lukacs and the Frankfurt school towards post-Enlightenment reason, which has missed its potential to act as a liberating tool. Instead it has been co-opted within specifically modern configurations and systems of power and oppressive administration (Adorno 2001; Horkheimer and Adorno 2002). Rationalisation has been operationalised as an instrumental process within all spheres of human experience—everything has been subjected to systematised logic. Even individual subjectivity, what for Kant ought to remain the inviolable sanctuary of private experience, has been externalised, publicised and rendered transparent to the machinations of modern systems—through, for example, the various concrete vehicles of the media, the professed wisdoms of popular psychology, the endless commodification of art, and the cult of celebrity. For Habermas, as for critical theory, this outgrowth of hyper-rationalisation has a corresponding corrosive and pathological effect on the 'lifeworld'—the phenomenological horizon experienced by individual subjects. Paradoxically, the domination of a singular form of rationality has also led to a fracturation and destabilisation of a social world into multiple systems. Such systems—at a macro level these include legal, economic, scientific and political systems—operate according to the internal dynamics of their particularist ends, and remain only loosely, if at all, coordinated within a social whole. Accordingly, conceptual schemes are segregated in a profound way within the system spheres in which they are engaged. Habermas describes this development:

> At the level of completely differentiated validity spheres, art sheds its cultic background, just as morality and law detach themselves from their religions and metaphysical backgrounds. With this secularisation of bourgeois culture, the cultural value spheres separate off sharply from one another and develop according to the standards of the inner logics specific to the different validity claims... In the end, systemic mechanisms suppress forms of social integration even in those areas where consensus-dependent coordination of action cannot be replaced, that is, where the symbolic reproduction of the lifeworld is at stake (Habermas 1987, p. 196).

However, this historical diversion is not irrevocable within Habermas' schema; the very conditions that effect the outgrowth of a particular form of rationalisation can also serve to corral it within its proper sphere of operation—that of scientific knowledge of the world. Provocations from the subjective sphere of experience, such as various inflections of Romanticism, are insufficient for this containment and merely serve to buttress the over-extended reach of systemic reason. Rather it is in the intersubjective sphere, where human agents engage in communication and dialogue, where reason can be directed towards not the achievement of specified functional ends, but the formation of social consensus, that functional ends can be re-evaluated within the context of society as a whole. The derivation of consensus through the pure consideration of better reasons—a never fully realised process, but nonetheless operating as a counterfactual ideal—acts as a mediating force between the private wants of subjective selves and the oppressive operations of hyper-rational systems of modernity. For Habermas communication offers the potential to arrest '*the uncoupling of the system and lifeworld*' and return from 'the threshold at which the mediatization of the lifeworld turns into its colonization' (Habermas 1987).

Habermas' analysis can be seen to supply the missing detail to Brandom's reference to the 'the social', which is posited as an 'unexplained explainer' in his account. The connection between Habermas and Brandom is not seamless, as a recent exchange attests. Despite many points of intersection, they differ precisely over the question of whether Kantian trichotomy precedes or is instead subject to the role of logic and inference—Brandom insists, contra Habermas, that specific domains sit downstream from the primordial experience of 'asking for and giving reasons' (Brandom 2000b). Broadly, though, Habermas can be seen as having developed an important and encompassing explanatory account of how specific schemes can be incommensurable. In spite of how language appears, even in the work of Brandom, to be an undifferentiated tool for establishing lines of inference between co-operative agents, social systems have in the course of modernity increasingly operated according to local teleological programs, which, through the operationalisation of specific language games and jargon, serve to blunt language's more incisive communicative potentials. Within the 'iron cages' of technocratic institutions, inter-system 'interfacing', using perfunctory rational procedures, has replaced genuine intersubjective dialogue. Within these differential ends and parametric conditions, unique morphologies of organisational cultures generate different conceptualisations of common entities. Even conceptualisations which are externalised and globalised—in the form of technology standards, for example—are typically adopted via rationalising fiat, either via conformance to *de jure* fiat or recognition of *de facto* network externalities—rather than because of an internally deliberated conclusion brought about by the force of better argument.

Unlike the accounts examined above, it is not a foregone conclusion that the conceptualisations produced within these spheres be radically incommensurable, however—only that it is possible to diagnose the potential causes, along lines of different cultural ends, procedures and intentions, when they are. Moreover the efficacy of idealised dialogue, of the kind both Habermas and Brandom are happy to countenance, and towards which actual communication constantly strives, can assuage the rougher edges of translation in practice. Brought back down to the technical domain of knowledge systems—and in lieu of any active participation between the cultures responsible for them—the role of the analyst is to ferret out both the points of differentiation and the potential conciliatory paths between them. This involves, practically, identification of salient dimensions against which such points and paths can be plotted, and a corresponding process of interrogation of the cultures responsible for the systems under review.

Habermas, then, does not endorse a romantic yearning for an over-arching metaphysics, a stable social order or a single governing conceptual scheme. Nor does he champion endless devolution into more granular, localised and ultimately untranslatable systems of meaning. His aim is rather to recuperate the promise of Kantian rationality by recalibrating the obsession of modernity with instrumental reason by emphasing the equivalence of ethical and aesthetic spheres. In practice this allows systems to proliferate in their respective manifold differences, but never so far as to negate the potentials of translatability and commensurability completely. Further consideration of the greater Habermasian project would take this discussion too far afield; here it suffices to provide a sociological and historical explanation of causative factors in the incommensurability of conceptual schemes, and thus serves to connect up Brandom's pragmatist analysis of linguistic meaning and Gardenfors' analysis of conceptual spaces to a broad historical context. Together these connections—linking up the linguistic, the cognitive and the social—develop an altogether more fluid and elastic conception of 'structure', one avowedly informed by materialist and pragmatist concerns, than those advanced by the earlier generation of theorists discussed above. A path has now been prepared for the description of such a rehabilitated structure, as it relates more directly to knowledge systems and the cultures responsible for them.

Towards a framework...

The early sections of this chapter outlined three broadly commensurate positions which can be broadly subsumed under the title 'conceptual perspectivism'. Though Foucault goes much further than Kuhn and Quine, little is articulated in these positions about *why* different perspectives take form—just *that* they do. Accordingly, these positions are all open to charges of relativism and incoherence, which Davidson and Derrida lay out powerfully. Hacking moves to outline a more nuanced position in the context of the recent 'science wars' of the 1990s, which demonstrates something of a dialectal force which motivates the staking out of positions and perspectives within, at least, the scientific domain. He demonstrates how the traditional debate between realism and nominalism has been resurrected in these contemporary discussions.

Habermas then supplies a more directed account—historically grounded and materialist in orientation— for how perspectives emerge and acquire currency through communicative practices. Brandom supplements this account with a more finely tuned analysis of linguistic utterances— paradigmatically, assertions—and how such utterances operate as more literal tokens within a dialogical game of 'giving and asking for reasons'. Playing the game—requesting and making assertions—offers language users endless opportunities to revise and correct a holistic conceptual network. Gardenfors, in turn, provides a more granular account still of the kinds of things which constitute a conceptual scheme—concepts, relations and properties—within an ostensibly pragmatist framework. Together these theories can be pieced together to formulate an explanatory device for conceptual schemes which is neither relativising nor succumbs to a purely representationalist thesis—'the myth of the given', in Sellars' words. In short, it is possible to construct on these theoretical underpinnings a framework which embraces correspondence, coherentist and consensual notions of truth. Or, it ought now be possible to describe a framework which examines conceptual translation in terms of denotation—whether two concepts refer to the same objective things in the world; connotation—how two concepts stand in relation to other concepts and properties explicitly declared in some conceptual scheme; and use—or how two concepts are applied by their various users. Moreover there is flexibility within the framework to lean towards either 'realism' or 'nominalism', since both can be accommodated—with varying degrees of approximation—within the kind of materialist and pragmatist orientation now developed.

References

Adorno, T.W. 2001. *The Culture Industry: Selected Essays on Mass Culture.* Abingdon: Routledge.

Austin, J.L. 1998. *How to Do Things With Words.* Abingdon: Routledge.

Bourdieu, P. 1990. *The Logic of Practice.* Stanford: Stanford University Press.

Brandom, R. 1994. *Making It Explicit.* Cambridge, MA: Harvard University Press.

—. 2000a. *Articulating Reasons: An Introduction to Inferentialism.* Cambridge, MA: Harvard University Press.

—. 2000b. 'Facts, Norms, and Normative Facts: A Reply to Habermas', *European Journal of Philosophy* 8, pp. 356–74.

Castells, M. 1996. *The Rise of the Network Society*. Cambridge, MA: Blackwell.

Davidson, D. 2006. *The Essential Davidson*. Oxford: Oxford University Press.

Derrida, J. 2001. *Writing and Difference*, A. Bass (tr.). Abingdon: Routledge.

Flyvbjerg, B. 1998. 'Habermas and Foucault: Thinkers for Civil Society?', *British Journal of Sociology* 49, pp. 210–33.

Foucault, M. 1965. *Madness and Civilization; A History of Insanity in the Age of Reason*. New York: Pantheon Books.

—. 1970. *The Order of Things: An Archaeology of the Human Sciences*. New York: Vintage Books.

—. 1980. *Power/Knowledge: Selected Interviews and Other Writings, 1972–1977*. C. Gordon (tr.). New York: Pantheon Books.

—. 2002. *Archaeology of Knowledge*. Abingdon: Routledge.

Gardenfors, P. 2000. *Conceptual Spaces*. Cambridge, MA: MIT Press.

Habermas, J. 1987. *The Theory of Communicative Action*, T. McCarthy (tr.). Boston: Beacon Press.

—. 1989. *The Structural Transformation of the Public Sphere*, T. Burger (tr.). Cambridge, MA: MIT Press.

Hacking, I. 1999. *The Social Construction of What?* Cambridge, MA: Harvard University Press.

—. 2002. *Historical Ontology*. Cambridge, MA: Harvard University Press.

Horkheimer, M. and T.W. Adorno. 2002. *Dialectic of Enlightenment: Philosophical Fragments*, E. Jephcott (tr.). Stanford: Stanford University Press.

Kuhn, T.S. 1970. *The Structure of Scientific Revolutions*. Chicago, IL: University of Chicago Press.

—. 2002. *The Road Since Structure: Philosophical Essays, 1970–1993*, with an autobiographical interview. Chicago, IL: University of Chicago Press.

Lakoff, G. and M. Johnson. 1980. *Metaphors We Live By*. Chicago, IL: University of Chicago Press.

Latour, B. 1993. *We Have Never Been Modern*. Cambridge, MA: Harvard University Press.

Medin, D.L. 1989. 'Concepts and Conceptual Structure', *American Psychologist* 44, pp. 1469–81.

Quine, W.V.O. 1964. *Word and Object*. Cambridge, MA: MIT Press.

—. 1980. *From a Logical Point of View*. Cambridge, MA: Harvard University Press.

—. 1992. 'Interview Between W.V. Quine and Yasuhiko Tomida', *http://www.wvquine.org/quine-tomida.html* (accessed 18 January 2010).

Pinker, S. 1995. *The Language Instinct*. New York: HarperCollins.

Rorty, R. 1982. *Consequences of Pragmatism*. Minneapolis, MN: University of Minnesota Press.

Rosch, E. 1975. 'Cognitive Representations of Semantic Categories', *Journal of Experimental Psychology: General* 104, pp. 192–233.

Sellars, W. 1997. *Empiricism and the Philosophy of Mind*. Cambridge, MA: Harvard University Press.

Wittgenstein, L. 1921. *Tractatus Logico-Philosophicus*. Mineola, IA: Dover Publications.

—. 1967. *Philosophical Investigations*, 3rd edn (first published 1953). Oxford: Basil Blackwell.

12

A framework for commensurability

Liam Magee

S: But you always need to put things into a context, don't you?

P: I have never understood what context meant, no. A frame makes
a picture look nicer, it may direct the gaze better, increase the value,
but it doesn't add anything to the picture. The frame, or the
context, is precisely the sum of factors that make no difference to
the data, what is common knowledge about it. If I were you, I
would abstain from frameworks altogether. Just describe the state
of affairs at hand (Latour 2004, p. 64).

The preceding chapter developed an implied theoretical approach to the
question of the commensurability of knowledge systems, one based around
the direct commitments expressed in the systems themselves, and of the
indirect and inferred commitments of the cultures responsible for them.
This chapter formalises and makes explicit that approach, by developing a
model for assessing the commensurability of knowledge systems. In
constructing a framework for assessing commensurability of ontologies,
this chapter cements several levels of argument expressed in this book
together. It presents, first, a speculative theoretical model of what it is that
is being investigated in a commensurability assessment—what sort of entity
underpins a formal knowledge system. Then the framework itself, designed
to profile and explore differences in these systems, is described. The
framework comprises a) a model of an idealised commensurability
situation, where two systems are to be aligned; b) a series of dimensions for
evaluating the cultures responsible for those systems; c) a quantification of
the assessment; and d) a procedure for applying the dimensions and
interpreting the results. Collectively these tools form part of what could be
considered an analyst's toolkit for evaluating the degree of fit between two
knowledge systems. This chapter, then, offers one possible practical
approach for working within the social web of knowledge.

What to measure—describing 'ontological cultures'

Having worked through a range of theoretical positions in the preceding chapter, it is now possible to put forward our own model of the kinds of conceptual entities which are both explicit in knowledge systems themselves, and implicit in the practices and beliefs of the people who design and use them. These 'entities' have so far been described through a series of near-cognate, proximally synonymous terms, ushered in throughout this study to denote both a given system or arrangement of concepts, and, on occasion, also the social environment, and the people who produce and consume them. Yet none of these terms—*perspectives, world views, paradigms, epistemes, conceptual schemes or spaces, historical ontologies, lifeworld, habitus*—seems quite adequate for the kinds of entities wanted here. The following account aims to characterise these entities in descriptive terms, before then offering a formalised account as a part of the framework further on below. The account may seem more dogmatic that is intended; just as Minsky notes in a similar framework endeavour, this account proceeds while 'pretending to have a unified, coherent theory' (Minsky 1974).

What is envisioned here, then, is an elastic, dynamic, fluid yet interconnected 'structure' shared across members of a group or organisation; neither a subjective, individual cognitive 'lifeworld', nor a stable, socialised epistemic 'system', but something at an intermediate and intersubjective level of granularity. 'Conceptual scheme' seems adequate though insufficient, as the sought-after concept must also embrace the structural conditions and social practices that give rise to such schemes. Stopping at the conceptual misses out on these elements. A more embracing term is needed, which directs attention out from subjective cognitive abstractions towards the objective and intersubjective spheres in which those abstractions are generated, and to which they correspond.

'Culture' is one possible term; it both signifies a collective group and, more remotely, connotes a homogenous, self-replicating organism. The term has the advantage of being at the right granular level, since it is elastic, and can be stretched and scaled along several dimensions; it can describe a large or small, short or long-lived, casually or formally, historically or spatially organised collective of individuals. One of the functions of the cultures considered here, though, is that they produce very particular kinds of artefacts—formal knowledge systems. To describe just those cultures engaged in the production of knowledge systems particularly, I have added the epithet 'ontological'. Taken literally, an 'ontological culture', then, is something which produces formal knowledge systems like semantic web ontologies—organisations, communities and other social groups who, as one of their practices, organise slices of the world into classificatory schemes. More tenuously, 'ontological culture' can also be taken in several other senses too: a culture which, to coin a neologism, *ontologises*; actively constituting its world and the beings in it (meaning something similar to Hacking's use of the phrase 'historical ontology'); or even as a biological 'culture', which is differentiated from more mundane microbial kinds of culture by being 'ontological' in the philosophical sense. The conjoined term, as a result, operates as a weak double pun, implying each of these meanings. Though concisely descriptive, this term does however strain at convention use; occasionally through the study the more conventional term 'knowledge cultures' has been preferred—though lacking in specificity the latter term also has an existing resonance in the sociology of knowledge and science, for instance, Knorr-Cetina (1999) and Peters and Besley (2006).

An 'ontological culture' inherits many of the characteristics ordinarily assigned to cultures generally. The remainder of this section presents a basic narrative, unfolding a series of terms as it develops a description of 'ontological culture'. These terms, in turn, are formalised into a more coherent model, which is employed in the more technical discussion of the framework further on.

The organic connotation of 'culture' implies a certain autonomy—that cultures are, like Luhmannian systems, first-order *sociological*, rather than psychological or biological entities. They are in some sense irreducible to the agents or actors who comprise them. Actors instead perform semi-deterministic roles in accordance with the functional goals of a culture, of which there can be many: for example, generating profits, delivering services, providing welfare and conducting research. A typical overriding goal is one of self-maintenance—one of the ways it achieves this goal is by replicating its beliefs and practices. This may happen in a more or less predatory fashion, and in part takes place through communicative practices which have the intended effect of norming participating agents—of fostering adherence to beliefs and practices. In a general sense, having goals gives a culture a quality of intentionality—its practices are directed and goal-oriented, much as those of a biological agent might be. Retaining the organistic analogy, cultures reproduce, evolve, inhabit spaces, communicate with other cultures, and ultimately expire. While analysable and modelable, this cultural activity is partly stochastic, predictable only within broader, non-deterministic and probabilistic parameters.

A culture also operates within a general environment—what it sees as its 'world'; or, in Habermasian terms, its 'lifeworld' (*Lebenswelt*). This environment supports other cultures; cultures can stand in structural relations to one another. Cultures can even be nested; for instance, when a greater culture harbours an embedded revolutionary cell. The relationships within and between cultures constitute semi-porous, permeable networks—sub-cultures, cross-cultures or 'hybrid cultures' are all examples. These structural delineations and permeations can be traced through the practices enacted within those cultures—canonically, within discursive practices. Discursive practices produce epistemic artefacts—representations of knowledge—which reflect the perspectival orientation of the culture towards the objects it encounters—or engenders—in its world. However, a perspective is not fixed—it reflects a point-in-time reification of a floating, variable conceptual scheme, which coordinates the production of beliefs within a culture. Other forms of practice, discursive or otherwise, are always 'kicking back' against a given perspectival view, which survives just so long as it can withstand or absorb these challenges. This is particularly the case in 'experimental' cultures such as scientific and, in the narrow sense exploited here, 'ontological' ones—cultures whose *a priori* rather than by-product function is the very production of knowledge. A characteristic of such cultures is their own self-explication of the beliefs and practices they engage in—formalised in rule-governing theory and rule-governed methodology respectively. This characteristic ensures repeatable observations—a kind of perspectival continuity across time, space and other cultural boundaries. Perspectives also, critically, remain one-sided; from any point of view there is always another, perhaps infinitely many other points of view available, through other accultured lens. Aspects of objects are both seen and occluded under a given perspectival lens; belonging to a culture, no matter how highly self-reflexively critical, means sharing both its insights and its blindnesses (de Man 1983).

Cultures, then, have conceptual schemes or, in Quine's other metaphor, a 'web of beliefs' (Quine 1964). These beliefs can be described as structured like a network, spanning from the concrete, synthetic and empirical through to the abstract, analytic and conceptual—some beliefs are closer to the world than others. Again following Quine's breakdown of the synthetic–analytic divide, a belief can be plotted along a scale of *ontological–epistemological*: *ontological*—here in the philosophical sense—to the extent that it refers to objects in the world; or *epistemological*—to the extent that it refers to other beliefs (or their expression in language). A belief is canonically expressed in a proposition, an assertion of a relationship between concepts, objects and properties. Together beliefs are mutually supporting, forming in the ideal system a coherent, consistent and non-contradictory whole. Within the semi-bounded environment of a culture, contradictions may nevertheless emerge in discursive practice between agents. One of the roles of discourse is to establish the grounds on which such intersubjective inconsistencies arise, to make assonance out of shared cognitive dissonance. Collectively, a network or web of beliefs constitutes a perspective—or, to use other common optical metaphors, an outlook, a point of view, a vantage point or an orientation. A perspective, however, is not here a passive lens through which the world is viewed; rather it actively constitutes, constructs and intends—in the active, phenomenological sense of 'intending'—how things are viewed and arranged. Actors partake or subscribe to belief networks to the extent they are imbricated in a culture, acquire its 'habitus', although this is never (quite) a total imbrication. Through the roles they play and practices they enact, actors rather develop more or less intensive, comprehensive and enduring commitments to a set of beliefs. Understanding epistemic extent—the degree to which a belief is taken to be knowledge—is an important part of developing a profile of a culture.

Beliefs are transmitted in language, via what Habermas terms communicative practices. Communicative practice generally serves to break down what are otherwise incommensurable divides between cultures, and permit actors to participate in the 'game of giving and asking for reasons', in Brandom's phrase. Hence assertoric utterances are paradigmatic instances of communicative practices—used to proclaim, query, test, revise, transmit, reconcile, and, in part, maintain cultural boundaries and integrity. Conveying of beliefs in language, while bearing the risk of a dissenting response, is above all an economic decision—it results in less work for belief transmission than other kinds of practices, of a presumably more coercive kind.

Beliefs form 'webs' in a less benign Quinean and more insidiously Foucauldian sense—as socially norming practices, discursive and otherwise (Foucault 1970). It might be possible in some cases to identify beliefs which are intrinsic and 'core' to a culture—those which motivate practices and subsidise ancillary beliefs, and which constitute the non-negotiable intransigent elements of a cultural 'perspective'. These are likely to be those which are practically intractable to empirical or communicative challenge, since their invalidation threatens maintenance of the identity and boundaries of the prevailing culture. Belief revision is consequently largely a piecemeal affair, at least within the confines of a given culture, as the 'carrying-out' of practices and even the revision of certain beliefs can only take place while the remainder of the belief system remains relatively stable. In this model, epistemic revolutions, as opposed to revisions, are rare.

Yet beliefs, as purely ideational and immaterial constructs, are essentially unknowable directly, and only can be inferred via the evidence of a culture's practices. For 'ontological' cultures—those that produce explicit representations of some slice of the world they are concerned with—a conceptual scheme can be directly interpreted in highly regulated ways, via the semantic specifications embedded in those representations. Such explicit representations cannot, however, be interpreted, purely and unreservedly, as the accomplished perspective of the culture which produces them. Rather they are narrow, restricted and temporarily discrete frames on an ever-changing flux of objects—or, in another formulation, sense-data 'perceivings' which only *a posteriori* congeal into the sorts of things conceptualisable as objects—subject to a continually changing dynamic process of theorisation and practice. Moreover they are also products with intended communicative effects. What is made explicit, then—the arrangement of concepts—needs interpreting not only in terms of its mode of explication, but against what remains tacit—a broader background of cultural beliefs and practices. Unlike the first kind of interpretation, operating directly on the axioms of a system itself and proceeding along set or model-theoretic— in other words, strictly analytical—lines, the second kind is necessarily dependent on exploratory, heuristic interpretive devices, using suggestive rather than direct forms of evidence. It is possible, then, to present knowledge systems generated by a culture as, instead of a stark unmediated delineation, a sort of highly detailed foreground, cast against a vague, impressionistic yet significant cultural backdrop. The resulting 'portrait' of a culture is then comparable with other depictions—partly in the precise quantitative sense of two geometric conceptual graphs being compared isomorphically, but also in the deliberately imprecise sense of two holistic images being comparing impressionistically.

Picking up methodological cues from Gardenfors (2000), to generate a portrait involves analysing cultures across any number of possible dimensions, some of which might be especially salient within a particular translation situational context. Generically, cultures can be described in a number of commonly occurring dimensions: size, rate of growth, 'core' or foundational beliefs, practices, perspectives, material and environmental conditions, influence, aggressiveness, health, longevity, maturity, internal organisational structure, relation to other cultures, organisational type and purpose (economic, political, legal), and so on. Other, specific variables relating to the situation in which translation takes place can be used as well. One possible formalisation of generic variables is described in the set of dimensions outlined below. Regardless of exactly which set of variables are selected, and how they are respectively weighted for saliency, what matters at this stage is that it is possible to describe, qualitatively and quantitatively, the explicit conceptualisations and tacit structures, beliefs and practices which underpin them, as a kind of portrait or profile. Commensurability of cultures involves, then, a comparison of the quantitative and qualitative profiles developed in this way. The 'tacit' part of a profile is not, of course, truly silent—it represents aspects of a culture which need hermeneutic or heuristic interpretation, typically kinds of discursive, textual practices in which conceptual commitments need to be 'drawn out' and inferred. Hence the methodological strictures about what counts as evidence, and what limits apply to the inferences drawn from it—this form of interpretation is necessarily suggestive and exploratory, rather than definitive and explanatory.

Presenting a framework for commensurability

The above characterisation is sufficiently abstract to describe the vague kinds of entities which reside behind knowledge systems. The remainder of the chapter now makes a sharp transition from theory to practice, from a theoretical model to a framework that might help an analyst work through practical problems of system translation. As indicated earlier, treatment of differences in knowledge systems takes place at least implicitly in several common information technology tasks—system integration, database design, information retrieval, decision support, resource planning, project management, and so on. A starting point for the framework is to describe what might be an idealised translation scenario, to serve as an approximation of the various real-world situations in which translation takes place. This provides a way of orienting the question of commensurability from the point of view of an analyst engaged in a translation process. The formalisation of the model also provides a way of moving from a qualitative to a quantitative characterisation of commensurability. From here, several generic dimensions for describing knowledge systems and their underlying cultures are proposed. A schematic procedure for applying the dimensions is then discussed, followed by some concluding notes on the interpretation of the commensurability assessment.

It is worth briefly reviewing the motivations for the framework. Referring back to Chapter 3, 'The meanng of meaning', there are broadly two ways of handling differences in knowledge systems. Computer science approaches focus on how to achieve individual concept alignment. They typically employ algorithms and external data definitions to match concepts from different systems. Matches can then be used to develop transformation rules to convert data from one system to another. These approaches can be broadly described as forms of semantic atomism— concepts are primary to the schemes containing them. Here by contrast system commensurability is considered in terms of plausible schematic alignment. This approach is fundamentally reliant on an interrogation of the cultural character of these systems. Following one of Brandom's key distinctions it can be considered a form of semantic holism, where the overall underlying cultural conceptual scheme is primary with respect to the individual concepts stipulated within it (Brandom 2000). Furthermore it can be described as predominantly interested in the pragmatic character of knowledge systems—what kinds of use they are put to. The difference in approach, then, is largely one of orientation and method; semantic holism as advocated here is consistent with algorithmic matching techniques described above, and it can be used as a supplementary heuristic to these techniques.

Modelling a commensurability scenario

Leading on from the preceding description, here a formal model of an idealised commensurability scenario or situation is presented. The scenario is idealised in that it may not correspond directly with the many actual contexts in which system translation, integration or alignment takes place, but it ought at any rate to capture key or exemplary features, which enable the model to be generalisable to those contexts. The model distinguishes between knowledge systems and the 'ontological cultures' responsible for authoring and using them. The model includes concepts explicitly defined by the system, as well those tacitly implied by it— background assumptions not evident in the system itself, but which can be inferred by the translating analyst. The model describes the differences between 'cultures', in the sense defined above, against several dimensions. It assumes that assessment of commensurability is for the purpose of aligning or harmonising two systems—or scoping out at any rate the work involved in such a task.

The model supports the idea of partial or gradual commensurability between systems. In the preceding chapter, the idea of 'commensurability' was picked up from Kuhn's account of scientific paradigms—there, commensurability is represented in all or nothing terms. I suggested that at face value this goes too far, leading to forms of linguistic or cognitive relativism, and begging the question of how communication across cultural or paradigmatic divides could happen at all. Commensurability then becomes a reified, ontological property of the systems; not, instead—and more helpfully—an analytic tool for describing their translatability relative to a context. If commensurability is considered in comparative rather than mutually exclusive terms, however, the ontological character and associated critique drops away. By extension, discussion of fine-grained, more or less commensurable cultural conceptual schemes can dispense with the charge of relativism. 'Local' schematic incommensurability, for example, can have reference to 'global' commensurability, and a mutually untranslatable pair of systems might well be translatable when transplanted to another situational context, with new goals, additional information, different translators and so on. This also accords with everyday intuition— language users frequently agree to disagree about their use of individual concepts, for instance, while still sharing sufficient common ground for these localised disagreements to be understood.

The model assumes the following scenario:

1. There are two formal systems which need to be aligned or harmonised, *Sys1* and *Sys2*, which ought to meet the following conditions (additional systems need to be considered as multiple pairwise comparisons):

   a. They are based on some more or less explicit formal language, with appropriate syntax and semantics (candidates are the relational model, XML schema, RDF and OWL).

   b. In the *term–assertion* distinction, the systems in question must include a non-empty set of *terms* (or concepts), but not necessarily *assertions* (or objects or individuals).

   c. The actual process of alignment or harmonisation is performed algorithmically, based on a series of transformational rules converting instances of concepts in *Sys1* to instances of concepts in *Sys2*. However, the details of this process are not relevant to the assessment of commensurability which precedes it.

2. There are two conceptual schemes, *Sch1* and *Sch2*, corresponding to the two formal systems. The schemes contain both explicit and tacit beliefs held by two 'cultures', *Cult1* and *Cult2*, in the broad sense described above.

3. There is at least one designated purpose for the alignment or harmonisation. Collectively the set of purposes is defined as *P* (individual purposes could be designated using lower-case and prime notation, for example, p', p'', etc.).

4. The purpose(s) are established within a situational context, *Cxt*. Assessment of commensurability can be viewed as a judgement on the relative fit of cultures for a given purpose. The degree of applicability of the judgement is thus relative to the dynamics of the situational context. Making explicit the context in the determination of commensurability promotes reusability—subject to contextual qualifications—of the assessment. This may for instance be a simple statement of the environmental or situational conditions in which the alignment or harmonisation process takes place, or a more formal analysis (SWOT and PESTLE analysis are examples of such formal contextual analyses).

5. There is some agent conducting the alignment or harmonisation, *Agt*. The agent is assumed to be a human individual or group, with appropriate techniques for characterising the formal systems.

6. Overall the alignment or harmonisation scenario consists of two systems (*Sys1* and *Sys2*), developed and used by two cultures (*Cult1* and *Cult1*), a set of purposes (*P*), a context (*Cxt*) and an agent (*Agt*).

7. Commensurability, *Cms*, can be defined as the *degree of conceptual fit* between two cultures, *Cult1* and *Cult2*, responsible for the knowledge systems *Sys1* and *Sys2* respectively, given *P*, within *Cxt*, by *Agt*.

The purpose of the model can be restated in plain language, assessing the commensurability for the 'ontological cultures' responsible for formal knowledge systems, suitable to particular purpose(s) within a context, and to be conducted by an agent(s). The problem is further refined after the model of commensurability (*Cms*) is further elaborated below.

The model contains a series of *semantic dimensions*, following Gardenfors (2000), which are applied to knowledge systems on the basis of interpretation of the cultures responsible for them. The model is therefore multi-faceted or multi-dimensional. Dimensions can be further characterised as follows:

- Dimensions (*Dims*) are salient properties of a 'ontological culture' (the word 'property' itself is deliberately not used, to avoid ambiguity with properties defined within the systems themselves).

- Collectively the defined dimensions of the model form a set of dimensions (*DimSets*).

- Dimensions can be grouped at multiple levels, thus forming a tiered hierarchy.

- Dimension values are interpretations of aspects of a system and the culture responsible for it, relative to the purposes and other systems specified in the situational context.

- Interpretations are in the first instance qualitative; they can also be converted to quantitative measures to support statistical analysis. This entails assumptions about the dimensions and their application—a point further expanded below.

Figure 12.1 shows the relationship between the major components of the model.

Figure 12.1 Commensurability model

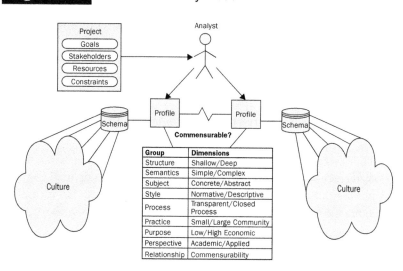

Quantifying commensurability

The qualitative measures can be interpreted quantitatively, as ordinal measures. Here dimensions are represented as integer values between 0 and 10—any scale can be applied, so long as it is consistent across all dimensions in the dimension set. Analysing commensurability then proceeds by assigning a value of 0 to 10 to each of the dimensions in the set for each of the systems being compared. This produces a set of values for *Sys1* and *Sys2*, respectively *V1* and *V2*, corresponding to each dimension belonging to the dimension set *DimSet*. Commensurability between *Cult1* and *Cult2* is then derived from the collection of values *V1* and *V2* taken for *Sys1* and *Sys2*, as follows:

1. The difference between two dimension values for *Sys1* and *Sys2* is defined as the semantic distance (d) for the dimension in question.

2. Based on the collective purposes, P, and situational context, *Cxt*, the agent can assign a weight, w, against each of the dimensions. The weight is considered to be some value between 0 and 1. By default the weight is assumed to be 0.5 (permitting a relative strengthening or weakening of the weight). Weighting permits differential emphasis on dimensions of relevance or saliency to a given context.

In a further refinement to the analysis, weights could also be applied against dimension groups. This could have the effect of either applying the weight to each of the dimensions within the group, or supplying a separate level of weighting. The first case is simply an overriding of the individual dimension weighting case; the implications of the second are not considered in detail here, but would have the effect of establishing multiple commensurability measures for different layers of the model.

3. Given n dimensions, three forms of commensurability measures can then be derived:

   a. The average of the semantic distances. This is the sum of the differences between the dimension valuations, divided by the number of dimensions. It ignores the weightings. Its formulaic expression is:

   $$\frac{\sum_{i=1}^{n} d_i}{n}$$

   b. The weighted average of the semantic distances. This is the sum of the weighted differences, divided by the sum of the weights. Its formulaic expression is:

$$\frac{\sum_{i=1}^{n} d_i w_i}{\sum_{i=1}^{n} w_i}$$

c. The square root of weighted average of squared semantic distances. This is the sum of the weighted squared differences, divided by the sum of the weights, from which the root is calculated. This measure accentuates the weighting effect. Its formulaic expression is:

$$\sqrt{\frac{\sum_{i=1}^{n} d_i^2 w_i}{\sum_{i=1}^{n} w_i}}$$

The second of these calculations, the weighted average, is the preferred formula for most purposes, since it is readily interpreted in relation to the unweighted average, but provides the benefit of differential assessment of dimension saliency. The derived value provides a quantifiable measure for the commensurability of the two cultural conceptual schemes, given the defined purpose(s) within a context, and as applied by the agent. The previous definition can now be restated more precisely:

1. Let *Sys1* and *Sys2* be two knowledge systems, and *Cult1* and *Cult2* be the cultures engaged with the respective systems.

2. An agent *Agt* is tasked with aligning or harmonising *Sys1* and *Sys2* in a given situational context (*Cxt*), for a set of stated purposes (*P*).

3. Let *Cms* be the unknown variable, the degree of conceptual fit or commensurability between *Cult1* and *Cult2*.

4. Then the calculation of commensurability, *Cms*, proceeds as follows:

    a. Define some set of dimensions, *DimSet*, for describing conceptual schemes.

    b. Interpret *Sys1* and *Sys2* against each of the dimensions, *Dim*, in the set *DimSet*.

    c. Take the semantic distance, *d*, as the absolute difference between each of interpreted valuations.

    d. Assign weights, *w*, against each of the dimensions, *Dim*, in the set *DimSet*, based on assessments of saliency of the dimension for the given purpose(s), *P*, within a context, *Cxt*.

    e. Sum the weighted distances (Σwd), and divide by the sum of the weights (Σw).

f. The resulting weighted average provides a measure of commensurability, *Cms*, for the cultures *Cult1* and *Cult2*, underlying *Sys1* and *Sys2*.

This measurement can be used in turn as an estimate for assessing the complexity of aligning or harmonising the two knowledge systems. Some further remarks about how the measurement is interpreted and used are warranted at this stage:

- Dimensions tend to be descriptive, rather than judgemental. However, judgement is usually involved in the assignment of values to dimensions, hence the overall assessment should not be presumed to be value-free—rather, the point is that such value judgements are made explicit.

- In certain cases, applying a quantitative scale may imply a false degree of precision, and require greater rigour than the context warrants. In these cases, it might be sufficient to rate the systems as either 'low' or 'high', or perhaps 'low', 'medium' or 'high'. In such cases, quantitative analysis can still be carried out by choosing appropriate values within the ranges set by dimensions with the greatest number of values. For example, if at least one dimension is scaled [0, 10], then other dimensions must have appropriate values within the lower and upper bounds (between 0 and 10), and an equivalent mid-way value. Value ranges such as [3, 7] and [2, 5, 8], for example, could be valid interpretations of the respective qualitative evaluations above.

- Dimension valuations can in some circumstances be added directly to the systems themselves. Most formal systems provide various metadata or annotation mechanisms. For instance, OWL provides annotation or metadata facilities which can be applied to the system as a whole, or to specific entities (classes or properties, for example) within it. Although the dimension valuations are related to a specific context, they may also be useful for future assessments of commensurability, or simply as annotated comments on the system itself.

- The set of dimensions constitute themselves a series of ontological claims about cultures and conceptual schemes. These claims are part, then, of a second-order conceptual scheme; the degree to which they require further explication and rationalisation will depend on context.

Contrasting ontology matching approaches

As discussed earlier, recent work in schema and ontology alignment views that task as a 'bottom-up' problem, that is, to be solved at the level of individual concepts (Shvaiko and Euzenat 2008). Designers of matching algorithms employ various strategies for determining matches. They generally take the form of generating a set of matches based on:

- A concept, *C1*, taken from *Sys1*
- A concept, *C2*, taken from *Sys2*
- A relation between concepts *C1* and *C2*: one of equivalence, generalisation, specialisation or disjointness
- A degree of confidence in the match.

It is clear why such approaches are semantically atomic, according to the terms outlined in this study. The degree of fit of the systems as a whole is derived from the completeness and precision of the set of matches obtained between individual concepts. Different strategies and algorithms can be compared with human interpretations in this regard. Nevertheless these approaches do not capture important contextual information about the knowledge systems, nor can they infer implicit information about the underlying cultural conceptual schemes. Rather this can only be inferred by a human agent who is capable of interpreting knowledge systems against a broader epistemological backdrop of purposes, contexts and other social agents. Such interpretation is argued here as a form of semantic *holism*—in which specific conceptual representations can only be understood within a general social whole of meaning production and consumption.

Interpretation, of the kind required to describe dimensions of a conceptual scheme, is, however, a notoriously arbitrary process. Obvious criticisms are that interpretation is at best partial, subjective, and in some cases irrelevant or not feasible given a cost-benefit analysis or other justificatory measures. There are several possible responses to these criticisms of the framework:

- It supplements rather than competes with alignment algorithms, so it can be regarded as a form of human rather than computer-aided design tool.
- It is intended as a heuristic aid to alignment activities, not as a definitive prescription, for tasks not amenable to algorithmic analysis.
- It merely formalises intuitions at work in everyday practice, albeit with a series of epistemological and methodological assumptions in tow.
- Its inclusion of an appropriate set of dimensions and application of method serves to corral the worst excesses of interpretive work.

The dimensions presented in the next section endeavour to perform some of this corralling work.

Describing commensurability—a generic dimension set

The framework also includes a default generic set of dimensions for describing knowledge systems and the cultures behind them. In practice, as the case studies bear out, the default set often needs revision, extension and weighting to fit the requirements of a given translation situation. By abstracting out the formal model and process for quantifying commensurability, it is possible to use *any* suitable dimension set, without loss of general applicability.

Inevitably the choice of dimensions appears arbitrary, and need justification on grounds of saliency and relevance to the systems under consideration. The dimensions have been selected on the basis of utility for determining commensurability. Some of the intrinsic dimensions seem logical for any kind of system analysis; others—particularly those relating to context—are governed specifically by the account of commensurability presented here. The dimensions are intended to draw out *salient* differences in systems and their underlying cultures and conceptual schemes.

The set presented here itself is intentionally abstract, and aims to capture the general tendencies of the culture responsible for a knowledge system. The set distinguished between intrinsic and extrinsic dimensions of systems. The intrinsic dimensions reflect the concepts, properties and individuals stipulated in the system itself, and its overall structural and stylistic features. Several of these have been extracted and simplified from schema and ontology metrics discussions mentioned in the literature review, notably in Tartir et al. (2005) and Yao, Orme and Etzkorn (2005). Unlike metrics, which can be computed just with reference to a single ontology, these dimensions are comparative—for example, the scope of a system can be judged to be general or specific only with reference to other systems under consideration.

The extrinsic dimensions aim to understand the implicit concepts that stand behind the system, which operate within the broader social environment in which the system is constructed. The distinction thus serves to differentiate a characterisation of the system itself from the characterisation of the environment in which it is constructed and used. A number of the extrinsic dimensions have been extracted or correlated to those developed in the standardisation and knowledge management literature discussed in Chapter 3, 'The meaning of meaning'. Others appear to be generic distinguishing traits differentiating knowledge systems, part of which has been borne out in the case studies which follow.

Intrinsic dimensions of a knowledge system

Intrinsic dimensions describe the knowledge system itself. There are four types of intrinsic dimensions:

- *structure*—describes structural characteristics of the system; for example, whether the system is relatively large or small, or detailed or sparse
- *style*—describes stylistic aspects of the system; for example, whether the system predominantly declares concepts or properties
- *scope*—describes the scope of the system; for example, whether the concepts concentrated on a particular area, or dispersed over several
- *subject*—describes the subject(s) dealt with by the system, and how these are characterised; for example, whether the concepts are relatively abstract or concrete.

Table 12.1 presents each of the dimensions with a brief explanation.

Table 12.1 Intrinsic dimensions of a knowledge system

Dimension group	Dimension	Description
Structure		Dimensions that describe the structural characteristics of the system
	Small–large	Whether there are a small or large number of concepts in the system.
	Light–dense	Whether the system contains a small or large number of properties and sub-classes for each class; this dimension corresponds to that of 'inheritance richness' mentioned by Tartir et al. (2005), and of 'Average Depth of Inheritance Tree of Leaf Nodes (ADIT-LN)' introduced by Yao, Orme and Etzkorn (2005).
	Self-contained–derivative	Whether the system uses only constructs defined internally, or makes use of imported constructs (can be determined by the presence of *owl:imports* declarations, and the extent to which imported constructs are used within the ontology).

Table 12.1	Intrinsic dimensions of a knowledge system (*Cont'd*)	
Dimension group	Dimension	Description
	Free–restricted	Whether the classes defined within the system have a small or large number of constraints applied to them; this dimension corresponds to that of 'relationship richness' mentioned by Tartir et al. (2005).
	Sparsely–heavily populated	Whether the system contains a small or large number of individuals.
Style		**Dimensions that describe the stylistic aspects of the system**
	Classificatory– attributive	Whether the system uses predominantly *sub-classes* or *properties/attributes* to describe relations between classes; this dimension corresponds to that of 'attribute richness' mentioned by Tartir et al. (2005).
	Literal–object composition	Whether the system uses predominantly data type literal or object type properties.
	Quantitative– qualitative	Whether the system uses predominantly numeric or textual values for its data type properties.
	Poorly–highly annotated	Whether the system is well described (uses a high number of metadata annotations).
Scope		**Dimensions that describe the scope of the system**
	Coherence– dispersion	Whether the concepts listed in the system belong to an existing coherent system, or are seemingly 'random' in their selection.
	Concentrated– diffused	Whether the concepts are tightly clustered around a particular area or field, or are diffused over a range of fields.
	General–specific	Whether the concepts are general in relation to a given field or fields, or are instead highly specific.
Subject		**Dimensions that describe features of the subject(s) dealt with by the system**
	Concrete–abstract	The degree the system relates to concrete objects (books, proteins, people) or tends towards abstract objects (space, time, substance). Ontologies are sometimes

Table 12.1 Intrinsic dimensions of a knowledge system (*Cont'd*)

Dimension group	Dimension	Description
		described as being 'upper-level', 'mid-level' or 'low-level' according to their level of abstraction—this dimension describes the same feature.
	Natural–social	Whether the system describes objects from a naturalistic or socialistic perspective (in philosophical terms, adoption of realist or constructivist perspective).
	Spatial–temporal	Whether the system describes predominantly spatial objects (books, people, organisations) or temporal objects (events, periods, durations).
	Phenomenalist–scientific	Whether the system describes objects from an everyday 'phenomenalist' perspective, or from the standpoint of science.

Extrinsic dimensions of a knowledge system

Extrinsic dimensions describe the social context in which the system is developed. As with the intrinsic dimensions, there are four types of extrinsic dimensions:

- *perspective*—describes the stated intention or purpose of the system; for example, whether the system represents an ideal or a pragmatic conceptualisation of a field or domain
- *purpose*—describes the underlying motivation (as best inferred) of the system; for example, whether strong financial or political motives underly the system's construction
- *process*—describes the process of the system's design and construction; for example, whether the system design was relatively centralised or distributed
- *practice*—describes how the system has been received; for example, whether the system is better characterised as a *de facto* or *de jure* standard.

Table 12.2 presents each of these dimensions.

Table 12.2 Extrinsic dimensions of a knowledge system

Dimension Group	Dimension	Description
Perspective		Dimensions that describe the general perspective or orientation of the system
	Pragmatic— idealistic	Whether the system is pragmatic— representing how concepts are presently represented in information systems—or idealist—suggesting how concepts ought to be represented.
	Academic— applied	Whether the system is intended for academic research or for 'real-world' applications.
	Serious— spurious	Whether the system is intended for serious use.
	Speculative— grounded	Whether the system is a speculative or hypothetical point of view about the objects it describes.
	Committed— uncommitted	Whether the system is committed to the conceptual scheme it operationalises.
	Compatible— independent	Whether the system is intended by design to be compatible with other systems.
Purpose		Dimensions that describe the underlying motivations and purposes of the system
	Financially motivated: weak–strong	Whether the system is motivated by financial considerations (for example, to promote related products and services, to cut costs of data management).
	Legally motivated: weak–strong	Whether the system is motivated by legal considerations (for example, to support particular licensing arrangements, or to work around legal obstacles).
	Politically motivated: weak–strong	Whether the system is motivated by political considerations (for example, to influence policy makers, or to form strategic alliances with organisations).
	Ethically motivated: weak–strong	Whether the system is motivated by ethical considerations (for example, to promote interoperability among non-profit organisations).
	Personally motivated: weak–strong	Whether the system is motivated by personal considerations (for example, to enhance individual career prospects).

Table 12.2 Extrinsic dimensions of a knowledge system (*Cont'd*)

Dimension Group	Dimension	Description
	Theoretically motivated: weak–strong	Whether the system is motivated by theoretical considerations (for example, to promote a given ontological orientation).
Process		**Dimensions that describe the process of the system's design and construction**
	Representative–unrepresentative of community	Whether the system is representative of the community that makes use of it.
	Central–distributed design	Whether the system is designed by a central body or via a distributed community.
	Closed–transparent process	Whether the system is designed in a way that elicits and incorporates critical review and feedback.
	Formal–informal construction	Whether the system uses a formal process, such as those used by international standards bodies.
	Explicit–implicit assumptions	Whether the system makes explicit background assumptions, as understood by those involved in its design.
	Rigorous–random method	Whether the system makes use of a rigorous method in its design.
Practice		**Dimensions that describe how the system is used**
	Active–inactive community	Whether the system is designed and/or used by an active community.
	Low–high adoption rate	Whether the system has a high adoption rate among its candidate users or market.
	Low–high maturity	Whether the system is mature—has gone through multiple iterative cycles or versions.
	Backward compatible–incompatible	Whether the system is compatible with earlier versions of the system.
	De facto standard: low–high	Whether the system is a *de facto* standard among its users.
	De jure standard: low–high	Whether the system is a *de jure* standard—has received ratification from appropriate standards bodies.

Table 12.2 Extrinsic dimensions of a knowledge system (*Cont'd*)

Dimension Group	Dimension	Description
	Industry support: low–high	Whether the system is widely supported within the industry (as evidenced by supporting documentation, tools, services, etc.).
	Documentation availability: low–high	Whether the system is supported by available documentation.

Pre-empting the methods discussion below, the extrinsic dimensions clearly require considerable interpretation. In contrast, some of the intrinsic dimension values may be derived algorithmically, especially in the case of the structural and stylistic dimensions. It is also clear that accurate evaluation of extrinsic dimensions may require considerable discovery effort. The extent of effort needs to be justified against the benefit of the assessment, on the basis of some kind of cost-benefit analysis. Nevertheless evaluation itself can be more or less formal or extensive—for certain purposes and contexts, existing knowledge or opinion may be sufficient, or the dimensions introduced here can be applied in an *ad hoc* fashion.

In conjunction the intrinsic and extrinsic dimensions provide a characterisation of the knowledge systems in their underlying conceptual scheme and the background cultures responsible for them. The intrinsic subject and extrinsic intention dimension groups do most to capture the implicit elements of the conceptual scheme; while the other intrinsic groups summarise what is already explicit but not immediately conveyed in the system; and the other extrinsic groups contextualise the system in ways that make more evident the causes behind the construction of the system itself. The next section outlines how the model can be applied in a given commensurability assessment scenario.

Assessing commensurability—applying the dimensions

As a final part of the overall framework, a basic procedure is proposed for the application of the dimensions to the systems. The method of construction can be minimal or highly sophisticated, depending on the context of the assessment. Nevertheless, some explicit treatment of method, in terms of how the model might be applied, is useful. The method assumes the idealised scenario presented in the discussion of the analytic procedure above—namely, *Sys1*, *Sys2* represent the two systems, *Cult2*, *Cult2* represent the underlying cultural schemes, *P* represents the purpose(s), *Cxt* represents the context, and *Agt* represents the agent.

First, the intrinsic character of *Sys1* and *Sys2* are described. This involves:

1. Surveying of parts or all of the definition of *Sys1* and *Sys2*; the 'definition' may be precisely specified in a formal language, or need to be inferred from secondary documentation. The following is a list of potential sources for analysing the definition:

   a. the source definition of the system: the concepts and properties declared in XML Schema files, RDF/OWL ontologies or relational models

   b. system documentation, which may be in the form of annotations to the source definition, external documentation or academic publications

   c. diagrammatic representations of the system, such as entity relational (E/R) or Unified Modeling Language (UML) diagrams

   d. available metrics summarising structural or stylistic aspects of the system

   e. secondary sources analysing or discussing the systems.

2. Analysing and rating the systems according to the intrinsic dimension groups *structure*, *style*, *subject* and *scope*. In the case of structural and stylistic dimensions, it may be useful to employ algorithms for counting numbers of concepts, properties, annotations, restrictions and individuals. The following list gives examples of how the given intrinsic dimension groups and dimensions might be analysed:

   a. *structural* dimensions—may involve counting the number of concepts and properties, finding 'import' declarations, and checking the extent of constraints applied to concepts and properties

   b. *stylistic* dimensions—may involve counting the relative number of concept and property declarations, examining property types (whether they are literal or relations), examining literal property types (whether they are numerical, textual or other), checking the internal documentation (whether the system entities are annotated), and examining whether there are multiple methods to describe an object

    c. *scope* dimensions—may involve interpreting whether the concepts are coherently grouped or seemingly random, concentrated around their subject matter or diffused, and general or specific

    d. *subject* dimensions—may involve interpreting whether concepts are concrete or abstract, temporal or spatially oriented, and refer to natural occurring or socially constructed objects.

3. Analysing the valuations and differences between the intrinsic properties of the system by grouping averages by dimension group.

Second, the extrinsic dimensions of the systems are analysed. This in turn involves:

1. Surveying the social environment in which *Sys1* and *Sys2* are developed. Depending on the scale of the method, availability of sources and nature of the systems, this could incorporate several different methods:

    a. interviews with the system designers and with other users of the system

    b. affiliation or participation in working groups, standards committees and design teams

    c. analysis of online social groups—blogs, wikis, forums, mailing lists—in which aspects of the system design are discussed or negotiated

    d. review of secondary materials: press, academic publications, conferences, journals and books that discuss aspects of the systems

    e. review of peripheral materials: government policies, company financial reports, industry group minutes, standard body procedures related to organisations sponsoring, advocating or using the systems.

2. Analysing and rating the systems according to the extrinsic dimensions. This requires interpreting the materials in dimension groups of perspective, purpose, process and practice. The following list gives examples of how the given extrinsic dimension groups and dimensions might be analysed:

    a. *purpose* dimensions—may involve examining the stated and implied intentions behind a system, including any economic, political, philosophical or technical rationales evident in the context of the presentation of the systems themselves (websites, accompanying documentation) and other sources (forums, commentaries, and so on)

b. *process* dimensions—may involve looking at how the system is developed: what explicit or implied policies determine how the system is designed, versioned, ratified and publicised

c. *practice* dimensions—may involve examining how the system is used within different environments; whether it is widely endorsed, supported and integrated within an ecosystem of other systems, standards and products

d. *perspective* dimensions—may involve direct interpretation or indirect sourcing of commentary about the general 'orientation' of the system: whether it is oriented towards everyday 'lay' or scientific vocabularies; whether it adopts a realist or constructivist position towards the objects it describes; or whether it uses existing vocabularies or enforces a new normative vocabulary of its own.

3. Separately analysing quantitatively the valuations and differences between the extrinsic properties of the system, to generate averages by dimension group.

Finally, the weighted average of all of the dimensional differences is obtained to provide a quantitative measure of commensurability, using the procedure outlined above. Any qualitative remarks, against dimensions or dimension groups, can also be summarised into an overall qualitative assessment.

Interpreting commensurability assessments

Qualitative and quantitative assessments need to be interpreted relative to the specific context in which the assessments have taken place. This is particularly the case for the quantitative measurement. Low values of in commensurability should correlate to quicker and less problematic alignments between the systems concerns; conversely, low values should indicate slower and more difficult alignments. High values might also suggest the need for various further activities: more consultation with those knowledgeable about the respective systems; iterative cycles of translation; more rigorous testing procedures; or, finally, that the task of translation is not viable within available constraints. In some situations, these determinations might have other, flow-on effects and impacts: the desirability for one system over another, for example, or even of the 'strategic fit' between two organisational cultures. Just as the background cultures responsible for two systems impacts on their relative commensurability, the 'embeddedness' of systems means their compatibility can be an indicator and even determinant for general questions of cultural alignment and affiliation. These, naturally, need to be asked with reference to specific operating conditions; so here no more than a vague indication can be provided for what commensurability assessments might mean, and how they ought to be interpreted, within those conditions. Some of these considerations are presented below in itemised form, however, to prompt this interpretative process:

- What does a high value, signalling a high degree of *in*commensurability, indicate? What if any consequences does this have?

  Does it mean that the systems are *radically* incommensurable, and any effort to align them will be in vain? Or does it entail practical consequences: a greater amount of work is required, additional resources or time need to be allocated, or further analysis or different approaches need to be explored? Or does it indicate a preferential choice of one system over another, where the dimensions have been interpreted as selection criteria?

  Conversely, what does a low value signify? That the systems are commensurable for the stated purposes, or that alignment or harmonisation of the systems is comparatively trivial?

- How do the quantitative and qualitative assessments compare? Are they consistent, and if not why not? Do some of the dimensions perhaps need to be re-weighted?

- How do the assessments fit with intuitive understandings of the general 'fit', or commensurability, of the systems concerned?

- What other steps or stages—consultation, testing, the alignment itself—need to be modified as a result of the assessments? Qualitative as well as quantitative findings could prompt particular decisions here.

- What follow-up actions or decisions might eventuate from these assessments? Do they indicate preference for one system over another? Are there alternate ways of achieving the ends to which the system alignment or translation is directed?

- Are there broader implications of these assessments? Do they reflect important 'extra-systemic' features, such as the 'strategic fit' between organisations or organisational units?

Applying the framework

Against the background of a broad charaterisation of the social web of knowledge earlier in this book, here we have proceeded to develop a general theoretical rubric and detailed framework for assessing the commensurability of both formal systems and the cultures responsible for them. The framework has four components: a model of an idealised commensurability scenario, a series of dimensions conforming to the demands of the procedure, a means for quantifying commensurability and a method for applying the framework and interpreting the results. The framework mobiles a series of analytic tools for understanding both the explicit and implicit commitments entailed by formal knowledge systems—those directly stipulated in the systems themselves, and those inferred through an examination of the background cultures in which they are produced and used. The series of dimensions uses the distinction between intrinsic and extrinsic dimensions to capture each of these types of commitments. The separation of the model and methodology permits the adoption of entirely different dimensions, allowing for considerable flexibility in how other criteria and even different ontological and epistemological assumptions come into play in the analysis.

Assessing the commensurability of systems is a necessary but ultimately insufficient step for building webs of meaning and knowledge around contemporary representations of knowledge. Assessment needs to be corroborated with specific pathways of concept transformation and translation; these, in turn, of course need to be guided by the kinds of methodological, heuristic and analytic rigour an assessment framework provides. However, inter-system translation threatens to become a task of exponential complexity as the number, size and underlying assumptions of these systems themselves proliferate. One way to corral such complexity—within arithmetically rather than geometrically growing bounds, at least—is to develop *interlanguages*— kinds of reference languages designed to guide translation between the micro-languages articulated (again, both explicitly and implicitly) within knowledge systems. The next chapter looks at the development of one such interlanguage, and how it helps with building the social web.

References

Brandom, R. 2000. *Articulating Reasons: An Introduction to Inferentialism.* Cambridge, MA: Harvard University Press.

de Man, P. 1983. *Blindness and Insight: Essays in the Rhetoric of Contemporary Criticism.* Abingdon: Routledge.

Foucault, M. 1970. *The Order of Things: An Archaeology of the Human Sciences.* New York: Vintage Books.

Gardenfors, P. 2000. *Conceptual Spaces.* Cambridge, MA: MIT Press.

Knorr-Cetina, K. 1999. *Epistemic Cultures: How the Sciences Make Knowledge.* Cambridge, MA: Harvard University Press.

Latour, B. 'On Using ANT for Studying Information Systems: A (Somewhat) Socratic Dialogue'. In C. Avgerou, C. Ciborra and F. Land (eds), *The Social Study of Information and Communication Technology: Innovation, Actors and Contexts.* Oxford: Oxford University Press, pp. 62–76.

Minsky, M. 1974. 'A Framework for Representing Knowledge', *http://dspace.mit .edu/handle/1721.1/6089* (accessed 19 January 2010).

Peters, M.A. and T. Besley. 2006. *Building Knowledge Cultures: Education and Development in the Age of Knowledge Capitalism.* Lanham: Rowman & Littlefield.

Quine, W.V.O. 1964. *Word and Object.* Cambridge, MA: MIT Press.

Shvaiko, P. and J. Euzenat. 2008. 'Ten Challenges for Ontology Matching'. In *OTM 2008: Proceedings of the 7th International Conference on Ontologies, Databases, and Applications of Semantics (ODBASE).* Berlin and Heidelberg: Springer, pp. 1164–82.

Tartir, S., I.B. Arpinar, M. Moore, A.P. Sheth and B. Aleman-Meza. 2005. 'OntoQA: Metric-Based Ontology Quality Analysis'. In *Proceedings of IEEE Workshop on Knowledge Acquisition from Distributed, Autonomous, Semantically Heterogeneous Data and Knowledge Sources.* IEEE Computer Society, pp. 45–53.

Yao, H., A.M. Orme and L. Etzkorn. 2005. 'Cohesion Metrics for Ontology Design and Application', *Journal of Computer Science* 1, pp. 107–13.

13

Creating an interlanguage of the social web

Bill Cope and Mary Kalantzis

The discursive practice of markup

Untagged digital text is a linear data-type, a string of sequentially ordered characters. Such a string is regarded as unmarked text. Markup adds embedded codes or tags to text, turning something which is, from the point of view of computability, a flat and unstructured data-type, into something which is potentially computable (Buzzetti and McGann 2006).

Tagging or markup does two things. First, it does semantic work. It notates a text (or image, or sound) according to a knowledge representation of its purported external referents. It connects a linear text with a formal conceptual scheme. Second, it does structural work. It notates a text with one particular semantics, the semantics of text itself, referring specifically to the text's internal structures.

In the first, semantic agenda, a tag schema constitutes a controlled vocabulary describing a particular field in a formally defined and conceptually rigorous way. The semantics of each tag is defined with as little ambiguity as possible in relation to the other tags in a tag schema. Insofar as the tags relate to each other—they are indeed a language—they can be represented by means of a tag schema making structural connections (a <Person> is named by <GivenNames> and <Surname>) and counter distinctions against each other (the <City> Sydney as distinct from the <Surname> of the late eighteenth-century British Colonial Secretary after which the city was named). Schemas define tags paradigmatically.

To take Kant's example of the willow and the linden tree, and express it the way a tagging schema might, we could mark up these words semantically as <tree>willow</tree> and <tree>linden tree</tree>. The tagging may have a presentational effect if these terms need highlighting, if they appear as keywords in a scientific text, for instance; or it may assist in search. This markup tells us some things about the structure of reality, and with its assistance we would be able to infer that a <tree>beech</tree> falls into the same category of represented meaning. Our controlled vocabulary comes from somewhere in the field of biology. In that field, a <tree> is but one instance of a <plant>. We could represent these structural connections visually by means of a taxonomy. However, <tree> is not an unmediated element of being; rather, it is a semantic category. How do we create this tag-category? How do we come to name the world in this way?

Eco (1999) provides Kant's answer:

> I see, for example, a willow and a linden tree. By comparing these objects, first of all, I note they are different from each other with regard to the trunk, branches, leaves etc.; but then, on reflecting only upon what they have in common: the trunk, branches and the leaves themselves, and by abstracting from their size, their shape, etc., I obtain the concept of a tree.

What follows is a process Kant calls 'the legislative activity of the intellect'. From the intuition of trees, the intellect creates the concept of tree. '[T]o form concepts from representations it is... necessary to be able to compare, reflect, and abstract; these three logical operations of the intellect, in fact, are the essential and universal conditions for the production of any concept in general' (quoted in Eco 1999, pp. 74–75).

Trees exist in the world. This is unexceptionable. We know they exist because we see them, we name them, we talk about them. We do not talk about trees because they are mere figment of conceptual projection, the result of a capricious act of naming. There is no doubt that there is something happening, ontologically speaking. However, we appropriate trees to thought, meaning, representation and communication through mental processes which take the raw material of sensations and from these construct abstractions in the form of concepts and systems of concepts or schemas. These concepts do not transparently represent the world; they represent how we figure the world to be.

And how do we do this figuring? When we use the concept 'tree' to indicate what is common to willows, linden trees and beeches, it is because our attention has been fixed on specific, salient aspects of apprehended reality—what is similar (though not the same) between the two trees, and what is different from other contiguous realities, such as the soil and the sky. But equally, we could have fixed our attention on another quality, such as the quality of shade, in which respect a tree and a built shelter share similar qualities.

Tags and tag schemas build an account of meaning through mental processes of abstraction. This is by no means an ordinary, natural or universal use of words. Vygotsky and Luria make a critical distinction between complex thinking and conceptual thinking. Complex thinking collocates things that might typically be expected to be found together: a tree, a swing, grass, flower beds, a child playing and another tree—for their circumstantial contiguity, the young child learns to call these a playground. From the point of view of consciousness and language, the world hangs together through syncretic processes of agglomeration. A playground is so named because it is this particular combination of things. The young child associates the word 'playground' with a concrete reference point. Conceptual thinking also uses a word, and it is often the same word as complex thinking. However, its underlying cognitive processes are different. Playground is defined functionally, and the word is used 'as a means of actively centring attention, of abstracting certain traits, and symbolising them by the sign' (Vygotsky 1962; also referred to in Cope and Kalantzis 1993 and Luria 1981).

Then, beyond the level of the word-concept, a syntax of abstraction is developed in which concept relates to concept. This is the basis of theoretical thinking, and the mental construction of accounts of a reality underlying what is immediately apprehended, and not even immediately visible (Cope and Kalantzis 1993). The way we construct the world mentally is not just a product of individual minds; it is mediated by the acquired structures of language with all its conceptual and theoretical baggage—the stuff of socialised worldviews and learned cultures.

Conceptual thinking represents a kind of 'reflective consciousness' or metaconsciousness. Markup tags are concepts in this sense and tag schemas are theories that capture the underlying or essential character of a field. When applied to the particularities of a specific piece of content, they work as a kind of abstracting metacommentary, relating the specifics of a piece of content to the generalised nature of the field. Academic, disciplinary work requires a kind of socio-semantic activity at a considerable remove from commonsense associative thinking.

Markup tags do not reflect reality in an unmediated way, as might be taken to be the case in a certain sense of the word 'ontology'. Nor do they represent it comprehensively. Rather, they highlight focal points of attention relevant to a particular expressive domain or social language. In this sense, they represent worldviews. They are cultural artefacts. A tag does not exhaustively define the meaning function of the particular piece of content it marks up. Rather, it focuses on a domain-specific aspect of that content, as relevant to the representational or communicative purposes of a particular social language. In this sense 'schema' is a more useful concept than 'ontology', which tends to imply that our representations of reality embody unmediated truths of externalised being.

Notwithstanding these reservations, there is a pervasive underlying reality, an ontological grounding, which means that schemas will not work if they are mere figments of the imagination. Eco characterises the relationship between conceptualisation and the reality to which it refers as a kind of tension. On the one hand

> being can be nothing other than what is said in many ways... every proposition regarding that which is, and that which could be, implies a choice, a perspective, a point of view... [O]ur descriptions of the world are always perspectival, bound up with the way we are biologically, ethnically, psychologically, and culturally rooted in the horizon of being (Eco 1999).

But this does not mean that anything goes. 'We learn by experience that nature seems to manifest stable tendencies... *[S]omething* resistant has driven us to invent general terms (whose extension we can always review and correct)' (Eco 1999). The world can never be simply a figment of our concept-driven imaginations. 'Even granting that the schema is a construct, we can never assume that the segmentation of which it is the effect is completely arbitrary, because... it tries to make sense of something that *is there*, of forces that act externally on our sensor apparatus by exhibiting, at the least, some resistances' (Eco 1999). Or as Latour says of the work of scientists, the semantic challenge is to balance facticity with social constructivism of disciplinary schemata (Latour 2004).

Structural markup

Of the varieties of textual semantic markup, one is peculiarly self-referential, the markup of textual structure, or schemas which represent the architectonics of text. A number of digital tagging schemas have emerged, which provide a functional account of the processes of containing, describing, managing and transacting text. They give a functional account of the world of textual content. Each tagging schema has its own functional purpose. A number of these tagging schemas have been created for the purpose of describing the structure of text, and to facilitate its rendering to alternative formats. These schemas are mostly derivatives of SGML, HTML and XHTML, and are designed primarily for rendering transformations through web browsers. Created originally for technical documentation, DocBook structures book text for digital and print renderings. The Text Encoding Initiative is 'an international and interdisciplinary standard that helps libraries, museums, publishers, and individual scholars represent all kinds of literary and linguistic texts for online research and teaching' (*http://www.tei-c.org/*).

Although the primary purpose of each schema may be a particular form of rendering, this belies the rigorous separation of semantics and structure from presentation. Alternative stylesheet transformations could be applied to render the marked up text in a variety of ways on a variety of rendering devices.

These tagging schemas do almost everything conceivable in the world of the written word. They can describe text comprehensively, and they support the manufacture of variable renderings of text on the fly by means of stylesheet transformations. The typesetting and content capture schemas provide a systematic account of structure in written text, and through stylesheet transformations they can render text to paper, to electronic screens of all sizes and formats, or to synthesised audio.

Underlying this is a fundamental shift in the processes of text work, described in Chapter 4, 'What does the digital do to knowledge making?'. A change of emphasis occurs in the business of signing—broadly conceived as the design of meaning—from configuring meaning form (the specifics of the audible forms of speaking and the visual form of written text) to 'marking up' for meaning function in such a way that alternative meaning forms, such as variable visual (written) and audio forms of language, can be rendered by means of automated processes from a common digital source.

In any digital markup framework that separates the structure from presentation, the elementary unit of meaning function is marked by the tag, specifying the meaning function for the most basic 'chunk' of represented content. Tags, in other words, describe the meaning function of a unit of content. For instance, a word or phrase may be tagged as <Emphasis>, <KeywordTerm> or <OtherLanguageTerm>. These tags describe the peculiar meaning function of a piece of content. In this sense, a system of tags works like a functional grammar; it marks up key features of the information architecture of a text. Tags delineate critical aspects of meaning function, and they do this explicitly by means of a relatively consistent and semantically unambiguous metalanguage. This metalanguage acts as a kind of running commentary on meaning functions which are otherwise embedded, implicit or to be inferred from context.

Meaning form follows mechanically from the delineation of meaning function, and this occurs in a separate stylesheet transformation space. Depending on the stylesheet, for instance, each of the three functional tags <Emphasis>, <KeywordTerm> and <OtherLanguageTerm> may be rendered to screen or print either as boldface or italics, or as an audible intonation in the case of rendering as synthesised voice.

Given the pervasiveness of structural markup, one might expect that an era of rapid and flexible transmission of content would quickly dawn. But this has not occurred, or at least not yet, and for two reasons. The first is the fact that, although almost all content created over the past quarter of a century has been digitised, the formats are varied and incompatible. Digital content is everywhere, but most of it has been created, and continues to be created, using typographically oriented markup frameworks. These frameworks are embedded in software packages that provide tools for working with text which mimic the various trades of the Gutenberg universe: an author may use Word; a desktop publisher or latter-day typesetter may use inDesign; and a printer will use a PDF file as if it were a virtual forme or plate. The result is sticky file flow and intrinsic difficulties in version control and digital repository maintenance. How and where is a small correction made to a book that has already been published? Everything about this relatively simple problem, as it transpires, remains complex, slow and expensive. However, in a fully comprehensive, integrated file flow, things that are slow and expensive today should become easier and cheaper—a small change by an author to the source text could be approved by a publisher so that the very next copy of that work could include that change.

To return to the foundational question of the changed means of production of meaning in semantic and structural text-work environment, we want to extend the distinction of 'meaning form' from 'meaning function'. Signs are the elementary components of meaning. And 'signs', say Kress and Leeuwen, are 'motivated conjunctions of signifiers (forms) and signifieds (meanings)' (Kress and van Leeuwen 1996). Rephrasing, we would call motivated meanings, the products of the impulse to represent the world and communicate those representations, 'meaning functions'. The business of signing, motivated as it is by representation (meaning interpreted oneself) and communication (meaning interpreted by others), entails an amalgam of function (a reason to mean) and form (the use of representational resources which might adequately convey that meaning).

The meaning function may be a flower in a garden on which we have fixed our focus for a moment through our faculties of perception and imagination. For that moment, this particular flower captures our attention and its features stand out from its surroundings. The meaning function is our motivation to represent this meaning and to communicate about it. How we represent this meaning function is a matter of meaning form. The meaning form we choose might be iconic—we could draw a sketch of the flower, and in this case, the act of signing (form meets function) is realised through a process of visual resemblance. Meaning form—the drawing of the flower—looks like meaning function, or what we mean to represent: the flower. Or the relation between meaning form and function may be, as is the case for language, arbitrary. The word 'flower', a symbolic form, has no intrinsic connection with the meaning function it represents. In writing or in speech the word 'flower' conventionally represents this particular meaning function in English. We can represent the object to ourselves using this word in a way which fits with a whole cultural domain of experience (encounters with other flowers in our life and our lifetime's experience of speaking about and hearing about flowers). On the basis of this conventional understanding of meaning function, we can communicate our experience of this flower or any aspect of its flower-ness to other English speakers.

This, in essence, is the stuff of signing, the focal interest of the discipline of semiotics. It is an ordinary, everyday business, and the fundamental ends do not change when employing new technological means. It is the stuff of our human natures. The way we mean is one of the distinctive things that makes us human.

One of the key features of the digital revolution is the change in the mechanics of conjoining meaning functions with meaning forms in structural and semantic markup. We are referring here to a series of interconnected changes in the means of production of signs. Our perspective is that of a functional linguistics for digital text. Traditional grammatical accounts of language trace the limitlessly complex structures and patterns of language in the form of its immediately manifest signs. Only after the structure of forms has been established is the question posed, 'what do these forms mean?'. In contrast, functional linguistics turns the question of meaning around the other way: 'how are meanings expressed?'. Language is conceived as a system of meanings; its role is to realise or express these meanings. It is not an end in itself; it is a means to an end (Halliday 1994). Meaning function underlies meaning form. An account of meaning form must be based on a functional interpretation of the structures of meaning. Meaning form of a linguistic variety comprises words and their syntactical arrangement, as well as the expressive or presentational processes of phonology (sounding out words or speaking) and graphology (writing). Meaning form needs to be accounted for in terms of meaning function.

Structural and semantic markup adds a second layer of meaning to the process of representation in the form of a kind of meta-semantic gloss. This is of particular value in the deployment of specialised disciplinary discourses. Such discourses rely on a high level of semantic specificity. The more immersed you are in that particular discourse—the more critical it is to your livelihood or identity in the world, for instance—the more important these subtle distinctions of meaning are likely to be. Communities of practice identify themselves by the rigorous singularity of purpose and intent within their particular domain of practice, and this is reflected in the relative lack of terminological ambiguity within the discourse of disciplinary practice of that domain. In these circumstances semantic differences between two social languages in substantially overlapping domains is likely to be absolutely critical. This is why careful schema mapping and alignment is such an important task in the era of semantic and structural markup.

Metamarkup: developing markup frameworks

We now want to propose in general terms an alternative framework to the formalised semantic web, a framework that we call an instance of 'semantic publishing'. The computability of the web today is little better than the statistical frequency analyses of character clusters that drive search algorithms, or the flat and featureless world of folksonomies and conceptual popularity rankings in tag clouds. Semantic publishing is a counterpoint to these simplistic modes of textual computability. We also want to advocate a role for conceptualisation and theorisation in textual computability, against an empiricism which assumes that the right algorithms are all we need to negotiate the 'data deluge'—at which point, it is naively thought, all we need to do is calculate and the world will speak for itself (Anderson 2009). In practical terms, we have been working through and experimenting with this framework in the nascent CGMeaning online schema making and schema matching environment.

Foundations to the alternative framework to the formalised semantic web

The framework has five foundations.

Foundation 1 Schema making should be a site of social dialectic, not ontological legislation

Computable schemas today are made by small groups of often nameless experts, and for that are inflexibly resistant to extensibility and slow to change. The very use of the word 'ontology' gives an unwarranted aura of objectivity to something that is essentially a creature of human-semantic configuration.

Schemas, however, are specific constructions of reality within the frame of reference of highly particularised social languages that serve disciplinary, professional or other specialised purposes. Their reality is a social reality. They are no more and no less than a 'take' on reality, which reflects and represents a particular set of human interests. These interests are fundamentally to get things done—funnels of commitment, to use Scollon's words (Scollon 2001)—rather than mere reflections of inert, objectified 'being'. Schemas, in other words, are ill served by the immutable certainty implied by the word 'ontology'. Reality does not present itself through ontologies in an unmediated way. Tagging schemas are better understood to be mediated relationships of meaning rather than static pictures of reality.

However, the socio-technical environments of their construction today do not support the social dialectic among practitioners that would allow schemas to be dynamic and extensible. CGMeaning attempts to add this dimension. Users can create or import schemata—XML tags, classification schemes, database structures—and establish a dialogue between a 'curator' who creates or imports a schema ready for extension or further schema alignment—and the community of users which may need additional tags, finer or distinctions or new definitions of tag content, and clarifications of situations of use by exemplification. In other words, rather than top-down imposition as if any schema ever deserved the objectifying aura of 'ontology', and rather than the fractured failure to discuss and refine meanings of 'folksonomies', we need the social dialectic of curator–community dialogue about always provisional, always extensible schemata. This moves the question of semantics from the anonymous hands of experts into the agora of collective intelligence.

Foundation 2 From a one-layered linear string, to a double-layered string with meta-semantic gloss

Schemas should not only be sites of social dialectic about tag meanings and tag relations. Semantic markup practices establish a dialectic between the text and its markup. These practices require that authors mark up or make explicit meanings in their texts. Readers may also be invited to mark up a text in a process of computable social-notetaking. A specialised text may already be some steps removed from vernacular language. However, markup against a schema may take these meanings to an even more finely differentiated level of semantic specificity. The text–schema dialectic might work like this: an instance mentioned in the text may be evidence of a concept defined in a schema, and the act of markup may prompt the author or reader to enter into critical dialogue in their disciplinary community about the meanings as currently expressed in the tags and tag relations. The second layer, in other words, does not necessarily and always formally fix meanings, or force them to be definitive. Equally, at times, it might open the schema to further argumentation and clarification, a process Brandom calls 'giving and asking for reasons' (Brandom 1994). 'Such systems develop and sustain themselves by *marking* their own operations self-reflexively; [they] facilitate the self-reflexive operations of human communicative action' (Buzzetti and McGann 2006).

In other words, we need to move away from the inert objectivity of imposed ontologies, towards a dialogue between text and concept, reader and author, specific instance and conceptual generality. Markup can stabilise meaning, bring texts into conformance with disciplinary canons. Equally, in the dialogical markup environment we propose here, it can prompt discussions about concepts and their relations which have dynamically incremental or paradigm-shifting consequences on the schema.

In this process, we will also move beyond the rigidities of XML, in which text is conceived as an 'ordered hierarchy of content objects', like a nested set of discrete Chinese boxes (Renear, Mylonas and Durand 1996). Meaning and text, contrary to this representational architecture, 'are riven with overlapping and recursive structures of various kinds just as they always engage, simultaneously, hierarchical as well as non-hierarchical formations' (Buzzetti and McGann 2006). Our solution in CGMeaning is to allow authors and readers to 'paint' overlapping stretches of text with their semantic tags.

Foundation 3 Making meanings explicit

Markup schemas—taxonomies as well as folksonomies—rarely have readily accessible definitions of tag meanings. In natural language, meanings are given and assumed. However, in the rather unnatural language of scholarly technicality, meanings need to be described with higher degree of precision, to novices and also for expert practitioners at points of conceptual hiatus or questionable applicability. For this reason, CGMeaning provides and infrastructure for dictionary-formation, but with some peculiar ground rules.

Dictionaries of natural language capture the range of uses, nuances, ambiguities and metaphorical slippages. They describe language as a found object, distancing themselves from any normative judgement about use (Jackson 2002). However, even for their agnosticism about the range of situations of use, natural language dictionaries are of limited value given discourse and context-specific range of possible uses. Fairclough points out that 'it is of limited value to think of a language as having a vocabulary which is documented in "the" dictionary, because there are a great many overlapping and competing vocabularies corresponding to different domains, institutions, practices, values and perspectives' (Fairclough 1992). Gee calls these domain-specific discourses 'social languages' (Gee 1996). The conventional dictionary solution to the problem of ambiguity is to list the major alternative meanings of a word, although this can only reflect gross semantic variation. No dictionary could ever capture comprehensively the never-ending subtleties and nuances ascribed differentially to a word in divergent social languages.

The dictionary infrastructure in CGMeaning is designed so there is only one meaning per concept/tag, and this is on the basis of a point of salient conceptual distinction that is foundational to the logic of the specific social language and the schema that supports it, for instance: 'Species are groups of biological individuals that have evolved from a common ancestral group and which, over time, have separated from other groups that have also evolved from this ancestor.' Definitions in this dictionary space shunt between natural language and unnatural language, between (in Vygotsky's psychological terms) complex association and the cognitive work of conceptualisation. In the unnatural language of disciplinary use, semantic saliences turn on points of generalisable principle. This is how disciplinary work is able at times to uncover the not-obvious, the surprising, the counter-intuitive. This is when unnatural language posits singularly clear definitions that are of strategic use, working with abstractions that are powerfully transferable from one context of application to another, or in order to provide a more efficient pedagogical alternative for novices than the impossible expectation of having to reinvent the world by retracing the steps of its every empirical discovery. Schemata represent the elementary stuff of theories and paradigms, the congealed sedimentations of collective intelligence.

Moreover, unlike a natural language dictionary, a dictionary for semantic publishing defines concepts—which may be represented by a word or a phrase—and not words. Concepts are not necessarily nouns or verbs. In fact, in many cases concepts can be conceived as either states or processes, hence the frequently easy transliteration of nouns into verbs and the proliferation in natural language of non-verb hybrids such as gerunds and particles. For consistency's sake and to reinforce the idea of 'concept', we would use the term 'running' instead of 'run' as the relevant tag in a hypothetical sports schema. In fact, the process of incorporating actions into nouns, or 'nominalisation', is one of the distinctive discursive moves of academic disciplines and typical generally of specialised social languages (Martin and Halliday 1993). As Martin points out, 'one of the main functions of nominalisation is in fact to build up technical taxonomies of processes in specialised fields. Once technicalised, these nominalisations are interpretable as things' (Martin 1992). This, incidentally, is also a reason why we would avoid the belaboured intricacies of RDF (Resource Description Framework), which attempts to build sentence-like propositions in the subject -> predicate -> object format.

Moreover, this kind of dictionary accommodates both 'lumpers' (people who would want to aggregate by more general saliences) and 'splitters' (people who would be more inclined to make finer conceptual distinctions)—to employ terms used to characterise alternative styles of thinking in biological taxonomy. Working with concepts allows for the addition of phrases which can do both of these things, and to connect them, in so doing adding depth to the conceptual dialogue and delicacy to its semantics.

Another major difference is that this kind of dictionary is not alphabetically ordered (for which, in any event, in the age of digital search, there is no longer any need). Rather, it is arranged in what we call 'supermarket order'. In this way, things can be associated according to the rough rule of 'this should be somewhere near this', with the schema allowing many other formal associations in addition to the best-association shelving work of a curator. There is no way you can know the precise location of the specific things you need purchase among the 110,000 different products in a Wal-Mart store, but mostly you can find them without help by a process of rough association. More rigorous connections will almost invariably be multiple and cross-cutting, and with varying contiguities according to the interest of the author or reader or the logic of the context. However, an intuitive collocation can be selected for the purpose of synergistic search.

Furthermore, this kind of dictionary does a rigorous job of defining concepts whose order of abstraction is higher (on what principle of salience is this concept a kind of or a part of a superordinate concept?), defining by distinction (what differentiates sibling concepts?) and exemplifying down (on what principles are subsidiary concepts instances of this concept?).

A definition may also describe essential, occasional or excluded properties. It may describe these using a controlled vocabulary of quantitative properties (integers, more than, less than, nth, equal to, all/some/none of, units of measurement etc.) and qualitative properties (colours, values). A definition may also shunt between natural language and more semantically specified schematic language by making semantic distinctions between a technical term and its commonsense equivalent in natural language.

Finally a definition may include a listing of some or all exemplary instances. In fact, the instances become part of the dictionary as well, thus (and once more, unlike a natural language dictionary) including any or every possible proper noun. This is a point at which schemata build transitions between the theoretical (conceptual) and the empirical (instances).

Foundation 4 Positing relations

A simple taxonomy specifies parent, child and sibling relations. However, it does this without the level of specificity required to support powerful semantics. For example, in parent–child relations we would want to distinguish hyponymy 'a kind of' from meronymy 'a part of'. In addition, a variety of cross-cutting and intersecting relations can be created, including relations representing a range of semantic primitives such as 'also called', 'opposite of', 'is not', 'is like but [in specified respects] not the same as', 'possesses', 'causes', 'is an example of', 'is associated with', 'is found in/at [time or place]', 'is a [specify quality] relation' and 'is by [specify type of] comparison'. Some of these relations may be computable using first order logic or description logics (Sowa 2000, 2006), others not.

Foundation 5 Social schema alignment

Schemata with different foci sometimes have varying degrees of semantic overlap. They sometimes talk, in other words, about the same things, albeit with varied perspectives and serving divergent interests. CGMeaning builds a social space for schema alignment, using an 'interlanguage' mechanism. Although initially developed in the case of one particular instantiation of problem of interoperability—for the electronic standards that apply to publishing (Common Ground Publishing 2003)—the core technology is applicable to the more general problem of interoperability characterised by the semantic publishing.

Developing an interlanguage mechanism

By filtering schemata through the 'interlanguage' mechanism, a system is created that allows conversation and information interchange between disjoint schemas. In this way, it is possible to create functionalities for data framed within the paradigm of one schema which extend well beyond those originally conceived by that schema. This may facilitate interoperability between schemas, allowing data originally designed for use in one schema for a particular set of purposes to be used in another schema for a different set of purposes.

The interlanguage mechanism means that metadata newly created through its apparatus to be interpolated into any number of metadata schemas. It also provides a method by means of which data harvested in one metadata schema can be imported into another. From a functional point of view, some of this process can be fully automated, and some the subject of automated queries requiring a human-user response.

The interlanguage mechanism, in sum, is designed to function in two ways:

- for new data, a filter apparatus provides full automation of interoperability on the basis of the semantic and syntactical rules
- for data already residing in an schema, data automatically passes through a filter apparatus using the interlanguage mechanism, and passes on into other schemas or ontologies even though the data had not originally been designed for the destination schema.

The filter apparatus is driven by a set of semantic and syntactical rules as outlined below, and throws up queries whenever an automated translation of data is not possible in terms of those semantic rules.

The interlanguage apparatus is designed to be able to read tags, and thus interpret the data which has been marked up by these tags, according to two overarching mechanisms, and a number of submechanisms. The two overarching mechanisms are the superordination mechanism and the composition mechanism—drawing in part here on some distinctions made in systemic-functional linguistics (Martin 1992).

The superordination mechanism constructs tag-to-tag 'is a...' relationships. Within the superordination mechanism, there are the submechanisms of hyponymy ('includes in its class...'), hyperonymy ('is a class of...'), co-hyperonoymy ('is the same as...'), antinomy ('is the converse of...') and series ('is related by gradable opposition to...').

The composition mechanism constructs tag-to-tag 'has a...' relationships. Within the composition mechanism, there are the submechanisms of meronymy ('is a part of...'), co-meronymy ('is integrally related to but exclusive of...'), consistency ('is made of...'), collectivity ('consists of...').

These mechanisms can be fully automated in the case of new data formation within any schema, in which case, deprecation of some aspects of an interoperable schema may be required as a matter of course at the point of data entry. In the case of legacy data generated in schemas without anticipation of, or application of, the interlanguage mechanism, data can be imported in a partially automated way. In this case, tag-by-tag or field-by-field queries are automatically generated according to the filter mechanisms of:

- taxonomic distance (testing whether the relationships of composition and superordination are too distant to be necessarily valid)
- levels of delicacy (testing whether an aggregated data element needs to be disaggregated and re-tagged)
- potential semantic incursion (identifying sites of ambiguity)
- the translation of silent into active tags or vice versa (at what level in the hierarchy of composition or superordination data needs to be entered to effect superordinate transformations).

The interlanguage mechanism (Figure 13.1) is located in CGMeaning, a schema-building and alignment tool. This software defines and determines:

- database structures for storage of metadata and data
- XML document inputs
- synonyms across the tagging schemas for each schema being mapped

Figure 13.1 The interlanguage mechanism

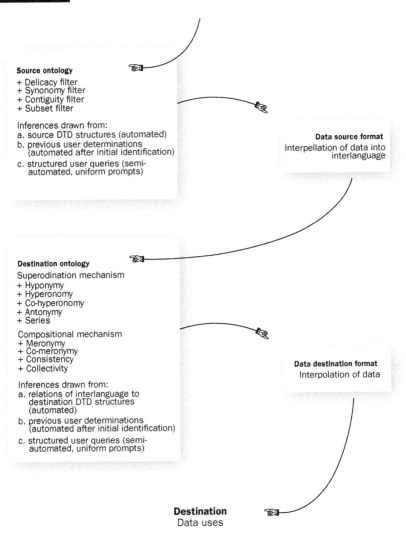

Source ontology
+ Delicacy filter
+ Synonomy filter
+ Contiguity filter
+ Subset filter

Inferences drawn from:
a. source DTD structures (automated)
b. previous user determinations
   (automated after initial identification)
c. structured user queries (semi-
   automated, uniform prompts)

Data source format
Interpellation of data into
interlanguage

Destination ontology
Superodination mechanism
+ Hyponymy
+ Hyperonomy
+ Co-hyperonomy
+ Antonymy
+ Series

Compositional mechanism
+ Meronymy
+ Co-meronymy
+ Consistency
+ Collectivity

Inferences drawn from:
a. relations of interlanguage to
   destination DTD structures
   (automated)
b. previous user determinations
   (automated after initial identification)
c. structured user queries (semi-
   automated, uniform prompts)

Data destination format
Interpolation of data

Destination
Data uses

- two definitional layers for every tag: underlying semantics and application-specific semantics; in this regard, CGMeaning creates the space for application-specific paraphrases can be created for different user environments; the underlying semantics necessarily generates abstract dictionary definitions which are inherently not user-friendly;

however, in an application, each concept-tag needs to be described and defined in ways that are intelligible within that domain; it is these application-specific paraphrases that render to the application interface in the first instance

- export options into an extensible range of electronic standards expressed as XML schemas

- CGMeaning, which manages the superordination and compositional mechanisms described above, as well as providing an interface for domain-specific applications in which interoperability is required.

Following are some examples of how this mechanism may function. In one scenario, new data might be constructed according to a source schema which has already become 'aware' by means of previous applications of the interlanguage mechanism as a consequence of the application of the mechanism. In this case, the mechanism commences with the automatic interpellation of data, as the work of reading and querying the source schema has already been performed. In these circumstances, the source schema in which the new data is constructed becomes a mere facade for the interlanguage, taking the form of a user interface behind which the processes of subordination and composition occur.

In another scenario, a quantum of legacy source data is provided, marked up according to the schematic structure of a particular source schema. The interlanguage mechanism then reads the structure and semantics immanent in the data, interpreting this from schema and the way the schema is realised in that particular instance. It applies four filters: a delicacy filter, a synonymy filter, a contiguity filter and a subset filter. The apparatus is able to read into the schema and its particular instantiation an inherent taxonomic or schematic structure. Some of this is automated, as the relationships of tags is unambiguous based on the readable structure of the schema and evidence drawn from its instantiation in a concrete piece of data. The mechanism is also capable of 'knowing' the points at which it is possible there might be ambiguity, and in this case throws up a structured query to the user. Each human response to a structured query becomes part of the memory of the mechanism, with implications drawn from the user response and retained for later moments when interoperability is required by this or another user. On this basis, the mechanism interpellates the source data into the interlanguage format, while at the same time automatically 'growing' the interlanguage itself based on knowledge acquired in the reading of the source data and source schema.

Having migrated into the interlanguage format, the data is then reworked into the format of the destination schema. It is rebuilt and validated according to the mechanisms of superordination (hyponymy, hyperonymy, co-hyperonomy, antonymy and series) and composition (meronymy, co-meronymy, consistency, collectivity). A part of this process is automated, according to the inherent structures readable into the destination schema, or previous human readings that have become part of the accumulated memory of the interlanguage mechanism. Where the automation of the rebuilding process cannot be undertaken by the apparatus with assurance of validity (when a relation is not inherent to the destination schema, nor can it be inferred from accumulated memory in which this ambiguity was queried previously), a structured query is once again put to the user, whose response in turn becomes a part of the memory of the apparatus, for future use. On this basis, the data in question is interpolated into its destination format. From this point, it can be used in its destination context or schema environment, notwithstanding the fact that the data had not been originally formatted for use in that environment.

Key operational features of this mechanism include:

- the capacity to absorb effectively and easily deploy new schemas which refer to domains of knowledge, information and data that substantially overlap (vertical ontology-over-ontology integration); the mechanism is capable of doing this without the exponential growth in the scale of the task characteristic of the existing 'crosswalk' method

- the capacity to absorb schemas representing new domains that do not overlap with the existing range of domains and ontologies representing these domains (horizontal ontology-beside-ontology integration)

- the capacity to extend indefinitely into finely differentiated subdomains within the existing range of domains connected by the interlanguage, but not yet this finely differentiated (vertical ontology-within-ontology integration).

In the most challenging of cases—in which the raw digital material is created in a legacy schema, and in which that schema is not already known to the interlanguage from previous interactions—the mechanism:

- interprets structure and semantics from the source schema and its instantiation in the case of the particular quantum of source data, using the filter mechanisms described above

- draws inferences in relation to the new schema and the particular quantum of data, applying these automatically and presenting structured queries in cases where the apparatus and its filter mechanism 'knows' that supplementary human interpretation is required

- stores any automated or human-supplied interpretations for future use, thus building knowledge and functional useability of this schema into the interlanguage.

These inferences then become visible to subsequent users, and capable of amendment by users, through the CGMeaning interface, which:

- interpellates the data into the interlanguage format
- creates a crosswalk from new schema into a designated destination schema, for instance a new format for structuring or rendering text, using the superordination and composition mechanisms; these are automated in cases where the structure and semantics of the destination schema are self-evident, or they are the subject of structured queries where they are not, or they are drawn from the CGMeaning repository in instances where the same query has been answered by an earlier user
- interpolates data into the destination schema
- supplies data for destination uses.

To give another example, the source schema is already known to the interlanguage, by virtue of automated validations based not only on the inherent structure of the schema, but also many validations against a range of data instantiations of that schema, and numerous user clarifications of queries. In this case, by entering data in an interface that 'knowingly' relates to an interlanguage which has been created using the mechanisms provided here, there is no need for the filter mechanisms nor the interpolation processes that are necessary in the case of legacy data and unknown source schemas; rather, data is entered directly into the interlanguage format, albeit through the user interface 'facade' of the source schema. The apparatus then interpolates the data onto the designated destination schema.

Schema alignment for semantic publishing: the example of Common Ground Markup Language

Common Ground Markup Language (CGML) is a schema for marking up and storing text as structured data, created in the tag definition and schema alignment environment, CGMeaning. The storage medium can be XML files, or it can be a database in which fields are named by tags, and from which exports produce XML files marked up for structure and semantics, ready for rendering through available stylesheet transformations. The result is text that is more easily located by virtue of the clarity and detail of metadata markup, and capable of a range of alternative renderings. CGML structures and stores data on the basis of a functional account of text, not just as an object but as a process of collaborative construction. The focal point of CGML is a functional grammar of text, as well as a kind of grammar (in the metaphorical sense of generalised reflection) of the social context of text work. However, with CGML, 'functional' takes on a peculiarly active meaning. The markup manufactures the text in the moment of rendering, through the medium of stylesheet transformation in one or several rendering processes or media spaces.

In CGML, as is the case for any digital markup framework that separates structure and semantics from presentation, the elementary unit of meaning function is marked by the tag. The tag specifies the meaning function for the most basic 'chunk' of represented content. Tags, in other words, describe the meaning function of a unit of content. For instance, a word or phrase may be tagged as <Emphasis>, <KeywordTerm> or <OtherLanguageTerm>. These describe the peculiar meaning function of a piece of content. In this sense, a system of tags works like a partial functional grammar: they mark up key features of the information architecture of a text. Tags delineate critical aspects of meaning function, and they do this explicitly by means of a relatively consistent and semantically unambiguous metalanguage. This metalanguage acts as a kind of running commentary on meaning functions, which are otherwise embedded, implicit or to be inferred from context.

Meaning form follows mechanically from the delineation of meaning function, and this occurs in a separate stylesheet transformation space. Depending on the stylesheet, each of the three functional tags <Emphasis>, <KeywordTerm> and <OtherLanguageTerm> may be rendered to screen or print either as boldface or italics, or as a particular intonation in the case of rendering as synthesised voice. Stylesheets, incidentally, are the exception to the XML rule strictly to avoid matters of presentation; meaning form is their exclusive interest.

CGML, in other words, is a functional schema for authorship and publishing. CGML attempts to align the schemas we will describe shortly, incorporating their varied functions. CGML is an interlanguage. Its concepts constitute a paradigm for representational work, drawing on a historically familiar semantics, but adapting this to the possibilities of the internet. Its key devices are thesaurus (mapping against functional schemas) and dictionary (specifying a common ground semantics). These are the semantic components for narrative structures of text creation, or the retrospective stories that can be told of the way in which, for instance, authors, publishers, referees, reviewers, editors and the like construct and validate text. The purpose of this work is both highly pragmatic (such as a description of an attempt to create a kind of functional grammar of the book) and highly theoretical (a theory of meaning function capable of assisting in the partially automated construction and publication of variable meaning forms).

In the era of digital media, the social language of textuality is expressed in a number of schemas. It is increasingly the case that these schemas perform a wide ranging, fundamental and integrated set of functions. They *contain* the content—the electronic files that provide structural and semantic shape for the data which will be rendered as a book. They *describe* the content—for the purposes of data transfer, warehousing and retrieval. They *manage* the content—providing a place where job process instructions and production data are stored. And they *transact* the content.

A number of digital tagging schemas have emerged which provide a functional account of these processes of containing, describing, managing and transacting text. More broadly, they provide a functional account of the world of textual content in general. Each tagging schema has its own functional purpose, or 'funnel of commitment', to use Scollon's terminology. We will briefly describe a few of these below, categorising them into domains of professional and craft interest: typesetting and content capture, electronic rendering, print rendering, resource discovery, cataloguing, educational resource creation, e-commerce and digital rights management. The ones we describe are those we have mapped into CGML.

Typesetting and content capture

Unicode (*http://www.unicode.org*) appears destined to become the new universal character encoding standard, covering all major language and scripts (Unicode 2010), and replacing the American Standard Code for Information Interchange (ASCII), which was based solely on Roman script.

A number of tagging schemas have been created for the purpose of describing the structure of text, and to facilitate its rendering to alternative formats. These schemas are mostly derivatives of SGML. HTML (W3C 2010a) and XHTML (W3C 2010b) are designed primarily for rendering transformations through web browsers. The OASIS/UNESCO sanctioned DocBook standard is for structuring book text, which can subsequently be rendered electronically or to print (DocBook Technical Committee 2010). The Text Encoding Initiative is 'an international and interdisciplinary standard that helps libraries, museums, publishers and individual scholars represent all kinds of literary and linguistic texts for online research and teaching' (*http://www.tei-c.org*).

Although the primary purpose of each schema may be a particular form of rendering, this belies the rigorous separation of semantics and structure from presentation. Alternative stylesheet transformations could be applied to render the marked up text in a variety of ways. Using different stylesheets, it is possible, for instance, to render DocBook either as typesetting for print or as HTML.

Electronic rendering

Electronic rendering can occur in a variety of ways—as print facsimiles in the form of Portable Document Format (PDF), or as HTML readable by means of a web browser. Other channel alternatives present themselves as variants or derivatives of HTML: the Open eBook Standard for handheld electronic reading devices (International Trade Standards Organization for the eBook Industry 2003) and Digital Talking Book (ANSI/NISO 2002), facilitating the automated transition of textual material into audio form for the visually impaired or the convenience of listening to a text rather than reading it.

Print rendering

The Job Definition Format (JDF) appears destined to become universal across the printing industry (*http://www.cip4.org/*). Specifically for variable print, Personalised Print Markup Language (PPML) has also emerged (PODi 2003).

Created by a cross-industry international body, the Association for International Cooperation for the Integration of Processes in Pre-Press, Press and Post-Press, the JDF standard has been embraced and supported by all major supply-side industry participants (equipment and business systems suppliers). It means that one electronic file contains all data related to a particular job. It is free (in the sense that there is no charge for the use of the format) and open (in the sense that its tags are transparently presented in natural language; it is unencrypted, its coding can be exposed and it can be freely modified, adapted and extended by innovators—in sharp distinction to proprietary software).

The JDF functions as a digital addendum to offset print, and as the driver of digital print. Interoperability of JDF with other standards will mean, for instance, that a book order triggered through an online bookstore (the ONIX space, as described below) could generate a JDF wrapper around a content file as an automated instruction to print and dispatch a single copy.

The JDF serves the following functions:

- *Pre-press*—Full job specification, integrating pre-press, press and post-press (e.g. binding) elements, in such a way that these harmonise (the imposition matches the binding requirements, for example). This data is electronically 'tagged' to the file itself, and in this sense it actually 'makes' the 'printing plate'.

- *Press*—The job can then go onto any press from any manufacturer supporting the JDF standard (and most major manufacturers now do). This means that the press already 'knows' the specification developed at the pre-press stage.

- *Post-press*—Once again, any finishing is determined by the specifications already included in the JDF file, and issues such as page format and paper size are harmonised across all stages in the manufacturing process.

The effects of wide adoption of this standard by the printing industry include:

- *Automation*—There is no need to enter the job specification data from machine to machine, and from one step in the production process to the next. This reduces the time and thus the cost involved in handling a job.

- *Human error reduction*—As each element of a job specification is entered only once, this reduces waste and unnecessary cost.

- *Audit trail*—Responsibility for entering specification data is pushed further back down the supply chain, ultimately even to the point where a customer will fill out the 'job bag' simply by placing an order through an online B-2-B interface. This shifts the burden of responsibility for specification, to some degree, to the initiator of an order, and records by whom and when a particular specification was entered. This leads to an improvement in ordering and specification procedures.

- *Equipment variations*—The standard reduces the practical difficulties previously experienced using different equipment supplied by different manufacturers. This creates a great deal of flexibility in the use of plant.

Resource discovery

Resource discovery can be assisted by metadata schemas that use tagging mechanisms to provide an account of the form and content of documents. In the case of documents locatable on the internet, Dublin Core is one of the principal standards, and is typical of others (Dublin Core Metadata Initiative 2010). It contains a number of key broadly descriptive tags: <title>, <creator>, <subject>, <description>, <publisher>, <contributor>, <date>, <resource type>, <format>, <resource identifier>, <source>, <language>, <relation>, <coverage> and <rights>. The schema is designed to function as a kind of electronic 'catalogue card' to digital files, so that it becomes possible, for instance, to search for Benjamin Disraeli as an author <creator> because you want to locate one of his novels, as opposed to writings about Benjamin Disraeli as a British prime minister <subject> because you have an interest in British parliamentary history. The intention of Dublin Core is to develop more sophisticated resource discovery tools than the current web-based search tools which, however fancy their algorithms, do little more than search indiscriminately for words and combinations of words.

A number of other schemas build on Dublin Core, such as the Australian standard for government information (Australian Government Locator Service 2003), and the EdNA and UK National Curriculum standards for electronic learning resources. Other schemas offer the option of embedding Dublin Core, as is the case with the Open eBook standard.

Cataloguing

The Machine Readable Catalog (MARC) format was initially developed in the 1960s by the US Library of Congress (MARC Standards Office 2003a; Mason 2001). Behind MARC is centuries of cataloguing practice, and its field and coding alternatives run to many thousands. Not only does MARC capture core information such as author, publisher or page extent. It also links into elaborate traditions and schemas for the classification of content such as the Dewey Decimal Classification system or the Library of Congress Subject Headings. MARC is based on ISO 2709 'Format for Information Exchange'. MARC has recently been converted into an open XML standard.

The original markup framework for MARC was based on non-intuitive alphanumeric tags. Subsequent related initiatives have included a simplified and more user-friendly version of MARC: the Metadata Object Description Schema (MARC Standards Office 2003c) and a standard specifically for the identification, archiving and location of electronic content, the Metadata Encoding and Transmission Standard (MARC Standards Office 2003b).

Various 'crosswalks' have also been mapped against other tagging schemas, notably MARC to Dublin Core (MARC Standards Office 2001) and the MARC to the ONIX e-commerce standard (MARC Standards Office 2000). In similar territory, although taking somewhat different approaches to MARC, are Biblink (UK Office for Library and Information Networking 2001) and Encoded Archival Description Language (Encoded Archival Description Working Group 2002).

Educational texts

Cutting across a number of areas—particularly rendering and resource discovery—are tagging schemas designed specifically for educational purposes. EdNA (EdNA Online 2000) and the UK National Curriculum Metadata Standard (National Curriculum Online 2002) are variants of Dublin Core.

Rapidly rising to broader international acceptance, however, is the Instructional Management Systems (IMS) Standard (IMS Global Learning Consortium 2003) and the related Shareable Content Object Reference Model (ADL/SCORM 2003). Not only do these standards specify metadata to assist in resource discovery. They also build and record conversations around interactive learning, manage automated assessment tasks, track learner progress and maintain administrative systems for teachers and learners. The genesis of IMS was in the area of metadata and resource discovery, and not the structure of learning texts. One of the pioneers in the area of structuring and rendering learning content (building textual information architectures specific to learning and rendering these through stylesheet transformations for web browsers) was Educational Modelling Language (OUL/EML 2003). Subsequently, EML was grafted into the IMS suite of schemas and renamed the IMS Learning Design Specification (IMS Global Learning Consortium 2002).

E-commerce

One tagging schema has emerged as the dominant standard for B-2-B e-commerce in the publishing supply chain—the ONIX, or the Online Information Exchange standard, initiated in 1999 by the Association of American Publishers, and subsequently developed in association with the British publishing and bookselling associations (EDItEUR 2001; Mason and Tsembas 2001). The purpose of ONIX is to capture data about a work in sufficient detail to be able automatically to upload new bookdata to online bookstores such as Amazon.com, and to communicate comprehensive information about the nature and availability of any work of textual content. ONIX sits within the broader context of interoperability with ebXML, an initiative of the United Nations Centre for Trade Facilitation and Electronic Business.

Digital rights management

Perhaps the most contentious area in the world of tagging is that of digital rights management (Cope and Freeman 2001). Not only does this involve the identification of copyright owners and legal purchasers of creative content; it can also involve systems of encryption by means of which content is only accessible to legitimate purchasers; and systems by means of which content can be decomposed into fragments and recomposed by readers to suit their specific needs. The <indecs> or Interoperability of Data in E-Commerce Systems framework was first published in 2000, the result of a two-year project by the European Union to develop a framework for the electronic exchange of intellectual property (<indecs> 2000). The conceptual basis of <indecs> has more recently been applied in the development of the Rights Data Dictionary for the Moving Pictures Expert Group's MPEG-21 framework for distribution of electronic content (Multimedia Description Schemes Group 2002). From these developments and discussions, a comprehensive framework is expected to emerge, capable of providing markup tools for all manner of electronic content (International DOI Foundation 2002; Paskin 2003).

Among the other tagging schemas marking up digital rights, Open Digital Rights Language (ODRL) is an Australian initiative, which has gained wide international acceptance and acknowledgement (ODRL 2002); and Extensible Rights Markup Language (XrML) was created in Xerox's PARC laboratories in Paulo Alto. Its particular strengths are in the areas of licensing and authentication (XrML 2003).

What tagging schemas do

The tagging schemas we have mentioned here do almost everything conceivable in the world of the written word. They can describe that world comprehensively, and to a significant degree they can support its manufacture. The typesetting and content capture schemas provide a systematic account of structure in written text, and through stylesheet transformations they can literally print text to paper, or render it electronically to screen or manufacture synthesised audio. Digital resource discovery and electronic library cataloguing schemas provide a comprehensive account of the form and content of non-digital as well as digital texts. Educational schemas attempt to operationalise the peculiar textual structures of traditional learning materials and learning conversations, where a learner's relation to text is configured into an interchange not unlike the ATM conversation we described in Chapter 4, 'What does the digital do to knowledge making?'. E-commerce and digital rights management schemas move texts around in a world where intellectual property rights regulate their flow and availability.

Tagging schemas and processes may be represented as paradigm (using syntagmatic devices such as taxonomy) or as narrative (an account of the 'funnel of commitment' and the alternative activity sequences or navigation paths in the negotiation of that commitment). Ontologies are like theories, except, unlike theories, they do not purport to be hypothetical or amenable to testing; they purport to tell of the world, or at the very least of a part of the world, like it is—in our case that part of the world inhabited by authors, publishers, librarians, bookstore workers and readers.

The next generation of ontology-based markup brings with it the promise of more accurate discovery, machine translation and, eventually, artificial intelligence. A computer really will be able to interpret the difference between Cope, cope and cope. Even in the case of the <author> with the seemingly unambiguous <surname> Kalantzis, there is semantic ambiguity that markup can eliminate or at least reduce, by collocating structurally related data (such as date of birth) to distinguish this Kalantzis from others and by knowing to avoid association with the transliteration of the common noun in Greek, which means 'tinker'.

In the world of XML, tags such as <author> and <surname> are known as 'elements', which may well have specified 'attributes'; and the ontologies are variously known as, or represented in, 'schemas', 'application profiles' or the 'namespaces' defined by 'document type definitions' or DTDs. As our interest in this chapter is essentially semantic, we use the concepts of 'tag' and 'schema'. In any event, as mentioned earlier, 'ontology' seems the wrong concept insofar as tag schemas are not realities; they are specific constructions of reality within the frame of reference of highly particularised social languages. Their reality is a social reality. They are no more and no less than a 'take' on reality, which reflects and represents a particular set of human interests. These interests are fundamentally to get things done (funnels of commitment) more than they are mere reflections of objectified, inert being. Schemas, in other words, have none of the immutable certainty implied by the word 'ontology'. Reality does not present itself in an unmediated way. Tagging schemas are mediated means rather than static pictures of reality.

Most of the tagging frameworks relating to authorship and publishing introduced above were either created in XML or have now been expressed in XML. That being the case, you might expect that an era of rapid and flexible transmission of content would quickly dawn. But this has not occurred, or at least not yet, and for two reasons. The first is the fact that, although almost all content created over the past quarter of a century has been digitised, most digital content has been created, and continues to be created, using legacy design and markup frameworks. These frameworks are embedded in software packages that provide tools for working with text which mimic the various trades of the Gutenberg universe: an author may use Word; a desktop publisher or latter-day typesetter may use Quark; and a printer will use a PDF file as if it were a virtual forme or plate. The result is sticky file flow and intrinsic difficulties in version control and digital repository maintenance (Cope 2001). How and where is a small correction made to a book that has already been published? Everything about this relatively simple problem, as it transpires, becomes complex, slow and expensive. However, in a fully comprehensive, integrated XML-founded file flow, things that are slow and expensive today should become easier and cheaper—a small change by an author to the source text could be approved by a publisher so that the very next copy of that book purchased online and printed on demand could include that change. Moreover, even though just about everything available today has been digitised somewhere, in the case of books and other written texts, the digital content remains locked away for fear that it might get out and about without all users paying for it when they should. Not only does this limit access, but what happens, for instance, when all you want is a few pages of a text and you do not want to pay for the whole of the printed version? And what about access for people who are visually impaired? It also puts a dampener on commercial possibilities for multichannel publishing, such as the student or researcher who really has to have a particular text tonight, and will pay for it if they can get it right away in an electronic format—particularly if the cost of immediate access is less than the cost of travelling to the library specially.

The second reason is that a new era of semantic text creation and transmission has not yet arrived. Even though XML is spreading quickly as a universal electronic *lingua franca,* each of its tagging schema describes its worlds in its own peculiar way. Tags may well be expressed in natural languages—this level of simplicity, openness, transparency is the hallmark of the XML world. But herein lies a trap. There is no particular problem when there is no semantic overlap between schemas. However, as most XML application profiles ground themselves in some ontological basics (such as people, place and time), there is nearly always semantic overlap between schemas. The problem is that, in everyday speech, the same word can mean many things, and XML tags express meaning functions in natural language.

The problem looms larger in the case of specialised social languages. These often develop a high level of technical specificity, and this attaches itself with a particular precision to key words. The more immersed you are in that particular social language—the more critical it is to your livelihood or identity in the world, for instance—the more important these subtle distinctions of meaning are likely to be. Communities of practice identify themselves by the rigorous singularity of purpose and intent within their particular domain of practice, and this is reflected in the relative lack of terminological ambiguity within the social language that characterises that domain. As any social language builds on natural language, there will be massive ambiguities if the looser and more varied world of everyday language is assumed to be homologous with a social language which happens to use some of the same terminology.

The semantic differences between two social languages in substantially overlapping domains are likely to be absolutely critical. Even though they are all talking about text and can with equal facility talk about books, it is the finely differentiated ways of talking about book that make authors, publishers, printers, booksellers and librarians different from each other. Their social language is one of the ways you can tell the difference between one type of person and another. These kinds of difference in social language are often keenly felt and defended. Indeed, they often become the very basis of professional identity.

This problem of semantics is the key dilemma addressed by this chapter, and the focal point of the research endeavour which has produced CGML. Our focus in this research has been the means of creation and communication of textual meaning, of which the book is an archetypical instance. Each of the schemas we have briefly described above channels a peculiar set of 'funnels of commitment' in relation to books—variously that of the author, typesetter, printer, publisher, bookseller, librarian and consumer. And although they are all talking about the same stuff—textual meaning in the form of books or journal articles—they talk about it in slightly different ways, and the differences are important. The differences distinguish the one funnel of commitment, employing its own peculiar social language to realise that commitment, from another. It is precisely the differences that give shape and form to the tagging schemas which have been the subject of our investigations.

The schemas we have identified range in size from a few dozen tags to a few thousand, and, the total number of tags across just these schemas would be in the order of tens of thousands. This extent alone would indicate that the full set of tags provides the basis for a near-definitive account of textual meaning. And although it seems as if these schemas were written almost yesterday, they merely rearticulate social languages that have developed through 500 years of working with the characteristic information architectures of mechanically reproduced writing, bibliography and librarianship, the book trade and readership. Given that they are all talking about authorship and publishing, the amount of overlap (the number of tags that represent a common semantic ground across all or most schemas) is unremarkable. What are remarkable are the subtle variations in semantics depending on the particular tagging schema or social language; and these variations can be accounted for in terms of the subtly divergent yet nevertheless all-important funnels of commitment.

So, after half a century of computing and a quarter of a century of the mass digitisation of text, nothing is really changing in the core business of representing the world using the electrical on/off switches of digitisation. The technology is all there, and has been for a while. The half-millennium-long shift is in the underlying logic behind the design of textual meaning. This shift throws up problems which are not at root technical; rather they are semantic. Interoperability of tagging schemas is not a technical problem, or at least it is a problem for which there are relatively straightforward technical solutions. The problem, and its solution, is semantic.

The commercial implications of the emergence and stabilisation of electronic standards are also enormous. These include:

- *Efficiencies and cost reduction*—Electronic standards facilitate cross-enterprise automation of file flow, including the process and commercial aspects of that flow—from the creator to the consumer. Efficiencies will also be created by B-2-B and B-2-C relationships based on standards, including error reduction, single entry of data and moves towards progressive automation of the production process.

- *Supply chain integration*—Electronic standards also mean that closer relationships can and should be built between the links of the publishing supply chain. For instance, a publisher ordering a print run of books can enter data into the printer's JDF via a web interface. It is also possible to transfer ONIX data automatically into this format, thus creating publisher–printer–bookseller supply chain integration. The key here is the creation trusted 'most favoured supplier' relationships and the development of a sense that the destinies of closely related enterprises are intertwined, rather than antithetical to each other's interests.

- *New business opportunities*—These will occur as new, hybrid enterprises emerge, which create links across the supply chain, offering services such as the multipurposing of content (for instance, to the web, to handheld reading devices and to digital talking book) and data warehousing. This will be supported particularly by the emergence of supply chain wide product identification protocols such as the Digital Object Identifier.

The key issue is the flow of business information and content between the various players in the text production and supply chain. Addressing this issue can produce efficiencies and competitive advantage for individual enterprises, and the whole industry. Many players are now arguing, in fact, that addressing this issue is not a choice—it is a necessity given the fact that standards are rapidly emerging, stabilising and gaining wide acceptance.

CGML is an attempt to address these semantic and commercial challenges. The aim of the CGML research and development endeavour has been to develop software that enables digital text production (electronic renderings and print renderings) using a markup language that offers stable and reliable interoperability across different standards. These standards include typesetting and text capture, electronic rendering, print rendering, B-2-B e-commerce, e-learning, digital rights management, internet resource discovery and library cataloguing.

CGML addresses one of the fundamental issues of the 'semantic web'—the problem of interoperability between different but overlapping and related electronic standards. Commercially and functionally, the intended result is a software environment in which texts render simultaneously to electronic and print formats (for instance, a bound book, computer screen, handheld reading device or synthesised voice) from a common source file. Metadata generated by this software is simultaneously able to create a library cataloguing record, an e-commerce record (automated entry to Amazon, international bookdata databases etc.) and make a published text an e-learning object and conform to the current and emerging digital rights management protocols.

At the time of writing, CGML consists of approximately 1,000 tags, interpolated into an XML schema. These tags are defined in the Common Ground Dictionary of Authorship and Publishing, which currently runs to some 25,000 words. CGML and the Dictionary are published dynamically (without 'editions' or 'versions'), with tags being constantly added and definitions refined as the Common Ground research endeavour proceeds. The Common Ground research and development team has created its own ontology-building software, CGMeaning, which houses CGML as well as providing a foundation for the export of data into a range of XML text and publishing schemas.

CGML takes the textual artefact of the written text as its point of departure. However, insofar as the digital medium also serves as a construction tool, repository and distributional means for audio, moving image, software, databases and the like, CGML also incorporates reference to these representational forms. CGML is designed to be fully extensible into all domains of creative media and cultural artefact.

From a technology point of view, CGML sets out to tackle one of the fundamental challenges of the 'semantic web'—the problem of interoperability between overlapping and related electronic standards. To this end, Common Ground researchers developed the 'interlanguage' mechanism (Common Ground Publishing 2003). This mechanism has the potential to extend the useability of content across multiple standards, XML schemas, ontologies or database structures. The approach taken by CGML may begin to address the enormous problem of interoperability in general, not just in publishing but in other areas of semantic publishing. Stated simply, electronic files do not flow well along production and distribution supply chains, because file formats vary, as does the metadata which defines file content format and uses. In the case of published material, there are enormous inefficiencies in file flow from author to publisher to printer to electronic rendering formats as well as the e-commerce mechanisms that deliver content from enterprise to enterprise and finally to consumers.

Even though each electronic standard or schema has its own functional purposes, there is a remarkable amount of overlap between these standards. The overlap, however, often involves the use of tags in mutually incompatible ways. Our extensive mapping of 17 standards in various text- and publishing-related fields shows that, on average, each standard shares 70 per cent of its semantic range with neighbouring standards. Despite this, it is simply not possible to transfer data generated in one standard to a database or XML schema using another. Each standard has been designed as its own independent, stand-alone schema. This, in fact, points to one of the key deficiencies of XML as a meta-markup framework: it does not in itself suggest a way for schemas to relate to each other. In fact, the very openness of XML invites a proliferation of schemas, and consequently the problem of interoperability compounds itself.

This produces practical and commercial problems. In the book publishing and manufacturing supply chain, different links in the chain use different standards: typesetters, publishers, booksellers, printers, manufacturers of electronic rendering devices and librarians. This disrupts the digital file flow, hindering supply chain integration and the possibilities of automating key aspects of supply chain, manufacturing and distribution processes. Precisely the same practical problems of interoperability are now arising in other areas of the electronic commerce environment.

Although our main interest is the world of authorship and publishing, the longer term possibilities technologies of interoperability such as CGML are in the areas in which the semantic web has so much—as yet unfulfilled—promise. This includes: indexing, cataloguing and metadata systems; product identification systems; systems for the production, manufacture and distribution of copyright digital content; knowledge and content management systems; systems for multi-channelling content and providing for disability access; machine translation from one natural language to another; and artificial intelligence.

More practically, the challenge of interoperability is this: in a scenario where there are many more than two parties, where the information is not covered by a single standard, where the resources and skills of the parties cannot facilitate costly and time-consuming integration, an approach is needed that caters for the complexity of the messages, while providing tools that simplify the provision and extraction of data and metadata. This is the crux of semantic interoperability. Such an approach involves providing a systematic mapping of associated XML standards to a common XML 'mesh', which tracks semantic overlays and gaps, schema versioning, namespace resolution, language and encoding variances, and which provides a comprehensive set of rules covering the data transfer—including security, transactional and messaging issues.

The idea of a 'meta-schema'—a schema to connect related schemas—was initially considered to be sufficient. Research has demonstrated, however, that this is not enough, being subject to many of the same problems as the individual schemas being mapped—versioning, terminological differences and so on.

The core operational principles of CGML are as follows: meaning form or rendering is rigorously separated from, yet reliably follows, markup tags expressing meaning function; interoperability of tagging schemas can be achieved by mapping through an interlanguage governed by a set of semantic and structural rules; a tag schema expresses paradigmatic relations; a tag thesaurus expresses relations between tagging schemas; a tag dictionary expresses semantics; interoperability mechanisms are automated or semi-automated; and tag narratives anticipate a range of activity sequences driven by funnels of commitment and realised through alternative navigation paths.

As a terminological aside, CGML deliberately recruits some quite ordinary concepts from the world of textual meaning, such as the ideas of a dictionary, thesaurus and narrative. If we are going to have what we have termed 'text-made text' in which markup is integral to textual reproduction, we might as well use these historically familiar devices—albeit with some refinement and levels of precision required by the logistics of digital meaning.

Interlanguage

Semantic publishing schemas promise to overcome two of the most serious limitations of the World Wide Web: searching involves simply identifying semantically undifferentiated strings of characters, and rendering alternatives is mostly limited by data entry methods—printed web pages do not live up to the historical standards of design and readability of printed text, and alternative non-visual renderings, such as digital talking books, are at best poor.

Specific schemas are designed to provide more accurate search results than is the case with computer or web-based search engines. Examples include the Dublin Core Metadata Framework and MARC electronic library cataloguing system. However, metadata harvested in one scheme cannot be readily or effectively used in another.

Specific schemas are also designed for a particular rendering option. For instance, among schemas describing the structure of textual content, HTML is designed for use in web browsers, DocBook for the production of printed books, Open eBook for rendering to handheld reading devices and Digital Talking Book for voice synthesis. Very limited interoperability is available between these different schemas for the structure of textual data, and only then if it has been designed into the schema and its associated presentational stylesheets. Furthermore, it is not practically possible to harvest accurate metadata from data, as data structuring schemas and schemas for metadata are mutually exclusive.

The field of semantic publishing attempts to improve on the inherent deficiencies in current digital technologies in the areas of resource discovery (metadata-based search functions) and rendering (defining structure and semantics in order to be able to support, via stylesheet transformations, alternative rendering options).

In support of semantic publishing, CGML attempts to inter-relate the principal extant in the tag schemas for the world of authorship and of publishing. However, unlike other tag schemas in this domain, it does not purport to be ontologically grounded. It does not attempt to name or rename the world. Rather, CGML builds a common ground between contiguous and overlapping tag schemas which already purport to name the world of authorship and publishing. It is not a language. It is an interlanguage (Figure 13.2).

The challenge of interoperability of tagging schemas (standards, application profiles or namespaces) has typically been addressed through schema-to-schema 'crosswalks'. A crosswalk is a listing of tag-to-tag translations not dissimilar from a language-to-language dictionary. For instance, as mentioned earlier, crosswalks have been created between MARC and ONIX (MARC Standards Office 2000) and between MARC and Dublin Core (MARC Standards Office 2001). As Paskin notes, when there are N schemas $(N/2)(N–1)$, mappings are required (Paskin 2003). For instance, as of writing, CGML maps to 17 schemas. For full interoperability, 136 'crosswalk' mappings would be required. Or, to take a natural language analogy, if there are 60 languages in Europe, translation between all 60 languages can be achieved with 1,770 language-to-language dictionaries—Italian–Gaelic, Gaelic–Vlach, Vlach–Italian and so on.

In fact, things are more complicated even than this. Each dictionary is, in fact, two dictionaries. Italian–Gaelic and Gaelic–Italian are not mirror inversions of each other because each language frames the world in its own semantically peculiar way. Similarly, the MARC to ONIX exercise (MARC Standards Office 2000) is quite a different one from the ONIX

Figure 13.2 CGML as an interlanguage

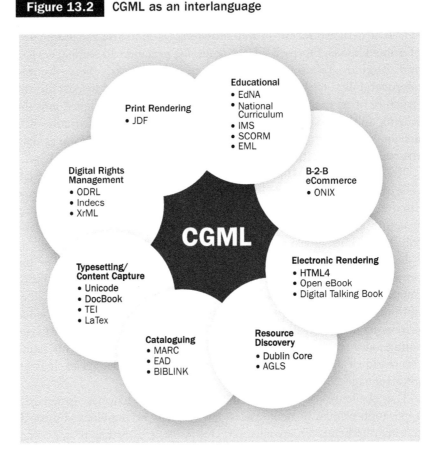

to MARC exercise (EDItEUR 2003). MARC to ONIX translates a library cataloguer's understanding of the nature and content of the book into a form intelligible to a publisher or a bookseller; and ONIX to MARC translates a publisher's or bookseller's understanding of the book into a form intelligible to a library cataloguer. In each case, the frame of reference or the starting point is defined in terms of a subtly distinctive social language. Each crosswalk is a separate intellectual and discursive exercise. So, we need to modify Paskin's crosswalk formula as follows: the number of mappings to achieve interoperability between N tagging schemas is $2[(N/2)(N-1)]$. In a terrain encompassed by the current version of CGML, 272 crosswalks would be required; Europe needs 3,540 dictionaries for comprehensive cross-translation of all its languages.

(And, while we are on this train of thought and although it is tangential to our point, cross-translation of all the world's estimated 6,000 languages would require a practically impossible 17,997,000 dictionaries.)

Creating a single crosswalk is a large and complex task. As a consequence, the sheer number of significant overlapping tagging schemas in a domain such as authorship and publishing presents a barrier to achieving interoperability—and this without taking into account the fact that the schemas are all in a state of continuous development. Every related crosswalk needs to be reworked with each new version of a single tagging schema. Moreover, new tagging schemas are regularly emerging and every new schema increases the scale of the problem exponentially. Five cross-translations require ten crosswalks; ten cross-translations require 90 crosswalks.

Paskin suggests that this level of complexity can be eased by mapping 'through a central point or dictionary' (Paskin 2003). This is precisely the objective of CGML, which is an intermediating language, or an interlanguage through which a full set of translations can be achieved. Tag by tag, it represents a common ground between tagging schemas. Tag <x> in the tagging schema A translates into tag <q> in CGML, and this in turn may be represented by <y> in tagging schema B and <z> in tagging schema C. The 'common ground' tag <q> tells us that <x>, <y> and <z> are synonyms. A theoretical 272 crosswalks are replaced by 17 thesauri of tag synonyms (Figure 13.3). If, by analogy, all European languages were to be translated through Esperanto, a language deliberately fabricated as a common ground language, 60 dictionaries would be needed to perform all possible translation functions instead of a theoretical 3,540. Even simpler, in theory just one dictionary would suffice, translated 60 times with 60 language-to-Esperanto thesauri. This is precisely what CGML does. It attempts to solve the semantic aspect of the interoperability problem by creating one dictionary and 17 thesauri of tag synonyms. (And, incidentally, returning to natural language for a moment, this technique can be used as a semantic basis for machine translation, bringing the inter-translatability of all human languages at least into the realm of possibility.)

Figure 13.4 shows the interlanguage approach—full interoperability between 17 schemas requires a thesaurus with just 17 sets of tag synonyms.

CGML has a number of distinguishing features, which means that it is constitutively a very different kind of tagging schema from all the others against which it maps. It is this constitutive character that defines it as an interlanguage, as distinct from a language.

Figure 13.3 Language pairs—full interoperability of 17 schemas requires 272 crosswalks

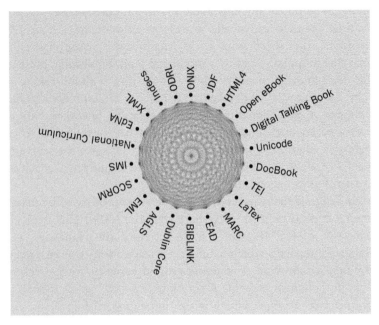

An interlanguage has no life of its own, no independent existence, no relation to reality other than a mediated relationship through other languages. We will outline the operational principles for the construction of such an interlanguage through the subsequent subsections of this chapter.

Before this, however, we want to mention some of the unique characteristics of an interlanguage such as CGML. As an interlanguage, CGML is designed to be open to the possibility of mapping new schemas that may emerge within or substantially overlapping its general domain. It is also designed to be able to absorb tagging that finely distinguishes conceptual subsets of certain of its core interests. In the case of authorship and publishing this might include, for instance, geospatial tags to define precise location, or tags representing controlled subject vocabularies in specific field-domains. By comparison with the crosswalk alternative, this mapping is achieved with relative ease.

Full subsumption and overlap are both cases of vertical integration of tagging schemas into CGML. However, CGML is also designed to be amenable to horizontal integration of schemas defining contiguous or complementary domains, such as the integration of other digital media or

Figure 13.4 The interlanguage approach to CGML

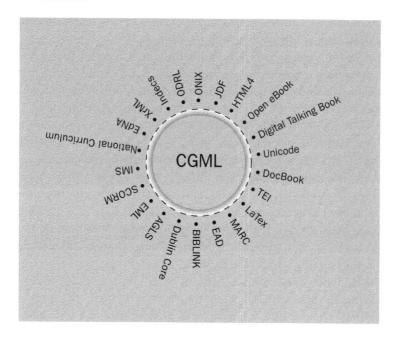

museum objects with the world of books. After all, books are routinely made into movies, bookstores sell DVDs and printed books and libraries store individual copies of rare and unique books as artefacts.

As an interlanguage, CGML is infinitely extensible, absorbing subsidiary, overlapping and contiguous schemas to the extent that seems necessary and useful. A the time of writing, CGML consists of nearly 1,000 tags—and these happen to be the tags for which there is the greatest degree of semantic common ground identifiable as synonyms across the interlanguage. The tags that represent the greatest degree of overlap also happen to be the most fundamental to the representational and communicative activities of authorship and publishing. However, there is no reason why CGML should not extend to 10,000 or a 100,000 tags as it describes progressively more arcane bywaters in each tagging domain (vertical integration) or as it spreads its range of reference into contiguous domains of meaning (horizontal integration).

To reiterate, CGML is an interlanguage which maps against any other related schema (or, as they are variously termed, standards, namespaces or application profiles) in the domain of authorship and publishing. It works through tag-to-tag translation links between schemas—be they competing within a substantially overlapping domain or serving varied functions in divergent but still overlapping domains. The CGML term is an intermediary or interlanguage term. CGML is not a schema in and for itself. Rather, it is a way of talking to schemas.

The conventional approach to evaluating the efficacy of alternative tag schemas within a particular semantic domain is to undertake a process of comparison and contrast, the purpose of which is to select the one that would, it seems for the moment at least, be most appropriate to one's expressive needs, or the one that appears to be the most internally coherent and robust, or the one that happens to be most widely used among the players within a particular community of practice.

As an interlanguage, however, CGML is entirely agnostic about the ontological validity of the schemas to which it maps. If they move a community of practice, or have the potential to move a community of practice, they are worth the trouble of mapping. New standards may emerge, and if they appear to be sufficiently cogent and practically useful, they are also worth the trouble.

CGML itself does not set out to be a competing or alternative standard. Rather CGML takes the approach that the prevailing uncertainty about which standards will predominate and the likelihood of the emergence of new standards is to a significant degree a diversion. In the interlanguage approach, standards are everything—CGML needs to talk with the main existing and emerging publishing standards from the pragmatic point of view of interoperability. Yet, in another sense, standards are nothing—it is immaterial if some standards fall into desuetude or if new standards emerge. Dogmatic debate about the value or lack of value of a particular schema or standard is of little value. Shoehorning social practices into ill-fitting received standards is also a fraught exercise. CGML cares about standards but eschews standardisation, or making things the same for the sake of sameness.

Our decision to take the interlanguage approach, paradoxically in the light of our scepticism about the ontological pretensions of tag schemas, is based on the stability inherent to the semantic ground, or a kind of ontological pragmatism. Behind the varied 'takes' on reality reflected by tag schemas, there is still a relatively stable and thus predictable material and social reality. The 'resistances' of which Eco speaks are at times insistent. Although we conceptualise the world paradigmatically through tag schemas and operationalise these schemas through activity narratives, these paradigms and narratives do have a reference point, and this reference point might reasonably be construed to be a matter of ontology. Ontology does not simply present itself; it is mediated by paradigms and narratives. However, ontology practically grounds paradigm and narrative. In fact, through language, paradigm and narrative make themselves integral to the ontological reality of society or culture.

This grounding provides stability and thus a certain predictability of paradigm and narrative within a particular semantic domain. If authorship and publishing is our domain of interest, for instance, this represents a set of social practices—practices of representation and communication—that have deep and only gradually changing roots. There are authors who write; these authors have names; their writings have titles; and these writings have characteristic generic structures and fields of representation or subjects. Any new tagging schema that turns up—no matter how fancy it is or how innovative its intentions and methodology (e-learning, digital rights management, variable rendering and the like)—is still going to have to name these insistent realities.

The basis of CGML, in other words, is in the semantic ground of publishing, and there is an essential stability in the everyday lifeworld of authorship and publishing. The technologies may be changing, but there are still creators (writers, editors, illustrators) creating works (books in print and electronic formats, chapters, articles and other written, visual and audio texts) that are subject to copyright agreements, which are then used by consumers (readers, learners). Schemas do no more than represent that lifeworld from a particular perspective—be that the perspective of the library, digital resource discovery, rights, commerce, education or rendering/production. Schemas may come and go, but the lifeworld they purport to represent and facilitate remains relatively stable. At most, it changes incrementally, despite even the large changes underway today in the new digital media.

The interlanguage approach of CGML also provides a tool for literature, science and curricula to be built in small languages and endangered languages, including, with the aid of Unicode, publication in any script. CGML can run in any language and any script, and this is achieved simply by translating the tags and tag definitions. This may seem a relatively small move in a practical sense. Conceptually, however, it is a huge move. In fact, it turns a linguistically expressed term into a mere 'token' of a core concept that exists above and beyond any particular language. And an indirect effect of this move is to add multilingual functionality to markup schemas which currently exist only in English. In addition, by virtue of its structural and semantic approach to markup, CGML could serve as an aid to effective and accurate human and machine translation. In other words, by these various means, CGML could literally find itself in the space of an interlanguage between various human languages.

In a globalised and multilingual world, Ron Scollon argues, social languages or discourses are more similar across languages than within languages (Scollon 1999). The way academics write for their particular discipline, for instance, whether it is in English or Japanese, is similar in terms of the structure of their texts and the ways those texts describe the world. A structural and semantic framework for structuring text such as CGML, which includes elaborate structural and semantic markup linked to controlled keyword vocabularies, will work across languages once the tags and the specialist vocabularies are translated, and this is because the most important thing about the discourse does not sit inside a particular language. Text structured and rendered in this way may become the platform for multilingual, multi-script publishing in communities more and more defined by their social language (what they want to do in the world, as expressed in peculiar ways of communicating about the world) than by the accident of mother tongue.

The CGML Dictionary does not purport to be about external referents as 'meaning'; rather, it is built via the interlanguage technique from other languages which purport to have external referents. Moreover, insofar as the semantic ground of CGML is meaning itself (and its instantiation in the practices of authorship and publishing), it is a kind of metasemantics, a language of meaning. It happens to be centred on the realm of semantics in general—the meaning of meaning—and within that realm the social practices and technologies of representation and communication stabilised in the historical practices of representation.

Furthermore, CGML is not an ordinary dictionary insofar as it develops a specialised 'take' on the world it purports to describe, the world of meaning. Its meanings are not the commonsense meanings of the lifeworld of everyday experience, but derivative of specialised social languages which speak in the refined and particularistic way characteristic of the professionals and aficionados of that domain. To apply a pair of concepts of Husserl's, commonsense language is shifting and ambiguous language of the lifeworld; social languages develop progressively refined (sedimented) and self-consciously reflective (bracketed) discourse more characteristic of science (Cope and Kalantzis 2000; Husserl 1970). CGML, in other words, derives from schemas developed in and for professions which have developed high levels of conceptual clarity about what authorship is and what publishing involves.

The CGML dictionary links a notation (the tag-concept), which may be used in practice as a label for a field in a database or as an XML tag, to a semantically explicit definition, as well as an annotation which explains and exemplifies the tag-concept in terms of subordinate tag-concepts in the taxonomy (the various logics of relation-inclusion discussed earlier), and provides advice where necessary on appropriate and well-formed data entry. The building blocks of the CGML dictionary are the other tag-concepts of the CGML schema, and these are connected by hyperlinks. The definition builds on parent tag-concepts; the annotation suggests the possible instantiations of a tag-concept by means of illustrative child tag-concepts. The dictionary is located in maintained in a purpose-build software application, CGMeaning. Figure 13.5 shows how it specifies the concepts of <creation> and <creator>.

The rules of CGML dictionary formation

The CGML Dictionary has been constructed using five semantic rules: minimised ambiguity, functional clarity, lowest common denominator semantics, the distinction of silent from active tag-concepts and comprehensive internal cross-reference.

Figure 13.5 Fragment of the CGML Dictionary of Authorship and Publishing specifying the concepts of <creation> and <creator>

NOTATION Tag-Concept.	DEFINITION Dictionary definition based on parent concepts.	ANNOTATION Examples, related child concepts, data entry advice.
CGCreation	The process of realising Meanings which serve particular communicative or representational Functions.	Involves Creators and Contributors, developing a Design, which is expressed as a Work and is manifest in the form of a Product, Event or Service. A Design has a Title and may vary in Status (as it evolves, for instance, from Proposal, to Draft, to Edition). It may have a Description which summarises or overviews its content. In the case of text, it will be expressed in a particular Language. It may sit in a defined Relation to other Designs, Works or Products, and this may be specified as a Source. Distribution may be the responsibility of a Publisher, on the basis of an assignment or licensing of Rights. It may have an Identifier in the form of a unique string of numbers and/or letters such as an ISBN or a URL. It will have a Format and an inherent and characteristic Structure, and also possibly Externals which exist specifically in order to relate to the Work, for example by way of Review or Promotional Matter.
CGCreator	A Person who, or an Organisation which, plays a primary role in the conceptualisation of a creative Design and the execution of a Work. An essential Party to the process of Creation.	Includes the roles of Author, Editor, Scriptwriter, Lyricist, Composer, Visual Artist, Photographer and Conference Presenter.

Rule 1 Minimise ambiguity

Digital expression languages such those captured by XML (of which CGML is an instance) use natural language tags in the interest of transparency. The appearance of natural language, however, simulating as it does everyday semantics, is deceptive. The further removed from everyday language a digital expression language, the more functionally effective it is likely to be. For instance, a <Work> may involve some very different kinds of 'editor', obscured by the ambiguity of that word in everyday parlance. CGML defines one kind of <Editor> as a primary <CreatorRole> in relation to a <Work>—a person who pulls together a number of texts by various <Author>s into a coherent work, and maybe writes an introduction. From a presentational point of view, the <Editor>s name will appear (via the stylesheet transformation process) on the cover and title page of a <Book>. This <Editor> is distinct from other types of 'editor', such as a <CommissioningEditor>—typically a person who works for a <Publisher> and who instigates the process which leads to the <Publication> of a <Product>. <Editor> is also distinct from a <CopyEditor> who identifies textual errors. These latter two kinds of people, frequently simply called 'editor' in everyday parlance, play a <ContributorRole> in the <Creation> process, and need to be clearly and unambiguously distinguished from an <Editor> who clearly and consistently has a <CreatorRole> in the process. In this way, the Dictionary draws explicit boundaries of distinction–inclusion between other tag-concepts, usually positioned as alternatives to each other at the same level in the taxonomy. Figure 13.6 shows how the Dictionary specifies the concept of <editor>.

CGML attempts to achieve a balance between domain-specific concepts, which are relatively free of jargon, and the precision characteristic of and necessary to technical and scientific discourses. Except when referring specifically to computers and computer-generated files, publishing terminology is preferred over computer terminology. For instance, <Edition> and <Draft> are preferred over 'version', not only for their familiarity to authors and publishers, but because they reflect an important distinction which is sometimes unclear in version enumeration.

In this process of removing ambiguity, at the furthest reaches of its taxonomic structure CGML may also absorb international standards and controlled vocabularies defining key features of the semantic ground such as ISO 3166 Territory Codes, ISO 4217 Currency Codes, ISO 639 Language Codes, ISO 8601 Standard Formats for the Description of Time and UCUM Unit of Measure Codes (International DOI Foundation 2002).

Fragment of the CGML Dictionary specifying the concept of <editor>

NOTATION Tag-Concept.	DEFINITION Dictionary definition based on parent concepts.	ANNOTATION Examples, related child concepts, data entry advice.
CGEditor	A Creator Role entailing the gathering together into a single, coherent Work, a number of Works by different Creators. Such a work may become a Product in the form of a Book or other, written Non Book Text.	Not to be confused with a Commissioning Editor, a Copy Editor or a Publisher.

Rule 2 Aim for functional clarity

The CGML Dictionary is not a description of things in themselves. Its purpose is functional—in a primary sense to provide an account of meaning functions, and in a secondary sense to provide a reliable basis for automated rendering through stylesheet transformation languages. Every definition and annotation explains in the first instance what an entity does, rather than what it is. Each tag-concept, moreover, can only do one thing. If a synonymous term in natural language does more than one thing, as was the case of 'editor' in the previous subsection, a specialised distinction needs to be made explicitly.

Rule 3 Use lowest common denominator semantics

As discussed earlier, CGML's interlanguage approach means that it takes the 'common ground' position between broadly synonymous concepts in the tagging schemas against which it maps. Every CGML term or tag translates into an equivalent term in the various other schemas, if and where there is an equivalent. However, these concepts are not always the same. In the nature of social languages characterised by their own particularised 'take' on the world, tag-to-tag equivalents are often not true synonyms. This places a particular semantic burden on the intermediate, interlanguage term and its dictionary definition within CGML. In the case of tag synonyms with roughly equivalent but not identical semantics, CGML either takes the narrower definition in cases when one tag represents a subset of another; or in the case of overlap, creates a new definition restricted to the semantic intersection between the functional referents of the two equivalent tags. This guarantees that data will always be created from within CGML which can be validly exported as content into the database field or XML-tagged content spaces markup by equivalent tag synonyms within the mapped schemas.

The key to CGML's functioning as an interlanguage, in other words, is its dictionary definition and data entry rules. If the rule of lowest common denominator semantics is rigorously applied, all data entered within the framework of this definition and data entry rules will produce valid data for each of the standards in which a synonymous term exists. Each interlanguage term represents a semantic common ground—defined in terms that are sufficiently narrow and precise to produce valid data for the tag synonyms in all other standards to which a particular term can be validly mapped at that particular semantic point.

Rule 4 Distinguish silent and active tag-concepts

Although certain tag concepts in CGML map against others successfully using the rule of lowest common denominator semantics, they cannot in practice be implemented at this level because they do not have a sufficient level of semantic delicacy to allow interoperability with schemas that require greater semantic delicacy than is possible at that level. Returning to the example provided in Figure 13.5, data cannot be entered at the CGML <Person> level even though that would be sufficient for certain schemas against which it is possible to map synonymous <Person> tag-concepts. Data entry must be broken up into the various name elements at the finest level of delicacy required by all of the mapped tag-schemas (active tag concepts); it can then automatically be recomposed to create valid data to populate the silent tag-concepts. Some of these silent concepts are purely theoretical. There will be very little practical need to 'climb out' to many of the highly abstracted first (root element), second and third level concepts. Indeed, some of them are well nigh useless in a practical sense. Their role is purely to provide an overall system and structure to the schema.

Rule 5 Develop a comprehensive internal cross-reference system

The key to building a resilient and functionally efficient tagging schema is to develop an interlocking system of cross-reference. This is rendered in the CGML Dictionary as hyperlinks. Every hyperlinked tag-concept in the dictionary definitions and annotations takes the user to a precise definition and annotation of that tag-concept. Cumulatively, the dictionary definitions and annotations build a systematic account of relations of relation-inclusion and distinction-exclusion, providing descriptive content to the abstract visual representation of paradigm in the taxonomy. The result is that the schema becomes less like a selection of concepts that seem useful to a domain, and more like a theory of that domain.

This is how CGML works as a functional schema of represented meaning. It attempts to create a sound basis for interoperability between the schemas it interconnects, incorporating their varied functions. CGML is an interlanguage. Its concepts constitute a paradigm for represented meaning, drawing on an historically familiar semantics, but adapting this to the possibilities of the internet. Its key devices are thesaurus (mapping against functional schemas) and dictionary (specifying a common ground semantics). These are the semantic components for narrative structures of text creation, or the retrospective stories that can be told of the way in which authors, publishers, referees, reviewers, editors and the like construct and validate text.

Paradigm

These, then, are the core concepts and principles of CGML: tags fit into schemas and these schemas function as paradigms. Tags mark up the narrative flow of activity sequences around the construction of meanings, and the architectures of meaning characteristic of specific social languages. Tagged narratives represent meaning functions and, in the rendering process, form follows function.

CGML's field is the ongoing and now—despite the disruptions of the new, digital media— relatively stable historical tradition text work. It provides an account of the internal information architecture of the textualities. It is a theory of text structure and the social world of creators, their creations, the relation of their creations to other creations in the world, and the referents in the world to which their creations refer.

CGML has two primary forms of expression, a paradigmatic expression in the form of the taxonomy of reprsented meaning (supported by a dictionary and a thesaurus) and an open framework for the construction of creative and publishing activity narratives, which link the CGML tag-concepts into activity sequences focused on products (the lifecycle of a work, for instance) or roles (the activity structures of authoring, publishing or browsing, for instance) (Common Ground Publishing 2003).

In terms of current computer science terminology (and even though we might question the use of the term) CGML is an ontology (Denny 2002). In a philosophical context this term has been described as follows:

In philosophy, an ontology is a theory about the nature of existence, of what types of things exist; ontology as a discipline studies such theories. Artificial-intelligence and web researchers have co-opted the term for their own jargon, and for them an ontology is a document or file that formally defines the relations among terms. The most typical kind of ontology for the Web has a taxonomy and a set of inference rules (Berners-Lee, Hendler and Lassila 2001).

In this specialised sense, computer science sense, CGML is an ontology—even though we would question the application of the word to computer science in the light of its philosophical connotations.

Represented as a taxonomy, CGML relates its 1,000-odd tags into eight orders of concept, or eight levels linked by branch or parent–child relationship—whichever metaphor one might use to choose to describe taxonomy. As is required by XML expression languages, there is a single first order concept or 'root element' (Harold and Means 2002). This root element is <Meaning>. <Meaning> has two children: <Function> and <Form>. As CGML has little interest in <Form>, no children are noted, although children could be added if and when there appeared to be a need to develop a new account of the realm of presentation and stylesheet transformation. This realm is taken as given within the realm of <Form>. In CGML, this is a space where existing stylesheet transformations can be applied as designed for the various structural and semantic tagging schemas with which CGML interoperates. We nevertheless include <Form> as one of our two second order concepts because it is of fundamental importance. From a representational or communicative point of view, <Function> remains unexpressed without a material realisation as <Form>. <Function> has no practical existence without <Form>.

At a taxonomic third level, <Function> splits into three: a <SemanticGround>, a process of <Creation> and the means of <Distribution>. The <SemanticGround> consists at a fourth level of the activities of a <Party> (a <Person> or <Organisation> at the fifth level), in a specifiable <Location>, at or during a point of <DateAndTime> and a <Subject> indicating the material, social or metaphysical referent of the creative work, to which a reader's or user's attention may be directed. The process of <Creation> consists at a fourth level of primary <Creator>s, ancillary <Contributor>s, whose creative efforts have an inherent <Design> (which at a fifth level becomes a <Work> and a sixth level becomes a <Product> such as, at a seventh level, a <Book> or a <Map>

for instance). The third level process of <Creation> may also involve ascribing a fourth level <Status> (such as <Proposal>, <Draft> or <Edition> at fifth level), providing a <Description>, noting the form of linguistic presentation in a natural <Language>, indicating <Relations> to encompassing or subsidiary <Works> or <Products>, naming a <Publisher>, defining <Rights>, ascribing a unique <Identifier> such as a product number or Digital Object Identifier, and describing <Format>. Still at a fourth level, the products of the <Creation> process have an inherent <Structure> or information architecture (covering everything from <MacroStructure> such as <Chapter> and <Index> and <LocalTextStructures> down to the level of <Paragraph> or <Emphasis> for words or phrases). These are supplemented by <Externals>, which refer to the <Work> in question, such as a <Review> or <RefereeReport>. The final third level concept <Distribution> provides a framework for the tagging of <Audience> (who a <Work> is meant for), <Availability> (where and how it can be found), <Consumer> (who reads or uses it), <Item> (an individual manifestation of a <Product>), <Transaction> (the legal basis of a particular <Consumer> use), <Delivery> (how the <Item> reaches the <Consumer>) and <Provenance> (where the <Item> has been during its life). This is the beginning of a paradigm which currently runs to 1,000 <Function>s within the field of <Meaning>, and whose main focus at this stage is the creative process of authorship and the publication of books. Figure 13.7 shows the CGML Taxonomy of Authorship and Publishing, first to fourth level concepts. The remaining approximately 1,000 tags add detail at the fifth level and beyond.

Within CGML, there are two types of tags: open tags and closed tags. Open tags mark up any content that they happen to enclose, for instance <MainTitle>Any Conceivable Title</Title>. In the XML expression format, these are called 'elements'. Closed tags specify a strictly defined range of content alternatives, and these take the form of a predetermined list of secondary tags. For example, in CGML as it currently stands, <MeaningMode> can only be defined among the alternatives <LinguisticMode>, <VisualMode>, <AudioMode>, <GesturalMode>, <SpatialMode> and <Multimodal>. In the XML expression format, these are called 'attributes'.

Paradigm is constructed in CGML by means of a number of taxonomic construction rules. Although CGML tags are written in natural language, this belies a level of precision not found in natural language. Natural language involves considerable semantic ambiguity, whereas a tagging schema needs to attempt to reduce this as much as practicable. It does this by rigorously applying two semantic logics that

Figure 13.7 First to fourth level concepts of the CGML Taxonomy of Authorship and Publishing

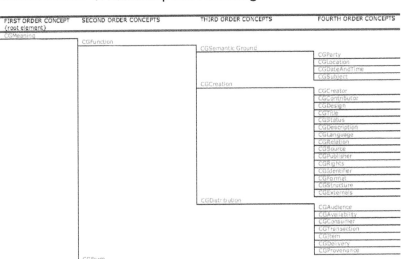

FIRST ORDER CONCEPT (root element)	SECOND ORDER CONCEPTS	THIRD ORDER CONCEPTS	FOURTH ORDER CONCEPTS
CGMeaning			
	CGFunction		
		CGSemantic Ground	
			CGParty
			CGLocation
			CGDateAndTime
			CGSubject
		CGCreation	
			CGCreator
			CGContributor
			CGDesign
			CGTitle
			CGStatus
			CGDescription
			CGLanguage
			CGRelation
			CGSource
			CGPublisher
			CGRights
			CGIdentifier
			CGFormat
			CGStructure
			CGExternals
		CGDistribution	
			CGAudience
			CGAvailability
			CGConsumer
			CGTransaction
			CGItem
			CGDelivery
			CGProvenance
	CGForm (-> stylesheets and rendering)		

exist somewhat less rigorously in natural language: the logic of distinction-exclusion and the logic of relation-inclusion. The logic of distinction-exclusion exists with parallel branches (sibling relations) in a taxonomy. A <Person> is not an <Organisation> because an <Organisation> is defined as a legally or conventionally constituted group of <Persons>. On the other hand, the logic of relation-inclusion applies to the sub-branches that branch off superordinate branches in a taxonomy (parent–child relations). A <Party> to a creative or contractual relationship can be either a <Person> or an <Organisation>.

'Meaning', says Gee, 'is always (in part) a matter of intended exclusions and inclusions (contrasts and lack of contrasts) within an assumed semantic field.' In natural language, we use rough and ready ways of working out whether another person means the same thing as we do by a particular word or phrase. One way is what Gee calls 'the guessing principle'—our judgement or 'call' on what a particular concept means. If we are in the same social, cultural or professional group or community of practice as the communicator of our particular concept, our guess is more likely to be congruent with the communicator's understanding. Another way is 'the context principle', or to add precision to the meaning of a work or phrase by deciphering it in the context of the text and social situation in which it appears (Gee 1996).

Domain-specific paradigms in the form of tagging schemas are designed to reduce the guesswork and contextual inference required in natural language. The solution we have proposed here is to build a social language that clarifies the exclusions and inclusions. This is achieved in CGML by three overlapping visual and textual techniques: taxonomy, thesaurus and dictionary.

Concentrating for the moment on the general rules of taxonomy or paradigm formation, we need to make distinctions between taxonomic processes of superordination and composition (Martin 1992). Superordination relations perform the function of sub-classification. They express an 'is a' relationship between one level in the taxonomic hierarchy and another. <Book> is a <Product>, as is an <AudioRecording>. Composition relations, by contrast, connect parts into wholes. They express a 'has a' relation between levels in the taxonomic hierarchy. A <GlossaryItem> and a <GlossaryItemDefinition> are both parts of a <Glossary>. Indeed, a <Glossary> is not functional without both of these parts.

To the superordination and compositional principles identified by Martin, we add the capacity of taxonomies to make a distinction of immanence. This expresses an 'underlies' relationship between contiguous levels in the taxonomic hierarchy. A <Design> underlies a <Work> and a <Work> underlies a <Product>. In CGML, <Design> has just one child, <Work>. However, <Design> and <Work> cannot be conflated even though there are no multiple children with whom composition (part/whole) or sub-classification functions can be performed. A <Design> may encompass the full scope and essential character of a <Work>. This may be prefigured at the planning or <Proposal> stage. However, a <Design> may never become a <Work>. If it does, however, it does not disappear; rather it is applied and adapted and remains immanent within the <Work>. Similarly, a <Work> such as the lyrics for a song, remains immanent within its various instantiations as a <Product>, such as a <Book> or an <AudioRecording>, or as a <Performance> at an <Event>. This logic of immanence in a creative work builds on, modifies and extends the entity–definition work of the International Federation of Library Associations (IFLA Study Group on the Functional Requirements for Bibliographic Records 1998).

Finally, taxonomies need to be cohesive if they are to provide an effective paradigmatic role for a field of practice. Such cohesion is created to a large degree by the proximity of concepts in contiguous levels in the hierarchy. Between one level and another, relations need to be tested to see whether a tag-concept on one level is experientially close enough to be presumed by a tag-concept on another (Martin 1992). <PrintedBook> and <Design> are not experientially close concepts, and thus would not form a cohesive parent–child relationship. However, the <Design>, <Work>, <Product>, <Book>, <PrintedBook> hierarchy involves contiguous items sufficiently close in an experiential sense to ensure taxonomic cohesion.

Thesaurus

The CGML taxonomy maps synonymous concepts from related tag schemas.

In Figure 13.8, the CGML open-element tags and CGML fixed-attribute tags are underlined. For each tag, synonyms are identified in the various tagging schemas against which CGML is currently mapped. The underlined concepts indicate levels of implementation. <Person> data,

Figure 13.8 Fragment of the CGML Taxonomy of Authorship and Publishing specifying the concept of <party> from the fourth to sixth levels

FOURTH ORDER CONCEPTS	FIFTH ORDER CONCEPTS	SIXTH ORDER CONCEPTS
CGParty XrML<principal> IN<party> SCORM<centity>		
	CGPerson IMS<person> ONIX<Name> XrML<commonName> IN<person> EAD<persname> MARC<100/700 I1 = 1; I2 = # ; $a,600 I1 = 1; I2 = 4; $a >	
		CGNameFunction CGNameForPublication CGLegalName CGMailingName
		CGHonorific ONIX<TitlesBeforeNames> DB<honorific> MARC<100/700 I1 = 1; I2 = # ; $a; $c,600 I1 = 1; I 2 = 4; $c >
		CGGivenNames ONIX<NamesBeforeKey> DB<firstName>,DB<othername> MARC<100/700 I1 = 1; I2 = # ; $a,600 I1 = 1; I2 = 4; $a > EML<Initials-prefix>
		CGSurnamePrefix ONIX <PrefixToKey>
		CGSurname ONIX<KeyNames> DB<surname> EAD<famname> MARC<100/700 I1 = 1; I2 = # ; $a; $b,600 I1 = 1; I 2 = 4; $a>
		CGNameSuffix ONIX<SuffixToKey> DB<lineage>
	V {to CGOrganisation}	

for instance, can only be collected in the smallest granular units required by any of the mapped tagging schemes. A valid CGML <Person> record (and the IMS, ONIX, XrML, indecs, EAD and MARC synonyms) can only be generated from data recomposed from smaller granular units including, for instance, <GivenNames> and <Surname>.

The CGML Thesaurus takes each tagging schema as its starting point, lists its tags and reproduces the definitions and examples as given by each tagging schema (Figure 13.9). In this way, CGML actually works with 17 thesauri, and each new mapping will require an additional thesaurus. Each thesaurus captures the way in which each tagging schema defines itself, and within its own terms. Against each tag, a direct CGML synonym is provided, whose semantics are coextensive with, or narrower than, the tag against which the mapping occurs. Unlike a conventional thesaurus, only one CGML equivalent is given for each mapped tag.

In combination with its dictionary, CGML uses what Martin identifies to be the two traditional approaches to the study of lexis in western scholarship: dictionary and thesaurus. Whereas dictionary 'purports to unpack the "meaning" [of lexical items] by means of paraphrase and exemplars', thesaurus is 'organised around meaning'; it 'purports to display the wordings through which meanings can aptly be expressed'. He concludes that '[b]ecause it is organised according to meaning, a thesaurus provides a more appropriate model of textual description for functional linguistics than a dictionary does' (Martin 1992). In the case of CGML, an additional layer of rigour is added by mapping the 17 thesauri into the paradigm-constituting taxonomy.

The effect of these cross-cutting processes is the systematic mapping of existing and emerging tagging schemas against each other, and the

Figure 13.9 Fragment of the Dublin Core to CGML Thesaurus

CGML Tag-concept	DC Tag-concept	DC Values, Qualifers
CGTitle CGPreviousTitle	DC<Title>	**Definition**: A name given to the resource. **Comment:** Typically, a Title will be a name by which the resource is formally known. **Exemplary Qualifiers:** **Label:** Alternative **Definition:** Any form of the title used as a substitute or alternative to the formal title of the resource. **Comment:** This qualifier can include Title abbreviations as well as translations. *MARC<245>*
CGCreator	DC<Creator>	**Definition**: An entity primarily responsible for making the content of the resource. **Comment:** Examples of a Creator include a person, an organisation, or a service. Typically, the name of a Creator should be used to indicate the entity. *MARC<100, 110, 111, 700, 710, 711,720>*
CGSubject CGLibraryOfCongressSubjectHeads CGMedicalClassification CGDeweyClassification CGLibraryOfCongressClassification CGUniversalDecimalClassification	DC<Subject>	**Definition:** The topic of the content of the resource. Comment: Typically, a Subject will be expressed as keywords, keyphrases or classification codes that describe a topic of the resource. Recommended best practice is to select a value from a controlled vocabulary or formal classification scheme **Exemplary Qualifiers:** **Label:** LCSH **Definition:** Library of Congress Subject Headings *MARC<600, 610, 611, 630, 650>* **Label:** MeSH **Definition:** Medical Subject Headings **See also:** http://www.nlm.nih.gov/mesh/meshhome.html *MARC<600, 610, 611, 630, 650>* **Label:** DDC **Definition:** Dewey Decimal Classification **See also:** http://www.oclc.org/dewey/index.htm *MARC <082>* **Label:** LCC **Definition:** Library of Congress Classification **See also:** http://lcweb.loc.gov/catdir/cpso/lcco/lcco.html *MARC<050>* **Label:** UDC **Definition:** Universal Decimal Classification **See also:** http://www.udcc.org/ *MARC<080>* *MARC<600, 610, 611, 630, 650, 653>*

stabilisation of synonyms between different markup languages through the medium of the CGML interlanguage tag. This has the potential to add functionality to existing schemas, not only by extension of new functionalities to otherwise separate schemas, but also by reinterpreting data created in one framework for (unanticipated) use in another. CGML thus has the potential to form the foundation for a broker software system within the domain of authorship and publishing.

Practically, this means that CGML provides a simple, transparent, clearly defined natural-language tagging framework, which will create data conforming to the schemas against which it is mapped. CGML data can be exported into any XML schema against which CGML has been mapped. The effect is to ensure interoperability between different data collection practices and frameworks—so, for instance, data collected with a CGML defined framework can simultaneously become a MARC library catalogue record and an ONIX record for a B-2-B e-commerce transaction. The reverse is only partly the case. Data formatted in any XML namespace against which CGML has been mapped can be imported into a CGML-defined database, and from this it can be exported into XML namespaces other than the one for which the data was originally defined, but only when that data enters CGML at the level granular delicacy required by the most delicately granular schema against which CGML has been mapped (identified by underlined tags, as illustrated in Figure 13.8). When a more granular mark up is required for interoperability than is available in imported data, this will usually have to be created manually—for example, breaking a <Person>'s name into <GivenNames> and <Surname>, part of which process will involve the complex and highly contextual business of interpreting whether the <Person>'s name appears in English or is structured in the traditional Chinese way.

In this sense, CGML is a resource for meaning, rather than a prescriptive activity sequence for authorship and publishing or a supplied structure of textual meaning. It is the basis for a process Kress calls transformation and design (Kress 2000, 2001). The design of meaning involves building on resources for meaning available in the world (the designed), appropriating and recombining the elements of those designs in a way that has never been done in quite the same way before (designing) and leaving a residue (the designed), which becomes a new set of resources for meaning, for the design process to begin afresh (Cope and Kalantzis 2000). This is also the way language itself works. Quoting Halliday, language is a 'resource for meaning making'; it is therefore a system that is open to choice, 'not a conscious decision made in real time but a set of possible alternatives' (Halliday 1994). This brings us back to the distinction we made earlier, between formal linguistics, which regards language as a system of rules, and functional linguistics, in which language is understood as a resource for meaning (Martin 1992). As a scaffold, paradigm is not restricting or constraining. Rather it is an enabling tool for widening the domain of expressive choice, for creating any number of narrative alternatives.

References

<indecs>. 2000. 'Interoperability Data in e-Commerce Systems', vol. 2003, '<indecs> Framework Limited'.

ADL/SCORM. 2003. 'SCORM Overview: Shareable Content Object Reference Model', vol. 2003, 'Advanced Distributed Learning'.

Anderson, C. 2009. 'The End of Theory: The Data Deluge Makes the Scientific Method Obsolete', *Wired*, 16 July.

ANSI/NISO. 2002. 'Specifications for the Digital Talking Book', vol. 2003.

Australian Government Locator Service. 2003. 'AGLS Metadata Standard', vol. 2003, 'National Archives of Australia'.

Berners-Lee, T., J. Hendler and O. Lassila 2001. 'The Semantic Web', *Scientific American*, May.

Brandom, R. 1994. *Making it Explicit: Reasoning, Representing and Discursive Commitment*. Cambridge, MA: Harvard University Press.

Buzzetti, D. and J. McGann. 2006. 'Electronic Textual Editing: Critical Editing in a Digital Horizon'. In L. Burnard, K.O.B. O'Keeffe and J. Unsworth (eds), *Electronic Textual Editing*. New York: Modern Language Association of America.

Common Ground Publishing. 2003. 'Method and Apparatus for Extending the Range of Useability of Ontology Driven Systems and for Creating Interoperability between Different Mark-up Schemas for the Creation, Location and Formatting of Digital Content'. Australia, US, Europe: Common Ground.

Cope, B. 2001. 'Making and Moving Books in New Ways, From the Creator to the Consumer'. In B. Cope and D. Mason (eds), *Digital Book Production and Supply Chain Management: Technology Drivers Across the Book Production Supply Chain, from Creator to Consumer*, C-2-C Project book 2.3. Melbourne: Common Ground, pp. 1–20.

Cope, B. and R. Freeman. 2001. *Digital Rights Management and Content Development: Technology Drivers Across the Book Production Supply Chain, from Creator to Consumer*, C-2-C Project book 2.4. Melbourne: Common Ground.

Cope, B. and M. Kalantzis. 1993. 'The Powers of Literacy: Genre Approaches to Teaching Writing'. London and Pittsburgh: Falmer Press (UK edition) and University of Pennsylvania Press (US edition), p. 286.

—. 2000. 'Designs for Social Futures'. In B. Cope and K. Mary (eds), *Multiliteracies: Literacy Learning and the Design of Social Futures*. London: Routledge, pp. 203–34.

Denny, M. 2002. 'Ontology Building: A Survey of Editing Tools', vol. 2002, 'XML.com'.

DocBook Technical Committee. 2010. 'DocBook Home Page', OASIS.

Dublin Core Metadata Initiative. 2010. 'Dublin Core Metadata Registry'.

Eco, U. 1999. *Kant and the Platypus: Essays on Language and Cognition*. London: Vintage.

EDItEUR. 2001. 'ONIX Product Information Standards 2.0', vol. 2003, 'International Group for Electronic Commerce in the Book and Serials Sectors'.

—. 2003. 'ONIX Mappings to MARC', vol. 2003, 'International Group for Electronic Commerce in the Book and Serials Sectors'.

EdNA Online. 2000. 'EdNA Metadata Standard', vol. 2003, 'Education Network Commonwealth of Australia'.

Encoded Archival Description Working Group. 2002. 'Encoded Archival Description Tag Library', vol. 2003, 'Society of American Archivists'.

Fairclough, N. 1992. *Discourse and Social Change*. Cambridge, UK: Polity Press.

Gee, J.P. 1996. *Social Linguistics and Literacies: Ideology in Discourses*. London: Taylor and Francis.

Halliday, M.A.K. 1994. *An Introduction to Functional Grammar*. London: Edward Arnold.

Harold, E.R. and W. S. Means. 2002. *XML*. Sebastapol, CA: O'Reilly.

Husserl, E. 1970. *The Crisis of European Sciences and Transcendental Phenomenology*. Evanston: Northwestern University Press.

IFLA Study Group on the Functional Requirements for Bibliographic Records. 1998. 'Functional Requirements for Bibliographic Records'. The Hague: International Federation of Library Associations and Institutions.

IMS Global Learning Consortium. 2002. 'IMS Learning Design Specification', vol. 2003.

—. 2003. 'Specifications', vol. 2003.

International DOI Foundation. 2002. *The DOI Handbook*. Oxford: International DOI Foundation.

International Trade Standards Organization for the eBook Industry. 2003. 'Open eBook Home Page', vol. 2003.

Jackson, H. 2002. *Lexicography: An Introduction*. London: Routledge.

Kress, G. 2000. 'Design and Transformation: New Theories of Meaning'. In B. Cope and M. Kalantzis (eds), *Multiliteracies: Literacy Learning and the Design of Social Futures*. London: Routledge, pp. 153–61.

—. 2001. 'Issues for a Working Agenda in Literacy'. In M. Kalantzis and B. Cope, *Transformations in Language and Learning: Perspectives on Multiliteracies*. Melbourne: Common Ground, pp. 33–52.

Kress, G. and T. van Leeuwen. 1996. *Reading Images: The Grammar of Visual Design*. London: Routledge.

Latour, B. 2004. 'Why Has Critique Run Out of Steam? From Matters of Fact to Matters of Concern', *Critical Inquiry*, pp. 225–48.

Luria, A. 1981. *Language and Cognition*. New York: John Wiley and Sons.

MARC Standards Office. 2000. 'ONIX to MARC 21 Mapping', vol. 2003, 'Library of Congress'.

—. 2001. 'MARC to Dublin Core Crosswalk', vol. 2003, 'Library of Congress'.

—. 2003a. 'MARC Standards', vol. 2003, 'Library of Congress'.

—. 2003b. 'Metadata Encoding and Transmission Standard', vol. 2003, 'Library of Congress'.

—. 2003c. 'Metadata Object Description Scheme', vol. 2003, 'Library of Congress'.

Martin, J.R. 1992. *English Text: System and Structure*. Philadelphia: John Benjamins.

Martin, J.R. and M.A.K. Halliday. 1993. *Writing Science*. London: Falmer Press.

Mason, D. 2001. 'Cataloguing for Libraries in a Digital World'. In B. Cope and D. Mason (eds), *Digital Book Production and Supply Chain Management: Technology Drivers Across the Book Production Supply Chain, from Creator to Consumer*, C-2-C Project book 2.3. Melbourne: Common Ground.

Mason, D. and S. Tsembas. 2001. 'Metadata for eCommerce in the Book Industry'. In B. Cope and D. Mason (eds), *Digital Book Production and Supply Chain Management: Technology Drivers Across the Book Production Supply Chain, from Creator to Consumer*, C-2-C Project book 2.3. Melbourne: Common Ground.

Multimedia Description Schemes Group. 2002. 'ISO/IEC CD 21000 Part 6: Rights Data Dictionary'. International Organisation for Standardisation, ISO/IEG JTC 1/SC 29/WG 11: Coding of Moving Pictures and Audio.

National Curriculum Online. 2002. 'The National Curriculum Metadata Standard'. London: Department for Education and Skills.

ODRL. 2002. 'Open Digital Rights Language', 'IPR Systems'.

OUL/EML. 2003. 'Educational Modelling Language'. Heerlen: Open University of the Netherlands.

Paskin, N. 2003. 'DRM Technologies: Identification and Metadata'. In E. Becker, D. Gunnewig, W. Buhse and N. Rump (eds), *Digital Rights Management: Technical, Economical, Juridical and Political Aspects*. Berlin: Springer.

PODi. 2003. 'Podi: The Digital Printing Initiative'.

Renear, A., E. Mylonas and D. Durand. 1996. 'Refining our Notion of What Text Really Is: The Problem of Overlapping Hierarchies'. In N. Ide and S. Hockey (eds), *Research in Humanities Computing*. Oxford: Oxford University Press.

Scollon, R. 1999. 'Multilingualism and Intellectual Property: Visual Holophrastic Discourse and the Commodity/Sign', paper presented at GURT [Georgetown University Round Table] 1999.

Scollon, R. 2001. *Mediated Discourse: The Nexus of Practice*. London: Routledge.

Sowa, J.F. 2000. *Knowledge Representation: Logical, Philosophical and Computational Foundations*. Pacific Grove, CA: Brooks Cole.

—. 2006. 'The Challenge of Knowledge Soup'. In J. Ramadas and S. Chunawala (eds), *Research Trends in Science, Technology and Mathematics Education*. Goa: Homi Bhabha Centre.

UK Office for Library and Information Networking. 2001. 'The Biblink Core Metadata Set', vol. 2003, 'Forum for Metadata Schema Implementers'.

Unicode. 2010. Unicode Consortium website, *http://unicode.org/*.

Vygotsky, L. 1962. *Thought and Language*. Cambridge, MA: MIT Press.

W3C. 2010a. 'HTML Specification', World Wide Web Consortium.

—. 2010b. 'XHTML Specification', World Wide Web Consortium.

XrML. 2003. 'Extensible Rights Markup Language', 'Content Guard'.

14

Interoperability and the exchange of humanly usable digital content

Richard Vines and Joseph Firestone

Throughout this book, it has been clearly articulated that the emergence and use of schemas and standards are increasingly important to the effective functioning of research networks. What is also equally emphasised is the danger posed if the use of schemas and standards results in excessive and negative system constraints—a means of exerting unhelpful control over distributed research activities. But, how realistically can a balance be facilitated between the positive benefits derived from the centralised coordination through the use standards versus the benefits from allowing self-organisation and emergence to prevail at the edge of organisational networks?

In this chapter we set out to explore how differing approaches to such problems are actually finding expression in the world. To do this, we have engaged in a detailed comparison of three different transformation systems, including the CGML system discussed at length in the previous chapter. We caution against any premature standardisation on any system due to externalities associated with, for example, the semantic web itself.

Introduction

In exploring the theme of interoperability we are interested in the practical aspects of what Magee describes as a 'framework for commensurability' in Chapter 12, 'A framework for commensurability', and what Cope and Kalantzis describe as the 'dynamics of difference' discussed in Chapter 4, 'What does the digital do to knowledge making?'. Magee suggests it is possible to draw on the theoretical underpinnings outlined in this book to construct a framework that embraces correspondence, coherentist and consensual notions of truth:

> it ought now be possible to describe a framework which examines conceptual translation in terms of denotation—whether two concepts refer to the same objective things in the world; connotation—how two concepts stand in relation to other concepts and properties explicitly declared in some conceptual scheme; and use—or how two concepts are applied by their various users (Magee, Chapter 11, 'On commensurability').

Cope and Kalantzis suggest something that could be construed as similar when they say that the new media underpinning academic knowledge systems requires a new 'conceptualising sensibility'.

But what do these things mean in the world of global interoperability? How are people currently affecting content exchanges in the world so that it proves possible to enter data once for one particular set of purposes, but be able to exchange this content for use related to another set of purposes in a different context?

In addressing this question, our chapter has four overarching objectives. The first is simple. We aim to make a small contribution to a culture of spirited problem solving in relation to the design and management of academic knowledge systems and the complex and open *information* networks that form part of these systems. For example, in the case of universities, there is the challenge of building information networks that contribute to two-way data and information flows. That is, a university information system needs to support a strategy of reflexivity by enabling the university to contribute to the adaptive capacity of the society it serves and enabling itself to adapt to the changes in society and the world.

The second objective is to facilitate debate about technical and social aspects of interoperability and content exchanges in ways that do not restrict this debate to information systems personnel only. As Cope, Kalantzis and Magee all highlight, this challenge involves the difficult task of constructively negotiating commensurability. This will require considerable commitment by all in order to support productive enagements across multiple professional boundaries.

The third objective is to highlight that new types of infrastructures will be required to mediate and harmonise the dynamics of difference. The reader will notice that a large part of the chapter draws on the emergence (and importance) of standards and a trend towards standardisation. A normative understanding of knowledge involves embracing the complex interplay between the benefits of both self-organisation and standardisation. Therefore, we think that a normative approach to knowledge now requires that the system patterns of behaviour emerge concurrently at different levels of hierarchy as has also been discussed extensively in Chapter 6, 'Textual representations and knowledge support-systems in research intensive networks', by Vines, Hall and McCarthy. Any approach to the challenge of interoperability has to take this matter very seriously—as we do.

The fourth objective is to highlight that in the design of new infrastructures, specific attention must be given to the distinctiveness of two types of knowledge—tacit and explicit knowledge. This topic has been well discussed throughout this book. We claim that an infrastructure that fails to acknowledge the difference between explicit and tacit knowledge will be dysfunctional in comparison with one that does. To this end, we are grateful to Paul David for suggesting the use of the phrase 'human interpretive intelligence', which we refer to extensively in this chapter. This phrase aims to convey that there is a dynamic interaction between tacit and explicit forms of knowledge representation. That is, explicit knowledge cannot exist in the first place without the application of human interpretative intelligence. We agree very much with Magee where in Chapter 3, 'The meaning of meaning', he expounds the idea that meaning is bound to the context within which content is constructed and conveyed.

The means by which we progress this chapter is by analysing one particular technical concern—the emerging explosion in the use of Extensible Markup Language (XML). The rise of XML is seen as an important solution to the challenges of automated (and semi-automated) information and data processing. However, the problem of interoperability between XML schemas remains a global challenge that has yet to be resolved. Thus this chapter focuses on how to achieve interoperability in the transformation of humanly usable digital content from one XML content storage system to another. We claim that it will be necessary to use human interpretive intelligence in any such transformation system and that a technology that fails to acknowledge this, and to make suitable provision for it, will be dysfunctional in comparison with one that does. We further claim that a choice about how such content is translated will have implications for whether the form of representation to which the content is transformed gives access to the meanings which users will wish to extract from it.

Our chapter examines three translation systems: Contextual Ontology_X Architecture (the COAX system), the Common Ground Markup Language (the CGML system) and Onto-Merge (the Onto-Merge System). All three systems are similar to the extent that they draw on 'merged ontologies' as part of the translation process. However, they differ in the ways in which the systems are designed and how the translation processes work. The CGML and COAX systems are examples of XML to XML to XML based approaches. The OntoMerge system is an example of an XML to Ontology (using web based ontology languages such as OWL) to XML approach.

We think that the leading criterion for selecting any XML translation system is the ease of formulating expanded frameworks and revised theories of translation that create commensurability between source and destination XML content and merged ontologies. We discuss this criterion using three sub-criteria: the relative commensurability creation load in using each system, the system design to integrate the use of human interpretive intelligence, and facilities for the use of human interpretive intelligence in content translations.

In a practical sense this chapter addresses the challenge of how to achieve interoperability in the storage and transfer of humanly usable digital content, and what must be done to exchange such content between different systems in as automated a way as possible. Automated exchanges of content can assist with the searching for research expertise within a university. Such search services can be secured by linking together multiple and disparate databases. An example of this is the University of Melbourne's 'Find an Expert' service hosted on the university's website (University of Melbourne 2010).

In this chapter we are concerned with requirements for the automated exchange of content, when this content is specifically designed for human use. As described by Cope and Kalantzis elsewhere in this book, interoperability of humanly usable content allows such content, originally stored in one system for a particular set of purposes, to be transferred to another system and used for a different set of purposes. We are concerned with the design of an efficient converter system, or translator system, hereafter referred to as a *transformation system*, that makes possible a compatibility of content across different systems.

Our interest in this subject arises because there are substantial sunk costs associated with storing humanly usable content in particular ways. There are also significant costs of translating content from one system to another. These costs will, in due course, become sunk costs also. Therefore, in addressing this topic, our expectation is that, over time, the costs incurred in the storage and transfer of humanly usable digital content will not be regarded as sunk costs, but as investments to secure the continued access to humanly usable digital content, now and into the future.

Many people, who are focused on their own particular purposes, have described *aspects* of the challenges associated with the need for exchanges of humanly usable content. Norman Paskin, the first Director of the Digital Object Identifier (DOI) Foundation, has described difficulties which must be faced when trying to achieve interoperability in content designed for the defence of intellectual property rights. These include the need to make interoperability possible across different kinds of media (such as books, serials, audio, audiovisual, software, abstract works and visual material), across different functions (such as cataloguing, discovery, workflow and rights management), across different levels of metadata (from simple to complex), across semantic barriers, and across linguistic barriers (Paskin 2006). Rightscom describe the need to obtain interoperability in the exchange of content, including usage rights, to support the continued development of an e-book industry (2006, p. 40). McLean and Lynch describe the challenges of facilitating interoperability between library and e-learning systems (2004, p. 5). The World Wide Web Consortium (W3C) is itself promoting a much larger vision of this same challenge through the semantic web:

> The semantic web is about two things. It is about common formats for integration and combination of data drawn from diverse sources, where on the original Web mainly concentrated on the interchange of documents. It is also about language for recording how the data relates to real world objects. That allows a person, or a machine, to start off in one database, and then move through an unending set of databases which are connected not by wires but by being about the same thing (W3C undated).

We argue that that there are two, deeper, questions relating to achieving interoperability of humanly usable content that have not been sufficiently discussed. The aim of this chapter is to show that these two challenges are interrelated.

First, we claim that it will not be possible to dispense with human intervention in the translation of digital content. A technology that fails to acknowledge this, and to make suitable provision for it, will be dysfunctional in comparison with one that does. The reason for this is that digital content is ascribed meaning by those people who use it; the categories used to organise content reflect these meanings. Different communities of activity ascribe different meanings and thus different categories. Translation of the elements of content from one set of categories to another cannot, we claim, be accomplished without the application of what we will call 'human interpretive intelligence'. (We particularly acknowledge Paul David's contribution and thank him for suggesting the use of this term, which we have adopted throughout this chapter.) In what follows, we will provide a detailed explanation of how this is achieved by one translation system, and will argue that any system designed to translate humanly usable content must make this possible.

Second, in order to achieve interoperability of digital content, we claim a choice about how such content is translated will have implications for whether the form of representation to which the content is transformed, gives access to the meanings that users will subsequently wish to extract from it. This has ramifications about the way in which translations are enacted. This, we argue, requires the application of human interpretive intelligence as described above in order that in the translation process content is mapped between the source and destination schemas.

We advance our general argument in a specific way—by comparing three existing systems which already exist for the abstracting of content to support interoperability. We have used this approach because these three different systems (a) make different assumptions about the use of interpretive intelligence, and (b) rely on different ontological and technical means for incorporating the use of this intelligence. The first system is the Common Ground Markup Language (CGML), whose component ontology has been used to construct the CGML interlanguage. We have termed this the CGML system. The second system is called the Contextual Ontology_X Architecture XML schema, whose component ontology is OntologyX. We have termed this the COAX system. The third system is called OntoMerge, whose architecture includes a means of merging and storing different ontologies (a feature referred to as the OntoEngine). We have termed this the OntoMerge System.

The ontological assumptions of these three different systems differ in that CGML system uses noun-to-noun mapping rules to link the underlying digital elements of content (we use the word 'digital element' in this chapter synonymously with the idea of a 'digital entity'). In contrast, the COAX system uses verbs and the linkages between digital elements that are generated when verbs are used (as we shall see below, it uses what we have termed 'verb triples'). OntoMerge also uses nouns, but these act as noun-predicates. In a way similar to the COAX system, these noun-predicates also provide linkages between digital elements in the same way as does the use of verb triples in the COAX system. The CGML system is built around the use of human interpretive intelligence, whereas the COAX and OntoMerge systems attempt to economise on the use of such intelligence.

We aim to show that points (a) and (b) above are related, in a way that has significant implications for how well exchanges of content can be managed in the three systems. We argue that choice of ontological and technical design in the COAX and the OntoMerge systems makes it much harder to apply human interpretive intelligence, and thus it is no surprise that these systems attempt to economise on the use of that intelligence. But we regard the use of such intelligence as necessary. We think this because explicit knowledge is reliant on being accessed and applied through tacit processes.

All three systems are still in their proof-of-concept stage. Because of this, a description of how all these systems abstract content is provided in the body of this chapter. We should not be understood as advancing the interests of one system over another. Rather, our purpose in analysing the systems is to highlight the possibility of locking into an inefficient standard. We agree with Paul David (2007a, p. 137) when he suggests that 'preserving open options for a longer period than impatient market agenda would wish is a major part of such general wisdom that history has to offer public policy makers'.

The outline of the remainder of this chapter is as follows. In the next section, we discuss the translation problem and outline a generalised model for understanding the mechanisms for translating digital content. This model is inclusive of two different approaches to the problem: what we have called the XML-based interlanguage approach and the ontology-based interlanguage approach. In the following sections we discuss these different approaches in some detail, using the three different systems—CGML, COAX and OntoMerge—as case study illustrations. Then we provide some criteria for how we might choose any system that addresses the XML translation problem. In the final sections we highlight some emergent possibilities that might arise based on different scenarios that could develop and draw our conclusions.

The transformation of digital content

With current digital workflow practices, translatability and interoperability of content is normally achieved in an unsystematic way by 'sticking together' content originally created, so as to comply with separately devised schemas. Interoperability is facilitated manually by the creation of procedures that enable content-transfers to be made between the different end points of digital systems.

For example, two fields expressing similar content might be defined as 'manager' in one electronic schema and 'supervisor' in another schema. The local middleware solution is for an individual programmer to make the judgement that the different tags express similar or the same content and then manually to create a semantic bridge between the two fields—so that 'manager' in one system is linked with 'supervisor' in the other system. These middleware programming solutions then provide a mechanism for the streaming of data held in the first content storage system categorised under the 'manager' field to another content storage system in which the data will be categorised under the 'supervisor' field. Such programming fixes make translatability and interoperability possible within firms and institutions and, to a lesser extent, along the supply chains that connect firms, but only to the extent that the 'bridges' created by the programmer really do translate two tags with synonymous content. We can call this the 'localised patch and mend' approach. And we note both that it does involve 'human interpretive intelligence', the intelligence of the programmer formulating the semantic bridges, and also that the use of such intelligence only serves to formulate a model for translation from one schema to another. And as should be plain to everyone, such models can vary in the extent to which they correctly translate the content of one schema to another.

Such an approach is likely to be advocated by practical people, for an obvious reason. The introduction of new forms of information architecture is usually perceived as disruptive of locally constructed approaches to information management. New more systematic approaches, which require changes to content management systems, are often resisted if each local need can be 'fixed' by a moderately simple intervention, especially if it is perceived that these more systematic approaches don't incorporate local human interpretive intelligence into information management architecture. We believe that such patch and mend approaches to translatability might be all very well for locally defined operations. But such localised solutions risk producing outcomes in which the infrastructure required to support the exchange of content within a global economy remains a hopeless jumble of disconnected fixes. This approach will fail to support translatability among conflicting schemas and standards.

The structure of the automated translation problem

In order to overcome the limitations of the patch and mend approach, we provide a detailed structure of the problem of creating more generalised translation/transformation systems. This is illustrated in Figure 14.1. This figure portrays a number of schemas, which refer to different ontological

Figure 14.1 Translation/transformation architecture

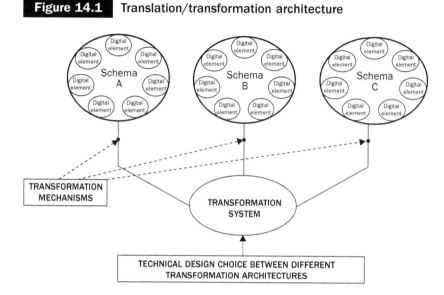

domains. For example, such domains might be payroll, human resources and marketing within an organisation; or they might include the archival documents associated with research inputs and outputs of multiple research centres within a university such as engineering, architecture or the social sciences.

Our purpose is to discuss the transfer of content from one schema to another—and to examine how translatability and interoperability might be achieved in this process. In Figure 14.1 we provide details of what we have called the 'translation/transformation architecture'.

To consider the details of this translation/transformation architecture, it is first necessary to discuss the nature of the various schemas depicted in Figure 14.1. Extensible Markup Language (XML) was developed after the widespread adoption of Hypertext Markup Language (HTML), which was itself a first step towards achieving a type of interoperability. HTML is a markup language of a kind that enables interoperability, but only between computers: it enables content to be rendered to a variety of browser-based output devices like laptops and computers. However, HTML does this through a very restricted type of interoperability. XML was specifically designed to address the inadequacies of HTML in ways which make it, effectively, more than a markup language. First, like HTML it uses tags to define the elements of the content in a way that gives meaning to them for computer processing (but unlike HTML there is no limit on the kinds of tags which can be used). This function of XML is often referred to as the semantic function, a term which we will use in what follows. Second, in XML a framework of tags can be used to create structural relationships between other tags. This function of XML is often referred to as the syntactical function, a term which we will also use. In what follows we will call a framework of tags an XML Schema—the schemas depicted in Figure 14.1 are simply frameworks of tags. The extensible nature of XML—the ability to create schemas using it—gives rise to both its strength and weakness. The strength is that ever-increasing amounts of content are being created to be 'XML compliant'. Its weakness is that more and more schemas are being created in which this is done.

In response to this, a variety of industry standards, in the form of XML schemas, are being negotiated in many different sectors among industry practitioners. These are arising because different industry sectors see the benefit of using the internet as a means of managing their exchanges (e.g. in managing demand-chains and value-networks) because automated processing by computers can add value or greatly reduce labour requirements. In order to reach negotiated agreements about such standards, reviews are undertaken by industry-standards bodies which define, and then describe, the standard in question. These negotiated agreements are then published as XML schemas. Such schemas 'express shared vocabularies and allow machines to carry out rules made by people' (W3C 2000). The advantage of the process just described is that it allows an industry-standards body to agree on an XML schema which is sympathetic to the needs of that industry and declares this to be an XML standard for that industry.

But the adoption of a wide range of different XML standards is not sufficient to address the challenge of interoperability in the way we have previously defined this. Obviously reaching negotiated agreements about the content of each XML standard does not address the problem of what to do when content must be transferred between two standards. This problem is obviously more significant, the larger the semantic differences between the ways in which different industry standards handle the same content. This problem is further compounded by the fact that many of these different schemas can be semantically incommensurable.

Addressing the problem of incommensurability

The problem of incommensurability lies at the heart of the challenges associated with the automated translation problem. Instances of XML schemas are characterised by the use of 'digital elements' or 'tags' that are used to 'mark up' unstructured documents, providing both structure and semantic content. At face value, it would seem that the translation problem and the problem of incommensurability could be best addressed by implementing a *rule based* tag-to-tag transformation of XML content. The translation 'rules' would be agreed through negotiated agreements among a number of localised stakeholders. This would make this approach similar, but slightly different from the 'patch and mend' approach discussed previously, where effectively the arbitrary use of the human interpretive intelligence of the programmer is used to resolve semantic differences.

However, in considering the possibility of either a patch and mend or a rule-based approach, we think there is a necessity to ask the question: do tags have content that can be translated from one XML-schema to another, through rule-based tag-to-tag transformations? Or put another way, do such transformations really provide 'translations' of 'digital content'?

To answer this question we have to be clear about what we mean by 'digital content'. This question raises an ontological issue in the philosophical, rather than the information technology, sense of this term. The sharable linguistic formulations about the world (claims and meta-claims that are speech-, computer- or artifact-based—in other words, cultural information used in learning, thinking, and acting) found in documents and electronic media have two aspects (Popper 1972, Chapter 3). The first is the physical pattern of markings or bits and bytes constituting the form of documents or electronic messages embodying the formulations. This physical aspect comprises concrete objects and their relationships. In the phrase 'digital content', 'digital' refers to the 'digital' character of the physical, concrete objects used in linguistic formulations.

The second aspect of such formulations is the pattern of abstract objects that conscious minds can grasp and understand in documents or other linguistic products when they know how to use the language employed in constructing it. The content of a document is the pattern of these abstract objects. It is what is expressed by the linguistic formulation that is the document (Popper 1972, Chapter 3). And when content is expressed using a digital format, rather than in print, or some other medium, that pattern of abstract objects is what we mean by 'digital content'.

Content, including digital content, can evoke understanding and a 'sense of meaning' in minds, although we cannot know for certain whether the same content presented to different minds evokes precisely the same 'understanding' or 'sense of meaning'. The same content can be expressed by different concrete objects. For example, different physical copies of *Hamlet*, with different styles of printing having different physical form, can nevertheless express the same content. The same is true of different physical copies of the American Constitution. In an important sense when we refer to the American Constitution, we do not refer to any particular written copy of it, not even to the original physical document, but rather to the pattern of abstract objects that is the content of the American Constitution and that is embodied in all the different physical copies of it that exist.

Moreover, when we translate the American Constitution, or any other document for that matter, from one natural language—English—to another, say German, it is not the physical form that we are trying to translate, to duplicate, or, at least, to approximate in German, but rather it is the content of the American constitution that we are trying to carry or convey across natural languages. This content cannot be translated by mapping letters to letters, or words to words across languages, simply because content doesn't reside in letters or words. Letters and words are the tools we use to create linguistic content. But, they, themselves, in isolation from context, do not constitute content. Instead, it is the abstract pattern of relationships among letters, words, phrases and other linguistic constructs that constitutes content. It is these same abstract patterns of relationships that give rise to the linguistic context of the assertions expressed as statements in documents, or parts of documents. The notion of linguistic context refers to the language and patterns of relationships that surrounds the assertions contained within documents. The linguistic context is distinct from the social and cultural context associated with any document, because social and cultural context is not necessarily included in the content itself. Rather social and cultural context if it is captured can be included in metadata attached to that content.

We think that it is linguistic context, in this sense of the term, which makes the problem of translation between languages so challenging. This principle of translation between natural languages is inclusive of XML-based digital content. With XML content it is the abstract patterns of objects in documents or parts of documents—combining natural language expressions, relationships among the abstract objects, the XML tags, relationships among the tags, and relationships among the natural language expressions and the XML tags—that give rise to that aspect of content we call linguistic context. This need for sensitivity towards linguistic context we think forms part of what Cope and Kalantzis extol as the need for new 'conceptualization sensibilities'. And we contend that a translation process that takes into account this sensitivity towards context involves what Cope and Kalantzis describe as the 'dynamics of difference'.

Once a natural language document is marked up in an XML schema the enhanced document is a meta-language document, couched in XML, having a formal structure. It is the content of such a meta-language document, including the aspect of it we have called linguistic context that we seek to translate, when we refer to translating XML-based digital content from one XML language to another.

So, having said what we mean by 'digital content', we now return to the question: do XML tags have content that can be translated from one XML-language to another, through rule-based tag-to-tag transformations? Or, put another way, do such transformations really provide 'translations' of 'digital content'? As a matter of general rule, we think not, because of the impact of linguistic context embedded in the content. We contend that this needs to be taken into account, and that tag-to-tag translation systems do not do this.

Therefore, we think something else is needed to alleviate the growing XML babel by means of a semi-automated translation approach. To address this matter and to set a framework for comparing three different transformation models and the way these different models cater for the application of human interpretive intelligence, we now analyse the details of the translation/transformation architecture outlined in Figure 14.1.

System components of a translation/transformation architecture

To address the challenge of incommensurability and linguistic context as described in the previous section, we argue that the design of effective transformation architecture must allow for the application of human interpretive intelligence. The fundamental concern of this chapter is to explore the means by which this can be achieved. Further details of the technical design choice outlined in Figure 14.1 are now summarised in Figure 14.2.

As a means of exploring aspects of the technical design choice when considering different transformation architectures, it is helpful to understand the 'translation/transformation system' as the underlying assumptions and rules governing the translation from one XML schema to another, including the infrastructure systems that are derived from these assumptions (see the later section where we discuss infrastructure systems in more detail). In turn, the transformation mechanisms are best understood as the 'semantic bridges' or the 'semantic rules' that create the connections between each individual digital elements within each

Figure 14.2 Outline of the technical design choice between different transformation architectures

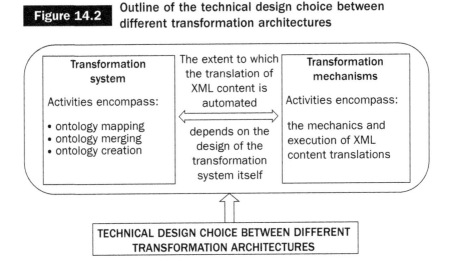

Transformation system	The extent to which the translation of XML content is automated	Transformation mechanisms
Activities encompass:		Activities encompass:
• ontology mapping • ontology merging • ontology creation	depends on the design of the transformation system itself	the mechanics and execution of XML content translations

TECHNICAL DESIGN CHOICE BETWEEN DIFFERENT
TRANSFORMATION ARCHITECTURES

XML schema and the translation/transformation system. In this chapter we refer to such connections as axioms. We now discuss the details of these concepts in turn.

The translation/transformation system

The design of a translation/transformation system involves the consideration of the means by which the entities that comprise multiple XML schemas are mapped together. This process is called ontology mapping. In this process, we think that in order to integrate incommensurable tags or fields and relations across differing XML schemas, human interpretive intelligence is required to create new ontological categories and hierarchical organisations and reorganisations of such categories. Importantly, when this happens, the ontology mapping process gives rise to the creation of an expanded ontology (ontology creation)—and results in what we will call a 'merged ontology'. We call this merged ontology an interlanguage.

This idea of a merged ontology (or interlanguage) we think has important implications for the role of categories. We are aware that many might think that the reliance on categories can lead to excessive rigidity in thought processes. However, we think that the use of human interpretive intelligence as a means of addressing incommensurable tags or fields and relations across differing XML schemas addresses this problem. The important point is that in explicitly addressing incommensurability, expanded ontologies with different categories and hierarchies of categories evolve, through time, according to very specific contexts of occurrence and application. Therefore, through time, we think that the growth of an interlanguage is best understood as an evolutionary process because its continued existence and expansion is reliant on the continued critiquing of its function and relevance by the human-centric social system that surrounds it.

The interlanguage approach to translation follows the pattern of the translation/transformation architecture presented in Figure 14.1. This is because in that architecture, the transformation system is the interlanguage. The interlanguage comprises the framework of terms, expressions and rules, which can be used to talk about documents encoded using the different XML schemas that have been mapped into the transformation system.

A key point is that an interlanguage can only apply to schemas whose terms, entities and relationships have been mapped into it and therefore are modeled by it. The model includes both the relationships among terms in the interlanguage and the mapping relationships between these terms and the terms or other entities in the XML schemas that have been mapped. The model expresses a broader framework that encompasses the ontologies of the XML schemas whose categories and relationships have been mapped into it—thus the term merged ontology.

An interlanguage model will be projectable in varying degrees to XML schemas that have not been mapped into it, provided there is overlap in semantic content between the new schemas and previously mapped schemas. Speaking generally, however, an interlanguage will not be projectable to other schemas without an explicit attempt to map the new schema to the interlanguage. Since the new schema may contain terms and relationships that are not encompassed by the framework (model, theory) that is the interlanguage, it may be, and often is, necessary to add new terms and relationships, as well as new mapping rules to the interlanguage. This cannot be done automatically, and human interpretive intelligence must be used for ontology creation. As we will see when we compare three different systems analysed in this chapter, there is potential to make the ontology merging process a semi-automated activity. We shall see that the OntoMerge system is an example of this.

The transformation mechanisms

Transformation mechanisms provide the semantic bridges and semantic rules between individual XML schemas and each translation/transformation system. As we shall see, the design of different transformation mechanisms is shaped by the assumptions or rules governing the transformation system itself. This includes whether human interpretive intelligence is applied during the content translation process itself, or whether the content translation process is fully automated. One of the key themes highlighted in this chapter is the extent to which the translation of XML content can be fully automated. In the examples we discuss, the COAX and OntoMerge systems are designed to automate the content translation process. In contrast, the CGML system builds within it the capacity to apply human interpretive intelligence as part of the execution of the translation process.

An interlanguage as a theory of translation

One way to look at the problem of semi-automated translation of XML content is to recognise that an interlanguage is a theory or model of a meta-meta-language. The idea of a meta-meta language arises because each XML schema defines a meta-language which is used to markup text and when different XML schemas are mapped together the framework for cross mapping these schemas becomes a meta-meta-language. The interlanguage is supplemented with translation/transformation rules, and therefore is constantly being tested, refuted and reformulated in the face of new content provided by new XML schemas. This is a good way of looking at things because it focuses our attention on the idea that an interlanguage is a fallible theoretical construct whose success is contingent on its continuing ability to provide a means of interpreting new experiences represented by XML schemas not encountered in the past.

We now turn to two different examples of addressing the translation/transformation challenge—the XML-based transformation approach and the ontology-based transformation approach.

The XML-based interlanguage approach: two examples

In the XML-based interlanguage approach, the transformation system or interlanguage is itself a merged ontology expressed as an XML schema. The schema provides a linguistic framework that can be used to compare and relate different XML schemas. It can also be used along with the transformation mechanisms to translate XML documents marked up in one schema into XML documents using different schemas.

We will now supplement this general characterisation of XML-based interlanguages with an account of two examples: the Common Ground Markup Language (CGML) and the Contextual Ontology_X Architecture (COAX). The theoretical foundations of the CGML system have been written up elsewhere in this book. CGML forms part of an academic publishing system owned by Common Ground Publishing, formerly based in Australia and now based in the Research Park at the University of Illinois in Champaign, Illinois. The foundations of the COAX system have been written up by Rightscom (2006). The COAX system forms part of an approach to global infrastructure which is being pioneered by the International Digital Object Identifier (DOI) Foundation. It uses an ontology called Ontology_X, which is owned by Rightscom in the UK.

The difference in ontological structure between the CGML and the COAX systems is visualised in Figure 14.3.

Figure 14.3   Comparison of the CGML and COAX systems

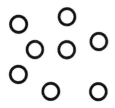 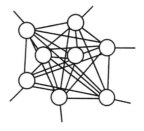

CGML SYSTEM	COAX SYSTEM
Digital elements are defined as nouns, or abstract nouns. These elements are connected by virtue of the CGML taxonomy, but no connection is created through the use of triples.	The lines represent the use of triples. Such triples are conceptualisations that display relationships between two digital elements.

The right hand side of this figure is referenced to the Universal Data Model (Rust 2005, slide 24)

The CGML translation/transformation architecture

With the CGML system, the digital elements that become part of this transformation system all emanate from the activities of practitioners as expressed in published XML standards. CGML uses semantics and syntax embodied in those standards. All digital tags in the CGML system define nouns or abstract nouns. But these are defined as a kind of a word. CGML tags can be understood as lexical items, including pairs or groups of words which in a functional sense combine to form a noun or abstract noun, such as <CopyEditor>.

A key element of the CGML system is the CGML 'interlanguage'. This is an 'apparatus' that is used to describe and translate to other XML-instantiated languages (refer to Chapter 13 for details). In particular, the CGML application provides a transformation system through which the digital elements expressed in one XML standard can be transformed and expressed in another standard. As Cope and Kalantzis highlight in Chapter 13, 'Creating an interlanguage of the social web', the interlanguage is governed by two 'semantic logics'. The first is that of distinction-exclusion. This helps identify tags whose meanings exist as parallel branches (sibling relations)—those tags which have synonymous meanings across different standards and, by implication, those that do not. For example, a <Person> is not an <Organisation> because an <Organisation> is defined as a legally or conventionally constituted group of <Persons>. The second logic is that of *relation-inclusion*. This determines tags contained within sub-branches (parent–child relations), which are semantically included as part of the semantics of the superordinate branch. For example, a <Party> to a creative or contractual relationship can be either a <Person> or an <Organisation>.

As outlined in Chapter 13, 'Creating an interlanguage of the social web', the impact of these two logics gives rise to the semantic and the syntactical rules that are embedded within the CGML tag dictionary and the CGML thesaurus. The CGML tag thesaurus takes each tag within any given schema as its starting point, reproduces the definitions and provides examples. Against each of these tags, a CGML synonym is provided. The semantics of each of these synonyms are coextensive with, or narrower than, the tag against which the mapping occurs. The CGML tag dictionary links the tag concept to a semantically explicit definition.

The CGML Dictionary does not purport to be about external referents as 'meaning'; rather, it is built via the interlanguage technique from other languages that purport to have external referents. As a consequence, its meanings are not the commonsense meanings of the lifeworld of everyday experience, but derivative of specialised social languages. In one sense, therefore, the dictionary represents a 'scaffold for action' with the CGML Dictionary being more like a glossary than a normal dictionary. Its building blocks are the other tag-concepts of the CGML interlanguage. A rule of 'lowest common denominator semantics' is rigorously applied.

Obviously, the contents of the thesaurus and the dictionary can be extended, each time a new XML standard or even, indeed, a localised schema is mapped into the CGML interlanguage. Thus, the interlanguage can continuously evolve through time in a type of lattice of cross-cutting processes that map existing and emerging tagging schemas.

By systematically building on the two logics described above, Cope and Kalantzis highlight that the interlanguage mechanism (or apparatus, as they call it) does not manage structure and semantics per se. Rather they suggest (in Chapter 13) that it automatically manages the structure and semantics of structure and semantics. Its mechanism is meta-structural and meta-semantic. It is aimed at interoperability of schemas which purport to describe the world rather than reference the world.

How the CGML system works

The key requirement for the CGML system to work on a particular XML document or content is that the XML standard underlying the document has already been mapped into the CGML interlanguage. The mapping process requires a comparison of the noun tags in the XML standard with the nouns or abstract nouns in the existing CGML ontology at the time of the mapping. This process requires the application of human interpretive intelligence. Generally speaking, there will be considerable overlap in noun tags between the CGML system and the XML standard: the 'common ground' between them. For the remaining tags, however, it will be necessary to construct transformation rules that explicitly map the noun tags in the standard to noun and abstract noun tags in CGML. Where this can't be done, new noun (or abstract noun) tags are taken from the standard and added to CGML, which means placing the new tags in the context of the hierarchical taxonomy of tags that is CGML, and also making explicit the translation rules between the tags in the standard and the new tags that have been added to the CGML system.

An overview of the resulting revised CGML translation/transformation system, as it is applied to XML content, is provided in Figure 14.4. We can describe how this system works on content as a two-stage process.

Figure 14.4 XML content translation using the CGML transformation system

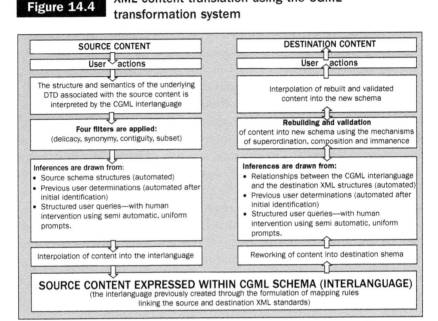

Stage 1 Merge the source XML content with the CGML XML schema

To begin with, the CGML interlanguage apparatus interprets the semantics and syntax of the source content. It is able to do this from the underlying XML standard (or schema) and the particular way the source content is expressed within the semantic and syntactic structure of the standard (or schema) itself. For this to be possible, it is, once again, necessary that each XML standard has already been mapped into the CGML interlanguage. The translation of the source content into the CGML interlanguage is then carried out by passing the source content through the delicacy, synonymn, contiguity and subset filters explained by Cope and Kalantzis in Chapter 13, 'Creating an interlanguage of the social web'.

The translation can at times occur in automated ways, when inferences can be drawn from the underlying XML standard. Where it is not possible to construe any direct relationships between content elements from the source standard and the interlanguage, a structured query is thrown up for the user to respond to. It is in this process that human interpretive intelligence is applied to enable translation. User responses to these structured queries become part of the accumulated 'recordings' of semantic translations. These responses are then built up into a 'bank' of previous translations. The results stored in this bank can be used to refine the operation of the filters so that as the transformation process is repeated fewer and fewer structured queries are thrown up for the user to respond to. It is possible, in principle, for the filters to be 'trained', in a similar way to that in which voice recognition software is trained to recognise the speech of particular speakers. The user responses grow the knowledge about translation contained in the translation system, and also grow the ontology resident in CGML. This shows that 'human interpretive intelligence' is about solving problems that appear in the translation system, and raises the question of whether such a hybrid approach might have an advantage over other XML-based systems that do not provide for human intervention in problem solving and the growth of translation knowledge.

Stage 2 Transform CGML XML content into the destination standard

Once the content is interpolated into the CGML interlanguage, the content is structured at a sufficient level of delicacy to enable the CGML transformation system to function. Some reconfiguration of the content is necessary so that appropriate digital elements can be represented according to the semantic and syntactic structures of the destination XML standard. This process involves passing the content 'backwards' through only two of the filters but with the backwards filter constraints set according to the requirements of the destination standard. Only the contiguity and subset filters are required, because when content is structured within the CGML interlanguage apparatus, the content already exists at its lowest level of delicacy and semantic composition and thus the delicacy and synonymy filters are not needed. The three mechanisms associated with this backwards filtering process are superordination, composition and immanence and a number of other 'sub-mechanisms'—as outlined by Cope and Kalantzis in Chapter 13, 'Creating an interlanguage of the social web'.

This translation can also occur in automated ways when inferences can be drawn from the destination standard. In the case where the filter constraints prevent an automated passing of content, then a structured query is thrown up for the user to respond to. User responses are then built up into a bank of previous translations. The results stored in this bank can also be used to refine the operation of the filters so that, as the translation process is repeated, fewer and fewer structured queries are thrown up for the user to respond to in this second stage as well as in the first stage.

The COAX translation/transformation architecture

The COAX transformation system differs from the CGML system principally in the importance that verbs play in the way in which the COAX system manages semantics and syntax: 'Verbs are… the most influential terms in the ontology, and nouns, adjectives and linking terms such as relators all derive their meanings, ultimately, from contexts and the verbs that characterize them' (Rightscom 2006, p. 46).

Rightscom gives the reason for this:

> COA semantics are based on the principle that meaning is derived from the particular functions which entities fulfil in contexts. An entity retains its distinct identity across any number of contexts, but its attributes and roles (and therefore its classifications) change according to the contexts in which it occurs (2006, p. 46).

The origins of this approach go back to the <indecs> metadata project. <indecs> was a project supported by the European Commission, and completed in 2000, which particularly focused on interoperability associated with the management of intellectual property. The project was designed as a fast track, infrastructure project aimed at finding practical solutions to interoperability affecting all types of rights-holders in a network, e-commerce environment. It focused on the practical interoperability of digital content identification systems and related rights metadata within multimedia e-commerce (Info 2000, p. 1).

The semantics and syntactical transformations associated with the COAX system depend on all tags within the source standard being mapped against an equivalent term in the COAX system. By working in this way, Rust (2005, slide 13) suggests that the COAX system can be understood as an *ontology of ontologies*. Rightscom explains the process by which an XML source standard is mapped into COAX:

> For each schema a once-off specific 'COA mapping' is made, using Ontology_X. This mapping is made in 'triples', and it represents both the syntax and semantics of the schema. For example, it not only contains the syntactic information that element X is called 'Author' and has a Datatype of 'String' and Cardinality of '1-n', but it contains the semantic information that 'X IsNameOf Y' and that 'Y IsAuthorOf Z'. It is this latter dimension which is unusual and distinguishes the COAX approach from more simple syntactic mappings which do not make the semantics explicit (2006, p. 27).

Even though we are describing the COAX system as an XML to XML to XML translation system, it is entirely possible that this methodology could emerge into a fully fledged semantic web application that draws on RDF and OWL specifications.

The ways in which the COAX system specifies the triples it uses is in compliance with the W3C RDF standard subject–predicate–object triple model (Rightscom 2006, p. 16).

How the COAX transformation system works

The COAX transformation system works as a two-staged process (Figure 14.5).

Stage 1 Merging the source XML content with the COA XML schema

To begin with, all 'elements' from the source content are assigned 'relators' using a series of rules which are applied using the COAX transformation system. A 'relator' is an abstraction expressing a relationship between two elements—the domain and range of the relator (Rightscom 2006, p. 57). The relators may be distinct for each different XML standard and all originate from the COAX dictionary. The relators and the rules for assigning relators will have been created when each

Figure 14.5   **XML content translation using the COAX transformation system**

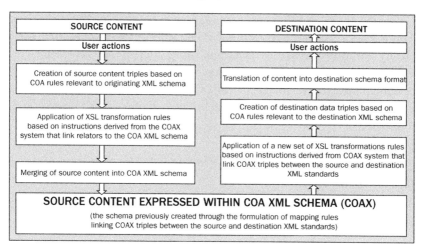

XML standard is mapped into the COAX system. Obviously for a user to be able to proceed in this way, it is necessary that each XML standard has already been mapped into the COAX system.

The linked elements created by the assigning of relators are expressed as XML structured triples. The COA model is 'triple' based, because content is expressed as sets of domain–relator–range statements such as 'A HasAuthor B' or 'A IsA EBook' (Rightscom 2006, p. 25). This domain–relator–range is in compliance with the W3C RDF standard subject–predicate–object triple model (Rightscom 2006, p. 16). These triples contain the semantic and syntactic information which is required for content transformation. Notice that relators must be constructed to express relationships between every pair of digital elements if these elements are to be used within the COAX transformation system. The aggregation of triples form the basis of the COAX data dictionary. Data dictionary items are created when the elements in the source and destination XML schemas are mapped against each using relators as the basis for mapping COAX triples.

Once the content is specified as a set of triples, then the COAX system uses the Extensible Stylesheet Language (XSL). XSL is an XML-based language, which is used for the transformation of XML documents (Wikipedia 2006) to further transform the source content, now expressed as triples, into a form whose semantics and syntax are compliant with the COAX schema. The XSL transformations (XSLTs) used to do this contain within them rules generated by Rightscom that are specific to the transformation of the content from the set of triples into the COAX interlanguage. For a user to be able to do this requires that the necessary rules and XSLT instructions have been mapped into the COAX system. Unlike the CGML XML content translation process, the COAX process of merging XML content into COAX is completely automatic and there is no facility for user queries to determine how content not represented in COAX may be integrated into the merged COAX ontology. Thus the use of human interpretive intelligence in COAX is limited to the contributions of Rightscom experts who create the bridge mappings of XML standards to COAX.

Stage 2 Transform the COAX content into the destination standard

Once the content is structured according to the COAX schema requirements, a new set of XSLTs is applied to the content in order to transfer the content from the COAX schema format into a set of triples which contain the semantic and syntactic information needed to convert the content into a form compatible with the destination XML standard. The new XSLTs used to do this also contain within them rules generated by Rightscom, and are specific to the transformation of COAX-formatted content to the destination standard. Again, for a user to be able to do this it is necessary that each XML standard has already been mapped into the COAX system.

A further series of rules are then applied using the COAX transformation system to translate the content, expressed as a set of triples, into the format of the destination XML standard. These rules will be different for each destination XML standard and are created when each XML standard is mapped into the COAX system. Again, for a user to be able to proceed in this way, it is necessary that the destination XML standard has already been mapped into the COAX system.

The ontology-based interlanguage approach: OntoMerge

In the ontology-based interlanguage approach, the transformation system or interlanguage (see Figure 14.1) is different from what we have described with CGML and COAX. This difference in approach arises because an ontology-based interlanguage approach does not result in an XML to XML to XML translation. Rather, it is an XML to ontology to XML translation. Like in the XML-based interlanguage approach, the transformation system is itself a merged ontology. But unlike the XML-based interlanguage approach the merged ontology is not expressed as an XML schema. In contrast, it is expressed as semantic web ontology through the use of object-oriented modelling languages such as Ontology Web Language (OWL). OWL is designed for use by applications that need to process the content of information instead of just presenting information to humans (W3C 2004a). Processing the content of information includes the ability to lodge queries across differing information systems that might be structured using different schema frameworks.

In achieving the objective of 'processing content' these merged ontologies, in turn can be used in two ways. First, they can assist with the translation of different ontologies through the continuous expansion of the transformation system to create larger, more expansive merged ontologies. Second, they can be used in the translation of one XML document to another. This highlights that XML schemas and ontologies are not the same thing. An XML schema is a language for restricting the structure of XML documents and provides a means for defining the structure, content and semantics of these documents (W3C 2000). In contrast, ontology represents the meaning of terms in vocabularies and the inter-relationships between those terms (W3C 2004a).

But despite the differences in the way the interlanguage mechanisms work, the overall system architecture is the same as that outlined in Figure 14.1. That is, the transformation system is the interlanguage, but the interlanguage is expressed as a semantic web ontology using object-orientated modelling languages. The ontology comprises a framework of terms, expressions and rules, which can be used as a basis for analysing documents encoded using the different XML schema that have been mapped into the transformation system and for supporting queries between different information systems that have been structured across different ontologies. To work through the differences in the ways the semantic web interlanguage systems work, we now turn to one example of such a translation/transformation architecture—OntoMerge.

OntoMerge: an example of an ontology-based translation system

OntoMerge is an online service for ontology translation, developed by Dejing Dou, Drew McDermott and Peishen Qui (2004a, 2004b) located at Yale University. It is an example of a translation/transformation architecture that is consistent with the design principles of the semantic web. Some of the design principles of the semantic web that form part of the OntoMerge approach include the use of formal specifications such as Resource Description Framework (RDF), which is a general-purpose language for representing information in the web (W3C 2004b); OWL and the predecessor language such as DARPA Agent Markup Language (DAML), the objective of which has been to develop a language and tools to facilitate the concept of the semantic web; Planning Domain Definition Language (PDDL) (Yale University undated a); and the Ontology Inference Layer (OIL).

To develop OntoMerge, the developers have also built their own tools to do translations between the PDDL and DAML. They have referred to this as PDDAML (Yale University undated b).

Specifically, OntoMerge:

> serves as a semi-automated nexus for agents and humans to find ways of coping with notational differences between ontologies with overlapping subject areas. OntoMerge is developed on top of PDDAML (PDDL-DAML Translator) and OntoEngine (inference engine).

> OntoMerge accepts:

> - a set of concepts or instance data based on one or more DAML ontologies
> - a target ontology

> and produces the concepts or instance data translated to the target ontology (Yale University undated c).

More recently, OntoMerge has acquired the capability to accept DAML+OIL and OWL ontologies, as well. Like OWL, DAML+OIL is a semantic markup language for web resources. It builds on earlier W3C standards such as RDF and RDF Schema, and extends these languages with richer modelling primitives (W3C 2001). For it to be functional, OntoMerge requires merged ontologies in its library. These merged ontologies specify relationships among terms from different ontologies.

OntoMerge relies heavily on Web-PDDL, a strongly typed, first-order logic language, as its internal representation language. Web-PDDL is used to describe axioms, facts and queries. It also includes a software system called OntoEngine, which is optimised for the ontology-translation task (Dou, McDermott and Qui 2004a, p. 2). Ontology translation may be divided into three parts:

- syntactic translation from the source ontology expressed in a web language, to an internal representation, e.g., syntactic translation from an XML language to an internal representation in Web-PDDL
- semantic translation using this internal representation; this translation is implemented using the merged ontology derived from the source and destination ontologies, and the inference engine to perform formal inference
- syntactic translation from the internal representation to the destination web language.

In doing the syntactic translations, there's also a need to translate between Web-PDDL and OWL, DAML or DAML+OIL. OntoMerge uses its translator system PDDAML to do these translations:

> Ontology merging is the process of taking the union of the concepts of source and target ontologies together and adding the bridging axioms to express the relationship (mappings) of the concepts in one ontology to the concepts in the other. Such axioms can express both simple and complicated semantic mappings between concepts of the source and target ontologies (Dou, McDermott and Qi 2004a, pp. 7–8).

> Assuming that a merged ontology exists, located typically at some URL, OntoEngine tries to load it in. Then it loads the dataset (facts) in and does forward chaining with the bridging axioms, until no new facts in the target ontology are generated (Dou, McDermott and Qi 2004a, p. 12).

Merged ontologies created for OntoMerge act as a 'bridge' between related ontologies. However, they also serve as new ontologies in their own right and can be used for further merging to create merged ontologies of broader and more general scope.

Ontology merging requires human interpretive intelligence to work successfully, because ontology experts are needed to construct the necessary bridging axioms (or mapping terms) from the source and destination ontologies. Sometimes, also, new terms may have to be added to create bridging axioms, and this is another reason why merged ontologies have to be created from their component ontologies. A merged ontology contains all the terms of its components and any new terms that were added in constructing the bridging axioms.

Dou, McDermott, and Qi themselves emphasise heavily the role of human interpretive intelligence in creating bridging axioms:

> In many cases, only humans can understand the complicated relationships that can hold between the mapped concepts. Generating these axioms must involve participation from humans, especially domain experts. You can't write bridging axioms between two medical-informatics ontologies without help from biologists. The generation of an axiom will often be an interactive process. Domain experts keep on editing the axiom till they are satisfied with the relation expressed by it. Unfortunately, domain experts are usually not very good at the formal logic syntax that we use for the axioms. It is necessary for the axiom-generating tool to hide the logic behind the scenes whenever possible. Then domain experts can check and revise the axioms using the formalism they are familiar with, or even using natural-language expressions (Dou, McDermott and Qi 2004b, p. 14).

OntoMerge and the translation of XML content

It is in considering the problem of XML translations that a distinguishing feature of the OntoMerge system is revealed when compared with the CGML and COAX approaches. OntoMerge is not reliant on the declaration of XML standards in order for its transformation architecture to be developed. This reflects OntoMerge's semantic web origins and the objective of 'processing the content of information'. Because of this, the OntoMerge architecture has developed as a 'bottom up' approach to content translation. We say this because with OntoMerge, when the translation of XML content occurs there is no need to reference declared in XML standards in the OntoMerge transformation architecture. Nor is there any assumption that content needs to be XML standards based to enact successful translation. In other words, OntoMerge is designed to start at the level of content and work upwards towards effective translation. We highlight this perceived benefit, because, in principle, this bottom-up approach to translation has the benefit of bypassing the need for accessing XML standards-compliant content. We say work upwards because, as we emphasise in the next paragraph, OntoMerge relies on access to semantic web ontologies to execute successful translations.

Within the OntoMerge system architecture there is a need to distinguish between a 'surface ontology' and a 'standard (or deep) ontology'. A surface ontology is an internal representation of the ontology derived from the source XML content when the OntoEngine inference engine is applied to the source content. In contrast, a standard ontology focuses on domain knowledge and thus is independent of the original XML specifications (Qui, McDermott and Dou 2004, p. 7).

Thus surface and standard ontologies in the ontology-based interlanguage approach appear to be equivalent to XML schemas and standards in the XML-based interlanguage approach. So, whereas with the XML-based interlanguage approach, there is a reliance on declared XML standards, with the ontology-based interlanguage approach there is a need to draw on published libraries of standard ontologies or semantic web ontologies. In translating XML content using the OntoMerge system architecture the dataset is merged with the surface ontology into what we have called a surface ontology dataset. In turn, this is subsequently merged with the standard ontology to create what we have termed a standard ontology dataset. The details of how this merging takes place are described in the following section. Once the content is expressed in the standard ontology dataset it can then be translated into a standard ontology dataset related to the destination content schema. The choice of the standard ontology is determined by its relatedness to the nature of the source content. In executing such translations of XML content, the OntoMerge system also uses bridging axioms. These are required in the translation between different standard ontology datasets. Thus with the OntoMerge system bridging axioms act as the transformation mechanisms and are central to the translation of XML content (Qui, McDermott and Dou 2004, p. 13). With both the CGML and COAX systems, the transformation mechanisms play a similar role to that of the bridging axioms in OntoMerge. In CGML, we saw that rules associating noun-to-noun mappings were critical to performing translations. For COAX, we saw that COAX triple to COAX triple mappings were the most influential terms in the ontology. In OntoMerge, the key to translation are the bridging axioms that map predicates to predicates in the source and destination standard ontologies respectively.

Predicates are terms that relate subjects and objects and are central to RDF and RDF triples. In RDF, a resource or subject (or name) is related to a value or object by a property. The property, the predicate (or relator) expresses the nature of the relationship between the subject and the object (or the name and the value). The assertion of an RDF triple says that some relationship indicated by the triple holds between the things donated by the subject and the object of the triple (W3C 2004b). Examples of predicates include: 'author', 'creator', 'personal data', 'contact information' and 'publisher'. Some examples of statements using predicates are:

Routledge is the **publisher** of All Life Is Problem Solving

John's **postal address** is 16 Waverly Place, Seattle, Washington

Michelangelo is the **creator** of David

With OntoMerge, then, predicates are nouns, and bridging axioms are mapping rules that use predicates to map nouns-to-nouns as in CGML. However, there are significant differences in approach because these nouns as predicates carry with them the inferred relationships between the subjects and objects that define them as predicates in the first place. This is the case even though the bridging axioms are not defined using triples mapped to triples as in the case of COAX.

The importance of predicates is fundamental to the OntoMerge inference engine, OntoEngine, because one of the ways of discriminating 'the facts' embedded within datasets loaded into OntoEngine is through the use of predicates. That is, predicates form the second tier of indexing structure of OntoEngine. This in turn provides the foundation for OntoEngine to undertake automated reasoning: 'When some dataset in one or several source ontologies are input, OntoEngine can do inference in the merged ontology, projecting the resulting conclusions into one of several target ontologies automatically' (Dou, McDermott and Qui 2004b, p. 8).

How the OntoMerge system works

There are some differences in the way OntoMerge is used to translate XML content versus how it is applied to translate ontologies. The general approach taken to XML content translation has been outlined by Dou, McDermott and Qi as follows:

> We can now think of dataset translation this way: Take the dataset and treat it as being in the merged ontology covering the source and target. Draw conclusions from it. The bridging axioms make it possible to draw conclusions from premises some of which come from the source and some from the target, or to draw target-vocabulary conclusions from source-language premises, or vice versa. The inference process stops with conclusions whose symbols come entirely from the target vocabulary; we call these target conclusions. Other conclusions are used for further inference. In the end, only the target conclusions are retained; we call this projecting the conclusions into the target ontology. In some cases, backward chaining would be more economical than the forward-chain/project process... In either case, the idea is to push inferences through the pattern (2004b, p. 5).

The details of this approach to translating XML documents into other XML standards are outlined in Figure 14.6. As with the CGML and COAX approaches, we have also described how this system works as a two-staged process.

Stage 1 Transform source content schema into the merged ontology data set

To begin with the OntoEngine inference engine is used to build automatically a surface ontology from the source XML content's Document Type Definition (DTD) file. A DTD defines the legal building

Figure 14.6 XML content translation using OntoMerge

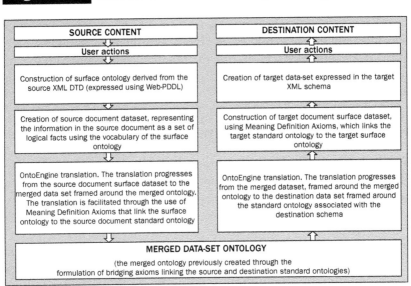

SOURCE CONTENT	DESTINATION CONTENT
User actions	User actions
Construction of surface ontology derived from the source XML DTD (expressed using Web-PDDL)	Creation of target data-set expressed in the target XML schema
Creation of source document dataset, representing the information in the source document as a set of logical facts using the vocabulary of the surface ontology	Construction of target document surface dataset, using Meaning Definition Axioms, which links the target standard ontology to the target surface ontology
OntoEngine translation. The translation progresses from the source document surface dataset to the merged data set framed around the merged ontology. The translation is facilitated through the use of Meaning Definition Axioms that link the surface ontology to the source document standard ontology	OntoEngine translation. The translation progresses from the merged dataset, framed around the merged ontology to the destination data set framed around the standard ontology associated with the destination schema

MERGED DATA-SET ONTOLOGY

(the merged ontology previously created through the formulation of bridging axioms linking the source and destination standard ontologies)

blocks of an XML document and defines the document structure with a list of legal elements and attributes (W3 Schools undated). The surface ontology is the internal representation of the ontology derived from the source DTD file and is expressed using Web-PDDL (mentioned previously). Drawing on the vocabulary of the surface ontology, OntoEngine is used to extract automatically a dataset from the original XML content and the surface ontology. Though Qui, McDermott and Dou (2004, p. 5) don't use this term, we call the new dataset the source document surface dataset.

This dataset represents the information in the source document 'as a set of logical facts using the vocabulary of the surface ontology'. The need then is to merge this dataset further into a standard ontology dataset. In order to accomplish this merging, there is a requirement that the surface ontology has been merged with the standard ontology through the formulation of different types of bridging axioms called Meaning Definition Axioms (MDAs) (Qui, McDermott and Dou 2004, p. 2). According to Qui, McDermott and Dou, MDAs are required to assign meaning to the source XML content. This is achieved by relating the surface ontology to the particular standard ontology. As in the case of formulating bridging axioms, these MDAs are created with the help of human interpretive intelligence. Once these MDAs are formulated, the merging process can proceed with an automatic translation of the source document surface dataset to a dataset expressed in the standard ontology. The translation is also undertaken using the OntoEngine inference engine. The translation is able to proceed because of inferences derived from logical facts that are accessible from the use of MDAs that link the surface ontology dataset to the standard ontology. We now call this the source document merged ontology dataset.

Stage 2 Transform the source document merged ontology dataset into the destination XML schema

The source document merged ontology dataset is then translated to the destination document merged ontology. This translation is executed using OntoEngine and once again this translation is conditional on the formulation of bridging axioms that link the source and destination standard ontologies. The translation results in the creation of a destination document merged ontology dataset. In turn, this is translated into a destination document surface ontology dataset also using OntoEngine. This translation is conditional on MDAs being formulated that link the destination standard ontology with the destination surface ontology. The destination document surface ontology dataset is subsequently used along with the DTD file for the destination XML standard or schema, to create a destination dataset expressed in the destination XML standard (or schema). This completes the translation.

Differences in approach

The OntoMerge approach to XML translation is different from the CGML and COAX approaches in that it is pursued in a much more bottom-up rather than top-down manner. That is, when someone is faced with an XML translation problem and wants to use the OntoMerge approach, they don't look to translate their surface ontologies to a single interlanguage model as represented by a model like the CGML or COAX systems. Rather, they first have to search web libraries to try to find a standard ontology (written in DAML, DAML+OIL or OWL) closely related to the knowledge domain of the surface ontology that has been merged with the surface ontology through the formulation of MDAs. Second, they also need to search web libraries for an earlier merged ontology that already contains bridging axioms linking the source standard ontology and the destination standard ontology. Third, they also need to search web libraries for previously developed ontologies that merge the destination standard ontology with the destination surface ontology through the formulation of meaning definition axioms. If no such merged ontologies exist, then no translation can be undertaken until domain experts working with OntoMerge can construct MDAs mapping the predicates in their surface ontologies to an ontology already available in DAML, DAML+OIL or OWL ontology libraries. Thus far, there appears to be no standard deep ontological framework that merges all the ontologies that have been developed in OntoMerge application work. There are many islands in the OntoMerge stream. But the centralised integration offered by CGML and COAX is absent.

Evaluating approaches to interoperability

In previous sections we have discussed the general nature of the transformation/translation problem from digital content expressed in one XML schema to the same digital content expressed in another. We have then reviewed three systems for performing such translations. Two of these systems originated in the world of XML itself and aim to transform the ad hoc 'patch-and-mend' and rule-based tag-to-tag approaches to transformation with something that would be more automatic, more efficient and equally effective. The third system originated in the world of the semantic web as a solution to the need for a software tool that would assist in performing ontology translations. The OntoMerge system was developed to solve this generalised problem and was found to be applicable to the problem of XML schema translations. As we have seen previously, all three systems rely on a merged ontology approach that creates either a generalised interlanguage, or in the case of OntoMerge a less generalised non-XML-based interlanguage that will work to translate one XML document to another.

In this section of the chapter we confront the problem of system choice. How do we select among competing architectures designed to enable XML translations? System selection, of course, requires one or more criteria, which we now proceed to outline and discuss. Then we illustrate the application of the criterion or criteria to the three illustrative systems reviewed earlier.

A generalised criterion for selecting among systems develops from the problem of semantic incommensurability that arises during the process of translating XML content between different schemas or standards. It is the criterion of ease of creating such commensurability (Firestone and McElroy 2003, p. 161; Popper 1970, pp. 56–57) where needed, so that transformations of XML content between one schema (or standard) and another can be implemented. In general, the system supporting the greatest relative ease and convenience in creating commensurability is to be preferred.

Another way to look at this arises from the recognition that the merged ontologies used in all three approaches may be viewed as fallible theories of transformation/translation among variant XML standards and schemas. Each time a dataset representing a new standard or schema is encountered that cannot be translated using a previously developed merged ontology, the theory of translation using that ontology is falsified by the new data that has been encountered, and there is a need to revise that theory of translation by creating an expanded merged ontology whether in CGML, COAX, OntoMerge or some other system.

Thus, to use such transformation/translation architectures, there is a continuing need to reformulate the embedded theories of translation and merged ontologies. Again, the system that makes it easiest to formulate expanded frameworks arising from revised theories of translation that create commensurability between source and destination XML content and merged ontologies is the system that should be selected among a number of competitors. We now apply this criterion to a comparison of the three transformation/translation systems reviewed above.

The commensurability creation load

We have coined the term commensurability creation load to describe the extent to which infrastructure is required to contribute to the means by which commensurability can be created between different ontologies. We are concerned here with the costs and complexity of establishing, administering and maintaining such infrastructure. In framing our discussions about such matters we recognise that different system architectures have significant impact on the nature of required infrastructure. Therefore, we discuss the issue of commensurability creation load under the headings of XML to XML to XML (CGML and COAX) and XML to ontology to XML (OntoMerge) infrastructure systems.

XML-based interlanguage infrastructure

With the two XML to XML to XML transformation architectures discussed in this chapter, the infrastructure requirements are similar to the extent that both require the creation, management and upgrading of interlanguage terms, including data dictionaries. In both cases, the origins of these terms are derived from declared XML standards. Therefore, one of the overarching infrastructure requirements of the XML-based transformation architectures is global agreements about protocols for the publishing of XML standards.

Beyond the publishing of XML standards we think that in the construction of interlanguage terms, including data dictionaries, the commensurability creation load of the CGML system architecture will prove to be significantly less than for the COAX system. We think this for two reasons. First, with CGML, all interlanguage terms are derived from published XML standards, with CGML's focus on noun mappings. Therefore with the CGML approach, the transformation architecture is grounded in a familiar social language of declared standards. This is not completely the case with COAX, where the verb triples are designed to be machine readable and not necessarily easily read by people. Second, there will need to be fewer interlanguage terms and data dictionary entries in CGML compared with the number of relators and triples within the COAX system dictionary. This claim is supported by some of the early figures, comparing the sizes of the data dictionaries of the two systems, and also by some simple arguments. We use their early figures (2005) below to make generalised comparisons—we have not been able to access more up-to-date figures.

In 2005 the COAX system was reported to have a dictionary of 27,000 terms, of which 23,000 were relators. It also included around 500,000 triples with a dozen standards being mapped into the system (Rust 2005, slide 13). The first reason for this difference in scale of approach between the COAX and CGML systems is apparent just from looking at Figure 14.3. Let us assume that this figure refers to one simple XML standard (and not multiple metadata elements from several different standards). If there are n circular objects in each of the pictures, then this requires that n items be defined in the CGML Dictionary. By contrast, the COAX dictionary requires that up to $n(n-1)/2$ triples be defined for every relator which is used to join n objects in the ontology. If n equals 10 and there are five relators in an ontology, then ten dictionary entries would need to be defined for CGML. But for COAX, there could be $10(10-1)/2$ or 45 triples for each of the five relators; altogether up to 225 triples that need to be mapped to the COAX system. As n increases linearly, the required number of COAX mappings explodes exponentially. Of course, not all objects will need relating to each other in triples, but the point that the number of COAX mappings necessary to create commensurability can explode compared to the number of CGML mappings remains a compelling one.

It is interesting to note that the infrastructure model related to the COAX system is continuing to evolve. For example, in December 2009 the University of Strathclyde Glasgow released a first stage report of a new Vocabulary Mapping Framework (VMF) project. The aim of this project, which includes proponents of the COAX system, is to:

> provide a freely available tool which can be used to automatically compute the 'best fit' mappings between terms in controlled vocabularies in different metadata schemes and messages (both standard and, in principle, proprietary) which are of interest to the educational, bibliographic and content publishing sectors (University of Strathclyde Glasgow 2009).

It is reported that the initial scope of the project has been to map <Resource categories> (eg CD, Ebook, Photograph), <Resource-to-Resource relators> (eg IsVersionOf, HasTranslation), <Resource-to-Party relators> (e.g. Author, EditedBy), <Party-to-Party relators> (eg AffiliatedTo) and <Party categories> (University of Strathclyde Glasgow 2009).

The initial report highlights some of the challenges associated with the commensurability creation load:

> As the VMF matrix will be freely available, there is no barrier to anyone attempting mappings or queries of their own for any purpose, and we encourage this to help in the development of the tool. However, it will not be sensible to allow mappings to be made in an ad hoc and unvalidated way if those mappings are going to be authoritative and used by others. A mapping represents a statement of equivalence between the concepts of two different parties or domains, and both parties, or representatives of the domains, should give their assent to them if at all possible (University of Strathclyde Glasgow 2009).

It also highlights that the VMF tool is not designed for human use:

> The matrix is a tool for computer, not human, use. It is a mapping tool, not a cataloguing tool or a public vocabulary. It is a very large network of terms whose job is to provide paths by which other terms may be connected: it is therefore not necessary for it to be generally accessible or 'user-friendly' to users of metadata in

general. It is also not a dictionary of the public meanings of words, or an attempt to provide definitive meanings for particular words. In the VMF matrix each term has one precise meaning, and so each word can be a label for only one VMF concept, whereas in the world at large the same name may be associated with a range of diverse or related meanings, as is reflected in the various controlled vocabularies being mapped to VMF. Names are invaluable clues to the meaning of a term, but the unique meaning of a term is built up, and therefore recognised, by its definition and the accumulation of logical relationships in the ontology. Because VMF must represent the sum of its parts, it also becomes necessary for term names in VMF (which have to be unique) to be more precise, and therefore less user-friendly, than in a smaller scheme (University of Strathclyde Glasgow 2009).

We think that this type of infrastructure is indicative of the type of commensurability creation load that the COAX system will require. That is, it appears to be moving in directions similar to the CGML approach, where the focus is on mapping the elements of published standards, but in the case of COAX it includes relators which can be expressed within the RDF framework and that as a result the notion of authority for cross-mappings will become an important consideration.

If the CGML system were to become a standard, in the way that the COAX system aspires to, it would be necessary to establish a governance infrastructure for such an approach. Institutionally, there is backing for the COAX approach through the International DOI Foundation. It has been a participant in and supporter of the <indecs> project and this vocabulary mapping framework.

Ontology-based interlanguage infrastructure

The infrastructure requirements associated with the XML to ontology to XML transformation architectures such as OntoMerge system will need to be consistent with the design principles of the semantic web. In order that functional outcomes are achieved, such requirements include the creation and publishing of, and access to, libraries of standard and merged ontologies: 'Ontology mappings will need to be published on the semantic web just as ontologies themselves are' (Bernstein and McDermott 2005, p. 1).

As we have also highlighted, the merged ontologies will need to reflect the underlying ontological structure of OntoMerge with its focus on semantic mappings of predicates and the formulation of bridging axioms and meaning definition axioms using these predicates. We think that the commensurability creation load of CGML will be less than for OntoMerge. This is because with CGML only the nouns are mapped from source and destination XML standards to the CGML interlanguage. In principle, once there are sufficient XML standards mapped into CGML, then possibilities associated with XML schema to XML schema translations could occur. In contrast, with OntoMerge the mapping and merging of ontologies involves the formulation of bridging axioms between the source and destination standard ontologies as well as the MDAs between the surface ontologies and the standard ontologies. On the other hand, OntoMerge does not require the mapping of triples and the creation and management of a large data dictionary as required by COAX. Therefore the commensurability creation load in OntoMerge should be much less than we find in COAX.

System provisions for the use of human interpretive intelligence for creating commensurability

Overlapping XML standards will all be 'rich' in their own distinctive ways. Some will be slightly different and some will be very different from each other, each for their own reasons. Because of this, judgements about semantic and syntactic subtleties of meaning will be required in order to revise and reformulate the interlanguages in all three systems. This means that human interpretive intelligence will, in principle, be necessary to enact the transformation of content from one storage system to another. So, a very important criterion for comparing transformation/translation architectures in general, and our three illustrative systems, in particular, is the provisions they make for incorporating the human interpretive intelligence needed for creating commensurability.

As we have seen, all three systems considered in this chapter incorporate human intelligence in the course of developing the various interlanguages. In the cases of CGML and COAX, human interpretive intelligence is incorporated when mapping rules are undertaken between the elements in different XML standards and the CGML or COAX interlanguages respectively. This principle could be extended beyond XML standards to XML schemas as well.

In the case of OntoMerge, human interpretive intelligence is central to the process of creating meaning definition axioms and bridging axioms.

Therefore, even though the three systems are alike in that they all incorporate human interpretive intelligence in the creation of each transformation system, we have already seen that they are not alike in the ways in which their respective transformation mechanisms work. In order to create a transformation architecture that is capable of handling the problem of incommensurability, there is a need to make a technical design choice about how to execute the semantic mappings and rules between the source and destination schemas. The ontological assumptions of the three different systems differ. The CGML system uses noun-to-noun mapping rules to relate the underlying digital elements of content. In contrast, the COAX system uses verbs and the linkages between digital elements that are generated when verbs are used (we have described these as 'verb triples'). Finally, OntoMerge also uses nouns, but these act as noun-predicates and thus the noun-to-noun mapping rules in OntoMerge are fundamentally different from CGML.

Facilities for the use of human interpretive intelligence in content translations

Facilities for human interpretive intelligence in COAX

The COAX system is not designed to facilitate human input. However, Rightscom admitted the problems associated with aspiring to a fully automated translation system by highlighting that the COAX system *should* (but by implication does not) facilitate what we perceive to be a type of human intervention:

> there is a strong argument for establishing an (optional) human interface for the management of default assumptions, or the making of ad hoc choices in specific cases. In principle, it is bad practice for defaults to be applied 'blindly': at the very least the user should be aware of the assumptions that have been applied. Each user may have different preferences, in accordance with their own practices, and so the provision of 'configurable' defaults and choices would support transparency and respects genuine variation in practice (Rightscom 2006, pp. 31–32).

We agree with everything in this quotation, except the word 'optional'. Note that this word has been placed in parentheses. The reasons for this are not clear.

To take this argument further, consider the right-hand side of Figure 14.3. If one circle is 'dog' and the other is 'cat' then a moment's thought reveals that a number of triples could emerge (the line connecting the circles). The cat can 'look at', or indeed 'spit at', a dog. But will a cat 'purr in the presence of' a dog? In some cases, this might in fact happen, but it will depend on context. We would expect difficulties like these to arise repeatedly. We suggest, therefore, that it will be a much more difficult task to describe all the triples in the COAX system than it will be to create data dictionary entries for the CGML system. We believe that this complexity is likely to be so great that, in the final analysis, the COAX system will need to rely on a mechanism whereby somebody defines allowable triples and then mandates their use in a standard.

Not surprisingly, something like this approach has already been proposed as part of the COAX system. It was the <indecs> metadata framework and the focus on rights and permissions associated with intellectual property management that has given rise to the notion of 'assertion': 'Assertions are the mechanisms in the <indecs> framework by which authority is established' (Rust and Bride 2000, p. 35). Rust makes this point clear: 'all triples are "asserted" by at least one authority' (2005, slide 13). Such a process of 'assertion' becomes a means by which standards are established.

It might be no accident that the authors of the COAX system think that triples will need to be 'asserted'. We think that defining triples will often—not always, but often—be difficult, and may require a great deal of human knowledge and judgement. Some human—indeed a whole team of humans—will, we think, probably need to manage the triple definition process. This essentially has become the role of the Motion Pictures Experts Group (MPEG-21) Rights Data Dictionary Registration (RDD) Authority (*http://www.iso21000-6.net/*). MPEG-21 is an open framework for multimedia delivery and consumption, developed under the joint standards framework of the International Standards Organisation (ISO) and International Electro-technical Commission (IEC) Joint Technical Committee. Two components of the MPEG-21 standards, a Rights Expression Language—REL—(ISO/IEC 21000-5) and Rights Data Dictionary (ISO/IEC 21000-6), provide the means for users to express rules about access and use of multimedia content. The REL provides the syntax and the RDD provides the semantics for the terms used in the REL. A methodology and structure for the (Rights Data) Dictionary is also standardised, along with the method by which further terms can be added to the dictionary through a registration authority. The methodology is based on a contextual ontology architecture, and was developed from earlier work on <indecs> (ISO/IEC 21000-6 Registration Authority 2007).

The World Intellectual Property Organisation has highlighted the importance of a rights expression language in the following way:

> A rights expression language requires extremely precise terms (semantics) in order to create precise, unambiguous expressions. However, it has long been recognized that natural language and computer language are two different things. The language of the everyday is far from precise in computer terms and society is built on the notion that the interpretation of the nuance of language is essential. For instance, all law is framed on the basis that it cannot be so precise as to exclude interpretation. Computers, on the other hand, cannot deal with imprecision. Given an ambiguous expression, computers will either fail to work or will function in an unpredictable manner. For this reason, it is necessary to create a set of terms (words) specifically for use in a rights expression language (WIPO 2003, p. 1).

We conclude from this that assertions result in the pre-specification of relationships between entities (as reflected in the lines in Figure 14.3). This pre-specification results in some user actions being allowable and others not, based on the notion of authority. This is the very basis of a licensing agreement itself. But we claim that the mechanism used to achieve this result (the use of verb triples) has an unintended consequence of imposing a constraining effect on the entire system. This flies in the face of one of the guiding principles of the internet itself—the principle of minimal constraint. Berners-Lee highlighted the principle of minimal constraint:

> as few things should be specified as possible (minimal constraint) and those specifications which had to be made should be made independent (modularity and information hiding). The independence of specifications would allow parts of the design to be replaced while preserving the basic architecture (1996).

Within this broad context, we believe that however important rights management issues are, they should not be allowed to dominate the interoperability agenda. In particular, a consequence of this view is that it will prove highly problematic to create a global interoperability architecture that is fully automated; we believe that any transformation system must build within it a provision to apply human interpretive intelligence, a point we will expand on below.

Rightscom has completed a project in which its transformation system has been piloted via real case studies. The published paper arising from this pilot project (Rightscom 2006) identifies a number of difficulties which the COAX system faces. The report is written in such a way that it appears that the authors are surprised by the difficulties they report. Indeed, they appear to believe that once teething problems are sorted out, all these difficulties will be eliminated. Rightscom found challenges associated with *semantic incommensurability*:

> Transformation can only preserve semantics: it cannot add semantic content which is not there to begin with. Where the semantics of two standards are incompatible with, or orthogonal to, one another, no transformation methodology can bridge the gap, and meaning will be 'lost' in transformation because it has nowhere to go (2006, p. 28).

The point here is that no automatic transformation methodology can bridge the gap because no wholly rules-based approach can formulate new rules. It takes 'human interpretive intelligence', or human creativity, to come up with new solutions to transformation problems, or, more generally, to come up with new theories of transformation that create commensurability.

Rightscom (2006, p. 31) also finds challenges associated with *semantic ambiguity*:

> Example 1: Dublin Core differentiates creator and contributor according to the importance of the role, whereas ONIX differentiates by the type of the creative role (for example, Author and EditedBy), so there is a semantic mismatch in mapping from ONIX to DC (though not vice versa).

> Example 2: To know whether an ONIX contributor is a Person or an Organisation, it is necessary to look first at the PersonalName and OrganisationName fields to see which one is populated. In this particular example, Rightscom reports that conditional rules are required in some instances to determine the semantics of particular fields to ensure transformations are achieved. In such circumstances, relators are not resulting in an unambiguous expression of meaning; rather it is the conditional rules applied to determine the semantics of the particular fields.

Rightscom also highlights challenges which appear to us to be the same as *semantic delicacy* in the CGML system. The COAX system does not always handle the breaking down of different fields and managing the relationships between the hierarchies of these fields:

> ONIX (like COA) separates out the quantity, the unit of measure and the type, so (for example) 'Height 25 cms' goes in three fields in ONIX (and COA) but only one (or sometimes two) in MARC and DC. Clearly, in one direction this is fine: accurate outputs for MARC and DC can be generated by producing a concatenated field from ONIX data within COAX. From the other end it is less straightforward, but where consistent practice is employed in MARC, it is possible to analyse 'Height 25 cms' into controlled value COAX fields. Comparable approaches can be taken for manipulating elements such as date/time variations, personal names and certain identifiers, with the likelihood of a high level of accuracy in results (2006, pp. 30–31).

In the COAX system, triples contain the semantic and syntactic information that is required for content transformation. It is clear that the use of triples was *designed* by the originators of the COAX system to store this kind of information, and so to automate content transformations as completely as possible. It is also clear that the use of triples is necessary to automate content transformations in COAX. Indeed, it is clear that triples will, in many cases, embody the kinds of information which would be stored in the four filters in the CGML system. As but one example, Rightscom (2006, pp. 54–55) stated:

> A COA ontology is built by creating hierarchies of specialized classes of Entity in the form of SubClasses or SubRelators to the Primary EntityTypes. For example:
>
> Entity HasSubClass Resource
> Resource HasSubClass Output
> Output HasSubClass Creation
>
> establishes this hierarchy:
> Entity
>   Resource
>   Output
>   Creation

This set of triples embodies the kinds of information contained within the super-ordination filter within the CGML system. As Cope and Kalantzis stated in Chapter 13, 'Creating an interlanguage of the social web':

Superordination relations perform the function of sub-classification. They express an 'is a' relationship between one level in the taxonomic hierarchy and another. <Book> is a <Product>, as is an <AudioRecording>.

If the COAX system meets the ambitions of its designers, then it does not matter how easy or how difficult it is to apply human interpretive intelligence. This is because—by assuming success in achieving complete automation in translation—such requirements will not be necessary. It is our judgement that some form of human intervention will be necessary to accomplish the continuous evolution of COAX. Further, currently, as we'll see below, COAX doesn't have the capability to receive and respond to the continuous human calibration that would allow it to change to move closer to a true transformation system.

In the face of this probable need for applying human interpretive intelligence in COAX we now point to a fundamental difficulty in applying it in the COAX system. In the COAX system, the means by which semantic and syntactic interpretation occurs will be via a two staged process. First the user will need to choose an appropriate triple that contains the subtleties of the semantic and syntactic information to support transformation. And second, the appropriate XSLT transformation mechanism will need to be applied to enact the transformation. We think that such a mechanism is likely to result in user resistance for the same reason that we have discussed previously—the notion of intangible knowledge. When choosing an appropriate triple, users will have to draw parallels between their accrued experiences of the domain in question and the triples that contain the semantic and syntactical subtleties associated with the users' interpretations of their experiences. But, triples used within the COAX system are not designed for human readability. Rightscom itself has highlighted this point:

> The COAX XML schema is built on this model, which allows for any semantic relationship at any level of granularity to be represented. The result is much more verbose than a typical metadata record, but as the purpose is for storing data for interoperability, and not human readability, this is not a problem (2006, p. 26).

Since, by its account, COAX triples are not designed to be readable by people, but only by machines, we believe that this system will face serious user resistance, and also won't be able to continuously incorporate the human interpretive intelligence needed to revise, maintain and recreate the merged ontology necessary for continuous successful translation of XML standards (and, by implication, XML schemas as well).

Facilities for human interpretive intelligence in OntoMerge

The OntoMerge system aims to maximise automation of ontology and content translations as much as possible. We choose the word *maximise* carefully because Dou, McDermott and Qui emphasise the importance of human interpretive intelligence: 'Devising and maintaining a merged ontology must involve the contribution from human experts, both domain experts and "knowledge engineers". Once the merged ontology is obtained, ontology translation can proceed without further human intervention' (2004a, p. 2).

Equally, Dou et al. highlight that OntoEngine provides a mechanism for automated translations through its automated reasoning function: 'We call our new approach *ontology translation by ontology merging and automated reasoning*. Our focus is on formal inference from facts expressed in one ontology to facts expressed in another' (Dou, McDermott and Qui 2004a, p. 2).

The overall objective of this approach is to provide automated solutions in the translation of datasets and queries: 'If all ontologies, datasets and queries can be expressed in terms of the same internal representation, semantic translation can be implemented by automatic reasoning' (Dou, McDermott and Qui 2004a, p. 16).

This automated reasoning function of the OntoMerge system architecture makes it fundamentally different from CGML and COAX. At base level, it is the reliance on bridging and meaning definition axioms, as predicate to predicate mappings, that forms the basis of the functionality of OntoEngine. This is because predicates are an important part of the OntoEngine indexing structure that allows it to find formulas to be used in inference (Dou, McDermott and Qui 2004b, p. 8).

Given the automated reasoning functions of OntoEngine, and the heavy reliance on these, we think there is little provision to integrate the use of human interpretive intelligence during the content translation querying process. However, we also conclude that there would appear to be little perceived benefit in this for the developers of OntoEngine because it would be contrary to the ambitions of the developers of OntoMerge. We have previously highlighted their overall objective of processing the content of information and maximising possibilities associated with automation.

It would be a mistake to conclude from this, however, that OntoMerge is an example of a system or architecture that does not result in the falsification of the underlying translation theory that makes up the architecture. The OntoMerge system does rely on the continuous merging of new ontologies and datasets to create a broader ontological framework. The ontology merging process in principle provides a means of falsifying and continuously expanding the underlying ontology and results in new solutions to the content translation problem as outlined in this chapter.

A question therefore arises from this. How easy is it for human interpretive intelligence to be incorporated into attempts made to automate the formulation of meaning definition and bridging axioms on which the OntoMerge system relies? Dou et al. address this question in the following way: 'We designed a semi-automatic tool which can help generate the bridging axioms to merge ontologies. It provides a natural-language interface for domain experts who are usually not good at logic formalism to construct and edit the axioms' (Dou, McDermott and Qui 2004b, p. 17).

The reliance on a natural language interface to support the integration of human interpretive intelligence into the OntoMerge system exposes two key differences of approach as compared to CGML. First, the creation of bridging (and meaning definition) axioms requires that the domain experts understand that they are mapping noun-predicates to noun-predicates as compared to nouns (or abstract nouns) to nouns or abstract nouns). Second, the underlying Web-PPDL language used by OntoMerge is difficult for lay users to understand—thus the primary reason for developing a natural language interface.

The integration of human interpretive intelligence into the OntoMerge architecture will result in the need for domain experts to understand something about the principles of semantic web ontologies. We think this problem will become compounded by the need to generate a distributed library of semantic web and merged ontologies to support OntoMerge. We note that, in contrast, XML standards are already being negotiated, published and used by industry practitioners—even though more needs to be done to provide protocols for how such standards should be published.

Facilities for human interpretive intelligence in CGML

The difficulties in the use of human interpretive intelligence found in COAX and to a lesser extent in OntoMerge are largely dealt with in the

CGML system. All CGML terms are defined drawing on the social languages of practitioners—because the CGML interlanguage terms are defined on the basis of their relatedness to digital elements of XML standards. The CGML filters—delicacy, synonymy, contiguity and subset—exist to expose areas of incommensurability that arise during XML content translations. When the filters expose areas of incommensurability, users are prompted via structured user queries to make choices and to take action. In other words they apply human interpretive intelligence during the content translation process.

With the application of such actions slight distinctions of semantic and syntactic differences between the tags within each XML standards become codified. If the 'digital tracks' of each transformation are archived, we have noted in the CGML system that the 'filters' can be 'trained' to respond appropriately to these differences. In this way, there will be a movement towards more successful automation, because human creativity is constantly being used to revise and improve the merged ontology underlying the translation system. However, such automation can only develop from the accumulation of digital tracks that develop from actions arising from human interpretation and choice. Over time, well-trained filters could, in principle, come much closer to automating the content transformation process.

Automation, in other words, will never be complete. Some human intervention in the form of semantic and syntactical interpretation will always be necessary. This follows from the idea that interlanguage is a theory about translation, and therefore is fallible and sooner or later will encounter a translation problem that is likely to falsify it. But since mediated actions revising such theories are part of the design of the CGML system itself, such design features allow many interpretive choices to be taken by users rather than programmers, and for the continuous revision of the transformation/translation theory that is at the heart of CGML.

We think that the need to apply human interpretive intelligence is also supported by another very important aspect of developing and revising theories of translation. This relates to the application of the user's intangible knowledge. In making choices associated with the subtleties of the semantic and syntactic distinctions when content transformation takes place via human intervention, users must and will draw on their own experiences and subject matter expertise associated with the domain of practice (the industry that the XML standard relates to). In this way, the personal knowledge of users themselves is available to support the 'intelligence' of the CGML transformation system, and to incorporate the capability of the users to revise, extend and recreate merged ontologies.

Conclusions on facilities for using human interpretive intelligence

Of the three illustrative systems, CGML provides a facility for using human interpretive intelligence, in principle, in both the ontology merging and the content translation processes. These processes can be supported through the use of a friendly interface so that users can be queried in order to resolve semantic ambiguities that arise in constructing transformation rules or executing translations.

In COAX the content translation is fully automated, but human interpretive intelligence is used in creating mapping rules using triples. Up until now, it appears that the process of creating these rules involves the need to be able to understand the meaning of triples. However, COAX triples are not easily read and understood by humans. This effectively constrains those involved in the COAX mapping rules to technical personnel.

In OntoMerge, like COAX, content translation is fully automated and provides no opportunity for human intervention. However, formulating bridging axioms and MDAs employs human interpretive intelligence in the form of domain experts whose participation is facilitated by an axiom generating tool. This tool provides a natural language interface that ensures users do not have to learn the underlying Web-PPDL software language.

Addressing the translation problem: emergent possibilities

We think that the evolution of information architectures required to generate solutions to the problem of translatability or interoperability of different XML languages, as outlined in this chapter, depends on how different approaches deal with the need to apply human interpretive intelligence where it is needed. In our view, a number of different outcomes might emerge; we think it will prove impossible to predict what architectures are likely to prevail. However, we discuss some of the possibilities in turn below.

Possibility 1 No choice—a patch and mend architecture prevails

A patch and mend (or rule based tag-to-tag) outcome is likely to evolve if no systematic effort is made to address the key challenges to achieving translation of humanly usable content addressed in this chapter. This outcome will depend on the kinds of unsystematic and localised approaches to interoperability we have discussed earlier. But, as we have suggested, such localised solutions risk producing outcomes in which the infrastructure required to support the exchange of digital content and knowledge remains a hopeless jumble of disconnected fixes. The reason for exploring more systematic approaches is a pragmatic one. The costs of reconfiguring content to a sustainable data structure are substantial. A global architecture to support translation and interoperability objectives would help to address the challenge of 'content sustainability' and to avoid the cost of reconfigurations required to keep content accessible and usable.

Possibility 2 Choice to maximise the automation of translations

A choice to pursue the use of system architectures that aim to minimise the need for human intervention and thereby maximise the potential for automation is likely to prove attractive, for obvious reasons. Within this choice, we see three potential scenarios unfolding.

Scenario 1

Scenario 1 is to find a technical solution to the translation and interoperability challenge. A system architecture that successfully solves the translation and interoperability problem will emerge if such problems can be addressed for one, or for a number of particular industries or related academic disciplines. This would give such a system(s) a critical mass from which further advances could be built. This would especially be the case if this type of functionality would suit a certain group of stakeholders. In the case of COAX, for example, those players that have control over aggregated quantities of copyrighted content in the digital media industries, such as publishing and motion pictures, would likely benefit from the successful implementation of COAX. This solution could also benefit a wide range of end users of content as well, on the basis that access to such content could be delivered online. End users such as university students might be able to access customised content such as book chapters on demand. Or current consumers of motion picture products would benefit from increased online access to copyright content, thereby by-passing current distribution retail channels. Owners of copyright content could leverage and protect the value of their content. Everyone would win. But, for reasons outlined above, we believe that the introduction of such solutions is likely to be met with resistance by the users of the systems, because of the constraining impact on the system. We suggest that as a result of this two different scenarios could unfold.

Scenario 2

In Scenario 2, in the end, the systems do not work. It is possible that a significant amount of resources are allocated to the development and roll out of system architectures of the COAX or OntoMerge type. OntoMerge, for example, forms part of the network structure of the semantic web initiative (an initiative that has already consumed vast resources). But, the more resources are expanded, it might well be that there is a continuing need to justify the expenditure of such resources. An historical example of this type of waste already exists—namely the EDIFACT story. In the mid 1980s work was undertaken in a UN-sponsored initiative called EDIFACT (David and Foray 1994). The objective of EDIFACT was to create a global standard to support computer-to-computer exchange of business documents. Now, 20 years later, these aspirations have not been achieved and a paperless trading system, operating by means of computer-to-computer exchanges—which EDIFACT was meant to help set up—has not been realised. EDIFACT is widely regarded as having been a failure. We are grateful to Paul David for helpful insights associated with the material in this section.

What emerged during the period in which EDIFACT was championed was the rise of a plethora of different local standards. Traders used file transfer protocols (FTPs) for specialised documents transmitted, for example, between marine insurers and customs brokers and their clients. Initially, this was conceived as an overlay on the telex and telephone communications messages, but such transfers eventually replaced the use of these technologies. The document formats substituted for and enriched the key bits of data that were conveyed using previous technologies. The striking of deals, and the enforcing of them, would have been much more difficult without such localised standards with which to specify what information was needed to support a deal, and in what way.

EDIFACT aspired to create much more of a system than this. But it turned out to be impossible for EDIFACT to play a role in supporting business exchanges, for two reasons which are of relevance to this chapter.

First, as already noted, standards which enable computer-to-computer exchange of important business information need to be developed in ways that reflect highly localised requirements of specialists. EDIFACT tried to create a universal document that could describe all the possible variations of transactions. But it turned out that the EDIFACT system took too long to develop and became too cumbersome. As a result such efforts were evaded by the use of highly localised standards, which reduced the costs of transactions that were already occurring without support of electronic networks, but which did not make use of proposed universal approaches.

Second, computer-to-computer interoperability of content and information usually becomes entangled with exchanges between the actual human beings who are operating the computers themselves. EDIFACT was conceived in ways that did not make it sufficiently flexible for this to be possible. David and Foray summarise the implications of this failure:

> According to our assessment of the European situation, the main mission of EDIFACT should not be that of displacing the local standards, but rather one of assisting their absorption within a unified framework. Increasing the flexibility of the language and tolerating a sacrifice of aspirations to rigorous universality may therefore prove to be the most effective long-run strategy. However, due to the persisting ambiguity that surrounds the goals of those charged with developing the standard, EDIFACT policy continues to oscillate between conflicting design criteria. This situation, in and of itself, should be seen to be working against the formation of greater momentum for EDIFACT's adoption and the diffusion of EDI (1994, p. 138).

We see a very real possibility that an attempt to create a global translation and interoperability agenda, based on either the system like the COAX or the OntoMerge type system, might end up with an outcome of this kind.

Scenario 3

In Scenario 3, ongoing resource allocations are made to gain a minimum level of functionality. If the resistance of users was not sufficient to cause the system to become dysfunctional, an alternative outcome might develop. This could involve the continuous investment of resources in system architecture to gain a minimum level of functionality, to the extent that this prevented other, more suitable, architectures from being established. The result might be a lock-in to an inappropriate system. This is like the outcome in video recording software where the poorer tape-recording system prevailed (the VHS tape-system rather than the BETAMAX tape-system). There is a famous historical example of this lock-in story—namely the story of the QWERTY keyboard. This keyboard was designed for good reasons—very common letters were separated on the keyboard, in order to prevent the jammed keys which were likely to arise, in a manual keyboard, if keys next to each other were frequently pressed one after the other. In 1935 the Dvorak Simplified Keyboard (DSK) became available and was a superior standard for keyboard design, leading to potential significant productivity improvements. David summarises what can happen in these cases as follows:

> Despite the presence of the sort of externalities that standard static analysis tells us would interfere with the achievement of the socially optimal degree of system compatibility, competition in the absence of perfect futures markets drove the industry prematurely into de facto standardization on the wrong system—and that is where decentralized decision-making subsequently has sufficed to hold it. Outcomes of this kind are not so exotic (1986, p. 14).

In the cases discussed in this chapter, where there is already a COAX or OntoMerge type architecture available, we argue that a similar story to the QWERTY one is a possible outcome. Suppose that a CGML type system has the potential to provide a better overall architecture. But such a system might not emerge unless enough users see the benefit of adopting it. However, this will not happen if translation or interoperability needs are already being met, more or less, by ongoing resource allocations to achieve minimum functionality requirements of competing type systems.

It is interesting to note that the COAX and OntoMerge systems are structured in ways that, in principle, form part of an approach to global interoperability infrastructure embedded within the semantic web vision. The semantic web vision is a significant one and already there are powerful networking effects arising from this global agenda. These network effects might provide a powerful rationale to persuade agents to adopt this approach. And they might do this, even if other approaches like the CGML system were superior. This type of constraining effects on standards setting has been described by David. His conclusion on the policy implications is as follows:

If there is one generic course that public policy should pursue in such situations, it would be to counter-act the 'excess momentum' of bandwagon movements in network product and service markets that can prematurely commit the future inextricably to a particular technical standard, before enough information has been obtained about the likely technological or organisational and legal implications of an early, precedent setting decision (2007b, p. 20).

Possibility 3 Embed human interpretive intelligence

A third possibility that could evolve is a system which systematically embeds the principle of human interpretive intelligence, such as the CGML system described in this chapter. The CGML transformation system architecture (for example) has the potential to evolve and develop because of its flexibility. This flexibility is derived from the fact that the system specifically contains within it a provision to facilitate the application of human interpretive intelligence during the content translation process via structured queries. We have argued that the ability to do this easily is linked to the technical design choice of focusing on nouns (in the case of CGML) versus verbs (in the case of COAX) and nouns as predicates (in the case of OntoMerge). User responses to structured queries become part of the accumulated 'recordings' of semantic translations. These responses might be built up into a 'bank' of previous translations. The results stored in this bank might then be used to refine the operation of the filters, which we have discussed previously, so that, as the transformation process is repeated, fewer and fewer structured queries are thrown up for the user to respond to. Thus, the more the system is used, the more automated the CGML system might become. This transformation system is premised on the principle of minimal constraint precisely because it aims to facilitate human intervention where necessary, but at the same time to do this in a way which might limit such intervention. And the flexibility of the design of the system is such that it also has the potential to be used as a universal application across multiple industries. This is because it would enable the absorption of the kinds of localised schemas within a unified framework.

There is, however, a significant challenge associated with the CGML system itself, or any other system that systematically takes into account the principle of human interpretive intelligence, which is that, at the current time, there are limited network externality effects available that would result in a widespread adoption of such an approach. Therefore, if such an approach to the problem of XML translation is to become widely adopted, the underlying theory of translation must not only withstand critical evaluation but also become a practical solution to the challenges of XML language translation and interoperability at both local and global levels.

In the case of Finland, for example, there are already efforts being made to respond to national cultural heritage challenges through the development of national semantic web content infrastructure. The elements of this infrastructure include *shared and open metadata schemas, core ontologies and public ontology services*:

> In our view, a cross-domain semantic cultural heritage portal should be built on three pillars. First we need a cross-domain content infrastructure of ontologies, metadata standards and related services that is developed and maintained on a global level through collaborative local efforts. Second, the process of producing ontologically harmonised metadata should be organised in a collaborative fashion, where distributed content producers create semantically correct annotations cost-efficiently through centralised services. Third, the contents should be made available to human end users and machines thought intelligent search, browsing and visualisation techniques. For machines, easy to use mash-up APIs and web services should be available. In this way, the collaboratively aggregated, semantically enriched knowledge base can be exposed and reused easily as services in other portals and applications in the same vein as Google Ads or Maps (Hyvönen et al. 2009).

This type of emergent semantic web infrastructure provides an example of what the future holds, if the challenge of interoperability and the exchange of humanly usable digital content are to be advanced in practical and useful ways.

However, we conclude that the new types of conceptualising sensibilities advocated by Cope and Kalantzis in this book are complex, and that significant consideration of these theoretical matters is required before the possibility of over investment in any one type of architecture occurs. We have demonstrated how different choices about aspects of infrastructure design will (and already are) unlock the emergence of new forms of complexity, particularly in the relationship between tacit and more explicit expressions of knowledge. We have concluded that the application of human interpretive intelligence must become an essential feature of any translation system, because explicit knowledge can only be accessed and applied through tacit processes. Thus, we claim that it will not be possible to dispense with human intervention in the translation of digital content. An infrastructure that fails to acknowledge this, and to make suitable provision for it, will be dysfunctional compared with one that does.

Conclusions

This chapter has discussed how to achieve interoperability in the transformation of XML-based digital content from one XML language to another. It is our view that it will prove impossible to create a transformation system that is fully automated. Any transformation system—we believe—must build within it a provision to apply human interpretive intelligence.

We have also highlighted that it will also be necessary to make a technical design choice about the means by which the translation process between different XML languages is achieved. In making such a claim, we have examined three transformation systems that have three entirely different ontological approaches to address the same translation problem: the Common Ground Markup Language (the CGML system), Contextual Ontology_X Architecture (the COAX system) and the OntoMerge system.

The important feature of the CGML system is that it specifically contains within it a provision to facilitate the use of human interpretive intelligence during the translation process by using structured queries and action response mechanisms. We have identified that the categories used in CGML make use of published XML standards used by the relevant user communities, and have shown that elements of the CGML interlanguage apparatus are derived from these standards. This is important because different users generate different ways of organising content which reflect localised and specific activities. We have shown how this system ensures that users can draw on their own particular knowledge. In this way, choices associated with the subtleties of the semantic and syntactic distinctions, which happen when content transformation takes place via human intervention, can enable users to draw on their own experiences.

In contrast, we have shown how the COAX system relies on the use of triples to contain the semantic and syntactic information required for content transformation. But, because we conclude that human intervention is required, we have considered how difficult this process will be to implement within the COAX system. We conclude that because triples are used and because triples are not designed to be readable by people—only by machines—the COAX system rules will not easily be applied to support mechanisms for the application of human interpretive intelligence. We therefore argue that the system will become more constraining, which is likely to result in user resistance.

We have also highlighted that in the OntoMerge system, a situation exists somewhere between the CGML and COAX systems. That is, like COAX, content translation aims to be fully automatic and provides no opportunity for human intervention. However, in constructing bridging axioms and MDAs that are required for automated content translations, human interpretive intelligence is employed in the use of domain experts whose participation is facilitated by an axiom generating tool that provides a natural language interface for use by human domain experts.

We have suggested that the primary criterion for comparing alternative translation/transformation systems for XML standards and schemas is the ease of formulating expanded frameworks and revised theories of translation that create commensurability between source and destination XML content and the merged ontologies. We have discussed this criterion using three sub-criteria: the relative commensurability creation load in using each system, the system design to integrate the use of human interpretive intelligence, and facilities for the use of human interpretive intelligence in content translations.

We believe that the two claims of this chapter—about the need for human intervention and about the need to make a technical design choice about the way in which content is translated—have important implications for the development of any global interoperability architecture. The means by which we have developed our argument—by comparing three systems—should not be understood as advancing the interests of one over another. We do note that both the COAX and OntoMerge systems are conceived in ways that are congruent with the design features of the semantic web initiative. We suggest this might give these approaches certain advantages arising from the externality effects that arise as a result of this. But in advancing our central claims, we wish to caution against premature standardisation on any particular system, before all potential systems have been properly compared. Such standardisation might lead to premature lock-in to inappropriate global interoperability architecture.

Our comparison of the three systems has suggested that there are essentially three outcomes possible depending on the choices made. The first outcome is that no choice is made at all about the inter-related question of human intervention and ontology. We have suggested that the actions that arise from such a choice will lead to a patch and mend architecture, one that will develop from unsystematic and localised approaches to interoperability. But, we believe that searches for more systematic approaches will prevail for pragmatic reasons, primarily because the costs of reconfiguring content in all sorts of different ways will eventually prove to be too great. We therefore suggest that a global architecture to support interoperability objectives is likely to become increasingly desirable. This is partly because of the need to address the challenge of 'content sustainability' and avoid the cost of reconfigurations required to keep content accessible and usable.

The second outcome is a choice for working towards the benefits of automated translation systems as much as possible. In the case of the COAX system this draws on the use of triples; in the case of OntoMerge it draws on the use of predicates (which might in their own right be defined as nouns). With this second choice, we suggest three scenarios could develop. The first is that the use of triples and or predicates could result in a workable system, with widespread benefits. But we have highlighted why both the COAX and OntoMerge solutions are likely to be constraining and why they might be met by resistance from users. A second scenario is that many resources could be allocated to the development and roll out of the COAX and OntoMerge type architectures, but that such resources could be wasted—primarily because, in the end, the systems prove to be dysfunctional. We have discussed a historical example of this happening—the EDIFACT story. The third scenario is that the resistance of users might not be sufficient to cause the system to become dysfunctional. Combined with the network externality effects of the COAX and OntoMerge systems being part of the International DOI Foundation and semantic web infrastructure, this might result in agents being persuaded to adopt a less than effective system, even if it is less desirable than a CGML-like system.

The third outcome is for something like the CGML system architecture to emerge. We have shown that this architecture has potential—because it offers a generalised solution which, at the same time, would allow particularised solutions to emerge, giving it some flexibility. We have highlighted how this flexibility is derived from the fact that the CGML system specifically contains within it a provision to facilitate human interpretive intelligence during the content translation process via structured queries and action responses.

Finally we note that our findings should not be interpreted as a 'product endorsement' of the CGML system. The CGML system, like the COAX and OntoMerge systems, is not, in its current form, an open standard. This is problematic, because if such a transformation system is to offer a solution to support global interoperability objectives, the CGML system will at the very least need to be positioned as a type of standard in ways similar to those in which the COAX system has become part of the International Organization for Standardization's umbrella framework.

Our aim in this chapter has been to suggest that there is a need for further thought before systems like the COAX and OntoMerge systems are adopted as the basis for any global interpretability architecture. Paul David has drawn out the lessons to be learned about the risks of premature lock-in to inappropriate standards. He suggests that: 'preserving open options for a longer period than impatient market agenda would wish is a major part of such general wisdom that history has to offer public policy makers' (2007a, p. 137).

We suggest that here too it would be desirable to preserve an open option for some time to come.

Acknowledgements

We are very grateful to Denis Noble and David Vines (Oxford University), Paul David (Oxford and Stanford Universities), David Cleevely (Chairman: CFRS—UK), Yorick Wilks (University of Sheffield) and Keith van Rijsbergen (University of Glasgow) for their helpful comments on early drafts of this chapter.

References

Berners-Lee, T. 1996. 'The World Wide Web: Past, Present and Future', *http://www.w3.org/People/Berners-Lee/1996/ppf.html*.

Bernstein, M. and D. McDermott. 2005. 'Ontology Translation for Interoperability Among Semantic Web Services', *AI Magazine* 26(1), Spring, pp. 71–82, *http://tinyurl.com/6ompvh*.

David, P. 1986. 'Understanding the Economics of QWERTY, or Is History Necessary?' In W.N. Parker (ed.), *Economic History and the Modern Economist*. Oxford: Basil Blackwell.

—. 2007a. 'Path Dependence, its Critics and the Quest for Historical Economics'. In G.M. Hodgson (ed.), *The Evolution of Economic Institutions: A Critical Reader*. Cheltenham: Edward Elgar.

—. 2007b. 'Path Dependence—A Foundation Concept for Historical Social Science', SIEPR Discussion Paper No. 06-08. Stanford Institute for Economic Policy Research, Stanford University, California, *http://tinyurl.com/3ylffnx*.

David, P. and D. Foray. 1994. 'Percolation Structures, Markov Random Fields and the Economics of EDI Standards Diffusion'. In G. Pogorel (ed.), *Global Telecommunications Strategies and Technological Changes*. Amsterdam: North-Holland.

Dou, D., D. McDermott and P. Qui. 2004a. 'Ontology Translation on the Semantic Web', *http://www.cs.yale.edu/~dvm/daml/ontomerge_odbase.pdf*.

—. 2004b. 'Ontology Translation by Ontology Merging and Automated Reasoning', *http://cs-www.cs.yale.edu/homes/ddj/papers/DouEtal-MAS.pdf*.

Firestone, J. and M. McElroy. 2003. *Key Issues in the New Knowledge Management*. Burlington, MA: KMCI Press and Butterworth Heinemann.

Hyvönen, E. et al. 2009. CultureSampo–Finnish Culture on the Semantic Web 2.0: Thematic Perspectives for the End-user. Museums and the Web International Conference for Culture and Heritage On-line, *http://tinyurl.com/38u4qqd*.

Info 2000. 2000. '<indecs>: Putting Metadata to Rights, Summary Final Report', *http://www.doi.org/topics/indecs/indecs_SummaryReport.pdf*.

ISO/IEC 21000-6 Registration Authority website, *http://www.iso21000-6.net/*.

Kuhn, T. 1970. *The Structure of Scientific Revolutions*, 2nd ed. Chicago, IL: University of Chicago Press.

MARC. 2006. 'Marc Standards: Library of Congress—Network Development and Marc Standards Office', *http://www.loc.gov/marc/*.

McLean, N. and C. Lynch. 2004. 'Interoperability between Library Information Services and Learning Environments—Bridging the Gaps: A Joint White Paper on Behalf of the IMS Global Learning Consortium and the Coalition for Networked Information', *http://www.imsglobal.org/digitalrepositories/CNIandIMS_2004.pdf*.

MPEG-21 Rights Data Dictionary Registration Authority website, *http://www.iso21000-6.net/*.

ONIX. 2006. 'Onix for Books', *http://www.editeur.org/onix.html*.

Paskin, N. 2006. 'Identifier Interoperability: A Report on Two recent ISO Activities', *D-Lib Magazine*, April, *http://www.dlib.org/dlib/april06/paskin/04paskin.html*.

Popper, K. 1970. 'Normal Science and its Dangers'. In I. Lakatos and A. Musgrave (eds), *Criticism and the Growth of Knowledge*. Cambridge, UK: Cambridge University Press.

—. 1972. *Objective Knowledge: An Evolutionary Approach*. London: Oxford University Press.

Qui, P., D. McDermott and D. Dou. 2004. 'Assigning Semantic Meanings to XML', *http://cs-www.cs.yale.edu/homes/dvm/papers/xmlMeaning.pdf*.

Rightscom. 2006. 'Testbed for Interoperability of Ebook Metadata: Final Report', *http://tinyurl.com/2ap4yt7*.

Rust, G. 2005. 'Thoughts from a Different Planet', presentation to the Functional Requirements for Bibliographic Recrods (FRBR) Workshop, Ohio, *http://tinyurl.com/2tsa9m*.

Rust, G. and M. Bride. 2000. 'The <indecs> Metadata Framework: Principles, Model and Data Dictionary', *http://www.indecs.org/pdf/framework.pdf.*

University of Melbourne. 2010. Find an Expert website, *http://tinyurl.com/38wnybw.*

University of Strathclyde Glasgow. 2009. 'The Vocabulary Mapping Framework: An Introduction', *http://tinyurl.com/2vkeblb.*

Victorian Council of Social Services. 2008. 'The Interoperability Challenge: A Draft Discussion Paper by the Interoperability Working Group', *http://tinyurl.com/8fhfhg.*

W3 Schools. Undated. 'Introduction to DTD', *http://tinyurl.com/dlx5tz.*

Wikipedia. 2006. 'XSL Transformations', *http://en.wikipedia.org/wiki/XSLT.*

World Intellectual Property Organisation. 2003. Current Developments in the Field of Digital Rights Management, Standing Committee on Copyright and Related Rights', *http://tinyurl.com/2do6apu.*

W3C. Undated. 'W3C Semantic Web Activity', World Wide Web Consortium, *http://www.w3.org/2001/sw/.*

—. 2000. 'XML Schema', World Wide Web Consortium, *http://www.w3.org/XML/Schema.*

—. 2001. 'DAML+OIL (March 2001) Reference Description', World Wide Web Consortium, *http://tinyurl.com/2bomon4.*

—. 2004a. 'OWL Web Ontology Language Overview', World Wide Web Consortium, *http://tinyurl.com/jgyd2.*

—. 2004b. 'Resource Description Framework: Concepts and Abstract Syntax', World Wide Web Consortium, *http://www.w3.org/TR/rdf-concepts.*

Yale University Computer Science Department. Undated a. 'Drew V. McDermott', *http://cs-www.cs.yale.edu/homes/dvm/.*

— b. 'PDDAML: An Automatic Translator Between PDDL and DAML', *http://www.cs.yale.edu/homes/dvm/daml/pddl_daml_translator1.html.*

— c. 'OntoMerge: Ontology Translation by Merging Ontologies', *http://tinyurl.com/399u3pv.*

15

Framing a new agenda for semantic publishing

Bill Cope and Mary Kalantzis

In 1686 Gottfried Leibniz finished the most comprehensive of his contributions to the field of logic, *Generales Inquisitiones de Analysi Notionum et Veritatum*, a work of formal logic focusing on the relationships between 'things' and 'concepts', truth and knowledge. His method was to develop a system of primitive concepts, to create compilations of tables of definitions, and to analyse complex concepts on the basis of a logical calculus. And his aim was to create an 'alphabet of human thought', using letters and numbers to denote concepts and to derive logical conclusions (Antognazza 2009, pp. 240–44). His intellectual ambition?:

> [G]o back to the expression of thoughts through characters, this is my opinion: it will hardly be possible to end controversies and impose silence on sects, unless we recall complex arguments to simple calculations, [and] terms of vague and uncertain significance to determine characters... Once this has been done, when controversies will arise, there will be no need of a disputation between two philosophers than between two accountants. It will in fact suffice to take pen in hand, to sit at the abacus, and—having summoned, if one wishes, a friend—to say to another, 'let us calculate' (quoted in Antognazza 2009, p. 244).

Over three centuries later, we live in a modernity in which we pervasively rely on calculation, often now in the form of computable information. And we're still debating the potentials of calculability. Leibniz may have been overly optimistic in his time, but are the aspirations to artificial intelligence and the semantic web still overly ambitious today? 'When will we be able to build brains like ours?', asks Terry Sejnowski, Francis Crick Professor at the Salk Institute in *Scientific American*. 'Sooner than you think' he replies, pointing to developments in computer and brain sciences (Sejnowski 2010). Pure fantasy, this is not going to happen anytime soon, replies John Hogan a couple of issues later (Horgan 2010). We still don't know whether Leibniz's aspiration for calculability can be realised.

The internet now constitutes a consolidated and widely accessible repository of a remarkable amount of human meaning. Yet, 'computers have no reliable way to process the semantics' of web content, lamented Berners-Lee, Hendler and Lassila in their seminal 2001 article introducing the semantic web. 'In the near future', they say, the semantic web 'will usher in significant new functionality as machines become much better able to process and "understand" the data that they merely display at present' (Berners-Lee, Hendler and Lassila 2001). A decade later, this promise was called Web 3.0 (Hendler 2010), but it remained little more than a promise. As we work over that now enormous body of represented human meanings which is the internet, we still have nothing much better than search algorithms which calculate statistical frequencies of character collocations, as if 'set' always meant the same thing every time the word is used.

The problem may be the extraordinary complexity of human meaning, as expressed in language, image, sound, gesture, tactile sensation and spatial configuration. The web may be able to record writing, sound and image, but our capacities to turn these into computable meanings is still limited. Meanwhile, the broader computer science agenda of artificial intelligence has become narrower as its results have proved disappointing. Hubert Dreyfus says that the roots of the problem are in the 'rationalist vision' of its research program, based on a 'symbolic information-processing model of the mind' and its incapacity to represent 'the interests, feelings, motivations, and bodily capacities that go to make a human being' (Dreyfus 1992, p. xi).

What then might be more modestly achievable in that peculiar discursive space, academic knowledge work?

The academic language game

Modern biological taxonomy orders life according to each lifeform's evolutionary relationship to a predecessor. Species are groups of biological individuals that have evolved from a common ancestral group and which, over time, have separated from other groups that have also evolved from this ancestor. In the taxonomic hierarchy established by Linnaeus in the eighteenth century, a species (for instance, 'sapiens') is a member of a genus (homo—hence the formal, Latin naming scheme creates the term 'homo sapiens'), a family (hominids), an order (primates), a class (mammals), a phylum (vertebrates) and a kingdom (animals). Living things are classified in this system in ways which, after careful application of definitional principle, are often contrary to commonsense. The everyday concept of 'fish' no longer works, since the systematic analysis of evolutionary variations in recent decades has shown that lungfish, salmon and cows all share a common ancestor, but lungfish and cows share a more recent common ancestor than lungfish and salmon (Yoon 2009, pp. 255–58). Commonsense semantics suggests that fish are more alike because they look alike and live in water. Careful semantic work, based on disciplinary definitions and principles, tells us something remarkably and revealingly different.

Creating systematic order is an old practice, as old at least as Aristotle's categories and logic (Aristotle 350 BCE). Markus, however, points out an enormous difference between modern disciplinary knowledge and earlier forms of philosophical wisdom, integrally related as they were to the persona or habitus of the thinker. Modern knowledge becomes objectified and made widely accessible in the form of disciplinary schemata:

> The idea of the system destroys this 'personalistic' understanding of the socially most esteemed form of knowledge which claimed to be an end in itself. It divorces philosophy—further regarded as a value in itself—from its direct impact upon the life of its practitioners (or recipients), from its personality-forming, illuminative influence, and thereby creates the conceptual preconditions within the framework of which the modern conception of the autonomy of cultural accomplishments first becomes intelligible (Markus 1995, p. 6).

In this view, the creation of disciplinary knowledge as an autonomous discursive space is a peculiar accomplishment of modernity which requires the development of shared schematic and discursive understandings.

In the founding moments of philosophical modernity, Kant speaks of an 'architectonic' or an 'art of constructing systems'. On the one hand, this is an *a priori* way of seeing: 'the idea requires for its realisation a schema, that is, a constituent manifold and an order of its parts'. On the other hand the process of construction of schemata is at times circuitous:

> only after we have spent much time in the collection of materials in somewhat random fashion at the suggestion of an idea lying hidden in our minds, and after we have, indeed, over a long period assembled the materials in a merely technical manner, does it first become possible for us to discern the idea in a clearer light, and to devise a whole architectonically in accordance with the ends of reason (Kant [1781] 1933, pp. 653–55).

In this tradition, the early Wittgenstein attributes these schematic qualities to language itself, positing the world as an assemblage of facts nameable in language, alongside a propositional facility which ties those facts together (Wittgenstein [1922] 1981). In other words, he attributes to natural language an intrinsic logic of categories and schematic architectonics. The later Wittgenstein claims that natural language works in much more slippery, equivocal ways.

Schematic conceptualisation becomes the stuff of 'ontology' in the world of the semantic web, as if such representations are unmediated or true expressions of empirical 'being'. As Bowker and Starr point out using as their case studies the disease classifications used on death certificates and the system of racial classification that was apartheid in South Africa, schemata do not unproblematically represent the world 'out there'. They also reflect 'the organizational context of their application and the political and social roots of that context' (Bowker and Star 2000, p. 61). How objective are the categories when much their definitional purport is contestable? And despite their promised regularities, they are fraught with irregularities in data entry—what 'goes' in which category? How does the context of application affect their meanings in practice? 'We need a richer vocabulary than that of standardization or formalization with which to characterize the heterogeneity and processual nature of information ecologies', they conclude (Bowker and Star 2000, p. 293).

The later Wittgenstein developed perspectives on language which were very different in their emphases from his earlier work. Meanings do not simply fit into categories. Apples and tomatoes are both fruit, but apples are more typically regarded as fruit than tomatoes. To this semantic phenomenon, Wittgenstein attached the concept 'family resemblance' as an alternative instead of strict definitional categorisation, a graded view of meanings where some things more or less conform to a meaning expressed in language. And instead of a world of relatively unmediated representational meanings, Wittgenstein proposed a world of 'language games... to bring into prominence the fact that the speaking of language is part of an activity, or a form of life' (Wittgenstein 1958, pp. 2–16). Something that means one thing in one text or context may—subtly or unsubtly—mean something quite different in another. As meanings are infinitely variable, we can do no better than pin specific meanings to situation-specific contexts.

Recently, Gunther Kress has argued—and we have argued similarly in the work on 'multiliteracies' we have undertaken with him and others (Cope and Kalantzis 2000, 2009)—that language is not a set of fixed, stable and replicable meanings. Rather, it is a dynamic process of 'design'. We have available to us 'resources for representation'—the Designed. These resources

> are constantly remade; never willfully, arbitrarily, anarchically but precisely, in line with what I need, in response to some demand, some 'prompt' now—whether in conversation, in writing, in silent engagement with some framed aspect of the world, or in inner debate (Kress 2009).

This is the stuff of Designing. And the consequence is a trace left in the universe of meaning in the form of the Designed, something that in turn becomes an Available Design in a new cycle of representational work. These, then, are Kress's principles of sign making: '(1) that signs are motivated conjunctions of form and meaning; (2) that conjunction is based on the interest of the sign-maker; (3) using culturally available resources'. The design process is contextually specific, dynamic and no two signs mean precisely the same thing:

> Even the most ordinary social encounter is never entirely predictable; it is always new in some way, however slight, so that the 'accommodations' produced in any encounter are always new in some way. They project social possibilities and potentials which differ, even if slightly, from what there had been before the encounter. As a consequence, the semiotic work of interaction is always socially productive, projecting and proposing possibilities of social and semiotic forms, entities and processes which reorient, refocus, and 'go beyond', by extending and transforming what there was before the interaction... It is work which leads to semiotic entities which are always new, innovative, creative; not because of the genius of the participants in the interaction but because of the very characteristic

forms of these interactions, in which one conception of the world—the 'ground' expressing the interest of one participant—is met by the different interest of the interlocutor (Kress 2009).

These things are true to the slipperiness of all language, and particularly so in the case of vernacular, natural language. In disciplinary work, however, we create a strategically unnatural semantics to reduce the contextual equivocations and representational fluidity of natural language. Disciplinary work argues about meanings in order to sharpen semantics—in discussions of what we are really observing, to define where one category of thing ends and other begins, to clarify meanings by inference and reasoning. These are peculiar kinds of semantic work, directing focused semantic attention to provisionally agreed meanings in a certain discipline. The peculiar insightfulness and efficacy of this semantic work is that it helps us do medicine, law, philosophy or geography in some relevant respects better than we could with mere commonsense expressed in natural language.

Of course, semantic slipperiness and fluid representational design is true of academic work, and even productively so when it becomes a source of generative dissonance and innovation. Our point here is the strategic semantic de-naturalisation in disciplinary work, the relative 'automomy' (to use Markus') word of disciplines from individual voice, and the comparative 'objectivity' of disciplinary discourses as communally constructed artefacts.

However, the prevailing temper of our times does not sit well with formal semantic systems. The postmodern language turn follows the later Wittgenstein into a realm of meanings which trend towards ineffability, and infinitely varied meanings depending for their semantics on the play of the identity of the communicator in relation to the 'role of the reader' (Barthes 1981; Eco 1981).

Disciplinarity, or the reason why strategically unnatural language is sometimes powerfully perceptive

The semantic web in the formal sense is the system of web markup practices that constitute RDF/OWL. This system, however, may prove just as disappointing as the results produced thus far by computer scientists working on artificial intelligence. It may bear as little fruit as earlier modern aspirations to create systems of calculable meaning on the basis of formal logic. The reason lies in part in the infinitely extensible complexity of human meaning, into which natural language analyses provide just one insight.

This book has suggested an approach to meaning which has the modest objective of doing a somewhat better job than search algorithms based on character collocations. Where the semantic web has thus far failed to work, we want to suggest a less ambitious agenda for 'semantic publishing'. By this, we mean the active construction of texts with two layers of meaning, the meaning in the text (the conventional stuff of representation in written words, pictures and sound) and, layered over that, a markup framework designed for the computability of the text whose effect is to afford more intelligent machine-mediated readings of those texts.

Academic knowledge is an ideal place to start to develop such an agenda. From here, the agenda may spread into other spaces in the web, in the same way that the idea of backward linking which weights search results in the Google algorithm derives from the idea invented half a century earlier by Eugene Garfield, the idea that citation counts could serve as a measure of intellectual impact.

Natural language is not readily computable because of its messy ambiguities, its context-variable meanings, and the vagaries of interest in which often dissonant nuances of meaning are loaded into the roles of meaning-makers and the different kinds of people in their audience. If language is itself semantically and syntactically endless in its complexity, then on top of that the infinite variety in contexts of expression and reception multiplies infinite complexity with infinite complexity. None of this complexity goes away in academic work. However, such work at times sets out to reduce—at least in part—the contextual slipperiness and semantic ambiguities of natural language. This is the one aspect of the practice of intellectual 'discipline'.

To define our terms and reflect on our context, an academic discipline is a distinctive way of making knowledge a field of deep and detailed content information, a community of professional practice, a form of discourse (of fine semantic distinction and precise technicality), an area of work (such as an academic department or a research field), a domain of publication and public communication, a site of learning where apprentices are inducted into a disciplinary mode, a method of reading and analysing the world, an epistemic frame or way of thinking, and even a way of acting and type of person. 'Discipline' delineates the boundaries of intellectual community, the distinctive practices and methodologies of a particular area of rigorous and concentrated intellectual effort, and a frame of reference with which to interpret the world.

Wherever disciplinary practices are to be found, they involve a kind of knowing that is different from the immersive, contextually embedded knowing that happens pervasively and informally in everyday life. Discplinarity deploys a kind of systematicity that does not exist in casual experience. Husserl draws the distinction between 'lifeworld' experience and what is in 'transcendental' about 'science' (Cope and Kalantzis 2000; Husserl 1970). The 'lifeworld' is everyday lived experience. It is a place where one's commonsense understandings and actions seem to work instinctively—not too much conscious or reflective thought is required. It is a place where the ambiguities of and ineffable complexities of natural language at once enlighten insiders and confound strangers. Knowledge in and of the lifeworld is amorphous, haphazard and tacit. It is relatively unorganised, acquired by accretion in incidental, accidental and roundabout ways. It is endogenous, embedded in the lifeworld to the extent at times that its premises and implications are often all but invisible. It is organic, contextual, situational.

The 'transcendental' of disciplinary knowledge is, by comparison, a place above and beyond the commonsense assumptions of the lifeworld. In counterdistinction to the relative unconscious, unreflexive knowledge in and of the lifeworld, science sets out to comprehend and create epistemic designs which are beyond and beneath the everyday, amorphous pragmatics of the lifeworld. Disciplinary knowledge work is focused, systematic, premeditated, reflective, purposeful, disciplined and open to scrutiny by a community of experts. It is deliberate and deliberative—conscious, systematic and the subject of explicit discussion. It is structured and goal oriented, and so relatively efficient in its knowledge work. It is exophoric—for and about the 'outside world'. It is analytical—abstracting and generalising to create supra-contextual, transferable knowledge. It is sufficiently explicit to be able to speak above and beyond the situation of its initial use, to learners and to other disciplinarians, perhaps in distant places or adjacent disciplines. All in all, disciplinary practice is more work and harder work than the knowing in and of the lifeworld.

The disciplinary artefacts of academic work are the result of deliberate knowledge design work, special efforts put into knowing. This work entails a peculiar intensity of focus and specific knowledge-making techniques, working at the interface of everyday life and specially designed efforts to elicit deeper knowledge. Disciplinary work consists of things people do that make their understanding more reliable than casual lifeworld experience. To become critically knowledgeable about phenomena of the embodied lifeworld, and in ways of knowing beyond taken-for-granted experience, requires systematic observation; the application of strategies for checking, questioning and verification; immersion in the culture of the way of knowing under examination; and the use of multiple sources of information.

More rigorous knowledge-making strategies include corroborating perceptions with others who have seen the same thing and which can be further tested and verified by others; applying insight and awareness based on broad experience that moderates emotions and feelings; justifying opinions and beliefs to oneself and others, including those whose judgement is to be respected based on their expertise; taking into account ideologies which represent interests broader than one's own and with a longer view than immediate gratification; taking into account statements whose logical consistency can be demonstrated; developing perspectives based on long, deep and broad experience and which are broadly applicable; grounding principles in critical reflection by oneself and others; and forming intelligence in the light of wary scepticism and an honest recognition of one's own motives. The knowledge that is founded on these kinds of knowledge-making practices and purposeful designs for engagement in and with the world help form a person who may be regarded as knowledgeable, a person who has puts a particularly focused effort into some aspects of their knowing.

Knowledge worthy of its name consists of a number of different kinds of action, which produce deeper, broader, more trustworthy, more insightful and more useful results. We have to concentrate on our ways of knowing to achieve this greater depth or expertise. We have to work purposefully, systematically and more imaginatively at it. What, then, do we do which means that our knowledge transcends the everyday understandings of the lifeworld?

Knowledge processes

Disciplinary work consists of a number of knowledge processes. It is not simply a process of thinking or a process of understanding in the cognitive sense. Rather it is a series of performatives—acts of intervention as well as acts of representation, deeds as well as thoughts, types of practice as well as forms of contemplation, designs of knowledge action and engagement in practice as well as concept. The deeper and broader knowledge that is the result of disciplinary work consists of the kinds of things we do (knowledge abilities) to create out of the ordinary knowledge. Fazal Rizvi calls the practices entailed in creating reliable knowledge 'epistemic virtues' (Rizvi 2007).

Figure 15.1 shows a schema of four-by-two knowledge processes.

Figure 15.1 A schema of knowledge processes

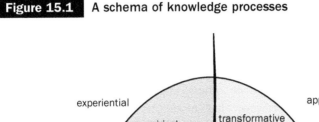

Experiential knowledge processes

Disciplinary practice has a basis in lived experience. Some of this may be bound up in the peculiar disciplinary and discursive practices of a field of endeavour (Cetina 1999; Latour and Woolgar 1986). In other respects it is bound up in personal experience, social background and socio-ethical commitments. In other words, the personal and professional profile of the person informs a certain kind of rhetorical stance (Bazerman 1988). In a work of academic representation this is noted explicitly in credits attributing institutional location and role, and biographical notation that sits alongside the text. The knowledge does not simply speak for itself. Its interlocutor needs to be trusted. And, more subtly, the experiential identity aspect of an authorial agenda is also to be found in the rhetorical structure of the text.

Disciplinary work may also have an empirical basis, either directly in the reporting of observations, facts and data or indirectly reporting on already published empirical material. Empirical work involves the experience of moving into new and potentially strange terrains, deploying the processes of methical observation, carefully regulated experimentation and systematic reading of experience. This involves refined processes of testing, recording, measurement, quantification and description. In the documentation of empirical data, clear coding and markup according to established and agreed disciplinary categories will facilitate more effective data mining. In some disciplines, the test of veracity is replicability, which requires clear documentation of empirical methods.

Conceptual knowledge processes

Academic disciplines use categorical frames of reference based on higher levels of semantic distinction, consistency and agreement within a community of expert practice more than is commonly the case in natural language. Here, we may make knowledge by grouping like and unlike on the basis of underlying attributes, and we may abstract, classify and build taxonomies (Vygotsky 1962). This kind of knowledge work includes defining terms, refining semantic distinctions and classifying empirical facts. This is what makes the language of the disciplines unnatural by comparison with the casual ambiguity of vernacular natural language. In the domain of digital text making, this is the space where specialist tags, dictionaries and glossaries are made.

Disciplines put concepts to work in theories that model the world and build explanatory paradigms. Theoretical work builds conceptual schemas capable of generalising from the particular, abstracting from the concrete and explaining processes whose workings may not be immediately obvious. Theory making involves building conceptual schemes, developing mental models, and conceiving and representing systems. It becomes the basis for the interpretative frames that constitute paradigms, and a reference point for confirmation or distinction of new work in relation to the generalisations that have hitherto been agreed. In the world of digital markup, this is the stuff of taxonomic and other concept-to-concept relationships.

Analytical knowledge processes

Disciplinary work involves developing frames of reasoning and explanation: logic, inference, prediction, hypothesis, induction and deduction. As a knowledge process, this involves making sense of patterns, analysing conceptual relations, and developing rules or laws which reflect regularities and systematic reasoning. In the world of markup, this is the stuff of conceptual dependency relations.

Disciplinary work also often analyses the world through the always cautious eye of critique, interrogating interests, motives and ethics that may motivate knowledge claims. It promotes, in other words, an ever-vigilant process of meta-cognitive reflection. This is represented in documentation via discussion of points of empirical, theoretical and ethical distinction of new work from earlier works.

Applied knowledge processes

Disciplinary work is also application-oriented, either directly or indirectly in the case of basic research. It is pragmatic, designing and implementing practical solutions within larger frames of reference and achieving technical and instrumental outcomes. What purpose knowing, after all, other than to have an effect on the world, directly or in the case of basic research, indirectly? This kind of knowledge process involves practical forms of understanding and knowledge application in a predictable way in an appropriate setting. In terms of markup practices, its referents of application might include time, place, industry or social sector—in which case it might be possible to come back at various times after initial publication to review the intellectual work against the measure of the text at the sites of its application.

In its most transformative moments applied disciplinary work is inventive and innovative—redesigning paradigms, and transforming social being and the conditions of the natural world. This kind of knowledge process may be manifest as creativity, innovation, knowledge transfer into a distant setting, risk taking, self-enablement, and the attempt to translate emancipatory and utopian agendas into practical realities. Among the measures of the impact of the work may be markup by other users of the sources of ideas, schemas and practices.

Some disciplines may prioritise one or more of these acts of knowing, these disciplinary moves, over others. In any event, these are the kinds of things we do in order to know in the out of the ordinary way of academic disciplines. Each step of the way, disciplinary work involves kinds of semantic precision which constitute a phenomenon we would like to call 'strategically unnatural language'. The dimensions of this unnaturalness become an agenda for semantic publishing.

Towards a new agenda for semantic publishing

The 'semantic web' conceived as a series of formalisms at the intersections of XML, RDF and OWL has not thus far worked, and postmodern sensibility may have forewarned the inevitability of its failure. However, if the semantic web has failed to realise its promise, rudimentary semantic publishing practices are in evidence everywhere.

For instance, semantic tagging has notably sprung to prominence in the world of the digital media. Soon after the appearance of the social bookmarking website Del.icio.us in 2004, the tagging practices of users came to be observed and commented on. Thomas Vander Wal called this practice 'folk taxonomy' or 'folksonomy'—in the case of Del.icio.us, tagging was designed to assist classification and discovery of bookmarks. David Weiberger characterised the difference between taxonomy and folksonomy as akin to the difference between trees and fallen leaves: 'The old way creates a tree. The new rakes leaves together' (Wichowski 2009).

If there is anything particularly semantic about the web today (beyond the text itself), it is this unstructured self-tagging practice. However, this practice has severely limited value as a support for online knowledge ecologies. At best, folksonomy is a flat world of semantic 'family resemblances'. Tags are quirkily personal. They mix terms which have semantic precision in disciplines with vague terms from natural language. They give no preference to disciplinary expertise over commonsense impressions. They have no dictionary or thesauri to specify what a person tagging really means by the tag they have applied. Tags are not related to tags. And to the extent that tag clouds add some grading of emphasis to the tags they represent, they simply provide a measure of lowest common denominator tag popularity, mostly highlighting the tediously obvious. Might folksonomy be just another moment of postmodern epistemic and discursive angst? Must we succumb to the anti-schematic zeitgeist?

We need schematic form, but with the rigidities of traditional taxonomy and logical formalism tempered by flexible and necessarily infinitely extensible social dialogue about meanings. We have attempted to create this in the infrastructure we described in Chapter 13, 'Creating an interlanguage of the social web'. Here, for now and by way of conclusion to this book, are our guiding principles, each of which corresponds to the 'knowledge process' ideas we introduced in the previous section of this chapter.

The principle of situated meaning

Disciplinary meanings are situated in communities of disciplinary practice. In this respect, there is more to knowledge than contingent language games (Markus 1986, pp 17–18) and the endlessness of variations in representational voice and reception. In fact, the struggle to agree on a strategically unnatural language entails ongoing debates to minimise these ever-present semantic contingencies. Communities of disciplinary practice are constantly involved in the critique of commonsense misconceptions (what you might have thought 'fish' to be) or ideological spin (on sources of climate change, for instance). This is not to say that individual members or even whole communities of disciplinarians are necessarily exempt from blindsighting by conventional wisdom or ideological occlusion. But the discursive work they do aims to refine meanings in order progressively to add perspicacity to their knowledge representations and extend them incrementally.

However, our digital knowledge infrastructures today do not provide disciplinarians with formal knowledge-representation spaces with which to refine the computable semantics of their domain. Static and ostensibly objective schemas are at times available—ChemML might be an archetypical case—but these do not have an organic and dynamic presence in the communities of intellectual practice they serve. They are not in this sense sufficiently situated. Operationally, they reflect a legacy of centralised and hierarchical knowledge systems, which needs to be opened out to the whole discipline.

Moreover, they need to be situated in another sense. Unlike Wikipedia, the authorial positions of people involved in the tag definition and schema formulation dialogue need to be made explicit in relation to the work they have done—the paradigm they represent, the empirical investigations they have done, the specific area in the subdiscipline. Suchman draws an important distinction between representationalism and situated action, the former purporting to represent the world in relatively unmediated ways (for instance, in our example, received 'ontologies'—the word itself is revealing), the latter constituting 'the cumulative durability of force and practices and artifacts extended through repeated citation and in situ re-enactment... It is only through their everyday enactment and reiteration that institutions are reproduced and rules of conduct realized' (Suchman 2007, pp. 15–16). Scollon recommends a focus on chains of mediated action (Scollon 2000, p. 20), in which terms, the discursive practices of schema formation need to be embedded in disciplinary work and an integral part of the chains of action characteristic of each discipline. Our informatic infrastructures must be built to support this (inter)action, rather than impose semantic rigidities.

The conceptual-definitional principle

If the situated is to extend its meanings beyond its sites of experiential depature, if our chain of mediated disciplinary action is to produce a body of knowledge autonomous of individuals and accessible to all, we need to provide our disciplinary communities with the tools for introducing concepts, defining their scope and exemplifying their contents. Rather than flat tags whose meanings are taken as given, disciplinarians need to be given spaces to add concepts, define concepts and exemplify them. Brandom calls this a process of 'making beliefs explicit', in which 'the objectivity of representational content is a feature of the practices of assessing the correctness of representations' consisting of a series of practices of giving and asking for reasons... and justifying beliefs and claims' (Brandom 1994, pp. 78, 89, 639). This is how dialogue is established about the relationships of concept to purported referrent.

The analytical principle

Then there is the question of relations of concept to concept. Deacon, following Pierce, speaks of two axes of meaning. The first is iconic and indexical representation, where signifier more or less reliably correlates with signified. Animals can do this. What is remarkable and unique about the words of human languages is that

> they are incorporated into quite specific individual relationships with all the other words in the language... We do not lose the indexical associations of words... [Rather we have a] sort of dual reference, to objects and other words... captured in the classic distinction between sense and reference. Words point to objects (reference) and words point to other words (sense)... This referential relationship between words—words systematically indicating other words—forms a system of higher-order relationships... Symbolic reference derives from the combinatorial possibilities (Deacon 1997, pp. 82–83).

Academic work takes this symbol-to-symbol work to levels of analytical delicacy and precision not found in natural language. This is one of the things we need to work on in communities of disciplinary practice, whether in the rhetorical flow of academic writing or in the schemas that also embody dependency relations. We need the simple dependencies implicit in taxonomies (parent, child and sibling concepts), and much more.

The transformational principle

Not only do we need schema infrastructures that push their markups out to the world; we need ways in which the world can speak back to these markups. Every markup is a documented instance of its concept. At every point the instance can throw into question the concept. Schemata must be designed not just to apply, but to allow that the application can speak back. Every concept and every concept-to-concept dependency is open for debate in every moment of tagging. Each tag is not simply a 'this is' statement. It is also an 'is this?' question. In this way, schemata remain always open to transformation—incrementally or even paradigmatically.

References

Antognazza, M.R. 2009. *Leibniz: An Intellectual Biography*. Cambridge, UK: Cambridge University Press.

Aristotle. 350 BCE. 'Categories'. The Internet Classics Archive, *http://classics.mit.edu/Aristotle/categories.html* (accessed 22 July 2010).

Barthes, R. 1981. 'Theory of the Text'. In R. Young (ed.), *Untying the Text: A Post-Structuralist Reader*. Boston: Routledge and Kegan Paul, pp. 31–47.

Bazerman, C. 1988. *Shaping Written Knowledge: The Genre and Activity of the Experimental Article in Science*. Madison, WI: University of Wisconsin Press.

Berners-Lee, T., J. Hendler and O. Lassila. 2001. 'The Semantic Web', *Scientific American*, May.

Bowker, G.C. and S.L. Star. 2000. *Sorting Things Out: Classification and Its Consequences*. Cambridge, MA: MIT Press.

Brandom, R. 1994. *Making it Explicit: Reasoning, Representing and Discursive Commitment*. Cambridge, MA: Harvard University Press.

Cetina, K.K. 1999. *Epistemic Cultures: How the Sciences Make Knowledge*. Cambridge, MA: Harvard University Press.

Cope, B. and M. Kalantzis. 2000. *Multiliteracies: Literacy Learning and the Design of Social Futures*. London: Routledge.

—. 2009. '"Multiliteracies": New Literacies, New Learning', *Pedagogies: An International Journal* 4, pp. 164–95.

Deacon, T.W. 1997. *The Symbolic Species: The Co-evolution of Language and the Brain*. New York: W.W. Norton.

Dreyfus, H.L. 1992. *What Computers Still Can't Do: A Critique of Artificial Reason*. Cambridge, MA: MIT Press.

Eco, U. 1981. *The Role of the Reader: Explorations in the Semiotics of Texts*. London: Hutchinson.

Hendler, J. 2010. 'Web 3.0: The Dawn of Semantic Search', *Computer*, January.

Horgan, J. 2010. 'Artificial Brains are Imminent... Not!', *Scientific American*.

Husserl, E. 1970. *The Crisis of European Sciences and Transcendental Phenomenology*. Evanston: Northwestern University Press.

Kant, I. [1781] 1933. *Critique of Pure Reason*, N.K. Smith (tr.). London: Macmillan.

Kress, G. 2009. *Multimodality: A Social Semiotic Approach to Contemporary Communication*. London: Routledge.

Latour, B. and S. Woolgar. 1986. *Laboratory Life: The Construction of Scientific Facts*. Princeton, NJ: Princeton University Press.

Markus, G. 1986. *Language and Production: A Critique of the Paradigms*. Dordrecht: D. Reidel.

—. 1995. 'After the "System": Philosophy in the Age of the Sciences'. In K. Gavroglu, J. Stachel and M.W. Wartofsky (eds), *Science, Politics, and Social Practice: Essays on Marxism and Science, Philosophy of Culture and the Social Sciences*. Dordrecht: Kluwer, pp. 139–59.

Rizvi, F. 2007. 'Internationalization of Curriculum: A Critical Perspective'. In M. Hayden, D. Levy and J. Thomson (eds), *Handbook of International Education*. London: Sage.

Scollon, R. 2000. 'Action and Text: Toward an Integrated Understanding of the Place of Text in Social (Inter)action'. In R. Wodak and M. Meyer (eds), *Methods in Critical Discourse Analysis*. London: Sage.

Sejnowski, T. 2010. 'When Will We Be Able to Build Brains Like Ours?', *Scientific American*.

Suchman, L. 2007. *Human-Machine Reconfigurations*. Cambridge, UK: Cambridge University Press.

Vygotsky, L. 1962. *Thought and Language*. Cambridge, MA: MIT Press.

Wichowski, A. 2009. 'Survival of the Fittest Tag: Folksonomies, Findability, and the Evolution of Information Organization', *First Monday* 14.

Wittgenstein, L. [1922] 1981. *Tractatus Logico-Philosophicus*. London: Routledge.

—. 1958. *Philosophical Investigations*. New York: Macmillan.

Yoon, C.K. 2009. *Naming Nature: The Clash Between Instinct and Science*. New York: W.W. Norton.

Index

academic discipline, 497
academic journal, 132–5
academic knowledge, 123–4
  books and journal articles, 123–43
    academic journal, 132–5
    future knowledge systems,
      135–7
    knowledge representation role in
      knowledge design, 123–6
    scholarly monograph, 126–8
  digitally mediated book
    production, 129–32
    authors, 130
    bookstores, 131–2
    publishers, 131
    readers, 132
  emerging knowledge ecologies,
    137–41
    disciplinarity and
      interdisciplinarity, 140
    distributed knowledge, 139
    globalism, 140
    intellectual property, 139
    knowledge making conditions
      for knowledge economy, 141
    post-publication knowledge
      validation, 138–9
    pre-publication knowledge
      validation, 138
    reconfiguring the university role,
      140

    representation and signification
      modes, 140
    sustainability, 139
  print-publishing system
    deficiencies, 128–9
    bookstores, 129
    publishers, 128
    readers, 129
    scholarly authors, 128
academic language game, 492–6
actor-network theory, 57, 307
ADIT-LN see Average Depth of
    Inheritance Tree of Leaf Nodes
Agreements, Treaties and Negotiated
    Settlements, 174–5
alignment, 68
Amazon, 20, 132
American Standard Code for
    Information Interchange, 110,
    391
An Investigation of the Laws of
    Thought, 203
analytical principle, 505
ANT see actor-network theory
article, 135
ASCII see American Standard Code
    for Information Interchange
assertions, 334
ATNS see Agreements, Treaties and
    Negotiated Settlements
attributes, 397

authors, 31–2
automated translation, 436–8
Average Depth of Inheritance Tree of
    Leaf Nodes, 72

Basic Formal Ontology, 237, 242–3,
    250, 293–4
belief, 346–8
BFO *see* Basic Formal Ontology
BioCyc, 291
bioinformatics, 298
biological cultures, 296–8
biological ontologies, 290–6
book publishing, 131
books
    academic knowledge textual
        practices, 123–43
    academic journal, 132–5
    digitally mediated book
        production, 129–32
    emerging knowledge ecologies,
        137–41
    future knowledge systems, 135–7
    knowledge representation role in
        knowledge design, 123–6
    print-publishing system
        deficiencies, 128–9
    scholarly monograph, 126–8
    definition, 126–7
    new, 127
    old, 126
    vs internet, 126–7
bookstores, 132
BULO *see* PROTo ONtology

Cartesian mind–body dualism, 50
cataloguing, 394–5
CGMeaning, 378, 381, 385–7,
    402
CGML *see* Common Ground
    Markup Language

Chemical Markup Language, 96, 504
ChemML, 96, 504
chronoid, 255
cinema, 82
class composition, 293
closed tags, 419
closed world assumptions, 223
COA mapping, 450
COA ontology, 472
COAX *see* Contextual
    Ontology_X_Architecture
cognitive semantics, 46–52
    categorisation theories, 46–9
    geometrics of meaning, 51–2
    semantics and the embodied mind,
        49–51
collaborative ontologies, 72
collaborators, 31–2
commensurability, 30–3, 303–41,
    343–69
    applying the framework, 369
    assessment, 227–9
    construction of science, 324–30
    creation load, 463–7
    de-structuring critiques, 319–24
        incommensurability of madness,
            321–3
        resurrecting structures, 323–4
    elastic structures, 330–40
        practising with concepts, 334–6
        socialising concepts, 337–40
        spatialising concepts, 331–4
    framework, 68–9, 340–1, 349–68
        assessment, 364–7
        generic dimension set, 358–64
        interpreting assessments, 367–8
        modelling a scenario, 350–3
        quantification, 354–8
    human interpretive intelligence,
        467–8
    material intangibles, 305–18

Foucauldian epistemes, 311–15
Kuhnian paradigms, 307–11
Quinean conceptual schemes, 315–18
ontological cultures, 344–9
quantification, 354–8
contrasting ontology matching approaches, 356–8
Common Ground Markup Language, 389–96, 401–2, 404–5, 431–2, 434, 445, 458, 466, 481
as an interlanguage, 405–25
approach, 409
language pairs, 408
paradigm, 417–22
schematic, 406
thesaurus, 422–5
cataloguing, 394–5
dictionary formation, 413–17
functional clarity, 415
internal cross-reference system, 416–17
lowest common denominator semantics, 415–16
minimising ambiguity, 414–15
silent and active tag-concepts, 416
Dictionary of Authorship and Publishing, 402
fragment specifying concept of <editor>, 415
fragment specifying concepts of <creation> and <creator>, 413
digital rights management, 396
e-commerce, 396
educational texts, 395
electronic rendering, 392
filters, 476
human interpretive intelligence facilities, 475–7
print rendering, 392–4

resource discovery, 394
Taxonomy of Authorship and Publishing
first to fourth level concepts, 420
fragment specifying concepts of <party>, 422
thesaurus, 422–5
fragment of Dublin Core, 423
translation/transformation architecture, 446–9
CGML XML content into destination standard, 449
how system works, 447–8
merging source XML content with CGML XML schema, 448–9
XML content translation, 448
typesetting and content capture, 391–2
vs COAX systems, 445
vs OntoMerge, 461–2
common knowledge, 158, 167–8
common-explicit knowledge, 159
communication, 376
communicative practices, 347
complete untranslatability, 320
composition, 421
computational semantics, 67–72
collaborative ontologies, 72
matching ontologies, 67–71
ontology metrics, 71–2
concept script, 204
concepts, 332
conceptual frames, 307
conceptual perspectivism, 304, 325, 330, 340
conceptual relativism, 304, 319, 325, 330
conceptual schemes, 306, 319, 338, 344
see also Quinean conceptual schemes

conceptual semantics, 334
conceptual spaces, 332–4
conceptual web, 51
conceptual-definitional principle, 505
configuroid, 255–6
connectionist model, 47
connotational meaning, 204
constructionist, 326
constructivism, 329
constructivists, 329
content capture, 391–2
context principle, 420
Contextual Ontology_X_Architecture,
    431–2, 434–5, 445, 458, 478–9,
    481
  human interpretive intelligence
    facilities, 468–74, 477
  translation/transformation
    architecture, 450–3
    content into destination
      standard, 452–3
    how system works, 451
    merging source XML content with
      COA XML schema, 451–2
  vs CGML systems, 445
  vs OntoMerge, 461–2
contingency, 329
continuants, 294
Convention T, 40, 320–1
crosswalks, 405–7
CUDOS, 173
culture, 65, 344–5
Cyc, 220, 239–40
Cycorp, 240

DAML see DARPA Agent Markup
  Language
DARPA see Defence Advanced
  Research Projects Agency
DARPA Agent Markup Language,
  220, 454–5

data dictionaries, 171
database, 20
  knowledge systems, 215–32
Database Task Group, 216
DEC see Digital Equipment
  Corporation
deep ontology see standard ontology
Defence Advanced Research Projects
  Agency, 216
definition, 383
Del.icio.us, 503
denotational meaning, 204
description logics, 219
Descriptive Ontology for Linguistic
  and Cognitive Engineering, 237,
  244, 250–1
design, 124
  (re)designed, 125–6
  available designs, 124–5
  designing process, 125
designing, 495
desktop, 3
desktop publishing systems, 92
digital content
  interoperability and exchange, 429–87
  interoperability approaches
    evaluation, 462–77
  ontology-based interlanguage
    approach, 453–62
  transformation, 435–44
    automated translation problem,
      436–8
    incommensurability, 438–41
    technical design choice, 442
    translation/transformation
      architecture system
      components, 441–4
  translation problem, 477–87
    automation, 478–82
    embedding human interpretive
      intelligence, 482–4

patch and mend architecture, 477–8

XML-based interlanguage approach, 444–53

Digital Equipment Corporation, 216

digital incunabula, 3

digital media, 140

effects in knowledge making, 81–120

knowledge representation, 82–4

old and new representation of meaning in digital reproduction era, 84–119

future knowledge systems, 135–6

digital print, 116

digital reproduction era

hype in hypertext, 85–119

changes in textwork since Gutenberg, 97

multimodality, 99–102

new dynamics of difference, 107–19

new navigational order, 97–9

parallels between old and new media, 104

recording and documentation ubiquity, 102–3

rendering mechanics, 87–96

representational agency shift in balance, 103–7

SGML markup for bungler definition, 93

knowledge representation work, 82–4

old and new representation of meaning, 84–119

virtual hyperbole, 84–5

digital rights management, 396

Digital Talking Book, 392, 405

digital text, 1–7

dimension set, 353–4

dimensions, 353

see also specific types

Dims see dimensions

DimSet see dimension set

disciplinarity, 496–502

dispositional knowledge, 156

distributed knowledge systems, 7–10

DocBook, 375, 392, 405

Document Type Definition, 171, 397, 459–61

documenting context, 179

dogmas of empiricism, 316

DOLCE see Descriptive Ontology for Linguistic and Cognitive Engineering

DOLCE ergo SUMO, 240

domain-level ontologies, 235–6

domains, 332

DSK see Dvorak Simplified Keyboard

DTD see Document Type Definition

Dublin Core, 394, 405, 471

fragment to CGML Thesaurus, 423

Dublin Core Metadata Framework, 404

Dublin Core Metadata Initiative 2010, 394

Dumontier ontologies, 291

Dvorak Simplified Keyboard, 481

e-commerce, 112–13, 396

e-Scholarship Research Centre, 174

EAC see Encoded Archival Context

EDIFACT, 479–80

EdNA Online 2000, 395

Educational Modelling Language, 395

educational texts, 395

EE see evolutionary epistemology

electronic rendering, 392

electronic standards

commercial implications of emergence and stabilisation, 400–1 efficiencies and cost reduction, 401

new business opportunities, 401

supply chain integration, 401

elements, 397, 419

Elements of Logic, 203

EML *see* Educational Modelling Language

Encoded Archival Context, 179

epistemes, 306

   see also Foucauldian epistemes

epistemic virtues, 499

epistemological, 346

errata, 2

eSRC *see* e-Scholarship Research Centre

evolutionary epistemology, 152

explicit knowledge, 157–8, 167

Extensible Hypertext Markup Language, 392

Extensible Markup Language, 7, 16, 18, 22–3, 93, 390, 397–9, 403, 419, 431–2, 437, 462–3

  content translation

    CGML, 448

    COAX, 451

    OntoMerge, 457–61

Extensible Rights Markup Language, 396

Extensible Stylesheet Language, 452

extrinsic dimensions, 358, 362–4

failure of translatability *see* untranslatability

family resemblance, 494–5

file transfer protocols, 479

FlyBase project, 294

FOAF ontology *see* Friend of a Friend ontology

folk taxonomy, 503

folksonomy, 503

form, 376

formal knowledge, 159

formal knowledge systems

  crises in modernity, 205–12

    towards a computational world, 211–12

    completeness, truth, decidability and computations, 208–10

    mathematical principles, 207

    thereof one must be silent, 207–8

  historical narrative, 197–212

    early modernity, 202–5

    pre-modernity, 200–2

formal semantics, 39–41

Foucauldian epistemes, 311–15

Foucauldian term, 21

foundational ontologies *see* upper-level ontologies

Friend of a Friend ontology, 237

FTP *see* file transfer protocols

function, 376

Gene Ontology, 290, 294–9

  factors in success, 296

General Formal Ontology, 237, 244–5

Generales Inquisitiones de Analysi Notionum et Veritatum, 491

GFO *see* General Formal Ontology

globalism, 140

Google, 9

Google Docs, 5

Google Scholar, 238–9

guessing principle, 420

Gutenberg's Bible, 1, 86, 107

Habermas, 337–8, 340

habitus, 337

hermeneutics, 41–3

hierarchically complex systems, 161–72

formal knowledge level, 168–70
  knowledge society level, 170
  social construction and
    knowledge formalisation, 169
individual researcher level, 165–7
  turning personal into explicit
    knowledge, 166
research knowledge and dynamics,
    164–72
  knowledge cycling hierarchical
    levels, 164
  research team or larger group
    level, 167–8
  socio-technical aspects of
    schema interactions, 170–2
theory, 161–3
  systems triad, 162
historical ontologies, 329
holon, 163
holonymy/meronymy, 38
homonymy/polysemy, 38
How to do Things with Words, 43
HTML *see* Hypertext Markup
  Language
human interpretive intelligence, 433,
  436, 447, 482–4
  facilities, 468–77
  CGML, 475–6
  COAX, 468–74
  OntoMerge, 474–5
  system provisions, 467–8
hypertext, 4, 85–119
Hypertext Markup Language, 7, 22,
  92, 127, 392, 405, 437

IBM *see* International Business
  Machines
Ideal Language Philosophy, 201
IFOMIS *see* Institute for Formal
  Ontology and Medical
  Information Science

illocutionary act, 44
incommensurability, 31, 309, 321,
  337, 351
  addressing problem in digital
    content, 438–41
  digital content transformation,
    438–41
  madness, 321–3
incunabula, 2, 91
inferences, 334
information infrastructures, 57
Institute for Formal Ontology and
  Medical Information Science,
  237
Instructional Management Systems
  Standard, 395
interlanguage, 369, 404–25
  ontology-based approach, 453–62
    (*see also* OntoMerge)
  social web, 371–425
    Common Ground Markup
      Language, 389–96
    discursive practice of markup,
      371–4
    interlanguage, 404–25
    mechanism, 384–9
    metamarkup, 378–84
    schema alignment for semantic
      publishing, 389–94
    structural markup, 374–8
    tagging schemas, 397–404
  theory of translation, 444
  XML-based approach, 435,
    444–53
interlanguage mechanism, 384–9,
  402
  schematic, 386
International Business Machines,
  206, 216
internet, 126–7
interoperability, 430–5

and exchange of humanly usable
digital content, 429–87
Interoperability of Data in
E-Commerce Systems, 396
intrinsic dimensions, 358–61
ISO 2709, 395
ISO website, 231
ISO/IEC 21000-5, 469
ISO/IEC 21000-6, 469–70

JDF *see* job definition format
JDF standard, 392
job definition format, 392–4
effects of wide adoption, 393–4
audit trail, 393
automation, 393
equipment variations, 394
human error reduction, 393
functions
post-press, 393
pre-press, 393
press, 393
journal articles
academic knowledge textual
practices, 123–43
academic journal, 132–5
digitally mediated book
production, 129–32
emerging knowledge ecologies,
137–41
future knowledge systems, 135–7
knowledge representation role in
knowledge design, 123–6
print-publishing system
deficiencies, 128–9
scholarly monograph, 126–8
journal peer-review process, 132–3
key flaws, 133

Kant, 371–2, 493
KL-ONE, 219

knowledge, 152
see also specific knowledge
contextual nature of personal
knowledge, 157
globalization and technologies, 56–7
in three worlds ontology, 155
management, 63–6
sociology, 52–5
knowledge domains, 289–300
biological ontologies, 290–6
biological/ontological cultures, 296–8
ontological objects, 298–9
ontologies in practice, 299–300
knowledge making
digital media effect, 81–120
knowledge representation work,
82–4
old and new representation
of meaning in digital
reproduction era, 84–119
knowledge processes, 499–502
analytical, 501–2
applied, 502
conceptual, 501
experiential, 500–1
schema, 500
knowledge representation
frameworks, 15–33
commensurability, 30–3
networked ontologies, 29–30
ontology computing, 25–6
Ontology Web Language, 27–9
order of things, 16–22
semantic web, 22–33
semantics framing, 33
knowledge society level, 170
knowledge support-systems
and textual representations in
research intensive networks,
145–88
knowledge systems, 15

changes in the era of social web, 1–10
  distributed knowledge systems, 7–10
  from print to digital text, 1–7
 extrinsic dimensions, 362–4
 intrinsic dimensions, 359–61
 relational database vs semantic web, 215–32
  ordering the world by relations, 215–18
  semantic web early threads, 218–20
  shifting trends or status quo, 221–2
  systems of knowledge, 222–4
 social context, 229–32
Kuhnian paradigms, 307–11

language games, 495
languages, 377, 505
Lebenswelt *see* lifeworld
libertarian technologies, 229
lifeworld, 338, 346, 498
lingua franca, 108, 114, 117, 140
lingua mundi, 108
linguistic semantics, 37–46
 formal semantics, 39–41
 hermeneutics and semantics, 41–3
 pragmatic semantics, 43–6
 semantics in language, 37–9
Linotron 1010 phototypesetter, 92
Linux operating system, 62
lithographic printing, 100
locutionary act, 44
logic, 303
 knowledge systems, 197–212
  crises in modernity, 205–12
  early modernity, 202–5
  pre-modernity, 200–2
 Second World War, 211
logic programming, 219

logical axioms, 25–6
 classes, 25
 individuals, 25
 properties, 25
logical positivism, 305
lower-level ontologies, 235
lumpers, 382

Machine Readable Catalog, 394–5, 404–5, 472
madness, 321–3
Madness and Civilisation, 321–2
MARC *see* Machine Readable Catalog
MARC Standards Office 2000, 405
markup, 371–4
 see also metamarkup
 schemas, 381
 tags, 373–4
Markus, 493
match, 68
material intangibles, 305–18
 Foucauldian epistemes, 311–15
 Kuhnian paradigms, 307–11
 Quinean conceptual schemes, 315–18
MDAs *see* Meaning Definition Axioms
meaning, 420
Meaning Definition Axioms, 460–1, 467
meaning form, 376–7, 390
meaning function, 376–7
MedicalWordNet, 291
merged ontology, 442–3
meta-meta language, 444
meta-schema, 404
metadata, 130–1
metalanguage, 38–9
metamarkup, 378–84

foundations to alternative
  framework, 379–84
  making meanings explicit,
    381–3
  one-layered linear string to
    double-layered string, 380
  positing relations, 383
  schema making as site of social
    dialectic, 379
  social schema alignment, 384
metamathematics, 212
micro-power, 337
Microsoft, 217
Microsoft operating system, 62
Microsoft Word, 101
monograph, 126
monotonic reasoning, 223
Motion Pictures Experts Group, 469
Mouse Genome Informatics project,
  295
MPEG-21 *see* Motion Pictures
  Experts Group
multiliteracies, 495
multimodality, 99–102

naive realism, 294
namespaces, 397
National Cancer Institute, 291
National Human Genome Research
  Institute, 295
natural semantic metalanguage, 38
network model, 216
Network Society, 18
networked ontologies, 29–30
NHGRI *see* National Human
  Genome Research Institute
NoL *see* number of leaf classes
nominalism, 325, 327–9
nonmonotonic reasoning, 223–5

NoR *see* number of root classes
NSM *see* natural semantic
  metalanguage
number of leaf classes, 72
number of root classes, 72

OAIPMH *see* Open Archive
  Initiative—Protocol for
  Metadata Harvesting
OASIS/UNESCO sanctioned
  DocBook standard, 392
OBO Foundry *see* Open Biological
  and Biomedical Ontologies
  Foundry
occurrents, 243, 294
ODRL *see* Open Digital Rights
  Language
OIL *see* Ontology Inference Layer
ONIX *see* Online Information
  Exchange
Online Information Exchange, 396,
  405, 471–2
OntoEngine, 434, 455–61, 474
Ontolog Forum, 280
ontological, 346
ontological cultures, 296–8,
  344–9
ontological objects, 298–9
ontological pluralism, 294
ontologies, 16, 22
  see also specific ontologies
  advantages, 26
  collaborative, 72
  computing, 25–6
  conceptual distinctions, 280–2
  networked, 29–30
  preliminary ontology for research
    knowledge support, 184–8
  upper-level, 235–85

Ontology Inference Layer, 220, 454–5

ontology mapping, 442, 466

ontology matching, 30, 33, 67–71

ontology merging, 456
 see also OntoMerge

ontology metrics, 71–2

Ontology Web Language, 7, 16, 22–3, 27–9, 41, 94, 220–1, 225, 227, 237, 263, 453
 language variants, 27

ontology-based interlanguage approach, 453–62

ontology-based interlanguage infrastructure, 466–7

OntoMap, 240

OntoMerge, 431, 453–62, 467–8, 479, 481
 differences in approach, 461–2
 human interpretive intelligence facilities, 474–5, 477
 ontology-based translation system, 454–6
 XML content translation, 457–61
  how system works, 459
  outline, 460
  source content into merged ontology data set, 459–61
  source document merged ontology dataset into destination XML schema, 461

Open Archive Initiative—Protocol for Metadata Harvesting, 179

Open Biological and Biomedical Ontologies Foundry, 290–4, 299
 foundational principles, 293–4

Open Digital Rights Language, 396

Open eBook, 392, 405

open tags, 419

open world assumptions, 223, 225, 228

Oracle, 217

Outlines of the Laws of Thought, 203

OWL *see* Ontology Web Language

OWLViz plug-in, 250

painting, 82

paradigms, 306
 see also Kuhnian paradigms
 Common Ground Markup Language, 417–22

partial untranslatability, 320–1

patch and mend approach, 436, 477–8

PDDAML, 454–5

PDDL *see* Planning Domain Definition Language

PDDL-DAML Translator *see* PDDAML

PDF *see* Portable Document Format

peer-review system, 138

perdurant, 243

perlocutionary act, 44

personal knowledge, 165–7

Personalised Print Markup Language, 392

perspectival specialisation, 255

perspective dimensions, 361, 367

perspectivism, 330

photoengraving, 100

photography, 82

Planning Domain Definition Language, 454

polylingual, 109

Portable Document Format, 3, 96, 126, 392

positivism, 318

post-press, 393

post-publication, 8

PPML *see* Personalised Print Markup Language
practice dimensions, 361, 367
pragmatic semantics, 43–6
pragmatism, 45–6
pre-press, 393
pre-publication, 8
press, 393
Principia Mathematica, 207, 209
print capitalism, 108
print rendering, 392–4
printing, 148
procedural knowledge, 158
process dimensions, 361, 367
properties, 332
Protégé, 27, 250
PROTo ONtology, 237, 245–6
PROTON *see* PROTo ONtology
public, 146
public knowledge space, 146, 151, 174–82
    contextual information management practices, 178–80
    knowledge brokering role, 180–2
    socio-technical aspects, 181
    notion and public knowledge, 174–8
publication, 8
purpose dimensions, 361, 366

quality dimensions, 332
Quine, 305–6
Quinean conceptual schemes, 315–18
QWERTY keyboard, 481

Ramus, Petrus, 2
RAND Corporation, 216
rationalisation, 337–8
rationalists, 329
RDD *see* Rights Data Dictionary

RDF *see* Resource Description Framework
realist perspectivalism, 242
reason, 322
referent, 37
REL *see* Rights Expression Language
relational database, 215–32
relational model
    advantages, 217
    key concepts, 217
relativism, 326, 330
relativists, 326, 344
relators, 451
representations, 332, 376
research enterprise, 150
research intensive networks
    cyclical model types with acquisition and growth of knowledge, 160–1
    John Boyd's OODA loop concept, 160
    hierarchically complex systems theory, 161–72
    research knowledge and dynamics, 164–72
    systems triad, 162
    implications for managing research enterprises in knowledge society, 172–82
    historical concern associated with open science, 172–4
    public knowledge space, 174–82
    knowledge as emergent property of evolutionary systems, 151–5
    knowledge in three worlds ontology, 155
    personal knowledge contextual nature, 157
    Popper's general theory of evolution, 153
    ontology of knowledge, 151–61

knowledge type emergence through time, 155–60
preliminary ontology for research knowledge support, 184–8
textual representations and knowledge support-systems, 145–88
Resource Description Framework, 7, 16, 22–3, 41, 94, 220–1, 225, 227, 263–4, 382, 454, 458
resource discovery, 394
Rights Data Dictionary, 469
Rights Expression Language, 469

Saccharomyces Genome Database project, 295
schema alignment, 384
  semantic publishing, 389–96
schemas, 148–9, 374, 379, 397
scholarly knowledge, 123–4
science, 307
Science Wars, 325
Scientific American, 201
Scientific Revolution, 148
scope dimensions, 359, 366
SEKT *see* Semantic Knowledge Technologies
semantic ambiguity, 471
semantic atomism, 350
semantic delicacy, 471
semantic dimensions, 352
semantic distances, 354–5
semantic frames, 219
  meaning of meaning, 35–72
    cognitive semantics, 46–52
    computational semantics, 67–72
    linguistic semantics, 37–46
    social semantics, 52–5
semantic function, 438
semantic holism, 350, 357
semantic incommensurability, 471

Semantic Knowledge Technologies, 237
semantic markup, 378, 380
semantic networks, 218–19
semantic primes, 38
semantic publishing, 7, 378, 405, 491–506
  academic language game, 492–6
  disciplinarity, 496–502
  new agenda, 502–6
    analytical principle, 505
    conceptual-definitional principle, 505
    situated meaning principle, 503–4
    transformational principle, 506
  schema alignment, 389–96
semantic tagging, 503
semantic web, 7, 16, 21–33, 212, 401–2, 433, 496–7, 502–3
  early threads, 218–20
  foundations to alternative framework, 379–84
  knowledge systems, 215–32
Semantic Web Interest Group, 258, 262
Semantic Web Interest Group and Ontology Forum
  author and subject counts, 260
  joint contributors to the ontologies surveyed, 260
  messages receive, 259
  ontology count, 262
  word frequency analysis, 283–5
semantic web ontology, 453
semantic web processing, 96
semantics, 19, 39, 41–3
  and the embodied mind, 49–51
sense-datum language, 316
SGML *see* Standardised General Markup Language

Shareable Content Object Reference
     Model, 395
sign, 37
sign making, 495
signified, 37
signifier, 37
signs, 376
situated meaning principle, 503–4
situoid, 256
Smart Web Integrated Ontology,
     247–8
SNOMED-CT *see* Systematised
     Nomenclature of Medicine-
     Clinical Terms
social constructionism, 324–5
social languages, 381
social semantics, 52–66
     critical theory as sociology of
          knowledge, 55–6
     globalization and technologies of
          knowledge, 56–7
     IT standardisation, 59–63
     knowledge management, 63–6
     sociology of knowledge, 52–5
     studies on technology and science,
          57–9
social web, 5
     changing knowledge systems, 1–10
          distributed knowledge systems,
               7–10
          from print to digital text, 1–7
     creating an interlanguage,
          371–425
          discursive practice of markup,
               371–4
          interlanguage, 404–25
          mechanism, 384–9
          metamarkup, 378–84
          schema alignment for semantic
               publishing, 389–94

structural markup, 374–8
tagging schemas, 397–404
Sokal hoax, 325
spatialising concepts, 331–4
splitters, 382
spreadsheet, 18
SQL *see* Structured Query Language
stabilists, 328
stability, 328–9
Standard Generalised Markup
     Language, 7
standard ontology, 457, 460
Standard Upper Merged Ontology,
     237, 246–7
Standard Upper Ontology, 239–40
standard wars, 62
Standardised General Markup
     Language, 92
     markup for bungler definition in
          Oxford Dictionary, 93
stimulus meaning, 317
structural dimensions, 359, 365
structural markup, 374–8
structuralism, 319
Structured Query Language, 217–18
stylistic dimensions, 359, 365
subject dimensions, 359, 366
subjective knowledge, 156
SUMO *see* Standard Upper Merged
     Ontology
SUO *see* Standard Upper Ontology
superordination, 421
surface ontology, 457, 460
Swoogle, 238–9
synonymy/antonymy, 38
syntax, 19
system of knowledge
     modern and postmodern
          assessing commensurability,
               227–9

closed vs open world
  assumptions, 223–4
comparison of knowledge
  systems, 228
modern grid, postmodern webs,
  225–7
System of Logic, 203
System R, 217
Systematised Nomenclature of
  Medicine-Clinical Terms, 291
systems of knowledge, 222–4

tacit knowledge, 157
tagging, 371
  see also markup
tagging schemas, 373, 379, 397–404,
  407
tags, 373, 375–6, 390, 399, 407,
  439, 503
Tarski's model theory, 41
taxinomia, 230
tensed intensional logic, 40–1
terminological logics, 219
text, 95
Text Encoding Initiative, 375, 392
textual representations
  and knowledge support-systems in
    research intensive networks,
    145–88
    hierarchically complex systems
      research knowledge and
      dynamics, 164–72
    hierarchically complex systems
      theory, 161–72
    ontology of knowledge, 151–61
The Archaeology of Knowledge, 312
The Concept of Truth in Formalised
  Languages, 209
The Cornucopia of Formal-
  Ontological Relations, 294

The Order of Things, 16, 311
The Origin of Species, 81
The Semantical Conception of Truth,
  209
The Social Construction of What?,
  324–5
*The Structure of Scientific
  Revolutions*, 307, 309
third dogma, 320, 338
topoid, 255–6
Tractacus, 207–8
transformation mechanisms, 443–4
transformational principle, 506
translation/transformation
  architecture, 437
  Common Ground Markup
    Language, 446–9
  Contextual Ontology_X_
    Architecture, 450–3
  system components, 441–4
    interlanguage as a theory of
      translation, 444
    system design, 442–3
    transformation mechanisms,
      443–4
Turing Test, 218
typesetting, 391–2
typography, 89–90

UK National Curriculum Metadata
  Standard, 395
UMLS *see* Unified Medical Language
  System
Unicode, 110–11, 391
ontology of knowledge, 151–61
Unified Medical Language System,
  291
Uniform Resource Identifiers,
  22, 26
universalis mathesis, 198, 200
universities, 7–10

untranslatability, 320
upper-level ontologies, 29, 70, 235–85
  assumptions, 241–8
    Basic Formal Ontology, 242–3
    Descriptive Ontology for
      Linguistic and Cognitive
      Engineering, 244
    extending the taxonomy, 248
    General Formal Ontology,
      244–5
    PROTo ontology, 245–6
    Smart Web Integrated Ontology,
      247–8
    Standard Upper Merged
      Ontology, 246–7
  background, 237–40
    Google Scholar results, 239
    Swoogie results, 238
  categories, 250–2
    Basic Formal Ontology, 250
    Descriptive Ontology for
      Linguistic and Cognitive
      Engineering, 250–1
    General Formal Ontology, 251
    PROTo ontology, 251–2
    Standard Upper Merged
      Ontology, 252
  commensurability, 271–7
    implications for general theory,
      275–7
    ontology commensurability
      matrix, 273–4
  conceptual distinctions between
    ontologies, 280–2
  foundational ontologies and their
    ontological choices, 248
  methodologies, 240–1
  ontology engineering dialogical
    account, 257–8
    mailing lists analysis, 258–9
    quantitative analysis, 259–62

work frequency analysis, 262–3
    qualitative analysis, 264–71
      Ontolog Forum dialogue map,
        264–7
      ontological dialogue, 264–7
      positions and distinctions,
        267–71
    Semantic Web Interest Group and
      Ontology Forum
      Author and subject counts, 260
      joint contributors to the
        ontologies surveyed, 260
      messages receive, 259
      ontology count, 262
      word frequency analysis,
        283–5
    structural features, 249–57
      classes, properties, concepts and
        ratios comparison within
        ontologies, 249
      orientation summary, 257
    supplementary data, 278–80
    survey, 237–57
    top-level classes representation
      Basic Formal Ontology, 278
      Descriptive Ontology for
        Linguistic and Cognitive
        Engineering ontology, 278
      General Formal Ontology, 279
      PROTo ontology, 279
      Standard Upper Merged
        Ontology, 280
URI see Uniform Resource Identifiers
US Patent Office, 231

VMF see Vocabulary Mapping
  Framework
Vocabulary Mapping Framework,
  465–6
voice-synthesised telephone banking,
  113

W2 *see* World 2
W3 *see* World 3
W3C *see* World Wide Web Consortium
Web 2.0, 7, 136
Web 3.0, 492
Web-PDDL, 455, 460
webometrics, 138
weighted average, 355
Wikipedia, 5, 9, 134
WIPO *see* World Intellectual
    Property Organisation
word processing, 3, 92
WordNet, 239–40
World 2, 154
World 3, 154
World Intellectual Property
    Organisation, 470
World Wide Web, 92–3, 220–1,
    404

World Wide Web Consortium, 220,
    433

Xerox, 216
Xeroxography, 116
XHTML *see* Extensible Hypertext
    Markup Language
XML *see* Extensible Markup Language
XML compliant, 438
XML Schema, 438
XML-based interlanguage approach,
    435, 444–53
XML-based interlanguage
    infrastructure, 463–6
XrML *see* Extensible Rights Markup
    Language
XSL *see* Extensible Stylesheet Language
XSL transformations, 452
XSLT *see* XSL transformations

Printed and bound by CPI Group (UK) Ltd, Croydon, CR0 4YY

03/10/2024

01040435-0018